SERGEI O. PROKOFIEFF, born in M
and art history at the Moscow School
posophy in his youth, and soon made th
He has been active as an author and lect___ ____ ____ 1982, and in 1991 he
co-founded the Anthroposophical Society in Russia. In Easter 2001 he
became a member of the Executive Council of the General Anthroposophical Society in Dornach. He is the author of many books, 21 of
which are now available in English translation.

By the same author:

THE EAST IN THE LIGHT OF THE WEST

Parts One to Three

Part One: The Teaching of Agni Yoga in the Light of
Christian Esotericism

Part Two: The Teaching of Alice Bailey in the Light of
Christian Esotericism

Part Three: The Birth of Christian Esotericism in the
Twentieth Century and the Occult Powers that Oppose it

SERGEI O. PROKOFIEFF

TEMPLE LODGE

Translated from German by Simon Blaxland-de Lange

Temple Lodge Publishing
Hillside House, The Square
Forest Row, RH18 5ES

www.templelodge.com

Published by Temple Lodge 2009
(Previously published edition of 1993 includes Part 1 only, translated from Russian)

This translation © Temple Lodge Publishing 2009

Originally published in German in three volumes under the title *Der Osten im Lichte des Westens*, Teil I–III by Verlag am Goetheanum, Dornach, in 1997 (with an earlier edition of Part I only published in 1992)

A catalogue record for this book is available from the British Library

ISBN 978 1 906999 06 3

Cover by Andrew Morgan Design
Typeset by DP Photosetting, Neath, West Glamorgan
Printed and bound by Cromwell Press Group Limited, Trowbridge, Wiltshire

Contents

Part One

THE TEACHING OF AGNI YOGA IN THE LIGHT OF CHRISTIAN ESOTERICISM

Preface to the Second German Edition

Since the time when the first part of this work appeared,[*] dedicated as it was to a consideration of the occult movement of 'Agni Yoga' or 'Living Ethics'—together with the history of its origin—in the light of Christian esotericism as represented in the twentieth century by anthroposophy or modern spiritual science, almost five years have gone by.

The promised second part about the occult movement of the so-called Arcane School founded by Alice Bailey was written shortly after the original publication of the first part. However, publication has been significantly delayed until now.

This delay was associated with the fact that, in the course of the author's work on the theme, a third part was appended to the second, where consideration was given to the question which evidently lived within many readers who had read the first part, namely that of the relationship between the Eastern and Western occult teachers and the occult streams that they represent.

As this question is so extraordinarily complicated, it was *consciously left unanswered* in the first part. For it soon became clear to me that merely the attempt to approach an answer to it required a broadly conceived independent investigation, and this could not be carried out within the framework of the first part as this was originally planned.

The decision to forego not merely a search for an answer to this question but also a posing of the question itself was expressed as follows in the first edition.

'In the present work the author has not considered it his task to identify the personalities of the theosophical teachers . . . His aim has simply been to indicate the quite particular intentions which have proceeded from those individualities (whoever they may have been) whom Helena Roerich (and also, as we shall see, Alice Bailey) called by those names (following Blavatsky), and whom she regarded as her "mahatmas". In an esoteric sense they are the founders of those occult streams to the study of which the present work is devoted.' (First English edition, p. 14.)

In other words, I wholly consciously declined to answer the question as to whether those Eastern mahatmas of whose existence Blavatsky, Olcott and Sinnett were the first to testify openly both verbally and in writing in

---

[*] The first English edition appeared the year after the first German edition in 1993.—Translator's note.

the Western world were the same individualities regarding whom Besant and Leadbeater, and also the Roerichs and Alice Bailey, were subsequently to speak and write about and with whom—as they frequently asserted—they associated.

The principal task both of this first part and of the subsequent second part was from the outset something quite different, namely to allow the Roerichs and then Alice Bailey to speak in their own words. For they were absolutely convinced that the occult teachers who inspired them were the same as those who first became known to the world through Helena Blavatsky.

Thus in accordance with the original plan these two parts consist mostly of quotations from the founders of the two occult streams (of Helena and Nicholas Roerich and also Alice Bailey), together with anthroposophical commentaries, intended to furnish the reader with the means of understanding these two streams in the light of modern Christian esotericism.

However, after the publication of the first part I was asked what could be said from the anthroposophical standpoint about the Eastern teachers (mahatmas) themselves and about their relationship to *Christian* esotericism. Because of this it became necessary to deal more thoroughly with this theme, which led to some specific research being undertaken and, hence, to a third, concluding part of the present work.

The main result of this research was that those occultists whom both the Roerichs and also Alice Bailey in the twentieth century named as their leaders have nothing in common with those Eastern mahatmas whose names were first made known by Blavatsky.

Hence in the case of both the Roerichs and also Alice Bailey one has to do *not* with the Eastern mahatmas but with quite different occultists who had illicitly appropriated their names and then tried—while deliberately misleading their followers—to attain their highly dubious occult political aims with the help of the occult movements which had already been initiated. It is true that Rudolf Steiner spoke in his lectures of the 'substitution' only of *one* of the two mahatmas who originally inspired Blavatsky. However, the further development of the Theosophical Society, especially under the leadership of Besant and Leadbeater, makes it clear that *both* mahatmas were replaced.

This substitution process of the Eastern mahatmas by occultists of a left persuasion began already during Helena Blavatsky's life. It was associated with the fact that the Eastern mahatmas gradually ceased inspiring the Theosophical Society, and finally turned away from it altogether. After their withdrawal, this vacant spiritual space was taken possession of by these other occultists. As a result the pre-Christian wisdom of the old Eastern religions, of which Helena Blavatsky had spoken under the inspiration of the Eastern mahatmas, gradually took on a distinctly antichristian character which distorted and worked destructively upon the very foundations of true Christianity.

The culmination of this process and the associated decline of the Theosophical Society in the twentieth century was represented by the attempt of Besant and Leadbeater to put the 14-year-old Krishnamurti forward as the reborn Messiah, whereupon the antichristian character which had already taken hold of the Theosophical Society was manifested in full measure. In the occult stream of Alice Bailey these preparations for the appearance of the 'Messiah' in a physical body were carried further and brought increasingly into connection with world development, thus intensifying their anti-Christian character.

Rudolf Steiner has, moreover, indicated that the original impulse for the founding of the Theosophical Society (1875) was given not by Eastern but by Western masters, indeed by the leading masters of Rosicrucian Christianity. On the basis of this fact, one can clearly distinguish three phases in the overall development of the Theosophical Society in the last quarter of the nineteenth century (still in Blavatsky's lifetime), which, while overlapping to some extent, nevertheless succeeded one another in time:

1. a Christian phase (of an esoteric Rosicrucian nature);
2. a pre-Christian phase (esotericism of the old pre-Christian religions of the East;
3. an antichristian phase (battle of left-oriented Eastern and Western occultists against Christianity).

If one is seeking to understand the subsequent destiny of the theosophical movement and the occult movements of the Roerichs and Alice Bailey, one must therefore keep these three elements very clearly distinguished.

Whereas the principal aim of the first of these three elements was to work for 'the essential *meaning of the earth*, which lies in the recognition and realization of the intentions of the *living Christ*', the second set itself the task of 'imprinting *their* form of spiritual knowledge, which had been preserved through the ages, on the Western world' in order to counteract 'the terrible danger' that threatens mankind in the event of an overall victory of Western materialism (see Appendix 5).

This is the source of the extraordinarily complicated and highly dramatic relationships between the Western (Rosicrucian) masters and the

Eastern mahatmas in the twentieth century, who were united by the common endeavour of overcoming the materialism that threatens humanity but who nevertheless had a different understanding of the Christ Being and of His central role in earthly evolution.

Finally, the third element of the left-oriented occultists had the aim of intensifying the already existing materialism by occult means, by extending it to the spiritual world and thus transforming it into an *occult materialism* posing particular dangers to contemporary humanity, in order that it might be used as an instrument of attaining their antichristian, occultly political aims.

It was in order to achieve this purpose that the occult movements of the Roerichs and also Alice Bailey, together with a whole series of other occultists who are characterized in the second part, were brought into being by these occultists of a left persuasion.

★

To conclude this Preface, it is necessary to draw the reader's attention to two further features of the present publication.[*]

Because of the way that this work has arisen, and also for technical reasons, it is being published not in one but in three volumes. This has led to some fundamental observations by Rudolf Steiner, which are necessary for an understanding both of the occult movements of the Roerichs and Alice Bailey and also of the highly complex relationships between the Western and the Eastern masters, being quoted in all three volumes.[†] For this reason, any of the three volumes can be read independently, without a knowledge of the other two.

The second feature is the following. In order that the anthroposophical reader may form his own judgement of the character and particular qualities of the occultism of the Roerichs and also Alice Bailey, a substantial number of quotations from their works have been made in all three parts of the present work. But since both the Roerichs and also Alice Bailey and the other occult authors with an affinity to them consistently referred—and still refer today—not only to the Eastern mahatmas, calling them by name, but also to the Western masters and even the founder of Christianity Himself, it was—in view of the frequent use of their names in the quotations—wholly impossible always to place the names cited by

---

[*] These observations refer to the publication of the German and Russian editions in three separate volumes.—Translator's note.

[†] This also applies to some of the characteristic observations of the founders of the two streams under consideration here.

them in inverted commas or in every case to add the words 'pseudo-', 'false' or 'alleged' and so forth.

Hence it must be reiterated here quite categorically: the use of the names referred to above in the occult streams of the Roerichs, Alice Bailey and others related to them has nothing in common with the true individualities of the masters of the East and the West who once bore—or continue to bear—these names.

Only if this reservation is taken into account can what follows be rightly understood.

In connection with the publication of this second German edition of the first part, it should be added that this edition has been thoroughly revised and extended, and supplemented by a whole series of new publications from the letters and literary and occult legacy of the Roerich family that have appeared in Russia in recent years.

The 'Preface' and 'Introduction' of the first Russian edition[*] have also been added to this second German edition, so that this expanded version corresponds to the Russian original.

Finally, it should be emphasized that the contents of this book derive from my personal research and therefore represent my own personal view.

Sergei O. Prokofieff
Stuttgart, December 1996

---

[*] Novikov Press, St Petersburg 1995.

Preface to the Russian Edition

Although this book, now being introduced to the Russian reader, on the occult stream founded in the first third of the twentieth century by Helena Ivanovna Roerich (1879–1955) and Nikolai Konstantinovich Roerich (1874–1947) was originally written in Russian, it first saw the light of day in German translation in 1992.* It was from the outset intended exclusively for readers already familiar with anthroposophy, the most important stream of Christian esotericism in the twentieth century.

In preparing the book for the Russian edition, it seemed necessary for me to introduce certain changes into its content. As I did not want to enter into some kind of polemics with the followers of other spiritual streams, in the present work I have merely set forth the anthroposophical view of the occult foundations of the teaching and activities of the Roerichs. It might be supposed that this view, together with the facts adduced in the book itself, could be of interest in Russia to a fairly wide circle of readers, for they are able to shed a new light upon the nature of the—now ended—Bolshevik epoch and furnish a better sense of orientation in the spiritual situation of today. From this standpoint, the book is addressed also to those readers who, while knowing little or even nothing at all about anthroposophy, are able to feel an affinity with certain essential aspects of its conception of the world. For them a whole series of explanations and additions have been given in the book which, however, are by no means able to be a substitute for an acquaintance with the numerous works of the founder of anthroposophy, Rudolf Steiner (1861–1925).

Further additions have been necessitated by the publishing of new materials from the literary legacy of the Roerichs, which made possible both a refinement and a further development of many of the statements of this book. All this material has served only to support the main conclusion of this book: the absence of any true knowledge of the Christ and of the central significance of the Mystery of Golgotha in earthly evolution leads man to a spiritual blindness, with—possibly—very dire consequences.

In conclusion it should be pointed out that the stream of Agni Yoga, despite its rapid spread in recent times in a number of countries within Europe, America and especially in the European East (Russia, Latvia, Belarus, Ukraine, Georgia and so forth), might not have achieved the

---

*To date, translations have also appeared in English and French.

attention that we have attributed to it in this book had it not been for its having been associated to a quite particular degree with another occult stream which has acquitted a considerable influence above all in the West (though it has latterly also penetrated into Russia)—the 'Group of the World Servers' or the 'Arcane School' founded by the Englishwoman Alice Bailey.

The fact is that both streams emanate from one and the same occult centre, whose leaders sent the Russian Helena Roerich to the East in order to spread its teachings from India via Tibet and Mongolia to Russia and the Englishwoman Alice Bailey at almost the same time to the West in order to achieve the same goals through America. (The occult stream of Alice Bailey will be considered in a separate volume in the second part of the present work.)

If we now consider the two streams as two complementary parts of one all-embracing plan, we may sense the true dimensions of the spiritual battle being waged in the twentieth century behind the scenes of outward events against the 'essential *meaning of the earth*, which lies in the recognition and realization of the intentions of the *living Christ*' (Rudolf Steiner).

And if anthroposophy is called upon in our time to help towards the urgent realization of these high intentions, the first step in this direction must necessarily be the clearest and deepest possible understanding of the significance and true meaning of this battle within which all anthroposophists now find themselves. Furthering the development of such a deeper understanding is the principal aim of the present work.

In the second and third parts of this trilogy, a number of questions posed or touched upon in the first part are developed further and sometimes also resolved.

Translator's Note

Nicholas and Helena Roerich wrote almost exclusively in Russian, and where their writings are quoted by the author of the present book they have been newly translated from the original Russian text, even where the initial publication was in English (although for ease of reference the titles of the published English translations are given). Readers wishing to consult such published English translations of these writings as are available are warned that in some cases the English editions contain omissions or have been abridged in some way (most strikingly in the case of the book *Community*).

Abbreviations in Part One

Works by Helena and Nicholas Roerich

AY   Helena Roerich, *Agni Yoga*. Complete Edition of all 14 books in three volumes, Samara 1992. (The number of the volume in question is given, followed by the relevant date—for the first volume—or, in the case of the other volumes, the part and section where the quotation appears.)

KV   Saint Iler Zh. (Helena Roerich), *Kriptogrammy Vostoka/Mir cherez kulkuru* ('Cryptograms of the East/Peace through Culture'), Sovyetsky Pisatel, Moscow 1990, pp. 123–60

NV   Helena Roerich, *Naputstviye Vozdyu* ('Parting Words to the Leader'), Leningrad–Izvara, 1990 (the number of the apophthegm or dictum is given)

OB   Helena Roerich, *Obshchina* ('Community'), *Agni Yoga*, Vol. III. Reprint of the first Ulan-Bator edition of 1927 in the journal *Tryezvost i Kultura*, Moscow 1989, nos 10–12, and 1990 nos 1–11

        Osnovy buddizma ('The Foundations of Buddhism'), N. Rokotova (Helena Roerich), Ulan-Udeh 1991

HR   *Pisma Eleny Rerich* ('Letters of Helena Roerich'), in three volumes, Novosibirsk 1992–3 (the number of the volume and the date are given)

UPNM   *U poroga novovo mira* ('At the Threshold of the New World'), Mezhdunarodny Tsientr Roerichov, Moscow 1993 (the date of the diary entry or letter is given) (also appears in Part 2)

PA   Helena Roerich, Letters to America in three volumes, Moscow 1996. Vol. I: 1929–1936; Vol. II: 1936–1946; Vol. III: 1948–1955

NR   Nicholas Roerich, Works in six volumes, Riga 1991–2: Vol. I, *Nerushimoye* ('The Indestructible'); Vol. II, *Tverdynya plamennaya* ('Fiery Stronghold'); Vol. III: *Vrata v budushcheye* ('The Door to the Future'); Vol. IV, *Altai-Gimalai* ('Altai-Himalaya'); Vol. V, *Derzhava svyeta. Svyashchenny dozor* ('The Kingdom of Light'); Vol. VI, *Tsvyety Morii. Puti blagoslovyeniya. Serdtse Asii* ('Flowers of Morya. Paths of Blessing. Hearts of Asia')

AG   Nicholas Roerich, *Altai-Gimalai* ('Altai-Himalaya'), Moscow 1974

ZS   Nicholas Roerich, *Zazhigaitye serdtse* ('Enkindle the Heart').
         Collection of articles and letters from his early years, Molodiya
         gvardiya, Moscow 1990

ShS   Nicholas Roerich, *Shamballa Siyayushchaya* ('Radiant Sham-
         balla'), *Uguns*, 1990

Theosophical Literature

HPB   H.P. Blavatsky, *The Secret Doctrine*. Quotations from this work
         are taken from the Adyar Edition, Theosophical Publishing
         House, Adyar, Madras, India, fourth edition 1938

EC   H.P. Blavatsky, 'The Esoteric Character of the Gospels' (from
         the journal *Lucifer*)

ML   *The Mahatma Letters to A.P. Sinnett*

Introduction

Amongst all the many occult streams which have in recent years become widespread and even officially acknowledged in Russia, the spiritual movement of 'Agni Yoga' (or 'Living Ethics') founded by the married couple Helena and Nicholas Roerich occupies a particular place.

The destiny of this movement in the final years of the Bolshevik dictatorship was remarkable. For in comparison with other occult and religious movements the position of its adherents—in the context of the total persecution of all dissidents—was relatively favourable. Monographs have appeared, dissertations have been published, exhibitions of Nicholas Roerich's pictures have been organized. It is true that the name of Helena Roerich, the founder of Agni Yoga, is seldom heard, and Nicholas Roerich is spoken of more as an artist and explorer or as a person in public life. But his literary works have been published, and those researching into his literary legacy have in the majority of cases been at the same time ardent followers and occult pupils of Helena Roerich, as can easily be deduced from their books (the names of P. Belikov, L. Shaposhnikova and V. Sidorov may be mentioned in this connection).

Helena and Nicholas Roerich's sons, Yuri and Svyatoslav, who have carried on their work and preserved their handwritten literary legacy, have not only maintained very active contacts with the various Roerich groups in the Soviet Union but also met several times with the Soviet leadership. Thus Yuri Roerich met Khrushchev in 1957 during the latter's visit to India, and shortly afterwards he settled permanently in the Soviet Union. Svyatoslav Roerich visited the Soviet Union for the first time in 1960 at Krushchev's invitation with an exhibition of his pictures and subsequently travelled there more than once, meeting with Gorbachev officially on two occasions.[1]

Such a mutual interest—however strange at first sight—between an occult stream and the Soviet regime cannot of course be explained by the significance of Nicholas Roerich as an artist (there were, after all, also artists whose work was banned!), nor even by the fact that Yuri and Svyatoslav Roerich were unremittingly full of praise for the structure of the Soviet Union. Indeed, this highly positive attitude of the entire Roerich family towards Bolshevism should not be regarded as fortuitous, for it was rooted in the teachings of Agni Yoga. We shall have full opportunity to convince ourselves of this when we enter directly into a consideration of the *occult* foundations of this evident sympathy of Agni Yoga for Bolshevism.

The teaching of Agni Yoga was initiated at the beginning of the 1920s by Helena Roerich. She expounded it in 14 volumes, 13 of which were published in Paris and Riga between 1924 and 1938. The final, fourteenth volume was incomplete and was published for the first time in New York in 1989. Together with the literary output of Nicholas Roerich, of which a good proportion is a kind of commentary on the actual body of the teaching, the literary legacy of the Roerichs encompasses 27 volumes, without taking into account several hundred unpublished manuscripts, occasional letters and articles.[2]

In recent years these have also begun to be published. Especially noteworthy in the present context is the third volume, containing Helena Roerich's letters to her pupils and presenting some more intimate aspects of the teaching that at the time were not included in the official books or in the two volumes of her letters which came out at the end of the 1930s or even in the anthology *U poroga novovo mira* ('At the Threshold of the New World'). This latter volume contains both autobiographical details and also extracts from Helena Roerich's occult diary, which affords insight into the character of her own development and her occult capacities.

The Roerichs started organizing the first groups for studying Agni Yoga already in the 1920s. Helena Roerich's letters make it apparent that by the 1930s such groups existed in many countries in Europe and America.* The Nicholas Roerich Museum in New York, founded in 1923, became its centre. Today there are similar groups in many of the towns of Russia and also Latvia, Belarus, Kazakhstan, Georgia and so on. Books on 'Living Ethics' are being published simultaneously in Moscow, Riga, St Petersburg, Novosibirsk, Samara, Tomsk, Tbilisi and Minsk. There is a Russian Roerich Society, an International Roerich Centre and an International Association 'Peace through Culture'. Newspapers such as *Znamya mira* ('Banner of Peace') and *Ozareniye* ('Enlightenment') appear regularly, as do the journals *Serdtse* ('Heart'), *Mir ognyonny* ('Fiery World'), *Voshozhdeniye* ('Ascent'), *Utrennyaya zvizda* ('Morning Star') and the journal *Uguns* ('Light of Fire'), which is brought out by the Latvian Roerich Society in Russian and Latvian. All these organs give regular reports of the Roerich Societies and of the many activities undertaken by

---

* Nicolas Roerich's book *Derzhava svyeta* ('The Realm of Light') (1931), which consists for the most part of his writings to these groups in various countries, also furnishes a good insight into the extent of the Roerich movement already in the 1920s. Nicholas Roerich was President of more than 80 Roerich societies in many countries.

the various groups towards spreading the teaching, together with the work which they carry out of developing their ideas and applying them practically.

The German translation (1989) of the American Jacqueline Decter's large monograph on Nicholas Roerich's life and work, *Nicholas Roerich. The Life and Work of a Russian Master* (Thames and Hudson, London 1989), also testifies to the growing interest in Nicholas Roerich's legacy in Switzerland and Germany, where a Roerich Society has existed for a number of years. On its initiative all the books and two volumes of letters have been translated into German. In America the museum dedicated to the artist's work in New York continues today to be the centre of the movement. Moreover, the majority of Helena and Nicholas Roerich's books have for some time been available in English, and many have been translated into other European languages and, in certain instances, even into Asiatic languages.

★

Agni Yoga, or 'Yoga of Fire'—the very name of the teaching is a clear testimony to its origin in Eastern esoteric tradition. This tradition was brought to the Christian West in the second half of the nineteenth century by Helena Petrovna Blavatsky (1831–91), the founder of the Theosophical Society. As will become evident from the present book, Blavatsky was herself for a time under the influence of Western, Christian esoteric tradition; but she later rejected this once she had come under the influence of a one-sided, Eastern, Tibeto-Indian occultism. Nevertheless, this brief, temporary contact on Blavatsky's part with the sources of Christian esotericism enabled the leading representative of this esotericism, Rudolf Steiner, to receive an invitation from German theosophists in the twentieth century and, in 1902, to take over the leadership of the German Section of the Theosophical Society. Through this the Theosophical Society, which was one-sidedly oriented towards Eastern and Asiatic wisdom, was given the unique opportunity to acquire a true knowledge of the mystery of the cosmic Christ and of the central significance of the Mystery of Golgotha for the whole of earthly evolution. However, the Theosophical Society not only missed this opportunity but even tried to oppose true Christian esotericism with the pathetic comedy of the Indian boy Krishnamurti, whom the then leaders of the Theosophical Society put forward as a new incarnation of the Christ. As Rudolf Steiner and his pupils categorically refused to recognize Krishnamurti as a new messiah and openly asserted that a profound occult error lay at the foundation of this claim, they were excluded from the Theosophical

Society and went on to found an independent Anthroposophical Society in 1913.*

From an inner point of view, however, the movement of modern Christian esotericism led by Rudolf Steiner was from the outset independent of Eastern esotericism (see further in Part Three). This is obvious to those who are familiar with Rudolf Steiner's extensive legacy; and no less obvious is the complete *misunderstanding* of the mystery of the living Christ displayed in *The Secret Doctrine*, Blavatsky's principal work, which was most valued by theosophists and especially by Helena Roerich. For Blavatsky, who had derived from Eastern religions a certain conception of the cosmic working of the Christ as Sun Logos *before* the Mystery of Golgotha, had absolutely no understanding of the central mystery of historical Christianity as expressed in the prologue to the Gospel of St John, 'And the Word became flesh', in that she (as did subsequently Helena Roerich) placed the Christ on a level with great initiates of mankind such as Gautama Buddha, Shankaracharya, Krishna and so forth.

What is at issue here is an aspect of concrete occult *knowledge*, that is, belonging to a category such as truth and error, where no compromise is possible; for this would be equivalent to a lie, which has a destructive power in any true occultism. Because of its consequences, it would from the standpoint of Christian esotericism be a particularly disastrous occult error if there were to be any confusion of the superhuman *divine* nature of the Christ, who lived only *once* in the physical body of a human being, with those elder brothers of humanity who are worthy of the highest respect and reverence and who as earthly human beings have attained true initiation in the course of many incarnations (in the East this would be called the bodhisattva or buddha stage) and are rightly the acknowledged leaders of mankind.

Where initiates are spoken of in Christian esotericism as spiritual leaders of mankind, their initiation is understood as a true knowledge of the cosmic Christ Being and also of the Mystery of Golgotha. 'And those who have understood that the future progress of humanity depends upon an understanding of the great Event of Golgotha are they who have united as the Masters of Wisdom and of the Harmony of Feelings in the great ruling lodge of mankind,' said Rudolf Steiner in this connection.[3]

The 'future progress of humanity' is, however, associated above all with

---

* For further details about the associated circumstances and for evidence that this was a matter of exclusion—as opposed to departure—from the Theosophical Society, see: S.O. Prokofieff, *Rudolf Steiner and the Founding of the New Mysteries*, second English edition, Temple Lodge, 1994.

the possibility being opened up to human beings, as a consequence of the Event of Golgotha, of a completely different kind of access to the principle of initiation to what was the case in pre-Christian times and continues to be the case in Eastern occultism. Two elements call for particular consideration here: an essentially new *method* of research into higher worlds and, resulting from this, wholly new *relationships* between teacher and pupil.

The foundations of the new method of spiritual research were laid by Rudolf Steiner in his early works, such as *A Theory of Knowledge Implicit in Goethe's World Conception, Truth and Knowledge* and especially *The Philosophy of Freedom.*[4] In these books the foundations of a wholly new *theory of knowledge* were established in the terms and categories of modern philosophy, such as can be applied to knowledge both of the physical world of the senses and also to the supersensible world. Thus this theory of knowledge, which from the outset has the strictly objective character as befits the natural sciences, can be used as a *practical method* also in the supersensible realms of existence and enables a person for the first time to investigate the higher worlds with the same precision, clarity and objectivity as characterizes scientific research of the sense-perceptible world—despite modern materialism, which would confine man's cognitive faculties to the sense-perceptible world alone.

This gradual overcoming of the limits to knowledge created by materialism, which as regards its nature is none other than the overcoming of that event in the sphere of knowledge referred to at the beginning of the Bible as the Fall of Man and which will gradually be followed by the overcoming of its consequences in all other spheres of human existence, would be altogether impossible had the Mystery of Golgotha not taken place on the earth at the beginning of our era and the possibility arisen for a new, conscious and free relationship to the higher worlds.

In other words, the anthroposophical method of spiritual research is founded upon the direct application in the realm of higher knowledge of those Resurrection forces which entered into earthly existence as a result of the divine Christ Being's passing through death and Resurrection. Hence the essential aim and the central experience of modern Christian initiation, as presented in Rudolf Steiner's books *Knowledge of the Higher Worlds* and *Occult Science* (the chapter entitled 'Concerning Initiation'),[5] is a conscious meeting with the Christ Being in the higher worlds similar to what was experienced by Paul the Apostle on the road to Damascus, thus bringing to realization his words 'It is no longer I who live, but Christ lives in me' (Gal. 2:20) in a new, modern form, that is, on the basis of full human freedom and in full consciousness. But bringing these words to realization in modern initiation does not mean that another ego takes the place of the human ego, nor that the human ego is subjected to some sort of external force that is alien to it; rather does it mean that this ego turns towards its heavenly archetype as a highest ideal, represented in our cosmos by the Christ Being. For only Christ's entering into the human ego or—which is the same thing—the awakening of a Christ consciousness within it can enable man to experience the true freedom that is expressed in the boundless love for this highest ideal of human evolution which the Christ manifested in all fullness during His *single* earthly life, while also granting him the possibility of entering consciously into higher worlds and there ascending in this Christ consciousness to the highest spheres of spiritual existence, as Rudolf Steiner has again and again succeeded in doing in his spiritual research.

Thus through being permeated by the forces issuing from the Mystery of Golgotha and, hence, freed from the consequences of the Fall in the sphere of knowledge, the modern Christian initiate is able to gain an experience of the supersensible in a form for which earthly human beings have no precedent. And it was out of such a Christ-filled spiritual experience, which can with justification be called the gift of the Holy Spirit promised by the Christ, that the modern science of the spirit or anthroposophy was founded by Rudolf Steiner. Even its very name—'wisdom about man'—is from an esoteric point of view an indication that, as a result of the divine Christ Being's having become man, or anthropos, the cosmic Theo-Sophia has become Anthropos-Sophia, for henceforth the highest ideal of earthly evolution will be made manifest by man on the earth.

The first step towards the actual fulfilment of this ideal in our time is when a person embarks upon the spiritual path of schooling described by Rudolf Steiner in the two books referred to above. The spirit-pupil traverses three stages of supersensible knowledge on this path: the stage of perceiving the spiritual world in pictures; then the stage of beholding actual events in the spiritual world deriving from the activity of spiritual beings out of which this world consists; and finally the intimate process of uniting with these higher beings, while maintaining one's individual ego-consciousness. These stages are called the stages of imaginative, inspirative and intuitive knowledge. One could also say that the first of these shows the pupil the spiritual world as it were from without, the second gives a full understanding of the processes in the spiritual world, while the third enables him to experience the essential nature of the higher beings of which the spiritual world consists, beings who in Christian esotericism are also called the divine-spiritual hierarchies or the ranks of Angels, through whose mediation the high Holy Trinity rules over our cosmos.

The new character of the relationship between teacher and pupil in Christian occultism is defined by what has been outlined here. The teacher becomes the pupil's leader in the same sense as, shall we say, the mathematics professor is for his students. For in the present epoch of human freedom the spiritual teacher can give his pupils no more than a description of the path into the supersensible worlds, he can characterize the conditions of this path, give warnings about the dangers and so forth. He can do this as much through books as through a personal encounter.[6] However, the pupil must in both cases take responsibility for his own spiritual development. The teacher can merely indicate the actual path that leads to the Christ, the *cosmic archetype* of all true teachers, to an experience of him at the stage of initiation. For in Christian occultism both teacher and pupil have this sole aim, whose fulfilment the former— by virtue of his higher development—has approached more closely than the latter.

In this sense Christ's saying 'You shall know the truth and the truth shall set you free' is the cornerstone of all Christian esotericism. The spiritual teacher merely presents the higher truths of the spiritual world to the pupil and describes the path whereby they are to be attained. Thus the relationship to these truths must unfold within the pupil above all on the foundation of his own feeling for truth, together with an all-round and unbiased thinking and not through the authority of the teacher who is imparting them. The same also holds good for the path described by the teacher which leads to a knowledge of the higher realms of existence. One can embark upon this and hence arrive at one's own experiences in this domain only out of one's own personal freedom and responsibility, not to the teacher but solely to the objective and purpose of this path—the Christ.

An altogether different relationship between teacher and pupil pertains in Eastern occultism. Helena Roerich forms no exception in this respect. The very fact that all the *Agni Yoga* books were not the work of Helena Roerich herself but were dictated by a certain occult teacher and were merely written down by her (which is why they all appeared without Helena Roerich's name on the cover) testifies to this. Her occult leader did of course have to prepare her sheaths and bring about certain changes in her psyche in order to achieve at the end the desired result of acquiring a compliant human instrument to which he could dictate his occult information. So whatever Helena Roerich may have said about her own higher faculties, from the standpoint of modern Christian esotericism they were and are merely a particular form of mediumism, which was developed to a higher degree in her predecessor, Helena Petrovna Blavatsky.

It is highly instructive to compare extracts from Blavatsky's letters to her sister Vera Zhelikhovsky about the way that her books came into being[7] with Helena Roerich's occult records, which were published in the anthology *U poroga novovo mira* ('At the Threshold of the New World'). The identical nature of the two phenomena is immediately apparent. Not without reason did Helena Roerich consider herself to be following in Blavatsky's footsteps. The numerous dreams, premonitions and visions of the future which the founder of Agni Yoga describes in the anthology, as a result of which she became wholly dependent upon the teacher controlling her steps and dictating all her books, are a clear testimony of Helena Roerich's telepathic, mediumistic faculties.

What has been said does not alter the fact that the founder of Agni Yoga sharply condemned mediumism and characterized her own faculties—in contrast to it—as clairvoyance.[8] However, this opinion proves to be wholly subjective, if one compares the anthology referred to with, for example, Rudolf Steiner's book *Knowledge of the Higher Worlds*. It also transpires that, on closer acquaintance with the books of Agni Yoga, a clear and systematic path to independently reaching higher worlds is lacking. The reason for this is that the entire teaching has not sprung from real spiritual experiences of Helena Roerich but represents the result of her teacher's dictating. 'The teaching is usually communicated by means of clairaudience,' she herself stated in a letter. This means that she heard the voice dictating to her and wrote down what she heard.[9]

The most important result of this constant occult 'whispering' from without, which originated from a certain secret inspirer and at times from an entire group of them, was—apart from a total misunderstanding of the Christ Being (following Blavatsky)—that she was unable to recognize the working of the powers of evil in the world or the forces of the Antichrist. Thus despite her favoured use of the word 'Armageddon', which she borrowed from the Book of Revelation, neither Helena Roerich nor the other members of her family could to the very end of their lives recognize one of the mightiest manifestations of the forces of evil in the twentieth century, namely Bolshevism, which cost the Russian people and the other nations that were subsumed under its rulership over 100 million innocent lives. This is why the Roerich family did not vary in its *positive* relationship both to the founder of Bolshevism and to the changes in Russia that followed in the wake of the Bolshevik Revolution of 1917, and above all—as will be shown subsequently—to Bolshevik ideology, whose foundation is a very radical materialism and atheism.

The reason for this blindness is, however, to be sought not so much in Helena Roerich herself as in the character of her relationship to her occult teachers. For her complete, unconditional acknowledgement of Bolshevism did indeed, as we shall see, spring directly from their inspirations and dictating. But since her relationship with them was from the outset based upon an unquestioning, blind obedience towards every word that they expressed or dictated (which Helena Roerich respected as a higher law), her positive relationship to Bolshevism and to its founder appeared to the entire Roerich family to be an ultimate 'truth' requiring neither consideration nor examination.

Thus the occult stream of Helena Roerich may serve as one of the most revealing examples in the twentieth century of how the absence of a true knowledge of the Christ leads inevitably to the impossibility of recognizing the working of the powers of evil in earthly evolution—those powers of evil spoken of so intimately in the Revelation of St John, or the Apocalypse, whose spiritual symbolism Rudolf Steiner explained in two mighty lecture cycles and in a number of individual lectures.

In this introduction, it is of course not possible to summarize even in its most general features the basic ideas of anthroposophical Christology and the teaching of evil. Some indications along these lines will be given in what follows. However, the full depth and significance of entering into this and many other spiritual regions of Rudolf Steiner's anthroposophy, derived as it was from the sources of true Christian esotericism, can be disclosed to the reader only if he makes himself familiar with Rudolf Steiner's own works.

Sergei O. Prokofieff
December 1993

Notes

1. See *Pravda*, issue of 15 May 1987. In this issue there is also a photograph of Gorbachev receiving Svyatoslav Roerich at the Kremlin. See Appendix 7.
2. See S.N. Roerich, *Stremitsa k prekrasnomy* ('Aspiring to the Beautiful'), Moscow 1993, pp. 48 and 70.
3. GA 107, 22 March 1909.
4. See GA 2, 3 and 4.
5. GA 10 and 13.
6. See the Appendix to Rudolf Steiner's book *Knowledge of the Higher Worlds: How is it achieved?* (GA 10).
7. See *Vestnik obshchestva druzhei H.P. Blavatskoi* ('Herald of the Society of Friends of H.P. Blavatsky'), second edition, Moscow 1992, p. 37.
8. HR 2, 4 February 1936.
9. HR 3, 12 July 1938.

1. The Sources of the Later Teachings of H.P. Blavatsky

The history of the founding of Helena Roerich's Agni Yoga is directly connected with the activity of another of her contemporaries, the well-known founder of the Theosophical Society, Helena Petrovna Blavatsky.

The first Russian lodge of this society was opened in 1908. As the American Jacqueline Decter wrote in her monograph on Nicholas Roerich, 'the Roerichs apparently joined it [the Russian branch of the Theosophical Society] prior to World War I'.[1]

As a result of becoming acquainted with theosophical literature and above all with the writings of Blavatsky herself, the Roerichs first came in contact with the ultimate source of her inspiration, which can be traced back to mysterious mahatmas or teachers of the East who lived somewhere in one of the remote valleys of the central Himalayas but who from time to time ventured to Europe and America.

According to Blavatsky—and Helena Roerich was to express herself in a similar way—she was not the author of the books that she had written, in particular the most important and far-reaching of her works, *The Secret Doctrine*. In the foreword to this book she indicates, quoting Montaigne: 'Gentlemen, I have here made only a nosegay of culled flowers, and have brought nothing of my own but the string that ties them.'[2] And in a letter to her sister Vera Zhelikhovsky she stated: 'Every time that I am commanded to write, I sit down, submit myself and am then freely able to write about virtually everything ... Why? Because He, who knows all, is dictating to me ... My teacher and also others whom I came to know during my years of travel ... If I write about any particular theme and I know very little about it, I turn to them and one of them ... inspires me ...'[3] Vera Zhelikhovsky recalled that Blavatsky reported to her on more than one occasion when they met personally that she had never arrived at the thoughts contained in her books 'with her own understanding'.[4]

Since Helena Roerich herself often pointed out that the inspirations that she received were derived from the same source as those of Blavatsky, it is necessary to attempt briefly to characterize this source from an anthroposophical point of view on the basis of Rudolf Steiner's spiritual-scientific research. Thus Rudolf Steiner characterized the inner nature of the Theosophical Society—which had been founded in New York in 1875—in a letter to the French writer and theosophist, Edouard Schuré.*

It is clear from this manuscript that Helena Blavatsky had originally been inspired by 'the great initiates of the West, who were also the initiators of Rosicrucian wisdom'. Her first substantial book, *Isis Unveiled*, was written out of this source of inspiration; and the Theosophical Society, 'which bears a Western [that is to say, Rosicrucian] character' and which initially had as its chief purpose the service of the highest ideals of humanity, was also founded in the spirit of Rosicrucianism.

However, because of her chaotic character, her lack of logical thinking and her inadequate control over her own considerable mediumistic faculties, Helena Blavatsky was only able, in the book referred to above, to give expression to Rosicrucian wisdom in a very incomplete, and in many respects even distorted, form.† That her conscious insight into this wisdom remained at a not very elevated level is, for example, evident from the fact that in *Isis Unveiled* there is no mention of reincarnation; for this truth was in the Rosicrucian mysteries accessible only at higher stages of inner development,[5] and these were beyond Blavatsky's reach.

When, shortly after the founding of the Theosophical Society, it became clear that high spiritual truths could only be communicated by Blavatsky in a distorted form, the Rosicrucian initiates ceased to inspire her and soon broke off all contact with her.

Nevertheless, Blavatsky's faculty for receiving higher inspirations—albeit in a mediumistic way—did not forsake her. The gates of her soul were now wide open and 'Eastern initiators were able to take hold of her'. 'Under the influence of this stream', the Theosophical Society took on its Eastern character, and Sinnett's *Esoteric Buddhism* and Blavatsky's *Secret Doctrine* were inspired by this same influence.

There were at least three reasons why, despite Blavatsky's estrangement from the sources of the Christian esotericism which belongs to all mankind, Rudolf Steiner was—especially in his early lectures—able to speak positively about the founder of the Theosophical Society. For in the first place much that Blavatsky imparted also in her later writings stemmed from her own occult experiences (for although her supersensible faculties

---

* Its complete text is reproduced in Appendix 5.

† In the lecture of 27 September 1911 (GA 130, *Esoteric Christianity and the Mission of Christian Rosenkreutz*), Rudolf Steiner spoke of how in addition to the Rosicrucian inspiration in *Isis Unveiled* there were also occult influences of quite a different kind which falsified the fundamentally Christian truths. Rudolf Steiner had previously expressed himself more fully about this in an esoteric lesson of 1 June 1907 (GA 264). These negative influences will be considered further below.

were of a mediumistic character, she was nevertheless able to perceive certain spiritual realities); and, in the second place, much of what is imparted in *The Secret Doctrine* regarding pre-Christian religions and the former conditions of the earth and humanity had objective philosophical value, on the grounds that it derived from the true mahatmas, the guardians of the ancient esoteric wisdom of the Asiatic East. Finally, considerable personal courage must have been necessary on Blavatsky's part to dare to speak publicly on occult themes at all in the second half of the nineteenth century, in the period when Euro-American materialism had reached its culmination, even if what she said was couched in a non-Christian form.

Gradually, however, the Eastern mahatmas began to distance themselves from the Theosophical Society (see Appendix 5), which had the consequence that the spiritual space that had become free was taken over by altogether different occult powers.

But when 'the ice was broken' from the Eastern side, Western—Christian—living occultism, 'which has been faithfully guarded in the Rosicrucian mysteries' was able to speak forth through Rudolf Steiner with full force.

'There is no such thing as an Eastern wisdom which is unknown to Western occultism, and in Rosicrucian teaching and research you will find to the last jot everything that has at one time or another been assimilated by the great sages of the East. Nothing of what it is possible to know from Eastern wisdom is lacking in the wisdom of the West ... It is simply that it [Western occultism] *had to renew all things through the rejuvenating spring of the Christ impulse.*'[6]

In the lectures that he gave in Dornach in October 1915 published under the title *The Occult Movement in the Nineteenth Century* (GA 254), Rudolf Steiner described—and this was after his separation from the Theosophical Society—the process of Blavatsky's coming under the influence of Eastern initiates. It follows from this description that, in addition to the true Eastern teachers (the real mahatmas), altogether different Eastern occultists with an open leaning to the left-oriented path and hence pursuing their own group-egoistic and therefore dubious occult-political aims were beginning to inspire Blavatsky more and more strongly.

According to Rudolf Steiner's description, Blavatsky came under their influence in the following way.

Because of her remarkable mediumistic faculties, soon after her appearance on the international scene she was admitted into a whole series of secret societies (brotherhoods) of Europe and North America. These brotherhoods tried above all to make use of her as a medium for the attainment of their group-egotistical and even political aims.

However, she gradually realized what a confused situation she was getting herself into, and she decisively refused to be a mere tool for alien purposes with which, as far as she was able to understand, she could not declare agreement. And since alongside her unusual mediumistic faculties she also possessed a strong and essentially honest character she eventually became altogether ungovernable by, and therefore highly dangerous to, the brotherhoods into whose many secrets she had been initiated. Because of the thoroughly confused and critical situation that had arisen, certain Western brotherhoods resolved upon the drastic remedy of subjecting Blavatsky to what in esoteric circles is called 'occult imprisonment'.

This essentially consists of the following. With the help of certain devices of ceremonial magic, the soul of the person concerned is surrounded on the astral plane by a supersensible sheath or aura, reflecting back all the impulses which the imprisoned soul wishes to send into the world. In other words, Blavatsky was inwardly placed in such a position that all her vast occult knowledge was thrust back into her soul by the spiritual sheath that had been formed around her. She was then rescued from this difficult situation by Eastern Indo-Tibetan occultists, by so-called mahatmas whose activity was, however, guided by specific group-egotistical interests rather than by those of a universally human dimension.* Henceforth Blavatsky became an obedient instrument in their hands, and subsequently the principal mediator between these Indo-Tibetan mahatmas and the leading members of the Theosophical Society: A.P. Sinnett, Colonel Olcott, C.W. Leadbeater, Annie Besant and others. This came symbolically to expression in that in 1879 the centre of the Theosophical Society was transferred from New York to India, to Madras, where Blavatsky herself now moved (she remained in India until 1886).

This situation was further complicated by the fact that, when they influenced Blavatsky and certain other leading members of the Theosophical Society, the left-oriented Eastern occultists referred to frequently used the names of the true Eastern teachers who inspired the early Blavatsky—the two so-called theosophical mahatmas.

Because of this all Eastern-oriented theosophical works derived essentially from this double source of inspiration, in that they originated partly from the true mahatmas and partly from the Eastern occultists of a left persuasion who also pretended to be mahatmas. Thus there appeared,

---

*See Appendix 1.

for example, Sinnett's *The Occult World*, which also contained a number of the mahatmas' letters to the author (1881); his *Esoteric Buddhism* (1883); and Blavatsky's *The Secret Doctrine* (1888). The chief quality of the latter two—the most authoritative books in theosophical circles—was their distinctive mixture of 'Indian esotericism' and 'modern materialistic science', a mixture which Rudolf Steiner, in the notes that he made for Schuré, called 'a barren hybrid'.

Thus the first component of this problematical mixture—Eastern wisdom—derived for the most part from the true Eastern mahatmas, whereas the transparently materialistic ideas contained in large measure in the books referred to—which were taken from the scientific theories of the nineteenth century—stemmed from the left-oriented occultists mentioned above.

As a result of this both works acquired a strongly materialistic timbre. Thus Rudolf Steiner says of Sinnett's *Esoteric Buddhism* that 'efforts were being made from a certain quarter to give an entirely materialistic form to [Eastern] spiritual teaching ... [In this book one finds] materialism in one of its very worst forms. The spiritual world is presented here in an entirely materialistic way ... The subject matter is, of course, very refined, but in Sinnett's book one cannot get away from materialism, however lofty the heights to which one may be led.'[7] Rudolf Steiner then goes on to speak about Blavatsky's principal work as follows: 'This [book], *The Secret Doctrine*, is written in the same style as *Esoteric Buddhism*.' And somewhat earlier in the same lecture he characterizes Blavatsky's situation in the following words: 'And so those who now were H.P. B[lavatsky]'s spiritual "proprietors"—forgive the materialistic analogy—not only had special aims connected with Indian interests but also made trenchant concessions to the materialistic spirit of the age.'[8]

A particular difficulty in distinguishing the true mahatmas from the left-oriented occultists who had for the time being taken their place was that the latter henceforth worked under the name of the former. However, Blavatsky and Sinnett were in no position whatever to recognize the deception, the first-named because of her natural naivety and trustful innocence and the second because he possessed no occult faculties.

As for the '*special* aims connected with Indian interests', which the Eastern brotherhood of occultists of a left persuasion pursued, they essentially consisted in that—in contrast to Blavatsky's first book, *Isis Unveiled*, where some esoteric truths about Judaism and Christianity are presented, albeit in a chaotic and distorted form—in *The Secret Doctrine* and in articles published at around the same time a distinctly anti-Jewish and anti-Christian sentiment appeared. Rudolf Steiner said in this connection: 'From this arose *The Secret Doctrine*, which with regard to everything that is not Christian contains great truths, but with regard to everything that is Christian contains nothing but utter nonsense.'[9] Moreover: 'The mystery of Sinai and Golgotha is not to be found in Madame Blavatsky, for she had a real antipathy towards it. Consequently, she was led towards such forces as were able—and with great power and clarity—to give what lay outside Christianity.'[10]* And so her 'special aims', in contrast to aims associated with humanity as a whole, lay in placing the national Eastern religions and their founders higher than the founder of Christianity, who is not only the leader of the *whole* of earthly humanity (and in an esoteric sense its higher Ego) but also the Spirit who gives life to and spiritualizes our entire solar system.[11]

We shall now mention some examples of Blavatsky's misunderstanding of the essence of Christianity. Thus by placing Lucifer above the biblical Jehovah in *The Secret Doctrine*, Blavatsky—under the influence of her Indo-Tibetan inspirers—distorted the true occult teaching about Jehovah, who, as one of the seven Sun Elohim, sacrificially left the sun for the moon in order to form out of the moon sphere a counterweight to the forces of Lucifer and at the same time to make ready for the preparation of the future incarnation of the Sun Logos, the Christ, on the earth.

Instead of this we read in *The Secret Doctrine*: 'The Devil is now called Darkness by the Church, whereas in the Bible, in the Book of Job, he is called the "Son of God", the bright star of the early morning, Lucifer. There is a whole philosophy of dogmatic craft in the reason why the first Archangel, who sprang from the depths of Chaos, was called Lux (Lucifer), the "Luminous Son of the Morning" or Manvantaric Dawn. He has been transformed by the Church into Lucifer or Satan, because he is higher and older than Jehovah, and had to be sacrificed to the new dogma.'[12]

Because of this erroneous understanding of the nature of Jehovah, Blavatsky was also unable to understand the prologue of St John's Gospel. Thus for her the light of the Logos is darkened by Lucifer as he approaches his incarnation and becomes darkness, whereupon the words of the Gospel that relate to the divine Word are interpreted by her as related to the darkness and she depicts them as follows: 'In him [in darkness] was life, and the life was the light of men.'[13]

---

*Rudolf Steiner said in addition: 'So it happened that Madame Blavatsky was increasingly compelled to experience a mist gathering around her [as regards the true knowledge of Christ] and was able clearly to see only what had been transmitted through so-called Aryan traditions ... outside the domain of Christianity' (8 May 1912, GA 143).

From this also stems her misunderstanding of the mystery that 'the Word became flesh', which is spoken of in the same Gospel. This is very clearly attested by an article of Blavatsky's with the title 'The Esoteric Character of the Gospels', which was published by her in the journal *Lucifer* which she founded at the end of the year 1887, that is, at the time when she was working on *The Secret Doctrine*. Blavatsky herself explained that in this article she 'praises Christ's preaching as God would grant any true Christian who hasn't been infected by Papism or by Protestant fantasizing'.[14] However, one may judge from the following what evoked this praise.

Blavatsky distinguishes between Chrestos and Christ. In her opinion the former name means 'lonely traveller', a pupil who is following a path of initiation;[15] whereas she characterizes the latter as follows: 'Christ—the true *esoteric SAVIOUR*—is no man, but the *DIVINE PRINCIPLE* in every human being.'[16] This name 'was never applied to any one man, but to every initiate at the moment of his second birth and resurrection'.[17] Or in other words, every Chrestos who has attained to higher initiation becomes a Christ, and this means that in the course of earthly evolution there are many such 'Christs', both before and also after the earthly life of Jesus Christ, who was therefore one of a whole series of similar initiates. The Christians have subsequently shifted all other initiates—Horus, Krishna, Buddha—artificially into the background only because they 'appeared to them as rivals of *their* Man-God'.[18] 'No wonder,' wrote Blavatsky, 'that the very meaning of the terms Chrestos and Christos, and the bearing of both on "Jesus of Nazareth" ... has now become a dead letter for all *with the exception of non-Christian Occultists*.'[19]

One can also find similar examples in *The Secret Doctrine*, such as for example: 'From Prometheus to Jesus, and from Him to the highest Adept as to the lowest disciple, every revealer of mysteries has had to become a Chrestos, a "man of sorrow" and a martyr.'[20] Or somewhat later: '... Was Jesus as "Son of God" and "Saviour" of Mankind, unique in the World's annals? ... Or was he only the "son of his deeds", a pre-eminently holy man, and a reformer, *one of many*, who paid with his life for the presumption of endeavouring, in the face of ignorance and despotic power, to enlighten mankind and make its burden lighter by his ethics and philosophy?' Only the latter alternative 'is suggested to everyone by reason and logic' (Blavatsky).[21]

However, that is only the first step in her considerations. If the historical Jesus was one among many initiates—adepts—who were there before him and will come after him, his own earthly life at the beginning of our Christian era has ultimately no particular significance. Thus

Blavatsky continues in the article referred to: 'To the true follower of the
SPIRIT OF TRUTH, it matters little, therefore, whether Jesus, as man
and Chrestos [that is, as a human being following a path of initiation],
lived during the era called Christian, or before, or never lived at all. The
Adepts, who lived and died for humanity, have existed in many and all the
ages, and many were the good and holy men in antiquity who bore the
surname or title of Chrestos before Jesus of Nazareth ... was born.'[22] It is
clear from these words that Blavatsky—at any rate when she was writing
The Secret Doctrine—did not have the slightest idea as to the central significance of the Mystery of Golgotha for the whole of earthly evolution.
Moreover, she believed that Christianity did not arise out of the earthly
life of the incarnated Logos and out of the fact that he passed through
death and Resurrection on Golgotha, as did all early Christians (see I
Corinthians 15:14, 17), but out of the old wisdom handed down from
pagan religions. 'The origin of all religions—Judaeo-Christianity
included—is to be found in a few primeval truths ... in the archaic
records of the Wisdom-religion.'[23] And then Blavatsky continues:
'Whence, then, the Gospels, the life of Jesus of Nazareth? Has it not been
repeatedly stated that no human, *mortal* [italics HPB] brain could have
invented the life of the Jewish Reformer, followed by the awful drama on
Calvary? We say, on the authority of the *esoteric Eastern* [italics SOP]
School, that all this came from the Gnostics, as far as the name Christos
and the astronomico-mystical allegories are concerned, and from the
writings of the ancient *Tanaïm*[*] as regards the Kabalistic connection of
Jesus or Joshua, with the Biblical personifications.'[24] In this quotation
there is a particular significance in Blavatsky's testimony that this and
similar views of Christianity and its founder derive from an *Eastern* esoteric school or, rather, from those of its representatives who were
Blavatsky's occult inspirers in the last period of her life.

Finally, we find in Blavatsky a yet further variation of her approach to
Jesus. Disparaging him as one of the (many) 'Christ' figures or an ordinary
Chrestos (a pupil of the Mysteries), and even altogether doubting his
earthly existence, she ends by identifying him with a completely different
individuality who lived at a different time: 'Thus Jesus, whether of
Nazareth or Lüd (Lydda) ...'[25]

In mentioning Lydda here Blavatsky is referring to the rabbinical
tradition about Jesus being the son of a man called Pandira and having
lived a century before the beginning of the events recorded in the Gos-

---

[*]Tanaïm, according to Blavatsky, was a Hebrew initiate, a predecessor of the old
cabbalists.

pels. In his youth he had lived for many years in Egypt, where he was initiated into occult Egyptian wisdom. When he returned to Palestine he reorganized the Essene order, in which he was active as a highly respected teacher until, under accusation by the Jews, he was stoned in his home town of Lydda on the eve of the Hebrew Passover and then nailed to the cross.

According to Rudolf Steiner's spiritual-scientific research,[26] Jeshu ben Pandira was actually not an incarnation of Christ but an incarnation of that high *human* individuality who in Eastern tradition is called the Maitreya Bodhisattva. Once the previous bodhisattva, Prince Gautama, had attained buddhahood, this individuality took over his place in the circle of the great masters and leaders of mankind. His task as Jeshu ben Pandira was to prepare the imminent coming of the Messiah, the incarnation of the Sun Logos on the earth, a century before the birth of Jesus of Nazareth. The Apostle Matthew, the author of the first of the four Gospels, was subsequently to emerge from the esoteric school that he founded.

Thus from the standpoint of Western esoteric tradition one is dealing here with two quite different individualities: Jeshu ben Pandira, the great reformer of the order of the Essenes, and Jesus of Nazareth, who was born later and received the divine Christ Being into himself at the Baptism in the Jordan.

For Blavatsky, however, these two altogether different Jesus individualities who were separated historically by a century gradually began to become one. Thus she explained quite decisively in an article from 1887: 'Jesus was a *Chrestos* ... who actually lived during the Christian era, or a century earlier ... in Lud [Lydda].'[27] And in a note to this quoted passage she expressed herself even more directly on this subject: 'I say that the scholars mention this, or they talk nonsense. *Our teachers* are the ones who confirm this. If the story of Jeshu or Jesu ben Pandira is an error, then the whole of the Talmud, the entire Hebrew canon, is an error. He was a follower of Jeshu ben Parashia, the fifth leader of the Sanhedrin after Ezra, who *rewrote* the Bible. Found guilty of participating in the uprising of the Pharisees against Jannaeus in the year 105 BC, he fled to Egypt and took the young Jesus with him. This story is much truer than the stories of the New Testament, of which history makes no mention.' And a year later in another article Blavatsky expressed her conviction in the following words: 'As I have shown on a number of occasions in my writings and notes, the [Christian] legend of which I am speaking is founded on a person called Jeshu (or Jesus), born in Lud or Lydda around the year 120 before the modern era.'[28]

According to Blavatsky, her occult inspirers therefore also infused in her the idea that Jeshu ben Pandira was the true, historical Jesus. From Blavatsky this wholly erroneous idea spread to Annie Besant and in time became an unshakeable matter of conviction in her soul. In her book *Esoteric Christianity or the Lesser Mysteries*—the greater mysteries were, according to Besant, not Christian but those of Egypt and Altar—she wrote about the birth of the Jesus of the Gospels, stating that it had taken place 'in 105 BC during the consulate of Publius Rutilius Rufus and Gnaeus Mallius Maximus';[29] and she went on to describe his life, which in her version is a mixture between two altogether different biographies, that of Jesus of Nazareth and that of Jeshu ben Pandira.

This had the consequence that Jesus Christ was from then on officially identified in occult contexts with the Maitreya Bodhisattva. But since according to Eastern tradition, and also confirmed by Rudolf Steiner's spiritual research, the bodhisattvas pass through many earthly lives—as do all other human beings—until they have reached buddhahood, the imminent incarnation of the 'Christ-Maitreya' as a world teacher was of course expected, not least within the Theosophical Society.[*]

And so we find already in Blavatsky's writings all the theoretical prerequisites for the familiar, sad episode with the Indian boy Krishnamurti. It needs merely to be added that the materialistic and antichristian tendencies, which began clearly to manifest themselves in the Theosophical Society shortly after its headquarters were transferred from America to Adyar in India and especially from the moment of the publication of the books of Sinnett and Blavatsky that have been referred to, were disseminated ever more widely in the years following Blavatsky's death. The culmination of this whole disastrous process was the attempt of Leadbeater and Besant from 1909 onwards to claim Krishnamurti as the new Messiah, as a reincarnation of Christ.

In the occult episode with Krishnamurti, in whose body—according to Leadbeater and Besant—the individuality of that 'world teacher' was to be incorporated, we have the grotesque fruit of a grave occult error, amounting to a complete misunderstanding of the Christ Being. However, the source of this materialistic, antichristian tendency in the theosophical movement can ultimately be traced back to that strictly enclosed group of Indo-Tibetan occultists of a left persuasion, as described above. Blavatsky and also Sinnett, on the other hand, were convinced that the source of their principal works—*The Secret Doctrine* and *Esoteric*

---

[*] Regarding 'the further incarnations which neither Buddhas nor Christs' can avoid, see *The Secret Doctrine*.

Buddhism—lay in the inspirations solely of the true Eastern mahatmas and, in particular, those two who in theosophical circles were known under the names of M.M. (Mahatma Morya) and M.K.H. (Mahatma Kut Humi). The former inspired the aforesaid book by Blavatsky, while the latter, through his correspondence with Sinnett, laid the foundation for his (Sinnett's) books. Portraits of both mahatmas—the higher patrons of the Theosophical Society—always hung at the premises of the Esoteric School founded by Blavatsky in the year of her publication of *The Secret Doctrine* (1888) and called by her the 'Eastern' school.

Thus already in *The Secret Doctrine* and *Esoteric Buddhism* there were actually two quite different inspirations coming to expression: the inspirations of the true mahatmas, which were receding ever more into the background, and the increasingly stronger inspirations of the occultists of a left persuasion, who were also called mahatmas.

It was with the latter, highly problematical source of inspiration that Nicholas and Helena Roerich linked themselves at the beginning of the twentieth century.

Notes

1. Decter, p. 107.
2. HPB I, p. 31 (quotations from *The Secret Doctrine* are taken from the Adyar Edition, Theosophical Publishing House, Adyar, Madras, India, fourth edition 1938—Translator).
3. 'Herald of the Society of Friends of H.P. Blavatsky', second edition, Moscow 1992, p. 37.
4. See the journal *Science and Religion*, 1991, no. 9.
5. See the lecture of 6 October 1911 (GA 131).
6. Lecture of 12 April 1909 (1) (GA 110).
7. Lecture of 11 October 1915 (GA 254).
8. Ibid.
9. Lecture of 23 October 1911 (GA 133).
10. Lecture of 8 May 1912 (GA 143).
11. See GA 15, chapter 3.
12. HPB I, p. 138.
13. Ibid.
14. Vera Petrovna von Hahn de Zhelikhovsky, *Radda-Bai—Biograficheski Ocherk* ('H.P. Blavatsky, A Biographical Sketch'), 1893.
15. 'The Esoteric Character of the Gospels' (EC), p. 18.
16. EC, p. 4.
17. EC, p. 13.
18. EC, p. 28–9.
19. EC, p. 37.
20. HPB 5, p. 105.

21. HPB 5, p. 155.
22. EC, p. 28.
23. EC, p. 32.
24. EC, p. 33.
25. EC, p. 17.
26. See GA 123.
27. *Le Lotus*, December 1887. [*Le Lotus* was published in Paris. The original pub-
    lication would have been in French.—Translator's note.]
28. *Le Lotus*, April 1888.
29. Annie Besant, *Esoteric Christianity or the Lesser Mysteries*, p. 96.

2. The Inspirers of Agni Yoga

From the time when they first became acquainted with the theosophical movement and above all with the works of Blavatsky and Sinnett, it was the chief aim of the Roerichs to enter into direct connection with its Eastern inspirers. This contact was indeed soon established.

Helena Roerich subsequently asserted that both the theosophical mahatmas appeared to her several times, not only in early childhood but also in a vision. However, only after the physical meeting with an Eastern mahatma (on 24 March 1920 in London), whom she did not hesitate to pronounce as being the theosophical Mahatma Morya, did she—in accordance with his telepathic dictation—begin to write down the teaching which soon received the name of 'Agni Yoga'.

Although Helena Roerich was subjectively convinced that she had a personal connection with the true theosophical mahatmas, she had in point of fact succumbed to the same fatal error as did Blavatsky in the latter part of her life, in that she considered the left-oriented occultists who had illicitly usurped their names to be the real mahatmas. The reason for this error can—as in Blavatsky's case—be ascribed especially to the purely mediumistic nature of Helena Roerich's faculties, which did indeed enable her to receive much information from the spiritual worlds but were not capable of distinguishing its sources, and also to the complete dependence of the pupil upon the teacher in the system of Agni Yoga. It will, moreover, be shown later on that the very intellectual content of Helena Roerich's teaching makes it perfectly clear that its source lay not in the true Eastern mahatmas but in the occultists of a left persuasion referred to by Rudolf Steiner.

When seen in this way, it transpires that Helena Roerich—in that she was constantly citing Blavatsky and seeing herself as her principal successor as regards her work—was actually a perpetuator of her errors and was ultimately no more than an obedient instrument in the hands of the aforesaid left-oriented occultists.

Only after these remarks can we now turn to what Helena Roerich wrote.

'It may be asked,' writes Helena Roerich in the eighth volume of *Agni Yoga* in accordance with the guidance of the mahatma who is dictating to her, 'what is the relationship of Our Teaching to that [teaching] given to

Us through Blavatsky? Shall we say that in every century there ensues, after a full exposition, a final culmination ... Thus Our Teaching includes [within itself] the *Secret Doctrine* of Blavatsky.'[1]

And in one of her letters Helena Roerich remarks in accordance with this indication: 'Now the Ocean of the Teaching of "Living Ethics" is being given, and whoever has studied it will be equipped for the further path ...'[2] For just as the ocean encompasses all seas and rivers and receives them into its bosom, so—in Helena Roerich's view—does the teaching of Agni Yoga embrace not only *The Secret Doctrine* but all Eastern teachings: 'Agni Yoga ... is the synthesis of all yogas.'[3]

Helena Roerich always wrote about Blavatsky full of praise, emphasizing in every conceivable way her own connection with her: 'I tell you, H.P. Blavatsky was a fiery messenger of the White Brotherhood,' she writes in one of her letters, 'she was in a quite particular way a bearer of the knowledge entrusted to it. Of all theosophists only H.P. Blavatsky had the good fortune to receive the teaching directly from the Great Teachers in one of Their Ashrams in Tibet ... Only through H.P. Blavatsky was it possible to approach the White Brotherhood, for she was a link in the hierarchic Chain ... For the good of the cause, the Mahatmas corresponded with some of her colleagues [for example, with Sinnett], but none [save Blavatsky] did they admit to pupilship ... H.P. Blavatsky was the hierarchic link whom to avoid or disregard would have signified total failure.'[4] And in another letter Helena Roerich described how Blavatsky after her three years in the ashram with the mahatmas 'was sent' by them 'into the world to give the great work *The Secret Doctrine* in order to bring about a change in the consciousness of a humanity that has arrived at an impasse'.[5]

In connection with Blavatsky, Helena Roerich referred very frequently also to her own alleged association with one of her (Blavatsky's) teachers, Mahatma Morya. 'I know that Mahatma M[orya] was not satisfied with all the biographies about Bl[avatsky].'[6] Or: 'In [19]25, it was indicated to N[icholas] K[onstantinovich Roerich] that he should paint the picture 'The Messenger' [*Vestnik*] and donate it for the founding of the Bl[avatsky] Museum. Through this gift and the founding of the museum the Gr[eat] Teacher M[orya] wished to perpetuate the name of her whose memory some of her successors have recently been trying to suppress.'[7] And in another letter she speaks even more openly about the occult source of her writings: 'Anyone who asks what relationship the G[reat] T[eacher] K[ut] H[umi] has to the teaching of "Living Ethics" evidently has no idea what the W[hite] Brotherhood is. Is it really possible that the one Brother [Kut Humi] would reject the teaching given by *the other Brother* [Mahatma Morya]?'[8*]

However, the clearest indication of the source of Helena Roerich's inspiration is the title of the first two volumes of *Agni Yoga*, published in Paris in 1924–5. They were both called 'Leaves of Morya's Garden', the first book being subtitled *Zov* ('The Call') and the second *Ozaryenie* ('Illumination'). They take the form of a day by day occult diary, in which Helena Roerich has written down what has been imparted to her by her teacher. The first entry is given as 'London, 24 March 1920'.[†] It begins with the words:

I am your well-being.
I am your smile.
I am your joy.
I am your peace.
I am your strength.
I am your bravery.
I am your knowledge.
Guard the precious stone, in its unique perfection, by holiness in life.[‡]
    Aum Tat Sat, Aum.[9]

The whole book is pervaded, as a leitmotiv, by the allegory of an esoteric garden of Eastern wisdom, whose guardian is the teacher guiding Helena Roerich; and the individual utterances are likened to the leaves and flowers that have been gathered in it and which the pupil is instructed to share with other human beings.[§] All in all, the content of the two

---

[*] In Helena Roerich's notes of the seances of her telepathic communication with Mahatma M. one may find the words: 'May Mara [H. Roerich] write and exert her spiritual hearing.' 'Mara, hear Our Singing, it exists.' 'May Mara know that I have endowed her with the capacity to hear the singing of the spheres' (*Serdtse*—'Heart'— 1993, no. 3, pp. 16–17). 'All the books of the Teaching [of Agni Yoga] bear witness to this direct contact,' states Helena Roerich in one of her letters. 'How could the experience of Agni Yoga be arrived at without direct contact with the Gr[eat] T[eacher]? All the books, after all, were and are given by the Great Teacher on the basis of this experience [of clairaudience]' (HR 2, 7 December 1935).

[†] According to H.P. Blavatsky her first meeting with Mahatma Morya in the physical body also took place in London.

[‡] Here for the first time there appears the theme of the stone, which was subsequently to be so important for Nicholas and Helena Roerich (see chapter 8).

[§] *Tsvety Morii* ('Flowers of Morya')—this is also the title of a volume of poetry by Nicholas Roerich, which appeared in 1921 in Berlin. It contains poems written between 1911 and 1921. The volume consists of four parts, in which the path that a person takes from the first steps of pupilship to the teacher, the guru, is described in poetic, allegorical form. It is, however, not clear whether Nicholas Roerich himself regarded his poems as being inspired by the Mahatma Morya or whether they were dedicated to him after the meeting in London.

volumes may be regarded more as second-rate poetry than true occult literature.

It is interesting that a mysterious name is constantly repeated in the book: it is denoted by the letter 'M ...' (with three dots). As the title of the book is *Listy sada Morii* ('Leaves of Morya's Garden'), the reader is bound to gain the impression that this is who is being spoken of.

This is seemingly further confirmed by the words at the beginning of the second volume of 'Leaves of Morya's Garden', 'Illumination': 'People will ask: who gave you this Teaching? Your answer should be: the Mahatma of the East,'[10] that is, Morya. However, it subsequently emerges that this is another individuality, in whose name and upon whose instruction Helena Roerich's teacher turns to her. The impression arises that this mysterious M ... of whom her occult leader repeatedly speaks can only be the highest lord of the Tibetan brotherhood of the mahatmas, and that is—according to the teaching of Agni Yoga—the Maitreya. Ultimately, however, the reader is unable to arrive at any real clarity with regard to the question as to whether Morya and the Maitreya are two different individualities for Helena Roerich or one and the same person. This had the consequence that many pupils of Helena Roerich came to the latter conclusion. Thus, for example, A. Ter-Akopyan writes in the notes to the anthology *Mozaika Agni Yogi* ('A Mosaic of Agni Yoga'), of which she was the editor: 'M ...—"Maitreya", he is Morya.'[11] G. Gorchakov also considers Mahatma Morya to be one of the earthly incarnations of the Maitreya.[12] And A. Klizovsky, a personal pupil of Helena Roerich, uses in his three-volume work ('The Basis for an Understanding of the New Epoch')[*]—which she fully recognized—quite simply the designation 'the Lord Maitreya-Morya' and calls him the source of all 'higher knowledge' contained in the books of *Agni Yoga*.[13][†]

Some concrete examples shall now be cited.

'Give repose to your spirit,' dictates Helena Roerich's occult leader to her, 'do not weary yourself with books, and love will pour forth in a radiant stream, revealing the wonders of the flowers of M ...' 'The

---

[*] See Bibliography, p. 182.

[†] On the basis of the published material it is difficult to draw an unambiguous conclusion as to whether Helena Roerich considered Morya and the Maitreya to be one individuality. It would appear that there was a certain development in this respect, and that in later years she equated the two, as can be seen for example from the following note: 'The Teacher initially appeared as a Hindu, but when the consciousness of the pupil expanded and learnt to encompass what was imparted, the Beautiful Countenance began gradually to change and finally took on the Sublime Countenance of Cosmic Meaning—the Lord of Wisdom and Beauty, the Lord of Holy Shamballa [the Maitreya]' (UPNM, p. 54).

flowers of M ... do not prosper in many gardens, but they even blossom in ice-floes,'[14] and so on.

Sometimes the 'dictation' takes more direct forms, as when the pronouns and adjectives 'Me' and 'My'—representing the dictating teacher—are written with a capital.

'My lotus is the joy of the visitors to My garden.' 'The fruits and flowers of My garden are accessible to all, be guardians of My garden.' 'But I shall augment the powers of My daughter, for she waits in My garden.' ('My daughter' here means Helena Roerich.)[15]

At times the 'dictation' acquires an openly authoritative form: 'I, I, I read your thoughts every day. The teacher verifies the creative work of his favourite pupils.' Or: 'My smile follows after you, My friends.'[16] And then the same teacher appears almost like a cosmic force:

> In the whispering of leaves,
> In the lapping of waves,
> In the wafting of the wind,
> I am with you.

Or:

> I am the burning heat of the sand,
> I am the flame of the heart,
> I am the all-consuming wave,
> I am the new-born earth.

And then:

> I am a valiant shield,
> I teach you My wisdom.
> I am not one who promises a bridge but who summons the light!
> I teach love.[17]

In some of these pronouncements the 'dictating teacher' is revealed as a member of the mysterious 'White Brotherhood' that lies hidden in inaccessible valleys of the Himalayas: 'Children, dear children, do not think that Our Brotherhood is hidden from humanity by impenetrable walls. The snows of the Himalaya which conceal Us do not hinder those who seek in truth.' Or: 'I taught you a happy knowledge, which thaws out the teaching of Tibet.' 'Exhaling fragrance from the mountains of Tibet, We bring to humanity tidings of the new religion of the Pure Spirit.'[18]

The mysterious 'M ...' also belongs to this brotherhood, and evidently occupies a central position in it. 'M ... has many watchtowers on the slopes of the Himalayas,' Helena Roerich's inspirer tells her; and he continues: 'M ... teaches you to entreat the pure Brothers that the stages of the mountain path may appear to you.' And then in the form of a command: 'Keep the others true to the ideas of M ...' 'Happiness comes to you through the shield of M ...' 'Be an Aeolian harp for the wafting of M ...' 'Study the manifestations of M ...' 'The mountains are clear, M ... is with you always.' 'Be bolder, be pupils of M ...' 'Follow the teaching of M ...' 'M ... protects.' 'If you believe Me,' continues the inspirer, 'know that you are surrounded by the care and protection of M ...' 'M ... is your smile, your well-being, your stronghold and knowledge.'[19] And so on. In these and many other pronouncements in the collection, dependence on the teacher as upon a higher divine power becomes truly absolute.

The mysterious significance of the subtitle of the first book, 'The Call', also becomes evident in the relevant statements. 'Do not tarry—M ... calls.' 'Gird up your strength and open up the path to Me.' Or:

In the forest seek My pointers,
In the mountains listen to My call,
In the murmuring of the stream attend to My whispering.

The teacher is always at your door,
But leave your doors open,
Await him and he will answer your call.[20]

The teacher now becomes everything for the pupil, even a father: 'Enter into life in My name and you will conquer the darkness,[*] for I am your protector, Friend, and Father.' 'I shall set you at My Gates and you will speak in My name. My Word will be with you.'[21]

And in the second book, 'Illumination', we find:

When a raindrop beats against the window—
This is My sign!
When a bird chirps—
This is My sign!
When leaves whirl like the wind—
This is My sign!
When the Sun melts the ice—
This is My sign!

---

[*] These words sound particularly disturbing if they are compared with the following words of Christ: 'I have come in the Name of my Father, and you do not receive me; but if someone else comes in his own name, him you will receive' (John 5:43).

When waves wash away the sorrows of the soul—
This is My sign!
When the wing of illumination touches the confused soul—
This is My sign!
Count the steps when you go to the Temple,
For every seventh step bears My sign!...
In the morning hours you labour,
In the evening rejoice in My name.
The new path!
My ray is your breath.
My hand—your banner.
My shield—your pride.
My house—your refuge.
My mountain—your wonder.
My wish—your law.
My manifestation—your happiness.
May the spirit of Our Brotherhood abide with you,'[22] and so forth.[*]

But not only does the problem of distinguishing between Morya and the Maitreya make these texts difficult to understand; there is also a second problem associated with it. For her total devotion to the teacher permeates Helena Roerich's teaching to the point that it is ultimately never possible to say with certainty whether she is speaking out of herself or whether the all-present mahatma or even the Maitreya himself has again begun to dictate. This ambiguity has, however, the quite concrete aim of endowing *every* word of Helena Roerich's with an indisputable authority which can ultimately be traced back to the 'Lord' of our planet. Extracts from 'Agni Yoga' books, frequently without reference to their origin, are constantly included by both the Roerichs in their letters and articles, so that the impression arises that at times they do not distinguish their own thoughts and words in any way from the thoughts and words imparted or dictated to them by the mahatmas. But is this actually possible in the case of telepathic, mediumistic communication? For in this

---

[*] Nicholas Roerich's article 'He' represents a particularly clear example of such an absolute, almost cosmic authority of the spirit-teacher on the Eastern path, which Agni Yoga also followed: 'The presence, the great presence fills nature. What makes the grass blades sway, why do the branches of the tree tremble, whence comes the crackling of fallen brushwood, why does sand break loose from the mountain, why and whither does the dog watch with intensity: He is going forth. He is approaching' and so on (N.K. Roerich, 'On', *Obitel' svyeta*, Moscow, the International Roerich Centre, 1992, p. 43). Similarly in the anthology 'Flowers of Morya' the teacher is called none other than Lord, Great, Mighty, All-Powerful.

impossibility of making a distinction lies the principle not so much of the occult but of simple suggestion.

We shall now again turn to that highest authority whence, in her own view, Helena Roerich received her knowledge—the Himalayan mahatmas. According to the teachings of Agni Yoga these mahatmas, who are members of the White Brotherhood, inhabit the mysterious land of Shamballa, whence—under the leadership of the Great Lord of Shamballa, the Maitreya—they guide the whole of earthly evolution. For the most part they appear in the dictated material as 'We'. Thus Shamballa is referred to by the dictating agent as 'Our place, Our towers, Our valley, Our mountains, Our stronghold', and so forth. And in the second volume of *Agni Yoga*, 'Illumination', it is described as follows: 'Shamballa is the place where the spiritual world is united with the material. Just as in a magnet there is a point with the greatest power of attraction, so are the gates of the spiritual world open to the Inhabitant of the Mountains.'[23]

Moreover, in for example the second volume of *Agni Yoga* there is much information about the inhabitants of Shamballa, including its buildings and the incredible technical achievements that exist there, and so on. Helena Roerich also reports about this land in her occult diaries in quite particular detail. Nicholas Roerich, too, speaks about the earthly Shamballa hidden somewhere in the depths of the Himalayas, about the mahatmas who live there and its emissaries who work throughout the world, in his works, above all in his article 'Radiant Shamballa' (this article comes at the beginning of his book *Shamballa*, which appeared in English—in America—in the year 1930) and also in the second part of his book *Heart of Asia* (*Serdtse Asii*), 1929, also called *Shamballa*.

In all these writings there is a description of the various kinds of help which the mahatmas of the Himalayan community and its numerous emissaries constantly make available to the rest of humanity in every continent. The influences can be psychic or completely material in nature. Meetings may come about, letters sent or large sums of money— but always from unknown sources. Mysterious unknown figures enter into conversation and give advice to politicians, artists and inventors. Sometimes the mahatmas appear to people physically, and sometimes—to more advanced pupils—in a more refined (astral) body. Finally, only the most advanced are found worthy to enter earthly Shamballa while still in a physical body.

The Roerichs were convinced that they had personally passed through all three stages of the approach to the mahatmas and to Shamballa. 'We met the teachers in their physical and their more refined bodies.'[24] And Nicholas Roerich, on being asked directly by one of his pupils, A.P.

Kheidok, after the latter had read his book 'Heart of Asia': 'Does such a place as Shamballa exist and are there really such Great Teachers? And have you actually been there?,' replied: 'Yes, I have been there.'[25]*

But who in Helena Roerich's view were these all-powerful mahatmas, these Great Teachers? Helena Roerich wrote about this question in one of her letters: 'Never lose sight of the fact that the Mahatma Brotherhood consists of those seven Sublime Spirits who came from the higher planets at the end of the third race [the Lemurian] to hasten the evolution of our humanity. Their spiritual power and their greatness are beyond comparison with any recognized human geniuses . . .'[26]

This assertion by the founder of Agni Yoga is, however, in complete contradiction not only with *true* Eastern tradition, according to which not only the mahatmas but even bodhisattvas and buddhas are highly developed human beings, but even also with her own book, *Osnovy buddizma* ('The Foundations of Buddhism'), where clear reference is made to the *human* nature of Gautama Buddha: 'The great Gautama gave the world the perfected teaching of life. Any attempt to make a god out of the great evolutionary will lead to nonsense.'[27]

The real reason why Helena Roerich exalted so highly the mahatmas who dictated the teaching of Agni Yoga to her was actually very simple, for as their *sole* chosen representative she was herself a participant in their 'incomparable greatness'.[†]

In this context, the last, fourteenth and most extensive volume (over five hundred pages long) of *Agni Yoga*—which remained unfinished and was therefore published only after Helena Roerich's death—is particularly characteristic. It bears the title 'The Superearthly' and consists of two parts which encompass 945 paragraphs, each of which is prefaced by the mahatma—together with a whole choir of mahatmas—who was dictating

---

* This can be compared with a similar episode involving Yuri Roerich: 'Once when Yuri Nikolaevich was leaving the exhibition hall, a lady came up to him and asked: "Have you seen the Teachers? Does Shamballa exist?" After a short silence Yuri Nikolaevich replied, looking her steadily in the eye: "Yes, I have been there" ' (Richard Rudzitis, *Zhizni Yu. N. Roericha—put' truda na obshcheye blago*—The Life of Yuri Roerich, a path of labouring for the general good,' p. 70).

† Helena Roerich's initiation either through the mahatma or even through the 'Lord of Shamballa' himself is reported at the end of the fourth volume of *Agni Yoga*: 'Given in the Brahmaputra valley, which has its source in the lake of the Great Nagas, where the covenants of the Rig Veda are guarded. "I laid the foundation of Agni Yoga on four ends like the pistil of a flower. I confirmed Agni Yoga with the pillars of my steps and received the Stone of Fire into my hands. I gave the stone to her who in accordance with Our resolve will be called the Mother of Agni Yoga" [henceforth the occult name of Helena Roerich]' (AY 4, p. 321). See further regarding the magic stone in chapter 8.

to her with a direct address to her personally and with a reference to her profound knowledge and highly developed faculties. Moreover, Helena Roerich is throughout called not by her ordinary name but by another, the Indian name 'Urusvati' (which, when translated out of the Sanscrit, means 'Light of the morning star' or 'Light of Venus'). After each such address there follows an explanatory commentary. We shall cite some examples of these addresses: '1: Urusvati knows the tower Chung [the tower in the Himalayan stronghold where the mahatmas' laboratory is situated]; 4: Urusvati knows how difficult it is to transmit thoughts over a distance; 5: Urusvati has seen Us both in the flesh and in a more refined form; 6: Urusvati can testify to the healing vibrations that are sent forth by Us; 7: Urusvati knows Our voices, both the silent and those that sound; 9: Urusvati has been in Our laboratory; 10: Urusvati knows Our language; 13: Urusvati can speak the Names of the Members of the Brotherhood...; 25: Urusvati has done much to explain why we are called the World Rulership; 31: Urusvati rightly understands the reason for the longevity of Our Manifestations; 48: Urusvati is in constant intercourse with Us;' and so on.[28] There is no doubt that this thousandfold repetition of what is essentially the same formula, by means of which the unknown mahatma (mahatmas)—as a voice behind the scenes—affirms the authority of Helena Roerich and the truth of all her communications, is in itself bound to have a powerful suggestive effect upon the reader.

And this is indeed what happened. For on account of the last volume of *Agni Yoga* many of Helena Roerich's pupils elevated her to the rank of a 'God-man', to a 'vessel of the World Mother' (a feminine hypostasis of the Logos according to the teaching of Agni Yoga), a 'daughter of the great Ruler who stands at the head of the Hierarchy of our planet' (that is, the Maitreya) and so on. In any case G. Gorchakov characterizes Helena Roerich with such words, referring to the last book of *Agni Yoga* and to certain of her as yet unpublished writings.[29] And L. Shaposhnikova, in her foreword to the anthology of Helena Roerich's writings 'At the Threshold of the New World', calls her quite simply 'the Great Cosmic Being' on whom depends 'the destiny of the Cosmic Evolution of the planet Earth'.[30]* Such a title was, surely, not even fitting for the mahatmas themselves. Indeed, Helena Roerich describes herself in this

---

*L. Shaposhnikova is here insistently comparing Helena Roerich's 'sacrifice' with the earthly life of Christ. A similar, direct comparison can also be found in another of her pupils, A.P. Kheidok. See A.P. Kheidok, 'Podvig materi Agni Yogi' (The Heroic Deed of the Mother of Agni Yoga), *Mater Agni Yogi. Materialy Konferentsü, posvyashchyonnoi 110-lyetu so dnya rozhdyeniya E.I. Roerich* ('Materials relating to the Conference in honour of the 110th Birthday of Helena Roerich'), Novosibirsk, 1989, pp. 8–13.

connection not with any particular modesty when she, as it were, quotes the Maitreya himself in one of her letters to America,[31] who lets it be known: 'As already said, Ur[usvati] is my representative.' And in another letter, written a year before her death and containing fragments of the teaching that were not included in the last volume of 'Agni Yoga', she cites inhabitants of the Himalayan fastness confirming: 'And out of the cosmic spaces we hear a choir of spiritual voices calling: "Mother of Agni Yoga!" in order then to declare: "You are our Mother and Daughter."'[32]

Notes

1. AY 8.
2. HR 2, 31 July 1937.
3. HR 3, 17 January 1934.
4. HR 1, 8 September 1934.
5. HR 1, 15 November 1934.
6. HR 2, 23 October 1936.
7. HR 2, 22 June 1936.
8. HR 2, 31 July 1937.
9. AY 1.
10. AY 2.
11. *Mozaika Agni Yogi*, Vol. 1, Tbilisi 1990 p. 5.
12. See G.S. Gorchakov, *Vyeliky Uchitel'. Zemniye zhizni Naivysshevo*, Tomsk 1994.
13. A.I. Klizovsky, *Osnovy miroponimaniya novoi epokhi*, Vol. 2, Riga 1990, p. 266.
14. AY 1, 18 July 1921 and 25 December 1921.
15. AY 1, 17 July 1922, 18 July 1922 and 4 April 1923.
16. AY 1, 3 April 1923 and 7 July 1921.
17. Ay 1, 13 April 1922, 27 May 1921 and 29 May–2 June 1921.
18. AY 1, 17 July 1922, 18 July 1921 and 2 July 1921.
19. AY 1, 2 December 1921, 23 January 1922, 23 July 1921, 17 August 1921, 20 August 1921, 31 October 1921, 31 August 1921, 30 January 1922, 30 March 1922 and 12 October 1921.
20. AY 1, 18 January 1922, 21 July 1922, 17 July 1922.
21. AY 1, 17 July 1922, 18 July 1922.
22. AY 2, Part 1, 1X 2–5.
23. AY 2.
24. AY 3, 12 July 1938.
25. A.P. Kheidok, 'Vstryecha s Uchitelem' (Meeting with the Teacher), *Rerikhovski Vestnik* ('Roerich Herald'), 1990, no. 3, p. 69.
26. HR 1, 21 May 1935.
27. *Osnovy buddizma* ('The Foundations of Buddhism'), p. 3.
28. AY 14, I: 4–7, 9, 10, 13, 25, 31 and 48.
29. G. Gorchakov, 'Pod zvezdoyu Materi Mira' (Under the Star of the World Mother), *Znamya Mira* ('The Banner of Peace'), 1993 nos. 3–4 (6–7).

30. L. Shaposhnikova, 'Ognyonnoye tvorchestvo Kosmicheskoi Evolyutsii' (The Fiery Creation of Cosmic Evolution), UPNM pp. 20, 13.

31. RA (Helena Roerich's Letters to America) I, p. 150, 12 April 1934.

32. RA III, p. 450, 15 September 1954.

3. The Asiatic Journey of the Roerichs. Conversations with the Mahatmas

The occult significance of the Roerichs' lengthy journey through Mongolia, Tibet and the Himalayas (1925–8) may be better understood if what has been said in the previous chapter is taken into account. The notes which Nicholas Roerich made during the journey and which he subsequently, in 1929, published in English under the title *Heart of Asia* are full of examples and stories of various people's meetings with the mahatmas. Summing up these stories, he writes: 'If you cross this remarkable Tibetan plateau with its magnetic waves and extraordinary optical phenomena,[*] if you hear testimonies of these things and witness them for yourself, you know about the mahatmas. I have no intention of trying to convince anyone of the existence of the mahatmas. Many people have seen them, conversed with them and received letters and material objects from them.'[1] And although the Roerichs only rarely mention their own meetings with the Himalayan mahatmas (in accordance with the strict direction 'not only not to give information about the teachers' whereabouts but even to speak about it'),[2] nevertheless—as will be apparent from what follows—they had a number of contacts with them.

Several conversations with the mahatmas were subsequently published in the third volume of *Agni Yoga*. This book, which bears the title *Obshchina* ('Community'), has the subtitle: *Listy besyed vysokovo obshchinnika vostoka* ('Leaves of Conversations of the High Member of the Community of the East'). It represents a direct continuation of the first two books of *Agni Yoga*, 'The Call' and 'Illumination'. Their common title is 'Leaves of Morya's Garden'. The authorship of the one and the same mahatma standing behind all three books is also confirmed at the beginning of the ensuing fourth volume, 'Signs of Agni Yoga'. There we read: 'The revered mahatma who gave the books "The Call", "Illumination" and "Community" transmitted many pieces of advice and signs of Agni Yoga. These practical indications have been collected by us for the use of those seeking knowledge.'[3] And in 'Community' the relationship between the first three books is expressed as follows: 'The book "The

---

[*] This is a reference to phenomena such as 'UFOs', the Unidentified Flying Objects which the Roerichs on more than one occasion observed and described during their journeys to the Himalayas. More will be said later about their occult origin.

Call" knew no obstacles. The book "Illumination" is like a stone. The book "Community" is like sailing before a storm, when every sail and every rope holds a life.'[4] Thus there is no doubt about the *occult* authorship of 'Community'.

Here too—as in the first two volumes—the style is couched in the form of direct dictation from one or several Eastern teachers: 'Your books are in our libraries,' they tell Helena Roerich; 'do you also have ours? ... Have you read them? ... Greetings [from] the Society of the East!'[5] The notes of the Roerichs' conversations with the mahatmas contained in this volume are at times written in very strange Russian—'with an Eastern accent', as A. Ter-Apokyan observes in her foreword, and then she continues: 'Helena Ivanovna [Roerich] is a very fine stylist, but here she wrote as she heard, with all the mistakes, repetitions ... [and] lack of articulation.'[6]

What, then, did Helena Roerich learn from her inspirers, the Eastern teachers, the inhabitants of earthly Shamballa in the ravines of the Himalayas? Here something most unexpected awaits the reader. In 'Community' we read: 'One may ask: "What characteristics do teachers value?" You know the qualities of action and are able to recognize new approaches to action. Preference should be given to that Teacher who followed new paths. In this respect the people of the Northern Land [Russia] have an excellent example—their Teacher Lenin [when referring to Lenin Helena Roerich everywhere without exception uses a capital for the word 'Teacher'] knew the value of new paths. Every word of his preaching, each of his actions, bore the stamp of unforgettable novelty. This difference from other men elicited a compelling power. He was no imitator, no interpreter, but a mighty moulder of new ore. The summons to innovation should be taken as a foundation.'[7] And then the Eastern mahatmas continue: 'The solidity of his fearless thought forged for Lenin an aureole from both left and right. His firm thinking did not desert him even in illness. His consciousness became concentrated as though in a cave, and instead of discontent and complaint he made remarkable use of his last days. He sent many silent emanations of will for the strengthening of the cause. His last hours were good. Even his last breath he sent to the people. In view of Russia's imperfection, one can accept much on Lenin's account, for there was no one else who could have taken upon himself a greater burden for the general good. It was not because of illness but out of a sense of justice that he would have spurned as would many other rulers. His books we love somewhat less, they are too long and what is most valuable about him is not expressed in his books. He did not love his books himself. Lenin is action rather than theory.'[8]

And then there follows something about his cosmic significance: 'Take the phenomenon of Lenin as a sign of the sensitivity of the cosmos ... Let us honour Lenin with our full understanding. Let us show affirmation of the Teacher who maintained a constant inner fire in both success and failure ... When he tore everything down, he created the people's consciousness.'[9] And then all the followers of Agni Yoga are invited to follow the 'leader': 'Lenin thought widely and understood matter. Can you not even to some extent follow the leader?' 'The teacher will be a natural leader. One may rejoice that Lenin is acknowledged to be such a teacher.' 'As pupils of Lenin, watch with the eye of an eagle, and with the leap of a lion claim the power that is yours. Don't miss the boat!'[10]

Finally, the Himalayan mahatmas tell the Roerichs what is of most importance: they speak about their meeting not only with Lenin but also with Marx: 'We know the monolithic way of thinking. We saw Lenin in Switzerland. Our colleague conversed with him in Moscow. He has not changed his views, nor is he unresolved. Everyone knew about the inexhaustibility of his convictions.'[11] And then about the contacts with the founder of Marxism: 'We know the books of Marx and Engels, and our representatives have even spoken with Marx. All their theses can easily be accepted by us. We do not find [in them] anything to ossify or deny matter. It is absurd that the West has not accepted our simple theses, which have been fortified by long experience.'[12] And then one of the mahatmas describes these meetings more fully to Helena Roerich: 'I have already said that our representatives met Marx in London and Lenin in Switzerland. Evidently the word Shamballa was spoken. At different times though independently, both leaders asked: "What are the characteristics of the age of Shamballa?" The answer was: "The age of truth and world community." Both leaders said independently: "May Shamballa come soon." We measure the successors by the words of the leaders. We cannot regard the narrowness of ignorance to be part of Marxism or Leninism. If an ignoramus dares to call himself a Marxist or Leninist, tell him sternly that this is a clear betrayal of the foundations of the community. Do you observe how the word Shamballa is pronounced in the East? Try even if only in a small way to enter into the ideology of this concept. Try to understand the rhythm of the way Shamballa is spoken about, and you will feel the great reality which will make mankind's strings tremble.'[13] Thus somewhere in the very heart of Asia, in the distant Himalayas, the Roerichs were able to learn some curious details about the occult foundations of Marxism–Leninism and even about its connection with 'Shamballa'.

However, the Roerichs first encountered the Himalayan mahatmas' positive relationship to Bolshevism and its victory in Russia in 1917 not in the Himalayas but seven years earlier in London.

As indicated above, Helena Roerich began to write down the teachings of Agni Yoga—which had their source in the 'dictate' of the mahatmas—in the Anglo-Saxon capital in the spring of 1920. At the same time the Roerichs also began to establish the first groups through which they might be studied. All this activity was the direct consequence of their first direct encounter with the mahatmas on the physical plane, which also took place in London. After this the mahatmas time and again furnished the Roerichs with, as they themselves expressed it, 'material' help. When they again met in the Himalayas, they reminded the Roerichs of this: 'Our community has sometimes been accused of seclusion and of being unwilling to help people. You yourselves know [the true state of affairs], having seen us in London, New York and Sikkim and our colleagues in Moscow.* It is for you to say that we were active as regards outward circumstances and clothing. We learnt in time about needs and new arrivals. You must admit that our London camouflage was resourceful, and our wish to furnish the greatest possible help was remarkable. Our material consignments to Paris and Sikkim were not small. You know that our letters arrive quickly and our messengers are never late. Say this to the young people' (this refers to the members of the Agni Yoga groups founded by the Roerichs).[14]

What were the words with which the exposition of the new teaching began, what was the first message of the mahatmas? We find the answer in the very first lines of the first volume of 'Leaves of Morya's Garden', which opens the 14-volume series of *Agni Yoga*. This book begins with the following remark on the part of the mahatma: 'My first message for the new Russia.' And then there follows an appeal to Nicholas and Helena Roerich:

You who have founded an ashram,
You who have bestowed two lives,† spread the word . . .[15]

And a promise of protection:

---

* This probably refers to certain Tibetans who appeared in Petersburg and Moscow at the end of the nineteenth century and before the Revolution and who tried to make contact with and exercise control over Nicholas II. (See further in Appendix 2.) Nicholas and Helena Roerich met them not only before the Revolution but also during their stay in Moscow in 1926. London, New York and Sikkim are the places where also Blavatsky had encounters with the mahatmas in her time.

† The Roerichs had two sons.

I shall enclose you with [my] shield—do your work.
I have spoken.

This command of the mahatma to found the doctrine of Agni Yoga and
to propagate it in future above all in 'the new [that is, Bolshevik] Russia'
was strictly followed by the Roerichs throughout their lives.[*]

A successful realization of this task was to be made possible primarily
through the fact that all 14 volumes of *Agni Yoga* were written in the
Russian language: 'Urusvati knows that when studying exhortations one
needs to have in mind not only their content but also the language in
which they are framed. A teaching is given not without reason in a
particular language. It is possible to study all teachings from ancient times
and understand that the language in question shows which people has the
task of bringing the next developmental stage to manifestation. Sometimes it may be thought that the Teaching is given in that language which
is closest to the one who receives it, but such an explanation is inadequate.
One needs to observe the reasons in their entirety. Nothing is accidental.
The recipient of the Teaching is not fortuitous, and the language is chosen
by necessity.'[16][†]

Moreover, the particular style of the presentation, which had become
established from approximately the fourth volume of the series onwards,
was intended—in the minds of those inspiring this work—to correspond
to the psychological characteristics of the Russian soul in order to direct its
evolution in a certain direction regarded by them as necessary. Agni Yoga
could, in its most essential features, be characterized as a purely Eastern
doctrine, though in a form adapted for the Slavonic soul and psychology.

Notes

1. NR 6, p. 246.
2. AY 2, p. 99.
3. AY 4, p. 283.
4. OB, Part 2, X. 1.
5. OB.
6. Ter-Akopyan, p. 3.
7. OB.
8. OB, Part 2, I. 1.
9. OB.
10. OB, Part 2, X. 7, Part 3, III. 7.

---

[*] See chapter 10.
[†] It is interesting that both Alice Bailey and E. Prophet spoke similarly about the English
language (see Part Two).

11. OB, Part 3, II. 22.
12. OB, Part 2, X. 19.
13. OB, Part 3, II. 26.
14. OB, Part 3, I. 16.
15. AY 1, p. 4.
16. AY 14, p. 468.

4. The Roerichs' Mission to Bolshevik Russia

The brief visit made by the Roerichs to Moscow in 1926, for the sake of which they interrupted their Himalayan expedition for a short while, acquires a particular significance in the context of our present considerations. This journey was made by them at the direct indication of the mahatmas and had as its aim the fulfilment of one important task assigned by them to the Roerichs.

It was preceded by a visit in December 1924 by Nicholas Roerich to the Soviet Embassy in Berlin. According to his own diary entry he had taken this step at the instigation of the mahatma in preparation for the impending journey to Bolshevik Russia. (The entry dated 28 July reads: 'You can carry out the task on the way home by not leaving out Berlin.'[1]

The direct contact with the official representatives of the Bolshevik Government is mentioned at some length in the biography of Roerich that appeared in Moscow in 1973. According to this source Nicholas Roerich reported to the Soviet consul in detail about his intimate acquaintance with the mahatmas and the potential leaders of India, who were in opposition to the English colonial powers. As Roerich explained to the consul, the mahatmas 'believed in the future of Soviet Russia, in its liberating mission and pinned great hopes on it'.[2] Nicholas Roerich also expressed his own 'sympathy for the Soviet regime and his conviction that progressive Communist ideas will establish new foundations for the entire social life of humanity'.[3]

The following detail is also mentioned in the biography: 'At Roerich's insistent request, his conversation was formally recorded and sent to Moscow,' and—in answer to this—an order of the Bolshevik Government arrived shortly afterwards at Berlin to the effect that Roerich 'can count on any necessary help on the part of the Soviet authorities.'[4]

It was in this way that the connection with the Bolshevik Government was established. Now the real task could be taken in hand.

The trans-Himalayan expedition began in March 1925 from Kashmir, in north-west India, whither the Roerichs had come directly from Sikkim where they had had meetings with the mahatmas. During their stay in Kashmir the Roerichs made an intensive study of the collection of legends and traditions according to which Jesus Christ did not die in Palestine on the Cross but was rescued and miraculously brought to the Himalayas by his spirit-teacher Chitan Natkhye, under whose instruction he had been in the period between his fourteenth and thirtieth years. Thereafter he lived for several years in Kashmir and died there. On his grave, which is still there today, the inscription can be read: 'Here lies Issa [Jesus], son of Joseph'.* The extent to which the Roerichs took these legends seriously is apparent from Nicholas Roerich's picture on this theme entitled 'Issa and the Giant's Head'.

From Kashmir the expedition moved on northwards through the western Himalayas. It was on this section of the journey that—according to what is said by the mahatmas—the third volume of *Agni Yoga*, *Obshchina* ('Community'), was written, although it is possible that its content originated in the meetings at Sikkim.† Moreover, the mahatmas now gave the Roerichs the wholly concrete commission of visiting Moscow and bringing their letter to the Bolshevik Government and the consecrated Himalayan earth to Lenin's grave. In fulfilment of the mahatmas' commission, the Roerichs directed their expedition— together with the letters and gifts—towards the Russian border and by 13 February were in Kashgar, which lies not far from it. There immediately followed a visit to the Soviet consulate and an extensive study of Soviet newspapers, under which impression Helena Roerich wrote in a letter: 'With great enthusiasm we read *Izvestiya*—what a magnificent project— and were especially moved by the veneration with which the teacher's name—Lenin—is surrounded ... This is indeed a new country, and the Dawning Light of the Teacher shines over it ...'[5] In the next big town, Urumqi, the Roerichs stayed several weeks waiting for their Soviet visas. Every evening they went to the Soviet consulate and read the consul excerpts from their book 'Community' about the mahatmas' relationship to Lenin and the Bolshevik Revolution.[6] For Lenin's birthday Nicholas Roerich, at the consul's request, in one night made a sketch for the pedestal of the bust of the 'leader' (newly brought from Moscow). The exhibiting of the bust before the Soviet consulate was, however, for-bidden by a personal instruction of the Chinese Governor General.[7] Roerich wrote at the time in his diary after one of his visits to the con-sulate: '... the truncated pyramid looks somewhat forlorn—the pedestal

---

* See Appendix 4.

† It is difficult to date the writing of 'Community' with any precision. L. Shaposhnikova says in her foreword to the 1992 Riga edition of 'Community' that the Roerichs took the completed manuscript of the book already to Moscow, but that they did not succeed in publishing it there. Z. Fosdik, on the other hand, who accompanied the Roerichs, wrote in her diary (that is, after the stay in Moscow): 'Now is given the third book amidst difficult conversations' (Fosdik, p. 69). It is, however, possible that the mahatma dictated the essential text of 'Community' *before* the Roerichs visited Russia and then completed it on the way to Mongolia.

of the forbidden Lenin monument. It is impossible to understand that, while all placards of Lenin are allowed and the Chinese authorities drink for the prosperity of Communism, the bust of Lenin cannot stand on a pedestal that has been prepared for it ... It is such a shame that they did not manage to write Lenin's name on the pedestal of the "forbidden" monument. Surely the entire thinking of the East will be drawn to this name and the most diverse people meet under this name.'[8]

This little episode merits particular attention, not only as yet another testimony of the Roerichs' veneration for the Bolshevik founder of 'the new Russia' but also for another reason.

The detail in this episode that is particularly interesting relates to the *form of the pedestal* as conceived by Roerich: a *truncated pyramid* with Lenin's head placed upon it. This form crops up again later in Roerich's life. In 1935, during his third and final visit to America, he gave the American state officials—through his friends—the idea of portraying a truncated pyramid on the one dollar note, which indeed happened.[9] Thus to this very day the design of these notes incorporates a *truncated pyramid*, on which, however, is placed not the head of Lenin but a triangle with the image of an eye, that is, the ancient symbol of the Father God, the great Creator of the Universe. But there can be hardly anyone in America who is now aware whose image Roerich had intended to crown his 'truncated pyramid'.

After receiving their visas the Roerichs could finally leave for Moscow by train via Omsk. Moreover, together with their permission to enter Bolshevik Russia there also came—evidently from central sources—a special instruction to the OGPU (which was what the KGB was called in the twenties) to help the Roerichs in every possible way on their journey to Moscow and to work with them.

In connection with this circumstance, Roerich noted in his diary: '9 June [1926], Omsk: We go to the OGPU to leave our weapons for safe-keeping. Again that same courtesy and solicitude. "How we help?" 10 June: We are on our way. The train leaves at midnight. The OGPU gave the order that we will be helped to find our seats ... At midnight the train [Omsk–Moscow] arrives. The OGPU agent goes past and indicates with his eyes that all is well.'[10]

In the capital they were officially received by two members of the Bolshevik Government—the People's Commissar for Foreign Affairs, G. Chicherin, and the People's Commissar for Education, A. Lunacharsky. In the course of a conversation of many hours with them, Roerich spoke at some length of 'the possibility of uniting Russia and the great world of Buddhism with the help of the mahatmas',[11] and gave Chicherin a casket from them containing the consecrated Himalayan earth and the letter.

'Half communist and half Buddhist', was how Chicherin described Roerich after the conversation. And in their letter the mahatmas write: 'We are sending the earth for the grave of our brother Mahatma Lenin, who has laboured so very hard for the general good.'* And the letter continues: 'In the Himalayas we know what you have accomplished. You have abolished the Church, which had become a breeding-ground of falsehood and superstition. You have wiped out the bourgeoisie, the source of prejudice. You have destroyed the prison of education. You have rooted out the seeds of hypocrisy. You have consumed the army of slaves with fire. You have crushed the spiders of profiteering. You have shut the gates of the dark dens of vice. You have liberated the earth from treacherous embezzlers. You have recognized that religion is the teaching of the all-embracing nature of matter. You have recognized the insignificance of personal property. You have discovered the key to the evolution of society. You have indicated the significance of knowledge. You have bowed down before Beauty. You have brought children the full might of the cosmos. You have opened the windows of the palaces. You have seen the urgency of building new houses for the common good.'

Then the mahatmas go on to speak about their own cause: 'We stopped an insurrection in India that was premature, we also recognized the timeliness of your movement and send you our help, thus affirming the Oneness of Asia. We know how much will happen in the years 1928–31–36. We greet you, who seek the common good!'[12]†

In addition to the gifts of the mahatmas, Roerich also presented the Bolshevik Government with gifts of his own. He gave to Lunacharsky a cycle of seven pictures under the general title of 'Maitreya', and also a large canvas entitled 'The time has come', where over a peaceful earth there appears the head of a giant bogatyr [knight] gazing towards the East, in whose face the features of Lenin are easily recognizable.[13] The artist defined the idea of the picture as follows: 'The time has come for the peoples of the East to awaken from their age-old sleep, to throw off the

---

* It may indeed be noted that no gravestone of Lenin existed. Moreover, there are in the available literature no indications as to what the Soviet Government did with the mahatmas' gift.

† In connection with this letter of the mahatmas to the Bolshevik Government, as with their indications contained in H. Roerich's letters to the American President, F.D. Roosevelt (see Appendix 3), one question remains unresolved: were these letters given to the Roerichs in a ready, handwritten form, or dictated by the mahatmas when they met, or communicated to them in a mediumistic way through occult dictation, as with all the volumes of *Agni Yoga*?

chains of slavery,' which, in his opinion, is to come about through the rapid spread of Bolshevism from Russia throughout the whole of Asia.

We shall now dwell at greater length upon the message of the mahatmas that was written in 1925 and endeavour to single out its most important elements. There are three. Firstly, the elevation of Lenin to the rank of mahatma and the allusion to the help afforded by the mahatmas to the Bolshevik Revolution of 1917 and the subsequent establishing in Russia of Bolshevik power and ideology: 'We send You our help.' Today one has to say retrospectively that this help was very effective. For in the years that followed all the basic propositions of this letter were fully implemented in the course of the Bolsheviks' programme of destruction, which the mahatmas so unconditionally approved of and also supported in their letter.[*]

Secondly, the prophetic allusion to the years 1928–31–36, in which period the Bolsheviks, under Stalin's leadership, made the transition to total terror: 1928, the preparation and beginning of forced collectivization, which was associated with the wholesale annihilation of the peasantry; 1931, the process of industrialization grips the entire country, gradually transforming it into a vast labour camp; 1936, the beginning of mass terror, which reached its peak in 1937, when millions of innocent people were without trial or investigation shot or sent away to camps (the so-called first wave of mass Stalinist repressions).

Finally, the third and perhaps most significant element. In the letter the following words are addressed to the Bolsheviks: 'You have recognized that religion is the teaching of the all-embracing nature of matter.'

In order that we may better understand this very strange 'revelation' of the mahatmas, it is necessary to turn to other, still stranger, 'revelations' as contained in the book *Obshchina* ('Community'). There the Himalayan mahatmas tell Helena Roerich: 'Collectivism and dialectivism[†] are two aids to thinking about materialism. The nature of materialism has a particular mobility, and does not fail to encompass any of life's phenomena. The teacher merely lays down the necessary landmarks. It is possible to develop principles for this manner of thinking. Materialism must become established to such a degree that all the scientific achievements of modern times are able to enter constructively into the understanding of it. We have spoken about astral bodies, magnets, the radiance of the aura, the

---

[*] 'The predictions have come true'—thus did Yuri Roerich, the painter's elder son, evaluate at the end of the 1950s what had taken place in Russia. (See the entry in R. Rudzitis's diary quoted on p. 135.)

[†] Meaning 'dialectic'. The word was incorrectly written by Helena Roerich.

emanation of every object, the shift of sensibilities, the change in grav-itational forces, the penetration of one layer of matter by another, the sending of thoughts through space, the feeling of centres, the under-standing of the word matter. Much that is invisible and discernible only by apparatuses must be grasped by one who wishes to introduce technology into life. It is necessary to replace idealistic blather by solid reasoning power. *We materialists* have the right to demand the respect and recog-nition of matter.'[14] 'Childish materialism is a narcotic for the people, but the materialism of enlightened knowledge will be a ladder to victory.'[15]

And then, probably recalling their meetings with Lenin in Switzerland, the mahatmas continue: 'We have already seen how a communist receives the teaching. We have already seen how easy it is to speak with a com-munist. For one we are mahatmas, for another we are scholars, for a third rebels, for a fourth a committee of revolutionaries, but the teaching itself encompasses all the hopes of the communists. Our conditions for colleagueship are a total wish to apply our principles to life, not theory but practice.'[16] And in this connection there is talk of the need to 'give instruction regarding the material nature of thinking'.[17]

Then the mahatmas go on to say: 'You rightly think that technology is impossible without communism ... As *practical materialists* we can boldly assert this.'[18] Lenin would also have been able to subscribe to this slogan, inasmuch as it even approximated to his style.

The mahatmas view the future age of the Maitreya (the age of Aquarius) in the same way: 'The Buddha has incorporated himself as a man, as the Teacher of affirmation. In this leonine, fiery affirmativeness he has attained to a preview of the Maitreya—*the age of the knowledge of the greatness of matter*. Affirm matter in all its manifoldness and oneness!'[19] Thus 'in the teaching of the Buddha we find not only materialistic philosophy but the practical improvement of each day ... Never do we call the Buddha meek, for on the contrary he is an intrepid leader, a fighter for community and matter, a hero of labour and unity.'[20]

And in the draft version of 'Community', from which first extracts have recently been published, these thoughts are expressed quite openly: 'The great Gautama gave the world the entire teaching of Communism ... A modern understanding of community forms an excellent bridge from Gautama Buddha to Lenin. We express this formula not in order to praise, not in order to revile, but as an evident, unchangeable fact ... We know that Lenin valued true Buddhism. We create the foundations of Buddhism out of the legacy that he has given. It is the one simple teaching that bears an affinity to the beauty of the cosmos. It holds itself aloof from any allusion to an idol, which would be unworthy of a teacher of the people.'[21]

In these and many other places in 'Community' one may be astonished by this mixture of Bolshevik terminology and Buddhist ideas. For example, there is the following observation in 'Community' about the first two volumes of *Agni Yoga*: 'If your thinking is not yet purified by the true hammer and sickle,* take up the book "Illumination" and the book "The Call".'[22] Or: 'One who wishes to devote himself to true communism acts in accordance with the principles of great matter.'[23] And then the mahatmas explain quite openly: 'Those who have understood reality and materialism can ally themselves with our community. It is impossible to think of a mystic or metaphysician as being behind our walls.' 'Communism, supported by technology, gives a mighty spur to knowledge.'[24] And all this they call 'the ideology of Shamballa'.

As with Bolshevik ideology, so is the 'ideology of Shamballa' dedicated to the 'new man' of whom Lenin dreamed, which is why he devoted particular attention to education. Thus the consequences of the mahatmas' indications in 'Community' regarding pedagogy and practical work with children are particularly dire, if one bears in mind that such work is being carried out today in many 'Roerich' groups.

The following utterances of the mahatmas in 'Community' can give a certain impression of their 'pedagogical ideas': 'It is necessary to examine the programmes of schools and strengthen the quota of materially reliable knowledge. The idealism of superstition drives people into abysses of horror. It is necessary to carry out this rectification of educational thinking with alacrity, otherwise yet another generation of imbeciles will disgrace the planet. Natural science must be strengthened, once the significance of this work has been understood. Biology, astrophysics and chemistry draw the attention of the youngest child's brain. Give children the opportunity to think!'[25]

And in another context: 'The education of the people must be introduced at the earliest possible age from the first lesson. The sooner the better. Be assured that an overstraining of the brain happens only through clumsiness. Every mother who approaches a child's cradle will express the first educational formula: You can do everything ... The awareness that "I can do everything" is not vainglory but merely a matter of becoming aware of the apparatus.'[26]

The mahatmas demand as much abstract, intellectual knowledge as possible at a very early age. The sooner it is begun the better. (Of particular importance is the work with children *before the age of three*, for 'only

---

* The 'hammer and sickle' were the chief symbols of the Bolsheviks, and were incorporated in the emblem of Soviet Russia.

a consciousness of below the age of three is readily receptive to the community.'[27]*

We shall confine ourselves to these quotations, which could be multiplied without any difficulty. Later on we shall examine the occult foundations of this remarkable devotion of the Himalayan mahatmas to Bolshevism. Meanwhile we need merely to observe that the mahatmas' acknowledgement of the central significance of materialism is by no means simply a 'discovery' on the part of Helena Roerich. For similar utterances can be found in a book already mentioned in these pages, *The Mahatma Letters to A.P. Sinnett*. These were letters received by the English journalist from the two theosophical mahatmas Kut Humi and Morya, with whom he had entered into contact through Blavatsky.

However, these letters, as we have seen, contain not only deep occult knowledge from the true mahatmas, who derived it from the treasures of wisdom of the old pre-Christian religions, but also highly problematic ideas of certain Eastern occultists of a left inclination. A particularly clear example of their correspondence is an extract from a letter to Hume, where the foundations of the teaching of the Himalayan mahatmas about matter are set forth. The source is a letter of Helena Roerich. Moreover, the reason why she quotes the mahatma and tries to defend his views is not without interest. Helena Roerich's letter is an answer to a letter from one of her pupils, who was troubled by the avowed materialism and even atheism contained in the mahatmas' teachings. Before answering her correspondent, Helena Roerich first once again quotes the portion of the mahatma's letter in question, having previously—as she says—verified it with the English original:[†] 'Then you refer to the *deeply philosophical* statement of the Elder Mahatma: "As to God—since no one has ever or at any time seen him or it—*unless he or it is the very essence and nature of this boundless eternal matter, its energy and motion*, we cannot regard him as either eternal or infinite or yet self-existing. We refuse to admit a being to an existence of which we know absolutely nothing, because ... there is no room for him in the presence of that matter whose undeniable properties

---

* These passages are in total contrast to the basic principles of the pedagogy founded upon an anthroposophical study of man, according to which the child should not be burdened with intellectual concepts in early childhood (let alone before the third year), since this makes a person inclined later to materialism. From the standpoint of anthroposophical pedagogy the child does not only have a physical brain that needs to be developed but it is a threefold being of body, soul and spirit which—on the basis of a true knowledge of its soul and spirit—should develop in its totality.

† The italics are in the original letter. A fuller extract from the letter is reproduced in Appendix 6.

and qualities we know thoroughly well . . . In other words, we believe in *matter* alone, in matter as visible nature and matter in its invisibility as the invisible omnipresent omnipotent Proteus . . .'' '[28]

These words of the 'mahatma' appear in a letter written by him to Hume in 1882.

In 1934 Helena Roerich tries to defend this as follows: 'You are disturbed by this glorifying of matter. But do you not know that in esotericism matter and spirit are one? That matter is merely a differentiation of spirit? Do you not know that matter is also energy, for one does not exist without the other? . . . Do you not know that Spirit, bereft of matter, does not have phenomenal form, in other words, does not exist? Indeed, in our actions and thoughts we cannot separate ourselves from matter. We are dealing with either the higher levels or the basest aspects of the same matter.' (The last two phrases are a quotation from 'Community'.)[29]

And in another letter, again responding to the same objections, Helena Roerich adds: 'Matter or the most refined substance of Spirit-Matter is infinite in its differentiations and in its visible and invisible manifestations, but it is impossible to do anything with pure spirit. Ignorance separates and analyses everything, but the Great knowledge of the East unifies and synthesizes everything.'[30]

From these quotations there unfolds a remarkable sequence in the activity of the mahatmas, from Blavatsky and Sinnett to Helena Roerich and her Agni Yoga.

In the following words, Helena Roerich speaks about the significance of the mahatma letters to A.P. Sinnett and their connection with the chief work of Blavatsky, on the one hand, and the teachings of 'Living Ethics' on the other: 'But it is useless and erroneous to condemn and deny the "Letters of the Mahatmas". Sinnett's *Esoteric Buddhism* was based on these "Letters". Their content—developed further—led to [Blavatsky's] *Secret Doctrine*. The volume of these "Letters" is a very great book, and it is highly esteemed in the West.[*] To deny it means to deny the whole teaching that was given through Blavatsky and also all the books of "Living Ethics".'[31]

But let us return to the Roerichs. Once he had discharged one commission of the mahatmas in Moscow, Nicholas Roerich immediately made it known to the members of the Ministry for Foreign Affairs that he had to return to India at once—and, moreover, via Mongolia—in order, as he said, to fulfil there further 'commissions of the mahatmas'.[32]

---

[*] Helena Roerich subsequently translated a portion of these letters into Russian and published them under the pseudonym of Iskander Hanum in 1925.

Whether because of the magic effect of the word 'mahatma' or for other reasons, the Roerichs obtained permission for their departure from Bolshevik Russia through Mongolia and China almost directly. Soviet expedition passes were given out to them, and they even received state help in equipping the expedition.

Just imagine the improbability of the situation! An expedition, journeying through Asia with secret aims, departing from an English colony under the American flag,* 'in the official documents' of whose members it is mentioned that they were making 'for Moscow as the mahatmas' special representatives, to fulfil their commission',[33] was permitted by the Bolshevik Government to enter Soviet Russia unhindered, and then just as freely allowed to leave the country and, moreover, in the direction chosen by the participants themselves. All this can only be explained if the 'representatives of the mahatmas' and their 'message' were taken far more seriously in the Kremlin than it might appear at a first glance.

A New York adherent of the Roerichs, Zinaida Fosdik, who had specially journeyed to Russia to meet them and then joined the expedition, wrote in her diary on the way to Mongolia: 'In the evening we discussed what I should say to the others on returning to New York. We were indicated to say that we had hardly arrived in Moscow when all doors were flung open to us, once we had merely uttered the name of N.K. [Roerich]. He arrived; and already on the first day there was a wonderful reception from Chicherin, and then at the homes of Lunacharsky, Kamenev and Krupskaya.† But the most remarkable meeting took place in the GPU,‡ where the names of the Maitreya and Shamballa were mentioned and where the name of M[orya] was in the air. Suggestions about collaboration were received with enthusiasm; on several occasions people were met with who hold power in their hands.'[34] Not only the immediate participants were satisfied with the meeting but also its secret directors: according to Zinaida Fosdik's diary, on 26 July 1926 in Novosibirsk, in the evening the mahatma said mediumistically to Helena Roerich: '... I think that the results achieved in Moscow will have historic significance.'[35]

---

* 'The very fact of a journey to Soviet Russia directly from British India was at that time an extraordinary phenomenon,' observes the Roerichs' biographer P. Belikov (Belikov, p. 34). See illustration no. 6, p. 186.

† L.B. Kamenev was at that time a member of the Politburo of the Bolshevik party; M.K. Krupskaya was Lenin's widow.

‡ With the head of the Foreign Office, Trilisser. See Y. Kobalidze: 'If Roerich had been our intelligence officer, we would have spoken about this with pride' (*Sobesednik*, 1944, no. 48).

Indeed, this successful visit by the Roerichs to Bolshevik Russia laid the foundation for the development of a whole programme for a new form of government in accordance with the 'Plan of the Rulers'. One result of this was the publication by Helena Roerich in 1933 in Riga, in an edition of 50 copies, of the book *Naputstviye Vozdyu* ('Parting Words to the Leader'), in which a picture of an 'ideal' ruler is depicted. While being separated from the people and elevated to the summit of power, with 'his every appearance being a festival for the people',[36] he will at the same time control all aspects of both the personal and social life of the citizens, in that he strictly regulates its economic, legal and cultural spheres. But his own intentions must remain an inviolable secret for all his subordinates. 'The nature of the Leader's intentions is a secret,' writes Helena Roerich.[37] Nevertheless the Leader does not have any independence. He is an obedient instrument of the 'Hierarchies' standing behind him and known to no one, who through him govern the people ('the Pearl of the Leader's power is alone intercourse with the Hierarchies'),[38] and—in the presence of many such Leaders in various countries—the whole of humanity.

Thus on the foundation of that 'ideal' socio-political order, which the teachers of Agni Yoga are preparing for humanity, there emerges a secret 'world government', working in the various countries through the 'Leaders' who are wholly subordinated to it. The mahatmas themselves do not conceal this: 'For you the decrees of the Invisible Rulership will be significant ... We do not bother about names; what is more essential for Us is that ... your brain remembers that there is an Invisible International Rulership ... The International Rulership has never denied its existence ... Not secret societies—which governments dread—but *visible persons*, who are sent by the decree of the Invisible International Rulership',[39] they openly declare in the fourth volume of *Agni Yoga*. Was not 'mahatma' Lenin such a leader—an instrument of the 'world rulership' of the mahatmas whom the 'Hierarchies' visited in Switzerland?* And was

---

*Was the American President Roosevelt intended to become such a 'leader' through Helena Roerich's mediation? It is known that Nicholas Roerich took a copy of *Naputstviye Vozdyu* ('Parting Words to the Leader') with him to America in 1934, and Helena Roerich wrote to Roosevelt in the same year in the mahatmas' name: 'The advice is ready for America ... You can be ... a truly great *Leader*' (see Appendix 3). It may be supposed that the advice from the mahatmas was ready not only for America. The following words from the book 'Parting Words to the Leader' are interesting in the light of this: 'One needs new methods for everything. It is possible to see how world events are forged with new swords. One needs to study International Law, so as not to fall back into old methods. You see what is happening in Germany, Italy and Turkey [that is, those countries where Fascist regimes came to power in the 1930s]—that is not foreseen in International Law. One can see that the path for the world lies outside the old law. We seek not laws but justice' (NV 157).

the message of the mahatmas from 1926 not a 'parting word' to the Bolshevik 'leaders'?

In Ulan-Bator, the capital of Mongolia, the Roerichs anonymously published the two books *Osnovy buddhizma* ('The Foundations of Buddhism') and, above all, the third volume of *Agni Yoga*, 'Community', with all the utterances of the mahatmas about Lenin, Communism, Bolshevik ideology, the Revolution of 1917 and so forth. There is no doubt that a significant part of the Roerichs' 'special mission' and the 'task of the mahatmas' entrusted to them consisted in their speedy publication in Mongolia. In Helena Roerich's recently published diary entries from that time can be found the following words, which were dictated to her by the mahatma on 1 July 1926: 'Yes, I charge that My book ['Community'] be given to those who seek community.'[40] Without doubt these publications, which rested on the authority of the mahatmas, were to serve to further strengthen and extend the power of Bolshevism in Mongolia and China.[*]

To be sure, Mongolia had by then already been under Bolshevism for three years. The Bolshevik Revolution there was carried out in 1924 by Sukhe-Bator, who had previously visited Lenin in the Kremlin. The result of the revolution was the destruction of all seven hundred Buddhist monasteries on Mongolian territory and also the killing or the incarcerating in camps of over a hundred thousand Buddhist monks. In his writings, Nicholas Roerich points out that the Mongolian soldier-revolutionaries were singing this song on the streets of Ulan-Bator (its words were written by Sukye-Bator):

The war of Northern Shamballa.[†]
Let us die in this war
To be reborn again
As Knights of the Ruler of Shamballa.[41]

Nor did Nicholas Roerich stand aside from these events. Before leaving Mongolia he presented its Bolshevik Government with the picture 'The Great Horseman'—painted in the traditional Mongolian style—which

---

[*] On 7 July 1926 the following words were dictated (by the mahatma): 'It is necessary to advance *the transformation of Buddhism into Leninism*. Endeavour to find a common chord with the Mongolian Government. You will need to move mountains. But it is not difficult to praise a young country. Action must lead the way, *everything for the action of 1917* [the year of the Bolshevik Revolution in Russia]. Try to succeed. I send you the ray' (*Rerikhovski Vestnik*, 'Roerich Herald', 1990 no. 3).

[†] By 'Northern Shamballa' is meant Bolshevik Russia. Roerich often employs this name for Russia in his books. See, for example, his *Heart of Asia* and *Shamballa*.

depicted 'The Ruler of Shamballa—the Maitreya', with the assembly of the 'Great Khural' (the higher organ of power in Bolshevik Mongolia) portrayed in its lower part. In presenting this picture to the leader of the Mongolian Government, Tserendorzh, Roerich explained: 'The Mongolian nation is building its radiant future under the banner of a new age. The Great Horseman of liberation is sweeping over the Mongolian expanses ... And loudly sounds the call of the *red*, beauteous Kingly Horseman [the Maitreya].'

In answer to these words, Tserendorzh—who had visited Lenin together with Sukhe-Bator, on the eve of the Mongolian revolution— said the following: 'May the idea of our common teacher Lenin spread throughout the world like the flame in this picture, and may the men who follow this teaching continue their work with the same sense of resolution with which the Great Horseman portrayed here gallops on his way.' As a result the Roerichs received from the Mongolian Government a charter of protection for their further expedition.

Now the Roerichs' path led through central Tibet back to India. At the Tibetan border a suburgan (sanctuary) to Shamballa was, in accordance with Nicholas Roerich's plans, established at the place where, according to tradition, one of the mahatmas had stopped for the night on his way to Mongolia. 'Behind the monument to Shamballa flies the American flag,' observes Roerich in his diary[43] (see Illustration 6).

Further diary entries by Roerich—in so far as these were published by him—contain a whole series of observations about direct contacts with the mahatmas and even a visit to their dwelling place in the Himalayas, Shamballa.*

The arduous expedition, in the course of which they had to cross several high passes with heights of up to 5000 metres, came to an end in May 1928 in the place where it had started: in the princedom of Sikkim in north-west India, which was where Mahatma Morya had visited

---

* 'On 20 July received indications of extraordinary significance. Difficult to implement, but pregnant with consequences. No one in the caravan has any inkling of the impending programme. The following day there is again important news, and again the companions know nothing. Check these dates with your events' (NR 4, p. 299): 5 August, episode with the flying fireball as a sign of 'Shamballa', the subject of further discussion below (see p. 100); then the expedition encounters a huge white block of Glauber's salt. 'Already the protected frontier,' notes Nicholas Roerich in his diary (NR 4, p. 302; cf. p. 87 and also NR 6, p. 245). This is the last entry before one and a half month's interruption: the period from the end of August until 6 October 1927 is not reflected in the published version of Nicholas Roerich's diary. One also has to bear in mind what Nicholas and Yuri Roerich asserted about their visiting Shamballa (see p. 42).

Blavatsky.* The Roerichs had spent two years here before the beginning of the expedition (1924–25). Moreover, it was here that the idea of it had been born, and where their own meeting with those whom they always called the mahatmas had taken place. Now, on returning there, Nicholas Roerich founds his institute of Himalayan research 'Urusvati', which means 'Light of the morning star' or 'Light of Venus', a name which was at the same time the title given by the mahatmas to Helena Roerich, who was chosen as its first and lifelong founder-president. In December 1928 the Roerichs again leave Sikkim and eventually settle in Kulu in north-west India, in the state of Kashmir, through which the mahatmas themselves passed.[44] The institute for Himalayan research is also trans-ferred there. Henceforth and until Helena Roerich's death in 1947, Kulu in Kashmir becomes their principal place of residence.

The geographical boundaries of the Roerichs' trans-Himalayan expedition are of particular interest, for an occult geo-political plan was associated with them behind which very real occult powers were stand-ing. This plan was effective already in Blavatsky's activity, in so far as in the last part of her life she came under the growing influence of the left-oriented Tibeto-Indian occultists, whom she faithfully regarded as mahatmas. Rudolf Steiner spoke in this connection about 'factors' standing directly behind her 'which wanted to link India to Asia [that is, to Mongolia, Tibet and China] in order to create an Asiatic-Indian Empire with the help of the Russian Empire'.[45]

India, Tibet, China,† Mongolia, Russia—this route of the Roerich expedition corresponds precisely to the boundaries of the vast 'Asiatic-Indian Empire' mentioned by Rudolf Steiner. And the pupils and fol-lowers of the Roerichs in Russia even today speak of this Russo-Indo-Tibeto-Chinese Empire. Thus the director of the Nicholas Roerich Centre and Museum in Moscow, L. Shaposhnikova, writes as follows in this connection: 'The Central Asian expedition was carried out to

---

* In connection with this Nicholas Roerich wrote the following in his diary during his first visit to Sikkim in 1923: 'There was in Sikkim one of the ashrams of the mahatmas. In Sikkim the mahatmas journeyed on mountain ponies. Their physical presence has endowed these places with a solemn significance. Of course, the ashram has now been moved from Sikkim. The mahatmas have, of course, left Sikkim. But they were here' (NR 4, p. 26).

† During their expedition through Central Asia the Roerichs only managed to visit the western fringes of China. Hence in 1934 and 1935 they organized a special expedition to China and Manchuria, during which they visited Peking and a number of areas of inner China, and also Japan. The Central Asian expedition of 1925–8 referred to above was also preceded by a journey to the south of India, in the course of which the Roerichs visited the island of Ceylon and the centre of the Theosophical Society in Adyar.

establish centres for a future civilization ... And if one considers the route of the Central Asian expedition from this point of view, it is possible to understand which countries entered into the system of the future civilization of our new evolutionary stage. These are India, China, Russia (in the first instance, Siberia), Mongolia and Tibet. This is that "lap of honour" which was undertaken by the Central Asian expedition.'[46] And A.V. Khramchenko, in an article entitled 'The International Mission of Helena Roerich', refers to 'an ancient Buddhist prophecy' in a certain sense fulfilled by the Roerichs through their expedition, 'that the epoch of the Maitreya will begin when four with the image of the Maitreya will pass through the territories of the future state where the Lord of Light will reign.'[47] It has to be said, however, that the 'ancient Buddhist prophecy' was derived by Khramchenko not from ancient Buddhist texts but from the book *Kriptogrammy Vostoka* ('Cryptograms of the East') published in 1929, that is, *after* the trans-Himalayan expedition.

Here are some extracts from this 'prophecy', whose publication has been antedated:[*] 'The occurrence will be clear, when I say—the path of the four to the East ...[†] Find the intelligence to encounter what has been prescribed, when in the fifth year [apparently, of the "new era" calculated from the Roerichs' meeting in London with Mahatma Morya in 1920, that is, in 1925, the year when the trans-Himalayan expedition began] the messengers of the warriors of Northern Shamballa will appear. Find the intelligence to encounter them and receive the New Glory! ... The Ruler Himself is hurrying, and His banner [this refers to the tangka, the banner of Shamballa with the figure of the Maitreya, which the Roerichs carried with them together with the American flag virtually throughout the expedition] already flies over the mountains! The blessed Buddha sends you the beloved Maitreya, so that you can approach the Community ... From the West, from the mountains, will my people come ... Northern Shamballa is on its way! ... When the procession with the Image of Shamballa passes over the lands of Buddha and returns to the Source, the time to utter the holy word "Shamballa" will come ... Thus the circle will be closed where the Image has been borne. "Kalagia" [a call meaning "Come to Shamballa"] has sounded. The Image has unfurled as a banner! That is as true as that the prophecy about Holy Shamballa lies beneath the

---

[*] In his book *Heart of Asia*, Nicholas Roerich also refers to the passage from 'Cryptograms of the East' quoted above simply as 'Tibetan prophecies about Shamballa and the Maitreya', without mentioning the source (NR 6, pp. 223–6).

[†] 'The four' being Helena and Nicholas Roerich and their sons Yuri and Svyatoslav.

Hum stone ...* The banner of the Maitreya will swell out like blood over the earth of the New World for the confused and like a red sun for those who understand!'[48]

These extracts can only be understood in the sense that the Roerich expedition, which encircled the borders of the future Russo-Asiatic 'Empire of the Maitreya', was thereby—in any event in the minds of the Roerichs—opening up a new epoch of earthly evolution, the epoch of Shamballa and the Maitreya, associated as it was with the arrival in Asia of 'people from Northern Shamballa'. These 'people from Northern Shamballa' were, however, the Bolsheviks, who at that very time were beginning to make their first attempts to spread Bolshevism throughout Asia and had already achieved some initial successes in this direction in Mongolia, where the Roerichs appeared immediately after their stay in Moscow as their direct ambassadors. Thus it was—as the Roerichs or, to be more precise, their Eastern inspirers thought—in Asia that the Bolshevism emanating from Russia was to become a movement of global or even planetary significance, inaugurating a new world epoch.†

This also enables one to gain a better understanding of the reasons for the highly positive attitude of the Eastern occultists standing behind the Roerichs' expedition to the Bolshevik powers in Russia, and also of the true aims of the expedition itself. Remarkably, this deep devotion to the East was even expressed in Nicholas Roerich's outward appearance; for towards the end of his life—despite all his Russian and Swedish ancestors—strongly Asiatic and Mongoloid features appeared in his face, just as happened in the case of him whom he and his inspirers so admired, 'Mahatma Lenin'.

---

* Cf. Nicholas Roerich's article 'Tainy' (Secrets), written in 1935 *during his second Asiatic expedition*: 'They say that at certain places, where new states are founded or great towns are built, or where great revelations and manifestations are to take place, parts of a great meteor, the messenger of distant heavenly bodies, are deposited. It was even the custom to attest the truth of phenomena by referring to such protected places. It was said: "What has been said is just as true as that at such a place this or that has been deposited"' (NR 1, p. 94). The Roerichs themselves in the course of the expedition probably in some way or other 'deposited' parts of the stone 'as a foundation stone', for they were convinced that they had received the stone from Himalayan Shamballa. (See further in the chapter 'Some Aspects of the Teaching of Helena Roerich'.)

† Despite the fall of Bolshevism in Russia and in other countries of Eastern Europe, it is still solidly adhered to in China, and its ideas are particularly popular in many Asian countries. Bearing in mind the colossal and exponentially increasing population of China, and also the extraordinary growth of its economic power, one has to acknowledge that Bolshevik ideas are still very far from disappearing from the historical stage of earthly humanity.

Notes

1. V. Khramchenko, *Mezhdunarodnaya missiya Eleny Roerich* ('The International Mission of Helena Roerich'), p. 17.
2. Belikov and Knyazeva, p. 166.
3. *Nicholas K. Roerich. Iz literaturnovo naslyediya* ('From Nicholas Roerich's Literary Legacy'), Moscow 1974.
4. Belikov and Knyazeva, p. 166.
5. Zarnitsky and Trophimova, p. 103.
6. Belikov and Knyazeva.
7. Belikov and Knyazeva.
8. AG, pp. 209–10, cf. NR 4, pp. 245–6.
9. Decter, p. 134.
10. AG, p. 237. Compare NR 4, pp. 277–8.
11. Zarnitsky and Trophimova, p. 104.
12. Zarnitsky and Trophimova, pp. 104–5.
13. Zarnitsky and Trophimova, p. 105.
14. OB, Part 2, X. 9.
15. OB, Part 2, X. 7.
16. OB.
17. OB.
18. OB, Part 2, X. 5.
19. OB, Part 2, XI. 2.
20. OB, Part 2, XI. 3.
21. *Rerikhovski Vestnik* ('Roerich Herald'), 1989, no. 1, pp. 37–8, published with the original handwritten text of Helena Roerich.
22. OB.
23. OB, Part 3, I. 12.
24. OB, Part 3, II. 14 and part 2, X. 7.
25. OB, Part 2, XI. 23.
26. OB, Part 2, X. 4.
27. Ibid.
28. HR 1, 12 September 1934.
29. Ibid.; OB, Part 2, X. 3; see also HR 1, 1 February 1935.
30. HR 2, 4 June 1937.
31. HR 2, 24 May 1936.
32. Zarnitsky and Trophimova, p. 105.
33. Sidorov, p. 381.
34. Fosdik, p. 69.
35. Fosdik, p. 67.
36. NV, 111.
37. Ibid., 98.
38. Ibid., 118.
39. AY 4, 24, 32.
40. *Rerikhovski Vestnik* ('Roerich Herald'), 1990, no. 3.
41. NR 6, p. 240.

42. Zarnitsky and Trophimova, p. 105.
43. NR 6, p. 243.
44. N.K. Roerich, *Urusvati*, Moscow, International Roerich Centre, 1993, p. 57, 1992, no. 2 (5).
45. GA 258, lecture of 14 June 1923.
46. *Ozaryenie* ('Enlightenment'), 1992, no. 2 (5).
47. Khramchenko, p. 20.
48. KV, ch. 10, 'Legends of the Stone', ch. 11, 'The Prophecy of Shamballa and the Maitreya'.

5. The Occult Foundations of the Teachings of Agni Yoga

Now that we have characterized certain aspects of the outer activity of the Roerichs and the teaching given through Helena Roerich, we must consider its occult foundations from an anthroposophical standpoint. In the first place we need to turn to the highly surprising fact of the deeply positive attitude of the Himalayan mahatmas to Bolshevism. There is doubtlessly a connection between this fact and their secret meetings with Marx in London and with Lenin in Switzerland, their pronouncement of the latter as a 'mahatma' and also their occult and political support of the Bolshevik Revolution of 1917 and of the subsequent rule of the Bolsheviks, of which they wrote in their letter to the Soviet Government, and so on. Whence came this evident interest on the part of the Eastern mahatmas in the victory and spread of Bolshevism not only in Russia and Asia but throughout the earth? Rudolf Steiner gives a very clear and simple answer to this question out of the sources of anthroposophical spiritual-scientific research: 'For these Eastern initiates the results of Leninism do not contain anything terrible, for these initiates say to themselves: If these institutions of Leninism are spread ever more widely over the earth, this will be the surest way of bringing doom to earthly civilization. But this will work to the benefit of precisely those people who through their previous incarnations have created for themselves the possibility of carrying their existence forward without the earth.'[1]*

In the above-quoted words of the spirit-researcher who derives his knowledge from modern Christian initiation, we have a clear indication of the sources of inspiration of these Eastern initiates or mahatmas. For the endeavour to draw humanity away from the earth *before* its earthly mission—as is made manifest through a true knowledge and a realizing of all the impulses springing from the Mystery of Golgotha—has been fulfilled is the central task of Lucifer with respect to earthly evolution as a whole. Rudolf Steiner had the following to say regarding these aims of

---

* Helena Roerich comforts her followers in a similar vein. In her opinion, 'all who are truly devoted to knowledge of the light [by which she means Agni Yoga] and the common good will [in the event of the earth's extinction] go on to higher planets. Sad will be the lot only of those who are left behind fluttering around the fragments of the disintegrated boat [the earth] or who have departed to Saturn' (HR 1, 21 May 1935).

Lucifer: 'From the very beginning of the evolution of the Earth, it was Lucifer's intention to lead men away from the earth into his spiritual kingdom. He had no interest in the rest of earthly evolution but wanted only to possess what the higher Gods had initiated [in earthly evolution] in connection with man ... In other words, he wished to lead the souls away and leave the earth to its fate.'[2]

In other words, the chief inspirers of the Eastern mahatmas in their efforts to attain this goal are luciferic spirits. This is also the source of the deep antipathy to Christianity with which Blavatsky had been inspired by the mahatmas, and of the unconditional devotion to Lucifer as 'the great benefactor of mankind'. It is true that in Helena Roerich's letters it is possible to find not infrequent references to Lucifer as an evil, negative spirit. However, these references actually relate to Ahriman, whom Helena Roerich always calls Lucifer.* This is made especially evident by her reference to the fall of Lucifer in the fourth root race, on Atlantis,[3] that is, in that period of earthly evolution when the ahrimanic spirits first entered into the evolution of humanity.[4] Moreover, in those same letters Helena Roerich describes 'Lucifer' or 'Satan', who tempted man in paradise and thereby endowed him with the gift of distinguishing between good and evil, as the great benefactor of humanity, 'since this gift could *not* be given by the power of darkness but was sacrificially bestowed by the Forces of Light. Hence the original name of this Emissary was Lucifer, the Light-bearer.'[5]

Thus as the knowledge of Christ, who brings the true balance between Ahriman's forces of darkness and Lucifer's one-sided forces of light, was inaccessible to Helena Roerich, the whole teaching of Agni Yoga is drawn into the opposition between these two categories of spiritual beings, which in many of her letters is characterized as the battle between the powers of light and the powers of darkness (also called Armageddon).

---

* According to modern spiritual science, evil in our world has a twofold nature, as represented by two different kinds of demonic beings, whose leaders are, respectively, Lucifer and Ahriman. The former seeks to tempt man mainly in his soul, making it inclined to pride, egotism and passions; and he tries to entice man into his own cosmic kingdom with the help of dazzlingly beautiful visions and illusion in order to attain the highest wisdom. Ahriman, in contrast, endeavours to tempt man with regard to his relationship to the outer world. He is the spirit of falsehood and denial, the true father of all materialism and of the assertion that matter is eternal. These two spirits and their forces generally oppose one another, but under certain conditions they can also work together. Thus Lucifer and Ahriman, albeit in utterly different ways, battle against the Christ impulse and the Mystery of Golgotha. Rudolf Steiner devoted dozens of lectures to a detailed characterization of these beings, their aims and their influence. See also GA 13.

However, this does not mean that we do not also find in Agni Yoga a significant ahrimanic influence. This is manifested with the greatest intensity in its teachings about matter and in its *occult materialism*, which is 'true and fearless', according to Nicholas Roerich.[6]

'We are materialists'; 'we are practical materialists', declare the mahatmas in the third book of *Agni Yoga*, 'Community'.

To the whole series of similar utterances of the mahatmas cited on p. 57, we shall add here one further remark which is particularly characteristic: 'Accept it when people call you materialists. In our thoughts and actions we cannot separate ourselves from matter. We are dealing with either the higher levels or the baser aspects of the same matter.'[7] However, similar ideas had lived in various forms within the Theosophical Society since the time of Blavatsky, when, for example, the wholly supersensible etheric body was conceived of as being similar to the physical, as simply being composed of 'more refined matter' or 'higher vibrations',[8] completely forgetting that the real transition from matter to spirit is not of a quantitive but of a *qualitative* nature. Rudolf Steiner indicated several times in his lectures that such notions of the supersensible are the residue of modern materialism.[*]

Further such 'residues' of materialism are the altogether false conceptions of certain theosophists regarding the 'permanent atom' which, as they would have it, passes as a constant particle of matter from one incarnation to another and so on.[9] This very evident inclination towards materialism, as we have seen, already appears in the mahatmas' letters to Sinnett. 'We believe only in matter ...' wrote the mahatma Kut Humi in one of these (see p. 60). And Helena Roerich wholly logically draws the following conclusion in her teachings from this proposition of the mahatmas: 'Outside matter, pure spirit is a nothing.'[10]

In order to understand this at first apparently so strange mixture of Eastern spirituality and Western materialism, which in 1907 Rudolf Steiner called a 'barren hybrid', it is necessary to turn once more to the

---

[*] This idea about more rarefied conditions of matter is entertained both by scientific and theosophical materialism; the conception is of ever further stages of rarefication. First there is dense matter; etheric matter is more rarefied, astral matter still more so, and then there are all these mental states of matter and everything to do with them—ever more rarefied [material] conditions. Such ideas are entertained just as much by theosophical as by scientific materialism, except that the former enumerates more stages of rarefication [of matter] than the latter. But the transition from ordinary weighable, ponderous matter to the ether has nothing to do with becoming more rarefied' (GA 201, 16 April 1920). (Later in the same lecture Rudolf Steiner fully characterizes what this transition is from a spiritual-scientific point of view.)

anthroposophical teaching about the eighth sphere and to dwell upon certain aspects of it.

According to Rudolf Steiner's spiritual-scientific research, the arising of the eighth sphere around the earth is connected with the *combined* activity of Lucifer and Ahriman, who, while being irreconcilable opponents on one level of world existence, can, nevertheless, on another level be entirely successful in uniting their efforts, as is indicated in the left-hand motif of the Sculptural Group.* This combined activity of theirs led to the gradual arising of the eighth sphere, which as regards its essential nature does not belong to any of the seven spheres, or planetary stages of development, through which man passes in the course of the complete cycle of world evolution from Saturn to Vulcan. Initially it arose through Lucifer—who always longs to conserve the past stage of earthly evolution with the aim of illicitly leading it over to the next stage—introducing into the present Earth evolution the forces of Old Moon, which in their original form can only be perceived in visionary, atavistic clairvoyance.

The Old Moon was formed in such a way that the higher spiritual worlds and their laws were continually reflected in its spiritual sphere as in a mirror; and it was through the permeation of Moon evolution by these reflections that Old Moon had by the end of its evolutionary cycle come to be transformed into the 'planet of wisdom', which then, after passing through a pralaya,† served as the foundation of the modern earth. It is this supersensible substance of Old Moon, containing in itself the imaginative reflection of the higher worlds, that Lucifer now illicitly introduces into earthly evolution. Here, however, he is joined by Ahriman, who endeavours to wrest from the earth sphere the dense, physical matter which has been legitimately formed within it and is connected only with its evolution in order to impregnate it with the cosmic imaginations preserved by Lucifer from Old Moon. These Moon imaginations which have been thus densified by earthly matter form the content of the eighth sphere.

'Thus,' says Rudolf Steiner, 'we are enclosed in a world of densified imaginations, which are not Moon imaginations for the simple reason that

---

* In the nine-metre high Sculptural Group, which depicts Christ overcoming Lucifer and Ahriman, there is a lateral motif where both spirits of opposition are shown combining their forces against the right evolution of mankind. The Sculptural Group was intended for the First Goetheanum, which was burnt down in 1922. It is at present in the Second Goetheanum.

† By 'pralaya' is meant the transition of a planet (or an entire solar system) for a certain period into a higher spiritual condition, at the end of which it again appears in physical form, though in a fully metamorphosed aspect. See GA 11 and 13.

they are densified by the material element of the earth. But they are spectres—that is, behind our world is a world of spectres created by Lucifer and Ahriman ... Thus into our fourth earthly sphere has been incorporated a sphere which is really a Moon sphere but which is wholly filled with the earthly material element [i.e. matter], and is, therefore, an utterly false phenomenon in the universe.'[11]

Rudolf Steiner goes on to speak about the goals which the opposing forces seek to attain with the help of the eighth sphere: 'According to the intentions of Lucifer and Ahriman, nothing less than the disappearance of the whole of human evolution into the eighth sphere is a prospect for humanity, as a result of which its entire evolution would have to take a different course.'[12]

In order that this should not happen, the Spirits of Form (Elohim) who guide earthly evolution sent one of their number, Yahweh or Jehovah, to the Moon, which he gradually permeated with such dense matter that Lucifer and Ahriman were unable to draw it away with them into the eighth sphere. Thus Yahweh became mankind's great defender from the forces of the eighth sphere, for he 'took pains to ensure in the physical domain that not the whole of the material realm could be sucked away by Lucifer and Ahriman [into the eighth sphere].'[13]

All the spiritual-scientific indications quoted regarding the eighth sphere have a direct relationship to the arising within the theosophical movement already at the time of Blavatsky and Sinnett of avowedly materialistic and antichristian tendencies.

Thus on the basis of information that he had apparently received from one of the mahatmas, Sinnett asserted in his book that the physical moon itself is the eighth sphere. Actually, the contrary is true. The physical moon orbits the earth precisely as a means of *countering* the evil forces of the eighth sphere. According to Rudolf Steiner, with this erroneous assertion of Sinnett 'materialism is introduced into the realm of occultism and occultism becomes materialism'.[14] 'And so it was easy for that individuality, whose interest lay in making use of materialism in a spiritual way for particular purposes of his own, to disseminate in Sinnett's *Esoteric Buddhism* an ostensibly spiritual teaching with a very strong materialistic hue.'[15]

Blavatsky, however—in contrast to Sinnett, who did not have any spiritual experience of his own—possessed real clairvoyant faculties, albeit of a mediumistic kind, and therefore 'was well aware that what Sinnett had written was untrue'.[16] And as she was essentially a deeply honest person (as has been pointed out), she could not agree with this. 'But on the other hand she was in the hands of those who desired that the false teaching [about the moon] should be inculcated into humanity.'[17] Nevertheless, even though she was 'in the hands of' the Indo-Tibetan occultists of a left inclination, she tried in her book *The Secret Doctrine* to rectify this error to some extent. But as Blavatsky was wholly inwardly dependent upon these occultists, she 'corrected [Sinnett's error] in a way that sought to reinforce the one-sidedness of the left-oriented Indian occultists'.[18] Having rectified (in her book) Sinnett's error by correctly pointing out that the moon is not the eighth sphere but has, on the contrary, been placed in the cosmos by the Gods as a counterweight to the forces of evil proceeding from the eighth sphere, Blavatsky was at the same time prepared 'in exchange', as it were, to yield to the left-oriented Indian occultists with respect to an even more important question. In the same book, *The Secret Doctrine*, she presented an altogether false teaching about Yahweh, that is, about that mighty being who—as the spiritual ruler of the moon—is also the chief antagonist of the eighth sphere and was the principal preparer for the appearance of Christ on earth.

As she had—under the influence of her Indo-Tibetan inspirers—completely distorted the truth about Yahweh, Blavatsky had actually ceased to be able to understand either Judaism or Christianity, despite the fact that in her first book, *Isis Unveiled*, she had already given expression to certain truths of esoteric Judaism and Christianity. The result of this was that 'in *The Secret Doctrine* she gave vent to a volley of abuse about everything to do with Judaism and Christianity.'[19]

Rudolf Steiner describes this process of Blavatsky's transformation into an implacable opponent of Judaism and Christianity in the following words: 'In order to establish on her own account something that would outweigh Sinnett's assertion [about the moon], she [Blavatsky] acceded to the proposals of the Indian occultists who were inspiring her. These occultists, being adherents of the left path, had no other aim than the promotion of their own specifically Indian interests. They had in mind to establish over the entire earth a system of wisdom from which Christ, and also Yahweh or Jehovah, were excluded. And so something which would gradually eliminate Christ and Yahweh had to be secretly interpolated in her teaching.'[20]

In order to understand how these intentions came to exist amongst the Eastern occultists, it is necessary to bear in mind that it was fundamentally impossible for the Eastern initiate to approach a true knowledge of the Christ Mysteries. Rudolf Steiner refers to this in the notes that he made for Schuré: 'For the Eastern initiations must necessarily leave the *Christ principle*, the central *cosmic* factor in evolution, untouched.' Thus 'they ['the revelations of Eastern initiation' and the mahatmas who stand behind them] can only hope for success in evolution if they can eradicate the Christ principle from Western culture. This would, however, be equivalent to nullifying the *meaning of the earth*, which consists in the knowledge and the fulfilment of the intentions of the *living Christ*.'*

As a means of achieving the purposes of the Indo-Tibetan initiates through Blavatsky, the attempt was made to replace the impulse of Christ-Yahweh by the impulse of Lucifer: 'The following method was adopted. It was said: If we consider Lucifer—nothing was said about Ahriman; so little was known about him that one name was used for both—we see what a great benefactor of mankind he is. He brings to human beings everything they have gained through the head: science, art, in short, all progress. He is the true spirit of light, and it is to him that we must adhere ... Hence, [Blavatsky's] assertion in *The Secret Doctrine* that human beings should not adhere to Yahweh, for ... the true benefactor of mankind is Lucifer. The whole of *The Secret Doctrine* is built up in such a way that this notion shimmers through it and is also clearly expressed in it. And so for occult reasons Blavatsky had to be made into someone who hated Christ-Yahweh. For in the occult domain this has exactly the same significance as the statement that the moon is the eighth sphere has in the realm that Sinnett was concerned with.' In other words, 'what it was desired to achieve through Blavatsky was, similarly, to mislead people into believing in the eighth sphere'.[21]

Thus through turning Blavatsky into an opponent of Christianity the Indo-Tibetan mahatmas managed to make the theosophical movement completely anti-Christian and avowedly *luciferic*. 'Of course, people were led in this way to the spiritual world; and this was *The Secret Doctrine*'s great merit ... But this path was such that it pursued only specific—as opposed to universally human—interests in the evolution of mankind.'[22]* The first part of this quotation may be taken as referring to the true mahatmas and the second part to the left-oriented occultists.

---

* In both quotations, the italics are Rudolf Steiner's. (See Appendix 5.)

† Bearing in mind the considerable importance of this process, let us now consider a further description of it, this time from the lecture of 27 November 1916: 'Blavatsky was misled by certain beings whose aim it was to allure her into replacing Christ by Lucifer; this was to come about through spreading ideas about the eighth sphere which were the complete opposite of the truth and through maligning the God, Yahweh, whom they made out to be a god of a lower order. Thus those cosmic powers that sought to further materialism were also working on behalf of materialism through what was called theosophy, for materialism would have plunged to the most abysmal depths if people had believed that the moon really is the eighth sphere ... and that it is necessary to do battle with Christianity.' (GA 172, 27 November 1916.)

Thus in the later theosophy of Blavatsky and to an ever greater degree in Helena Roerich's Agni Yoga, because of the total misunderstanding of the Christ Being evoked by the influence of the pseudo-mahatmas there came into being what the adversarial powers were putting into effect together on a cosmic level for the strengthening of the eighth sphere, with Lucifer bringing the imaginations of Old Moon, and Ahriman permeating them with earthly matter. And as these Moon imaginations, as has been shown, contain the reflections of higher spiritual worlds, through their being permeated by earthly matter these higher worlds themselves begin to appear to a human individual who beholds them in the reflections of the eighth sphere as though they are permeated by ever more refined matter. Thus Agni Yoga teaches: 'We are dealing with either the higher levels or the baser aspects of the same matter' and 'outside matter, pure spirit is a nothing'. Such utterances can indeed spring only from inspirations from the eighth sphere.

All this enables us to understand more clearly a further thesis of Agni Yoga ('Leaves of Morya's Garden', Vol. 2, 'Illumination'): 'Astral bodies have volume and weight and possess many of the qualities of earthly life.'[23] Behind such a statement lies the following reality. If a human individual begins to develop an inclination towards occult materialism during his life, after the death of such a person Lucifer acquires the possibility of bringing part of his astral body into the eighth sphere, and Ahriman of impregnating this astral body with earthly matter. In this new spectral existence it then actually acquires certain attributes of the physical world, 'volume and weight', as it were.

From what has been said it becomes more possible to understand the significance, as described by Rudolf Steiner, in the books of Sinnett and Blavatsky between Eastern esotericism and Western materialistic science. In an occult sense this union is none other than the concrete expression of the combined activity of Lucifer and Ahriman in the process of creating and strengthening the eighth sphere. As already said, the beginning of this barren 'synthesis' came with the books of Blavatsky and Sinnett under the influence of the left-oriented Eastern occultists referred to. This highly problematic trend (and not the esoteric wisdom of the true mahatmas) is directly continued with redoubled force in Agni Yoga, which—in the words of its founder—aspires to find 'connecting links between the ancient traditions of the Vedas and the formulas of Einstein.'[24] The architecture of the Roerich Museum in New York was to become a visible symbol of these 'connecting links'. The artist himself conceived it in the form of a 24-storey skyscraper, crowned by a round Buddhist stupa.

Notes

1. GA 196, 9 January 1920.
2. GA 172, 27 November 1916.
3. HR 2, 3 December 1937 and 5 April 1938.
4. See Rudolf Steiner, *Occult Science* (GA 13), the chapter entitled 'Man and the Evolution of the World'.
5. HR 2, 3 December 1937.
6. NR 4, p. 318.
7. OB, Part 2, X. 3.
8. Similar descriptions can be found in the books of A. Besant and C. Leadbeater.
9. See GA 258, 15 June 1923.
10. HR 1, 1 February 1935.
11. GA 254, 18 October 1915.
12. Ibid.
13. Ibid.
14. Ibid.
15. GA 254, 17 October 1915.
16. Ibid.
17. Ibid.
18. Ibid.
19. Ibid.
20. GA 254, 18 October 1915.
21. Ibid.
22. Ibid.
23. AY 2, Part 2, IV. 10.
24. NR 6, p. 221.

6. The Macrocosmic Christ Being and the Microcosmic Being of the Bodhisattvas

Now that we have, with the help of anthroposophy, considered the occult foundations of Agni Yoga's devotion to Bolshevism and materialism, we must turn to the central error of this teaching, to its inability to recognize the Christ Being and His whole significance for world evolution. This lack of understanding, however, can be traced not only to the left-oriented Eastern occultists who inspired Helena Roerich but extends also to the true Eastern mahatmas,* whose initiation Rudolf Steiner described as follows: 'The Eastern initiations must necessarily leave the *Christ principle*, the central *cosmic* factor of evolution, untouched.'†

From an esoteric point of view this inner blindness with regard to a true understanding of the Being of the Christ stems from the fact that the spiritual experience of the Eastern initiates extends only to the lunar and planetary spheres and not to that of the sun and the fixed stars.

The Eastern mahatmas give indications of this limitation in their knowledge to what is *within the bounds of the solar system* on several occasions in their letters to Sinnett and other theosophists. Thus the mahatma Kut Humi writes: 'You were told that our knowledge was limited to this our solar system.'‡ And then in other letters: 'What lies beyond and outside the worlds of form, and being, in worlds and spheres in their most spiritualized state ... is useless for anyone to search after, since even Planetary Spirits have no knowledge or perception of it. If our greatest adepts [of the East] and Bodhisattvas have never penetrated themselves beyond our solar system ...'[1] 'No adept has ever penetrated beyond the veil of primitive Cosmic matter. The highest, the most perfect vision is limited to the universe of *Form* and *Matter*.'[2] And finally in yet another letter: 'Not even a Dyan Chohan of the lower orders could approach it without having its *body* consumed, or rather annihiliated. Only the highest "planetary" can scan it.'[3]

It follows clearly that for the Eastern mahatmas direct access to the inner *mysteries of the sun*, to its deepest, 'starry' secrets, remains closed. This means that their occult knowledge embraces only the world of the planets

---

* See further in Part Three.
† See Appendix 5.
‡ See Appendix 6.

which make up our solar system, and 'the higher *planetary spirits* which rule them—'the only "spirits" we believe in', write the mahatmas.[4] As for the sun, the spiritual focus of our cosmic world, it is perceived by them merely in its lower, 'planetary' aspect, that is, as an integral *part* of the solar system and not as a mediator for, and a gate into, the higher spiritual worlds lying beyond it, which in an occult sense corresponds to the higher aspect of the sun not as a 'planet' but as a 'star'. Thus their higher occult knowledge is confined to what can be received by initiates who in their spiritual development have risen to the bodhisattva stage, that is, beings 'who have never penetrated themselves beyond our solar system'.

The Christ Being is at an opposite pole to the bodhisattvas. Whereas a bodhisattva is a highly developed *human being*,[*] Christ is a cosmic divine Being. In other words, whereas a bodhisattva, in becoming a buddha, *ascends* to the outer limits of the solar system, that is, to the 'mantle' of the starry mysteries of the sun, Christ, as an exalted divine-cosmic Being, *descended* from the worlds lying *beyond its bounds*, uniting first with the higher 'starry' aspect of the sun which the Planetary Spirits serve and then with its planetary aspect to which they themselves belong, in order from thence to descend to earth for the fulfilment of the central event of earthly evolution—the Mystery of Golgotha.[†]

Thus from the sources of Christian initiation Rudolf Steiner speaks about him as follows: 'Christ, who now reveals himself as the Being who at the beginning of our era passed through the Mystery of Golgotha, *descended to the sun from still greater heights.*'[5]

At the boundary between the 'starry' and 'planetary' aspects of the sun a meeting takes place between the descending Christ and the ascending bodhisattvas, who together form there a high spiritual lodge, with Christ representing the central sun or starry principle and the bodhisattvas the planetary or moon principle. For, just as the moon reflects sunlight, transmitting it from itself to the earth, so do the bodhisattvas receive in this exalted sphere, and then bring to all mankind, the light and knowledge of the central Being of our cosmos, its spiritual Sun—the Christ.

Rudolf Steiner unfolded this highly important mystery of esoteric

---

[*] The human nature of the Buddha was acknowledged in the Theosophical Society. Its co-founder, Olcott, for example, expressed this in a short Buddhist catechism which he compiled for schools in southern India. See also the quotation from *Osnovy buddizma* ('The Foundations of Buddhism') by Helena Roerich on p. 42.

[†] See further regarding the two aspects of the sun and also the descent of Christ through the various cosmic spheres in: S.O. Prokofieff, *The Twelve Holy Nights and the Spiritual Hierarchies*, Temple Lodge Publishing, second edition 1993 (reprinted 2004).

Christianity from the sources of Christian-Rosicrucian initiation. In a whole series of lectures given in 1909–10 he referred to the circle of twelve bodhisattvas who in the sphere of Buddhi or Providence surround the higher source of their inspirations, their knowledge and their life—the Cosmic Christ: 'Thus to Christ there belong twelve bodhisattvas, who have the task of preparing and further establishing what He [the Christ] has brought as the greatest impulse of our cultural development . . . By this means we have risen to the sphere of the bodhisattvas and have entered a circle of twelve stars with the sun at its centre, illuminating and warming them. This Sun is that source of life which they will then bring down again to the earth.' This is the true relationship between Christ and the bodhisattvas: 'Christ at the centre of earthly evolution, and the bodhisattvas as His predecessors and successors, who have the task of renewing humanity's relationship with His work.'[6] Thus in another lecture Rudolf Steiner calls the bodhisattvas the 'emissaries of the moon (lunar sphere)' or, which is the same thing, the representatives of the 'Moon Logos', which in the spiritual spheres of the moon and the planets is 'the reflection of the Sun Logos' or the Christ.[7]

However, *this* aspect of the activity of all *true* bodhisattvas remains completely closed to the Eastern mahatmas, with the result that they apparently know nothing of their higher aim of serving the Sun Logos— the central Being of our cosmos, who on one single occasion became flesh in Jesus of Nazareth.[*] This becoming flesh of the Logos (John 1:14) opened up to earthly humanity for the first time in its whole existence the possibility of gaining *direct* knowledge of the most hidden essence of the Sun mysteries in their higher, 'starry' aspect—which unites our solar system with the entire universe, extending even to the regions of the highest spirituality, that is, those divine-spiritual worlds which are in Christian esotericism rightly called the worlds or kingdom of the Divine Father—not through the mediation of the bodhisattvas, that is, not through the reflection of the Sun Logos (as was the case in pre-Christian religions), but from the Christ Himself, who passed through the Mystery of Golgotha and has since that time been united with the whole of earthly evolution.[†] Herein lies the esoteric significance of Christ's words: 'No one has ever seen God; the only-begotten Son, who is in the bosom of the Father, he has made him known' (John 1:18). In other words: the

---

[*] In the thick volume of the mahatmas' letters to Sinnett with its 500 pages of small script, letters which form the basis not only of his book *Esoteric Buddhism* but also of Blavatsky's book *The Secret Doctrine*, Christ is not mentioned at all.

[†] 'Lo, I am with you always, until the closing of the age' (Matthew 28:20).

mysteries of the spiritual cosmos lying beyond our solar system were not accessible to any of the earth's initiates until the coming of Christ. Now, however, through union with the Christ impulse, they have become accessible to all who follow the path of Christian initiation.

In our time the revelation of these Sun mysteries of the Christ takes place in anthroposophy. Through his knowledge of them Rudolf Steiner, as the modern Christian initiate, was in a position to penetrate in his spiritual research into the evolution of our solar system not only to the limits of the Earth aeon but also to the limits of the aeon which preceded it, that of the Moon, and to the aeons of Ancient Sun and Ancient Saturn—of which Eastern wisdom knows virtually nothing.*

Thus everything that the Eastern mahatmas were able to dictate to Sinnett and Blavatsky, especially in *The Secret Doctrine*, remains almost entirely within these limits: 'By far the greater part of what was given by Helena Petrovna Blavatsky in *The Secret Doctrine* is derived from this consciousness which reaches back only to Ancient Moon. This is known by all occultists who have investigated these matters. Thus if you study *The Secret Doctrine* you will find in its great, all-encompassing panorama of primal beginnings precious little about a more distant past than the [Ancient] Moon condition, which preceded the present Earth condition.'[8]

In this sense, what Rudolf Steiner imparted in his book *Occult Science* about the two more ancient cosmic conditions, and also about the three future aeons of world evolution, those of Jupiter, Venus and Vulcan, represented a truly colossal step forward. Rudolf Steiner subsequently spoke about this as follows: 'So when—this was between 1906 and 1909—in my book *Occult Science* I described the Earth in its earlier incorporation of Ancient Moon, in its still earlier incorporation of Ancient Sun and finally in its earliest incorporation of Ancient Saturn, you will see that I did not stop at its incorporation of Ancient Moon but went further back to the condition of Ancient Saturn;† whereas all the initiates who spoke about these matters came to a halt between moon and sun and, hence, went back only to the moon sphere.‡ They became unin-

---

*Knowledge of these is attainable for Eastern wisdom only indirectly, through their microcosmic repetition at the very beginning of the Earth aeon (see GA 13 and 11).

†In the lecture of 31 October 1911 Rudolf Steiner speaks of how in the course of his spiritual research he was able to reach the sources of existence of the very first aeon of our cosmos, that of Saturn, only because he 'was borne by the Christ Being', 'felt at one with the Christ Being' (GA 132).

‡As is clear from the context of this lecture, this refers mainly to the *Eastern* initiates standing behind and inspiring Blavatsky.

terested and even at times disturbed if it were suggested that they look
further back into the past. They declared this to be impossible, for there
one encounters a barrier, *in the form of a veil*, beyond which one cannot
penetrate.'[9]

These words of Rudolf Steiner have a remarkable amount in common
with the following passage from a letter of the mahatma Kut Humi
(September 1882), where he similarly speaks of the 'veil' which forms the
limit of the 'correct' knowledge of the mahatmas: 'So far—We KNOW.
Within and to the utmost limit, to the very edge of the cosmic veil we
know the fact to be correct—owing to personal experience, for the
information gathered as to what takes place beyond we are indebted to
the planetary spirits, to our blessed Lord Buddha. This of course may be
regarded as second-hand information.'[10] Modern Christian-Rosicrucian
initiation, however, makes it possible for this 'information' to be received
at *first* hand. In the lecture of 13 April 1912 Rudolf Steiner fully characterizes the relationship of Gautama Buddha to the Planetary Spirit of
Mercury who inspires him and then to Christ. Here, too, there is on the
one hand the ascent of the spiritual consciousness of Gautama—when he
became a Buddha—to the sphere of the Planetary Spirit of Mercury, who
in his turn serves still more exalted Sun Spirits belonging to the 'starry'
aspect of the sun, and on the other the descent of the Cosmic Being of the
Christ through the upper, 'starry' gates of the sun, first to the sphere of the
higher Sun Spirits, that is, the rulers of the *entire* solar system as a single
entity, and then to the sphere of the Spirit-rulers of the individual planets.

On this level the Cosmic Christ, as the Ruler of the entire Kingdom of
the Sun amidst the Planetary Spirits who serve Him, is like a radiant sun
encircled by the choir of the planets; and this is repeated nearer the earth,
when Christ appears not only to the Planetary Spirits but also to the
bodhisattvas who are guided by them, and who contemplate and serve the
Cosmic Christ as was described above.

Thus in characterizing Buddha's relationship to Christ at the end of the
lecture referred to above, Rudolf Steiner says: 'When Blavatsky identified
Buddha with Mercury, she was expressing a profound truth which can be
better understood to the extent that one grasps the relationship of Buddha
to Christ in the occult sphere, just as cosmic relationships are best
understood if one comprehends the relationship of the planet Mercury to
the fixed star of the sun. These things cannot be dismissed from view out
of human prejudice; for they can work rightly in the cultural process only
if we confront them directly and in an unbiased way.'[11] In these words
Rudolf Steiner is referring to the endeavour to place Buddhism higher
than Christianity, and Buddha higher than Christ—which is ultimately

based upon a complete ignorance of the true Christian mysteries. For Eastern initiation affords access only to an understanding of beings of the rank of bodhisattva and Buddha and also of the higher Planetary Spirits who guide them, whereas the mysteries of the Cosmic Christ, the Sun Logos who rules our cosmos, remain completely beyond its ken. And so the central event of earthly evolution—the incarnation on earth of the Sun Logos and his passage through the death and Resurrection on Golgotha, an event which signified the beginning of a new world epoch and laid the foundations of a completely new relationship of the earth and humanity with the whole spiritual cosmos—is wholly beyond its capacity to grasp.

Since this time it has been the principal task of true Rosicrucians to unfold the entire earthly and cosmic significance of this central event to all people of good will. Rosicrucians work in the world out of the direct inspiration of Christ, who is served in the supersensible worlds not only by all true bodhisattvas but also by all Planetary Spirits (provided they are not of a luciferic nature[*]). For, in Rudolf Steiner's words, 'the deepest purpose of Rosicrucianism is to reveal ... the intentions of the *living Christ* ... in a form that is filled with wisdom, beauty and active strength'.[†]

These masters of esoteric Christianity (at whose head stands Christian Rosenkreutz), who have in the deepest sense understood the full cosmic significance of the Christ impulse and the Mystery of Golgotha, were the inspirers of the modern science of the spirit, or anthroposophy, founded by Rudolf Steiner at the beginning of the twentieth century, the principal task of which is to make the true knowledge of Christ accessible to the whole of mankind.[12]

Notes

1. ML 22.
2. ML 9.
3. ML 23b.
4. ML 6.
5. GA 211, 24 April 1922.
6. GA 116, 25 October 1909; see also lectures in GA 113, 114, 116, 130.
7. GA 227, 29 August 1923.
8. GA 137, 12 June 1912.

---

[*] In the lecture of 13 April 1912 quoted above, Rudolf Steiner also speaks about retarded, luciferic Planetary Spirits.
[†] See Appendix 5.

 9. GA 243, 20 August 1924.
10. ML 22.
11. GA 136, 13 April 1912.
12. See GA 113, 31 August 1909 and GA 264, Esoteric Lesson of 1 June 1907.

7. The Principal Error of Agni Yoga

Whereas the true mahatmas in their endeavour to counteract Western materialism with the Eastern wisdom, which they had preserved from olden times, for the reasons mentioned above scarcely touched upon the esoteric mysteries of Christianity, from a certain moment onwards the Eastern occultists of a left inclination who had taken their place began immediately to distort these truths. We encounter such a distortion of Christianity throughout the writings of the founder of Agni Yoga.

As we turn directly to the teaching of Agni Yoga and consider its ideas about the Christ from the standpoint of esoteric Christianity, we must emphasize from the outset that it is not simply a question here of an outward respect or disrespect towards the founder of Christianity but—and it is worth repeating this—of actual *spiritual knowledge* and a strict difference between truth and error in this realm. For quotations from the Gospels and references to the Founder of Christianity are met with fairly often in Helena Roerich's books and letters. This fact is often cited by her followers as proof of Agni Yoga's positive relationship to Christianity. However, if one examines such instances more carefully it immediately becomes obvious that Christ is regarded there merely as one of the many teachers of humanity, of the same rank as Gautama Buddha.

For example, in a letter of 24 May 1936 Helena Roerich writes: 'You are right that Jesus [Christ] is a remarkable phenomenon in history, but one should add that all the Kumaras and God-men were no less remarkable. And only a conceited ignoramus will begin to weigh up which of these sublime Spirits is higher or lower. For an excellent formula has been given to us in the Teaching.[*] If the question arises as to who is higher, Christ or Buddha, answer that it is impossible to measure the distant worlds, we can only take delight in their glory' ('Leaves of Morya's Garden', Vol. 2, 'Illumination').[1] And in another letter, Helena Roerich develops the thought of her occult inspirer with the words: 'The future epoch [of the Maitreya] will stand under the rays of the Three Lords—the Maitreya, the Buddha and the Christ.'[2] However, even this answer is actually only a subterfuge for 'non-initiates'. In Helena Roerich's true opinion, or rather in the opinion of the Eastern occultists standing behind

---

[*] By 'teaching' here is meant the books of *Agni Yoga* written by Helena Roerich. Objectifying it in this way is indicative that the content of these books originates not from her but from the mahatmas who dictated to her.

her, the Maitreya is above everyone else. Thus she wrote in another letter: 'In the esoteric Teaching three World Leaders are indicated [by the mahatmas]: Buddha, Christ and Maitreya. *The Maitreya is the Oldest, the First and the Last* [that is, Alpha and Omega, one of Christ's designations, Rev. 1:8–10], *the Lord of Lords* [another name for Christ, Rev. 19:16], *the Teacher of Teachers.*'[3] Being the 'Oldest', he has therefore taken upon himself 'the responsibility for our planet',[4] which is to say, he is today its highest occult leader.

However, Helena Roerich's 'revelations' about the Christ Being are not confined to this. Thus in a letter of 24 September 1935, again after referring to the words quoted above from the 'Leaves of Morya's Garden', Helena Roerich elucidates them as follows: 'Indeed, Christ and Buddha are such distant stars of the spirit in comparison with us earthly [people]. Let us not forget that They and the Lord Maitreya came from Venus* at the dawn of the birth of physical man, and are hence our Divine Fore-fathers and Teachers.'[5]

From the standpoint of Christian esotericism, however, the only element in these words which corresponds to the truth is the indication that the Buddha originally came from Venus. Nevertheless, in the light of Rudolf Steiner's spiritual-scientific research even this fact has a completely different significance and different causes. For after the gradual separation of Venus and Mercury from the sun, Christ, the Sun Logos and sublime Ruler of the Sun Kingdom, sent the future Gautama Buddha as his messenger first to Venus and from thence to the earth: 'This individuality of the [future Gautama] Buddha had already been sent from the sun, from the hosts of Christ, to the Venus men before they—as is recounted in my *Occult Science*†—returned to the earth, so that that individuality which lived in Buddha was Christ's messenger from the sun to Venus. He [the future Gautama Buddha] descended to the earth with the Venus men; but because of the circumstances indicated he so outstripped the other [men]

---

* Helena Roerich conceives of Venus in a highly fantastic and materialistic way, as a kind of upgraded version of the earth. In a letter of 13 August 1938, drawing either upon the mahatmas or Blavatsky's *Secret Doctrine*, she writes about it as follows: 'It is said that on higher planets there are fewer animals and that they are far more perfect. Thus on Venus there are no insects or beasts of prey at all. People fly, birds fly and even fish. Moreover, the birds understand human speech . . .' and so on (HR 2).

† What is meant here is the former period of Earth evolution—described in *Occult Science*—in the course of which it was impossible to find on earth suitable bodies for incarnation and many human souls were forced to seek further possibilities of evolution on other planets of the solar system (including Venus). Subsequently, when the conditions on earth had reverted to a more favourable aspect, they again returned to it.

that during Atlantean times and on into the post-Atlantean age he was able to develop to Buddhahood, attaining this stage before Christ's appearance on the earth. He was, so to speak, a Christian before Christ . . . Accept this result [of occult research], that Buddha was an emissary of the Christ and as such initially lived on Venus.'[6][*]

On the basis of these words we may characterize Gautama Buddha as the last preparer of Christ's incarnation on the earth. But the bodhisattva who in the distant future will reach the stage of buddhahood and, as the new Maitreya Buddha, 'will become the bearer of goodness . . . and will place his words of goodness at the service of the Christ impulse' is to a still higher degree a pupil and follower of the Christ.[7][†]

As for Helena Roerich, access to these truly central mysteries of earthly evolution remained closed to her, as it remained closed to her Eastern inspirers. Thus all the statements of the mahatmas standing behind Helena Roerich to the effect that they are carrying out some sort of 'plan of Christ', on the grounds that over the course of several incarnations they have been his pupils and are in constant intercourse with him—they even indicate to Helena Roerich that Christ abides with them in their Himalayan stronghold (Shamballa)[8]—merely testify from the standpoint of Christian esotericism that they are actually regarding some altogether different being as Christ or calling him by His name.

We shall now present some characteristic examples of such a substitution. In her notes of the seances where her telepathic communication with the mahatmas took place, Helena Roerich tells the mahatmas how a lama gave her an image of the Buddha, explaining that 'Tara' (a female deity) appeared to him in a dream and ordered him to do this.[‡] The mahatma then clarifies this episode as follows: 'Do not suspect the lama [that he is mistaken], for by order of the Christ Sister Or. [Oriona, one of

---

[*] Compare with another lecture: 'The Christ first sent him [the future Buddha] to Venus . . . Thus you have in the Buddha an old emissary of the Christ, who had the task of preparing for Christ's work on the earth' (GA 137, 12 June 1912).

[†] That this mystery of the relationship between Christ and the bodhisattvas was known to Rudolf Steiner from the very beginning of his activity as a teacher of Christian esotericism is evident from the fact that one of his first lecture cycles, given before he became the leader of the German section of the Theosophical Society, bore the title *From Buddha to Christ* (24 lectures given between October 1901 and March 1902). In his autobiography, *The Course of My Life*, Rudolf Steiner writes in recollection of this: 'In these lectures I tried to show what an immense advance the Mystery of Golgotha represents in comparison to the Buddha event and how the evolution of humanity, in that it aspires towards the Christ Event, arrives at its culmination' (GA 28).

[‡] This episode appears in Helena Roerich's account in the book *Altai-Himalaya* (NR, p. 33).

the members of the Himalayan community] sent him in order that the new fire of the Buddha might be kindled beside Christ. The lama is right, for our Eastern Brothers call the Sisters Tara.'[9] On another occasion Helena Roerich said that she had herself heard 'the voice of Christ', whereupon the mahatmas, confirming her experience, reply that his voice is easier to listen to than the voice of Gautama Buddha.[10] Whoever's occult voice this was, to whichever supersensible or earthly being it belonged, one thing can be said with absolute certainty—it was *not* the voice of Christ.

As a result of hearing all these 'voices' and dictating, Helena Roerich's ideas about Christ reach a level of total absurdity. In the last book of *Agni Yoga*, 'The Superearthly', we literally read the following: 'The Great Teacher Himself had the wisdom of Pericles in not expecting justice from the crowd ... The century of Pericles was one of the most refined of phenomena ... Pericles knew both the delight and the blows of fate. The best minds were gathered around him. Philosophers such as these bequeathed to mankind a whole era of thought. *Among the friends of Pericles may be counted also the Great Traveller*, who *absorbed* the unforgettable fascination of the century of knowledge and beauty. Such basic principles also strengthen selflessness and *aim towards heroic deeds*. One may see how the best spirits gather together, in order that they may meet one another in the field of work.'[11] However, as is explained, *this 'Great Traveller' is Christ*, which amidst all these veiled hints is confirmed by two direct statements by Helena Roerich: 'I have already sent you pages from the life of the Great Traveller, or J. Chr.'[12] 'The Great Traveller is of course Christ ...'[13]* Thus in the opinion of Helena Roerich's inspirers, the Christ lived in his previous (pre-Gospel) incarnation in the fifth century before our era in ancient Greece and was one of the friends of Pericles. The extract quoted is not only grotesque but directly blasphemous, if one considers that Helena Roerich, according to her letters, regards the Mahatma Kut Humi as a reincarnation of Pericles ('Pericles and the Gr[eat] T[eacher] K[ut] H[umi] are one individuality)'[14] and herself and her husband as reincarnations of, respectively, the second wife of Pericles, the hetaera [mistress] Aspasia, and the great sculptor Phidias,† who was also part of the circle of Pericles.[15]

---

* In the designation 'Great Traveller' lies a conscious distortion of words that Christ uttered about himself, 'I am the Way' (John 14:6), that is, representing his Being as *the Way itself* rather than as an anonymous 'lonely traveller' (cf. p. 28).

† Helena Roerich considered Leonardo da Vinci to be a previous incarnation of Nicholas Roerich (RA II, p. 74, 24 June 1937).

In the next paragraph of 'The Superearthly', Helena Roerich's inspirer opens up for her the curtain veiling the mystery as to who the 'Great Traveller' was at the time of Pericles: 'Urusvati knows how scanty is the information about the most remarkable of statesmen . . . Let us turn to the great philosopher Anaxagoras. The foundations of His teaching, which were new for many centuries, are well known. Even today the teaching about the *indestructibility of matter* as a basic substance cannot be considered outmoded.* Similarly, His idea of the Highest Reason can be regarded as a wholly new teaching. One can see how the description of the philosopher's life was indicative of His character as a man. Mind you, He was a representative of a remarkable century. He *imbibed* the refinement of Greek thought. He valued art and *on several occasions helped Pericles with advice.* He was the key inner factor in many undertakings. He had sufficient dignity to protect a friend and preferred exile to being deprived of honour. I maintain,' dictated the mahatma, 'that one can give the most brilliant examples of what He did, although He did not want to give a fixed description of forthcoming events. *Already then, in the depths of His heart, He had a presentiment of a future heroic deed.*'[16] And somewhat later she writes in a similar spirit about the 'Great Traveller': 'Difficult is the task of the Teacher and all the more difficult, in that the Hierarchy is erroneously construed by the majority of people. The Great Traveller knew all this and *hastened towards the fulfilment of the heroic deed.* One heroic deed took place in the course of a century, the other during several years.'[17]

This extract cannot be understood other than in the sense that the previous incarnation of Jesus Christ was Anaxagoras, the creator of the first materialistic teaching in the ancient world. He denied the gods, taught the eternity of matter, that it is composed of small particle-like atoms (apeirons) and that all things originate in various combinations of them. He also wrote about 'reason' (nous) as the lightest and purest substance of all substances, about the mechanical evolution of the universe, anticipating in his conclusions modern materialistic psychology, the cosmological theory of Kant-Laplace and the general principle of the conservation of matter and energy.

Thus amongst the founders of the *occult materialism* lying at the foundation of the teaching of Agni Yoga, having as it does a wholly antichristian character, there suddenly also appears the Founder of Christianity himself. And his followers and pupils are all the Eastern mahatmas: 'We knew much, but he could do everything. We accordingly decided to serve his teaching.'[18]

---

* Compare with the text of the letter, written supposedly by K.H., in Appendix 6.

We find the description of how this came about in the second volume of *Agni Yoga*: '... The star of Allagabada* pointed the way, and so we visited Sarnat and Gaia.† Everywhere we found a mockery of religion. On the way back, at new moon, a memorable saying of Christ's was expressed. During the night's expedition the leader lost his way. After some searching I found Christ sitting on a sandy hillock, looking at the moon-spangled sand. I said: "We have lost our way, we must look to the positions of the stars." "Rossul Morya, what is the way to us when the whole of the earth is waiting for us ... ?"

'Taking a bamboo cane, he drew a square around the impression of his footprint, and added: "Verily I say—a human foot." Then, making a print with his palm, he enclosed it with a square. "Verily I say—a human hand." Between the squares he drew some similarly shaped columns and covered them as it were with a hemisphere. He said: "O, how Aum will enter into human consciousness! There, I have drawn a pistil with an arc above it, and have created a foundation for it with four sides. When the Temple where my pistil is blossoming has been built with human feet and human hands, may the builders follow my path. Why do we wait to find a path when it lies before us?" Then he stood up, erasing with the cane what he had drawn.'[19]

This extract from *Agni Yoga*, where Mahatma Morya gives an account of his meeting with Christ, was illustrated by Nicholas Roerich in 1924. In his painting the seated figure of Christ (the face is not visible, and there is no halo) is portrayed with his back to the spectator, and behind him, though at the same time as it were towering *over* him, is the larger figure of the seated Morya, covered from head to foot by a cloak from beneath which only the sharp outlines of a nose and a dark beard are visible. Both figures are bending over the drawing described above on the earth. The figure of Christ is pointing at it with a small cane and is evidently already preparing to 'erase what he had drawn'. The picture bears the title, 'The Signs of Christ'. (See Illustration 16 on p. 190)

Whether this description has a bearing on the Kashmir legends about Christ-Issa's stay in India after his flight from Palestine, or—which is more likely—has to do with a contemporary meeting of Mahatma Morya with

---

* Allagabada is a town in southern Nepal, on the Ganges.
† The places mentioned in the passage cited here lie not far from Sikkim and are associated with the earthly life of the Buddha. The Roerichs visited them at the end of 1923. In his diary Nicholas Roerich makes the following observations in this connection: 'Sarnat and Gaia—places associated with personal exploits of the Buddha—lie in ruins. They are merely places of pilgrimage, just as Jerusalem is not more than a place of pilgrimage to Christ...' (NR 4, p. 42).

the Founder of Christianity, now reincarnated and concealed somewhere in the Himalayas, is left wholly unclear in the book of *Agni Yoga*. However, this passage appeared in a later book by Helena Roerich called *Kriptogrammy Vostoka* ('Cryptograms of the East'), published under the pseudonym G. Saint-Iler in 1929. In this book the passage likewise bears the title 'Signs of Christ', as with Nicholas Roerich's picture; and it is included in the section 'From the Life of Christ', which consists of a whole series of similar descriptions. Although the passage itself is unaltered, much in it now becomes more clear. We shall cite the passage that precedes it in the book, which as regards its content forms with it a single whole. It is called 'The Coming of Christ'. It runs as follows: 'Christ, who only gave, took nothing. This resolution from His early years led Him through a burning hot desert, and His feet burned like those of a simple drover. We awaited Him, but, as always happens, the moment of His coming was unexpected. My horse was brought forward for me, and I was preparing to bid farewell to my family when the servant noticed a ragged *traveller*. His long face was pale, and His hair hung in thin strands over His shoulders. And only a grey linen cloth covered His body.' This is how the mahatma describes Christ's arrival in India. 'Thus we waited every day for three years, and the light of the star shone over us ...'

'I [who is meant here and earlier on in this section is unclear] was also told to lead Him where I myself was unable to go. We rode by night on a white camel and by nightly stages arrived at Lagor,[*] where we found, as though awaiting us, a follower of the Buddha [possibly the Maitreya himself]. We had never seen such resoluteness, for we had been on our way for three years. And *for three years* He had been there, where I was unable to go. We waited for Him and led Him to the Jordan.'[20]

It is clear from these extracts that Nicholas and Helena Roerich were convinced that Jesus visited India and Tibet between the ages of 12 and 30, where over the course of *three years* he was under the tutelage of the Maitreya Buddha or Gautama Buddha himself in his secret sanctuary (Shamballa), which was not accessible to his companion and whence he was to derive his wisdom.[†] Moreover, as is apparent from Helena Roerich's occult diary, these reports about Christ's visiting India and Tibet, which were subsequently included in the second volume of *Agni*

---

[*] The former centre of the Indian province Punjab and now a town in Pakistani territory.

[†] Helena Roerich also confirmed her conviction that the Founder of Christianity visited Tibet and India in one of her letters: 'Read,' she wrote, 'in "The Coming of Christ" in the "Cryptograms of the East" from the thirteenth chapter onwards. I do not doubt, or rather I know, that Chr[istos] was in India ... Rossul M[orya] was already getting on in years when Chr[istos] went out to preach' (HR 3, 24 May 1938).

Yoga and in 'Cryptograms of the East', were originally *dictated* to her by
the Mahatma Morya in two telepathic seances, taking place on 25 April
and 6 May 1924. In the diary there are also certain phrases which did not
find their way into these books. 'More needs to be said about the 30 years
than about the three years of Service' suggests the mahatma to Helena
Roerich.* '... Thus we begin with the Description [capital letter] of his
[small letter] Life, in order that no distorted word may be inscribed on the
earth.'[21] All the 'writings about Christ' which then appeared five years
later in 'Cryptograms of the East' may be seen as a testimony to the
obedient fulfilment of this indication of the mahatma.

The extent to which the views of Helena Roerich about this question
changed in the course of her life is borne out by the following extract
from a letter that she wrote two years before her death and in which she—
in contrast to everything that she had written previously—referred to
Jesus not as a teacher but as a pupil of Morya: 'We know that Jesus also
received instruction from the Great Sage of the East, Rossul Morya, and
remained with him for no less than seven years, after which they travelled
together in India; and then Jesus left with the blessing of the L[ord]
Maitreya for his own country. But He was unable to complete his Task
there; He became terribly overtired and fell ill; and at the threshold of
yonder world there appeared before him the great Sage [Maitreya?] in a
refined form and suggested to him that He conclude His Task by entering
into his body. Of course, agreement was given with joy!'[22]

The significance of the second theosophical mahatma K.H. grows in a
similar way in the last years of Helena Roerich's life. He appears as none
other than Jesus of Nazareth himself. Thus she writes in one of her late
letters to America: 'In theosophical literature one can find the indication
that Jesus was an incarnation of the Teacher Kut Humi, but when the
time came for the Way of Sorrows and the Crucifixion, a still higher Spirit
entered into him.'[23]

As for the story about Anaxagoras, it leaves the possibility of further
incarnations of Christ also after his life in Palestine open. The following
extract from the second volume of *Agni Yoga* seems to bear this out: 'After
Augustus the church began to plunge into the darkness of the Middle

---

*By this means Helena Roerich consciously transfers her attention from the three years
that the Cosmic Christ Being spent on earth (from the Baptism in the Jordan to the
Mystery of Golgotha) to the 30 years of the life of Jesus of Nazareth, the meaning and
substance of which did not actually consist of journeys to the East in search of ancient
wisdom but in preparing to receive the divine Christ Being, as Rudolf Steiner has
described in detail in the lectures on the 'Fifth Gospel', that is, the Gospel events inscribed
for all time in the Akashic Chronicle.

Ages, and Christ seemed locked in a golden cage. In order to break out of it, Christ Himself even passed among demeaned figures, merely to show the greatness of communion in unity.'[24] For the same reason Helena Roerich valued Annie Besant's *Esoteric Christianity* highly, although it had served as the theoretical basis for the scandalous history around Krishnamurti and she condemned this adventure. 'Of Besant's books,' writes Helena Roerich in one of her later letters, *Esoteric Christianity* is, of course, the best.'[25]

All in all, however, the theme of the various physical incarnations of Christ is only sketchily presented in *Agni Yoga*, which is understandable since in reality its occult interests were not directed towards the Founder of Christianity but towards another far higher and more significant a figure—with a stature of the 'hierarchy of the Himalaya'—deemed to be the 'oldest of the Rulers', the Maitreya.

As a consequence, the figure of the Maitreya gradually acquired a truly cosmic stature in Helena Roerich's consciousness as her teaching developed from the first volume of *Agni Yoga* to the last. Thus she wrote in the seventh volume: 'For some the Ruler of Shamballa is a painted Idol, for others the Ruler of Shamballa is the *Leader of all planetary spirits* ... The Ruler of Shamballa lives and breathes in the heart of the Sun.'[26] He is in addition the lord of the earth, who unites in himself all impulses of his predecessors and above all Buddha and Christ: 'The Great Spirit standing at the head of the New Cycle must encompass within himself the whole synthesis, *all* the great Figures of the past Cycle. Hence the Synthesis of the Maitreya encompasses *all* Rays.'[27]

Thus for Helena Roerich everything, including the Christ, is united in this high individuality: 'Everything that is Greatest and Highest is contained in this individuality. There is no higher expression of the Great Mystery of Existence than in the Sun Hierarchy, the L[ord] Maitreya, the Lord Christ. He is the Great Preserver and Creator. He is *Everything*!'[28] (italics by Helena Roerich).

According to Helena Roerich, the Maitreya was from the very beginning the one who gave all higher revelations to humanity: 'Our G[reat] L[ord] is the Sun Hierarch, and His *Will*, His *Voice* sounded in all eternal Precepts of Wisdom, imprinted upon the most ancient Tables. Open the Bible and hear this Voice in all Proclamations and Prophecies. Also Moses heard it as the Voice of his Spirit' (italics by H.R.).[29]

While at the end of her life, the Maitreya became for Helena Roerich that highest being of the universe who holds in his hands the life-threads of all human beings. Thus in 1954 she writes to her pupils in America:

'My brothers and sisters, our life is in the hand of the L[or]d. He knows when the thread connecting us to the earth should be cut.'[30]

This endless elevation of the Maitreya, which contradicts all notions of classical Eastern religions about him and behind which lies the clear endeavour to belittle the Christ and reduce him to the second rank, has been taken further by various pupils of Helena Roerich. Thus for example G. Gorchakov, in his recently published book *Vyeliky Uchitel'. Zemniye zhizhni Naivyshevo* ('The Great Teacher. The Earthly Lives of the Most Exalted One'), not only maintains—following the founder of Agni Yoga—that the 'Most Exalted One', that is, the Maitreya, is the head of the entire hierarchy but also 'the focal point of all life, at any rate within the confines of our solar system',[31] for 'the heart of the Maitreya is like the Fire of the Sun'.[32] According to Gorchakov, the Maitreya is the 'One Giant who bears the earth',[33] of whom ancient traditions speak; moreover, he is also 'the Great Sacrifice' (this is actually the esoteric name of Christ[34], the being 'who had the power to *create* the world'.[35] And his 'titles' become for Gorchakov still more dazzling. The Maitreya is already the 'Creator of the solar system',[36] but he is also its 'Eldest Logos'.[37] But even this is not enough. He is 'Infinity itself' and the 'Heart of the Cosmos'.[38]

And finally the Maitreya is the Father God himself: 'It is complicated and highly responsible to speak about the individuality of the Maitreya,' writes Gorchakov, 'for He is the One Whom We call God!'[39]

It troubles Gorchakov little that such a relationship to the Maitreya as to God can hardly be reconciled with the majority of his many incarnations as a human being, to the description of which his book is devoted. On the basis of Helena Roerich's letters (especially those collected in the third volume) Gorchakov cites the following incarnations: Krishna, Hermes Trismegistos, Capila, Menes, Ramases II, Enoch, Abraham, Moses, Solomon, Zoroaster, Orpheus, Apollonius of Tyre, Sheikh Rossul Morya, Origen, Prester John, Sergei Radonezh, Akbar and even Mahatma Morya . . .[*]

And after all this there follows Gorchakov's conclusion, evidently based on the passages from 'Community' that we have already been considering: 'The Maitreya is—if one may put it thus—a SPIRITUAL MATERI-ALIST.'[40] [The capitalized letters represent Gorchakov's emphasis.]

---

[*] In Helena Roerich's letters to America one can also find indications to the effect that in previous lives the Maitreya was also Rama (according to Indian beliefs an avatar of the god Vishnu) and that he will in future be the Manu of the sixth *and* seventh root races (RA I, 7 June 1934; 4 October 1934).

Thus 'the One Whom We call God' ultimately turns out to be a 'spiritual materialist'. Moreover, the word 'We'—written by Gorchakov with a capital letter—is intended to refer not so much to the followers of Helena Roerich and to her herself as to the entirety of the Himalayan hierarchy of teachers.

But let us return to the writings of the founder of Agni Yoga herself. In her letters a whole series of observations can be found which touch upon the shortly imminent and—by all world religions—long awaited appearance of the Messiah. But Helena Roerich does not await the appearance of Christ; she considers the Maitreya to be the 'true' Messiah. Thus she writes, for example: 'Also in the name of Truth one must say that Christ was not really the one promised to them [the Hebrew people] by the Scriptures as the Messiah. The Messiah of the Jews is identical with the Maitreya, the Kalki Avatar [of the Hindus], Muntasar [of the Muslims] and so on—with that sublime figure who is to appear at the change of the Races in order to bring the new Tidings and establish that vibration at which the spiritual evolution of the New Cycle will sound.'[41] This idea is also supported by Nicholas Roerich in a number of his articles, where he repeats, with a few variations, the same series of names, 'which express in a manifold way the same secret and heartfelt aspiration of mankind': 'the Messiah, the Maitreya, Muntasar, Mitolo ...'.[42] The appearance of the Maitreya among human beings is, however, represented by the Roerichs not as a physical phenomenon, but similar to the second (supersensible) coming of Christ described in the Gospels (Matthew 24:30, Mark 13:26, Luke 21:27). In this connection Helena Roerich writes to her correspondent: 'It was also strange to read [in his letter] that "if the Lord Maitreya is to become a Buddha, He will probably come in a physical body". That Individuality who according to the Eastern conception has the Aspect of the Maitreya became a Buddha long ago, that is, he attained a high Enlightenment, with the result that the reason which you have given for physical incarnation no longer applies.'[43] And in another letter: 'The whole of the East believes in a Coming of the L[ord] Maitreya, but those who know are aware that the L[ord] Maitreya now bears the Form of the Lord of Shamballa,* and of course His Coming cannot be understood as a manifestation of His flesh amidst earthly conditions and earthly inhabitants.'[44]

---

* And this means *in a physical body*: 'The L[ord] Maitreya still now bears a physical body for particular purposes, but not for an encounter with crowds' (HR 3, August/September 1934, p. 57). Or in another letter: 'For our Teaching derives from a Teacher who dwells in a physical body' (RA II, 2 April 1938).

These remarks are sharply at variance not only with classical Buddhist tradition but also with the spiritual-scientific research of Rudolf Steiner, according to which the true Maitreya Bodhisattva, like his predecessor, the Gautama Bodhisattva, will incarnate on earth again and again until after three thousand years he attains the stage of Buddhahood, in order as the first *Christian Buddha* 'to place all that he has at the service of the Christ impulse'.[45]

One can also discern the activity of this new bodhisattva in the twentieth century. It is associated with the central spiritual event of our time, the new appearance of Christ in the etheric body, which— according to Rudolf Steiner—modern spiritual science or anthroposophy is called upon to proclaim and prepare for: 'Without books and docu- ments this great event—the second coming of Christ—will take place for those who have made themselves worthy of it. It is the obligation of anthroposophy to proclaim this.'[46] For 'it is the mission of the anthro- posophical movement to create, first of all, the conditions that make understanding of Christ possible on the physical plane, and then to furnish the power to behold Him'.[47]

And if, on the one hand, the *whole* of anthroposophy is intended to serve as a means of preparing mankind for this highly important event, on the other hand the beginning of its proclamation—which Rudolf Steiner embarked upon in 1910—was accomplished by him out of the direct inspirations of the Maitreya Bodhisattva. He himself spoke of this in the tenth lecture of the cycle on the Gospel of St Matthew: 'And this bod- hisattva will inspire us by making us aware that the time is approaching when the Christ will . . . appear as an enlivening force to human beings in a new form, in an *etheric* body.'[48]

★

The inner blindness of Agni Yoga towards the spiritual sphere of Christ that we have characterized is manifested with particular clarity in one of its central teachings, that about Shamballa. Its foundations are contained in Nicholas Roerich's conversation with the Tibetan lama. This was pub- lished in the article 'Radiant Shamballa', in which Roerich clearly dis- tinguishes between two aspects of Shamballa, the earthly and the heavenly. Addressing the lama he says: 'Lama, we know the majesty of Shamballa. We know that this is indeed an indescribable kingdom. But we also know of the reality of earthly Shamballa. We know that certain high lamas went to Shamballa, and that on their way they saw familiar physical objects. We know stories about the Buryat lama, that he was led by a very narrow secret path. We know that a fellow traveller saw a caravan of mountain-folk with salt from the lakes on the border of Shamballa.[*] Moreover, we have ourselves seen the white frontier post of one of the three frontiers of Shamballa. So do not speak with me only about the heavenly Shamballa but also about the earthly Shamballa; for you know just as well as I that the earthly Shamballa is connected with the heavenly Shamballa. And by means of this link both worlds are united.'[49]

Much is said in a whole series of other books by Nicholas Roerich[†] and in Helena Roerich's letters about the earthly Shamballa, which is also called the 'Trans-Himalayan Stronghold' or the 'Stronghold of Light' and is situated somewhere in one of the inaccessible valleys of the Himalayan mountains. According to her testimony, the earthly Shamballa—now led by the Maitreya Bodhisattva—is the hidden abode of that secret 'community' where all the mahatmas live in physical and 'refined' bodies. From there they visited H.P. Blavatsky, and from there they wrote the letters to her and to Sinnett which were to form the foundation of their books. In a letter of 23 July 1936 Helena Roerich writes about the way to it: 'Many miles from that town [she is referring to one of the towns in Tibet] lies the Stronghold of Light. The approaches to this stronghold are well guarded.[‡] There are various ways to it, and it is often necessary to follow subterranean paths and go under rivers in order to reach the hidden heights. But there are landmarks for those who have been called.'[50] Or in another letter: 'The Himalayan Mahatmas live in total seclusion and admit into their Stronghold one, or at the most two, candidates in a century.'[51] In this same letter, the Mahatmas Kut Humi and Morya are named as inhabitants of this 'stronghold'.

According to Helena Roerich, Apollonius of Tyre,[52] Paracelsus[53] and the Count of Saint-Germain[54] were formerly in the 'Trans-Himalayan Stronghold'. From this same 'spiritual sanctuary in the heart of Asia' there also worked the mysterious Prester John, the last guardian of the Holy Grail.[55] Furthermore, in one of the ashrams of the 'Trans-Himalayan Stronghold' H.P. Blavatsky was prepared for the writing of her book The Secret Doctrine. Helena Roerich writes of her: 'Sometimes the Mahatmas summon brethren for a certain time to one of their Ashrams and prepare

---

[*] Roerich experienced all this through a 'very intelligent buryat' (see NR 6, p. 239; NR 4, p. 99).

[†] Thus, for example, in Heart of Asia: 'Shamballa is a holy place, where the earthly world makes contact with a higher state of consciousness. In the East they know that two Shamballas exist: one earthly and the other invisible' (NR 6, p. 250). Compare with the definition of Shamballa in the second volume of Agni Yoga (see above p. 41).

[‡] See the reproduction of Nicholas Roerich's painting 'The Guardians of Himalaya', Illustration 18, p. 191.

their organisms for [otherwise] hidden perceptions of refined energies and give them instructions. Thus it was in the case of H.P. Blavatsky, who spent three years in their Ashram before sending *The Secret Doctrine* out into the world,'[56] and so on.[*]

Finally, the Roerichs themselves were convinced that during their trans-Himalayan expedition in 1927 they visited Shamballa.

Helena Roerich describes earthly Shamballa or the 'Trans-Himalayan Stronghold' in a highly materially real way. Thus in the second volume of *Agni Yoga* ('Leaves of Morya's Garden', Vol. 2, 'Illumination'), the mahatmas tell her about 'our laboratories and observatories', 'our prismatic mirrors', 'our telescopic apparatuses'.[57] And in a letter of 24 June 1935 Helena Roerich mentions 'an apparatus that collects psychic energy' and 'apparatuses which measure the tension of the fire of space', and adds: 'All these apparatuses work not only on a refined level but also on the physical plane in the Fortress of the Great Brotherhood.'[58]

In her occult diary Helena Roerich also reports about her visiting the astral body of a huge 25-storey 'museum' of the occult history of mankind, which was hewn out of the rock underground in the valley in the Himalayas where the mahatmas live. While in the museum, '[Helena Roerich] spent a particularly long time in the lower galleries devoted to

---

[*]The extent to which these and similar communications on the part of Helena Roerich may be questionable is shown very clearly by her own allusion to the subsequent spiritual destiny of Blavatsky. Hence in Helena Roerich's opinion, Blavatsky, who died in 1891, reincarnated on the earth 'almost immediately after her death' in earthly Shamballa in the Himalayas (HR 1, 8 September 1934).

This assertion, however, is in complete contradiction with Rudolf Steiner's spiritual research, according to which the soul of the founder of the theosophical movement was still in the spiritual world between death and a new birth in 1910–12. Thus in a whole series of lectures Rudolf Steiner refers to the importance *for Blavatsky's after-death existence* of correcting the errors that she had made on earth as quickly as possible, and particularly all those which had sprung from her complete misunderstanding of and negative attitude towards the Christ impulse. For example, in the lecture of 8 May 1910, which was dedicated to the 'day of the white lotus', that is, the festival of Blavatsky's birthday in the Theosophical Society, Rudolf Steiner says: 'Thus in H.P. Blavatsky we see the bringer of a new dawning light. But what good would that light be if it had no wish to illumine the most important thing that mankind has ever had? A theosophy which does not have the means to understand Christianity [and Blavatsky's theosophy was of such a kind] has absolutely no value for the culture of today' (GA 116).

And then Rudolf Steiner goes on to say that those of Blavatsky's followers who reject the true knowledge of Christianity 'impede the activity of her spirit in our age! ... This spirit is now working in the spiritual world ...' (ibid.). He also spoke in a similar way in the lectures of 27 September 1911 and 8 May 1912, that is, on the 'day of the white lotus'.

the life of Christ'.[*] In the course of this, the mahatma who was dictating to her warned that the entire underground museum was saturated with 'protective gases', which were not without danger even for *astral* visitors.[59] For the astral body of the person concerned entered into a materialization process there and hence became accessible to earthly, physical influences.

In all these and similar descriptions, which are repeated again and again in the pages of *Agni Yoga*, we encounter in a sense a kind of spectre of the eighth sphere: all the 'visions' of Helena Roerich are hopelessly impregnated by the conceptions of modern materialistic science and appear in a highly material form. It is possible that this is associated with the fact that during the great Himalayan journey (1925–8) the Roerichs continually encountered phenomena in the mountains of which little was known or spoken about at that time but which have since the middle of our century become accessible to many hundreds of people in various continents and have received the name of 'unidentified flying objects'. In his book on Shamballa Nicholas Roerich recalls the 'remarkable plateau of Tibet with its magnetic waves and miracles of light'. Nicholas Roerich himself reports to the Tibetan lama about such a phenomenon: 'Lama, not far from Ulan-Davana [a place near the northern border of Tibet] we saw an enormous dark vulture . . . It crossed the path of something radiant and beautiful which was moving southwards over our camp and shining in the rays of the sun. The lama's eyes lit up: "O, Shamballa is protecting you . . . The protective power of Shamballa is accompanying you in the form of this Radiant Matter . . . Did you notice the direction in which this sphere was moving?" '[60][†]

What the Roerichs on several occasions observed in the twenties in the Himalayas and is now observable throughout the world in the form of 'flying saucers' has in fact nothing to do with the true Shambhala but has its origin in the eighth sphere, which since the middle of our century has been strengthened and densified to such an extent that its phenomena have become accessible to an ever-growing number of people. Lucifer-ized imaginations of Old Moon, which in their original form can be apprehended only through imaginative consciousness, are permeated to such an extent by matter that has been wrested from earthly evolution and

---

[*] Probably to his life in the Himalayas. See Appendix 4.

[†] This episode is described not only in Nicholas Roerich's book *Shamballa Siyayushchaya* ('Radiant Shamballa') but also in his books *Heart of Asia* (NR 6, p. 244) and in *Altai-Himalaya* (NR 4, pp. 299–300), where the following comment was added: 'Energy A. Brother D.K. [Djwhal Khul?], marvellous!'

has been taken hold of by Ahriman that they become visible to man's outward, physical sight in the form of hallucinations.

Rudolf Steiner characterizes this combined work of Lucifer and Ahriman in the following words: 'Ahriman interferes with our perception of outer phenomena and deceives us with regard to them. Nevertheless, we could unmask his intentions if Lucifer did not awaken certain inner longings and incite us towards such materialistic notions in our view of the world.'[61] And then Rudolf Steiner indicates in connection with these processes that the principal source of the matter which the opposing forces are continually trying to gain mastery over in order to draw it into the eighth sphere is the human head, the human brain, the most perfect and spiritualized part of the physical body. Thus when people think only materialistic thoughts, as is currently the case for a large number of those belonging to modern Western civilization, the possibility of Lucifer and Ahriman taking hold of the matter of the brain becomes far greater. When, however, a human being begins 'to seek [and think about] the spiritual world in the form of materialism',[62] that is, by extending materialistic ideas directly to the occult realm, he becomes an 'occult materialist', and thereby creates particularly favourable conditions for strengthening the eighth sphere. Thus the constant growth of its forces in our time—as is shown in the form of physically visible phenomena—is the direct consequence of the general *materialistic character* of the modern era.

Modern spiritual science derives its information about the true Shamballa from altogether different, *purely spiritual* sources. It also reveals the true significance of the ancient Eastern teaching regarding the heavenly Shamballa. For this is that ancient spirit-land which with the coming of Kali Yuga and with the disappearance of the atavistic clairvoyance became invisible for earthly human beings but which will, from our time onwards, become accessible in a still greater majesty and glory to man's spirit-vision, appearing before him as that etheric sphere surrounding the earth where the Etheric Christ can now be experienced: 'The appearance of Christ in His etheric form will be amongst the first things that human beings will perceive when Shamballa again becomes manifest. There is no one else who can lead mankind into the country which oriental writings declare to have vanished other than the Christ. Christ will lead human beings to Shamballa ... Thus the new Christian confession will arise through our growing into that realm where we will first meet Him: through growing into the mysterious land of Shamballa.'[63]

This central reality of Shamballa—the living Christ, who in his etheric body leads humanity into it and reveals himself therein—was altogether unknown to the Roerichs. Their 'earthly Shamballa', lost somewhere in the inaccessible valleys of the Himalayas, has, in contrast, a wholly material character and is ruled by mahatmas for whom the mysteries of true Christianity are as yet beyond their reach. Hence the 'heavenly Shamballa', too, is for the Roerichs merely a repetition of ancient Shamballa, which in former times disappeared from human sight. The decisive metamorphosis through which it passed as a result of the Mystery of Golgotha, leading it to become in our time the spiritual sphere of activity of the Etheric Christ, was inaccessible and unknown both to the Roerichs and to the mahatmas who inspired them.

It follows from this that that other 'heavenly Shamballa', to which the Roerichs aspired, is none other than the realm of Lucifer—where Christ is not recognized—and his luciferic 'hierarchy of light'. For after the Mystery of Golgotha and Christ's union with the earth, *everything* in earthly evolution that has not gained access to the sphere of Christ will inevitably sooner or later fall prey to Lucifer and Ahriman. It is in this sense that we should understand Helena Roerich's words that 'there is only one Hierarchy of Light, and this Hierarchy is of course the Trans-Himalayan Hierarchy',[64] that is, the hierarchy which serves Lucifer and, hence, knows nothing of either the true significance of the Mystery of Golgotha or the new etheric appearance of Christ.

Moreover, Helena Roerich's assertion—quoted above—that the Lord of Shamballa, the Maitreya, has already attained the stage of buddhahood and will never appear on earth again in a physical body but will only work in a spirit-body is very clearly an attempt to replace the Etheric Christ by that luciferic being whom she acknowledges as the Maitreya and as her, and her teaching's, inspirer.[*]

---

[*] This falsehood has its source in one particular circumstance which Rudolf Steiner considers at some length in the lecture of 9 January 1912. There he speaks of how the chief purpose and ultimate significance of the evolution of the present earth is the full development by man of the *fourth* principle of his being, the principle of the ego. Thus Christ, in descending to the earth, brought this central principle to mankind, though in its *macrocosmic* form, as the World Ego, which is the archetype of every human ego and at the same time its highest ideal. In contrast, the luciferic spirits will ever and again try to entice man towards the premature development of his higher principles: the Spirit Self, the Life Spirit and even the Spirit Man, that is, the fifth, sixth and seventh principles, though only in their *microcosmic* form. If the luciferic spirits succeed in obscuring the fundamental difference between macrocosmic and microcosmic evolution, they will be able to impress upon human beings the idea that the fifth, sixth and seventh principles are 'higher' than the fourth, which is to say that the false messiahs and teachers whom they possess are higher than the Christ.

And it is ultimately this luciferic being, who only in her consciousness took the form of the Maitreya and who was inimically disposed towards Christianity and, hence, made every effort to prevent the arising of a true knowledge of Christ amongst mankind, who was the actual occult source of the teaching of Agni Yoga.

It is a real life's tragedy of Helena and Nicholas Roerich that they entrusted themselves to the guidance of the Eastern occultists of a left inclination and were accordingly not in a position either to distinguish the macrocosmic nature of the Christ from the microcosmic nature of the bodhisattvas or true Shamballa from the luciferic Shamballa.

This principal error of Agni Yoga was the source of all other errors, some of which are considered in the chapter that follows.

Notes

1. HR 2, 24 May 1936, quotation from AY 2, Part 3, IV. 8.
2. HR 2, 31 July 1937.
3. HR 3, 4 July 1936.
4. HR 3, 10 March 1936.
5. HR 2.
6. GA 133, 20 June 1912; see also GA 137, 12 June 1912. For further details about the participation of Buddha in the preparation of the earthly life of Christ, see GA 114.
7. GA 131, 14 October 1911.
8. See, for example, UPNM, 9 June 1924.
9. UPNM, 9 April 1924.
10. UPNM, 24 June 1924.
11. AY 14, 164, 165.
12. HR 3, 8 February 1938.
13. UPNM, 28 June 1948.
14. HR 3, 17 March 1938.
15. See Khramchenko, pp. 13, 15. This testimony comes from an unpublished statement by Helena Roerich.
16. AY 14, 166.
17. AY 14, 173.
18. UPNM, 25 April 1924.
19. AY 2, Part 2, V. 5.
20. KV, p. 132, chapter 2 'From the Life of Christ'.
21. UPNM, 13 January 1948.
22. RA III, p. 342, 13 April 1953.
23. RA III, p. 341, 13 April 1953.
24. AY 2, Part 2, III. 18.
25. UPNM, 13 January 1948.
26. AY 7.5.

27. HR 1, 8 August 1934.
28. RA III, p. 360, 5 August 1953.
29. RA III, p. 206, 28 November 1950.
30. RA III, p. 410, 5 March 1954.
31. Gorchakov, p. 205.
32. Ibid., p. 213.
33. Ibid., p. 215.
34. See GA 102, 27 January 1908.
35. Gorchakov, p. 219.
36. Ibid., p. 235.
37. Ibid., p. 93.
38. Ibid., p. 237.
39. Ibid., p. 211.
40. Ibid., p. 206.
41. HR 3, 30 June 1934.
42. NR, p. 59.
43. HR 1, 12 April 1935.
44. HR 2, 4 November 1935.
45. GA 131, 14 October 1911.
46. GA 118, 10 May 1910.
47. GA 130, 21 September 1911.
48. GA 123, 10 September 1910.
49. ShS.
50. HR 2.
51. HR 2, 7 December 1935.
52. See HR 1, 6 May 1934.
53. See HR 1, 25 March 1935.
54. Ibid.
55. Ibid. and HR 2, 30 March 1936.
56. HR 2, 7 December 1935.
57. AY 2.
58. HR 1.
59. UPNM, 15 May 1924.
60. ShS.
61. GA 254, 17 October 1915.
62. Ibid.
63. GA 118, 6 March 1910.
64. HR 2, 30 August 1935.

8. Some Aspects of the Teaching of Helena Roerich

In this chapter we shall consider some other aspects of the teaching of Agni Yoga.

The relationship of Agni Yoga to the luciferic realm as it has been characterized here is confirmed by one fact of interest, from which it is apparent that in the light of luciferic inspirations many truths can acquire a diametrically opposite meaning. Thus Helena Roerich transfers the dwelling place of the last guardian of the Grail, the mysterious Prester John or 'the sage of the great mountain', to 'earthly Shamballa', from where he sent news and messages to various earthly rulers, amongst whom was the conqueror, Genghis Khan: 'This Genghis Khan received advice from the Sage of the great Mountain,' writes Helena Roerich in the eighth volume of *Agni Yoga*.[1]

The fact that the direct inheritor of the impulses of Genghis Khan, his grandson Khan Batu, destroyed and burnt virtually the whole of Russia in 1238–40 and then subjected it to 250 years of slavery in all probability disturbed the Roerichs but little. After all, Nicholas Roerich dedicated a whole series of his pictures to Genghis Khan.

The reasons for this unusual sympathy for someone who was one of the cruellest conquerors in the entire history of humanity lie in the occult sphere. Thus in order to understand them it is necessary to turn to what has been given through modern spiritual science.

In the lecture of 17 September 1916 Rudolf Steiner indicated that it was Genghis Khan who in the twelfth century received through a priestly emissary of a secret mystery centre in the depths of Asia a *luciferic* initiation of unusual intensity and, associated with it, the task of 'gathering together everything that it was possible to gather from the forces of Asia and using this for the dissemination of what could lead the fifth post-Atlantean epoch back into a luciferic mould'. In other words, the mission of Genghis Khan was 'the great attempt—originating from Asia—to "visionize" [that is, give a visionary, atavistic character to] European culture and thereby cut it off from the conditions of further evolution, so as in a certain sense to draw it away from the earth'.[2] Does not this aspect of the mission of Genghis Khan correspond to the underlying aspirations of the Roerichs in the twentieth century?

In this same spirit the Roerichs also interpret the Grail, which for them is no more than a meteorite that fell to earth from Orion and is now preserved in Shamballa, as a great stone, the Chintamani Stone, in which 'magic powers' are concentrated.[3]

'After all, the legend of the Grail Chalice came from the East and is one of the numerous accounts of that same Shamballa,'[4] writes Helena Roerich in a letter.[*]

The Roerichs carried a fragment of this stone, which—as they repeatedly asserted—they had received from Shamballa, during their trans-Himalayan expedition through Asia. According to them, it can, as an occult talisman, connect the one who possesses it with the 'Himalayan fortress'. Helena Roerich claimed that Moses, Solomon, Alexander the Great, Tamerlane, Napoleon and also her family in previous incarnations had possessed this stone.[†] On another occasion the stone becomes for the Roerichs 'the chalice of Amrita', the sacred drink of the East, with a similarity to soma. 'Thus in its time [the Chalice] was brought to the Lord Buddha ...', writes Helena Roerich. 'After the death of the Buddha, the Chalice was for a while in a Temple in Karashar, from whence it disappeared. Since this time it has been kept in Shamballa.'[5][‡]

There is no mention here of the connection of this chalice with Christ. Hence the communion Chalice, hewn from the sacred stone, the 'Lapis Exillis', remains empty for the Roerichs, bereft of its true content—the blood of Christ. And this means that the stamp of Lucifer is also imprinted upon the Roerichs' 'Grail': this is an old chalice which has not become the Grail ...

According to the inspirer of Helena Roerich, the point at issue here is that the Himalayan brotherhood has as its principal object a meteorite stone which fell to the earth from Orion. As a powerful magnet it connects the earth in a plane of energy with this distant constellation. Her inspirer spoke to Helena Roerich about it as follows: 'The stone that fell from Orion is preserved within the Brotherhood. A fragment of it is sent

---

[*] And in a letter of 1 October 1935 to Rudzitis she informed him: 'The Grail brotherhood guards the Grail which was sent from Orion.' (Quotation from *Zhivaya etika: izbrannoye*—'Living Ethics: An Anthology', Moscow 1992, p. 398.)

[†] The Roerich family possessed a fragment of this stone while they were incarnated in the third century BC in China (see the collection of poems by Helena Roerich entitled 'Flowers of Morya', Moscow 1984, the poem 'Zaklyatye' (Invocation) and likewise in thirteenth-century Germany, see below in the same chapter.

[‡] One of Helena Roerich's pupils, R. Rudzitis, the president of the Roerich Society in Riga in the thirties and forties, wrote a work by way of further development of these indications of hers under the title of 'Brotherhood of the Grail', in which he tried on the basis of historical and literary material to prove the Eastern Asiatic (Himalayan) origin of the whole cycle of legends of the Grail and even of the Arthurian knights. Extracts from it were recently printed in the journal of the Latvian Roerich Society, *Uguns*.

out into the world to accompany world events and maintains through its inner magnetic power a connection with the Brotherhood where the main body of the Stone lies. This is the principle of a simple magnet.'[6] In antiquity this stone was originally received by Jason: 'Jason, the Hierophant, received Orion's gift in Asia.'[7] And in another context the mahatma dictates to Helena Roerich: 'In it [the stone] is contained a portion of the Great Breath—a portion of the soul of Orion ...'[8] and confirms: 'Morya knows the habits of the stone.'[*] Fragments of this 'holy' stone have been sent to many people in the course of earthly history. In the nineteenth century, for example, Napoleon received one; and it remained with him for as long as he obediently implemented the mahatmas' plans.[9] In the nineteenth century the Roerichs reported of this in a letter: 'There are many marvels in our lives, many affirmations. Thus the last message signifying the beginning of the Century of the Maitreya arrived in January [19]34. The S[tone] came on 6 Oct[ober] [19]23...'[10] 'The stone is assimilated to your rhythm,' dictated the mahatmas to Helena Roerich, 'if it remains with you; and it strengthens its connection with the predetermined path through the constellation of Orion.'[11] It was with this stone that the Roerichs completed their three-year trans-Asiatic journey, bearing it throughout the future earthly domain of the Maitreya.[†]

In 1935 Helena Roerich even sent a photograph of it to her followers in Europe. She wrote about this in one of her letters: 'In the photograph the S[tone] is resting in a shrine on an ancient piece of fabric, in which is embroidered in shining radiance the ancient inscription "With it you will conquer".'[12] Nicholas Roerich on several occasions depicted the shrine with the stone in his paintings, for example in the picture 'Treasure of the World', which is kept in the Roerich Museum in New York. Moreover, according to information that they received from their inspirer, the Roerichs possessed this magic talisman already in one of their previous lives, when they were incarnated in Germany in the thirteenth century as the Naumburg princess Margravine Uta and her husband Ekkehard.[13] Nicholas Roerich represented them in his picture 'Long live the King!', where the figure of Mahatma Morya appears between them holding the stone in his hands.[14]

---

[*] This same 'mahatma' tells Helena Roerich what the actual stone that is preserved in the subterranean temple of the Himalayan brotherhood looks like, and also informs her of the 'nightly services' of the mahatmas 'around the stone' (UPNM, p. 90). Nicholas Roerich depicted such a 'divine service' in the picture 'Sokrovishchye gor' (Treasure of the Mountains). (The picture is in the Roerich Museum in New York.)

[†] See also Appendix 2.

Whatever may actually have been behind this stone totem, one thing is clear: the Roerichs, who were convinced that 'the Christ and His Great brothers'[15] were living somewhere in Himalayan Shamballa, received their magic stone from there in 1923. And in the same year Rudolf Steiner, no more than two months later, spoke at the Christmas Conference in Dornach about an altogether different *supersensible stone*, which had not a physical but an etheric reality and was therefore called an 'imaginative form of love'.[16] This supersensible stone is, indeed, connected with the true *spiritual* Shamballa, that is with the etheric sphere surrounding the earth where the Christ is made manifest in etheric form from the twentieth century onwards.[17]

Thus there are in reality two stones: the supersensible (imaginative) Foundation Stone of which Rudolf Steiner spoke, and the material magnetic stone which the Roerichs carried with them everywhere as a talisman—two polar symbols of a true and a false understanding of the Second Coming, the coming of Christ in etheric form and the coming of the false messiah who is now still concealed in *a physical body* in the ravines and subterranean temples of the Himalayas and who is therefore in need of the magical powers of the magnetic stone.

A further detail needs to be considered. In her letters and articles Helena Roerich mentions on more than one occasion that this meteoric stone from Orion was also formerly in the guardianship of the Grail brotherhood.[18] In this connection it is instructive to call to mind a profound occult legend, according to which the stone whence the holy chalice was fashioned did not come from Orion but fell from the crown of Lucifer when the Archstrategist Michael cast him down from heaven to the earth.[19] And when the blood of the Divine Redeemer was collected on Golgotha in this chalice, the holy blood gradually spiritualized it and transformed it into an *etheric* vessel, into a radiant supersensible form which thenceforth became the bearer of the spiritual forces able to overcome the *objective* consequences of the Fall in the individual human ego. As a result of this total transformation the chalice with its holy contents could be taken up again to heaven and was to be found there in the care of the angels and certain chosen souls of the dead,[20] until in the eighth century it was once more entrusted to human beings in order to prepare for the future epoch of human freedom, but entrusted to them not as a physical but as an imaginative reality, as a purely supersensible form which preserves the etherized blood of Christ that is untouched by the consequences of the Fall.[21]

At that time the great initiate Titurel founded the Grail brotherhood, whose members were able in the course of their initiation into the mysteries of esoteric Christianity to partake in an etheric communion from the supersensible chalice and thereby experience an actual meeting with Christ in the spiritual world.

Helena Roerich, however, as has already been shown, spoke merely of a stone which in spite of everything did not become the Grail and, hence, retains even today its material and, from an occult point of view, luciferic nature.* Hence the founder of Agni Yoga was so disturbed by the very thought that Christ had through his sacrificial death on Golgotha redeemed mankind from original sin as to refer to this idea as 'a terrible suggestion'.[22] For neither she nor her secret inspirer were able to understand in what sense the atonement by Christ of original sin is an objective reality and in what sense every human being has to atone for his *individual* sins by means of the law of karma and reincarnation. In this total inability to understand the essential nature of the Mystery of Golgotha, in this utter lack of awareness of its real consequences for earthly evolution as a whole, there comes to expression the dark magical influence upon Helena Roerich's mind of the stone which did not become the Grail.

It should merely be added that Rudolf Steiner devoted a whole cycle of lectures to precisely this highly important theme, the theme of objective and subjective sin and the various ways of atoning for them, under the title *Christ and the Human Soul* and also the lecture 'The Concepts of Original Sin and Grace',[23] where he shed light upon the essence of this question from the standpoint of esoteric Christianity. One can also learn about the destiny of the true Grail mysteries and their modern continuation in anthroposophical spiritual science from his numerous lectures, and also from his book *Occult Science*.[24]

To conclude this theme of the magical magnetic stone in the destiny of the Roerichs it is impossible to fail to notice its distinctive connection with Nicholas Roerich's artistic legacy, where the influence of the magical stone was present from the outset. It was possibly Maximilian Voloshin who best characterized this principal quality of Roerich the painter's creative work in his article 'Archaizm russkoi zhivopisi' (Archaism in Russian Painting), published already in 1909, that is, long before Roerich came into direct contact with the Himalayan occultists.

---

* One could also say that what in the purely imaginative fabric of the legend still bore a luciferic character subsequently, through being deprived of any real connection with Christ, succumbed to an ahrimanic influence and—once having become materialized— was transformed into a magical magnetic stone (magnetism is always associated with ahrimanic forces).

Voloshin wrote: 'He [Roerich] is truly a painter of the Stone Age,[*] and not because he sometimes tries to portray the people and constructions of this epoch but because—of the four elements of the world—he recognized only earth, and in earth only its bony foundation—the stone. Not mineral, not crystal, which gives back to the sun its light and flame, but the heavy, solid and opaque stone of erratic blocks. As one looks at his pictures, one involuntarily recalls all the Celtic traditions of evil stones which lead a bewitching life ... And in everything else in the world that grows, sings, shines and speaks, Roerich sees only what is blind, dumb, deaf and stony. The sky for him becomes an opaque stone, glowing red at times during a purple sunset, and beneath the dull red vault he depicts intense, stone clouds. Both people and animals are visible for him only from the standpoint of a stone. That is why his people do not have faces ... And not only does Roerich see the air, trees, man and the surging sea in terms of stone, but even fire becomes for him the biting teeth of a yellow stone.'[25]

This fossilized picture of a formerly living world is, however, represented in Roerich's paintings in the reflection of a cold, utterly luciferic, enchanting beauty that is devoid of any inner warmth and soul substance. This illusory beauty, akin to the beauty of theatrical scenery and a decorativeness that merely imitates nature, precisely because of its luciferic quality does not allow the beholder to perceive at once the occult reality that is concealed *behind it*, a mystery which Roerich, without wishing to do so, betrays in his canvasses. What is actually manifested in them is a reflection of that spiritual sphere whence Ahriman is making preparations today for his imminent incarnation, where, in Rudolf Steiner's words, 'the atmosphere ... becomes like granite, very dense and stonelike'.[26] For 'it is the endeavour of the ahrimanic powers to reduce the earth to a state of complete rigidification. Their victory would be won if they succeeded in bringing earth, water and air into this rigidified state.' This victory of the ahrimanic powers in earthly evolution becomes manifest in Roerich's paintings. In them a wholly stonelike universe is depicted, where Lucifer and Ahriman reign harmoniously together: the spirit of a cold, fascinating beauty and the spirit of an eternally 'dead matter'.[27]

---

[*] Nicholas Roerich himself expressed his relationship with the art of the Stone Age as follows: 'It is strange to think that, quite possible, the legacy of the Stone Age approximates more closely to the searchings of our time' (article entitled 'Radost iskusstva' [Joy of Art], 1908). When he subsequently found the magical totem stone, Roerich thus finally achieved the purpose of his search.

Another central idea of Agni Yoga—in addition to the teaching of the eternity of matter and of Shamballa—is that of fire. Hence its name: 'Yoga of Fire'. The fourth volume of the teaching bears this title, and its eighth, ninth and tenth volumes have the collective title of 'Fiery World'.

In Agni Yoga the universe is divided into three levels: the 'world of density', corresponding to the physical plane; the 'refined world', which corresponds to the etheric and sometimes to the astral world; and the 'fiery world', corresponding to the mental or spiritual plane (the 'Devachan' of theosophy).* The kindling of fire in the innermost heart is regarded by Agni Yoga as the entry into the sphere of cosmic fire, the fiery world. But here too the basic inadequacy of Agni Yoga becomes apparent: its total blindness to the sphere of Christ. For since the Mystery of Golgotha the twofold mystery of fire in the cosmos and in man has been inseparably connected with the mystery of the Living Christ. Christ brought the true 'heavenly fire' to the earth and, after passing through death and the Resurrection, appeared clothed in fire to the Apostle Paul on the road to Damascus: 'Christ appeared to Paul's enlightened gaze out of spiritualized fire.' Henceforth 'Paul knew that Christ is alive when he saw Him manifested in spiritualized, blazing heavenly fire,' said Rudolf Steiner.[28][†]

This central experience of Paul acquires a particular significance in our epoch of Christ's etheric revelation to mankind, which begins in the twentieth century and will become increasingly widespread in the course of the next two and a half thousand to three thousand years.[29] Hence Rudolf Steiner speaks of the 'Christians of the future': 'They will understand not only the Christ who passed through death but also the triumphant Christ of the Apocalypse, who resurrected in spiritual fire and whose coming has been foretold ... Thus the Christ is manifested ... in

---

* A. Klizovsky, a pupil of Helena Roerich's, who set forth the foundations of the teaching of Agni Yoga in his three-volume work (see chapter 9), characterizes these three worlds as follows: 'After the physical [world] there follows the astral world, consisting of *less dense matter*, or, as the Teaching of Living Ethics calls it, the Refined World ... After this comes the mental world, or the Fiery World. The still higher worlds and the *still finer conditions of matter* are inaccessible to our understanding' (Klizovsky, Vol. 2, p. 242).

† 'I came to cast fire upon the earth; and would that it were already kindled!' (Luke 12:49): these words of Christ Jesus, which he spoke before the Mystery of Golgotha, refer to this mystery. It is this 'heavenly fire' or fire of Devachan which was kindled by Christ in the supersensible sphere of the earth as a result of the Mystery of Golgotha. Through his passing through death and Resurrection this spiritual fire transformed ancient Shamballa into the cosmic sphere of Resurrection forces, into the source of the arising of the new cosmos of which Rudolf Steiner speaks at the end of his book *Occult Science* (GA 13).

the spiritualized fire of the future. "He is with us always until the end of the world", and will appear in spiritual fire to those who allow their eyes to be illumined by the Event of Golgotha. Human beings will behold Him in spiritual fire. They will have first seen Him in another form, and only thereafter will they see the true form of Christ in spiritual fire,'[30] that is, the Christ as the highest Lord of a transformed Shamballa that is henceforth permeated by the new fire of the spirit.

This allusion to the general spiritualization of the earth, which began as a result of the Mystery of Golgotha through the spiritualizing of the substance of fire (to be followed in future by the spiritualizing of denser substances), is directly connected with the process whereby our earth gradually becomes a new sun, the radiant, fiery focus of the future cosmos. For now that he has as a result of the Mystery of Golgotha become the Spirit of the Earth, the Christ has kindled at its centre a new source of spiritual fire and spiritual light.[31]

But it is not only the macrocosmic mystery of 'heavenly fire' that is connected with the Event of Golgotha and the new etheric appearance of Christ. With them is also connected its microcosmic reflection in the human heart. For this organ is by no means merely what modern science considers it to be. From earliest times the mysterious process of the etherization of earthly blood—a process which in occultism is also associated with fire—has been taking place in the human heart. The stream of this etherized blood flows from the heart to the head, and from thence out into man's spiritual environment. Thus one can say: the fire mystery which is continually being enacted in the human heart unites man with the higher supersensible world. However, this is not all there is to the fire mystery of the heart. For according to the testimony of modern spiritual research, since the Mystery of Golgotha another stream, that of the etherized blood of Christ, has flowed in every human being together with his own etherized blood from the heart to the head.[32]

In an ordinary human being these two etheric streams are not united, since in our time their union is inseparably connected with the assimilation of the true knowledge of Christ such as is given to modern man through anthroposophy. But if such a union is achieved, it leads to a direct contemplation of the Etheric Christ in the spiritual world nearest to the earth.[33] Thus the rightly understood and experienced microcosmic fire mystery, the mystery of the heart, leads man to an initiation into the macrocosmic fire mystery, to a contemplation in the macrocosm of Christ clothed in 'spiritualized heavenly fire', the source whereby the earth will become in future a new sun.

The fire mystery of the heart, in its old, pre-Christian form, is also spoken of—albeit in a very vague and confused way—in *Agni Yoga*, especially in the seventh volume, which is entitled 'The Heart'. However, Helena Roerich knows nothing about the mystery of the presence and influence in the human heart of the etherized blood of Christ, or the change that has come about in the relationship of the earth and humanity to cosmic or heavenly fire as a result of the Mystery of Golgotha. Thus the fire that is spoken of in Helena Roerich's books is merely that primordial fire which—untouched by the transforming power of the Christ impulse—is in our time only capable of leading a human being who experiences it into the cosmic sphere of Lucifer, as is indicated in the central motif of the south green window in the First Goetheanum.

In Helena Roerich's books and letters, many additional examples can be found which testify to the complete inability of this occult stream to gain even a remote understanding of the truths of esoteric Christianity. Thus, for example, it is said of the present abode of Gautama Buddha that 'the Great Individuality of Buddha, His Fiery Ego, clothed with Materia Lucida [primal matter], dwells today in the spheres surrounding our planet'.[34] That the real Gautama Buddha, who has long been 'the most intimate pupil and friend of Christian Rosenkreutz',[35] was sent by him at the beginning of the seventeenth century to Mars, where he continues to abide even now for the fulfilment of a highly important spiritual mission, is something of which Helena Roerich—understandably enough—has no knowledge.

Similarly, she regards Christian Rosenkreutz himself—this high initiate and leader of the whole stream of Christian esotericism—as merely one of the many teachers who tried to bring to Europe those same ancient teachings of the East, though outwardly endowing them with a 'semi-Christian aspect'. 'Thus, when Christian Rosenkreutz, the founder of the Rosicrucian Order, returned from Asia, he had to impart the Teaching of the East in a semi-Christian form, in order to defend his pupils from the persecution and vengeance of fanatics and hypocrites.'[36][*] In other words, Christian Rosenkreutz had in Helena Roerich's view no direct relationship either to esoteric Christianity or even to Christianity at all. A greater misunderstanding of the nature and task of this greatest of esoteric Christian initiates would be difficult to imagine. Christian esotericism is viewed here merely as a protective cloak that has been cast over the

---

[*] These are actually not Helena Roerich's words but a free rendering of an extract from the letters of the mahatmas to Sinnett (see Appendix 6).

treasures of Eastern knowledge for the purpose of diverting the attention of 'fanatics and hypocrites'.[*]

In conclusion, a few words need to be said about the style in which the 14 volumes of *Agni Yoga* are couched. Their principal feature is a strongly expressed poetic or mantric character, with numerous repetitions and variations of what is for the most part a simple selection of the same images and ideas, which with repeated reading over a long period—as is recommended—inevitably leads to one's waking, thinking consciousness being lulled to sleep. This effect is further intensified through the almost total absence in the text of concrete, cognitive elements or of the slightest aspiration towards a consistent logically ordered manner of exposition, such as the reader might be able to grasp with his individual cognitive faculties.

The endless kaleidoscope of separate thoughts, incomplete images, frequently broken-off phrases, endless repetitions, the piling up of the same metaphors, and so on, eventually calls forth in the reader the feeling that he is in a surging and ceaselessly changing sea of images and rhythms, where any conscious control on the part of the individual ego is almost completely lost. And then the content can work in an unimpeded way upon the soul, like a hypnotic dream.

It is true that one can experience an inner world, a soul satisfaction, even bliss, but at the same time one is—imperceptibly—increasingly subject to the real danger of the uncontrollable influence of those forces and beings of whose nature one cannot gain the least idea from Agni Yoga. Thus it must be said that by excluding individual consciousness the content of Agni Yoga endeavours to exert a direct influence upon the deep, unconscious regions of the human soul, thus making man to a very high degree dependent upon this teaching and the mysterious mahatmas concealed behind it. In this sense its effect is comparable to a refined soul narcotic. And souls that have been prepared in this way are best able to

---

[*] Two further examples shall be cited, which have to do with temporal distortions in Agni Yoga. Thus the end of the dark age of Kali Yuga, which began in the year 3001 BC and ended—according to Rudolf Steiner's spiritual-scientific research—in 1899, is postponed by Helena Roerich until 1942: '[Nineteen] forty-two is in all the ancient writings reckoned to be the end of Kali Yuga and the beginning of the new cycle of splendour' (HR 2, 23 April 1938). And in another letter she writes: 'The year [19]36 is denoted in all prophecies as the year of the beginning of the personal battle between the Arch[angel] Michael and the dragon' (HR 2, I October 1935; compare also 24 May 1936). Whereas in Rudolf Steiner's spiritual-scientific research it is indicated that this battle began in 1841 and culminated in 1879 with Michael's victory and the beginning of the *modern epoch* of his rulership amongst mankind. (See GA 177.)

serve as unconscious tools for the attainment of those goals which the Eastern mahatmas seek to reach with respect to the Slavonic and especially the Russian peoples.

These goals, as is clear from what has been said hitherto, are associated with the endeavours of certain left-oriented occult brotherhoods of the Asiatic East—under whose influence the Roerichs had fallen—to replace true Christianity at any price with a new world pseudo-religion, consisting of a mixture of ancient Eastern wisdom and occult materialism,* in order by this means to prevent the arising in the sixth post-Atlantean period of the universally human Christian culture which will be wholly founded on a new cosmic understanding of the Christ impulse, the establishing of which will be the task of the Slavonic nations of Europe.

As was indicated at the beginning of this present work in the course of considering the first volume of *Agni Yoga*, its teaching is based on the absolute authority of the teacher. Helena Roerich emphasizes this on several occasions in her letters: 'Yes, the Teaching of Living Ethics is based upon devotion to the Hierarchy of Light, upon a recognition of the high authority of the Teachers.'[37] From a practical point of view this increasingly leads modern man into a situation whereby he loses the most precious gift of earthly evolution, his free will, which can then be seized hold of by the opposing forces and drawn into the eighth sphere. For 'Lucifer and Ahriman are endeavouring to swallow man's free will up into the eighth sphere ... And this means that man is continually subject to the danger that his free will is taken away from him and swallowed up in the eighth sphere.'[38]

Thus everyone who becomes acquainted with Agni Yoga should know that although it originates from a luciferic source it nevertheless—because of the blind adherence to the authority of teachers and the strong inclination towards the occult materialism developed under their influence—serves not only the aims of Lucifer but also of Ahriman, and that it is one of the very evident manifestations of their *combined* activity in the twentieth century. This combination of forces can be withstood only by the true knowledge of the mysteries of the Living Christ revealed in our time by anthroposophy, which alone are capable of leading mankind into a future that is free from the forces of both Lucifer and Ahriman.

---

*These secret intentions of the left-oriented occultists referred to are even more clearly in evidence in the teaching of Alice Bailey (see Part Two).

Notes

1. AY 8, 295.
2. GA 171.
3. ShS.
4. HR 2, 30 March 1936 (2).
5. HR 2, 2 April 1936.
6. UPNM, pp. 84–5.
7. Ibid., p. 85.
8. Ibid., p. 58; the following quotation p. 60.
9. Ibid., pp. 58 and 83–4.
10. HR 1, 1 October 1935.
11. UPNM, pp. 84–5.
12. HR 1, 1 October 1935.
13. See the article by V. Khramchenko, 'Mezhdunarodnaya missiya Eleny Roerich' (The International Mission of Helena Roerich), *Serdtse* ('Heart'), Moscow 1993, no. 1 (3).
14. See illustration no. 20 on p. 192.
15. HR 1, letter of 7 May 1939.
16. See GA 260, and also S.O. Prokofieff, *Rudolf Steiner and the Founding of the New Mysteries*, second English edition, Temple Lodge, 1994.
17. See GA 118.
18. See for example HR 1, 19 December 1939.
19. See GA 113, 23 August 1909.
20. See GA 214, 23 July 1922.
21. See GA 112, 24 June 1909 and GA 109, 11 April 1909.
22. HR 1, p. 121.
23. See GA 155; GA 127, 3 May 1911.
24. See GA 13, the chapter entitled 'The Present and Future Evolution of the Earth and Mankind'.
25. M.A. Voloshin, *Liki tvorchestva* ('Faces of Creativity'), St Petersburg 1988.
26. GA 191, 15 November 1919. The following quotation is from the same source.
27. From the article by M. Voloshin, op. cit., note 25.
28. GA 109/111, 11 April 1909.
29. See regarding this in GA 118, 130, 131.
30. GA 109/111, 11 April 1909.
31. See GA 112, 6 July 1909.
32. See the lecture of 1 October 1911 (GA 130), 'The Etherization of the Blood. The Entry of the Etheric Christ into the Evolution of the Earth'.
33. Ibid.
34. HR 1, 30 April 1935.
35. GA 130, 18 December 1912.
36. HR 1, 21 May 1935.
37. HR 2, 31 July 1937.
38. GA 254, 18 October 1915.

9. Agni Yoga Versus Anthroposophy

The contrast between anthroposophy as representative of modern esoteric Christianity and the teachings of Agni Yoga, the source of which is an Indo-Tibetan occultism of a left orientation, is clear from the facts adduced in the present work.

This contrast is confirmed by the three-volume work by A. Klizovsky, *Osnovy miroponimaniya novoi epokhi* ('Foundations of World Understanding in the New Epoch'), republished in Riga (in Russian) in 1991. It contains a general exposition (almost 1000 pages) of the teachings of Agni Yoga, over half of which consists of quotations from its founder. Klizovsky himself—a personal pupil of Helena Roerich—was in the thirties an executive member of the Latvian Roerich Society, and originally published his work in Riga in 1934 and dedicated it to his teacher. All three volumes, therefore, appeared during Helena Roerich's lifetime (she died in 1951).

Klizovsky devoted the last nine pages of the first volume to an analysis of anthroposophy, and especially the personality of Rudolf Steiner, from the standpoint of Agni Yoga. They contain powerful attacks upon anthroposophy and its founder. Attacks upon Rudolf Steiner are also contained in the recently published third volume of Helena Roerich's letters. Helena Roerich's opinion of Klizovsky's book has also been recorded.

But before giving the not merely positive but openly enthusiastic opinion of this book on the part of the founder of Agni Yoga, we shall cite here a few of its author's observations. It should be pointed out beforehand that in the following quotations Agni Yoga is completely identified with the third period of Helena Blavatsky's theosophy,[*] inasmuch as Helena Roerich regarded her teaching as a continuation of Blavatsky's mission in the twentieth century.

Klizovsky begins the section on anthroposophy with the words: 'Apart from its overt and obvious enemies, theosophy has others who are secret and, hence, more dangerous. Amongst these foes are anthroposophy and its followers.' The reason for this is that 'shortly before Mrs Besant's death, the powers of darkness succeeded in recruiting Rudolf Steiner to the ranks of the Theosophical Society'. According to Klizovsky, this happened in the following way. Rudolf Steiner 'reckoned that after

---

[*] See the foreword to the Russian edition and also Part Three.

Blavatsky's death he would be chosen as president of the Theosophical Society', whereas the mahatmas of the White Brotherhood chose not him but Annie Besant. 'As a result ... of this insult to his pride ... he abandoned theosophy and founded anthroposophy,'[*] which was 'the first victory of the dark powers over Steiner'. For 'having gained mastery over such a capable colleague as Steiner, the dark powers gave their teaching [that is, anthroposophy] to the world by using Steiner as their instrument'.

There then follows a thoroughly incompetent criticism of certain aspects of anthroposophical cosmology, a criticism which Klizovsky does not base on the works of Rudolf Steiner himself—most likely he has never even read them—but, in his words, on 'a wholly objective judgement' which he has derived from a book written against anthroposophy by a certain V. Goldenberg, *Antroposophskoye dvizhyeniye i yevo prorok* ('The Anthroposophical Movement and its Prophet').

However, all this is merely the prelude to addressing what is from the standpoint of Agni Yoga the principal 'error' of anthroposophy and its founder. 'The Western world'—Klizovsky continues—'believes that Christ is the Only Son of the One God. *Steiner fully complies with this error...*' (italics S.P.). And then he goes on: 'People may say that it is hardly possible to regard anthroposophy as a teaching of darkness when it has so high an estimation of Christ, when anthroposophists are zealous Christians and make efforts to combine Christianity with anthroposophy. But the recognition of Christ by the powers of darkness is a generally known fact, for how could they fail to recognize Him? They have recognized Him post factum, but they have recognized Him in such a way as to shut out the possibility of recognizing the next Teacher, for the formula that "One such as Christ there has never been and will never be again" shuts man off from all further progress, and this is all that is needed by the powers of darkness, it is for this reason that they recognize Him.'

It is evident from these words that it is precisely the principal result of Rudolf Steiner's spiritual-scientific research, with its testimony of the central significance of the Christ Being, as the Sun Logos, for our whole cosmos and of the Mystery of Golgotha for the whole of earthly evolu-

---

[*] The 'explanation' that Klizovsky gives here as the reason for Rudolf Steiner's 'departure from theosophy' is actually part and parcel of that slander which Annie Besant unleashed against Rudolf Steiner in the first decade of the century. In the lecture of 18 March 1916 (GA 174a) Rudolf Steiner called these fabrications of hers a 'conscious lie', inasmuch as in 1909 he had personally and in the presence of witnesses '... clearly explained to her that ... [he] did not *under any circumstances* want to be more than the General Secretary of the German Section, or something along those lines' (GA 174a; see also GA 167, 28 March 1916).

tion, which represents the main stumbling-block in anthroposophy for the followers of Agni Yoga. For them, Christ is merely one of the many teachers of mankind for whom they have equal reverence, merely the precursor of the 'next teacher' in the endless chain which Helena Roerich calls the 'Hierarchy of Light'. What she means by this she states in one of her letters: ' . . . there is only one Hierarchy of Light, and this is the Trans-Himalayan Hierarchy,'[1] unaware that she is in point of fact speaking about the pseudo-hierarchy of the left-oriented occultists.

In Klizovsky's opinion, Rudolf Steiner fell from this 'hierarchy': 'In calling anthroposophy a teaching of the powers of darkness, the epithet of dark power must also be applied to the founder of this teaching. That this is neither calumny nor an insinuation is evident from the fact that Steiner rejected the heavenly Hierarchy that rules the world and did this wholly consciously, for Steiner—as a former theosophist—could not fail to know of its existence and that it rules the world. By rejecting the Hierarchy of Light he thereby acknowledged the hierarchy of darkness.'

Yes indeed, by rejecting the hierarchy of the Indo-Tibetan mahatmas, which pursued only group and egotistically national interests, Rudolf Steiner was from the outset acknowledging only the true 'heavenly hierarchy' that serves the Cosmic Christ, of which Dionysius the Areopagite wrote out of the sources of esoteric Christianity. All the leading teachers of esoteric Christianity have always been directly associated with this true heavenly hierarchy, whose impulses they have endeavoured to bring to realization amongst mankind, in the knowledge that 'Christ is the Ruler of *all* the beings of the higher hierarchies',[2] that is, of the hierarchies both within and outside our solar system.

As has been shown, the founder of Agni Yoga regarded Christ as a being who came—together with Gautama Buddha and the Maitreya Bodhisattva (in her opinion, the latter had long since attained the stage of buddhahood)—from the planet Venus (see p. 87), that is, she saw in him a being who as regards his spiritual significance had not gone beyond the rank of Buddha. Her pupil Klizovsky adds to this series of teachers 'Mohammed, Confucius' and, at one stroke, 'all the past and future Teachers of humanity'. In other words, according to the conception of Agni Yoga Christ is not a *Cosmic Being* who lived *only once* on the earth but merely one of many human initiates who, like them, has passed through many earthly incarnations before and since his life in Palestine at the beginning of the Christian era.

Once one has become familiar with this attitude of Agni Yoga to the Founder of Christianity, it is not difficult to distinguish the true sources of such ideas. In his descriptions in his lectures of how the luciferic and ahrimanic powers battle against the Christ impulse (which is to say, against the true evolution of humanity), Rudolf Steiner often spoke of the way in which Lucifer tries to represent Christ's earthly life in Palestine as a kind of illusion or beautiful legend, whereas Ahriman endeavours to portray Christ merely as one of many earthly initiates, as a being who does indeed stand at a higher level in his development than 'Socrates or Plato' but who nonetheless belongs wholly to the human race.

But this conception of Christ, according to which His higher cosmic, divine nature completely disappears and only the human, earthly aspect remains, is not simply a special form of modern materialism but is, in Rudolf Steiner's words, one of the most effective means whereby Ahriman is in our time preparing for his future incarnation amongst mankind, in order—by appearing on earth as a new and higher teacher—to attempt to lead earthly evolution in the direction that he desires.[*]

Klizovsky's criticism of anthroposophy springs ultimately from these overtly ahrimanic influences—which are also the source of its manifest coarseness. Not mincing his words, over the course of barely nine pages he calls anthroposophy a 'human fabrication', a 'distortion', a 'falsification', 'lie', coarse imitation', 'mystification', the 'ravings of a disordered imagination', 'a cunningly conceived net to catch people in', 'a great deception', 'tares which the enemy of humanity has sown amongst the wheat', and so on.

This stream of hostile remarks reaches its culmination in the following words: 'Steiner's yielding to dark powers proceeded slowly, but with surety towards the end of his life. They finally overwhelmed him in the six years before his death. According to highly authoritative sources, for the last six years of his life Steiner was no longer Steiner. Some kind of dark power, which continued his activity in the direction that suited it, entered into the bodily sheath of Steiner.' Two statements from this passage are particularly striking: the reference to 'information from highly authoritative sources' and the indication regarding the last six years of the earthly life of Rudolf Steiner.

In the context of Klizovsky's treatise, this 'highly authoritative source' can only be Helena Roerich herself, the founder of Agni Yoga. And indeed, Helena Roerich wrote to Klizovsky in one of the letters recently published in Russia as he was working on his book: 'Steiner did indeed at

---

[*] Rudolf Steiner tells of Ahriman's incarnation on earth, which is to come about at the beginning of the third millennium, and about the preparation for this incarnation in our time in the lectures published in GA 191 and GA 193. There it is indicated that this incarnation will take place in the American West.

the end of his life abandon the path of Light, and his temple was destroyed by the destroying Ray.'[3] Moreover, in one of her letters to America Helena Roerich indicates that, in certain occult circles with which she is associated, this event 'of the destruction of this highly important temple by the pure Ray was known already beforehand'.[4] By 'pure Ray' one is to understand, in the terminology of Agni Yoga, the light of the ruler of Shamballa—the Maitreya.[5]

It is obvious how false this assertion is, since the first Goetheanum was actually destroyed by the most irreconcilable of enemies of the spirit, whose names have long been known. The main reason for this attack on the part of dark powers was that the last six years of Rudolf Steiner's life were the time when he embarked upon the revelation in all their depth of the Michael mysteries of our cosmos. Precisely from this period (1919–25), his relationship with the high sphere of the Time Spirit, Michael, acquired such a concrete and intense character that it can be said in full accord with the occult reality that through Rudolf Steiner, the modern Christian initiate, Michael, the cosmic 'Countenance of Christ', was active to an ever greater degree from this time onwards, and through his greatest pupil founded on earth the new Christian mysteries, whose task it is to serve the true heavenly hierarchy led in the spiritual world by Christ Himself.[*]

And as from Ahriman's point of view everything coming from the sphere of Michael is seen as darkness, in that he is spiritually blind to its influences, it is completely clear that this activity of Michael as expressed through Rudolf Steiner must be perceived by Ahriman as 'darkness' or as a 'power of darkness'.

This also sheds light upon the real inspirer of those 'highly authoritative sources' upon which Klizovsky and his guru, Helena Roerich, drew in their spiritual blindness. Thus Helena Roerich writes to him in a letter from India after she became acquainted with the text of the work whence all the remarks about anthroposophy and its founder quoted above are taken: 'Your excellent work has brought great joy. This is what is so urgently necessary now, for we must do all we can to stir the awareness that has been buried in musty prejudices and crushed by the horrors of this terrible age. The light of the new era is dawning, and we must be able to

---

[*] This period begins with the lecture cycle *The Mission of the Archangel Michael, the Revelation of the Essential Secrets of Man's Being* (November 1919, GA 194), and ends with the articles on 'The Michael Mystery' (August 1924–March 1925, GA 26). For further details regarding the last years of Rudolf Steiner's life and his relationship to the sphere of Michael in this period, see S.O. Prokofieff, *Rudolf Steiner and the Founding of the New Mysteries*, Rudolf Steiner Press, 1986.

meet it with an awake spirit. I await with impatience the continuation of your work, which should be printed and widely disseminated. Your work, which so clearly sets forth the problems of Existence, is of the greatest value, and we hope that you will continue in this direction. The Teaching of Life contains so many new themes which have not as yet been touched upon!'[*]

And in a further letter to America Helena Roerich indicates that the Maitreya has, so to speak, personally helped her to verify the correctness of what her pupil had written: 'Our colleague from the Latv[ian] Soc[iety], Al[exander] Iv[anovich] Klizovsky, is currently writing a book along these lines and has sent it to me in chapters to peruse; with the L[ord's] help I am able to complete, and, where necessary, correct it. His work is very valuable, it gives what is now so urgently necessary, namely, the Foundations of a new World Conception.'

Bearing in mind what has been said so far, it might be supposed that the hateful attacks brought 'with the approval of' the mother of Agni Yoga, Helena Roerich, by Klizovsky against anthroposophy would only be encountered by Russian-speaking readers, since his three-volume work was written and published in Russian. But this is not so. For Klizovsky's book is also well known in the circles of Central European devotees of Agni Yoga and is actively used in the battle against anthroposophy. This is especially the case with an Austrian from Linz, Leopold Brandstätter (pseudonym Leobrand, 1915–68), who, as a new 'teacher' of Agni Yoga who saw himself as spiritually carrying on Helena Roerich's work, had become her pupil and successor. In a series of articles by Brandstätter, which were published by him in the Munich-based Agni Yoga Verlag under the title *Briefe über Lebendige Ethik. Einführung in Agni Yoga* ('Letters on Living Ethics. Introduction to Agni Yoga'), a four-and-a-half-page section on anthroposophy was included in number 31 (new edition 1980) entitled 'Occultism—Yes or No?' This brochure (like all following ones) bears the inscription: 'The new Gospel for the coming age. Only through this can Christ's teaching be rightly understood in its original sense!' And at the end of this series of 36 articles, Klizovsky's book is included in the list of literature consulted, alongside the works of Helena Roerich herself.[†]

However, this reference to Klizovsky is not simply of a formal nature,

---

[*] This quotation is cited in the publisher's foreword to the first volume of Klizovsky's work.

[†] To each of the 36 instalments is appended a list of the basic books of Brandstätter and Helena Roerich published in German translation by the Agni Yoga Verlag in Munich.

for if one familiarizes oneself more closely with Brandstätter's attacks on anthroposophy and especially on its founder, Rudolf Steiner, it becomes apparent that he repeats virtually *all* 'arguments' of his East European precursor, 'arguments' which in the case of both him and his predecessor flow from the fact that today '[Blavatsky's] theosophy and [Helena Roerich's] *Living Ethics*, which derive from the same Holy Source and *do not entice human beings with Christ's name*' (italics S.P.), therefore 'clash' with 'anthroposophy' as do 'light and darkness'.

The only difference between Brandstätter and Klizovsky is that the former, as a Mid-European, makes the claim to be somewhat better informed about anthroposophy. Thus in his attacks he does not merely repeat what Klizovsky has already asserted but adds some new details, probably in order to show that he is 'more fundamentally' familiar with the subject. For example, he mentions the Goetheanum in Dornach—unsurprisingly of course as an 'ugly building'—and even refers to the previous incarnations of Rudolf Steiner, who, in his opinion, was a plagiarist in ancient Greece, a 'bastion of church dogmatism' in the Middle Ages, and so forth.

Out of his irreconcilable hatred towards anthroposophy and above all towards Rudolf Steiner, Brandstätter tried—as though not simply to copy Klizovsky—to outdo him in his choice of negative epithets. Thus for Brandstätter the founder of anthroposophy is a direct tool of 'Satanists', one who acknowledged Christ's central significance in our cosmos 'along Satan's lines' and therefore became 'the great Judas of the new age' or even worse, for—according to Brandstätter—by founding anthroposophy Rudolf Steiner took a step that 'even Judas Iscariot did not dare [to take]' and which 'cannot be rectified for several millennia ...'

As in the case of Klizovsky, in the coarse and mocking tone of Brandstätter it is not difficult to recognize the voice of Ahriman, who clearly is appearing here as an author.* For by remaining unrecognized by spiritually blind human beings he can all the more successfully make use of them in the battle with his deadly enemies, the earthly representatives and servants of Michael, the greatest supersensible leader and inspirer of the stream of esoteric Christianity in the modern epoch.

Coarse criticism based on obvious lies is, however, in spite of everything, not the strongest weapon of the ahrimanic spirits of darkness. For

---

* In the lecture of 20 July 1924 (GA 240) Rudolf Steiner spoke at some length of how from our time onwards Ahriman will appear all the more frequently as an author, in that he works through people who are blinded and beholden to his power: 'Human hands will write the books, but Ahriman will be the author.'

by working through his earthly, human instruments Ahriman is resorting to a far more effective method which he has used many times, consisting of the following. As Ahriman is not by nature a creative spirit, he is not capable of creating anything new in the world but can only copy—albeit in a distorted, demonic form—the deeds of the divine Hierarchies ('Satan is God's monkey', according to a medieval saying). Not direct lying but the constant falsifying of truths turns out to be his best method.

In Brandstätter and his followers we have, so to speak, a classic example of this. For he calls his teaching—despite actually completely negating true Christianity—'the new Gospel for the coming age', which makes 'Christ's teaching' in the 'original sense' comprehensible for the first time. For this reason Brandstätter, in keeping with the indications of anthroposophy, 'recognizes' the Archangel Michael as leader of the present epoch, albeit in an ahrimanic way, in that instead of the true, spiritual Archangel Michael he proposes an altogether different, 'human' (that is, false) being.

Thus in the monthly journal *Welt-Spirale* ('World Spiral') founded by Brandstätter in 1961 (1986, no. 12), which was published by the Ethical Society for Progress and World Renewal established by him in Linz and also by the Agni Yoga Society based in Munich, one can read the following announcement at the end of his article: 'All sources of spiritual and religious Christian culture refer with full clarity to St Michael, the spiritual leader of the part of humanity to which the future is revealed in the fulfilment of qualitative demands, in the improvement of one's own character and in the raising of consciousness. Living, actual Christianity takes this fact into account and brings Michael's message to realization.' And in the accompanying letter added to the free third issue of *Welt-Spirale* for 1988, V. Augustat—Brandstätter's successor and current editor of the publishing house—writes as follows: 'Please do not regard the enclosed journal as an advertisement! The call goes out to serious people who also in the Christian sense respond to the spiritual summons of the Archangel MICHAEL and seek to prepare for the [Aquarian] age to come.'

It becomes clear from closer study of this and other issues of *Welt-Spirale* that the being in question here is not Michael, the Archstrategist of the heavenly powers, who originally belonged in the heavenly hierarchy to the rank of Archangel, but someone quite different. In order to see through the evident distortion and deceit that is going on here, one needs to consider the following.

On reading the first book of the 14-volume series of *Agni Yoga*, 'The Call', the reader has a certain difficulty in distinguishing the Mahatma

Morya, who had supposedly dictated the book to Helena Roerich, from the Maitreya.* Hence the firm conviction arose in Helena Roerich's lifetime among her pupils that one and the same person is meant here. This is borne out by Klizovsky's book, whose manuscript was personally examined and approved by Helena Roerich before it appeared in 1934. He writes at the end of the second volume about 'the books of the teaching [of Living Ethics] which was given for the incipient epoch [of Aquarius] of the future *Lord Maitreya-Morya*'.

In spite of the fact that this view completely contradicts traditional theosophical teaching, which goes back to Blavatsky's works and the letters of the mahatmas to Sinnett and also to other early theosophists, it has become firmly entrenched both amongst present-day followers of Helena Roerich in Russia and also beyond its borders. Thus, for example, A. Ter-Akopyan and G. Gorchakov, modern pupils of Helena Roerich, write along these lines.[6]

The same view is also shared by Brandstätter, though he goes even further in this respect. In the third issue of *Welt-Spirale* from 1988 an article was published by him with the title 'The Older Brothers of Mankind and the Guidance of the World', in which he wrote: 'He [Master Morya], as the ... world teacher for the Aquarian Age, provides guidance now for the evolution of the newly forming world religion ... In this capacity he [Morya] was already foreseen by Gautama Buddha as the coming Maitreya ... Thus it is that Morya receives the [honorary] title Maitreya.' And in the same third issue of the journal *Welt-Spirale* for 1988 the portrait of Morya familiar in theosophical circles was reproduced, with the caption 'Maitreya Morya'. If the reader then turns to the contents page of the same issue, he finds to his astonishment a completely different name for this same portrait of the mahatma: 'a picture of Morya-Michael'.

Brandstätter himself resolves the riddle contained in these words in the article about this portrait. There he writes: 'Since Morya, as the master of the first ray of will and power and at the same time also the highest

---

*Thus, for example, in the following passage from the second volume of *Agni Yoga*, 'Leaves from Morya's Garden', it is very difficult to be sure in whose name Helena Roerich is speaking and who is meant by the pronouns written with capital letters: 'The Maitreya sends boldness. The Maitreya will take the gift. The Maitreya, love has a premonition of him. The Maitreya sends blessings for joyful work. The Maitreya transmits work to the earth to achieve miracles.—Go light-filled on your way.—Joy for *Me* to maintain the smiling ones. The teaching of light arises in every phenomenon. Finding oneself is the quality of *My* pupils. *I* am showing you how a miracle that the people need may be beheld...'

commander of the angel hosts—identical with the Archangel Michael—and likewise ruler of the Holy City of Shamballa, is in the physical realm of the earth, he is now leading the final battle against Lucifer in the Armageddon of culture' (ibid.). In stating this, Brandstätter evidently seems to be unaffected by the complete contradiction of his assertions with what the mahatmas say in, for example, the letters to Sinnett; for they regard themselves without doubt as highly developed *human* and not supersensible or superhuman beings like the Archangel Michael.

And in another issue of *Welt-Spirale*[7] Brandstätter's pupil and the present editor of the journal, V. Augustat, in an article about 'The Guidance of Mankind', adds the following etymological 'discovery' in confirmation of what had been communicated to him by his teacher: 'The Maitreya is identical with the Archangel MICHAEL, as the Sanscrit name "Morya" when translated means "Michael".'[*] And since Brandstätter together with his pupils—following Helena Roerich—is convinced that for the preparation of the future root race 'the teaching of Agni Yoga was given by Master Morya through the mediation of his pupil Helena Roerich',[8] the reader must conclude that the teachings of Agni Yoga—as imparted both by Helena Roerich herself and her follower Brandstätter—derive from none other than the Archangel Michael himself!

This is also confirmed by the following words of Brandstätter's pupil Augustat: '. . . when on 24 March 1920 the initiate Helena I. Roerich, standing on the level of a Master of Wisdom, received the first proclamation of the Agni teaching from the Archstrategist Michael/Maitreya Morya.'[9][†]

If, however, the reader would like to know the sort of facts underlying the 'living, currently relevant Christianity' that comes to manifestation through 'the present Michael proclamation',[10] it is enough to turn to the article by Brandstätter which has already been quoted, 'The Older Brothers of Mankind and the Guidance of the World', where it is stated that the Christ has risen from the bodhisattva to the buddha stage, that

---

[*] Here the Russian pupil of Agni Yoga G. Gorchakov repeats Brandstätter and Augustat. In his book dedicated to Helena Roerich, *Vyeliki Uchitel. Zemniye zhizni Naivysshevo [Maitreyi]* ('The Great Teacher. The Earthly Lives of the Most High [Maitreya]'), he writes: 'The Great Teacher and the Archstrategist Michael or George Pobedonosyets [the Victorious] have met in personal single combat, He is the Maitreya, and the Prince of darkness' (Gorchakov, p. 202).

[†] As the reader may recall, the inspirer of Agni Yoga begins this 'first proclamation of the teaching of Agni Yoga' with the words: 'To the new [that is, Bolshevik—S.P.] Russia—My first proclamation.' (See chapter 10.)

Buddhism—nevertheless—far exceeds Christianity 'in depth and wisdom' and that, of course, the teaching of Agni Yoga stands above everything else.[11]

To conclude, we shall now cite some further words from Brandstätter himself: 'The Christ of the fifth root race ... was already initiated as a Buddha, as proclaimed from a higher source [as with Klizovsky, in all probability this refers to Helena Roerich] ... For Christians it may sound strange that there are still higher stages of initiation than those of a Christ; nevertheless someone who is philosophically and logically trained will have to admit without hesitation that Buddha's teaching significantly surpasses Christian teaching in depth and wisdom, just as Dynani Yoga—the esoteric foundation of Buddhism—has a deeper spiritual foundation than Bhakti Yoga, the esoteric foundation of Christianity and Islam. The synthesis of all yoga systems, so far as they are still confirmed by the radiant hierarchy, is Agni Yoga.'

This final sentence is, as the reader may recall, a quotation from *Agni Yoga*. The true character of this synthesis and all the consequences resulting from it has already been sufficiently discussed in this book.

Notes

1. HR 2, 30 August 1935.
2. GA 129, 21 August 1911.
3. HR 3, 30 June 1934.
4. RA 1, p. 131, 17 February 1934.
5. RA 1, p. 170, 6 May 1934.
6. See p. 37.
7. No. 12, 1986.
8. *Welt-Spirale* ('World Spiral'), 1988 no. 3.
9. Ibid.
10. 'World Spiral', 1986 no. 12.
11. 'World Spiral', 1988 no. 3.

10. Helena and Nicholas Roerich as Representatives of Occult Bolshevism

As is fully clear from the content of the present book, one of the principal qualities shared by the Roerichs was a deeply positive attitude to Bolshevism in Russia and above all to its leader and chief ideologue—Lenin. From a certain moment and until the very end of their lives this positive attitude remained unchanged, and even the passage of decades was not able to affect it in the slightest.

However, Helena and Nicholas Roerich did not immediately come to such a complete and unqualified acceptance of Leninist Bolshevism. To begin with, after the October Revolution of 1917, guided by the natural feelings of educated and culture-loving people, they had a negative attitude to the Bolsheviks' seizure of power, reckoning them to be barbarians and destroyers of all culture. Only after their meeting in London in 1920 with that individuality whom they were subsequently to venerate as their spiritual teacher did their opinion of the Bolsheviks and of everything that was taking place in Russia change completely.[*]

As we have already seen, the Roerichs were convinced until the end of their lives that the personality who had taken up contact with them was Mahatma Morya, and everything that they did and wrote after their meeting with this figure was done and written on his behalf and with his agreement and for the most part under his dictation. That in reality their secret inspirer was an altogether different individuality, who belonged to the occultists of the left path and merely used the name of the true mahatma in order to achieve his highly dubious aims, was not something that Helena and Nicholas Roerich recognized.

This is still not understood by their followers even today; for they continue more or less openly to support and glorify Bolshevism until the present time, especially its 'great' founder.

In the weekly journal *Znamya mira* ('Banner of Peace') recently founded in Tomsk by the adherents of Agni Yoga, in the April issue for 1993, an article appeared—according to the editorship only the first of a whole series—which was devoted to a study of Lenin's mission from the

---

[*] Nicholas Roerich's critical remarks about Bolshevism, which he wrote down before his meeting with the occult leaders, were published in the Petrozavodsky journal *Nabat Severo-Zapada* ('Toxin of the North-West'), 12 June 1992.

standpoint of Agni Yoga.* The article is accompanied by a portrait of the leader, and its title is a quotation from Helena Roerich's book *Obshchina* ('Community'): 'Take the appearance of Lenin as a sign of the sensitivity of the cosmos'—an unambiguous indication of the 'cosmic' dimensions of its mission.

In the article there appear the following words: 'The Mission of Vladimir Ilich Lenin (Ulyanov) is so complex that even the Roerichs were only able to understand it from the Highest Plane. It is known that even in 1919 N.K. Roerich supposed the Bolsheviks to be "destroyers of culture". It is also known that after 24 March 1920 the Roerichs became ardent "reds" [that is, Bolshevik in their sympathies]. On this day there took place their meeting with Mahatma M. Evidently, their initiation into the Plan of the Rulers [the mahatmas] had begun.'[1]

And then the author of the article turns to a question put by him to an old pupil of N.K. Roerich: 'How can the New Epoch and the coercive means of inaugurating the new order in 1917 be reconciled with one another?' The pupil's answer was brief and clear: 'Not to accept Lenin's Mission is not to accept the Plan of the Rulers [the mahatmas].'[2]

However people today may relate to these words, spoken at the end of 1989, they could when applied to the Roerichs fully serve as a leitmotif of their entire lives *after* their first meeting with the mahatma.

Indeed, already in 1924 Helena Roerich—while she was abroad—brought out the first volume of *Agni Yoga* under the title *Listy sada Morya* ('Leaves of Morya's Garden'), Part I, *Zov* ('The Call'). On the second page of the book a date is given: 'London. March 24th, 1920'—that is the day of the meeting with the mahatma. And on the first page are the words with which the book itself begins: 'To the new Russia—My first proclamation.'† The word 'My' is printed with a capital and refers to the mahatma who—according to Helena Roerich's conviction—dictated to her not only this first but also all the subsequent 13 volumes of *Agni Yoga* by mediumistic means.

---

* In 1995 an entire volume was published on this theme by Roerich adherents in Russia: V. Kleshchevsky, *Taina Lenina* ('The Mystery of Lenin'), Tomsk 1995.

† Subsequent foreign editions of Helena Roerich's works, obviously not wishing to compromise themselves by openly manifesting sympathy for the Bolsheviks, generally omitted or metamorphosed this first phrase. Thus V. Sidorov, a contemporary adherent of Agni Yoga, wrote in this connection in his Afterword to the book *Living Ethics—An Anthology* (Moscow 1992): 'It is curious and, of course, characteristic that in virtually all western publications of the books of Living Ethics the theme of Russia is toned down and obscured. The first phrase of the first book is here either omitted or edited as follows: "To the New Land—My first proclamation"' (Sidorov, p. 387).

The Roerichs henceforth had to serve this new Russia, and in 1926 their spiritual teacher sent them to its rulers. On the way there, while they were crossing the Himalayas, he dictated to Helena Roerich the third volume of *Agni Yoga*, *Obshchina* ('Community'), together with the letter to the Bolshevik Government, which the Roerichs were to pass on to its representatives in Moscow. Then the same mahatma ordered the Roerichs to return to India via Mongolia, where they were also entrusted with carrying out a certain task.

In the Mongolian capital of Ulan-Bator, Helena Roerich personally published the text of 'Community' in Russian (anonymously, without any indication of the author's name)[*] in a small edition of 200–300 copies. It was in this book, which was first dictated by the Eastern mahatma and then, in accordance with his indication, published in the Mongolian capital, that all the positive statements about Lenin, Bolshevism and its materialistic world-view—and also its remorseless battle against the church and religion—are contained, some of which have already been cited in the present work (see p. 60).

Thus in 'Community' reference is made to 'the particular criminality of the church, which is a repository of dark traditions', to the need to 'strengthen [in schools] the lines of materially authentic knowledge'; also to 'pseudo-communists', who must be 'avoided like an infection of syphilis', to 'the dissemination of vanity, ignorance and fear', to the overcoming of the dark legacy of the past; then to the battle against hypocrisy and falsehood (of course with those who sully the radiant form of Leninist Communism); and again and again mention is made of the significance of matter and materialism as the principal forces of the epoch that is to come, by which is meant its higher religion, and so on—that is, the themes are the same as those about which the whole Bolshevik press in Russia was writing in those years and with virtually the same attitudes.[3]

During her stay in Mongolia Helena Roerich anonymously, and also in Russian, published one further book, *Osnovy buddizma* ('The Foundations of Buddhism'). In it can be found a whole series of thoughts which almost literally coincide with many places in 'Community'. For example, she writes of Gautama Buddha that he was a 'fighter for community and matter', or that 'in the teachings of Buddha we find ... materialistic philosophy', 'the living creativity of great matter'. There one can also read

---

[*] This anonymity, apart from possible considerations of personal safety, had above all an occult significance. For Helena Roerich considered that the author of this and all the subsequent books of *Agni Yoga* was not herself but the mahatma who dictated their content to her.

that the Buddha 'attained to a premonition of the Maitreya—the symbol of the age of knowledge about the greatness of matter . . .' Finally, in the same book, Helena Roerich cites a long quotation from a certain professor from Petrograd (his name is not given*), who gave expression in his lecture to a 'universe without God' and called this one of the basic features 'both of Buddhist and of our modern, most recent [meaning Bolshevik] world-conception', a view with which Helena Roerich wholly agrees, criticizing in the section that she quotes only the pupil's denial of freedom of the will but not his denial of God.[4]

Only when the tasks of the mahatma had been accomplished and both books were published did the Roerichs leave Ulan-Bator and follow the caravan road to the south, back to India. This took place on 13 April 1927. The same year is also of significance as the year of the first edition in a jacket of 'Community'. Subsequently, however, on its republication in Europe in 1936 the year 1926 was inscribed on it,[5] which refers not to the year of the book's first publication but to the year of its dictation by the mahatma. The new edition again came out with the mahatma's approval, as Helena Roerich indicated in a letter to her colleagues in Riga: 'I cannot express to You our joy that the members of the Riga [Agni Yoga] Society have so idealistically and ardently responded to the Wish of the L[ord] M[orya]† that the third part of the 'Fiery World' and 'Community' could be published as soon as possible.'[6]

If we turn from a reading of 'Community' and 'The Foundations of Buddhism' to the 'Letter of the Mahatmas' to the Bolshevik Government (see p. 55), we may be particularly struck by their similar style, even to the extent that in some places there are individual expressions and turns of phrase which correspond with the text of 'Community'. So there is little doubt that both documents, the book and the letter, were composed by one and the same personality and at approximately the same time. This was indeed the case. As has been said, both the letter and 'Community' were dictated by the mahatma to Helena Roerich at the end of 1925 and the beginning of 1926 during the expedition from India to Russia. The Roerichs' deed of bringing soil from the Himalayas for Lenin's grave merely ratified—as though with a symbolic seal, and thus confirmed—the sole authorship of all the quoted statements. All in all, 'Community'— both through its content and the coarseness of its style (strongly

---

* The person in question is possibly the orientalist F.I. Shcherbatsky (1866–1942). See M. Tsybikov, 'Za mir na zemlye i v dushye kazhdovo chelovyeka' ('For Peace on Earth and in the Soul of Each Human Being'), *Osnovy buddizma* ('Foundations of Buddhism'), p. 70.
† Or even the Maitreya?

reminiscent of that of the writings of Lenin himself)—is none other than an expanded commentary on the 'Letter of the Mahatmas' to the Bolshevik Government, with which it forms a single whole.

In his acknowledgement of Lenin as a cosmic phenomenon Nicholas Roerich was the equal of Helena. In 1926 he wrote: 'He [Lenin] incorporated and circumspectly fitted every material into the world order. This opened up to him the path into all parts of the world. And people have formed a legend not only as a record of his deeds but also as a mark of his aspirations. Behind us lie twenty-four countries [he here refers to all the countries through which the Roerichs have travelled, especially those in Asia], and we have seen for ourselves how the nations have understood the magnetic power of communism. Friends, the worst counsellor is negativity. Behind every negation ignorance is concealed. And in ignorance is the hydra of counter-revolution.'[7]

These words were most likely written by Roerich during his stay in Bolshevik Russia. Shortly before this, while he was in Urumqi—within the territory of China—awaiting permission to depart, he wrote in his diary some words of E. Chin-Ben, who on the occasion of Lenin's death compared him with no less than 'Shakya-Muni [Buddha] and Christ'. Roerich was in complete agreement with this, and for this called its author a 'light-filled, brave and honourable Chinaman'.[8][*]

This frank acknowledgement of the rightness of such a comparison represents the culmination of the relationship between the Roerichs and Lenin. Despite its blasphemous character and its obvious absurdity, it is fully compatible with the content of 'Community', where Lenin is spoken of as a cosmic phenomenon ('a sign of the sensitivity of the cosmos'), and with the 'Letter of the Mahatmas' to the Bolshevik Government and, finally, with the Himalayan soil brought by them for the grave of 'Mahatma Lenin'.

After all that has been said above the reader will not be surprised about the following extract from the will of Nicholas Roerich recently published for the first time in Russia, which he wrote down in 1926 in Xinjiang not long after his visit to Moscow: 'Herewith I bequeath all my property, paintings, literary rights ... to the use for as long as she lives of my wife Helena Ivanovna Roerich. After her I bequeath *the aforesaid*

---

[*] In the Soviet edition (AG, p. 203), the censor omitted from E. Chin-Ben's words the names of the founders of Buddhism and Christianity—probably because he reckoned the comparison to be inappropriate (after all, Lenin was a convinced materialist and an enemy of any religion). However, in 1993, in the post-Bolshevik era, they could be published in full, without cuts, and were even included as the epigraph to an article by V. Kleshchevsky on the relationship of the Roerichs to Bolshevism.

property to the Communist Party of the Soviet Union, with the sole request that a worthy place—corresponding to the *high tasks of communism*—is allotted to the objects of art.'[9] *

As for the Roerichs, subsequent years did not fundamentally alter their relationship to Lenin's mission, to Bolshevism and to all 'successes' of the Russian people in building up a 'radiant future'. It is true that Helena Roerich made some significant revisions to 'Community' for its republication in Riga (1936) and removed the most pro-communist portions, which is, however, wholly understandable. For to bring it out openly in Europe and America in the mid-1930s with its adulations of Lenin and the Bolsheviks without ruining her reputation and being branded as an 'agent of the Reds' was virtually impossible.

Nevertheless, in her letters to America she continued to praise Bolshevik Russia or 'the New Land', as she called it. Thus, for example, she wrote in June 1937: 'Yur[i]—Helena Roerich's oldest son] is at present developing a remarkable insight into the affairs of the New Land; after a few days he knows what is going on there. This gift should be regarded as a blessing, it stands him in such good stead in life; and what is particularly gratifying is that he accepts all these Indications in full confidence.'[10]

These words leave one dumbfounded. For in 1937 the first great wave of Stalinist repressions was beginning, costing millions of innocent people their lives. This sinister wave of bloody terror was still continuing when Helena Roerich in 1938 wrote the following in letters to America: '. . . We often recall a prophecy that we wrote *in [19]22*, that soon the New Land will be the best place for life—so it will be,' (italics by Helena Roerich).[11] In other words: 'Leninist Russia' will in the years of the most awful repressions be the 'best place for life'!

Then from another letter to America: 'The changes in the New Land are amazing and precipitous. Truly, the temple of the Spirit will soon be

---

* On this account Jacqueline Decter remarks: 'This seeming gesture of good will was undoubtedly the artist's way of ensuring a safe sojourn in his native land, because the expedition's property in fact belonged to the museum in New York' (Decter, *The Life and Work of a Russian Master*, p. 163). It is, however, noteworthy that almost all Roerich's biographers who mention this will omit the words about the Communist Party and replace them with the Russian state or the Russian people, as Decter also does. In A. Shchupev's recent comment, 'Nicholas Roerich was not an agent of Ogpu [United State Political Administration, the organization active from 1923 to 1934 to combat counter-revolutionary activity in the Soviet Union—Tr.]' (*Izvestiya*, 22 October 1993), a curious additional light is shed upon Roerich's will. Roerich asks for his property to be disposed of by 'Chicherin, Stalin, Bystrov or whomsoever they indicate'; but even Shchupev is silent about the Communist Party, and the 'worthy place' is mentioned without the 'high tasks of communism'.

established. Truly, all events will be only for the best of the New Land.'[12] Or, in another letter to America from the same year, this time signed by both the Roerichs: 'The stars predict eternal prosperity for the New Land, which is why we take all outward appearances calmly; for the essential reality will remain unchanged.'[13]

Again one asks: what are these 'events' which in the years of bloody terror are 'only for the best of the New Land'? Which outward appearances are we to 'take calmly', for their 'essential reality'—Leninist and Bolshevik—'will remain unchanged'?

The immovable position adopted by the Roerichs over this question is borne out above all by their numerous articles, letters and diary entries from the thirties and forties. Thus, for example, Helena Roerich wrote in one of her letters from 1935: 'Our homeland has already embarked upon the path of healing and is searching for a new and glorious path. It is particularly gratifying to see that the masses have awakened to conscious life.'[14] Similar thoughts were also expressed by Nicholas Roerich. He wrote in 1940: 'The Russian people have put down great stones. To everyone's astonishment what has been erected is not a Babylonian but a Russian tower. A hundred-towered Kremlin of sun-bearers! ... Listen, this is the future, and how radiant it is!'[15] Or from 1941: 'The whole world is being drawn towards Armageddon. All are confused. All are unsure about the future. But the Russian people have found their course and with a mighty torrent are aspiring towards their radiant future;'[16] and in 1943 he calls: 'May the Leninists remember the legacy of dialectical materialism,'[17] and so forth.

The Roerichs' followers in Russia tried several times after the so-called Khrushchev thaw to publish material about the relationship of the Roerichs to Lenin, with the object of proving the complete loyalty of the founders of Agni Yoga to the ruling regime. They hoped thereby to gain for themselves the possibility of a more legal existence and indeed made some progress in this respect.

The deeply positive attitude of the Roerich family to Bolshevism and to all its 'achievements' is also attested by their efforts already in 1936 to return not merely to Russia but precisely to the 'new' Bolshevik Russia. Nicholas Roerich takes up connections with Soviet diplomats in Paris and Riga, prepares the dispatch of his archive via Latvia to the Soviet Union, asks his colleagues in Riga to see to it that in Soviet Russia 'nothing bad is written about us [Roerichs]'[18] and makes the plea in almost every letter to 'go with the "New Land"'.[19] As P. Belikov relates, 'more than four hundred paintings ... were packed in boxes for their transporting by sea via Bombay'[20] to Russia; and only Nicholas Roerich's death in 1947 prevented the implementation of these plans. However, Helena Roerich on her death made her eldest son Yuri (1902–60) promise to return without fail to Russia, which he did in 1957.

Indeed, the Roerichs remained to the end faithful in their family to the legacy of the Eastern occultists guiding them. This lived on as a deeply rooted tradition. In his 'Memories of Yuri Roerich' G.F. Lukin reports of a general conversation with him in Moscow, where Yuri Roerich—after sharp criticism of the West (England, Germany, North America)—explained that, in contrast to the West, as regards man's path of evolution 'we in the Soviet Union are experiencing a sudden upsurge', especially among young people, for 'nowhere in the world is there a younger generation such as in the Soviet Union, which would aspire so ardently and selflessly to follow the new [i.e. the Bolshevik] path'.[21] And Yuri Roerich said this at a time when Khrushchev was mobilizing all forces, and especially young people, for a battle against any manifestation of religion and religiosity, closing thousands of churches throughout Russia. R. Rudzitis likewise cites statements of a similar nature by Yuri Roerich in his diary, where he recorded the substance of his personal conversations with Yuri Roerich in the last years of his life: 'The youth of Russia is a circle of interests and endeavours aspiring towards heroic deeds. Much here is taking place as foreseen by the Teaching ... In Russia much is happening according to the Plan [of the mahatmas]. Predictions are coming true, although not exactly as was envisaged.'[22]

Helena and Nicholas Roerich's younger son Svyatoslav (1904–93) maintained this family tradition unchanged until the end of his life. After Yuri's departure for Rome he was the sole guardian of the literary and artistic legacy of his parents and the person who most strongly continued their work. As their successor he personally visited the editors of the journal *Trezvost i kultura* ('Temperance and Culture'), which had undertaken to reprint 'Community' in its original Ulan-Bator edition, and signed with his own hand a copy—from which the republication was made—for all the Roerichs' followers in Russia.

The fact of such a signing *after* the fall of Bolshevism in Russia of the most pro-Bolshevik book by Helena Roerich is an eloquent testimony of the faithfulness of *all* the members of the Roerich family until the very end of their lives to the 'Mission of Lenin'. And indeed, how could this be otherwise, if its 'cosmic' significance was once revealed to Helena and Nicholas Roerich by their spiritual teachers, whom they regarded as infallible?

The foreword to the reprinted edition of 'Community' was written by V. Sidorov, the President of the Commission for the Literary Legacy of

N.K. Roerich, who gave it the title 'Don't miss the boat!'. This foreword, written by a well-known pupil of the Roerichs in the post-Bolshevik era, perhaps best reflects the present mood of the majority of the pupils and followers of the Roerichs in Russia who, despite all the terrible lessons of Russian history, want to remain consistently loyal to the Bolshevik precepts of the founder of Agni Yoga. And whereas in the West the followers of the Roerichs do, as a rule, keep an embarrassed silence about their open sympathy for Bolshevism, thus not only manifesting an inner inconsistency but quite consciously deluding the entire Western public, in Russia this legacy of the Roerichs is honoured by their pupils even today, in that they view it as an indication of the mahatmas given through the Roerichs and not subject to doubt.

We shall not quote Sidorov himself here. For if we turn to the context out of which he took the title for his introductory article, it speaks for itself and further commentaries are unnecessary. Sidorov concludes his foreword with it. 'As pupils of Lenin, watch with an eagle eye, and with the leap of a lion claim the power that is yours. Do not miss the boat!'

To conclude this chapter, which has led the reader back to the occult sources of Bolshevism and to the relationship to it and to its founder of the Eastern occultists,[*] it is necessary to speak also about the relationship to it of Western, that is, Christian-Rosicrucian occultism as represented in the twentieth century by Rudolf Steiner.

Thus only a year after the Bolsheviks came to power in Russia, Rudolf Steiner indicated 'that in them [Lenin and Trotsky] the greatest, most intense enemies of the spiritual evolution of mankind could be seen',[23] in whom 'there lives ... hatred for the supersensible, even if this comes to expression ... in other words'.[24]

Subsequently, as he gazed ever deeper into the Russian tragedy, Rudolf Steiner in 1919 came to pronounce an even sterner sentence. He called Lenin 'the hangman' and 'gravedigger of all spiritual life', in whom was manifested the aspiration towards 'wild destruction of everything of a spiritual nature'.[25] And then in the same year: 'I know that what lies at the foundation of his [Lenin's] view of the world is not the creating of a new culture but the murder of a culture.'[26] A year later he explains this destructive power of Bolshevism in the following way: 'Bolshevism is so destructive for mankind because it is a creed purely of the brain, the *material* brain,'[27] that is, of matter alone. This thought has much in

---

[*]Regarding the *Western* occult sources of Bolshevism, see the present author's book *The Spiritual Origins of Eastern Europe and the Future Mysteries of the Holy Grail*, Temple Lodge, 1993.

common with these words from 'Community': 'In our acts and our thoughts we cannot separate ourselves from matter,' after which one is told about the need for 'a training in the materiality of thinking'.

In this connection, the following words of Rudolf Steiner about the Bolsheviks' ideas on education acquire a special significance: '... Lunacharsky's educational reform* is something quite terrible. It is the death of all culture! And although so much that is bad has already emerged for the rest of Bolshevism, the worst will be the Bolshevist methods of education.'[28]

Rudolf Steiner gives the following characterization of what awaits our earth in the event of the universal spread of Leninism: 'Mankind would then, beginning with Russia, be mechanized in spirit, vegetabilized in soul and animalized in body,'[29] as a result of which all 'human society over the entire earth would necessarily be transformed into a herd of animals *with no more than a refined thinking capacity*.'[30] For 'in Leninism the *cleverness of the human animal*, the cleverness of the human animality, comes to the surface of human evolution'.[31]†

Finally, Rudolf Steiner touches upon the occult nature of Bolshevism. He calls Leninism 'the ahrimanic form of antichristianity';[32] and he continues: 'Lenin, Trotsky and others like them *are the tools of ahrimanic powers*. This is an ahrimanic initiation, which quite simply *belongs to a different cosmic sphere from ours*. But it is an initiation which bears in its depths the power to efface human civilization from the earth, to wipe out everything that has been formed by way of human civilization.'[33]‡

The answer to the question as to what these words about 'Bolshevist initiation' belonging to 'another cosmic sphere' from the human sphere signify has already been given in the pages of this book. Bolshevik initiation has its origin and is inspired out of *the eighth sphere* and would lead the whole of earthly evolution to it.

Thus already in 1919 Rudolf Steiner said that 'if things were to go

---

* The Roerichs met with Lunacharsky in 1926 in Moscow and had many hours of conversations with him. He also took part in the ceremony of the handing over of the 'message of the mahatmas' to the Bolshevik Government and the Himalayan soil for Lenin's grave. Probably as a result of being inspired by this conversation, Nicholas Roerich also recorded in his notebook a long quotation from Lunacharsky with references to Marx, Lenin and the Communist Party. (NR 4, pp. 289–90.)

† This characterization by the modern Christian initiate of the inner nature of the occult phenomenon of Bolshevism is directly related to the corresponding passage in the Book of Revelation, where St John writes about the beast from the abyss along with the 'human' number 666 (Revelation, 13:18).

‡ Compare with Rudolf Steiner's words about the reasons for the so positive relationship of Eastern initiates to Bolshevism quoted on p. 71.

further in the way that they have now begun in Russia, this would signify that the earth would lose its task, would be deprived of its task, would be wrested from the universe and be ahrimanized'.[34]

Bearing in mind what has been said, it is not difficult to understand that Bolshevism as a social and occult phenomenon is—first and foremost—deeply alien to all the true tasks of Russia, to the whole of its future mission in the evolution of humanity. Rudolf Steiner referred also to this in 1918, when he said that 'never have such great contrasts collided with one another than the soul of the European East and the anti-humanity of Trokskyism and Leninism'.[35] And two years later he formulated this thought as follows: 'There are many people who think that what is to arise in the East has something to do with Leninism and Trotskyism. They have nothing whatever to do with what is to arise in the East [of Europe] but only with what will perish there and what will be further doomed to perish because of Leninism and Trotskyism. These are purely destructive forces, and what is to arise in the East [of Europe] must develop there in spite of these destructive forces.'[36]

'There are many people ...' Amongst these 'many people' were the whole Roerich family, who were misled by the left-oriented Eastern occultists calling themselves mahatmas and who until the very end of their lives preserved an unshakeable belief in the deep-down affinity between Bolshevism and the true tasks of Russia.

All their lives they wanted not to 'miss the boat', but that is exactly what they did.

Notes

1. V. Kleshchevsky, 'Poyavlenie Lenina primitye kak znak chutkosti Kosmosa', *Znamya mira* ('Banner of Peace'), 1993, nos. 7–8 (9–10), p. 10.
2. Ibid.
3. OB.
4. 'Foundations of Buddhism'.
5. See the editor's Foreword to OB.
6. HR 3, 24 February 1936 (1).
7. AG, p. 246, compare also NR 4, p. 290.
8. NR 4, pp. 238–9.
9. Quoted from A.D. Alekhin, *Trud, podvig, krasota* ('Labour, heroic deeds, beauty'), ZS, pp. 13–14.
10. RA II, p. 74, 24 June 1937.
11. RA II, p. 254, 10 December 1938.
12. RA II, p. 280, 26 July 1939.
13. RA II, p. 299, 28 July 1939.
14. HR 2, 17 December 1935.

15. N.K. Roerich, *Iz literaturnovo naslyediya* ('From the literary legacy'), p. 210.

16. ZS [*Zazhigaitye serdtse*, 'Enkindle the heart'].

17. Ibid.

18. Quoted from P.F. Belikov and L.B. Shaposhnikova, 'Urusvati' Institute, *Urusvati*, Moscow 1993.

19. G.R. Rudzitis, *Perepiska semyi Roerichov c Obshchestvom imeni H.K. Roericha v Latvii*. (Correspondence of the Roerich Family with the Nicholas Roerich Society in Latvia), Roerich Readings, 1979, Novosibirsk, p. 304.

20. Belikov, p. 44.

21. G.F. Lukin, 'Vospominaniya o Yuri Nikolaeviche Roeriche', *Rerikhovski Vestnik* ('Roerich Herald'), 1992, 5th issue, p. 65.

22. Rudzitis, see note 19, pp. 83–4.

23. GA 181, 9 July 1918.

24. GA 181, 30 July 1918.

25. GA 192, 13 July 1919.

26. GA 192, 3 August 1919.

27. GA 198, 3 April 1920.

28. GA 293, 25 August 1919.

29. GA 192, 29 June 1919.

30. GA 197, 13 June 1920.

31. Ibid.

32. GA 198, 3 April 1920.

33. GA 197, 13 June 1920.

34. GA 294, 22 August 1919.

35. GA 182, 30 April 1918.

36. GA 199, 7 August 1920.

Appendices

Appendix 1. H.P. Blavatsky and Eastern Occultism

Rudolf Steiner spoke as follows about Blavatsky's liberation from her occult prison by Indian occultists: 'Certain Indian occultists now came to know of the affair [that Blavatsky had become occultly imprisoned], occultists who on their part tended strongly to the left [which in occult terminology means those who belonged to the "left", egotistical path], and whose prime interest it was to direct the occultism which was to be given to the world through H.P. Blavatsky in such a way that it could influence the world in line with their special aims' (GA 254, 11 October 1915).

The occult reasons for Blavatsky's gradual shift from the Rosicrucian masters towards the Eastern mahatmas and subsequently in the direction of the left-oriented Eastern occultists who took their place lay not merely with the subjective qualities of her soul nature and with her mediumistic gifts but also had their deeper roots in the karmic guilt of the West for the 'innumerable injustices' that it had inflicted over the centuries upon the Asiatic East. Rudolf Steiner said of this: 'India, whose occult endeavours had been suppressed, took karmic revenge by impregnating the first manifestation of occultism in the West with its own egotistic, national occultism. This took place in the time of H.P. Blavatsky . . . Her first work, *Isis Unveiled*, shows her to be a person of a thoroughly chaotic, illogical, passionate and confused nature, but it also shows that behind her there stood guiding forces[*] wanting to direct her towards universally human concerns. In *The Secret Doctrine*—quite apart from its very evident stature—everything is dominated by narrowly human interests, interests stemming from certain occult centres which in our time do not concern themselves with affairs of a universally human nature but only with a certain specific aspect. Both the Tibeto-Indian and the Egyptian initiation of modern times[†] always only have specific, limited interests in view; they want to avenge themselves upon the Western world for having suppressed Eastern occultism, for having overwhelmed the world of the East with materialistic influences' (address to Russian members, GA 158, 11 April 1912).

---

[*] Associated with true Rosicrucianism—see Appendix 5.

[†] In the fourteenth book of *Agni Yoga* the Eastern occultist dictating to Helena Roerich indicates that 'also the last Egyptian ashram had to be moved to the Himalayas'. (AY 14.19)

E.F. Pisareva, Blavatsky's follower and biographer, active theosophist and translator into Russian of many theosophical works, describes *from theosophical sources* the history of Blavatsky's selection by the mahatmas as the mediator between them and Western humanity: 'This question [regarding the spread of Eastern occult teachings to the West] was discussed in the lamaist monastery of Halaring Sho near Shigatse, which is on the border between China and Tibet.* The people who resolved this question were philosopher-ascetics with a deeply meditative life, who in the hierarchy of humanity stand far higher than us . . .' However, most of the participants—according to Pisareva—did not support this idea and only two of those who were present were in favour of it happening. 'These were the voices of two Hindus: Morya, a descendant of the rulers of Punjab, and Kut Humi, who came from Kashmir. They took upon themselves the responsibility for choosing the emissary and directing her to the West, in order that she might disseminate there *the philosophy of Brahmanism* and reveal a portion of the secrets concerning the nature of man . . . And the choice fell upon H.P. Blavatsky . . . Why was she chosen and not someone endowed with a more even temper, the power to convince, disciplined intellectual capacities and an absence of passion— qualities which H.P. Blavatsky has always lacked?' Pisareva herself gives the following answer to this question: 'She [Blavatsky] was chosen because of her unusual mediumistic gifts and her paranormal faculties, which she had had since childhood. These faculties enabled her teachers, Morya and Kut Humi, to communicate easily with her at a distance by means of telepathy, that is, to impart higher knowledge to her by means of mediumistic dictation and astral demonstration, which played an important part in the writing of her *Secret Doctrine* and in the origin of the so-called 'Letters of the Mahatmas'. (E.F. Pisareva, 'The Mission of H.P. Blavatsky, Theosophy and the Theosophical Society', article in the collection entitled *Aum*, New York-Moscow 1989.)

By 'theosophical sources' Pisareva probably meant the following letters of the mahatma. In autumn 1881 the Mahatma K. H. wrote to Sinnett: 'This state of hers [the chaotic soul condition of Blavatsky, of which her colleagues so often complained] is intimately connected with her occult training in Tibet, and due to her being sent out alone into

---

*Subsequently, the Roerichs visited these places during their Himalayan expedition. In the book *Heart of Asia*, published in New York in 1930, Nicholas Roerich—without, it is true, mentioning the monastery of Halaring Sho—writes: 'Near the region of Shigatse, on the picturesque banks of the Brahmaputra . . . there still were until quite recently ashrams of the Himalayan Mahatmas.'

the world to gradually prepare the way for others. After nearly a century of fruitless search, our chiefs had to avail themselves of the only
opportunity to send out a *European body* upon European soil to serve as
a connecting link between that country and our own.' (ML 26) And in
February 1882 the Mahatma M. explored this theme further in his letter to Sinnett: 'One or two of us [probably M. himself and K.H.]
hoped that the world had so far advanced intellectually, if not
intuitionally, that the Occult doctrine might gain an intellectual acceptance, and the impulse given for a new cycle of occult research.
Others—wiser as it would now seem—held differently, but consent
was given for the trial.' (ML 44)

But it was precisely these remarkably developed mediumistic faculties
that Blavatsky herself could not control which served as the open door
whereby left-oriented occultists were gradually able to master her. That
Blavatsky herself was hardly in a position to distinguish the one from
the other (for, as we have seen, they very quickly adopted the names of
the true mahatmas) is evident, for example, from the following episode
from her journey to India. In her book *From the Caves and Jungles of
Hindustan*, which consists of travel notes written by Blavatsky for a
Russian journal in the 1880s, she gives a detailed description of her
meetings and conversations with one of the mahatmas, who accompanied her and her companions during part of the journey in India. In
the book he is presented under the name of Gulab Lall Singh, behind
whose identity is concealed the Mahatma Morya, although Mahatma
Kut Humi in the letters to Sinnett often signed with the name Lall-
Singh.[*]

In a conversation with an American, a member of the expedition,
whom she calls 'Colonel O' (presumably Olcott), Blavatsky says of
Morya-Lall Singh: 'I know him better than you … Let us thank destiny
that he, who sees better than any other that we—despite belonging to the
"white race" which he hates and despises—are ardently devoted to him
and, perhaps even more important, have a sincere sympathy for his people
and a respect for his country, makes for us a unique exception [accepts
two 'whites' as his occult pupils]. Do not demand of him what he cannot
and will be unable to give us, and be content with the crumbs [of wisdom]
which he throws to us on the road.' (H.P. Blavatsky, *From the Caves and
Jungles of Hindustan*, ch. xxix, London 1892.)

These words about the 'white race' which the mahatma 'hates and
despises' (by which is meant Euro-American humanity) fully correspond

---

[*] See Helena Roerich's comment about this in HR 2, 14 August 1936.

in their meaning and especially in their emotional mood to Rudolf Steiner's remark quoted above about the efforts of Tibeto-Indian initiates to take vengeance upon the Western world on behalf of suppressed Eastern occultism.

Appendix 2. Russia and Tibet (Badmayev, Dorzhiyev, Helena and Nicholas Roerich)

The attempts of certain Tibetans to enter Russia and gain influence over its policy with regard to Asia and Europe are attested by the following facts.

In the last third of the nineteenth century two brothers of Buryat origin came to St Petersburg from Tibet. They were direct descendants of Genghis Khan; one of them was a lama and the other was a doctor, a specialist in Tibetan medicine. The Russified name of the latter was Pyotr Badmayev (1851–1919). In St Petersburg the brothers established the first Tibetan pharmacy and opened a medical practice. Between 1875 and 1892 P. Badmayev had almost a quarter of a million patients, which led to the Tsar, Alexander III, granting him the title of Privy Councillor.

Having thus developed a connection with the Petersburg court, Badmayev soon submitted a written proposal to the Tsar for a plan for a bloodless union of the Russian Empire with China, Mongolia and Tibet, merely requesting the necessary support for this—to begin with, the two million gold roubles by means of which, for the fulfilment of his intentions, Badmayev proceeded to found the Russo-Asiatic firm of P.A. Badmayev and Co. The plan itself was as follows: to profit from the discontent with the ruling Manchurian dynasty that was at the time widespread amongst the Chinese people and, with the help of clever propaganda and bribery and if necessary with the support of a small contingent of the Russian army, 'to capture the strategic point [the town of Lan-chou-fu] without bloodshed. [For] from this point it is very simple to extend influence throughout China, Tibet and Mongolia' (from Badmayev's memorandum to Tsar Alexander III of 13 February 1893 entitled 'The Tasks of Russia in the Asiatic East').

The Minister of Finance, Witte, who initially supported Badmayev's plan, wrote to Alexander III as follows about the Badmayev project: 'The whole undertaking, as said, must have a completely private character and be conducted in an entirely unofficial way, with no more than material support' (memorandum of 27 February 1893). And he continues in the same vein: 'If the enterprise yields the results expected by Mr Badmayev, Russia—from the shores of the Pacific Ocean and the heights of the Himalayas—will hold sway not only in Asiatic but also in European affairs.'[*]

---

[*] Subsequently, on the eve of the First World War, Witte came out against Badmayev's plans.

However, it appeared that there was not enough money for the fulfilment of Badmayev's plan, and so after a certain time he again turned to the Tsar for financial help, this time to Nicholas II, who in the meantime had ascended the throne. In a letter of 19 December 1896 Badmayev, endeavouring in every way he could to convince the Tsar of the political advantages of his enterprise, wrote to him: '... my activities have the aim that Russia should have greater influence than other powers upon the Mongolian-Tibetan Chinese East.' Badmayev made particular efforts to oppose the English in the East. In connection with this he even sent the Tsar a special memorandum entitled 'On Opposing the English in Tibet', where he wrote, in particular: 'Tibet, which—as the highest plateau of Asia—rules over the Asiatic continent, must without doubt be in the hands of Russia. By commanding this point, Russia will surely be able to make England more compliant.'

In addition to writing secretly to the Tsar, Badmayev also represented his ideas in the official press; and in 1905 an article of his appeared in an anthology entitled *Rossiya i Kitai* ('Russia and China'). Nevertheless, the enterprise soon folded up, since Badmayev was unable to obtain money from Nicholas II for the further implementation of his project. It is not impossible that a significant part was played in this by Rasputin, who did all he could to oppose the influence of the Tibetans on the Tsar.

In St Petersburg Badmayev had an association with a highly placed Tibetan, the lama Agvan Dorzhiyev (1854–1938), the tutor and principal confidant of the 13th Dalai Lama. Dorzhiyev subsequently recalled that when before the threat of Anglo-Chinese occupation 'secret deliberations started to take place in the higher spheres of Tibet about the need to have recourse to the protection of some foreign state or other', at one of these conferences he 'expressed the opinion that it was necessary to give preference to Russia'. In 1898 Dorzhiyev came for the first time to St Petersburg as a plenipotentiary of Tibet. Through the protection of Prince E.E. Ukhtomsky, who was a Buddhist, he succeeded in 1900 in being granted an audience with Nicholas II, and in the following year he journeyed at the head of a Tibetan delegation with gifts from the Dalai Lama and with an official written request for protection. The delegation was favourably received but it did not achieve its object. That Dorzhiyev's activities were not merely of a diplomatic or missionary nature is borne out by the 'Memorandum regarding a more intimate connection of Russia with Mongolia and Tibet' that he presented in November 1907 in the name of the Vice-President of the Russian Geographical Society P.P. Semenov-Tyan-Shansky, where projects of a 'great Buddhist confederation', distinguished from those of Badmayev by no more than economic details, were quite openly drawn up.

Through Dorzhiyev's efforts and with the Dalai Lama's blessing, a Buddhist temple was opened in St Petersburg—the first in European Russia. Its construction was actively supported by Nicholas Roerich, whom Dorzhiyev included in his construction committee. The temple was dedicated to 'Kalachakra', which according to Tibetan tradition is an occult teaching and derives from Shamballa itself. It was oriented towards the north, in the direction of Shamballa, and the statue of a standing Maitreya Bodhisattva was solemnly erected within it. It was from Dorzhiyev that Nicholas Roerich had for the first time heard of the existence of Shamballa and also of the mysterious 'valley of the mahatmas' which can be found somewhere in the depths of the impenetrable mountains of the Himalayas. Roerich said of this: 'I heard for the first time about Shamballa during the construction of the Buddhist temple in the Russian capital. As I was a member of the construction committee, I got to know a very learned Buryat lama who for the first time mentioned the name Chan Shamballa [Northern Shamballa]. It will one day become more widely known why this name, uttered under such circumstances, has so great a significance.'

However, both Badmayev and Dorzhiyev saw the principal guarantee for the success of their enterprise in the wide diffusion in Mongolia, China and Tibet of the legends about the 'white tsar' who was to come from the north (from 'Northern Shamballa') and restore the violated and now decadent traditions of true Buddhism. In his memorandum to Alexander III quoted above ('The Tasks of Russia in the Asiatic East'), Badmayev cites some of these legends. One of these is of particular interest, and in the memorandum there is the following observation about it: 'In the seventh century after the death of Genghis Khan, who died in 1227, a white standard is expected to appear in Mongolia from Russia.'

If we add 700 years to 1227 we arrive at 1927, at the beginning of which the trans-Himalayan expedition under Roerich's leadership, which had left Moscow under the tangka (banner) of Shamballa, finally reached the Mongolian capital, Ulan-Bator. Here Helena Roerich published the third volume of *Agni Yoga*, 'Community', with all its adulations of Lenin and Bolshevik ideology by the Himalayan mahatmas, and also the book 'The Foundations of Buddhism', which portrays Gautama Buddha as a materialist. If we now recall that Nicholas Roerich said that he went to Mongolia in order to fulfil certain 'assignments on behalf of the mahatmas', we have here a definite connection between the activities of Badmayev and the Roerichs, behind whom in both cases there stood one and the same impulse of the Himalayan occultists.

Finally, Roerich's great plan of 'uniting Russia and the vast world of Buddhism with the help of the mahatmas', which—at the behest of the latter—he explained at some length in a conversation with the People's Commissar for Foreign Affairs, Chicherin, in 1926 in Moscow and regarding which (albeit in different words) Helena Roerich wrote in her letters to President Roosevelt, can in all essentials be found in Badmayev's letters to the Russian tsars.

Probably before the beginning of the First World War, an even more significant figure of the Tibetan world, the lama Lubsan Sandal Tsydenov (born 1842), who bore the very rare title of 'Dharma Radzhi' (tsar of learning), visited St Petersburg at the head of a Buryat delegation through the mediation of lama Dorzhiyev. It could be supposed that the negotiations were most likely conducted along the same lines as those of Badmayev. However, they did not lead to any perceptible success, as the following episode—in particular—makes manifest. During the official reception at the Winter Palace, when Nicholas II entered the reception-room where the Buryat delegation was waiting with Tsydenov at its head and all those present immediately knelt according to etiquette, the 'tsar of learning' alone remained standing. His answer when asked about such incivility was: 'A spiritual tsar does not bow down before a worldly tsar.' As a result the Buryat delegation had to pay a substantial penalty, and nothing further is known about the subsequent negotiations.

Probably on the eve of the Bolshevik Revolution it was decided in the occult circles of Tibet to achieve the aims referred to above not through the 'white' but through the 'red tsar', as is attested by the fact of the mahatmas' timely visit to Lenin in Switzerland and also their letter sent in 1926 through Nicholas Roerich to the Bolshevik Government.

In the same sense Dorzhiyev continued to exert an influence after the 1917 Revolution in Russia, in that over the course of many years (1920–30) he played the role of principal mediator between Tibetan Lhasa and the Bolshevik Government in Moscow (he was the 'Plenipotentiary of the Tibetan Government in the USSR'). Thus Dorzhiyev regarded 'the teaching of the great Gautama Buddha as identical in its essentials to that of the great Marx and Lenin', asserting that 'Buddhism is above all an atheistic religion'.

Helena and Nicholas Roerich met Dorzhiyev during their stay in Moscow in 1926. At that time a big exhibition of Buddhist art was being prepared. When it was opened Dorzhiyev had to give a talk where, in complete accord with the ideas of Agni Yoga, he spoke about the cultural and ideological affinity between Indo-Buddhist culture and European culture—the culture of the exact sciences and technology. Subsequently, in the 1950s, Yuri Roerich on returning to Russia became a member of a group of activists trying to reopen the Buddhist temple which had for some time been closed by the Bolsheviks. He also wrote a special research project about 'Kalachakra'.

It should also be pointed out that what is said here does not relate to the traditional Eastern religions as such but only to the so-called 'left-oriented' streams, which concern themselves with occult politics and strive towards the spiritual conquest of the Christian West

All this enables one to have a better understanding of the positive attitude of the left-oriented Eastern occultists who stood behind the Roerichs' expedition to the Bolshevik powers in Russia. For this union between Russia and Asia could only happen in the event that Christianity were wiped out in Russia, which would be equivalent to a denial of its true mission in the sixth cultural epoch (see Appendix 5). The Bolsheviks had in mind to bring about such an extinction of Christianity in Russia, so that a Russia thus 'purified from any religious superstition' could be flooded by the one-sided wisdom of the East, above all Buddhism, as the Roerichs sought to achieve under the guidance of the aforesaid Eastern occultists.

This over-estimation of Buddhism calls to mind Rudolf Steiner's words spoken in 1912 in Helsinki to the group of Russian anthroposophists who had gone there to hear them, when he referred to the second great temptation threatening Russia (in addition to the first, as represented by Western materialism): 'The second temptation will be from the East, if the power of spiritual culture dawns. Then it will be one's duty to know that, for all the greatness of this spiritual culture of the East, people in the present time need to say to themselves: it is not the past that we have to carry into the future but new impulses. It will not be a question of simply receiving some sort of spiritual impulse of the East but of cultivating what the Christian West can itself bring forth out of spiritual sources', that is, out of the spiritual sources of esoteric Christianity, as it is represented today in modern spiritual science or anthroposophy. (GA 158, 11 April 1912.)

References

Andreyev, A.I., *Buddhiskaya svyatynya Petrograda* ('The Buddhist Sanctuary of Petrograd'), Ulan-Ude: Agency EkoArt, 1992.

Andreyev, A.I., *Buddhiskiye lamy iz Staroi Deryevni* ('The Buddhist Lamas from the Old Village'), Nevsky Archive, Moscow-St Petersburg 1993.

Andreyev, A.I., 'Iz istorii peterburgskovo buddhiskovo khrama' (From the History of the Petersburg Buddhist Temple), *Minuvsheye: Istoricheski almanakh* ('The Past: Historical Almanac'), issue 9, Moscow: Phoenix, 1992 pp. 380–405.

Andreyev, A.I., 'Sankt-Petersburgsky buddhisky khram' (The St Petersburg Buddhist Temple), *Rerikhovski Vestnik* ('Roerich Herald'), SPb 1991, no. 3.

Gusyev, B.S., 'Pyotr Alexandrovich Badmayev'; Badmayev, P.A., 'Osnovy vrachebnoi nauki Tibeta Zhud-shi' (Foundations of the Tibetan Medicine Zhud-Shi), Moscow: *Nauka* ('Science'), 1991.

Gusyev, B.S., *Za kulissami tsarisma (Archiv tibetskovo vracha Badmayeva)* ('Behind the Scenes of Tsarism, the Archive of the Tibetan Doctor Badmayev'), Leningrad 1925.

Kulshov, N.S., *Rossiya i Tibet v nachalye XX vyeka* ('Russia and Tibet at the Beginning of the 20th Century'), Moscow: Eastern Literature, 1992.

Appendix 3. Helena and Nicholas Roerich and America

In addition to the occult connections of Nicholas and Helena Roerich with the Asiatic East, their occult relationship with the American West is also of interest, although little is known about this.

If one considers the positive attitude of the Eastern mahatmas towards Bolshevism and the part they played in preparing for the Bolshevik Revolution, the question arises as to the possibility of contacts—even if only of an indirect nature—between them and those secret societies of the West in which the idea of the 'socialist experiment' in Eastern Europe was born in the last quarter of the nineteenth century.[*] Nicholas Roerich, who lived for many years in America and subsequently visited it several times, meeting there a number of highly placed individuals, was able to serve as an ideal mediator for these contacts.[†]

The succession of journeys made by the Roerichs to India and America is therefore not without interest. Thus in 1919–20 the Roerichs lived in London, and then between 1920 and 1922 in America, for the most part in New York. From there in 1923 they made their first visit to Sikkim. In 1924 the Roerichs were again in New York, where they had no difficulty in gaining permission to undertake the great Himalayan expedition that they were planning.

The expedition was undertaken under two signs or symbols: the American flag and the tanka of Shamballa bearing the image of the Maitreya Bodhisattva. Every evening both emblems were raised over the camp. In Asia Nicholas Roerich again and again looked for features that give it an affinity with the civilization of America. 'What a lot of similar spaces there are in America and Asia,' he writes in his diary. 'And now, at the moment of rebirth, Asia recalls its distant connections. Greetings to America!' (NR 4, p. 209). In Mongolia Roerich shows the local inhabitants photographs of New York skyscrapers. The Mongolians 'exclaimed: "The land of Shamballa!"' and rejoiced at each pin, button or

---

[*] Regarding the secret societies of the West and their part in preparing the 'socialist experiment' in Russia which began with the Bolshevik Revolution of 1917, see further in the present author's book *The Spiritual Origins of Eastern Europe and the Future Mysteries of the Holy Grail*, Temple Lodge, 1993. There will also be found most of Rudolf Steiner's observations on this subject.

[†] As a rule, the occultists who enter the Western secret societies are in a state of 'secret warfare' with Eastern occultists. However, it seems as though for the purpose of carrying out the socialist experiment first in Russia and then in certain other countries they have managed to reach a compromise and even for a short time—albeit for different reasons—to combine their efforts.

tin can'. 'The heart of these people of the desert is open to the future,' concludes Nicholas Roerich (NR 6, p. 193). Tibetan architecture likewise reminds him of American skyscrapers: 'Are not such dwellings suitable for the latest improvements and do they not extend their hands to our [i.e. American] skyscrapers?' (NR 6, p. 209). In Moscow they were paid a visit by the Lichtmanns, the future curators of the Roerich Museum in New York, who had come from the United States especially for this purpose. Shortly after the end of the expedition, in June 1929, the Roerichs again travelled to New York. 'I am happy to bring to America the vision of Asia—Agni Yoga ...' writes Nicholas Roerich in his article 'Radost tvorchestva' (The Joy of Creation). 'What a joy to see again the towers [skyscrapers] of New York! How often in the deserts of Asia and especially in Tibet we have recalled the skyscrapers ... And among old friends I have noticed so many new strongholds [skyscrapers] which have arisen during the last five years. Such ceaseless creation evokes real joy' (N.K. Roerich, *Vostok-Zapad* ('East-West'), Moscow: International Roerich Centre, 1994, pp. 70–1). One of these new skyscrapers must have become the Roerich Museum in New York, whose construction must just have been completed then. In 1934 the Roerichs visited America for the last time.[*]

Nicholas Roerich found influential sponsors, patrons and followers in North America. The circle of his acquaintances there included President Hoover, the Mayor of New York Jimmy Walker, the Minister for Agriculture and later Vice President Henry Wallace,[†] the governors of many American states and so on. Roerich's fame is also apparent from the proposal in 1929 to put him forward for the Nobel Prize, alongside the then American Secretary of State, the British and French Prime Ministers and a French senator (Decter, p. 131).

The question of Nicholas Roerich's possible contacts with those secret societies of the West that Rudolf Steiner speaks of as being the real 'fathers' of the socialist experiment in Eastern Europe must, in the absence of any direct proof, be left open. Nevertheless, all the Roerichs' attempts to unite the ancient spirituality of Tibet and India with the materialism

---

[*] In the course of this last journey, certain disagreements emerged between Roerich and his American patrons.

[†] Decter relates the following facts about Nicholas Roerich's acquaintance with Henry Wallace. It began when Roerich travelled to America in search of financial support. This led to the expedition being furnished with supplies from the American Ministry of Agriculture, which Wallace led. In time Wallace himself became a devotee of Agni Yoga, as is proved by his letters of 1933–4 to Roerich, which begin with the mode of address 'Dear Guru!' (Decter pp. 134–6).

and one-sided scientific and technological progress of the West, whose symbol may rightly be regarded as North America, were only one form of that union of luciferic and ahrimanic powers which appeared in a somewhat different aspect in that socialist experiment to which from 1917 onwards Eastern Europe and subsequently many other countries in various parts of the world were subjected.

The correspondence which Helena Roerich conducted with the American President F.D. Roosevelt in the period between October 1934 and January 1936 acquires a particular significance in this connection. Nine of these letters to the President were recently published in translation from English (the originals are kept in the Franklin D. Roosevelt Library in New York).[*] Despite their pathetic style and thoroughly muddled content, the large number of vague allusions and areas of incomprehensibility, one aspect at any rate presents itself in them with sufficient clarity. It is, moreover, apparent from the beginning of Helena Roerich's second letter that there must have been answering 'messages' on the part of the President, though it is not clear whether they were written or merely in verbal form through intermediaries. It was when the correspondence was in full swing that Roosevelt signed the cultural pact of Nicholas Roerich in the White House on 15 April 1935, a deed which was doubtlessly the expression of the influence of these letters.

Already in the first and longest of the letters (dated 10 October 1934), which was written shortly after the Roerichs' return from America to India, to the Kulu valley, there is a very clear indication that these letters were written at the behest, and at times according to the direct dictation, of the mahatmas standing behind Helena Roerich (these parts of the letters are in inverted commas in the original).

The first letter begins thus: 'Mr President, at this weighty hour, when the whole world stands at the threshold of reconstruction and the destinies of many countries hang in the Cosmic Balance, I write to you from the heights of the Himalayas in order to offer you Help from Above: Help from that Source which since times immemorial has been ceaselessly on the alert, observing the course of world events and directing it along paths of salvation.' And the letter goes on to enumerate a whole series of examples, where mysterious individuals have been sent by the Himalayan brotherhood to Europe and America in order to exert an influence upon the historical destiny of mankind. Thus the 'first Habsburg' was visited by a certain knight-troubadour; the Norwegian King Knut by an unknown figure in a pilgrim's garb; and Marie Antoinette by the Count of Saint-

---

[*] The present renderings have been made from the Russian translation—Translator's note.

Germain, who was, according to Roerich, also 'a member of the Himalayan brotherhood'.[*]

Then the letter mentions some warnings given by certain mysterious individuals to Napoleon, Queen Victoria and the Swedish King Charles XII; reference is made to a 'grave warning' which was given from the same source to the government of Russia and to the 'sad consequences of its being ignored' and so on. Then it speaks of the advice which was given to George Washington by an anonymous professor; and of the decisive appearance of a mysterious stranger when America adopted the Declaration of Independence, and so forth. And this lengthy catalogue ends with the words: 'Thus in the course of history it is possible to be a witness of the various ways in which Help, Warnings and Advice from higher sources have been manifested. And this advice issuing from the Great Source was always easy to carry out and has never harmed the country for which it was intended.' Today 'advice has been made ready for America, and it would be well to accept it, for there are many examples of the sad consequences of rejection'. After this long introduction Helena Roerich now turns directly to the President himself: 'You can be not only a Ruler but a truly great leader.[†] From now on the Mighty Hand extends Help to you from this One Source and the Fiery messages can again reach the White House.'

In the next letter, of 15 November 1934, Helena Roerich writes: 'My heart has joy in transmitting the following Great Words to you: "Despite the opposition the Country has not known a better loved President. His fame will grow. That is predestined." ' And then she continues: 'And now I shall quote verbatim the indications that I have received …'

The following picture gradually emerges from this and subsequent letters of the nature of the secret intentions of the 'One Source' standing behind Helena Roerich, a picture which consists of certain elements:

(a) 'The country [the USA] should not disarm but, on the contrary, its power shall make itself felt. And although the nation may be against armaments, one should not defer to this, since no one will dare to attack a powerful ruler' (letter of 15 November 1934). And in another letter (of 27 December 1935): 'America must stand as a power that is mightily armed and equipped.'

(b) 'All Cosmic conditions are favourable to the secret negotiations of

---

[*] Blavatsky erroneously considered Saint-Germain to be an 'Eastern agent'—see H.P. Blavatsky, *Teosofsky Slovar* ('Theosophical Dictionary'), Moscow 1994.

[†] Compare with what was said on p. 62 about Helena Roerich's work *Naputstviye Vozhdyu* ('Parting Words to the Leader').

the President, negotiations which should not be divulged by the press nor by those surrounding him. The President must therefore work through those who are devoted to him and are sincerely disposed towards him. Thus we look towards the establishing of a Union, which will in future unite S[outh] A[merica] with the USA and Pr[esident Roosevelt] will become the founder of this Great State. This Great Union is already determined and will come about' (letter of 27 December 1934). Then in the same letter Helena Roerich again turns to the President: 'May the Pr[esident] be the Great Uniter of this mighty Country, which is destined to play a Great part in the Cosmic Balance. This vital question will be resolved, and Help will be granted to the Pr[esident].'

(c) 'But the President's attention must be turned towards the East. In speaking of the East, We also mean Russia ... A Great State is arising in the East. This new beginning will bring that equilibrium which is so urgently necessary for the building of the great Future ... And so the time has come for the reconstruction of the East and may there be friends of the East in America. The union of the peoples of Asia is something that has been decided, the union of the tribes and peoples will gradually come about, it will be something akin to a Federation of countries. Mongolia, China and the Kalmuks will form a counterweight to Japan, and for this union of peoples Your Good Will is necessary, Mr President' (letter of 4 February 1935). This 'good will' of the President was in particular, in the opinion of the mahatmas standing behind Helena Roerich, to serve to 'save [from hunger] the needy of China' (letter of 15 April 1935).

From the sections that have been quoted there is evidence of a need for the maximum possible military strengthening of North America and the subjection of South America to its power. Thus united, America was—in the minds of the mahatmas—to represent a Western world bloc. On the other hand, an Eastern world bloc—consisting of Russia, China, Mongolia and the Kalmuks (including Tibet, see Appendix 2)—was also to arise.

The relationships between these two world blocs are then characterized in a thoroughly contradictory way. On the one hand, 'so-called Russia will be a counterbalance to America, and only through such an order will the problem of World Peace be solved' (letter of 4 February 1935). And, on the other hand, we read in the same letter: 'America has already long been connected with Asia. The old connections were strengthened under favourable configurations of the Stars. What has been foreordained by Cosmic Laws will inevitably be accomplished. To no one is it given to hamper or block the path of the Enlightened Ones. Consequently, everyone must acknowledge the truth that the peoples who occupy the greater part of Asia are destined to respond to America's friendship. The President can receive the counsel of happiness. May the President's powers be employed in consolidating the situation. The President can at the designated hour direct his peoples with a firm hand towards the Union which will establish equilibrium in the World. One may employ small-scale measures, but must aspire to greater things. We send this message which can strengthen the President's will and bring it into accordance with the rays of the Enlightened Ones.' This is reminiscent of Nicholas Roerich's words from his book *Heart of Asia*: 'The heights of Asia and the heights of America will reach out their hands to one another...' (NR 6, p. 256).

And at the end of her message Helena Roerich communicates to the president the following words of the mahatmas standing behind her: 'Our Ray is over President Roosevelt. A new dawn rises over America' (letter of 4 February 1935), and from herself personally she sends him 'an ancient symbolic image of the Lord of Shamballa', with the request that he accept this 'Image which is sacred to me [Helena Roerich] and remember that the Ray of the Great God will accompany You ...'*

Despite the confused and contradictory nature of what is expressed, there nevertheless emerges from the letters—as has been said—a pretty clear picture of the opposition, and at the same time the common ground (perhaps first the one and then the other), between the Western and Eastern worlds. The result and ultimate goal of such a constellation—although of course this is not spoken of directly in the letters—must be *the exclusion of the creative middle, expressed by Christian Europe,* from human evolution and the establishing of an at times mutually antagonistic and at times mutually unifying *world dualism,* in the sense of the fundamental principle of Agni Yoga: the uniting of the materialistic West with the ancient, pre-Christian spirituality of the East, which on an occult plane signifies the realization of a synthesis—embracing the entire planet—of

---

* One year later there appeared altogether different observations regarding the President in Helena Roerich's letters. Thus in a letter of 19 August 1937 she suddenly mentions his 'hate campaign' in the Russo-Japanese War and writes in this connection about the 'personal hatred of Roosevelt and his helpers—Jew[ish] bankers—against Russia' (*Letters,* Vol. 3). It would appear that Helena Roerich's inspirers were not altogether happy with the results of their pupil's influence upon the American President.

ahrimanic and luciferic forces with, if possible, the total exclusion of the Christian impulse of the middle (see chapter 10).

The only thing that can withstand this is a true esoteric knowledge of the cosmic significance of the Christ impulse, as has now been given to humanity in anthroposophy. For only through attaining a completely new and fully conscious relationship to the Christ impulse is it possible to establish a real balance in the world between the luciferic and ahrimanic forces and thus furnish humanity with the opportunity for further evolution on earth. 'On the scales of world existence we have the luciferic element, representing the one arm, and the ahrimanic element, representing the other arm, while the Christ impulse represents the state of equilibrium.' (GA 194, 21 November 1919.)

Appendix 4. Helena and Nicholas Roerich and 'The Story of Issa, the Son of Man'

Legends about a visit to India by Jesus during his youth, about his life after the crucifixion and his death in India became known in the West for the first time at the beginning of the twentieth century through the publication of a book by the Russian journalist Nikolai Notovich containing Christ legends, which Notovich is said to have found in 1887 in an ancient manuscript in the Buddhist monastery of Chemi in Ladakh. As one of the lamas of this monastery expressed it (according to Notovich), the legends were written in Pali, presumably still in Jesus's lifetime, and had been preserved in a monastery in Lhasa. In Chemi there is a translation into Tibetan that was made around the year 200.

The persistence and consistency displayed by the Roerichs not only in collecting legends but also in their quest for the secret manuscript which is said to confirm the 'fact' of Jesus Christ's presence in India and Tibet are confirmed by the following notes written by Nicholas Roerich in his own hand in the diary that he kept of his journey.

'If it is difficult to discern the high Countenance of Buddha the Teacher behind an idol of the Buddha, it is even more unexpected to encounter and get to know beautiful lines about Jesus in the Tibetan mountains. A Buddhist monastery preserves the teaching of Jesus, and lamas offer their respect to Jesus, who passed through here and taught.

'The writings of the lamas report that Jesus was not killed by the Jews but by representatives of the Roman Government. The Empire and the rich, the capitalists, killed the Great Community Builder, who brought light to the poor and those who laboured.'

Referring to manuscripts that were over 1500 years old, Nicholas Roerich goes on to present two versions, an Indian and a Tibetan, of the story of Jesus' time in India, Nepal, the Himalayas and Tibet before his thirtieth year.

Nevertheless, Roerich is still not satisfied and continues in his search for manuscripts: 'The existence of manuscripts about Jesus is at first completely denied. To our astonishment the denial springs primarily from missionary circles. Then, by degrees, fragmentary and tentative information gradually emerges which is arrived at only with great difficulty. Finally, it transpires that some old people in Ladakh (northern Kashmir) have heard of and know the manuscripts. Such documents as the manuscripts about Christ and the book about Shamballa lie in a very "dark" [secret] place.'

'Three pieces of information in one day about a manuscript concerning Jesus ... This is how people talk about the manuscript. Thus news gradually comes to light. But the main thing is the extraordinary profundity of the text and the intimate relationship to it of lamas throughout the East! A good and sensitive Indian speaks in a remarkable way about the manuscript, about the life of Issa [Jesus]: "Why is Issa always sent to Egypt during [his] absence from Palestine? The years of his youth were, of course, devoted to study ... It is incomprehensible why Issa's journey on the caravan route to India and to the region we now call Tibet is so fiercely denied!"'

'An old lama-king arrived [from Ladakh] ... It transpired in the course of conversation that the family of the king knows the manuscripts about Issa. They even said that many Muslims would wish to possess this document.'

Finally on 17 September 1925 the Roerichs become completely convinced of the existence of the manuscript in question: 'We have recognized the authenticity of the manuscript about Issa. In Chemi there in indeed an old Tibetan translation of the manuscript that was written in Pali and is in a well-known monastery not far from Lhasa ... Stories about a forgery have proved unfounded.'

All the more incomprehensible is Nicholas Roerich's reaction to the rumours—which had reached Moscow—that he had finally found the secret manuscript: 'The Moscow papers say that we have "found" the manuscript about Christ [Issa]. Where does this notion come from? How could we find what has long been known? But we have found more. We have been able to establish that the notion of Issa as a member of the community is accepted and lives throughout the East. The text of the manuscript lives on the borders of Bhutan, in Tibet, on the hills of Sikkim, on the heights of Ladakh [that is, in all regions where the Himalayan mahatmas are most in evidence], and in the Mongolian khoshuns [tents] and in the Kalmuck ulus [yurts]. It lives there not as the sensationalism of Sunday newspapers but as a firm and calm awareness. What for the West is sensationalism is for the East ancient knowledge. As one travels through Asia one may become convinced of how these people think.'

And in a later article from 1931, 'Legenda Asii' (The Legend of Asia), Roerich gives the assurance that 'Notovich's notorious book[*] probably derives from various traditions', and he is inclined to see ill-intent in what

---

[*] Notovich had published the text of the so-called 'Tibetan Gospel' in Russia at the beginning of the century. Its true origin is unknown.

has been written about the manuscript: 'People ask what ill-intentioned mind forms the legend from these notes [he refers here to his—at that time—already published books *Altai-Gimalai* ('Altai-Himalaya') and *Heart of Asia*, which contain the notes and other similar material that we have been quoting from] that I have found some kind of manuscript from the time of Christ. Instead of rejoicing with us at the wide, all-embracing extent of the great understanding of Christ the Redeemer, instead of marvelling in one's heart at the incomprehensible and unfathomable ways in which the name of Christ has spread through all deserts, someone merely wants to obscure and belittle this out of some kind of ill-will.'[*]

Subsequently, in the 1950s Nicholas Roerich's eldest son Yuri, who had been a participant in the expedition, brought all these conflicting pieces of information together in a conversation with Richard Rudzitis: 'He [Yuri Roerich] supposes,' wrote Rudzitis in his diary, 'that Notovich added something on his own account. [Yuri Roerich] asked the rinpoche of the monastery [Chemi] where this manuscript was found. [The rinpoche] replied that such a manuscript exists ... N.K. [Roerich] did not personally find anything, but wrote about Jesus and the signs on his [small letter] Way [capital letter] to Asia' (Rudzitis p. 87).

Whether the Roerichs in the end found the mysterious manuscript or merely heard of it remains unclear. For our present purposes this question is of secondary importance. Indeed, the existence of the manuscript is of less significance than the Roerichs' unshakeable conviction of the truth of the 'facts' that find expression in it. Whether all these legends about Jesus's time in the East derive from a mysterious manuscript or are to be traced back to inspirations of the mahatmas, they are from the standpoint of Christian esotericism *wholly erroneous*, as is clear primarily from Rudolf Steiner's lectures on *The Fifth Gospel* (GA 148), where he describes Jesus'

---

[*] Despite what Roerich says here, several authors continue to assert that this manuscript about Issa had been found. Thus in 1988, a book came out in Srinigar (India) by the Kashmir historian F. Chassanaiya entitled *Fifth Gospel*, where the testimonies, legends and traditions about Jesus's time in India before and after his three-year period of activity in Palestine are collected. In his book the Indian scholar claims that the principal source for his research was a Tibetan manuscript discovered in 1925 by the Russian artist Nicholas Roerich. L.V. Shaposhnikova, Director of the International Roerich Centre in Moscow, asserts that she saw the manuscript of the 'Tibetan Gospel' in 1979 but lack of time prevented her from making a translation: she estimated the age of the manuscript at five to six hundred years old. Another book that should be mentioned is *The Last Years of Jesus* by Elisabeth Claire Prophet (1984), where the author does not only refer to Nicholas Roerich but also cites many passages from his books and articles accompanied by several reproductions of his paintings (see further about her in Part Two).

life between his twelfth and thirtieth years. In the legends referred to, there comes to expression the secret endeavour of certain occult circles in the East to put it about that the wisdom of Jesus, and, with it, of Christianity, ultimately derives from India and Tibet and so contains nothing new.

References

NR 4, see pp. 82–6, 101, 104–6, 110–11, 115, 204, 237, 242, 277.

NR 6, see pp. 169, 173, 178–9, 227, 230.

NR 2, pp. 140–74.

HR 3, pp. 264–5.

'Iisus Khristos v Indii: legendy i skazaniya' (Jesus Christ in India: Legends and Tales), *India*, Moscow 1991.

Lazarev, H., 'Tibetan Stories about Jesus', *Nauka i religiya* (Science and Religion), 1989, no. 7.

Mitrochin, L.V., *Kashmirskiye legendy ob Iisuse* ('Kashmir Legends about Jesus'), Moscow 1990.

Appendix 5. Rudolf Steiner on Western and Eastern Occultism (The So-called Barr Manuscript)

The following notes were written by Rudolf Steiner himself in 1907, while he was staying in Barr (Alsace) as a guest of the French writer and occultist Edouard Schuré at his country home.

Making use of a rare opportunity, Schuré asked his guest three questions: about the spiritual development of Rudolf Steiner himself; about Christian Rosenkreutz; and about the Theosophical Society. He received his answers in written form. That is the reason for their particular trustworthiness, inasmuch as all possibility of inaccurate transmission of meaning or incorrect understanding is completely excluded—which is not the case with lectures recorded in shorthand, still less if they have not been revised by the lecturer.

In 1907 this manuscript, which reveals the occult foundations of the arising and development of the theosophical movement and the Theosophical Society, was intended solely for Schuré's personal use. Subsequently however—after his withdrawal from the Theosophical Society—Rudolf Steiner returned on several occasions to this theme in his lectures, especially in 1915 (see GA 254). Thus Rudolf Steiner's literary estate considered it possible in 1967 to publish these notes within the framework of the complete edition of his works (in GA 262), and their final part is reproduced here in its entirety.[*]

The Theosophical Society was first established in 1875 in New York by H.P. Blavatsky and H.S. Olcott, and had a decidedly western nature. The publication *Isis Unveiled*, in which Blavatsky revealed a large number of esoteric truths, has just such a western character. But it has to be stated regarding this publication that it frequently presents the great truths of which it speaks in a distorted or even caricatured manner. It is similar to a visage of harmonious proportions, appearing distorted in a convex mirror. The things which are said in 'Isis' are true, but *how* they are said is a lopsided mirror-image of the truth. This is because the truths themselves are *inspired* by the great *initiates of the West*, who also inspired the Rosicrucian wisdom. The distortion arises because of the inappropriate way in which H.P. Blavatsky's *soul* has received these truths. The educated world should have seen in *this* fact alone the evidence for a higher source of

---

[*] Translation by Christian and Ingrid von Arnim from *Correspondence and Documents 1901–1925, Rudolf Steiner and Marie Steiner-von Sivers*, Rudolf Steiner Press and Anthroposophic Press, 1988.

inspiration of these truths. For no one who rendered them in such a distorted manner could have created these truths himself. Because the western initiators saw how little opportunity they had to allow the stream of spiritual wisdom to flow into mankind by this means, they decided to drop the matter *in this form* for the time being. But the door had been opened: Blavatsky's soul had been prepared in such a manner that spiritual wisdom was able to flow into it. *Eastern* initiators were able to take hold of her. To begin with these eastern initiators had the best of intentions. They saw how Anglo-American influences were steering mankind towards the terrible danger of a completely materialistic impregnation of thinking. They—these eastern initiators—wanted to imprint *their* form of spiritual knowledge, which had been preserved through the ages, on the western world. Under the influence of this stream the Theosophical Society took on its eastern character, and the same influence was the inspiration for Sinnett's *Esoteric Buddhism* and Blavatsky's *Secret Doctrine*. But both of these became distortions of the truth. Sinnett's work distorts the high teaching of the initiators through an extraneous and inadequate philosophical intellectualism and Blavatsky's *Secret Doctrine* does the same because of her chaotic soul.

The result was that the initiators, the eastern ones as well, withdrew their influence in increasing measure from the official Theosophical Society and the latter became the arena for all kinds of occult forces which distorted the great cause. There was a short pause, when Annie Besant entered the stream of initiators through her pure and elevated mentality. But this phase came to an end when Annie Besant gave herself up to the influence of certain Indians who developed a grotesque intellectualism derived from certain philosophical teachings, German ones in particular, which they misinterpreted. This was the situation when I was faced with the necessity of joining the Theosophical Society. True initiators stood at its cradle and *that is why* it is *at present* an instrument of current spiritual life, even if subsequent events have resulted in certain imperfections. Its continued fruitful development in western countries is dependent completely on the extent to which it shows itself capable of assimilating the principle of western initiation among its influences. For the eastern initiations must of necessity leave untouched the *Christ* as the central *cosmic* factor of evolution. But without this principle the theosophical movement will have no decisive influence on western cultures, which trace their beginnings back to Christ's life on Earth. If taken on their own, the revelations of oriental initiation would have to stand aside from the living culture in the West in a sectarian manner. They could only hope for success within evolution if the principle of Christianity were to be eradicated from western culture. But this would be the same as eradicating the essential *meaning of the Earth*, which lies in the recognition and realization of the intentions of the *Living Christ*. To reveal those intentions in the form of complete wisdom, beauty and activity is, however, the deepest aim of Rosicrucianism. Regarding the value of eastern wisdom as the subject of study, one can only say that this study is of the highest value, because western cultures have lost their sense of esotericism, while the eastern ones have preserved theirs. But equally it should be understood that the introduction of a correct esotericism in the West can only be of the Rosicrucian-Christian type, because this *latter* gave birth to western life and because by its loss mankind would deny the meaning and destiny of the Earth.

The harmonious relationship between science and religion can flower only in this esotericism, while every amalgamation of western knowledge with eastern esotericism can only produce such unproductive mongrels as Sinnett's *Esoteric Buddhism*. The correct way can be represented schematically as:

> Original revelation Evolution Indian esotericism Christ Esoteric Rosicrucianism Modern western scientific materialism Synthesis: productive modern Theosophy

The incorrect way, of which Sinnett's *Esoteric Buddhism* and Blavatsky's *Secret Doctrine* are examples, would be represented as:

> Original revelation Evolution Indian esotericism Development in which the eastern world has not taken part Modern scientific materialism Synthesis: Sinnett, Blavatsky

Appendix 6. The Letters of the Mahatmas

The following excerpt from a letter signed with the initials of the Mahatma Kut Humi, which was sent in September 1882 to a friend and colleague of A.P. Sinnett, the Christian A.O. Hume, bears the title 'Notes by K.H. on a "Preliminary Chapter" headed "God" by Hume, intended to preface an exposition on Occult Philosophy'.

This letter, which is known in theosophical and Roerich circles as the 'letter about God', might more appropriately be called the 'letter against God'. It is quoted here because of its obvious affinity—as regards both content and style—to Helena Roerich's book *Obshchina* ('Community') and to the 'Letter of the mahatmas' to the Bolshevik Government. Thus we have in it a concrete testimony of a consistent and uninterrupted flow of development from 1882 to 1927. For in this letter are contained all the foundations of the new understanding of 'religion' as the teaching of the all-embracing nature of matter' spoken of in the 'Letter of the Mahatmas' (see p. 56) and further developed in 'Community'.

On becoming generally familiar with the content of this collection of selected letters from the mahatmas, which were translated into Russian and published by Helena Roerich under the title *Chasha vostoka* ('The Chalice of the East') in 1925 (reprinted in 1926), one is struck that the translator has chosen those letters which are as regards their content especially close to the book 'Community' (whose appearance was in the following year), inasmuch as they often speak of the eternity of matter, of reason as a manifestation of the activity of the brain, of the significance of materialism, of religion, of the source of evil and illusion as begotten of human ignorance—and so on. Many of these utterances are in their style and content strangely reminiscent of certain statements of Marx and Lenin, which in itself lends support to what the mahatmas communicate in 'Community', namely that their emissaries visited the former in London and the latter in Switzerland.

This choice of letters is, of course, not fortuitous, for according to Helena Roerich she received indications regarding both the translation of the letters into Russian and the content of the book 'Community' (though with an interruption of almost a year) from one and the same mahatma whom the Roerichs met in 1925 and then again in 1926, on their way from India to Bolshevik Russia.

After the long quotation from the letter to Hume there follow some short extracts from other letters chosen by Helena Roerich. The number of similar utterances could be considerably augmented without any difficulty.

The passages from the 'Mahatma Letters' quoted below show clearly that many of these letters were partly, or even at times wholly, written not by the true theosophical mahatmas but by left-oriented occultists pursuing quite different aims, the members of a particular Eastern brotherhood. As, however, these latter individuals signed with the falsified names of the true mahatmas (Morya and Kut Humi) who were well known in theosophical circles, it was in fact extremely difficult to distinguish between the true and the falsely attributed letters.

As a general criterion we have Rudolf Steiner's indication that the true theosophical mahatmas had as their goal from the very beginning the *overcoming* of Western materialism with the help of the ancient wisdom of the East which they had preserved (see Appendix 5), whereas the aforesaid occultists of a left persuasion were trying to achieve a mixture of Eastern wisdom with one-sided scientific ideas of the nineteenth century capable of transforming ordinary materialism into a far more dangerous *occult materialism*, in order to make use of this in their battle against a true knowledge of Christ and the significance of the Mystery of Golgotha for earthly evolution as a whole.

In this *twofold source* of the 'Mahatma Letters' (as with the principal works of Blavatsky and Sinnett) we have the explanation of why Rudolf Steiner in several instances spoke very positively about them and in others disparagingly (compare for example what he says in GA 143, 8 May 1912 and in GA 258, 12 June 1923). His positive remarks concerned the deep Eastern wisdom in the 'letters' (albeit with the reservation that, since they derived from *pre-Christian* religions, they could not communicate anything about esoteric Christianity), whereas the negative comments had to do with the falsely attributed letters, of which some clear examples now follow in this appendix.

★

By way of a conclusion to this introduction, it is necessary to append a few statements which may serve as a counterbalance to the content of the letter which follows.

In St John's Gospel Christ says: 'God is spirit, and those who worship him must worship in spirit and truth' (4:24). And as man was originally created 'in the image and likeness of God' (Genesis 1:27), we should in this same sense understand the following words of the modern Christian initiate, Rudolf Steiner: 'Man is a spirit; and *his* world is the world of spiritual beings' (GA 26, article of 12 October 1924). But the world of spiritual beings is, from the standpoint of Christian esotericism, none other than the world of the nine higher hierarchies, from the Angels to the Seraphim (see GA 13), with whom—when the ultimate goal of earthly evolution has been attained—human beings will be united as pure spirits to pure spirits, as a new, *Tenth* Hierarchy, which will represent in our cosmos the principles of *freedom and love* (see GA 110, 18 April 1909 (II)). Thus freedom and love, which in their highest and most spiritual form were revealed to humanity in the Mystery of Golgotha, have since that time come to represent the holiest and most exalted ideals which humanity has on earth. However, their fulfilment—that is, the fulfilment of *the intentions of the living Christ*—is strongly opposed by all forms of the materialism which is being disseminated throughout the cosmos. Thus 'anyone who speaks out of some world-conception or other about the eternity of matter destroys, on the one hand, freedom and, on the other, a fully developed capacity for love' (GA 202, 19 December 1920). For 'wherever people are lost in contemplation of matter, Ahriman is indeed present'—he who is the greatest opponent of earthly evolution (GA 145, 28 March 1913).

Text of Letter No. 10

Neither our philosophy nor ourselves believe in a God, least of all in one who necessitates a capital H. Our philosophy falls under the definition of Hobbes.* It is pre-eminently the science of effects by their causes and of causes by their effects, and since it is also the science of things deduced from first principle, as Bacon† defines it, before we admit any such principle we must know it, and have no right to admit even its possibility. Your whole explanation is based upon one solitary admission made simply for argument's sake in October last. You‡ were told that our knowledge was limited to this our solar system: ergo as philosophers who desired to remain worthy of the name we could not either deny or affirm the existence of what you termed a supreme, omnipotent, intelligent being of some sort beyond the limits of that solar system. But if such an existence is not

---

* Thomas Hobbes (1588–1679), English philosopher and materialist, pupil of Francis Bacon.

† Francis Bacon (1561–1626), English philosopher, father of English materialism.

‡ Emphasizing the passage from here until the end of the paragraph, Roerich quotes this letter in his book *Altai-Gimalai* ('Altai-Himalaya'). The context in which he places it is characteristic. 'There are not so many creators of life who inwardly correspond to the meaning of future evolution,' writes Roerich; and after his thoughts about Issa, Origen and Sergei of Radonezh 'continuing the list until modern times', he directly turns to this letter 'from one of the great mahatmas of India' (NR 4, pp. 87–8).

absolutely impossible, unless the uniformity of nature's laws breaks at those limits we maintain that it is highly improbable. Nevertheless we deny most emphatically the position of agnosticism in this direction, and as regards the solar system. Our doctrine knows no compromises. It either affirms or denies, for it never teaches but that which it knows to be the truth. Therefore, we deny God both as philosophers and as Buddhists. We know there are planetary and other spiritual lives, and we know there is in our system no such thing as God, either personal or impersonal. Parabrahm is not a God, but absolute immutable law, and Iswar[*] is the effect of Avidya and Maya, ignorance based upon the great delusion. The word 'God' was invented to designate the unknown cause of those effects which man has either admired or dreaded without understanding them, and since we claim and that we are able to prove what we claim—*i.e.*, the knowledge of that cause and causes—we are in a position to maintain there is no God or Gods behind them.

The idea of God is not an innate but an acquired notion, and we have but one thing in common with theologies—we reveal the infinite. But while we assign to all the phenomena that proceed from the infinite and limitless space, duration and motion, *material, natural, sensible and known* (to us, at least) causes, the theists assign them *spiritual, supernatural* and *unintelligible* and unknown causes. The God of the Theologians is simply an imaginary power, *un loup garou* as d'Holbach[†] expressed it—a power which has never yet manifested itself. Our chief aim is to deliver humanity of this nightmare, to teach man virtue for its own sake, and to walk in life relying on himself instead of leaning on a theological crutch, that for countless ages was the direct cause of nearly all human misery. Pantheistic we may be called—agnostic NEVER. If people are willing to accept and to regard as God our ONE LIFE immutable and unconscious in its eternity they may do so and thus keep to one more gigantic misnomer. But then they will have to say with Spinoza[‡] that there is not and that we cannot conceive any other substance than God; or as that famous and unfortunate philosopher says in his fourteenth proposition, "praeter Deum neque dari neque concipi potest substantia"—and thus become pantheists. Who but a Theologian nursed on mystery and the most absurd

---

[*] Iswar—a concept of Vedantic philosophy, close in meaning to the concept of the 'creative Logos'.

[†] P.A. d'Holbach (1723–89), French philosopher. One of the principal founders of French materialism. Criticized religion from a position of extreme atheism.

[‡] B. Spinoza (1632–77), Dutch philosopher and pantheist. Did not acknowledge Christianity.

supernaturalism can imagine a self-existent being of necessity infinite and omnipresent *outside* the manifested *boundless* universe. The word infinite is but a negative which excludes the idea of bounds. It is evident that a being independent and omnipresent cannot be limited by anything which is outside of himself; that there can be nothing exterior to himself—not even vacuum, then where is there room for matter? for that manifested universe even though the latter [be] limited? If we ask the theist is your God vacuum, space or matter, they will reply no. And yet they hold that their God penetrates matter though he is not himself matter. When we speak of our One Life we also say that it penetrates, nay is the essence of every atom of matter but has all its properties likewise, etc.—hence *is* material, is *matter itself.* How can intelligence proceed or emanate from non-intelligence?—you kept asking last year. How could a highly intelligent humanity, man the crown of reason, be evolved out of blind unintelligent law or force?! But once we reason on that line, I may ask in my turn: how could congenital idiots, non-reasoning animals, and the rest of 'creation' have been created by or evoluted from, absolute wisdom, if the latter is a thinking intelligent being, the author and ruler of the Universe? How? says Dr Clarke in his examination of the proof of the existence of the Divinity. 'God who hath made the eye, shall he not see? God who hath made the ear, shall he not hear?' But according to this mode of reasoning they would have to admit that in creating an idiot God is an idiot; that he who made so many irrational beings, so many physical and moral monsters, must be an irrational being.

We are not Adwaitees, but our teaching respecting the one life is identical with that of the Adwaitee with regard to Parabrahm. And no true philosophically trained Adwaitee will ever call himself an agnostic, for he knows that he is Parabrahm and identical in every respect with the universal life and soul—the macrocosm is the microcosm and he knows that there is no God apart from himself, no creator as no being. Having found Gnosis we cannot turn our backs on it and become agnostics.

Were we to admit that even the highest Dyan Chohans are liable to err under a delusion, then there would be no reality for us indeed and the occult sciences would be as great a chimera as that God. If there is an absurdity in denying that which we do not know it is still more extravagant to assign to it unknown laws.

According to logic 'nothing' is that of which everything can be truly denied and nothing can truly be affirmed. The idea therefore either of a finite or infinite nothing is a contradiction in terms. And yet according to theologians 'God, the self-existent being, is a most simple, unchangeable, incorruptible being; without part, figure, motion, divisibility, or any other such properties as we find in matter. For all such things so plainly and necessarily imply finiteness in their very notion and are utterly inconsistent with complete infinity.' Therefore the God here offered to the adoration of the 19th century lacks every quality upon which man's mind is capable of fixing any judgement. What is this in fact but a being of whom they can affirm *nothing* that is not instantly contradicted. Their own Bible, their Revelation, destroys all the moral perfections they heap upon him, unless indeed they call those qualities perfections that every other man's reason and common sense call imperfections, odious vices and brutal wickedness. Nay more, he who reads our Buddhist scriptures written for the superstitious masses will fail to find in them a *demon* so vindictive, unjust, so cruel and so stupid as the celestial tyrant upon which the Christians prodigally lavish their servile worship and on which their theologians heap those perfections that are contradicted on every page of their Bible. Truly and veritably your theology has created her God but to destroy him piecemeal. Your church is the fabulous Saturn, who begets children but to devour them.

There then follow some answers to certain questions posed to the mahatma by Hume in his letters:

(*The Universal Mind*)—A few reflections and arguments ought to support every new idea—for instance we are sure to be taken to task for the following apparent contradictions. (1) We deny the existence of a thinking conscious God, on the grounds that such a God must either be conditioned, limited and subject to change, therefore *not* infinite, or (2) he is represented to us as an eternal unchangeable and independent being, with not a particle of matter in him, then we answer that it is no being but an immutable blind principle, a law. And yet, they will say, we believe in Dyans, or Planetaries ('spirits') also, endow them with a universal mind, and this *must be explained*.

Our reasons may be briefly summed up thus:

(1) We deny the absurd proposition that there can be, even in a boundless and eternal universe—two infinite eternal and omnipresent existences.
(2) Matter we know to be eternal, *i.e.* having had no beginning (a) because matter is Nature herself (b) because that which cannot annihilate itself and is indestructible exists necessarily—and therefore it could not begin to be, nor can it cease to be (c) because the accumulated experience of countless ages, and that of exact science

show to us matter (or nature) acting by her own peculiar energy, of which not an atom is ever in an absolute state of rest, and therefore it must have always existed, *i.e.*, its materials ever changing form, combinations and properties, but its principles or elements being absolutely indestructible.

(3) As to God—since no one has ever or at any time seen him or it— *unless he or it is the very essence and nature of this boundless eternal matter, its energy and motion,* we cannot regard him as either eternal or infinite or yet self-existing. We refuse to admit a being or an existence of which we know absolutely nothing; because (a) there is no room for him in the presence of that matter whose undeniable properties and qualities we know thoroughly well (b) because if he or it is but a part of that matter it is ridiculous to maintain that he is the mover and ruler of that of which he is but a dependent part and (c) because if they tell us that God is a self-existent pure spirit independent of matter—an extra-cosmic deity—we answer that admitting even the possibility of such an impossibility, *i.e.*, his existence, we yet hold that a purely immaterial spirit cannot be an intelligent conscious ruler nor can he have any of the attributes bestowed upon him by theology, and thus such a God becomes again but a blind force. Intelligence, as found in our Dyan Chohans, is a faculty that can appertain but to organized or animated being—however imponderable or rather *invisible* the materials of their organizations. Intelligence requires the necessity of thinking; to think one must have ideas; ideas suppose senses which are physical material, and how can anything material belong to pure spirit? If it be objected that thought cannot be a property of matter, we will ask the reason why. We must have an unanswerable proof of this assumption, before we can accept it. Of the theologian we would enquire what was there to prevent his God, since he is the alleged creator of all, to endow matter with the faculty of thought; and when answered that evidently it has not pleased Him to do so, that it is a mystery as well as an impossibility, we would insist upon being told why it is more impossible that matter should produce spirit and thought than spirit or the thought of God should produce and create matter.

We do not bow our heads in the dust before the mystery of mind—for we *have solved it ages ago.* Rejecting with contempt the theistic theory we reject as much the automation theory, teaching that states of consciousness are produced by the marshalling of the molecules of the brain; and we feel as little respect for that other hypothesis—the production of molecular motion by consciousness. Then what do we believe in? Well, we believe in the much laughed at *phlogiston* (see article 'What is force and what is matter?' *Theosophist*, September), and in what some natural philosophers would call *nisus*, the incessant though perfectly imperceptible (to the ordinary senses) motion or efforts one body is making on another—the pulsations of inert matter, its life. The bodies of the Planetary spirits are formed of that which Priestley[*] and others called Phlogiston and for which we have another name—the essence in its highest seventh state forming that matter of which the organisms of the highest and purest Dyans are composed, and in its lowest or densest form (so impalpable yet that science calls it energy and force) serving as a cover to the Planetaries of the 1st or lowest degree. In other words we believe in *matter* alone, in matter as visible nature and matter in its invisibility as the invisible omnipresent omnipotent Proteus with its unceasing motion which is its life, and which nature draws from herself since she is the great whole outside of which nothing can exist. For as Bilfinger[†] truly asserts, 'motion is a manner of existence that flows by its own peculiar energies; that its motion is due to the force which is inherent in itself; that the variety of motion and the phenomena that result proceed from the diversity of the properties of the qualities and of the combinations which are originally found in the primitive matter' of which nature is the assemblage and of which your science knows less than one of our Tibetan Yak-drivers of Kant's[‡] metaphysics.

The existence of matter then is a fact; the existence of motion is another fact, their self-existence and eternity or indestructibility is a third fact. And the idea of pure spirit as a Being or an Existence—give it whatever name you will—is a chimera, a gigantic absurdity.

The letter ends with the mahatmas' views on evil. They see one third of the problem in man himself, in his selfishness, and the other two thirds in religion.

Therefore it is neither nature nor an imaginary Deity that has to be blamed, but human nature made vile by *selfishness*. Think well over these few words; work out every cause of evil you can think of and trace it to its origin and you will have solved *one third* of the problem of evil. And now,

---

[*] Joseph Priestley (1733–1804), English chemist and philosopher.
[†] Georg Bernhard Bilfinger (1693–1750), German academic, professor of philosophy and teacher of mathematics.
[‡] Immanuel Kant (1724–1804), German philosopher.

after making due allowance for evils that are natural and cannot be avoided—and so few are they that I challenge the whole host of Western metaphysics to call them evils or to trace them directly to an independent cause—I will point out the greatest, the chief cause of nearly two thirds of the evils that pursue humanity ever since that cause became a power. It is religion under whatever form and in whatsoever nation. It is the sacerdotal caste, the priesthood and the churches, it is in those illusions that man looks upon as sacred, that he has to search out the source of that multitude of evils which is the greatest curse of humanity and that almost overwhelms mankind. Ignorance created Gods and cunning took advantage of the opportunity. Look at India and look at Christendom and Islam, at Judaism and Fetishism. It is priestly imposture that rendered these Gods so terrible to man; it is religion that makes of him the selfish bigot, the fanatic that hates all mankind out of his own sect without rendering him any better or more moral for it. It is belief in God and Gods that makes two thirds of humanity the slaves of a handful of those who deceive them under the false pretence of saving them. Is not man ever ready to commit any kind of evil if told that his God or Gods demand the crime—voluntary victim of an illusionary God, the abject slave of his crafty ministers? The Irish, Italian and Slavonian peasant will starve himself and see his family starving and naked to feed and clothe his padre and pope. For two thousand years India groaned under the weight of caste, Brahmins alone feeding on the fat of the land, and today the followers of Christ and those of Mahomet are cutting each other's throats in the names of and for the greater glory of their respective myths. Remember the sum of human misery will never be diminished unto that day when the better portion of humanity destroys in the name of Truth, morality, and universal charity, the altars of their false gods.

If* it is objected that we too have temples, we too have priests and that our lamas also live on charity ... let them know that the objects above named have in common with their Western equivalents but the name. Thus in our temples there is neither a god nor gods worshipped, only the thrice sacred memory of the greatest as the holiest man that ever lived [Buddha].

From Letter No. 9

... For I trust you have given up the queer idea—a natural result of early Christian training—that there can possibly be *human* intelligences inhabiting *purely spiritual* regions?'

---

*Significantly, this passage was omitted in Nicholas Roerich's translation.

However ethereal and purified of gross matter they may be, the pure Spirits are still subject to the physical and universal laws of matter.

From Letter No. 13 from Mahatma M.

Your 'Lord God,' says Bible, chapter 1, verses 25 and 26—after having made *all* said: 'Let us make man in our image,' etc., and creates man—an *androgyne ape*! (extinct on our planet) the highest intelligence in the animal kingdom and whose descendents you will find in the anthropoids of today.

From Letter No. 22

... we say this perpetual motion is the only eternal and uncreated Deity we are able to recognize.

But of that which lies within the worlds and systems, not in the trans-infinitude (a queer expression to use) but in the cis-infinitude rather, in the state of the purest and inconceivable immateriality, no one ever knew or will ever tell, hence it is something non-existent for the universe. You are at liberty to place in this eternal vacuum the intellectual or voluntary powers of your deity—if you can conceive of such a thing.

A pure yet volitional spirit is an absurdity for volitional mind. The result of organism cannot exist independently of an organized brain, and an organized brain made out of nihil is a still greater fallacy. If you ask me 'Whence then the immutable laws?—laws cannot make themselves'—then in my turn I will ask you—and whence their supposed Creator?—A Creator cannot create or make himself if the brain did not make itself for this would be affirming that brain acted before it existed, how could intelligence, the result of an organized brain, act before its creator was made.

The conception of matter and spirit as entirely distinct, and both eternal could certainly never have entered my head, however little I may know of them, for it is one of the elementary and fundamental doctrines of occultism that the two are one, and are distinct but in their respective manifestations, and only in the limited perceptions of the world of senses.

... matter *per se* is indestructible, and, as I maintain, coeval with spirit— that spirit which we know and can conceive of.

From Letter No. 23B

Spirit, life and matter, are not natural principles existing independently of each other, but the effects of combinations produced by eternal motion in space.

From Letter No. 49

These [the Rosicrucian MSS] expound our eastern doctrines from the teachings of Rosencrauz, who, upon his return from Asia dressed them up in a semi-Christian garb intended as a shield for his pupils, against clerical revenge.

Appendix 7. Gorbachev, Bolshevism and the Roerich Family

The friendly relations between the Gorbachevs and the last representative of the Roerichs' family are not fortuitous. For in one particular area their opinions strongly coincide. This concerns the relationship of both M. Gorbachev and S. Roerich to the mission of Lenin, the events of 1917 and the subsequent 75 years of Bolshevik rule in Russia.

That Gorbachev has not altered his convictions on this matter—convictions which he has previously expressed more than once as General Secretary and as President—now that he has for some time been merely a private individual is apparent from his last interview, given to the German newspaper *Der Spiegel*. This interview was published in January 1993 (issue no. 3, 1993) and gives further confirmation of the fact that, from the very beginning of *perestroika*, Gorbachev did not want to abolish but merely to reform Bolshevik socialism in Russia, by restoring it to its sources—that is, to its original Leninist principles to which Gorbachev, like S. Roerich and his parents, remained faithful to the end. We shall cite some extracts from this interview.

Der Spiegel: For three generations Russia was a field of experiment for state socialism. Why Russia: historical accident, or was there a national predisposition for this?

Gorbachev: We should not become mystical about it, but set 1917 in its real context. And then we must ask ourselves what was wrong . . . and why it was with us . . . that the Bolsheviks came to power. Because the alternative was military dictatorship.

This completely mythical justification for the Bolsheviks coming to power has been reiterated by Gorbachev also while he was General Secretary and President of the USSR, seemingly forgetting that from 1917 onwards the Bolsheviks established in Russia a dictatorship which in its cruelty and criminality surpassed all dictatorial regimes that have ever existed in the history of mankind.

Later in the interview, when asked about the past 75 years of Bolshevik rule, Gorbachev replied: 'I would not wish to dismiss these seven and a half decades as a period when nothing positive or democratic occurred, when there was no freedom or social justice . . .'

The German correspondent, doubtless astonished at such a candid remark, could not restrain himself from asking a direct question: 'Can it be that you are still a communist?' Gorbachev's answer is somewhat evasive, but sufficiently clear in its meaning: 'I shall simply say that there are things which should not be forgotten and which the people do not wish to renounce.'

One might well suppose that these words would be completely sub-scribed to by not only all the members of the Roerich family but also by their Himalayan inspirers.

Appendix 8. A Successor to the Roerichs: the Neo-Pagan Movement of the Bazovtsy

The neo-pagan movement of the 'Bazovtsy'[*] takes its name from the Soviet Russian author Pavel Petrovich Bazov (1879–1950). He was born in Yekaterinenburg in the Urals and completed his course at the seminary in Perm. However, this did not prevent him from becoming a member of the Communist Party already in 1918. After the Revolution he collected folk tales and legends from the Ural region, which he published under his own editorship in various publications. In 1939 he brought out his magnum opus, the collection of folk tales *The Malachite Casket*. Since then the Bolshevik Government supported the hitherto hardly known author. In 1943 he received the Stalin Prize, the highest recognition possible at that time. Above all he was praised for his efforts to place the popular heritage of the Urals at the service of Soviet Realism. This is not to say that the source of Bazov's stories cannot be traced back to the folk tales of the Urals, which—as do all true folk tales—have a spiritual significance. But since they were heavily edited and turned into stories of magic by Bazov, it is extremely difficult to distinguish the authentic element from the later additions.

At the centre of his collection of folk tales is the figure of the 'Lady of the Copper Mountain', who—half goddess, half lizard—exercises a magical authority not only over the metals and gemstones of the Urals but also over human beings. Through magic power all ores and stones, but above all malachite, are able to work in a healing or a destructive way upon human beings and their surroundings. In the Bazov movement this collection of folk tales is regarded as 'holy', as it forms the movement's spiritual foundation.

The Bazov movement originated in Chelyabinsk (Urals) and—apart from the book referred to—is based on the occult heritage of Helena and Nicholas Roerich. Modern pseudo-scientific ideas—such as science fiction—also play a significant part with the 'Bazovtsy'. Thus their movement consists of two components: the shamanic, magical ideas of the East are—through the mediation of the occult teaching of Helena Roerich—linked with Western scientific thinking (oriented as it is explicitly towards the materialistic and sense-perceptible) and brought to a kind of 'marriage'.

The founder of this new movement is Vladimir Sobolev, who is still

---

[*] This is what the followers of this movement call themselves.

active today. On the basis of Helena Roerich's teaching, he developed the following occult picture of the world. 'The highest reason of the universe' is designated as the 'Logos' and the cosmic Father of the earth as 'Lucifer', the great leader and educator of mankind. On behalf of the 'Logos' a number of highly developed beings came to the earth from Venus eight million years ago. However, 'Lucifer' did not want to share his power over mankind with them and decided to destroy the earth. Thereupon the 'Reason of the universe' gave the earth a new father (the great 'Leader') and a mother (the 'Mother Earth'). Then at the beginning of the nineteenth century Lucifer constructed a 'hell machine' capable of gathering up the psychic energies of all evil, immoral human beings in order to destroy the earth. As a counter-reaction there ensued in 1928 the first 'Second Coming of Christ', which had the aim of creating the new humanity of the Aquarian Age. These human beings were to have developed three centres within themselves: the intellect, heart and will. The raw material for this was to be made available by the 'Rossiyans' (Russians), who consist of three folk groups: Russians, Jews and Tatars, with the Russians representing the goodness of the heart, the Jews the intellect and the Tatars the will. From this, Christ on his reappearance in 1940 created a new 'Aquarian race'. According to Sobolev, 1999 will be the next appearance of Christ and after this the Last Judgment will take place. After this Last Judgment the long-lost legendary people of the Chuds were to reappear in the Ural region, thus representing the beginning of the resurrection of the dead. According to the 'Bazovtsy', the Chuds are a dark-haired people who will possess magic, shamanic powers in the sense of the 'Lady of the Copper Mountain'.

Among the essential characteristics of the Bazov movement is the central role of the Ural region as a threshold between Europe and Asia, not only for Russian but for the whole of human history. Not far from the town of Magnitogorsk is the small township of Arkaim. There were discovered the ruins of a temple of the god Tengri, who was a chief god of the Turanian race of the Chuds who lived there in ancient times. Thus the 'Bazovtsy' believe that this nomadic people in its time had a direct connection with Tibet and above all with the wise people of 'Shamballa' or the land of 'Belovodye' (the land of the white waters). In this way the 'Bazovtsy' refer back to the same source of inspiration for their teachings as do the Roerichs.

After the Last Judgment, which consists of several natural catastrophes, Arkaim will become the centre not merely of Russia but of the entire earthly planet. Bazov's book of folk tales will then be the new 'Bible' of the new Aquarian race and the 'Lady of the Copper Mountain' will be its senior goddess. She will then endow those human beings who are devoted to her with magical shamanic power over all the earth.

In addition to Bazov's book, a religious ritual known as the Bazov Festival, which has taken place annually since 1993 at the summer solstice, also plays an important role for the 'Bazovtsy'. It is celebrated over several weeks at Lake Chebarkul, not far from Chelyabinsk. It represents a reflection of the 'thousand-year empire' which, according to the belief of the 'Bazovtsy', indeed existed in Bolshevik Russia for over 30 years from the end of the Second World War until *perestroika*. For according to the leader of the movement, V. Sobolev, this 'blossoming time of developed socialism' corresponds to the 'thousand-year empire' which is to precede the Last Judgment. The ritual of the festival consists of various elements, all of which derive from rites of pre-Christian shamanism: jumping over fire, ritual night bathing, the burning of straw dolls, the erecting of idols carved out of wood and so forth. All this is supposed to invoke and bring to life the 'spirit' of the 'thousand-year empire', that is, the 'spirit' of the 'blossoming time of developed socialism'.

In the year 1996 over six thousand people took part in this festival. The festivities were supported by the Russian cultural fund and the authorities of the region of Chelyabinsk together with the ministers for education and cultural affairs in the neighbouring states of Kazakhstan and Bash-kortostan. In particular, many scientists, writers, astrologers, UFO experts and Roerich adherents participated and augmented the programme through their lectures and working groups.

In the Ural region the influence of the Bazov movement is growing rapidly in cultural and political life as a whole, especially in the education system. This aim is furthered by the 'Bazov Academy for Occult Knowledge', which has a great influence upon the fund for culture, the College of Education, the town council and the military training centres in Chelyabinsk. Thus all doors are open to the spread of the teachings of Bazov. This stream has also been filtering increasingly into the politics of the region. The 'Ural Eurasian Club' was founded for this purpose, an organization which gives advice and recommendations to the Chelya-binsk town administration for developments in the Ural region. In addition to people with esoteric knowledge, astrologers, UFO experts and so forth, many influential officials including even the chairman of the town *duma* are members of this club. The movement has its own journal (*Atlantida*), publishes books, advertises in the local newspapers and is connected to the Internet.

As the Bolsheviks did in their time, the 'Bazovtsy' endeavour to make their teachings generally understandable through propaganda. For schools and making publicity in the town illustrated displays and other exhibition material are put together, even to the extent of painting the special train running between Chelyabinsk and Moscow. Through the initiative of the movement a monument to the conqueror of Siberia, the Cossack leader Yermak (sixteenth century), is to be erected in the near future. Yermak, who initiated the conquest of Siberia, stands for the 'Bazovtsy' as a 'great incarnation', who united Europe and Asia and therefore also opened up the path to Tibetan Shamballa.

★

In this outline of the Bazov movement it is not difficult to recognize the basic principles of the teaching of Helena and Nicholas Roerich: the great wise beings coming from Venus and founding Shamballa in Tibet (Nicholas Roerich made a particular point of identifying the 'Land of the White Waters' described in the Russian legends with Tibetan Shamballa); the endeavour to unite Western science with Asiatic occultism (in this case with northern Asiatic shamanism), even to the extent of renewing its rituals under the pretext of nurturing ethnographic traditions; replacing Christianity through a series of 'Second Comings' (although, as with Helena Roerich, it remains unclear whether they are thought of in a physical or spiritual sense); and as a facet of the whole an aspiration to invigorate and maintain Bolshevism as an occult, political phenomenon.

It would perhaps not be necessary to mention all this within the compass of this book were it not for the fact that the Bazov movement derived from the Ural region, regarding which Rudolf Steiner made some important pronouncements from his spiritual research in his lecture of 15 July 1923 (GA 225).[*] Here Rudolf Steiner described how to the west of the Urals and the Volga certain luciferic beings have gathered in the astral world bordering upon the earth who possess the refinements of the Western scientific intellect, directed as it is solely towards the physical world of the senses. In contrast, the beings who have gathered to the east of the Urals and the Volga basin have, as the metamorphosed satyrs and fauns of ancient Greece, taken on a wholly ahrimanic character and have therefore become the inspirers of northern Asiatic shamanism, which draws the spiritual down to the earth 'in stone, in blocks of wood', in order to portray the true deeds of the Gods 'as the deeds of physically perceptible idols'. Thus 'the magical enchantment of the shamanism' of northern Asia and extending to Siberia stands today under the influence of these 'terrible ahrimanic, etheric-astral beings'. From these two kinds of

---

[*] All the quotations that follow are from this lecture.

beings whose influence lies 'eastwards and westwards from the region of the Urals and the Volga a marriage is being sought between magical arts and Bolshevism ... because the luciferically spiritual [pseudo-idealistic] qualities of Bolshevism are forming a union with the now wholly decadent forms of shamanism that are approaching the Urals and the Volga and are increasingly pervading this region'.

Rudolf Steiner characterizes this marriage in such a way that there arises from it an altogether new kind of being, whose head manifests an almost superhuman but also lustful, sense-bound intellectuality and whose lower portion has adopted the form of a goat or bear. Such beings are today 'the tempters and seducers of physical human beings, because they can cause human beings to be possessed by them ... Then it comes about that people believe that what they do is done by themselves, is wrought by their own nature, whereas in truth what people do in this realm often only comes about because they are inwardly in their blood infiltrated by such a being who has from the East come to manifest a goat's body that has taken on the form of a bear and a European human head as metamorphosed in the West into something of a superhuman nature.' Prominent amongst those who were most strongly possessed by such beings was the founder of Bolshevism and his comrades: 'And there arose beings such as those who from the astral plane have come to possess the Lenins and their companions.'

In the same lecture Rudolf Steiner indicates that the task of those human beings who live in this region today is to recognize these truths and counteract these demonic beings. By this means they will fulfil their task not only with respect to Russia but also to 'the evolution of humanity as a whole, whereas if they were to divert their attention from it they will be inwardly infiltrated and possessed in their souls by these influences'. These words of the modern Christian initiate show where the occult foundation of a movement such as that of the 'Bazovtsy' is to be sought. For it tries—without those who profess allegiance to it noticing—to divert attention from a knowledge of the true spiritual facts and lead all the more surely to the sphere of influence of the demonic astral beings.

If precisely in the Ural region such movements are widely disseminated, there is a real danger that virtually insuperable difficulties will arise for Russia in the path of suffering leading to its deliverance from the soul-destroying power of Bolshevism. The knowledge and the inner courage that are necessary for overcoming these difficulties are available today only through anthroposophy, as the modern stream of esoteric Christianity.

Reference

The article by Alexander Shchipkov published in *Literaturnaya Gazeta* on 4 September 1996 served as a source of information about the Bazov movement.

Bibliography

See pages 11–12 for list of works by Helena and Nicholas Roerich and theosophical literature for which abbreviations are used in the text.

Belikov, P.F. (ed.), *N.K Rerich, Iz literaturnovo naslyediya* ('From Nicholas Roerich's Literary Legacy'), Moscow 1974

Belikov, P.F. and Knyazeva, V.P., *Rerich*, Molodiya gvardya, Moscow 1973, in the series 'Lives of Prominent People'

Decter, J., *The Life and Work of a Russian Master*, in collaboration with the Nicholas Roerich Museum, Thames and Hudson, London 1989

Fosdik, Z., 'V Moskvye i na Altae s Rerichami' (In Moscow and in Altai with the Roerichs), *Svyet ognya*, November 1990. From the diaries of Zinaida Fosdik, summer 1926

Gorchakov, G.S., *Vyeliki Uchitel. Zemniye zhizni Naivysshevo* ('The Great Teacher. The Earthly Lives of the Highest One'), Tomsk 1994

von Hahn de Zhelikovsky, Vera Petrovna, *Radda-Bai—Biograficheski ocherk* ('H.P. Blavatsky—A Biographical Sketch'), 1893

Khramchenko, V., 'Mezhdunarodnaya missiya Eleny Rerich' (The International Mission of Helena Roerich), *Serdtse*, 1993, no. 1 (3)

Klizovsky, A.I., *Osnovy miroponimaniya novoi epokhi* ('The Basis for an Understanding of the New Epoch'), Vols I–III, Riga 1990

Rudzitis, R., 'Yuri Rerich: Iz dnyevnikov Richarda Rudzitsa' (From the Diaries of Richard Rudzitis), *Svyet ognya*, November 1990

Sidorov, V., 'Provozvyestie XX vyeka' (Proclamation of the 20th Century), in *Zhivaya ethika: izbrannoye* ('Living Ethics: An Anthology'), Moscow 1992

Ter-Akopyan, A.K., Foreword and Notes to *Mozaika Agni Yogi* ('A Mosaic of Agni Yoga'), Vol. I, Tbilisi 1990.

Zarnitsky, S. and Trophimova, L., 'Pyt k Rodine' (The Path to the Fatherland), *Mezhdunarodnaya zhizn*, 1965, no. 1

Illlustrations

1. *Helena Roerich, beginning of the 1920s*

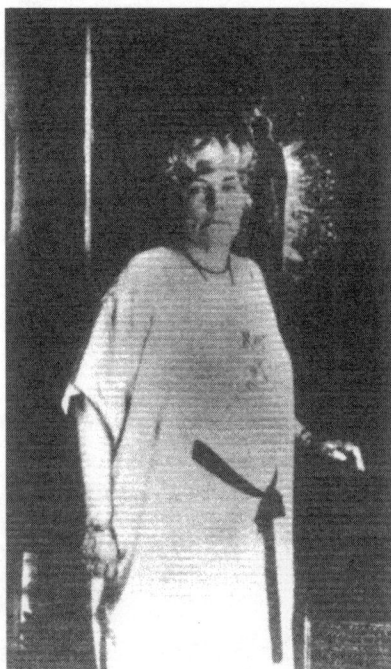

2. *Helena Roerich in the 1940s in her house in Kulu (India). In the background is the middle part of the triptych with the figure of Mahatma M. (See illustrations 20 and 21.) The handwritten words beneath the photograph read: 'In the spirit, Your Helena Roerich.'*

3. Nicholas Roerich

4. Nicholas Roerich with his sons Yuri and Svyatoslav in Kulu, India

5. *The trans-Himalayan expedition (1925–8). Nicholas Roerich with the tangka (banner) of Shamballa, Mongolia 1926*

6. *The trans-Himalayan expedition. View of the camp in Sharugan (Tibet). On the left is the tangka of Shamballa, on the right is the American flag. The photograph was taken on the way back from Bolshevik Russia to India*

7. Nicholas Roerich, The Roerich Museum in New York, *sketch from the end of the 1920s. At the top of the skyscraper a Buddhist stupa can be clearly discerned*

9. Nicholas Roerich in the Roerich Museum in New York in the 1920s. (The museum was opened on 17 October 1929)

8. Nicholas Roerich in the pose of an archer, 1928, India

10. Nicholas Roerich, 1933, Kulu

11. *Jawaharlal Nehru, Indira Gandhi, Nicholas Roerich (from the left) in front of the Roerichs' house in Kulu, May 1942*

12. *Nicholas Roerich in his house in Kulu in the 1940s. Above him on the cloth is the red emblem of Roerich's 'Cultural Pact' (pact for the protection of cultural treasures)*

13. *Svyatoslav Roerich,* Portrait of Helena Roerich, *1937. In the foreground is the iron casket in which the fragment of the meteorite from Shamballa was given to the Roerichs*

14. *Svyatoslav Roerich, portrait of his father,* Nicholas Roerich as the Ruler of Tibet, dressed as the Dalai Lama. *In the background is the Dalai Lama's palace in Lhasa, the capital of Tibet. The picture is in the Roerich Museum in New York*

15. *Nicholas Roerich,* The Burning of Darkness, *1924. (The mahatmas from the Himalayas bring a fragment of the meteorite from Shamballa in a casket, in which it was subsequently given to the Roerichs)*

16. *Nicholas Roerich,* The Signs of Christ

17. Nicholas Roerich, The Treasure of the World, *1924 (the further journey of the casket containing the stone to the Roerichs)*

18. Nicholas Roerich, The Guardians of Himalaya *(at the entrance to Shamballa)*

19. *Nicholas Roerich,* Agni Yoga. *Helena Roerich as the 'mother' of Agni Yoga)*

20. Long Live the King! *triptych. In the middle is Mahatma M. holding the meteorite fragment which the Roerichs possessed already in the thirteenth century. At that time, they believed, they lived in Germany as Eckhard and Uta von Naumburg (portrayed on the left and right parts of the triptych)*

21. Nicholas Roerich; in the background is the middle part of the triptych, Kulu 1937

22. Meeting in the Kremlin (Moscow) between Mikhail Gorbachev and Svyatoslav Roerich, the son of Helena and Nicholas Roerich, in May 1987

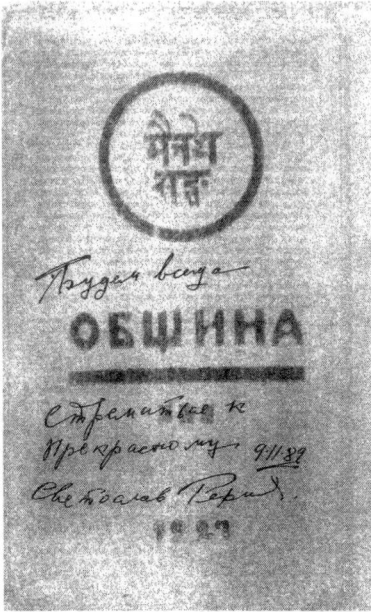

23. Title-page of the first edition of the book Obshchina ('Community') by Helena Roerich (Ulan Bator 1927), which contains all the positive remarks about Lenin and Bolshevism quoted in the present book. This book was signed by Svyatoslav Roerich at the time of perestroika (1989) for the adherents of his father with the words: 'Let us constantly aspire to the good'

24. President Franklin D. Roosevelt in a high-grade lodge. (From the book by T. Nage, Jesuiten und Freimauer ('Jesuits and Freemasons'), Vienna 1969)

Part Two

THE TEACHING OF ALICE BAILEY IN THE LIGHT OF CHRISTIAN ESOTERICISM

'It is the Mystery of Golgotha that has to be rescued today.'
Rudolf Steiner, 30 October 1920

'Among all the battles of our time, rich as it is in hard struggle, the battle for God, for Christ, has a primal place. It is the deep undercurrent in all tragic events, which are but the outward breaking of the waves.'
Marie Steiner, 1933

'From the vantage-point whence we have hitherto been enabled to proclaim supersensible truths, it has been incumbent upon us to point out that man's supersensible body will be imbued with a supersensible experience in the course of the twentieth century: human beings, as if through a natural occurrence, will find the reappearing Christ. So much were we able to point out. But this reappearing Christ will not sail the sea in ships, nor travel in trains, nor airships; rather will he be recognized, with the means appropriate to the etheric realm, within the individual being of man, in what—in accordance with the way human souls are themselves constituted—passes from one human soul to another. What we are thus enabled to say about the way in which the reappearing Christ will be manifested seems feeble as compared with what will approach the human soul directly from the supersensible world. For human beings would love to see with physical eyes the Mighty Being who is to come; they would love to conceive of him as flying in an aeroplane or travelling by sea, they would want to be able physically to touch and take hold of him who is to come. Why is this? Because they dread coming into actual contact with the supersensible worlds. Such phenomena appear to the occultist as disguised fear and a dread of truth. This is said quite dispassionately, merely as an objective statement.'
Rudolf Steiner, 31 August 1912 (GA 138)

Preface

The second part of *The East in the Light of the West. Two Twentieth-century Eastern Streams in the Light of Christian Esotericism* is intended specifically for the anthroposophical reader. This second part is likewise the result of my own research and hence reflects my personal viewpoint. Its subject is the occult stream of the so-called Arcane School founded by Alice Bailey, considered from an anthroposophical standpoint; it appears now five years after the publication of the first part [in German], which was devoted to the teaching of Helena Roerich's Agni Yoga.

This long-awaited second part was written soon after the publication of the first part but could only appear now [in 1997] after considerable delay. It began to become clear in the course of working with this theme that a third part had to be added in order to consider the question which had obviously stirred in the minds of many who had read the first part, namely the question of the relationship between the Eastern and Western occult teachers and the occult streams that they represented.

Since this question is extremely complicated and multi-layered, it was *consciously left unanswered* in the first part. For it soon became clear that even the mere attempt to approach an answer to it required an independent investigation. However, this could no more be carried out within the compass of the second part than within the first.

Thus initially there was no attempt to investigate whether the Eastern mahatmas, of whose existence not only Blavatsky but also Olcott and Sinnett publicly reported in the Western world, were those same individualities of whom Besant and Leadbeater and also Alice Bailey and the Roerichs were subsequently to speak and write and with whom, according to their repeated assertions, they were in occult communication.

The task of the first and now the second part consists, rather, in allowing first Helena and Nicholas Roerich and then Alice Bailey to speak in their own words. They were convinced that the occult teachers who inspired them were the same as those who were made known to the world for the first time by H.P. Blavatsky.

Thus in accordance with the original plan, this second part also consists in the first instance of statements by the founder of the Arcane School and of anthroposophical commentaries on them, which may serve to help the anthroposophical reader to understand this stream in the light of modern Christian esotericism.

Since after the publication of the first part I have been repeatedly asked what can be said from an anthroposophical standpoint about the Eastern teachers (mahatmas) and their relationship to *Christian* esotericism, it seemed to me to be necessary to deal more thoroughly with this theme. This led to my own study of it and hence to a third, concluding part of this present work.

The main conclusion of this third part is that those occultists whom both Alice Bailey and also Helena and Nicholas Roerich called their leaders have nothing in common with those Eastern mahatmas whose names H.P. Blavatsky was the first to make known.

And so in the case of both Alice Bailey and the Roerichs one is concerned *not* with the Eastern mahatmas but with altogether different occultists who had illicitly appropriated their names and then tried—to the utter confusion of their followers—to attain their highly dubious occult-political aims with the help of the occult movements which the Eastern mahatmas had brought into being. It is true that Rudolf Steiner spoke in his later lectures of the 'substitution' of just *one* of the two mahatmas who had originally inspired Blavatsky. However, the further development of the Theosophical Society, especially under the leadership of Besant and Leadbeater, makes it plain that *both* mahatmas were substituted.

This process of substituting the Eastern mahatmas by left-oriented occultists began already during Blavatsky's life. It was associated with the fact that the Eastern mahatmas were gradually ceasing to inspire the Theosophical Society, and eventually distanced themselves altogether from it. After their withdrawal, occultists with a left inclination soon seized hold of the spiritual space that had become vacant. As a result the pre-Christian wisdom of the ancient Eastern religions, of which Blavatsky had spoken and written out of the inspirations of the Eastern mahatmas, gradually acquired a distinctly antichristian character, which distorted and destroyed the foundation of true Christianity.

The climax of this process, and the associated decline of the Theosophical Society in the twentieth century, was represented by the attempt of Besant and Leadbeater to promote the 14-year-old Krishnamurti as the reborn 'Messiah', whereupon the antichristian character that had already taken hold of the Theosophical Society became fully manifest. Subsequently, these preparations for the appearance of the 'Messiah' in the physical body were taken further in the occult stream of Alice Bailey and placed within an even broader world context. In this way the antichristian character of this stream became still more pronounced.

Since it follows from further indications by Rudolf Steiner that the original impulse to found the Theosophical Society (1875) was given not by Eastern but by Western masters and, moreover, by the leading masters of Rosicrucian Christianity, one can by taking this fact into account clearly distinguish three elements in the overall development of the Theosophical Society in the last quarter of the nineteenth century (still in Blavatsky's lifetime). These overlapped in a temporal sense; all in all, however, they followed on one from another:

1. a Christian impulse (Rosicrucian, esoteric Christianity);
2. a pre-Christian impulse (esotericism deriving from the ancient pre-Christian religions of the East);
3. an antichristian impulse (battle of left-oriented Eastern and Western occultists against Christianity).

If one is seeking to understand the subsequent destiny of the theosophical movement and the occult streams of Alice Bailey and of Helena and Nicholas Roerich that are associated with it, one needs strictly to distinguish these three impulses.

Whereas it was the main aim of the first impulse to work for the 'essential *meaning of the earth*, which lies in the recognition and realization of the intentions of the *living Christ*', the second set itself the task of 'imprint[ing] *their* form of spiritual knowledge, which had been preserved through the ages, on the Western world', in order to counteract 'the terrible danger' threatening mankind in the event of an overall victory of Western materialism (see Part One, Appendix 5).

It was from all this that the extraordinarily complex and highly dramatic relationships between the Western (Rosicrucian) masters and the Eastern mahatmas in the twentieth century resulted, characterized by on the one hand a common endeavour to overcome the materialism threatening mankind and, on the other, by a different understanding of the Christ Being and his central role in earthly evolution.

Lastly, the third impulse of the left-oriented occultists had set itself the goal of occultly intensifying the already existing materialism by extending it to the spiritual world and turning it into an *occult materialism* with a particular danger to modern man, in order to use it as an instrument for the attainment of their antichristian political aims.

The occult movements of Alice Bailey and of Helena and Nicholas Roerich, together with a whole series of other occult streams characterized in this part of the present book, were brought into being by the aforesaid occultists of a left inclination in order to achieve this.

★

Two features of the present study still need to be characterized.

Because of the way that this book has appeared [in German], and also for technical reasons, it has been published not in one but in three volumes. This has led to some basic statements by Rudolf Steiner that are necessary for an understanding both of the occult movements of Alice Bailey and the Roerichs and also of the very complex character of the relationship between the Western and Eastern masters being quoted in all three volumes. (The same also applies to some of the characteristic statements by the founders of the two streams under consideration here.) Because of these repetitions, each of the three volumes can be read independently without a knowledge of the other two.

The second feature consists of the following. In order that the anthroposophical reader may form his own judgement of the character and the particular qualities of the occultism of Alice Bailey and also of Helena and Nicholas Roerich, a large number of quotations from their works have been included in all three parts of the present work. But since both Alice Bailey and the Roerichs and also the occult authors who were connected with them were constantly referring—and continue to refer even today— not only to the Eastern mahatmas and called them by their names but also to the Western masters and even to the founder of Christianity Himself, it was because of the frequent use of their names in the quotations completely impossible always to put the names cited by them in inverted commas or simply to add the words 'pseudo', 'false' or 'allegedly' and so forth.

Thus it must be reiterated here with full emphasis: the use of the above names in the occult streams of Alice Bailey, the Roerichs and other streams affiliated to them has nothing in common with the true individualities of the masters of the East and the West who once bore, or still bear, these names.

★

In conclusion, the question should be asked why it is altogether necessary to concern oneself with the occult stream of Alice Bailey from an anthroposophical standpoint. The answer is that we are dealing here with the most dangerous and widespread distortion of Christianity; and the future of the evolution of humanity depends in no small measure upon whether this distortion is implemented or destroyed.

When the affair of Krishnamurti as the 'Messiah' appearing in a physical body emerged from within the Theosophical Society, Rudolf Steiner did not reach a compromise with it but spoke increasingly more loudly and sharply about the falsification that had been brought about of the fundamental truths of Christianity.

Today at the end of the century it is one of our tasks as anthroposophists to take stock of the century also occultly and to recognize that the stream of Alice Bailey represents a direct continuation and far-reaching intensification of this antichristian tendency.

Rudolf Steiner has in this regard himself given us the task of guarding the fundamental truths of esoteric Christianity and of raising our voices clearly and without compromise wherever such distortions appear.

The present book has been written in the light of this task.

Sergei O. Prokofieff
Stuttgart, December 1996

Abbreviations Used in Part 2

1. Alice Bailey. The Story of a Medium

The outward life of Alice Ann Bailey—her maiden name was La Trobe-Bateman—was simple and unremarkable.[1] Alice was born on 17 June 1880 as the daughter of a prosperous owner of a construction firm in Manchester. When she was six years old her mother died, and her father also died two years later. Thus it was that Alice and her younger sister lived for a time with various relations, while also attending a boarding school. According to her own testimony, Alice lacked for nothing until her twenty-eighth year. However, after she had married Walter Evans, a priest of the Episcopal Church, and had left with him for America, a decisive change came about. She gave birth there to three daughters. Her husband suffered from mysterious fits of rage, during which he became a danger to his surroundings; and in the end this led to their separation. The family was living at the time in California, and Alice began to work in a factory in order to support herself and her daughters. In the same period she came in contact for the first time with the Theosophical Society and became a member in 1915. In theosophical circles she met her second husband, Foster Bailey, in 1919; at this time he had just become the General Secretary of the Theosophical Society in America. In 1920, however, she—together with her husband—left the Theosophical Society, as its leadership in Adyar was against her new 'revelations'. In 1922 she and her husband founded the 'Lucis [Lucifer] Trust' Company[*] for the purpose of publishing her books and the journal *The Beacon*, which appeared bi-monthly in London. In 1923 she opened her own occult school under the name of the 'Arcane School', thereby fulfilling a wish that Blavatsky had expressed already in her time, namely to call the Esoteric School of the Theosophical Society that she had founded by this name. Subsequently, Alice Bailey brought a number of occult movements into existence in 1932/33, which she called the 'New Group of the World Servers' and the 'Group of the All-Encompassing Good Will' and also (in 1937) the movements of the so-called 'Triangles'.[†]

Alice Bailey wrote books until the end of her life (in all there are 24 volumes, some of which are fairly extensive). She died on 15 December 1949 in New York, soon after completing her work on her final book,

---

[*] Its name was originally the 'Lucifer Publishing Company'.

[†] See further regarding these movements later in this chapter and in chapter 4.

written together with 'the Tibetan',[*] and without having brought her autobiography to a conclusion. Her second husband wrote: 'When this had been accomplished, and within thirty days after that period, Mrs. Bailey gained her release from the limitations of the physical vehicle'.[2]

It is evident from *The Unfinished Autobiography*, which Alice Bailey was writing in the last years of her life, that she was a difficult, very wilful child who was inclined to melancholy and depression. She found learning difficult, and she evidently suffered for a long time under the complex of being of less worth than her pretty and clever younger sister. As she herself wrote, she tried on three occasions in her childhood to end her life and later suffered at times from 'acute psychical disturbance'.[3] In the girls' boarding school in London, where she was sent at the age of 18, it was not possible for her—not even in accordance with the level of a 12-year-old child—to learn to read, so that those who ran the boarding school eventually exempted her from this subject altogether. Only *when she was 35* did Alice Bailey discover that she *could think*. 'Yet I was 35 years old before I really discovered that I had a mind and that it was something which I could use. Up to that time, I had been a bundle of emotions and feelings; my mind—what there was of it—had used me and not been used by me.'[4]

Together with this evident backwardness in her intellectual development and her total lack of independence in her thinking, Alice Bailey was 'deeply religious' and 'imbued by the mystical consciousness', which at times—when intensified—led to a 'morbidly sensitive ... conscience', which for example came to expression in that she was unable to decide to sit next to someone at table 'without ascertaining whether they were "saved" or not'. Such states of religious exaltation were succeeded by others of profound melancholy and a heavy emotional state. 'Life was not worth living. There was nothing but sorrow and trouble on every hand.'

When Alice Bailey was 15 years old she met for the first time the person whom since then and to the end of her life she called her teacher and whom she subsequently identified as the Mahatma K.H. (Kut Humi). This happened in the following way. One Sunday morning, when all others living in the house were at church, a tall Indian dressed like a European but with a turban on his head entered the living room in which Alice Bailey was sitting. He told her that she must take herself in hand and fundamentally change her character, for upon this would depend the possibility of her being able to serve the world and in particular 'doing

---

[*] This is the way that Alice Bailey's occult leader Djwhal Khul (D.K.) was referred to in her circles.

your Master's work all the time'. Before this stranger departed he went on to say that he would 'be in touch with me at intervals of several years apart', whereupon he cast her a glance which made a deep impression on her soul and took his leave.

The stranger kept his word. Alice Bailey wrote: 'As the years went by I found that at seven years intervals (until I was thirty-five) I had indications of the supervision and interest of this individual.' In due course the telepathic connection with him became so strong 'until today I can, at will, contact Him'. Nevertheless, it was only after over 20 years that she learnt who her mysterious visitor was. This happened in 1918 in California, when Alice Bailey had been received into the Esoteric School of the Theosophical Society and when during the first lesson she saw a portrait of Mahatma K.H. Then she had no doubt: the portrait depicted her mysterious visitor. Now she knew who her spiritual teacher was.

The first meeting with Mahatma K.H. in 1895 had a further quite particular occult consequence which is of great significance for a true understanding of all that was to follow. She herself described what happened soon after the meeting referred to: 'Twice I had a dream in full waking consciousness. I called it a dream because I could not imagine at that time what else it could possibly be. Now I know that I participated in something that really took place.' Thus as she herself described, Alice Bailey was after the mahatma's visit able to take part in a ceremony whose significance and meaning she grasped only after 20 years. This ceremony took place in a remote Himalayan valley and was associated with the great Buddhist festival of Wesak, when at the first full moon in May Gautama Buddha's birthday is celebrated both in southern Asia and also in Tibet. According to Alice Bailey, what she experienced was an annual ritual which was celebrated in an altogether real way *on the physical plane*. It came about in full consciousness, amidst a great crowd of people, consisting for the most part of people from the Orient but 'with a large sprinkling of occidental people'. In this way she knew from the outset that the place that she occupied amongst all these people corresponded precisely to the stage of her own spiritual development.

The valley in which Alice Bailey found herself was enclosed by high mountains. It became narrower towards the East and culminated in a funnel-shaped crevice in front of which there was a large rock resembling a table on which stood a large crystal chalice a metre in width and filled with water to the brim. The big crowd of people was walking towards it, giving rise to various symbolic forms: a cross, a circle, a five-pointed star and so on. At the head of the whole procession Alice could distinguish three figures: 'They formed a triangle and, to my surprise, the one at the apex of the triangle seemed to me to be the Christ.' Then she continued: 'Suddenly, the three Figures before the rock stretched out Their arms towards the heavens. The crowd froze into immobility. At the far end of the bottleneck a Figure was seen in the sky, hovering over the passage and slowly approaching the rock. I knew in some subjective and certain fashion that it was the Buddha. I had a sense of recognition.'

In this description the moment that needs particular attention is where Alice Bailey, who was brought up in the Christian tradition, saw nothing demeaning in the fact that she saw Christ raising his hands and praying to the Buddha: 'I knew at the same time that in no way was our Christ belittled.' Furthermore, as a result of this experience she 'got a glimpse of the unity and of the Plan to which the Christ, the Buddha and all the Masters are eternally dedicated . . . I grasped—faintly—that human beings needed the Christ and the Buddha and all the Members of the planetary Hierarchy . . .' Nevertheless, wrote Alice Bailey, 'I was left bewildered' by this vision, 'because to me (at that time) the heathen were still heathen and I was a Christian. Deep and fundamental doubts were left in my mind.'

The years went by, and gradually Alice Bailey's doubts were allayed under the influence of her teacher. The Buddha and the Christ became for her representatives of equal standing of the Eastern and Western paths to God, and her whole life henceforth consisted of serving her teacher, the Mahatma K.H., for whom she had, according to her own conviction, worked without interruption since her fifteenth year.[5] It is true that the greater part of Alice Bailey's work had been carried out under the influence of another teacher, who had previously been a pupil and thereafter an independent collaborator and helper of Mahatma K.H. With this we have arrived at the next section of Alice Bailey's life, her encounter with the 'Tibetan' or the Mahatma D.K. (Djwhal Khul).

Before we describe this meeting, however, the vision of Alice Bailey described above must be considered more closely. We learn more about it in C.W. Leadbeater's 1929 publication *The Masters and the Path*.[6] There Leadbeater devotes a whole chapter to the Buddhist Wesak festival in the Himalayas that Alice Bailey experienced in her vision, describing in particular detail the spiritual aura of the Buddha as he appeared out of the heavens. A coloured picture in the frontispiece of the book entitled 'A Wesak Blessing' serves as an illustration to this chapter. It portrays a mountain valley over which a gigantic Buddha figure hovers in the lotus position, his right hand raised in blessing, surrounded by a mighty coloured aura filling the whole sky, while beneath him is a procession of people clothed in white who are in comparison to his gigantic figure barely visible and who form a five-pointed star, enclosing a circle. At the upper point of the star is a clearly rising figure who is leading the procession depicted with raised hands and in front of it a white form— probably the altar rock referred to by Alice Bailey. All in all this picture may be regarded as a sort of illustration of her vision.

But Leadbeater, who—like Alice Bailey—called himself a pupil of Mahatma K.H. and quite especially of the latter's companion D.K.,[7] was not the only one to speak about this festival. D.K. himself also did so several times. He subsequently dictated the following to Alice Bailey: 'This is the Festival of the Buddha, the spiritual Intermediary between the highest spiritual centre, Shamballa, and the Hierarchy.'[8] (According to D.K., Christ is leading the latter today, as we shall see later.) 'The Wesak Festival has been held, down the centuries, in the well-known valley in the Himalayas ... in order: [firstly] to substantiate *the fact of Christ's physical existence among us* ... [and secondly] to prove (on the physical plane) the factual solidarity of the Eastern and Western approaches to God. Both the Christ and the Buddha are then present.'[9]

D.K. explained the significance of the events at this festival, that is, the scene that Alice Bailey perceived in her vision, in such a way that 'the distribution of spiritual energy ... will be direct from the Buddha ... to the Christ, and then from the Christ to those disciples in every country who can be overshadowed, and so act as channels for the direct current of energy'.[10] However, the Buddha in turn receives this energy from a still higher being, who in the teaching of the 'Tibetan' is called the 'Lord of the World' (more will be said about him later on): 'Once a year, at the Wesak Festival, the Lord Buddha, sanctioned by the Lord of the World, carries to the assembled humanity a dual stream of force ... This dual energy He pours out in blessing over the people gathered at the ceremony in the Himalayas, and from them in turn it flows out to all peoples and tongues and races.'[11] But as for the *three figures* 'beheld' by Alice Bailey at the head of the procession, the 'Tibetan' writes to his pupil about them as follows: 'There and at that time [at the Wesak festival], the three Representatives of Shamballa within the Hierarchy—the Manu, the Christ and the Mahachohan—invoke the Buddha, Who in His turn is the transmitter of still higher forces.'[12]

Particularly symptomatic in this connection is the fact that Alice Bailey was shown in the vision already at 15, when of course she did not have the slightest conception of these things, what she was to describe at greater length in her books over 20 years later under the dictation of the Mahatma D.K., so that in writing his words down she could say to herself: this is how it is, for I was present at the time and know it from my own experience.

Now we shall return to the beginning of Alice Bailey's collaboration with the Tibetan mahatma, which lasted for 30 years. The first contact with him took place in November 1919 in California. The children were at school, and Alice was walking up a small hill that lay behind her house. As she was climbing the hill, she suddenly heard a voice which was clearly directed to her. The voice said: ' "There are some books which it is desired should be written for the public. You can write them. Will you do so?" '[13] Alice Bailey was frightened, and answered categorically: ' "Certainly not! I'm not a darned psychic and I don't want to be drawn into anything like that." ' She was astonished 'to hear myself speaking out loud' with no one. However, the mysterious voice did not let up but assured her 'that I [Alice Bailey] had a peculiar gift for the higher telepathy . . .' After further protests Alice Bailey finally explained that she would think about it, and the voice informed her that it would speak with her again in three weeks. Precisely three weeks later, when the children were already asleep, the voice spoke to her once more, as predicted. This time Alice Bailey suggested the experiment of working with it for two or three weeks and then deciding. In this way the collaboration began. As Alice Bailey reports, she initially only heard the voice dictating to her and wrote down what was dictated to her without allowing the smallest alterations in what she wrote down, despite the fact that the quality of the English of the 'person dictating to her' was not particularly good. Quite soon, however, she no longer needed his voice. She had merely to concentrate sufficiently and she 'could register . . . the thoughts of the Tibetan' which, as she writes, 'are dropped one by one into my brain'.

Although her curiosity was aroused, she again began to feel a certain anxiety, and she shared with the 'voice' that she feared 'if I were [to become] ill or . . . crazy'; also she had to care for three children and therefore she wasn't going to do any more writing for him. Thereupon the voice suggested getting in touch telepathically with its teacher K.H. and talking the matter over with him. Alice Bailey consented, and with the help of 'the very definite technique that He had taught [her]' discussed the whole situation with him. Through this she was assured that she had nothing to fear, since the voice that had spoken to her—so K.H. assured her—belonged to his collaborator and former pupil, the Mahatma D.K. (the 'Tibetan') and that he himself had suggested that K.H. should help her. In an occult sense she would however continue to be his pupil and not D.K.'s, of whom she should avail herself only for helping her work.

Thus in the course of 30 years 18 books came into being, written by Alice Bailey under the direction of Mahatma D.K. in the manner referred to, many amounting to over a thousand pages and dealing with the most diverse realms of occultism and the conduct of life, including themes such as: initiation, white magic, evolution of the cosmos and humanity, the teaching of the new epoch, the tasks of nations, telepathy, education, esoteric psychology, astrology, the art of healing and so forth.[14]

As the obedient executor of D.K.'s will Alice Bailey never claimed authorship of these books but expressly emphasized each time that not she but her inspirer was the true author. '... The books are His, not mine, and basically the responsibility is His,'[15] she wrote in her autobiography.*

The at first sight so unusual story of the origin of her books is in point of fact nothing new. The book that Krishnamurti wrote in 1911 after his first 'initiation', *At the Feet of the Master*, came about in the same way. 'These are not my words; they are the words of the Master [K.H.] who taught me,' he wrote in the foreword.[16] And his mentor Leadbeater describes the arising of this book as follows: 'Every night I had to take this boy in his astral body to the house of the Master, that instruction might be given to him.' After he awoke the young author wrote down what he had heard, and Leadbeater corrected his mistakes in English. When the task was finished the manuscript was typed, sent to K.H. for correcting and, once he had revised it, sent to the printers. The same thing happened in Alice Bailey's case, for D.K. himself 'does not permit me to make mistakes and watches over the final draft with great care'.[17] The only difference between Krishnamurti and Alice Bailey was that Krishnamurti received his instructions at night and Alice Bailey by day. In this case, however, the difference is not of any particular significance. For the result was ultimately the same.† In Alice Bailey's case it is also interesting that she only had telepathic and not clairvoyant faculties. 'She was not either clair-audient or clair-voyant and never would be,' said the 'Tibetan' of her.[18] In this respect Alice Bailey clearly differed from her predecessor H.P. Blavatsky, who was highly endowed both with clairaudience and clair-voyance, albeit in a mediumistic, atavistic form. Her well-known biographer, H. Pisareva, explains why it was precisely she who was chosen by the mahatmas for fulfilling their aims: 'She was chosen because of the remarkable capacities that she had shown from her childhood. These

---

* Here Alice Bailey introduces a humorous detail. For some time the well-known psychologist C.G. Jung had been studying the way that she wrote her books, and he sought to explain the phenomenon of the 'dictating Tibetan' by identifying him with Alice Bailey's 'higher self' and the writer herself with the 'lower self'. Whereupon Alice Bailey replied, not without a certain humour, that were she to meet Jung she would ask him how she might from time to time receive parcels sent from India by her 'higher self'.

† See further in chapter 4 regarding the 'Tibetan's' positive attitude to the 'experiment' with Krishnamurti, which had the aim of making a world teacher out of him.

capacities enabled her teachers, Morya and Kut Humi, to contact her easily from a distance by means of telepathy [the transference of thoughts].'[19] But what both women had in common was their *lack of understanding* of much of what was dictated to them. Blavatsky wrote on several occasions along these lines to her sister V. Zhelikovskaya,[20] and Alice Bailey mentioned it in her autobiography: 'I do not always understand what is given [dictated]. I do not always agree. But I record it all honestly and then discover it does make sense and evokes intuitive response [in me].'[21] And in another context: 'The assumption that I know all that is given in His books is a false one.' Of course, neither Blavatsky nor Bailey or Helena Roerich, whom one should by virtue of her capacities place somewhere between the other two,[*] were ordinary, simple mediums, while nevertheless their occult capacities were of a mediumistic, atavistic nature and were dependent upon what the mahatmas or the spiritual beings standing behind them dictated or manifested in the spiritual worlds.

All this is fundamentally different from the method of *fully conscious, individual spiritual research* that Rudolf Steiner expounded in his books and himself practised throughout his life, and 'took thorough account of modern scientific methods, which merely needed to be developed in such a way as to make ascent to the spiritual realms possible'.[22] 'In this connection, the introduction of our spiritual-scientific direction of work [into theosophy] represented from the outset something entirely new as compared with the methods of the Theosophical Society.' For in this latter context, since the time of Blavatsky virtually all occult facts 'had been obtained in the Theosophical Society . . . by means of a certain kind of mediumistic investigation'. This was also true of Alice Bailey, although she, as has been said, did not possess any clairvoyant faculties. Her apparent inability to think independently, and her tendency to emotional states in the course of which her own thoughts were easily turned into other people's—in this case into the thoughts of her inspirer, which very often she did not even understand—are typical traits of mediumism. However, the fact that Alice Bailey constantly maintained her normal consciousness testifies to the extent to which she herself *was not conscious* of

---

[*] As was shown in Part One, chapter 2, Helena Roerich likewise did not consider herself to be the author of the books of *Agni Yoga*. She was convinced that they were dictated to her by Mahatma Morya, which is why they were published without her name. However, she did not consider herself as a medium but as a bearer of new spiritual capacities. But what she wrote about Blavatsky shows with full clarity that her own capacities derived from the same plane, even though they were far less developed.

herself, as did indeed happen with her, that is, the extent to which her own ego became a kind of continuation of the ego of her inspirer and came fully into his power.

To conclude this brief biographical survey one further distinctive quality of Alice Bailey's books needs to be considered. Originally these books were written and published under her own name, although from the outset she explained that they were dictated to her by the mysterious initiate who functioned in them under the name of 'the Tibetan'. Subsequently, from 1934 onwards, all these books were provided with a brief foreword entitled 'Extract from a Statement by the Tibetan',[23]* in which he proclaimed the following about himself.

'Suffice it to say, that I am a Tibetan disciple of a certain degree, and this tells you but little, for all are disciples from the humblest aspirant up to, and beyond, the Christ Himself. I live in a physical body like other men, on the borders of Tibet, and at times ... preside over a large group of Tibetan lamas, when my other duties permit ... Those associated with me in the work of the Hierarchy ... know me by still another name and office. A.A.B. knows who I am and recognizes me by two of my names. I am a brother of yours, who has travelled a little longer upon the path than has the average student ... I am not an old man ... yet I am not young or inexperienced. My work is to teach and spread the knowledge of the Ageless Wisdom wherever I can find a response, and I have been doing it for many years. I seek also to help Master M. and the Master K.H. whenever opportunity offers, for I have been long connected with Them and with Their work.'

Thus the reader of Alice Bailey's books could initially learn only little about their occult inspirer. But to the extent that the books of the 'Tibetan' become more widespread, more and more people throughout the world tried to fathom the mystery of his true name. Despite this, Alice Bailey and a small circle of pupils, following the strict order of their teacher, assiduously guarded the mystery of his name. And it would probably have remained unknown to the general public if Alice Bailey had not herself given it away. This happened in the following way. When in 1943 Alice Bailey was editing an article by D.K. for the journal *The Beacon*, signed with his own name Djwhal Khul, she forgot to delete a sentence which made it clear that he was the mysterious 'Tibetan' and the true author of all her books. Thus through this mistake of Alice Bailey the name of her inspirer was revealed. Thereafter it could no longer be

---

* Apart from four books, which, as she herself asserted, were written by her without her inspirer's participation.

concealed, and D.K. henceforth signed his books with his own name; and he even wrote about the history of his connection to Alice Bailey and briefly characterized the content of his books. (This story was published in an enclosure to Alice Bailey's *Autobiography* under the title 'My Work'.)

Now the reader of his books could, after this misadventure had revealed the true name of the 'Tibetan', turn especially to the first book, which bears the title *Initiation—Human and Solar*, and there read the following: 'The Master Djwhal Khul, or the Master D.K. . . . is the latest of the adepts taking initiation, having taken the fifth initiation in 1875 . . . He is a Tibetan. He is very devoted to the Master K.H. and occupies a little house, not far distant from the larger one of the Master . . . He is particularly learned, and knows more about the rays and planetary Hierarchies of the solar system than anyone else in the ranks of the Masters.'[24] One could also learn from this book that he inspired many doctors and therapists and also various philanthropic movements, for example the Red Cross. It also says that over the past decade (1910–20) he has taken upon himself part of the teaching work of the Masters M. and K.H., beginning with the instruction of their pupils. Moreover, it was he who dictated to Blavatsky a large part of the *Secret Doctrine* and had shown her many pictures in the spiritual world which she then used in her books. Whoever it was who was concealed behind the name D.K., it is none-theless a fact that this individuality according to his own statement, when he was working through Blavatsky or Bailey, always used them as mediums, even though in a higher way. In a similar connection, Rudolf Steiner refers in a lecture from the year 1915 to two basic rules which anyone who takes a serious interest in modern spiritual science should take into account when confronted by such a phenomenon, since the luciferic powers manifest themselves with considerable power in such a situation. 'From this will follow an infinitely significant and important law for the dissemination of spiritual-scientific truths and for working in the spiritual-scientific stream: one should be aware that all direct belief in the authority of a human being must be diminished to the extent that this person shows signs of being a medium.'[25] And as an example of such a medium Rudolf Steiner went on to cite H.P. Blavatsky.

'This personality shows strong traits of mediumship, hence it is impossible to attribute to her an authority, or at any rate it is only possible to attribute authority to her to a very small degree.' In the light of these words the fact that Djwhal Khul himself described the works that he himself telepathically dictated to Alice Bailey as a continuation and further development of Blavatsky's *Secret Doctrine* and she herself as Alice Bailey's 'predecessor' acquires a particular significance.[26]

Rudolf Steiner formulated the second rule as follows: 'For the imparting of [spiritual-scientific] teaching it is therefore really important that anyone who communicates the teaching out of the sources takes full responsibility for the teachings with his own personality and through the way he stands within the physical world rather than referring to unknown masters.'[27] And somewhat earlier in the same lecture: 'Similarly it is, I would say, an axiom in the dissemination of spiritual-scientific truths that, when the truths are published, there should never be any reference to unknown masters or mahatmas.'*

These two basic rules for the dissemination of occult knowledge *in the epoch of the consciousness soul* were not only completely ignored by Alice Bailey and also by her inspirer but were even turned into their opposite, into a new rule or a new method in accordance with which, as they said, all pupils of occultism must learn in future. Thus D.K. wrote in his book *A Treatise on White Magic* (1934) 'that I was an initiate of a certain standing but that my anonymity would be preserved'.[28] Hence it was only because of a mistake by Alice Bailey that his name inadvertently became known to a wider public. This happened at a time when her books had already reached millions of people, the meditations of the 'Tibetan' had been

---

* In the same lecture Rudolf Steiner went on to say that this second rule does not in any way mean that nothing from the teachings of true teachers should be imparted. This is not at all what is meant, but rather that anyone who imparts occult knowledge in our time *must bear full personal responsibility for it*, that is, stand openly before the world and only speak or write out of his own personal experience and not under the dictation of an anonymous mahatma concealed somewhere in the Himalayas. Thus Rudolf Steiner said: 'In the moment when there is a question of the publication of an [occult] teaching—not where one is simply saying in a small circle that something or other has been communicated to oneself and one believes it is true: these are things that can be shared between one person and another and that is an entirely different matter—in the moment, then, when there is a question of presenting an [occult] teaching to the world, the person who is presenting it has to take responsibility for it. And only someone who makes it clear through the manner of his being that he is not referring to untrue or unknown mahatmas when he is seeking to establish what he is sharing makes it understandable, makes it clearly apparent, that he as a personality living firmly on the physical plane feels a full obligation to take complete responsibility for his teaching.' Rudolf Steiner also spoke throughout his life about teachers of Christian esotericism and their deeds only in accordance with this rule and the strict occult obligation arising from it (ibid.). In complete contrast, Alice Bailey, as we have seen, in her capacity of medium rejected all responsibility for the books dictated to her and passed this on to a teacher who was unknown to everyone, whose name she and her closest pupils did all they could to keep secret to people in general. Moreover, Rudolf Steiner's further indication needs to be considered, that any anonymous dissemination of occult teaching in our time (or carried out under a pseudonym) is inspired by Lucifer (see GA 130, 17 June 1912).

translated into 16 languages and approximately 30,000 people had visited
the 'Arcane School' (by 1949).[29] Even after the secret had been exposed
D.K. never appeared in public but continued to remain in the shadows
and merely entered telepathically into contact with his pupils, maintaining that from our time 'disciples are now being trained telepathically
and the actual presence of a Master is no longer necessary'. Furthermore,
in the 'Arcane School' established by D.K. it was, as Alice Bailey reports,
the case that the individual development of pupils took second place to
cultivating group initiation: 'The old personal development is no longer
emphasized ... Disciples are being taught today to work together in
groups with the possibility of group initiations held before them, an
entirely new idea and vision.'* And in another work D.K. both imparts
and tries to establish the idea: 'Initiation is today concerned with the
group and not with the individual.'[30]

To conclude this chapter a further extract from the same lecture by
Rudolf Steiner needs to be cited which characterizes the *nature* of the
relationship between Alice Bailey and her inspirer with remarkable
exactitude, although the words to be quoted below were spoken in 1915,
that is, four years before the beginning of their collaboration. It is clear
from the context of the lecture that this extract refers mainly to one of the
numerous inspirers of Blavatsky who, at a definite point in time, took the
place of another of her inspirers whose name was 'Mahatma K.H.'.
Something similar also happened, as we have seen, in the case of Alice
Bailey, whose occult guidance also passed at a certain moment from K.H.
to another mahatma. However, the question as to whether the 'false
K.H.' of whom Rudolf Steiner spoke in his lecture is identical or not with
Alice Bailey's inspirer must remain open, as it goes beyond the limits of
the present study. What is of significance here is the extent of the correspondence between what is expressed by Rudolf Steiner and the nature
of the relationship between Alice Bailey and her inspirer. For this reason
the relevant portion of the lecture will despite its length be quoted in full.

Rudolf Steiner starts by characterizing two personalities, the 'first' of
whom has mediumistic faculties and the 'second' has a measure of occult
knowledge which he does not want to use for the good of humanity as a
whole but for certain special, national egotistic aims by means of the first
personality. And then Rudolf Steiner continues: 'Let us suppose that this
second person is not inclined to use everything that has come to him
through such a consciousness in the pure sense of universal spiritual

---

* A thorough examination of this theme can be found in the book *Discipleship in the New
Age* by Alice Bailey.

science, in the sense, moreover, of a Christian spiritual science, but he has his particular purposes in the world; let us suppose that this person belongs to a region of the world which has developed a particular world-conception in the course of its historical development and that this person has grown up within this region of the world with this world-conception; let us also suppose that he has quite particular egotistic reasons to bring this world-conception into effect in the world and with full intensity. The true occultist has no wish other than to bring into effect what can be of benefit to all humanity, he has no desire for power of any sort. But let us suppose that a person of the second kind does indeed have such desires and has the need to extend the world-conception of a limited region so that it dominates other regions of the world. If he simply goes there and implants the world-conception that he wants to bring into a dominant position, there will be some who will believe him and others who will not. Those who are of a different viewpoint will not believe him and will resist what he is doing . . .

'This is one way that the person of this second kind might behave. But he could also take another path. Through being conscious of this whole process [of how one can exert an occult influence upon other people], he has the power, for example, of exerting an influence on a person of the first kind, and if he does not merely work through his intellect but through his whole being, he can work upon his mental faculties.

'If the other person is endowed with mediumistic faculties, that is, he is able to take something in without apprehending it in the normal way, so that he receives it as a truth because it has been advanced to him by the second person, then the world-conception living in the second person streams from him to the first, who allows it to pass through his unsophisticated intellectual powers. When the first appears before mankind, what should come to light appears in an altogether different way. Where the second kind of person is concerned people would notice that he is merely representing his own views in the world, and he has the power to clothe what arises from within his being in an intellectual system, for what he gives out is also his own possession. The ego of the first person does not have it as his own inner possession but takes it from the other as something objective and represents it with his intellect—since he has not made it his own personal possession—in such a way that it has more the character of something universal. As viewed from the unsophisticated intellect of the first person it seems as though something of a universal nature were being enunciated.

'This is how it can arise that one-sided information can be brought into the world from a grey or black source. The way that it is brought into the world is not that the grey or black spiritual scientists concerned one-sidedly present it and represent their views; rather does it enter through a personality with mediumistic gifts. Such a person takes it in, passes it on and lets it work through other people. This is why such grey or black spiritual scientists are often working as mahatmas in the background, and those who appear in the world say that behind them stands the mahatma and they impart what they have to relate as a message of the mahatma.'[31]

Anyone reading these words of Rudolf Steiner who is only superficially familiar with Alice Bailey's work may counter that the mahatma dictating to her was not pursuing any specially formulated aims but was, on the contrary, merely speaking of what can be of benefit to all humanity, such as the uniting of all religions and emphasizing that love and brotherhood between all people, irrespective of their nation or race, is necessary. And could one describe his teaching as antichristian if he throughout pays Christ the fullest respect and called him 'the supreme Head of the ... spiritual Hierarchy' of the planet,[32] 'the great Lord of Love and of Compassion',[33] 'the Master of all the Masters and the Teacher alike of angels and of men'[34] and spoke of himself as no more than a humble and devoted pupil? And can one really call this mahatma, who claimed to have no aim other than that of serving Christ, a grey or black occultist?[35]

The answer to all these and similar retorts is that in true and serious occultism it is not a matter of fine words and pious assertions but of concrete, occult facts, and in the present case these give an entirely different picture. To be sure, certain aspects of the teaching of the 'Tibetan' and also various organizations and movements brought into being by him seem—especially to someone knowing nothing about occultism—very attractive and evidently capable of bringing good to the world, quite particularly because words such as 'love', 'willingness to make sacrifices', 'goodness', 'altruism' and so forth appear again and again on the pages of the books of the 'Tibetan'. And yet, as will be shown in the further pages of this book, the strongest antichristian impulses are hidden behind this façade.

We shall allow D.K. himself to speak in his own words and see how he describes the principal tasks and aims of his activity: 'The two major ideas which it was my task to bring to the attention of humanity everywhere throughout the world have been securely anchored (if I may be permitted to use such a term), and these constitute by far the most important aspect of the work which I have done. These formulated ideas are:

1. The announcement of the existence (hitherto unrecognized) of the *New Group of World Servers*. This is an effective group of

workers, intermediate between Humanity and the Spiritual Hierarchy of the planet.

2. The statement, sent out lately, in connection with the *Reappearance of the Christ*, and for the immediate consolidation of the work in preparation.

'All else that I have done in the service of the Hierarchy is of secondary importance to these two statements of spiritual *fact*.' (Italics Alice Bailey.)[36]

D.K. goes on to speak of the 'Arcane School' founded by Alice Bailey in 1933 and spiritually controlled by himself, 'its aim is to train those disciples who can implement the Plan and thus prepare for the reappearance of the Christ'. For, as he said: '. . .—with due preparation and the establishment of a pronounced tendency towards right human relations— the time had come when the Christ could again appear and take His rightful place as World Teacher.' Herein also lies the purpose of the organization 'World-Encompassing Good Will'. Alice Bailey even considers this as a special branch of the movement of the 'New Group of World Servers', which D.K. characterized as follows: 'The general staff of the Christ is already active in the form of the New Group of World Servers.' And in another context D.K. formulated his task in this respect as follows: 'That preparatory work [for the reappearance of Christ] is the major incentive lying back of all that I do, and was the prime reason for the formation of the group in the early part of this century.'[37] And finally in the year 1937 Alice Bailey and D.K. founded the so-called movement of the 'Triangles', in which the members join together in groups of three people daily at a definite time corresponding with all other triangles in the whole world and at the same time they meditate 'The Great Invocation', where the Christ is summoned to return in the *physical body* on Earth (for its text, see below).

The 'Tibetan' himself represented the system of the organizations founded with his help in the following way:

THE SPIRITUAL HIERARCHY OF THE PLANET
working through
/
THE NEW GROUP OF WORLD SERVERS
using many agencies, among them
/
THE ARCANE SCHOOL
working through
/

THE SERVICE ACTIVITIES
the Triangles, the Goodwill work, the Invocation work* allied with

/

THE LUCIS PUBLISHING COMPANY
[the books of the 'Tibetan' and Alice Bailey].

Directing his remarks to his pupils, D.K. characterizes his participation in the founding of these organizations with these words: 'Here you have a brief account of the work which I undertook on behalf of the Hierarchy and for the Christ, whom I most reverently regard as my Master.'[38] As regards the literary works of the 'Tibetan', 'other work awaits me under the reorganization of all the hierarchical efforts incident to the reappearance of the Christ and the closer relationship which will then be established between humanity and the Hierarchy' after these literary works were concluded in the year 1949.

That all the organizations enumerated and all movements of the 'Tibetan' together with the books that he dictated ultimately served the one principal purpose referred to above is confirmed by words spoken by Alice Bailey's closest collaborator, her second husband Foster Bailey. In the lecture that he gave in May 1950 in New York at the annual conference of the 'Arcane School'—whose theme was 'The Arcane School—its Esoteric Origins and Purposes'[39] he said that the 'Tibetan' in addition to writing books also concerned himself with 'inaugurating certain spiritual activities in the world which conform to the plan of operations of the Hierarchy, as worked out by them in their effort to *hasten the reappearance of the Christ*'. And he continued: 'It is only in these later years that we have come to understand how this return of the Christ has, in fact, been the keynote and climaxing objective of all that has been done.'

All this can be confirmed by the following passage from a letter of D.K.'s to his advanced pupils: 'As disciples, your place is in the senior ranks of the New Group of World Servers and your responsibility as a group is to aid a phase of the work to be done which is strictly the project of the Hierarchy as a whole. I ask you to throw your efforts into the work of preparation for the reappearance of the Christ, to further in all possible ways the distribution both of the pamphlet so entitled and the book which deals with His reappearance. The world must be flooded with the information and through the hope and expectation thus engendered may move forward into greater light, better human relations and a newer happiness.'[40]

---

*See regarding this pp. 274–8.

Thus all the movements founded by the 'Tibetan' in the first half of the twentieth century through the medium Alice Bailey had essentially *two* occult purposes: firstly, to prepare humanity for a second coming of Christ in the *physical body*, with which on this occasion all the masters of the 'Hierarchies from the Himalayas'—likewise in the physical body—will appear in order to help him to bring his 'mission' on earth to its ultimate conclusion;[41] and secondly, to reveal to humanity the mystery of this 'Hierarchy from the Himalayas', which consists in that within its context the Christ is equal to the Buddha and the Buddha to the Christ, for they each belong to one and the same hierarchic level.

Notes

1. See AU.
2. CF, p. vi.
3. AU, p. 86.
4. AU, p. 12; the following quotations ibid., pp. 33, 34, 36, 37, 38, 39, 39–40, 40.
5. AU p. 37.
6. MP.
7. See C.W. Leadbeater, *How Theosophy Came to Me*, Adyar 1986.
8. RC, p. 155.
9. EH, p. 699.
10. EH, p. 553.
11. I, p. 105.
12. EH, p. 160.
13. AU, pp. 162–3. The quotations that follow are from the same source, pp. 163, 167, 164, 166.
14. See the complete list of Alice Bailey's/the Tibetan's works on p. 359.
15. AU, p. 168; see also note 14.
16. Op. cit., p. 1; the following quotation comes from MP, p. 52.
17. AU, p. 168.
18. AU, p. 245.
19. H.P. Pisareva, 'Missiya E.P. Blavatskoi, teosophiya I Teosophskoye Obshchestvo' (The Mission of H.P. Blavatsky, Theosophy and the Theosophical Society), *AUM*, no. 3, Moscow, p. 38.
20. See Vera Petrovna von Hahn de Zhelikhovsky, *Radda-Bai—Biograficheski ocherk* ('Radda-Bai, A Biographical Sketch'), and Marie K. Neff, *Personal Memories of H.P. Blavatsky*, Rider, 1937.
21. AU, p. 164. The quotations that follow are from p. 192.
22. GA 254, 11 October 1915, likewise the quotations that follow.
23. I, p. ix, also the following quotation.
24. I, p. 57.
25. GA 162, 1 August 1915, also the following quotation.
26. AU, p. 255.
27. GA 162, 1 August 1915, also the following quotation.

28. AU, p. 254.
29. AU, pp. 193, 257, 289, also the following quotations from p. 240.
30. D–2, p. 333.
31. GA 162, 1 August 1915.
32. EH, p. 612.
33. I, p. 43.
34. RC, p. 170.
35. See EH, p. 635 and RI, p. 755.
36. EH, p. 632; the following quotations ibid., pp. 633, 634, 598.
37. D–2, p. 231; the following quotation ibid., p. 88.
38. EH, p. 635; the following quotation ibid., p. 632.
39. AU, p. 297; the following quotation ibid., p. 299.
40. D–2, p. 89.
41. See RC and EH.

2. Alice Bailey's Teaching of the Hierarchies

The Lower Hierarchy

The first indications about the Hierarchy from the Himalayas, which according to the 'Tibetan' is the only Hierarchy of our planet, can be found already in Blavatsky's *Secret Doctrine*, albeit in a thoroughly indefinite and unsystematic form. A second source is Krishnamurti's account of his supersensible experiences during his so-called first initiation.[1] A first attempt to disseminate the teaching about the hierarchy thoroughly and systematically was the first book that D.K. dictated to Alice Bailey, *Initiation, Human and Solar*, published in 1922 in America.[2] This was followed by Leadbeater's book published in Adyar in 1925, *The Masters and the Path*.[3] They all harmonize in their general features and are distinguished only in certain details. Finally, the following works by D.K. contain a whole quantity of information which essentially merely adds to what was presented in the first book.[4]

According to the sources mentioned the highest leader of the planetary hierarchy is a being called *Sanat Kumara*. As D.K. says,[5] this being came to the earth for the first time in the middle of the Lemurian epoch roughly 18 million years ago. According to Blavatsky and D.K. he came at that time from Venus.[*] He is for D.K. an incarnation of one of the seven 'heavenly human beings' or 'planetary Logoi' who stand before the throne of our solar system. Thus Sanat Kumara is the highest representative of the entire fullness of the forces of the planetary Logos, for he 'holds the same place in connection with the Planetary Logos as the physical manifestation of a Master holds to that Master's Monad'.[6][†] As to his incarnation in the Lemurian epoch, D.K. said that he did not work through a body similar to our physical body but through an etheric body. The etheric body was, however—as we shall see later—regarded in the occult system of the 'Tibetan' as a form of the most refined *physical matter*,

---

[*] With regard to the acknowledgement of this fact as the starting point of the planetary Hierarchy, Blavatsky, Bailey and Helena Roerich are all in agreement.

[†] Regarding the relationship of the planetary Logos of the Earth in this sense to that of Venus, the 'Tibetan' says that 'its [Venus'] planetary Logos is in a more advanced group of students in the cosmic sense than is our planetary Logos' (CF, p. 1179). From this one may conclude that Sanat Kumara was formerly one of the students of the planetary Logos of Venus.

which is why in another context D.K. also remarked that Sanat Kumara 'took upon Himself a physical form and was made in the likeness of man'[7] and somewhat later: 'The decision of the Planetary Logos to take a physical form produced an extraordinary stimulation in the evolutionary process.' As the highest being of our planet he bears the title 'Lord of the World' (of the universe), who is 'relatively sinless', who is also 'the greatest of all Avatars', 'the Great Sacrifice', 'the Ancient of Days' and 'the One [highest] Initiator' who guides the evolution of humanity on earth.[*] In another book D.K. also characterizes him with the words: 'Sanat Kumara has created this planet and all that moves and lives therein'.[8] Outwardly he looks like an immature 16-year-old youth, which is why he is also often called 'the Youth of Endless Summers'[9] (see his description in the vision of Krishnamurti[10]) or the ' "Eternal Youth", the One Who holds all men in life and Who is carrying His whole creation along the path of evolution to its consummation'.[11] Six of his pupils or kumars, who bring to expression the 'triple nature of the Planetary Logos', came with him from Venus to the earth.[12] They form two groups: an exoteric and an esoteric, each consisting of three members, each of whom represents one of the three principal aspects of the planetary Logos: the will or strength; love-wisdom and the active reasoning power (intelligence). Thus these seven as a whole have since this time served as the actual mediators for the working of the planetary Logos on the earth. The result of their coming to the earth and their ensuing activity was the gradual emergence of the human kingdom (that is, of man as a 'self-conscious, functioning, rational entity') out of the man-animals who had hitherto inhabited our planet.

The second consequence of their coming was the establishing of the earthly Hierarchy or the 'Hierarchy of Brothers of Light', whose midpoint is in Shamballa, which lies in a 'centre in the Gobi desert' but 'in etheric matter' and which consists of 'the matter of the second ether'. D.K. says of this: 'Shamballa, as it constitutes the synthesis of understanding where our Earth is concerned, is also the centre where the highest Will of the Solar Logos is imposed upon the Will of our planetary Logos [Sanat Kumara].'[13] Hence Sanat Kumara can also 'be regarded as a personal disciple of the Solar Logos',[14] who is, however, 'only a centre in His greater body of manifestation'.[15]

Sanat Kumara and the higher part of the members of the Hierarchy dwell constantly in Shamballa. The lower part lives in dense physical

---

[*] A reader familiar with anthroposophical literature will be struck that three in particular of these epithets, 'he who is without sin', 'the greatest of all avatars' and 'the great sacrifice', correspond to those that Rudolf Steiner gives to the Christ.

bodies in one of the Himalayan valleys inaccessible to human beings (Shigatse), or it is active as the emissary of Shamballa in the most diverse regions of the earth. In a temporal sense, however, the centre in the Himalayas is not the first centre of Shamballa on the earth. For as D.K. indicates, this was preceded by a still older centre, which emissaries of Shamballa founded in South America under the name 'Temple of Ibez', the source of the Maya culture.[16]

Of the historically familiar members of the Hierarchy who have acted openly in the past, D.K. mentions the names of Jesus of Nazareth, Shri Karachariya and Krishna, and of those belonging to the lower stage he refers to the Apostle Paul and Luther.[17]

As has already been explained, Sanat Kumara forms the head of the Hierarchy, he is the personification of the planetary Logos. He it is whom, according to D.K., Christ called his 'Father', and Shamballa, where Sanat Kumara dwells, he called the 'Kingdom of the Father': 'Frequently we read in the New Testament that "the Father spoke to Him", that "He heard a voice", and that the seal of affirmation (as it is occultly called) was given to Him. Only the Father, the planetary Logos, the Lord of the World [Sanat Kumara],[*] enunciates the final affirmative sound.'[18] Or in another context: 'The Lord of the World, the Ancient of Days, Sanat Kumara, the planetary Logos, Melchisedek.[†] He to whom Christ referred when He said, "I and My Father are One." ' [19][‡]

The closest disciples of Sanat Kumara are three of his exoteric pupils, or the three 'Pratyeka Buddhas', also called the 'Buddhas of Activity'. Together with their leader they embody the 'active, intelligent loving will'[20] of the planetary Logos on our earth. Besides them there dwell in Shamballa the three other 'esoteric Kumaras' or Buddhas; however the nature of their activity remains hidden. All seven *guide* the energy of the seven spirits before the throne of the Logos of our solar system to the earth, with the exception of Sanat Kumara, who, as already said, is a

---

[*] In the moment of the initiation of his pupils Sanat Kumara, according to D.K., identifies himself fully with the planetary Logos.

[†] In his lectures Rudolf Steiner refers to Melchisedek as an altogether different individuality who through his appearance to Abraham had the task of preparing for the appearance of Christ on the earth (see GA 123, 4 September 1910).

[‡] In one of his books D.K. draws a parallel between Sanat Kumara, who permeates the whole earthly planet with his 'energy', and the Christ, who in a similar way 'though on a much smaller scale . . . permeates, energizes and holds in coherent expression the Christian Church' (RI, p. 205). This teaching totally contradicts the results of modern spiritual research, according to which Christ has since the Mystery of Golgotha been the new guiding Spirit of the *entire earth* (GA 103, 26 May 1908).

'physical incarnation of one of the planetary Logoi' (or of the spirits before the throne). In addition to these seven there are four additional guiding 'Maharajas' or rulers of the karma of our solar system who belong to the leadership or the 'Council Chamber at Shamballa'.

Thus all in all, according to D.K., the guidance of the earth is enacted on three different, but connected planes: Shamballa—Hierarchy—Humanity,[21] forming 'the three major centres in the body of the planetary Logos'[22] corresponding to the 'head', 'heart' and 'throat centres'. Through these three centres are also active three principal rays: 'the 1st Ray of Will', 'the 2nd Ray of Love Wisdom' and 'the 3rd Ray of Active Intelligence', which represent the revelations of the three highest aspects of the Solar Logos.[23] These three principal rays are supplemented by four more: the 'Ray of Harmony through Conflict',[24] the 'Ray of Concrete Science or Knowledge', the 'Ray of Idealism or Devotion', and the 'Ray of Order or Ceremonial Magic'. Thus the totality of the seven rays is the revelation of the seven highest spirits who stand before the throne of the Solar Logos and, from thence, permeate the entire solar system.[25]*

D.K. devoted five extensive books under the general title *A Treatise on the Seven Rays* to a description of the various aspects of the working of these rays in earthly evolution and in the various spheres of human activity.

All other lower-ranking members of the Hierarchy are divided in accordance with the working of the rays into three principal and four subsidiary groups. At the head of the first three are three teachers, who, at a lower level than the 'Buddhas of Activity' referred to, represent the same threefoldness of the planetary Logos: the aspect of will, of love–wisdom and reason (intelligence). The first main group is led by 'Vaivasvata Manu'[26] or the 'Manu of the fifth root-race', the 'ideal man or thinker ... [He has] presided over its destinies since its inception nearly one thousand years ago' and took on this task shortly before the decline of Atlantis. Hence his place will shortly be taken on by the next Manu, while he is elevated to a still higher stage of development. With him also works the Manu of the fourth root race. He 'has His centre of influence in China'. (His predecessor, the Manu of the third race, has left the earth.) According

---

* At the lowest level every ray is represented by a particular master of the Himalayan Hierarchy. These seven masters are also the seven masters of theosophical teaching. Hence Josephine Ransom also begins her *A Short History of the Theosophical Society* (Adyar 1989) by characterizing this. Similarly, Leadbeater writes about the seven rays and their connection with the masters in his book *The Masters and the Path* (1925).

to the conviction of D.K. Vaivasvata Manu is physically incarnated and 'has his dwelling place in the Himalaya mountains'. From thence he 'is largely concerned with government, with planetary politics'. As he is the representative of the aspect of will and strength of the planetary Logos, he 'rais[es] and lower[s] continents'. Moreover 'He works in closer co-operation with the building devas than does His Brother, the Christ', who stands at the aforesaid level of the second aspect of the planetary Logos, that of love-wisdom.

But we shall let D.K. speak in his own words: '[The main] group two has the World Teacher for its presiding Head. He is that Great Being Whom the Christian calls the Christ; He is known also in the Orient as the Bodhisattva, and as the Lord Maitreya, and is the One looked for by the devout Mohammedan, under the name of the Iman Mahdi. He it is Who has presided over the destinies of life since about 600 BC[*] and He it is Who has come out among men before, and Who is again looked for. He is the great Lord of Love and of Compassion, just as his predecessor, the Buddha, was the Lord of Wisdom. Through Him flows the energy of the second aspect [of the planetary Logos], reaching Him direct from the heart centre of the Planetary Logos via the heart of Sanat Kumara.' As with his 'brother Vaivasvata Manu', he has—according to D.K.'s stated view—his dwelling-place in the Himalayas: 'in a physical body He can be found by those who know the way, dwelling in the Himalayas, and working in close co-operation with His two great Brothers, the Manu and the Mahachohan. Daily He pours out His blessing on the world, and daily He stands under the great pine in His garden at the sunset hour with hands uplifted in blessing over all those who truly and earnestly seek to aspire.' His most familiar past incarnation was his incarnation as Krishna in ancient India. Thus if, says D.K., 'Shri Krishna is shown to be an earlier incarnation of the Lord of Love, the Christ,'[27] this serves the union between East and West.

The third group is led by Mahachohan or the 'Lord of Civilization',[28] who has led it for considerably longer than 'His two brothers'. He has led it since the time of the second sub-race of Atlantis, whereas Manu took over the leadership of his group only at the end of Atlantis and 'Christ' 600 years before the birth of Jesus. He is the 'head of all the Adepts'.[29] He implements the forces of nature; according to D.K. He 'is largely the emanating source of electrical energy as we know it'.[30]

---

[*] That is, since the time of the Buddha's enlightenment. D.K. says in this connection: 'This office was originally held by the Buddha, but His place was taken (after His Illumination) by the Christ' (CF, p. 120).

All three of these leaders of the principal aspects of the Hierarchy are, according to D.K., *living* together with Gautama Buddha *in the physical body* somewhere in the Himalayas[*] as the principal representatives of Sanat Kumara on the earth, who with them and with their help fashions a kind of energy form which shapes the whole of humanity today: '... via His [Sanat Kumara's] four Representatives: the Buddha, the Christ, the Manu, and the Mahachohan [arise] the five points of energy which are creating the five-pointed star of Humanity at this time'.[31][†]

In all there are 63 adepts (7 × 9) in the three groups, including their three leaders, a number that is necessary for effective work on the evolution of earthly humanity.[32] Forty-nine of these are working exoterically amongst mankind and 14 esoterically. They have all reached the *fifth* initiation, which makes direct access possible to the three groups. D.K. also gives a brief characterization of some of them. Thus to the first group, the one led by Manu, belongs the 'Master Jupiter'.[33] He is the 'Regent of India [and] is looked up to by all the Lodge of Masters as the oldest among Them'. In this way the priority and supreme position of India in all spiritual matters is emphasized. He lives in the Nilgherria mountains in southern India and does not at present receive any pupils. The Mahatma Morya also belongs to this group. By descent he is a Rajput prince. 'He works in close co-operation with the Manu, and will Himself eventually hold office as the Manu of the sixth root-race. He dwells, as does His Brother, the Master K.H., at Shigatse in the Himalayas.' From there he guides the implementing of the plans of the present Manu on the earth, in that he inspires in particular various members of governments with respect to these aims.

The leading master of the second group is the Mahatma Kut Humi, who is likewise an Indian from Kashmir; he received an excellent education in England and speaks fluent English. 'The Master K.H. is in line for the office of World Teacher when the present holder of that office vacates it for higher work, and the sixth root-race comes into being'. His house in the Himalayas is near to that of the Mahatma Morya, and they work in the 'closest association'. K.H. sees the uniting of humanity as a whole as his task, and quite particularly the uniting of Western and Eastern spirituality and the great religions.

---

[*] According to D.K. Gautama Buddha is also 'physically present' in human evolution (RC, p. 46). That this assertion completely contradicts the classical Buddhist conception apparently does not trouble D.K.

[†] As in many other cases the significance of this 'five-pointed star of mankind' is never explained.

The leading teacher of the third group or the group of Mahachohan is the Master Jesus. He is 'the focal point of the energy that flows through the various Christian churches'. He is incarnated in the body of a Syrian and lives in a secret place in Palestine, from whence he inspires today many dignitaries of the Churches. D.K. then refers to several of his previous incarnations.[34] Thus he was incarnated in the Hebrew people first as Joshua, son of Nun (Navin), a helper and follower of Moses, then as Jeshua at the time of Ezra, when he received his third initiation. Then when he incarnated as Jesus of Nazareth and 'handed over [his body]' for the Christ he achieved his fourth incarnation, and, finally, when he had incarnated as Apollonius of Tyana, he received the *'fifth* initiation' and entered the circle of the 'Masters of Wisdom'.

Apart from the contradiction that the Master Jesus was supposed to be both Jesus of Nazareth and also Apollonius, who were historical contemporaries,[*] there is something else of significance in these indications. This is the relationship which in D.K.'s view existed between Jesus of Nazareth and Christ. Thus the 'Tibetan' apparently knows nothing of how the human ego of Jesus left his sheaths during the Baptism in the Jordan and offered them up to the cosmic Ego of the Christ, in which this Ego was active for three years. D.K. on the other hand speaks of their combined activity in the course of all 33 years, and nothing is said here about an incarnation but merely that the Christ 'overshadowed' Jesus, which ultimately made it possible for the Master Jesus to reach the *fifth* stage of initiation,[†] and Christ the *seventh*. But we shall let D.K. speak for himself: 'The Master Jesus crucified there [on Golgotha], felt the agony of human need and renounced His own life, and gave His all (again symbolically speaking) to meet that need. The Christ, at that time overshadowing His great Disciple, also passed simultaneously through a great initiatory experience.'[35] Thus 'at the Crucifixion initiation, the Master Jesus took the fourth initiation and the Christ took the sixth initiation'.[‡]

---

[*] It is, however, not impossible that D.K. also accepted that the historical Jesus was not born at the Turning Point of Time in Palestine but earlier, and that he was therefore not a contemporary of Apollonius. In any event, a remark of D.K.'s which will be quoted later confirms this supposition.

[†] Probably D.K. learnt only later that Jesus of Nazareth and Apollonius of Tyana were contemporaries, and then explained in later books that Jesus attained his fifth stage already during his Palestinian incarnation.

[‡] Elsewhere in the same book D.K. completely reverses the roles of the Master Jesus and the Christ: 'Forget not that in the interim between the tomb experience and the appearance in living form to His disciples, the *Master Jesus* went down into hell (figuratively speaking), carrying release for those to be found there.'

After the Crucifixion there then followed the Resurrection and Ascension, as a result of which Jesus received the fifth and Christ the seventh initiation (even though not fully). D.K. says of this: 'There are five obvious crises of initiation which concern the Master Jesus as step by step He took or re-enacted the five initiations. But lying behind this obvious and practical teaching lies an undercurrent or thread of higher revelation. This is concerned with the realizations of the overshadowing Christ as He registered the voice which is heard at the third, fifth, sixth and seventh initiations of the Master Jesus, beginning with the first and ending with the fifth. But it also gives the initiations of the Christ, starting from the second and ending with the seventh. The latter is left incomplete, and the voice is not recorded, because at the Resurrection and Ascension we are not told of the hearing of the affirmative sound. That will be heard when the Christ completes His work at the time of the Second Coming. Then the great seventh initiation, which is a dual one (love-wisdom in full manifestation motivated by power and will), will be consummated, and the Buddha and the Christ will together pass before the Lord of the World, together see the glory of the Lord, and together pass to higher service of a nature and calibre unknown to us.'

Without considering D.K.'s system of initiation in detail, one thing is fully clear from the quoted passage: the difference between the Master Jesus and the Christ consists merely of two—or to be more precise not quite two—initiatory stages.* Moreover, once he will as a result of his second appearance in the physical body have reached the full initiation of the seventh stage, the Christ will merely have become equal in rank to Gautama Buddha, who attained the seventh stage under the bodhi tree 600 years before the birth of Christ. Thereupon he will work together with him on the fulfilment of tasks which will lie beyond the bounds of earthly evolution.

It should at this point be briefly asserted that for D.K. there is, in addition to the so-called 'planetary' initiation which has for some while been the subject of discussion, the considerably higher 'cosmic' initiation, which leads not to Shamballa but much higher 'to the greater lodge of Sirius' (which is on the star of Sirius). Thus the relationship between the two kinds of initiation is of such a form that the fifth stage of the first kind corresponds to the first stage of the second kind, the sixth stage to the second and so forth.[36] This means that the Master Jesus (as also all the other masters referred to above) is at the first stage

---

* Thus D.K. said in another book: 'The sixth initiation marks the point of attainment of the Christ' (I, p. 17).

in the Sirius lodge and the Christ somewhere between the second and third stages.

To be sure, D.K. is not very consistent in formulating the planetary initiation stage of Christ. Thus later in the same book he speaks with regard to 'the story of the resurrection', 'in which the Master Jesus arose out of the tomb; [for] the chains of death could not hold Him.'[37] At that time of His "rising",* a far more important event took place and the Christ passed through the seventh Initiation of Resurrection ... The Son of God has found His way back to the Father and to His originating Source, that state of Existence to which we have given the name Shamballa.'[38] And so this path of Christ back to Shamballa is for D.K. 'the true and last resurrection'. In his view, this is where the true meaning of this event lies. 'Yet two thousand years ago the Christ did not rise out of a rocky sepulchre and reassume His discarded body. He passed through the great seventh initiation,' which 'gives the initiate the right to "come and go *in the courts of* Shamballa" [that is, in the forecourt of the kingdom of the 'Father' in the sense of D.K.].'

All that has been said makes it very apparent that the 'Tibetan' has no clear conception of the Mystery of Golgotha and hence seeks to claim this central deed of Christ as his *teaching*. Thus he writes to his pupils: 'It must be remembered that it is the teaching given by the Christ which serves humanity—not any *symbolic* death upon a cross ... This is a point which should be forcefully instilled by all of you ... This must be brought today to the consciousness of as many human beings as the followers of the Christ can reach.'[39]

Whether the Christ belongs, in D.K.'s view, to the sixth or seventh stage of initiation does not in this case have any particular significance. For in the Hierarchy there is a whole group of so-called 'Contemplative Initiates'[40] (in the East they are called 'Nirmanakayas'), who 'function in deep meditation at a point midway between the Hierarchy and Shamballa', and a still 'much higher group', consisting of still more highly developed beings, who 'function in the deepest cosmic meditation between our planet, the Earth, and our sister planet, Venus'. Moreover, 'most of the Nirmanakayas have taken the sixth and seventh initiations, while the group which functions midway between the Earth and Venus have all taken the eighth and ninth initiations'.

D.K. then refers to a category of still more sublime beings who come to

---

*It is not fortuitous that D.K. put this word in inverted commas, for the death of Jesus Christ on Golgotha is for him merely 'symbolic' (EH, p. 635; see further below), which could only be followed by a symbolic 'resurrection'.

Shamballa as emissaries from worlds lying wholly beyond the bounds of our solar system. Pre-eminent amongst these is the so-called 'Avatar of Synthesis', who is specified here because of his participation in the Second Coming (see further about this below). D.K. has this to say about him: 'The Avatar of Synthesis, Who is working in co-operation with the Christ, is one of Them. Bear in mind that these extra-planetary Avatars have not arrived at Their high state of spiritual unfoldment on our planet or even in our solar system. Their origin, source and spiritual relationships are a great mystery even to the planetary Logoi—to Whose help They go...'

By referring to beings who stand even higher than Sanat Kumara, we have departed from the logical order of our analysis. Hence before moving on to a consideration of these and other cosmic beings in the occult system of the 'Tibetan' we must conclude the description of the masters of the 'earthly' Hierarchy who are at the fifth stage of initiation and mention at least some of them.

The last of whom we spoke above was the *Master Jesus*. Even if one only fleetingly compares what D.K. says about him with the results of Rudolf Steiner's spiritual research, the impression arises that D.K., while using the same name, is really speaking about someone else. For he knows nothing—whether it be of his incarnation as Zarathustra (Zarathustra is not mentioned by him at all in the sequence of members of the Hierarchy) or as Zarathos, the teacher of Pythagoras, or of his other incarnations as spoken of by Rudolf Steiner, or, most importantly—of his true role in preparing the descent of Christ to the earth (together with Gautama Buddha).[41] Moreover, D.K.'s statement that 'the Mahommedan faith will be found to be linked to the Christian faith because it embodies the work of the Master Jesus as He overshadowed one of His senior disciples, a very advanced initiate, Mahomet'[42] seems particularly strange.

With this we arrive at a consideration of the next master, with the name of *Saint Germain*. According to D.K., he lived in the Carpathians in the physical body of a Hungarian from the lineage of the Rakoczys. D.K. mentions only two of his previous incarnations, which clearly indicate that—as in the case of the Master Jesus—there is agreement with what Rudolf Steiner said about Saint Germain only with regard to the name, behind which someone entirely different is concealed. These two incarnations are Francis Bacon and Roger Bacon. D.K. does not even suspect that Saint Germain has nothing in common with the individualities referred to, of whom the former—according to Rudolf Steiner's spiritual research—was formerly incarnated in the Arabic world and, as a result, in his incarnation in the sixteenth century as Francis Bacon brought a highly materialistic impulse to Europe,[43] whereas Roger Bacon in the thirteenth century was under the influence of the impulse of Gond-hishapur, the strongest demonic impulse in human history.[44] The true Saint Germain, in contrast, was—if one separates this personality from all the fabrications and legends associated with this name—in the eighteenth century the exoteric reincarnation of Christian Rosenkreutz, the greatest representative of Christian esotericism,[45] of which D.K. knows nothing, for his name is not mentioned among the members of the Hierarchy.

In his book[46] D.K. also mentions the Master Hilarion, who is known in theosophical circles and is said to be living today in Egypt in the physical body of a Cretan. According to D.K. he was incarnated formerly as the Apostle Paul.[*] Similarly, the Master Serapis—likewise known in theosophical circles—is living in an Egyptian physical body, whose whereabouts on the earth cannot be disclosed. All four of these masters, the Master Jesus, St Germain, Hilarion and Serapis, belong to the third group led by Mahachohan. To this group there also belongs the so-called 'Venetian Master',[47] and two 'English Masters', one of whom lives in England and 'has in hand the definite guidance of the Anglo-Saxon race ... He is behind the Labour movement throughout the world, transmuting and directing.' The last master belonging to this group is a Master P., who lives in North America and is of Irish descent. He is the inspirer of various sciences of the spirit, such as for example the Christian Science founded by Mary Baker Eddy, regarding whose illusory character Rudolf Steiner spoke on several occasions.[48]

However, it is not so very important to characterize the influence of *all* these masters of the fifth stage but, rather, the aim of their *overall* influence. Their aim and task are as follows: 'First, the work of training Their pupils and disciples to be of use in [preparing for] ... the coming of the World Teacher towards the middle or close of this present century ... Secondly, the preparation of the world on a large scale for the coming of the World Teacher, and the taking of the necessary steps before They Themselves come out among men ... The Master M., the Master K.H. and the Master Jesus will be specially concerned with the movement towards the last quarter of this century. Other Masters will participate also, but these three are the [main] ones ... '[49]

---

[*] This assertion does not prevent D.K. in his later books from making numerous sharply negative comments about Paul. Thus for example: 'In the past, the keynote of the Christian religion has been death, *symbolized* for us in the death of Christ and much distorted by St. Paul in his effort to blend the new religion which Christ brought with the old blood religion of the Jews' (RC, p. 30). And this is said of the great 'Apostle of the Gentiles', who proclaimed that without the Resurrection there is no Christianity!

Especially the following must happen through the efforts of all members of the Hierarchy: 'Prior to the coming of the Christ, adjustments will be made so that at the head of all great organizations will be found either a Master, or an initiate who has taken the third initiation. At the head of certain of the great occult groups, of the Freemasons of the world, and of the various great divisions of the Church, and resident in many of the great nations will be found initiates or Masters.'[50] 'Very definitely may the assurance be given here' that all this will happen, asserts D.K. in 1922.[*] The situation in 1995 does, however, leave one with some doubt about this.

The Higher Hierarchy

Before we address the theme of the 'Second Coming', we must turn briefly to another aspect of D.K.'s teaching about the Hierarchy. For after considering its 'lower' or 'planetary' aspect, extending from Shamballa and its Lord (Sanat Kumara) to earthly humanity, we need now to consider its 'higher' or 'cosmic' aspect, which so to speak lies 'above' Shamballa.

D.K. says of this: 'The line of relationship then extends [from Shamballa] . . . to the *life* at the very centre of our Earth's "alter ego", the planet Venus, to Jupiter and from thence to the solar Lord Himself and on to a point in the Sun, Sirius.'[51]

In his books D.K. divides the planetary Hierarchy into three stages: the highest stage of Shamballa or the 'Holy City'; the middle stage, the actual Hierarchy as such or the 'New Jerusalem'; and the lower stage of earthly humanity or 'the City, standing foursquare'.[52] The regent of the first is Sanat Kumara, he is Melchisedek,[†] the regent of the second in our time is Christ, the regent of the third is Lucifer.[‡] Between the third and the second stages (of humanity and the Hierarchy) lies the activity of D.K. himself and all the organizations that have arisen through his influence. Between the second and the first stages (the Hierarchy and Shamballa) Gautama Buddha appears as the principal mediator. As D.K. has said, his

---

[*] It is interesting that roughly at the same time (the 1920s) Leadbeater was also pursuing this aim, when he was seeking to prepare humanity for the appearance of the World Teacher in the form of Krishnamurti, making use not only of the Theosophical Society as an 'occult group' but also of Freemasonry and even the Catholic Church (see Part Three, ch. 13).

[†] See footnote on p. 223.

[‡] All this is presented in a summarizing diagram. Lucifer's significance in it is not, however, explained anywhere in the text.

task consists in 'the establishment of a more easily achieved relation between the Hierarchy and Shamballa'. But as he himself has actually completed his earthly evolution, he appears to human beings only once a year—during the Wesak festival in the Himalayas.

The highest leader of Shamballa, Sanat Kumara, who is the supreme head of the entire 'planetary Hierarchy',[53] as the physical manifestation of one of the planetary spirits or 'Logoi' belongs at the same time to a higher Hierarchy, that of the sun, and with him also the other six planetary spirits.[54] In their totality they represent the seven 'centres ... of the body'[55] of the Sun Logos. This latter, however, manifests itself not at once as a sevenfoldness but initially as a threefoldness. D.K. characterizes this as 'Will or Power', 'Love-wisdom' and 'Active Intelligence' and compares it both with the Christian trinity and also with the Indian.[56] Thus for D.K., in contrast to the traditional conception, it is not the creator of the world, Brahma, who is the highest Godhead but her destroyer, Shiva.[57] All three persons are in their capacity as the highest manifestations of the Sun Logos connected above all with the sun itself, with regard to which D.K. distinguishes three aspects or three 'solar mysteries'.[58] The first is the 'mystery of Christianity' or the 'mystery of Brahma', which is 'latent in the physical Sun'; the second is the 'mystery of Polarity or of the universal sex impulse' (Vishnu), which 'is latent in the Heart of the Sun, or the subjective Sun', and the third is the 'mystery of Fire' or the destroying Shiva, which is latent 'in the Central Spiritual Sun'. This connection of Shiva with the 'spiritual Sun' has, however, nothing in common with anything spiritual on the sun but only with purely material processes, albeit of a very highly refined composition. For what is being spoken of here are increasingly refined layers of matter, which extend from below to above, from the physical, earthly world through the seven levels of our solar system to the sphere of the Sun Logos itself. Thus according to D.K. the etheric world still belongs wholly to the physical level.* But the same is true of the astral level, the mental (lower and higher Devachan), the Buddic, the Nirvanic (Atma), the Anupadaka plane (Para-Nirvana) and also the realm of the appearance of the Sun Logos itself or the Adi plane (Maha-Para-Nirvana).[59] D.K. designates these *seven* levels as the 'cosmic-physical level'.[60] At the maximum subdivision that gives rise to them each of these levels has a 'permanent atom' of matter, corresponding to the

---

*Thus when he enumerates the members of man's becoming nature, D.K. defines the physical body as at once 'the dense physical and the etheric body' (I, p. xv) and the incorporation of Sanat Kumara as 'in physical form', where he has 'not taken a dense physical body' (CF, p. 753).

level: a physical-etheric permanent atom, an astral, mental and so forth right up to 'atomic matter'[61] or the 'permanent atom'[62] of the highest plane of Adi or Maha-Para-Nirvana. And so D.K. demands of his reader that he imagines the Sun Logos in the following way: 'Seen from cosmic levels, the sphere of the Logos can be visualized as a vibrating ball of fire of supernal glory, containing within its circle of influence, the planetary spheres likewise vibrating balls of fire [punctuation *sic*]. The Grand Man of the Heavens vibrates to a steadily increasing measure . . .'[63]

This movement of matter brought about by the Sun Logos on the highest plane of our solar system (Adi or Maha-Para-Nirvana) broadens out from thence to all other six planes down to the material world, becoming slower in the process: 'This sevenfold vibratory measure is the key of the lowest cosmic plane.'*

And even on the next level that is still higher than all the *cosmic* levels referred to (the Adi plane) D.K. conceives of the threefold Logos as being weighed down by matter. Thus the highest aspect of its Trinitarian manifestation contains the unity of spirit and matter, the second aspect their separation, the third the furnishing of matter with those principal qualities which enable it to become the 'atomic matter' or the 'permanent atom' of the next lower level (Maha-Para-Nirvana).

There then follow further ascending levels of the cosmos, which are already beyond our solar system. There are again seven of these, of which the lowest is the one described above as the 'cosmic-physical level' (with its seven great subdivisions from the physically earthly world to the Maha-Para-Nirvana). D.K. calls these levels 'cosmic astral',[64] 'cosmic buddhic', cosmic atmic', 'cosmic monadic' and 'cosmic Adi'. Still higher is a being whom D.K. calls 'cosmic Parabrahman', who is manifested initially in the trinity of the *cosmic* Shiva, Vishnu and Brahman, corresponding to the first cosmic Logos who does not reveal himself and consists of spirit-matter, and to the second cosmic Logos, the bearer of wisdom, and also to the third cosmic Logos, the bearer of creative power. This cosmic trinity then develops into a sevenfoldness and becomes the 'seven spirits before the throne of God' at the underlying stage, the 'cosmic Adi' level. Each of these seven spirits, as the centre of its energies, bears within itself seven higher Sun Logoi, each single one of whom is subdivided on the under-'lying' six cosmic planes into seven further Logoi, so that at the lowest cosmic plane (the cosmic-physical) there are ultimately 7 to the power of

---

* In all such descriptions D.K. uses the concept 'atom'. The sun, the centre of the planetary system, is by analogy the core in the midst of the atom; all beings of the solar system are separate atoms in the 'body of manifestation' of the Sun Logos and so on (CF, p. 255).

7 or 823543 Sun Logoi, *one of whom* is the Logos of our solar system,[*] who is surrounded by 5,764,801 planetary Logoi, *one of whom* descended to the earth and guides earthly evolution under the name Sanat Kumara.[65] As was said above, he is—according to D.K.—the being whom Christ in the Gospels calls His heavenly Father.

All this is clearly indicative of two tendencies. On the one hand there is a consistent belittling of the Christ Being, through the fact that He has been allotted a more than modest role in the cosmic ordering of the world only in the context of the next Earth evolution (see the next chapter), and on the other there is a maximum extension of the cosmos lying *above Him*, which turns into an inferior sort of 'infinity'. For ultimately there is nothing to suggest that the highest cosmic level of 'Parabrahman' is not in its turn the lowest level of a yet higher sevenfoldness, of, so to speak, a 'super-cosmic' or 'para-cosmic', which again forms the lowest stage of a still higher 'maha-para-cosmic' seven-foldness and so forth. Thus at each stage three arise from one layer and, from three, seven layers, and this is repeated ad infinitum. This purely mechanically numerical stacking of ever new layers upon others in a wholly abstract cosmic layered 'puff-pastry pie' does not contain on any single level a *qualitative metamorphosis* but only an ever greater refining or condensing, speeding up or slowing down of the vibrations of con-stantly the same 'cosmic material' or 'permanent atom'. It is true that D.K. speaks of matter in the same narrower sense only with regard to the seven levels of the solar system (from the physical level to Adi), which in their totality form only the lowest of the seven cosmic levels, the 'cosmic-physical'.

As regards what lies beyond the limits of the solar system, only little is said in D.K.'s books, since in his view the worlds corresponding to this lie beyond the limits of human evolution as such. From there, however, *energies* of various kinds have been constantly flowing into our solar system which support and invigorate the working of the Sun Logos. Whether these 'energies', however, are spiritual or material remains in the end an unresolved question. Thus in her own book, *The Consciousness of the Atom*,[66] consisting of lectures that she gave herself soon after the begin-ning of her collaboration with the 'Tibetan', Alice Bailey presents the following scenario:[†]

---

[*] In D.K.'s view he is connected in particular with the seven stars of the Great Bear, with the seven stars of the Pleiades and also with Sirius (see further below regarding this).

[†] In a simplified form this progression reproduces the teaching that can be found in D.K.'s book *A Treatise on Cosmic Fire* (CF, p. 1045).

First, the atom of the chemist and physicist.

Secondly, the human atom, or man.

Thirdly, the planetary atom, energized by a planetary Logos, or the Heavenly Man.

Fourthly, the solar atom, indwelt by the solar Logos, or the Deity.

For Alice Bailey has derived from her collaboration with D.K. the conviction that the material atom is not only endowed with life and consciousness but also represents the foundation of man's being, whereas man for his part must be understood as an atom within the complex body of the planetary Logos, the latter again as an atom within the body of the Sun Logos and this as an atom of still higher beings.[67] She said in this connection: 'We have for several weeks been considering the evolution of the atom from stage to stage, until we included the entire solar system under the term "atom".'[68] With this she comes to the conclusion 'that [also] the solar Logos reaches out to a consciousness beyond His own analogous to that which stretches between the atom in your body and Him'. This means that, according to Bailey's logic, the Sun Logos is merely a 'solar atom' in the body of a still higher cosmic being. D.K. describes this in the following way: '*The solar Atom*, also an individualized Life, the Son in incarnation, through the medium of the Sun [that is, the second Person of the Trinity], pursuing its own inherent cycle, yet spiralling in cyclic fashion through the heavens, and therefore, progressing through the effect of the extra-cosmic active Lives who either attract or repulse it [that is, themselves function as atoms].'[69]

This atom or cell nature, when manifested by the Sun Logos, is called by D.K. the 'cosmic Logos'. For just as human beings are cells in the body of the 'heavenly man' or one of the seven planetary Logoi, so is the latter a cell or a centre of power in the body of the 'solar Logos' and the latter a cell or atom of the 'cosmic Logos': 'The cosmic Logos of our system . . . utiliz[es] seven solar systems (of which ours is one), for the distribution of His force and [has] myriads of sevenfold groups as the cells of His body.'

In accordance with the structure of the cosmos as described above the 'cosmic Logos' exerts an influence in the next cosmic level that lies *above* the realm of the Sun Logos, designated above as the 'cosmic-astral'. (It is not difficult to calculate the number of these cosmic Logoi: 7 to the power of 6 = 117,649.)

If one takes this thought further one must accept that also the 'cosmic Logos' in the following next level above is merely a 'cell' or an atom of the super- or para-cosmic Logos and this in its turn is a part of the maha-para-cosmic Logos and so on. One indication regarding this can be found in D.K.'s teaching, that the cosmic Logos, of which our Sun Logos forms a 'cell', is the Logos of Sirius, above which are beings of the constellation of the Pleiades and above them the beings who form the constellation of the Great Bear. But what in that case can be said about less highly evolved beings such as the mahatmas or the adepts of the various stages and even the Buddha and Christ? For according to this logic they are merely atoms or cells in the body of a planetary Logos (of which there are 5,764,801 in the cosmos), which itself is only a lower member (an atom) in the endless sequence of ever more grandiose and more ghostly cosmic beings.[*]

What D.K. is trying to achieve with these highly abstract constructions is the following. If the modern reader compares in an abstractly intellectual way the structure of the cosmos as the 'Tibetan' describes it for example with the content of the book *Theosophy* by Rudolf Steiner, he must come to the conclusion that Rudolf Steiner is describing only three worlds, the physical, astral and mental,[70] whereas D.K. is speaking not only of four additional higher worlds *within* the 'cosmic-physical' level but of six further *cosmic levels*, each of which consists of seven worlds (the small levels)—similar to the three described by Rudolf Steiner. Thus Rudolf Steiner speaks only of three, whereas D.K. speaks in addition of about 46 worlds beyond these ($6 \times 7 = 42 + 4 = 46$).

The contrast between the two actually rests on something quite different. For both the supersensible worlds described in *Theosophy* are *not material*, whereas for D.K. all seven ($3 + 4$) worlds (from the physical to Adi) are material, and the 42 lying above them he describes analogously to the seven lower ones, that is, he judges the 'spiritual' on the basis of the material world which is alone accessible to him and as a result endows all further cosmic levels with the same material attributes, which are therefore distinguished from those of the 'cosmic-physical' level only quantitatively and not qualitatively. Viewed in this way D.K. would probably have also acknowledged the validity of G. Gurdjieff's[†] aphorism: 'The difference between a microbe and God consists only in the number of centres.'

Modern spiritual science has nothing in common with these and materialistic conceptions similar to them in nature. For the 'soul world'

---

[*] Atomistic thinking sits so firmly in the head of the 'Tibetan' that even the group-work of his pupils is conceived of in atomistic categories: 'This law [the third law of group-work or 'the law of service'] concerns the identification of an atom [of a member of the group] with the group interest, and the steady negation of the atom's own material interests.'

[†] With respect to both the content and also the extreme abstractedness of their cosmologies, D.K. and Gurdjieff resemble one another in many ways.

and the 'spirit world' with their seven subdivisions is in Christian esotericism not a further variation of the abstract constructions of theosophists and the 'Tibetan' but a modern presentation of that higher reality of
the *spiritual world* which Dante had described in his *Divine Comedy*. Thus
according to the context of the supersensible research carried out by
Rudolf Steiner himself and described in his *Theosophy*, the soul world
extends to the sun sphere and the 'spirit world' from the sun to the world
of the fixed stars, while the 'world of archetypes' that is to be found above
them lies *beyond the limits* not only of our solar system but of the entire
visible cosmos, even beyond the zodiac in that sublime spiritual sphere
whence the Elohim in the process of the creation of earthly man brought
the forces that are necessary for the arising of his individual ego[71] and from
whence the archetype of this ego was brought by the Christ to the earth.

Thus Rudolf Steiner describes in his books and lectures not the
quantitative structure of the astronomical cosmos but the *qualitative*
experiences arising from it of the actual path leading beyond the limits of
the visible universe, where beyond space and time lies the One Threefold
Source of all Being.

This highest divine source comes to manifestation in the created universe through the ninefold Hierarchy that serves It. In its first triad of the
Angeloi, Archangeloi and Archai that lies closest to man the creative
forces of the Holy Spirit are revealed, awakening consciousness in all
beings; in the second or middle triad of the Mights, Powers and
Dominions there is revealed the Divine Son or the Divine Word (Logos),
who through them guides the life of the solar system from the sun; and
the divine Father comes to revelation through the third, highest hierarchic triad of the Thrones, Cherubim and Seraphim, granting being to all
that exists in the created universe.

This hierarchic order can also be considered from the cosmic standpoint. Thus the first triad, working within the limits of the planetary
spheres, accomplishes the guidance of the historical development of
mankind: the Angels as the guiding spirits of individual human beings, the
Archangels as the folk spirits of individual peoples and the Archai as the
guides of successive historical epochs. The second triad, working from the
sun, imprints all beings and processes of the solar system with their
spiritual form, guiding their development from within, giving them their
faculty of movement and filling them with a higher meaning that is
permeated with wisdom. The spirits of this second hierarchic triad—since
they give form, movement and wisdom to all that exists within the
bounds of the solar system—are in spiritual science also called the Spirits
of Form, Movement and Wisdom. In this way they guide the entire solar

system from the sun. Finally the third and highest triad encompasses the whole starry cosmos beyond the limits of the solar system, filling it with the will of the divine Creator, bringing all its individual parts into harmony and imbuing all that has being with the boundless, all-embracing love of the Creator for his creation, for all the beings inhabiting it. Hence the spirits of this highest Hierarchy are in spiritual science also called Spirits of Will, Spirits of Harmony and Spirits of Universal Love.*

Thus modern spiritual science speaks out of the sources of Christian esotericism not of abstract levels, planes and subdivisions of the visible cosmos—still less of various forms of ever more refined matter and also various kinds of material forces and energies, of electricity, magnetism and countless atoms—but of the actual influence of *spiritual*, and not refined material beings in the cosmos, on earth and within man.

The same also applies to the Christian-Rosicrucian path of knowledge given by modern spiritual science. Here too it is not a question of a number of stages (Rudolf Steiner describes seven of these,[72] D.K. nine†), but of the *qualitative metamorphosis* through which the stages of imaginative, inspirative and intuitive knowledge that follow the first stage of study lead correspondingly to knowledge of the three categories of the heavenly Hierarchies and thereby to a union with the planetary, solar and starry aspects of our cosmos. However, at the centre of this path of initiation lies a knowledge of the Christ Being and of the significance of the Mystery of Golgotha for the earth. For with this cosmic-earthly event a direct connection was forged for the first time between the earth—and also the humanity that inhabits it—and the sphere of the highest spirituality lying beyond the created cosmos. Hence the modern Christian-Rosicrucian path of initiation is based from the very outset upon the experience of a relationship with the living Christ, which is only possible because of His having passed through the Mystery of Golgotha; and the aim of this path is to guide the individual human ego under the guidance of Christ upwards on the same path down which the Christ descended from the heights of spirit to the earth for the sake of this individual human 'I'.[73]

Thus Christian esotericism speaks out of actual spiritual experience of various aspects of the all-encompassing Christ Being, who is revealed

---

* See further regarding the activity of the Hierarchies in GA 13, 110 and 137 among others.

† If one takes into account certain particular aspects of initiation, nine or even twelve stages can be spoken about also from an anthroposophical standpoint (see for example the lecture of 9 February 1906, GA 97). What is, however, decisive is not the number of stages that one or another path of inner evolution has but where it is leading.

beyond the limits of the created cosmos as the divine Son or the Second Person of the Holy Trinity, *within* the cosmos as the creative Word or the Sun Logos and *on the earth* as the sole God-Man, Christ Jesus, whose divine Spirit passed on His path to the earth in the spiritual worlds through all the nine divine-spiritual Hierarchies who serve him.[74]

It would seem highly likely that Alice Bailey's secret inspirer concealed somewhere in the Himalayan foothills knows nothing about all of this. The mystery of the historically real presence of Jesus Christ and also of the Sun Logos and the Son of God remained inaccessible both to him and to the other members of his occult brotherhood. And so the path of initiation described by him—although the characterization of its individual stages bears some affinity to certain elements in the earthly life of Christ Jesus[75]—leads *not to a true knowledge of Christ's Being* but diverts his pupils along another path, which, despite the large number of its subdivisions, planes and levels does not go beyond the limits of the *physically visible cosmos* with its atomic and energy based structures but makes the transition *within the latter's bounds* to a 'Sirius path', whose significance consists in showing its followers that 'the Christian resurrection is, however—from the angle of the great Lodge on Sirius—only a minor one and a passing resurrection, though the revelation subsequently accorded is lasting and permanent in its effects'.[76] In reality, however, the Mystery of Golgotha unites the earth and the human beings inhabiting it with the highest spiritual sphere, which lies outside all categories of space and time and is, hence, *beyond the limits* of the entire starry cosmos, including Sirius and all other stars and constellations.

Thus in D.K.'s cosmological constructions we have none other than a transference into the spiritual world of that infinity of the visible worlds (the solar system) of which modern materialistic science speaks on the physical plane. Between one dimension and another there is no *qualitative metamorphosis*, which is to say, no real conception of spirit and of the spiritual world as such. This leads to the earth and its human inhabitants becoming even in a 'spiritual' respect like a particle of dust, like a microscopic atom, whereby the earth is—according to the conceptions of modern materialistic science—portrayed as being in a boundless world of space full of countless stars, galaxies, nebulas and so forth.

In his Leading Thought 'What is the Earth in Reality within the Macrocosm?' and also in his lectures Rudolf Steiner reiterates[77] that the earth, amidst the old macrocosm that surrounds us, together with man who dwells upon it will through the union of the divine Christ Being with it as a result of the Mystery of Golgotha become the seed of a new future macrocosm. For 'to the consciousness of the seer this "speck of dust", the earth, is revealed as the germ and beginning of a new-rising macrocosm, while the old macrocosm appears as a thing whose life has died away'.[78]

It appears characteristic of D.K.'s books that he describes in detail only the influence and the beings of the seven *material* planes, which in their totality constitute the 'cosmic-physical' level, whereas he offers the reader information about the higher worlds in what are for the most part wholly abstract patterns and diagrams, generally without precise elucidations.[*] From the context of his descriptions one can derive the explanation that the evolution of earthly man is confined to the framework of the present solar system, in which, moreover, the earth does not by any means occupy a high place. This follows from the ninefold structure of man's being presented by D.K.,[79] which he divides into three categories. The first category, which he also calls 'Monads', 'pure Spirit' or 'Father in Heaven', relates to the three highest aspects of man's being. It is the reflection in it of Father, Son and Spirit or of Shiva, Vishnu and Brahma. These three highest aspects are 'Will or Power', 'Love-wisdom' and 'Active Intelligence'. Then comes the second category or middle triad, also called 'the Higher Self or the Individuality'. It consists of Atma, Buddhi and the higher Manas and correspondingly to the 'Spiritual Will', 'Intuition or Love-wisdom' (which D.K. also relates to the 'Christ principle') and the 'higher or abstract Mind'.[†] Then follows the lower triad, which is called 'the Personality or the lower self'. It is formed by the lower manas, the astral body and finally the 'dense physical and the etheric body' bound together in a unity.

This structure of man's being is contrasted with a conception whereby his nine members are linked with the seven subdivisions (planes) of our solar system.[80] Its highest level (Adi or Maha-Para-Nirvana), the level of the revelation of the Sun Logos,[‡] is not attainable for man, since his highest triad as enumerated from above is only at the second level (that of the monad). At the three levels that follow in a descending succession— the atmanic, the buddhic and mental (Higher Devachan)—can be found a correspondence with the middle triad, and to the three lower levels (Lower Devachan), the astral and 'physical-etheric' level, belong corre-

---

[*] Most of these are not even original, but are simply taken from old issues of the journal *Theosophist*.

[†] In another context this is called the '*atomic* sub-plane' of the cosmic-physical level (CF, p. 327).

[‡] According to D.K. the fulfilment of the highest triad is possible for man only at the fourth to seventh stages of initiation, and of the middle triad at the first three stages.

spondingly the three members of the lower threefoldness. In this way, as has been said, *all* seven levels of our solar system referred to together form—according to D.K.—only the one lower level or layer of the cosmos, namely the '*cosmic-physical*', which is to say, they all represent a *material* layer in his occult system. (Leadbeater also presents a similar scheme in his writings, for example in his book *Man Visible and Invisible*.)

This particular form of occult materialism, which Rudolf Steiner encountered at the beginning of the twentieth century in the Theosophical Society, was characterized by him in these words: 'Materialism is still very busy with this perpetual "rarefying" [of matter], both the materialism of natural science as well as the materialism of theosophy. It distinguishes first dense matter; then etheric matter, more rarefied; and then there is the "mental" and I do not know what else—always more and more rarefied! The only difference (in this theory of rarefying) between the two forms of materialism is that the one recognizes more degrees of rarefaction than the other.'[81]

Or: 'Call it Kama-manas, or what you will, it is not spiritual, but remains materialistic!'[82]

What has been disseminated by the 'Tibetan' and before him by Leadbeater about virtually the whole visible and invisible world is indeed an occult materialism of this kind. This absolute materiality on all levels— even *beyond the limits* of our solar system—is indirectly asserted by general statements on the part of D.K. such as: 'spirit and matter are a unity'[83] or 'matter is spirit at its lowest point and spirit is matter at its highest'.[84]

These statements by D.K. correspond fully with the views of his teacher, the Mahatma K.H., who expounded them in his letters to Sinnett. There the following statements may be found: 'Spirit and matter are *one*, being but a differentiation of states not *essences*.'[85] 'In the book of Kin-te, Spirit is called the unultimate sublimation of matter, and matter the crystallization of Spirit,' whereupon the radical conclusion is expressed: 'The idea of pure spirit as a Being or an Existence—give it whatever name you will—is a chimera, a gigantic absurdity.' For 'matter *per se* is indestructible, and as I maintain coeval with spirit—that spirit which we know and can conceive of. Bereaved of Prakriti [matter], Purusha (Spirit) is unable to manifest itself—hence ceases to exist— becomes *nihil.*'

In the sense of these words the existence of 'pure spirit'—wherever in the cosmos it may be—even outside our solar system is hardly likely from the standpoint of the occult conceptions of the 'Tibetan'. For according to his teaching, *all* the levels lying above it, that is, above the cosmic-physical level of the cosmos within which the solar system lies, consist merely of etheric, astral, mental (and so forth) qualities projected into the realm of the cosmic qualities which D.K. has already defined as *material* on the lower levels of cosmic existence.

Thus the words with which Rudolf Steiner characterized Sinnett's book based upon his correspondence with the mahatmas apply entirely to D.K.'s teaching: 'It is materialism in its very worst form. The spiritual world is presented in an entirely materialistic way. No one who gets hold of *Esoteric Buddhism* can shake himself free from materialism. The subject-matter is very subtle; but in Sinnett's book one cannot get away from materialism, however lofty the heights to which it purports to carry one.'[86]

Particularly the last sentence characterizes with the greatest precision the teaching of the 'Tibetan', which when compared with Sinnett was indeed hugely intensified, so that the materialism of *Esoteric Buddhism* as seen from the heights of D.K.'s occult materialism comes to resemble a naive, childlike toy.[*]

In the scheme of the occult structure of man's being that has been outlined, two things are particularly striking. The first is the non-existence of the ego-principle in it as such, that is, the centre and inner focus of the whole of man's being which, according to Rudolf Steiner, derives from the world of the highest spirituality lying *above* the sphere of activity of all nine Hierarchies.[87]

Instead of this 'veiled holy of holies within man',[88] D.K. speaks only of the dualism of the higher and lower ego, of which the former is represented in man by the middle triad (Atma-Buddhi-Manas) and the latter by the lower triad (lower manas, astral and etheric-physical bodies). That which constitutes a link *between them* and would have to correspond to the idea of the individual ego is mentioned in the scheme merely as an 'egoic or causal body',[89] regarding whose destiny in the course of the initiation depicted by the 'Tibetan' one is told: 'Then [from the third stage of initiation onwards] disintegration or destruction ensues; the causal body

---

[*] Here is a further example from the life of the soul after death. The extent of the materialistic way that D.K. viewed the soul's existence after death may be seen from indications such as this: 'As regards the use of radio as a means of communication with the "spirit world" [here D.K. appropriately puts these words in inverted commas], the present electrical instruments are too slow in vibratory activity ... to do the work ... Yet the first demonstration of existence after death, in such a way that it can be registered upon the physical plane, will come via the radio' (P, p. 104). This is the new possibility—contacting the dead by radio! The question is, what kind of dead would these be? Souls who have wholly succumbed to Ahriman or even ahrimanic spirits who have been erroneously taken to be souls of dead people?

vanishes in a blaze of *electrical fire* and the real "man" or self [that is, the totality of the middle triad] is abstracted from the three world-bodies.'[90]

As one considers further that this causal body in D.K.'s teaching is the principal bearer or 'the centre of the egoic consciousness',[91] the process referred to of the 'destruction' of the former necessarily also means the extinguishing of the latter. This then has the consequence that the higher consciousness that man attains on the path of initiation described by the 'Tibetan' indeed becomes cosmic but is no longer individual.

This initiation process then also applies for D.K. automatically to all higher-sounding beings of the solar system. He continues: 'So will it be seen in the body of a Heavenly Man [a planetary Logos], a planetary scheme, and so likewise in the body of the [Sun] Logos, a solar system.'[92]

This omission of the ego-principle from the human organization, as happens through the 'Tibetan', is not fortuitous. It is a consequence of the fact that in the teaching of the 'Tibetan' a connection with the living Christ who passed through the Mystery of Golgotha is wholly lacking. But it is the Christ who represents the principle of the ego—the I am—of our cosmos and at the same time the macrocosmic archetype of the essential nature of the individual human being.

In this connection Rudolf Steiner referred to how the luciferic spirits will in future try to endow man prematurely with the higher members of his nature (Manas, Buddhi and Atma), while *evading* the true ego principle.[93] This would have the consequence that the higher members of man's being would remain deprived of any connection with their macrocosmic archetypes, since a connection with them is achievable only through the collaboration of the Christ, and they would therefore remain for ever *microcosmic* in their nature. Then despite certain higher faculties which those people endowed with them may attain, the possession of these higher members would not be fruitful either for the earth or for man's individual development, unless he wrests them from the luciferic spirits and places them at the service of Christ, that is, imbues them with the purest, spiritualized ego-impulse—in the sense of the words of the Apostle Paul: 'Not I, but Christ in me' (Gal. 2:20).

The second peculiarity of the scheme delineated by the 'Tibetan' is the fact that all seven cosmic levels depicted in it, corresponding as they do to the ninefold structure of man, together form only its lowest, *material* level; and this means that, according to D.K., the whole ninefold being of man as an integrating part of this aspect of the cosmos is also *itself of material nature*. And even if pure spirit exists somewhere in the cosmos (which, as we have already seen, is barely probable), this would in any event be only in the cosmic spheres lying *beyond the limits of our solar system*, and this means also beyond the limits of the earthly evolution of mankind, the effect of which would be that pure spirit would be unable to gain contact with it. Thus according to D.K. even the highest earthly adept who has attained all seven stages of initiation, that is, who in his evolution stands higher than Christ and Buddha, would have no access to it. Hence in D.K.'s scheme the 'permanent atoms', which have their origin in the seven levels referred to and are filled with 'atomic matter', also correspond to *all* seven members of man's being.[*]

Because of the inaccuracy and the materialistic nature of such ideas, Rudolf Steiner spoke several times at the end of the nineteenth century about these 'permanent atoms' which played a large part in theosophical teachings as 'something quite dreadful'.[94] Thus what are called in anthroposophy *Spirit* Self, Life *Spirit* and *Spirit* Man become in the system of the 'Tibetan' *material* members, consisting of mental, buddhic and atmanic 'permanent atoms', of energy and, as we shall see, of various kinds of electricity.

Also in this case the reader may, from an intellectual standpoint, come to the conclusion that D.K. is in his description furnishing man with a higher 'monadic triad' of which Rudolf Steiner says nothing in *Theosophy*. However, this has to do with the fact that, in the present cosmic aeon, man can only rise to Atma or Spirit Man, while his higher members as yet belong not to him but to the higher Hierarchies, which Rudolf Steiner also mentions in connection with their influence.[95] The real problem here consists in that, according to D.K., also this highest triad of man's being belongs to the material part of the cosmos, consisting purely of 'atomic matter', which is itself material in its nature. In other words, even that which D.K. calls 'pure Spirit' or the 'Father in Heaven' (see p. 241) is of *material* nature in man.

D.K. similarly thinks in a wholly material way about the three forms of fire,[†] of which the 'permanent atoms' on all seven planes of our solar system consist;[96] in the centre is 'electric fire', around this centre is 'solar fire' and at the periphery 'fire by friction', which D.K. compares as regards their cosmic aspect with the Christian Trinity: 'electric fire' is the 'Father', 'solar fire' is the 'Son' and 'fire by friction' the 'Holy Spirit'.[97] As regards

---

[*] It is true that the connection of man's higher triad with the 'permanent atom' of the monadic level is lacking in the scheme, but it can be deduced from another diagram, according to which all seven levels of the 'cosmic-physical level' consist of 'atomic matter' (I, p. xiv and CF, pp. 56 and 94).

[†] An allusion to these three forms of fire can also be found in Blavatsky's *Secret Doctrine*, to which the 'Tibetan' refers several times regarding this question.

their inner nature, however, all three forms of fire are merely three variations of one and the same omnipresent *electricity*, which represents the *energy* of Shiva, Vishnu and Brahma, that is, the energy of all three countenances of the revealed Sun Logos.[98] Of these three 'macrocosmic' forms of fire the highest is the energy of Shiva or the energy of electricity par excellence. D.K. says of this: '*Electric fire*, or the logoic Flame Divine. This flame is the distinguishing mark of our Logos, and it is that which differentiates Him from all other Logoi.'[99] Hence this Sun Logos on all levels of our solar system consists purely of electricity. Thus D.K. gives the following set of relationships in this regard:

> The Solar Logos:
> Electrical vibration . . . the plane logoic or adi [Maha-Para-Nirvana]
> Electrical light . . . . the plane monadic or anupadaka [Para-Nirvana]
> Electrical sound . . . . . . the plane of atma [Nirvana]
> Electrical colour . . . . . the plane of buddhi[100]*

After this there follow two lower forms of electricity, as appropriate for the expressions of the working of the Sun Logos on the astral and the physical-etheric level. And so D.K. can state: 'Electricity in the solar system shows itself in seven major forms . . .' according to the seven principal levels. And the sun is for D.K. merely 'a gigantic ball of electro-magnetic Forces, the store-house of universal Life and Motion', and this feeds 'the smallest atom as the greatest genius' with the 'same material'.[†] D.K. finally calls the three highest kinds of electricity the 'threefold Sacred Word',[101] whereby the second kind is '*electricity as Light*, causing spheroidal objectivity', and that is, in the opinion of D.K., 'the birth of the Son'.

It follows from further descriptions by D.K. that by the Son here he means the Sun Logos of our system, who is sometimes also called the 'cosmic Christ'. (In D.K.'s system this is, however, a completely abstract concept which has no direct relation to the real Christ, who lived in Palestine at the beginning of our era.) As regards his development, he is not at a very high cosmic stage. For 'from the cosmic point of view, as we know, our Sun is but of the fourth order [that is, it has only reached the fourth evolutionary stage] and on the lowest cosmic plane'. D.K.

---

* The same subdivision of electricity into four parts is then repeated in the planetary Logos and in man.

† D.K. has taken this description of the sun from one of the letters of Mahatma K.H. to Sinnett. It corresponds to another indication of the mahatma, that 'electricity . . . is life' (ML, p. 140).

described the birth of the Son (the Logos) in the following words: 'The Son is the product of the electrical union of "fire by friction" and electric fire, and is Himself "solar fire" or the manifestation of the other two.' And in another context D.K. says that 'the solar Logos is an Intelligence as relatively low in the order of cosmic consciousness as man is in relation to solar consciousness.* *He is but a cell* in the body of the ONE ABOUT WHOM NAUGHT MAY BE SAID [this refers to the cosmic Logos and yet higher beings].' This also concerns all planetary Logoi or 'heavenly men' who serve him, of whom one—and by no means the most advanced—is the one who guides the whole of earthly evolution, the Supreme Lord of Shamballa, Sanat Kumara: 'Each Heavenly Man is consequently the embodiment of a particular kind of electrical force which flows through His scheme ...'

The occult significance of this teaching of the 'Tibetan' concerning the atomic and electrical structure not only of the entire visible, but also the invisible, that is, 'spiritual' cosmos and its company of 'spiritual' beings including the Sun Logos and those who go beyond him together with all the Hierarchies who serve him may become more comprehensible to us if we consider what Rudolf Steiner said about electricity and magnetism.

He spoke out of the sources of modern Christian esotericism of how in the universe alongside the good or super-material (supersensible) astral and mental worlds there also exist their demonic reflections in the sub-material world, one created by Lucifer and the other by Ahriman: 'The evil astral world is the province of Lucifer, the evil Lower Devachan the province of Ahriman ...'[102] And Rudolf Steiner continued: 'When chemical action [the chemical ether] is driven down beneath the physical plane, into the evil devachanic world, magnetism arises; and when light is thrust down into the sub-material—that is to say, a stage lower than the material world—electricity arises.'

In this connection the description of the so-called 'mystery of electricity'[103] by the 'Tibetan' is particularly characteristic; for according to his teaching it consists of a knowledge of the 'threefold type of electricity' which is administered in earthly evolution by the three Buddhas of Activity or Pratyeka Buddhas standing before the throne of Sanat Kumara in Shamballa (see p. 223). The first kind of electricity 'concerns the secret of that which "substands" or "stands back", of all that is objective'; the

---

*The same applies to the 'cosmic Christ', whom D.K. occasionally equates with the Sun Logos (but never with Christ Jesus who lived on the earth) and of whom he says: 'The cosmic Christ must measure up to the stature of a "full-grown man".' (This is how D.K. interprets the Letter to the Ephesians, 4:13.)

second kind 'energizes and produces the activities of all atoms'; and the third 'deals with the electrical phenomenon which finds expression in ... light'. Thus for D.K. light is engendered from electricity, whereas from the standpoint of Christian esotericism electricity is none other than original light which Lucifer has stolen and has then been bound by him to the 'evil' (sub-sensible) astral plane. 'Electricity,' as Rudolf Steiner has said, 'is light in the sub-material state. Light is there compressed to the utmost degree.'[104] Magnetism is similarly a manifestation of the chemical ether, which Ahriman has stolen and bound to the 'evil' (sub-sensible) Lower Devachan.[*]

Thus the universe of the 'Tibetan' with all the beings inhabiting it including and extending beyond the Sun Logos who leads our system, consisting as it does purely of forces of electricity and magnetism, is none other than a reflection of the true spiritual world in the luciferic-ahrimanic mirror of the sub-physical astral and mental world.

In addition the sun is for D.K. merely 'a gigantic ball of electro-magnetic Forces, the store-house of universal Life and Motion'.[105] Moreover, these electric and magnetic forces manifest themselves on *all* levels of cosmic existence and likewise permeate all its beings: 'These three electrical manifestations—vitality, magnetism, and fohatic impulse—are to be seen at work in a solar Logos, a Heavenly Man [planetary Logos] and a human being.' And the inner connection between electricity and magnetism in the cosmos D.K. characterized as follows: '*Magnetism* is the effect of the divine ray in manifestation in the same sense that electricity is the manifested effect of the primordial ray of active intelligence.'

In reality, however, it is the chemical and light ether which correspond to earthly manifestation and intelligence and not magnetism and elec-tricity. And so this characterization harmonizes with the above description of the working of Lucifer and Ahriman, that Ahriman brings the world to its sub-physical manifestation[106] and Lucifer endows man with the abstract intellect which consists only of electrical-magnetic-atomic forces.

D.K. then makes a further quotation from the Letters of the Mahatma K.H. to Sinnett, where it is stated that electricity is the 'alter ego' of magnetism.[107] This reference to the 'similarity in nature' between the two forces brings the relationship between Lucifer and Ahriman in earthly

---

[*] In the same lecture Rudolf Steiner also spoke of the forces of the life-ether which, stolen by the Asuras and held fast by them to the 'evil' (sub-physical) Higher Devachan, will appear on earth as 'terrible destructive forces', as life-destroying atomic power. More will be said about D.K.'s relationship to these forces in chapter 5.

evolution precisely to expression. For the former entered into this evolution in the Lemurian epoch and thereby karmically brought about the entry into it of the latter in the Atlantean epoch.[108] In this sense Lucifer can rightly be called Ahriman's 'alter ego' with regard to their influence upon world evolution.[*]

Finally, D.K. also depicts the 'destruction'—described above—of individual ego-consciousness in the course of the disappearance of the 'causal body' (see pp. 243–4) as a result of the *electrical manifestation of magnetism*.[109] This destruction of the causal body is according to D.K. preceded by a further process whereby *'the entire causal body becomes radioactive* [!]', whence it follows that its destruction, in the opinion of the 'Tibetan', is like the explosion of a kind of inner atom bomb or at any rate like a gradual radioactive decomposition, which in this case takes place within the being of man himself. (From this it becomes understandable that the 'Tibetan' has a positive attitude not only to atomic energy in general but also to the dropping of the atom bomb at the end of the Second World War, which will be spoken of in chapter 5.)

In conclusion, a further feature of D.K.'s cosmological teaching needs briefly to be considered. In this teaching there are not only endless cosmic planes but also endless and ever higher stages of 'initiation'. Thus, for example, it was mentioned above that the fifth stage of earthly initiation is the first stage of initiation in the Sirius Lodge and so forth. Moreover, an initiate or supreme hierophant is necessary for each initiation. And so 'for the first two [earthly] initiations the Hierophant is the Christ, the World-Teacher',[110] then from the third to the seventh initiation Sanat Kumara appears, who is an earthly manifestation of the planetary Logos. However, he too for his part goes through a whole series of initiations, in which the solar Logos plays the role of hierophant.[111] Thus for example the planetary Logos of a less developed or 'non-sacred planet', as our earth is,[†] goes through three cosmic initiations and can as a result through the mediation of the solar Logos enter into union with 'the quality of Life which informs the Sun, Sirius'.[112] The Logos of a 'sacred' or more highly evolved planet such as Venus has already passed through five cosmic

---

[*] This is again repeated in post-Atlantean times, in that whereas the period preceding the Mystery of Golgotha was more under the influence of the luciferic powers, the period subsequent to it has been more under the influence of the ahrimanic powers (see GA 191, 1 November 1919 and 15 November 1919).

[†] The fact that through the Mystery of Golgotha the earth has been 'initiated'—in that the highest divine Being of the cosmos united himself with it—is unknown to the 'Tibetan'.

initiations and therefore not only is it 'conscious of or virtually responsive
to the life of Sirius [but] is beginning to respond consciously to the [fixed
stars'] vibratory influences of the Pleiades'. The Sun Logos too goes
through a whole series of initiations and his hierophant is a still higher
'cosmic Logos'. By virtue of his initiation the Sun Logos can not only
reach the sphere of Sirius and the Pleiades but also the still higher sphere
of the Great Bear and so forth.[113]

D.K. also connects his teaching about avatars or 'messengers' with these
ideas about initiations. He begins his description with the 'cosmic avatars',
who participate in the 'initiation of the solar Logos'.[114] Only once, at the
beginning of his development, did such an avatar visit our solar system.
D.K. calls him 'the Avatar from Sirius'. This is followed by a series of 'solar
Avatars'. They are the teachers or 'Gurus' of the planetary Logoi, and they
are also, like the previous category, 'extra-systemic visitors [i.e. from
outside our system]'. (One such is also the present 'visitor' whom D.K.
calls an 'Avatar of Synthesis', and who was referred to above.) Under these
stand the 'interplanetary avatars' and under them the 'planetary avatars' or
beings like Sanat Kumara.* At the lowest stage of this hierarchic ladder
stand finally the so-called 'human avatars'. To them belong all bodhisattvas and also the Christ, 'the coming Avatar' who in the very near
future will appear on earth in the *physical body*. Hence D.K. says: 'The
Avatars most easily known and recognized are the Buddha in the East and
the Christ in the West.'[115]

From this brief list its actual significance becomes clearly apparent: it is
that of transforming the highest divine avatar, the Christ, into the last of
the ascending sequence of illusory beings of whom the reader is unable to
form any precise conceptions from the uninformative and fragmentary
information given by the 'Tibetan'. This has the consequence that, in the
place of the actual spiritual reality of the Christ, a shadowy pseudo-reality
appears which blinds the soul and fascinates the abstract intellect but from
which there is no way of gaining access to the true sphere of the spirit,
where alone the real Christ can be found in his relationship with the
whole cosmos, the earth and mankind.

From the standpoint of spiritual science the Christ is not only the leader
of the Sun Spirits or Elohim but immeasurably more: 'Elohim is the
collective name for the Sun Beings; they had ... chosen the Sun as their

---

* The appearance of all these avatars is accompanied in its turn by a periodic influence on
the part of various 'streams of energy' in the cosmos, of which D.K. again enumerates a
whole hierarchy, consisting of planetary, interplanetary, systemic (giving rise to solar
systems), cosmic and intercosmic streams.

dwelling-place ... Christ, the highest of the Elohim, is their regent. *However, he belongs not to the Hierarchies but to the Trinity.'*[116]

If one considers D.K.'s teaching as a whole, three themes have very little place in it: the life of the soul after death in the spiritual worlds between two incarnations; the problem of evil; and a clear consideration of the questions of karma and reincarnation.

It is no accident that these three themes—to which Rudolf Steiner devoted hundreds of his lectures—are not dealt with, for they are all directly related to the mysteries of the living Christ. A true knowledge of the Mystery of Golgotha, through which the forces that can conquer death were brought to earthly evolution for the first time, has given man a new consciousness in the existence after death. For when the Christ appeared in yonder world after His sacrificial death, He filled it with that 'lightning flash of spirit' which filled it with a new light.[117] Since then the modern *Christian* initiate has been able to follow the soul of someone who has died in full consciousness through the cosmic worlds of all nine heavenly Hierarchies, whose outer expression are the spheres of the planets and the fixed stars, to the highest point of the ascent after death, the so-called 'world midnight', after which begins the descending path of the soul to the next earthly incarnation.[118]

Just as the Mystery of Golgotha is connected with the unveiling of the mysteries of death, so can the appearance of Christ in the etheric gradually endow people today with a true knowledge of the forces of evil in our cosmos and, with this, enable the foundation to be laid for their conscious overcoming.[119]

Finally, the laws of karma and reincarnation—to the knowledge of which Rudolf Steiner devoted quite especially the last year of his earthly life—are a direct result of the fact that the Christ, from our time onwards, has become the 'Lord of Karma' of the whole of earthly evolution.

Thus only their uniting with the forces of the living Christ in modern Christian initiation can provide the key to a true knowledge of these three most important mysteries of human existence.

Notes

1. See Part Three, ch. 13.
2. I.
3. MP.
4. See e.g. CF and EH.
5. See I, pp. 28–9 and pp. 38–9.
6. I, p. 29.
7. I, p. 29; the following quotations ibid., pp. 31, 28, 29.

8. RI, p. 717.
9. I, p. 38.
10. See Part Three, ch. 13.
11. EH, p. 464.
12. I, p. 29; the following quotations ibid., pp. 31, 32–3.
13. EH, p. 534.
14. RI, p. 421.
15. EH, p. 534.
16. WM, p. 379.
17. I, p. 38.
18. RI, p. 83.
19. EH, p. 287.
20. I, p. 39; the following quotations ibid., pp. 39, 40.
21. D–2, p. 214 and RI, p. 551.
22. RI, p. 551, likewise the following quotation.
23. See I, p. 49.
24. RI, p. 558 and the following quotations.
25. See I, p. 49.
26. I, pp. 41–2; the following quotations ibid., pp. 42, 43, 43–4.
27. RI, p. 254.
28. I, p. 45.
29. CF, p. 120.
30. I, p. 45.
31. RI, p. 90.
32. See I, p. 51.
33. I, p. 46; the following quotations ibid., pp. 53, 54, 56.
34. See I, p. 56.
35. RI, pp. 523–4, and the following quotations ibid., pp. 524, 86–7, 83–4.
36. I, pp. 17–18.
37. RI, p. 730.
38. RI, p. 730; the following quotations ibid., pp. 730, 730, 735.
39. EH, p. 635.
40. RI, p. 734; the following quotations ibid., pp. 734, 735, 734.
41. See GA 109, 25 May 1909, and GA 114, 19 September 1909.
42. RI, p. 254.
43. See GA 240, 27 August 1924.
44. See GA 184, 12 October 1918.
45. GA 130, 27 September 1911.
46. I.
47. I, p. 59; likewise the following quotation ibid., pp. 59–60.
48. See GA 199, 21 August 1920.
49. I, pp. 60–1.
50. I, pp. 61–2 and the following quotation.
51. D–1, p. 768.
52. EH, p. 107; the following quotations ibid., pp. 107, 348.
53. I, p. 49.

54. See I, p. 28.

55. CF, p. 256.

56. I, p. 49 and pp. 152–3.

57. I, pp. 152–3 and CF, p. 94.

58. I, p. 168; likewise the following quotation.

59. CF, p. 94. Rudolf Steiner also mentions this structure of the universe in GA 93a, 30 September 1905 and 4 October 1905.

60. I, p. xiv.

61. CF, p. 94.

62. I, p. xiv.

63. CF, p. 256; the following quotation ibid., p. 256.

64. CF, p. 344; the following quotations ibid., pp. 344, 1230.

65. See CF, pp. 344 and 347.

66. CA, the following quotation pp. 79–80.

67. CF, p. 293.

68. CA, p. 143, and the following quotation ibid., p. 154.

69. CF, p. 1045; and the following quotations ibid., pp. 353, 571, 572, 1053 and 1216.

70. GA 9, chapter 3, 'The Three Worlds'.

71. See GA 122, 22 August 1910.

72. See GA 13, the chapter 'Knowledge of Higher Worlds. Concerning Initiation', and GA 99, 6 June 1907.

73. See further in S.O. Prokofieff, op. cit. in note 44, chapter 1.

74. See further in S.O. Prokofieff, *The Twelve Holy Nights and the Spiritual Hierarchies*, ch. 2, 'The Starry Script as a Key to Anthroposophical Christology'.

75. See RI, second section, 'The Aspirant and the Great Initiations'.

76. RI, p. 741.

77. See GA 26, Letters of 1 February 1925 and 8 February 1925 and also GA 13, the chapter entitled 'Present and Future of the Evolution of the World and of Mankind', and GA 219, 31 December 1922.

78. GA 26, Leading Thought no. 154 published 1 February 1925.

79. I, p. xv and the following quotation.

80. I, p. xiv.

81. GA 201, 16 April 1920.

82. GA 201, 24 April 1920.

83. I, p. 35.

84. D–2, p. 163.

85. ML, p. 63; the following quotations ibid., pp. 141, 142, 56, 142.

86. GA 254, 11 October 1915.

87. GA 122, 22 August 1910.

88. GA 9, 'Body, Soul and Spirit'.

89. I, p. xiv.

90. CF, p. 315.

91. I, p. 217.

92. CF, p. 315.

93. See GA 130, 9 January 1912.

94. GA 258, 15 June 1923.
95. See GA 99, 2 June 1907 and GA 102, 27 January 1908.
96. CF, p. 762; and the following quotation.
97. CF, p. 4.
98. See CF, pp. 38, 41, 42 and also I, p. 153.
99. CF, p. 38.
100. CF, p. 331; and the following quotations ibid., p. 310.
101. CF, p. 319; and the following quotations ibid., pp. 319, 230, 229, 295, 230, 357.
102. GA 130, 1 October 1911, the question and answer session after the lecture.
103. CF p. 873 and the following quotation.
104. See note 102.
105. CF, p. 311; and the following quotations ibid., pp. 313, 44.
106. See GA 145, 28 March 1913 and GA 194, 23 November 1919.
107. CF, p. 311.
108. See GA 13, the chapter entitled 'The Evolution of the World and of Mankind'.
109. CF, p. 315; and the following quotation ibid., p. 543.
110. I, p. 88.
111. See CF, p. 348.
112. EA, p. 504 and the following quotation.
113. See CF, pp. 348, 349, 1052–3.
114. CF, p. 723; and the following quotations ibid., pp. 724, 722, 724, 722, 747.
115. RC, p. 10.
116. GA 110, from the question and answer session following the lecture of 21 April 1909.
117. GA 13, the chapter entitled 'Present and Future Evolution of the World and Mankind'.
118. From numerous lectures on this theme see especially GA 140, 153, 227, 231 and the karma lectures GA 235–240.
119. See GA 185, 25 October 1918. Rudolf Steiner devoted several dozens of lectures to the revelation of the mysteries of evil out of the sources of Christian-Rosicrucian esotericism. (See e.g. GA 107, 22 March 1909, and also GA 177, 184, 191, 194 and many others.)

3. The Occult Sources of Alice Bailey's Teaching of the Hierarchies

Before we consider the main theme of D.K.'s teaching, that of the Second Coming, we would like to make the attempt to form a brief summary of what has been said so far.

At the beginning of chapter 2 it was mentioned that Sanat Kumara came to the earth from Venus as the physical manifestation of the planetary Logos:[*] 'The planetary Logos of this scheme is called "the first Kumara", the One Initiator, and the statement is made[†] that He came to this planet from Venus, Venus being "the Earth's primary".'[1] D.K. goes on to explain that an incarnation of Sanat Kumara on the earth in the Lemurian epoch would have been impossible 'had not the planetary Logos of the Venus scheme been in a position to link up closely with ours'. For just as the Sun Logos received his faculty of thinking or his 'Manas' from the star Sirius and the seven Logoi (heavenly human beings) standing before him from the Pleiades, so did the planetary Logos of the earth (Sanat Kumara) receive his Manas from Venus: '*The sun "Sirius" is the source of logoic manas* in the same sense as the Pleiades are connected with the evolution of manas in the seven Heavenly Men, and Venus was responsible for the coming in of mind in the Earth chain.' D.K. explains as follows how this statement is to be understood: 'In an occult sense, Venus is to the Earth what the higher Self is to man.' For 'the coming of the Lords of Flame [Sanat Kumara and his followers] to the Earth was all under law and not just an accidental and fortunate happening',[‡] for through this fact 'is a channel being built by collective man on this planet [the earth] to its primary, Venus'.[§] And so

---

[*] H.P. Blavatsky had already referred to this in *The Secret Doctrine*.

[†] D.K. does not disclose the mystery as to from what authority he received this information, but one may suppose that it came from high-ranking members of the 'Himalayan hierarchy'.

[‡] According to information which D.K. received from his teachers, Sanat Kumara came to the earth with a large retinue: 'It has been stated that one hundred and four Kumaras came from Venus to the Earth; literally the figure is one hundred and five, when the synthesizing Unit, the Lord of the World Himself, is counted as one. There remain still with Him the three Buddhas of Activity.'

[§] For this reason 'Venus is a sacred planet and the Earth is not', according to D.K. As for what it means for a planet to be 'sacred', he explains thus: 'This means that certain of the planets are to the Logos what the permanent atoms are to man.'

since then the high 'Venusian energy' has permeated the entire planetary hierarchy of the earth. D.K.: 'Within the Hierarchy itself, the two great Messengers who have embodied the dual Venusian energy were the Buddha and the Christ.'[2]*

What is the significance of the characterization of Venus in this context as the 'Earth's primary'[3] and even as its 'higher self', whereas from the standpoint of Christian esotericism this is not Venus but the sun? In his lectures Rudolf Steiner gives an unambiguous answer to this question; he said: 'Venus is . . . the realm of Lucifer.'[4] And he continued: 'From Lucifer we learn [from spiritual research] that his domain is Venus and that the . . . physical rays of Venus which are emitted into cosmic space are symbols of the physical influence of Lucifer upon human beings.' Thus Venus is none other than the *luciferic double* of the true higher ego of the earth which originally dwelt on the sun and was wholly united with the earth only through the Mystery of Golgotha. 'The meaning of the earth [that is, its higher ego] was on the sun before the Mystery of Golgotha,' said Rudolf Steiner. 'Since the Mystery of Golgotha the meaning of the earth has been united with the earth itself.'[5]

Once we have realized this, we need to turn our attention to the Lemurian epoch and consider what actually happened at that time. Rudolf Steiner describes *two* important influences which were exerted upon earthly humanity at that time from the cosmic regions beyond the earth. Firstly there was the influence of the Spirits of Form,[†] of the seven Sun Elohim who were endowing mankind with the ego principle, making possible a union with man of the higher, spiritual triad, which consists of the germinal elements of the Spirit Self, the Life Spirit and the Spirit Man (according to theosophical terminology, Manas, Buddhi and Atman), whereas until then man had consisted only of the physical, etheric and astral bodies.

This most important event of the first half of earthly evolution happened in the following way. After the separation of the sun from the earth in the previous epoch, the moon likewise separated from it at the beginning of the Lemurian epoch.[‡] The seven Sun Elohim went to the

---

* Helena Roerich also spoke about the descent of Buddha and Christ (see Part One).

† The Spirits of Form (Powers) occupy the fourth place in the cosmic hierarchy. Beneath them stand the Angels, Archangels and Archai, above them the Spirits of Movement (Principalities), the Spirits of Wisdom (Dominions), the Spirits of Will (Thrones), the Spirits of the Harmony of the Universe (Cherubim) and the Spirits of Universal Love (Seraphim). These nine cosmic Hierarchies are also divided into three triads. The Spirits of Form stand at the lowest stage of the second triad (see *Occult Science*, GA 13, and the Foundation Stone Meditation in GA 260).

‡ See further in GA 11 and 13.

Sun as its leaders, as the Bible speaks of in the plural (Book of Genesis). Then one of them sacrificially transferred his activity to the close proximity of the earth, to the moon. He subsequently received the name Jehovah or Yahweh. In this way conditions for a state of equilibrium between the spiritual forces of the sun and the moon—forces which bring about a developmental process which is, respectively, too fast or too slow—were established for the further evolution of earthly humanity. This state of equilibrium formed at that time the indispensable precondition for the integration of the individual principle into man.

This latter process unfolded in two stages. First the six Sun Elohim again united, though on a higher level, with the Eloah Yahweh working from the moon, and so for some time they developed into what the Bible calls their higher unity or 'Yahweh-Elohim'. This had the consequence that, as Rudolf Steiner said, they 'grew beyond themselves';[6] and in order that all their creative deeds might be crowned by bestowing on man his individual ego, they were enabled to receive an impulse from the realm *above* the hierarchic cosmos, that is, from the realm *beyond* the starry worlds. For the working of the combined hierarchic cosmos, of all the Hierarchies up to the Seraphim, was not sufficient to endow man with the ego principle, that is, with what alone makes him the 'image and likeness of God', but the creative impulse had to come from the Holy Trinity that abides *above* the created cosmos, that is, from that highest sphere whence the Christ subsequently descended to the earth. Rudolf Steiner described this in the following words: 'But then help had to come [to the Yahweh-Elohim] from a realm to which we can only raise our spiritual gaze in dim apprehension, it had to come from a sphere really above that of the Seraphim.'[7] Thus the creation of earthly man as an ego being has its origin in the activity of the six Spirits of Form dwelling on the sun who, as they created man, were supported by the Eloah Yahweh from the moon and who received help for this deed from the spheres above the created cosmos. This was the first extraterrestrial influence exerted upon man in the Lemurian epoch.

The second influence was exerted soon after man had been endowed with the ego principle, and it came from a completely different direction. For hardly had earthly humanity received the gift of the independent ego principle from the Elohim than altogether different spirits immediately took an interest in it. These spirits had been retarded in their own development in the previous cosmic aeon (albeit at a stage much higher than the human level of development), and they now decided to make up for what they had failed to achieve with, as it were, the help of earthly human beings.

This second influence is also described in the Bible, in this case as the entering into earthly evolution of luciferic forces symbolized by 'the subtle serpent' in Paradise, tempting the still young ego-humanity in the form of Adam and Eve *prematurely* to taste the fruit of the Tree of Knowledge of Good and Evil. In other words: these luciferic powers sought to awaken the earthly faculty of reason, the abstract intellect within youthful humanity from the very outset. However, they did this not for man's sake but for themselves, that is, *before* the due time and in a form such as contradicted his true task and must ultimately lead mankind away from its divine creators into a particular luciferic kingdom. These luciferic beings who entered into earthly evolution in the Lemurian epoch came from the planet Venus. For all physical planets form the body of spiritual beings who, under certain circumstances, can also act independently from it, that is, they can leave it and move to other heavenly bodily vessels. When favourable conditions for this came about on the earth, 'Lucifer became independent of his [planetary] body, Venus, and [lives] on in our earthly evolution.'[8] This entry of Lucifer and his hosts into earthly evolution necessarily, of course, evoked resistance on the part of the spirits following a legitimate path of evolution, above all by the Eloah Yahweh, who of all the Spirits of Form guiding earthly evolution was the closest to mankind, since he dwelt in the moon sphere. And so from this moment there commenced the battle for mankind between Yahweh and Lucifer which has ever since run like a red thread through earthly evolution. 'So that we ... can point to the moon as the bearer of the opponent of Lucifer,' said Rudolf Steiner. For 'Yahweh or Jehovah is the opponent of Lucifer.'[9] However, in this resistance to the luciferic powers Yahweh does not by any means represent the moon principle as such but the sun principle. For just as the moon sends to the earth not its own light but sunlight that has been radiated back from it, so did all six Elohim left behind on the sun exert their influence in pre-Christian times upon mankind *through* Yahweh and were in their totality the servants and mediators of the forces of the Sun Logos. Thus the Sun Logos was able gradually to prepare His coming to the earth through Yahweh by forming the physical sheaths for His incarnation amongst the ancient Hebrew people,[*] the incarnation that was to become the turning point of earthly evolution and to give mankind the possibility of ultimately overcoming Lucifer's power. This explains why the Eloah Yahweh, from an esoteric

---

[*] The forming of these sheaths came about under the guidance of Yahweh through the forces of heredity, which he guided from the moon sphere and to which he denied Lucifer access.

standpoint, must be regarded as the servant and emissary of the Sun Logos, as one who went to the moon from the sun not for his own sake but as a deed of sacrifice and whose task it was to prepare the incarnation of the Sun Logos on earth by maintaining there a constant resistance to the power of Lucifer. Hence a lack of understanding for this cosmic mission of Yahweh must also lead to a failure to understand the mystery of the incarnation of the Sun Logos, the Christ, on the earth.

This is what happened with Blavatsky. For her the true benefactors and guides of mankind were not Yahweh and the Sun Elohim standing behind him but Lucifer, who came from Venus, and the spirits who serve him.* Thus she wrote in *The Secret Doctrine*: 'The Devil is now called Darkness by the Church, whereas in the Bible, in the *Book of Job*, he is called the "Son of God", the bright star of the early morning,[†] Lucifer ... He has been transformed by the Church into Lucifer or Satan, because he is higher and older than Jehovah and had to be sacrificed to the new dogma.'[10] This had the consequence that Blavatsky was not in a position to distinguish light from darkness, and finally their places changed. Thus she rewrote the words from St John's Gospel 'In it [the Word] was life, and the life was the light of men' as follows: 'In him (in darkness)[‡] was life; and the life was the *light* of men', for she was convinced 'Light was created out of darkness' and this light is the 'first Archangel who sprang from the depths of Chaos, [and] was called Lux (Lucifer)'.[§]

Thus under the occult influence that had been exerted upon her, Blavatsky had to come to the conclusion that *human* evolution on earth only began through luciferic spirits coming to it from Venus and endowing man with the earthly faculty of reason. She wrote: 'Lucifer, or "Light-Bearer" ... is our *Mind*—our tempter and Redeemer, our intelligent liberator and Saviour from pure animalism. Without this principle ... we would be surely no better than animals.'[11] The most important event that this endowment of mankind with reason brought about was the coming to earth of Sanat Kumara and his followers in the Lemurian epoch. Subsequently this theme also appears in D.K.'s works, and not without reason he regards himself to be the inspirer of a 'significant part' of *The Secret Doctrine*.[12]

---

* See further regarding Blavatsky's positive relationship to Lucifer and her negative relationship to Yahweh and Christ in Part One.
† That is, Venus.
‡ Blavatsky added the words in round brackets.
§ Helena Roerich agreed in her letters that '[Lucifer] is in accordance with cosmic law the leader of our planet' (letter of 10 May 1937).

In order to underline the inner connection and the spiritual relationship between Blavatsky's principal work and his own works, D.K. does
the following. For a start he dedicates to Blavatsky not only his most
extensive work (it amounts to nearly 1500 pages and gives the fullest
overview of the cosmology of the 'Tibetan'—it was called *A Treatise on
Cosmic Fire*) but he considered on her own admission that it was a continuation and further development of *The Secret Doctrine*,[*] that is, of the
book of which Rudolf Steiner said many times that it lacked any
understanding of the Christ Being.[†] Secondly, D.K. speaks in another
book about the three stages in the development of the teaching of wisdom which is given to humanity at the behest of the 'Himalayan hierarchy': 'The teaching planned by the Hierarchy to precede and condition
the New Age, the Aquarian Age, falls into three categories:

1. Preparatory, given 1875–1890 ... written down by H.P.B.
2. Intermediate, given 1919–1949 ... written down by A.A.B.
3. Revelatory, emerging after 1975 ... to be given on a world wide
   scale via the radio.

In the next century and early in the century an initiate will appear and will
carry on this teaching. It will be under the same "impression", for my task
is not yet completed.'[13]

While we shall not consider the third point further here, on the
grounds that it has not hitherto come to fulfilment, one can merely say
that there is complete consistency between points 1 and 2 with respect to
the question whether Sanat Kumara and his retinue came from Venus in
the Lemurian epoch as representatives of the luciferic impulse; and the
planetary Hierarchy described by D.K. has to be characterized as a luciferic impulse, consisting of luciferic beings who have entered into earthly
evolution.

Of particular importance here is the oft-repeated assertion of
Blavatsky's that 'Venus–Lucifer [is] the occult sister and alter ego of the
Earth'.[14] The problem of the 'alter ego'[15] has already been considered
above (see pp. 248–9) in connection with the occult relationship which,
according to D.K.'s teaching, exists between electricity and magnetism. In
both cases the expression 'alter ego' refers to the original source of luci-

---

[*] In the foreword to *Cosmic Fire*, Foster Bailey wrote that Blavatsky herself predicted the
appearance of a book in the twentieth century which would be like a 'psychological key'
to her own principal work. Possibly it was for this reason that D.K. began his book, as had
Blavatsky herself, by publishing some new 'Stanzas of Dzyan' (CF, p. viii and 11).
[†] See Part One and Part Three.

feric powers, to the 'other'—that is, not yet filled by the Christ impulse—'ego of the earth'.

Blavatsky characterizes Venus in its relationship to the earth in this sense: 'Venus, or Lucifer ... the planet, is the light-bearer of our Earth, in both its physical and mystic sense.'[16] For 'every world has its parent star and sister planet. Thus Earth is the adopted child and younger brother of Venus.'

In reality, however, the earth in its evolution is not associated with Venus but with the sun, that is, not with Lucifer but with Christ. But both have from the outset been in opposition to one another, and since ancient times a ceaseless battle has been waged between the good sun gods and their luciferic adversaries. (We have a reflection of this battle in Yahweh's opposition to the luciferic powers in the course of the historical preparation for the incarnation of the Sun Logos on the earth.) The leader of the good sun gods is the Archangel Michael, who as the heavenly arch-strategist and sublime servant of the Christ wages the battle on the one hand with the luciferic 'alter ego of the earth' and, on the other, with its 'false ego' or the illicit prince of this world (that is, with its luciferic and its ahrimanic double), in the name of the ultimate conqueror of the *higher ego* of the earth, which until the Mystery of Golgotha abided on the sun.[*]

Blavatsky also mentions this battle in *The Secret Doctrine* and refers in this respect specifically to the 12th chapter of the Book of Revelation, while placing herself wholly on the side of the Morning Star of Lucifer who is so appealing to her. She wrote: 'Hence also the War in Heaven of Michael and his Host against the Dragon (Jupiter[†] and Lucifer-Venus) ...'[17]

Regarding this battle upon which the destiny of earthly civilization depends, Rudolf Steiner had the following to say: 'There are intelligences [Spirits of Venus] which live in a continual conflict with, or I should say a continual opposition to, the intelligences of the sun. This conflict between the Venus intelligences and those of the sun played a considerable part in the ancient mysteries. People spoke with a certain justification of an on-going battle of the Venus intelligences against the sun intelligences. There were the starting points of such battles, when the Venus intelligences began to battle against the sun intelligences. There have been intensifications and culminations, there have been catastrophes

---

[*] From this also derives the opposite gesture of the symbols for the earth and Venus, the first of which points towards the victory of the Christ impulse in earthly evolution and the second to its defeat, which the luciferic spirits aim to achieve in whatever way they can.
[†] In her only dim awareness of the twofold nature of evil, Blavatsky erroneously confuses Jupiter with Ahriman.

and crises … Successive phases can be observed in everything that has been going on. And no one can understand what lives on earth as the inner impulse of history unless he knows about the battle between Venus and the sun. For battles that take place here on earth and what otherwise unfolds in the evolution of civilization—all this is an earthly reflection of this battle between Venus and the sun. This was known in ancient mysteries.'[18]

These words make it more possible to understand the source of the two hierarchies on the earth: on the one hand the one which has from the outset been oriented around the Christ and regarding which Rudolf Steiner speaks out of the sources of Christian esotericism, and on the other that which is oriented around Lucifer and of which D.K. and also his secret inspirers speak in his books.

Here, however, the question arises as to how one may reconcile the transparently luciferic source of D.K.'s inspiration with the clearly ahrimanic form of its expression, why the whole planetary Hierarchy— and indeed all D.K.'s ideas about the cosmos and its inhabitants—have such a material and physical character. In his teaching there are constant references to atoms, electricity, magnetism, energy, endless stages of ever more refined and more rapidly vibrating etheric, astral, mental material and so forth. Even Sanat Kumara appears as though incarnated in a ghostly etherically material or etherically physical body.

Before we enter into this question, we wish still to bring some actual examples from the teaching of the 'Tibetan' relating to the past and near future of human evolution. According to D.K. it was in the past the task of the adepts of the Temple of Ibez, this 'first outpost for the Shamballa Fraternity' on the earth, 'to stimulate mysticism and the stimulating of the kingdom of God within the human atom'.[19] And today in his view what is happening is the following: 'One of the results of the world condition at this time is the speeding up of all the atomic lives upon and within the planet [the earth]. This necessarily involves the increased vibratory activity of the human mechanism, with a consequent effect upon the psychic nature,* producing an abnormal sensitivity and psychic awareness.'[20] And somewhat later in the same book he says: 'We are on the verge of new breakthroughs and the atoms of the body are being tuned up for reception [of the knowledge appropriate for the Aquarian Age]. Those atoms which are predominantly Piscean are beginning to slow down their activity and

---

* Is this not like an illustration of the Marxist-Leninist thesis that matter determines consciousness? Compare also with the letter of Mahatma K.H. to Sinnett in Part One, Appendix 6.

to be "occultly withdrawn", as it is called, or abstracted, whilst those which are responsive to the New Age tendencies are, in their turn, being stimulated and their vibratory activity increased."[*] And so on.

These examples, the number of which could easily be augmented from D.K.'s works, make it clearly apparent that in this case a curious union of the efforts of both kinds of adversarial forces, the luciferic *and* the ahrimanic, is taking place. Rudolf Steiner described this phenomenon in the following manner: 'A remarkable trend has developed, namely to harbour fallacies which indeed could flourish only in the age of materialism—one might say in the age of ahrimanic deception—because Lucifer helps from within. Ahriman insinuates himself into the concepts formed of outer phenomena [such as, for example, the atom, electricity and so on] and deceives one about them. But one would see through these wiles if Lucifer did not awaken certain longings to lend force to such materialistic notions in one's [spiritual] view of the world.'[21]

As a result of such a combined working of Lucifer and Ahriman, man will 'be forced to give the spiritual itself a materialistic form'.[22] In this way, 'materialism is raised to the occult sphere, it *becomes occult materialism*',[23] or, to use another word of Rudolf Steiner's, materialism is 'super-materialized'.

However, D.K., with his atomic notions, was by no means the first. For in addition to Sinnett and to an extent also Blavatsky,[†] Leadbeater had also been particularly 'productive'. As Rudolf Steiner said, 'Leadbeater constructs spiritual worlds, spirits, angels and so forth out of . . . atoms,'[24] and he continues: 'He has done something horrible by conceiving of the spiritual world in an atomistic way, that is, the materialistic mode of thinking is introduced into the spiritual world.'[25] Thus already at the turn of the nineteenth century Leadbeater and other well-known theosophists were speaking and writing much about the 'permanent atom' and were publishing various diagrams in theosophical journals which depicted the influence of atomic matter and the permanent atom upon the various levels of cosmic existence and of which D.K. republished a whole number in his books.[26] Did he borrow these ideas from Leadbeater, or was he indeed, as he asserted, already then Leadbeater's inspirer?[27] In any event those who spoke in the Theosophical Society about the 'permanent atom' and about atoms in general had—as Rudolf Steiner formulated it—'no idea that they had simply brought materialism into the spiritual concep-

---

[*] These words were written at the beginning of 1934, that is, at the beginning of the epoch of Christ's appearance in the etheric body.
[†] See Part One.

tion of the world!'[28] The same is true of the teachings mentioned above of the etheric and astral body, of Manas, Buddhi and Atman as merely ever more refined kinds of matter. For all these teachings are simply indicative of the fact that the 'theosophists' 'did not have the will ... to make the transition from conceiving of the material to conceiving of the spiritual'.

From the occult standpoint, what is contained in this fundamental error of the theosophists—which D.K. fully shares and which he significantly intensifies in his books—is the problem of the eighth sphere or the sphere of evil in our cosmos already briefly mentioned above. We shall now consider this at greater length. According to Rudolf Steiner's spiritual-scientific research,[29] it consists in that Lucifer, since his development was retarded with respect to cosmic evolution as a whole in the aeon of Old Moon, endeavours illicitly to bring imaginations in the way that they were formed on Old Moon into present earthly evolution, and that Ahriman, working in this particular context with Lucifer, seeks to fill these imaginations out with matter which he purloins from the earthly sphere, as a result of which they acquire a shadowy, material character. The eighth sphere, into which Lucifer and Ahriman would like to draw the whole of earthly evolution, consists of this ghostly matter or imaginations that have been condensed into materiality. Viewed in this way it is not physical matter which consists of atoms but the illusory matter of the eighth sphere. 'Were it [the earth] really to consist of atoms, all these atoms would still be impregnated by formations belonging to the eighth sphere—which are perceptible only to visionary clairvoyance. These formations are present everywhere; so too is the spectre-like content of the eighth sphere which can therefore be perceived just as actual spectres are perceived. All earthly being and existence are involved here. Lucifer and Ahriman strive unceasingly to draw from the earth's substances whatever they can snatch, in order to form their eighth sphere.'[30] And so in actual fact 'wherever man dreams of matter, there in reality is Ahriman. And the atomic theory ... is grossly misleading; for the material atoms are simply the forces of Ahriman.'[31]

All the more does this apply to the notion of atoms and matter in the *spiritual* cosmos, as D.K. portrays this in his books. For all these endlessly extending planes and levels of the cosmos are none other than an 'evil infinitude' of atavistic imaginations from the time of the Old Moon conjured up by Lucifer in order to demonstrate to man the spiritual insignificance of the earth and quite especially of the coming of Christ and the Mystery of Golgotha in comparison with the bewildering and dazzling sublimity of the countless (though wholly illusory) luciferic worlds. While on the other hand Ahriman appears and tries to impregnate these luciferic worlds to their very extremities with earthly matter which he has snatched for himself. Because of this all seven levels of our solar system, from the physical to the Maha-Para-Nirvana level, appear to the 'Tibetan' to be filled with atomic matter, that is, seized hold of and permeated by ahrimanic forces, while Ahriman himself is revealed at the highest level of Adi (Maha-Para-Nirvana) as the leading *first* person of the Sun Logos or *Shiva*, the cosmic destroyer.[32]*

As for the further, yet higher levels of the cosmos, D.K. uses in describing them the concepts of 'energy' and 'forces' rather than 'matter' and 'atoms'; and this means that these still higher worlds, which are like a stairway stretching into infinity with virtually identical steps and the same ever-repeating features, still belong to Lucifer. For 'where force and matter are depicted as the constituents of the world, in the twentieth century we must substitute for them Lucifer and Ahriman; for Lucifer and Ahriman are identical with what are described as force and matter'.[33] Of particular importance here is the fact that the nine-membered being of man—as D.K. conceives of it—inclusive of his threefold monad lying above Atma, *belongs wholly to the domain of the cosmos conquered by Ahriman* (to the so-called cosmic-*physical* level), and this means that it has no direct access to the still higher cosmic-astral, cosmic-mental and so on levels at which, it is supposed, the 'pure spirit' dwells, where, however, in reality Lucifer abides with his countless illusory worlds which mirror one another endlessly and repeat one another.[†] And man, who according to D.K. with his highest, ninth member[‡] reaches the monad level, has immediately above him, at the next Adi level, Shiva,[§] who permeates *the whole cosmic existence of man with atomic matter* from above to below, *that is, with the ghostly matter of the eighth sphere.* And there is for man no way out of this ghostly matter.

---

* Rudolf Steiner speaks of Shiva as a manifestation of Ahriman in the modern world in the lecture of 27 March 1913 (GA 145). In the past, luciferic beings were revealed to humanity in the figure of Shiva.

† Beside a diagram in one of the 'Tibetan's' books one may read: 'The sub-divisions throughout the Seven Kosmic Planes [our Sun Logos is the lowest of these] must be imagined as going on *ad infinitum*' (CF, p. 1230).

‡ Paradoxically D.K. calls these three higher members of man his 'monads or the pure spirit' which, in contradiction to his definition, is nevertheless wholly made up of monadically atomic matter (see CF, p. 94).

§ It is also characteristic of D.K.'s teaching that Shiva-Ahriman appears in it not only as the highest manifestation (the first person) of the Sun Logos but also as the highest manifestation of the cosmic Logos or 'Para-Brahma', who is revealed at the *seventh cosmic level* (whereas only the first and lowest cosmic level corresponds to the Sun Logos) (see CF, pp. 818 and 1230 and also I, p. 153).

In reality the point at issue here is not that Lucifer and Ahriman have already sucked the whole cosmos into themselves (although they are trying to do so) but that their endeavour gradually to draw earthly humanity into the eighth sphere is projected on the whole cosmos, and from this sphere the cosmos must look approximately as the 'Tibetan' describes it in his books. For 'no less a prospect looms as a consequence of this intention of Lucifer and Ahriman than that the whole evolution of humanity may be allowed to disappear into the eighth sphere, so that this evolution would take a different course'.[34] This picture of the future of humanity as the eighth sphere sucks it into itself is also portrayed in D.K.'s occultly materialistic ideas about the cosmos, according to which it is filled with electromagnetic atomic substances, that is, dense ghosts of the eighth sphere. Hence taking in these ideas—to the extent that those studying them do so consistently—must slowly and incessantly lead to a kind of incarceration or imprisonment of their souls (initially, of course, wholly imperceptibly), to a kind of occult imprisonment akin to the first stage on the path to the eighth sphere. 'Such a danger of a general occult imprisonment lies in the surrounding of people everywhere with atomistic and molecular pictures. The imprisoning effect of these pictures is such that it is impossible to look at those of the *free* spirit and the stars; for the atomistic picture of the world is like a wall around man's soul—the spiritual wall of a prison house.'[35] 'Lucifer and Ahriman are engaged perpetually in shackling man's free will and in getting him to believe all sorts of things [especially ideas about atoms, energies and so forth] in order to snatch away what he makes out of these things and let it disappear in the eighth sphere.'[36] But as the soul has already been living with these ghostly luciferic and ahrimanic pictures, a corresponding 'part ... of their souls [is] wrested away and prepared for the eighth sphere'.

Both Lucifer and Ahriman understand very well that they can never wholly conquer the human soul for the eighth sphere without destroying its connection with the living Christ. The destruction of this connection is therefore their principal task. To this end, Lucifer, as we have seen, endeavours to conjure up an endless chain of ascending worlds before the human soul, in the light of which earthly history and its focal point—the Mystery of Golgotha—must appear to man as something altogether insignificant and the coming to earth of Christ at the Turning Point of Time not as an incarnation but merely as an 'overshadowing' of the human being Jesus by Him.

Ahriman, in contrast, tries to distort truth in the opposite direction by leading the human soul to believe an idea of the Christ as an initiate of the rank of a bodhisattva, who before incarnating at the Turning Point of

Time had, like Gautama, already incarnated several times amongst mankind and attained only the sixth or seventh initiation with the Mystery of Golgotha, as countless adepts on the earth or on other planets have done before him.[*] With the help of this false picture Ahriman imperceptibly prepares within the human soul an even more fatal (because of its consequences) error, namely the idea that Christ lives today somewhere in the Himalayas and that he will appear to mankind in the very near future physically as a new world teacher, in order to lead humanity during a certain time-span in its earthly history and, through this, himself to attain the next stage of initiation, which again endless streams of anonymous, but far more advanced, beings have attained before him.[†]

'Ahriman cannot get rid of Christ; but what he can do is so to transform the concept, the mental picture of Christ in the human intellect that man experiences not the Christ impulse but a mask that veils it. This means that he creates a false picture of Christ. People are exposed to the danger that, while they may talk about Christ, their intellectual picture is inspired by Ahriman ... By no means is it always the real Christ whom the adherents of Christianity call Christ.'[37]

Both the pictures of the world that we have presented as being drawn up by, respectively, Lucifer and Ahriman complement one another very well. With their help Lucifer tries to destroy a true understanding of Christ as regards His connection with the earth and the evolution of mankind, and Ahriman endeavours to annul an understanding of Christ as regards His connection with the spiritual cosmos. A person who is dazzled by Lucifer's deceptive pictures will inevitably fall into the hands of Ahriman and necessarily take refuge in the redemptive idea that Christ's coming in the physical body is imminent and that, as with a magic wand, he will from one moment to another solve all the present problems of mankind.

This state of affairs can be characterized more precisely as follows. If he succumbs to the luciferic powers, it ultimately seems to man as though the Sun Logos has absolutely nothing in common with the incarnation of Christ on the earth, that is, as though the 'Word' spoken of in the pro-logue of St John's Gospel did not 'become flesh' in Christ on the earth. This true standpoint of the *pre-Christian* mysteries, however, proves *after* the Mystery of Golgotha to be wholly luciferic, for it is in Lucifer's nature

---

[*] As we have seen, D.K. even reckons Christ among the 'pupils' (see p. 211).

[†] Compare, for example, what was cited on p. 229 about Nirmanakayas, who, according to D.K., have long reached the seventh stage of initiation.

to want to conserve the past in an illicit way in order then to carry it into the future.[38]

Ahriman, on the other hand, tries by using the fruits of Lucifer's influence to arouse in man the thought that Christ is a new 'world teacher' or another human initiate who, in common with all human beings, has had many incarnations and will appear on the earth in a physical body, in order to accomplish what he did not manage to achieve in the past because of his inadequate spiritual development.[*] It is Ahriman's ideal, one with which—especially from modern times onwards—he tries to tempt mankind ever and again anew, to put Christ forward as one of the great earthly teachers who will shortly come again magically to establish 'the kingdom of God *on earth*—thus contradicting the words 'My Kingdom is not of this world'.

For the Christ, however, a return in the physical body would imply a rejection of that high meaning of the earth with which He imbued it through the Mystery of Golgotha. Rudolf Steiner said of this: 'If Christ wanted wholly to deny Himself and regard the Mystery of Golgotha as something that never happened, He would have to incarnate [again] in a physical body of some sort ...' Hence the Christ will never again appear in a physical body, but from our time onwards He will reveal himself to humanity initially in an etheric body and subsequently in a still higher way.[39] Only the false Messiah (Antichrist) of whom He foretold, or one of the demonic beings who serve him, will appear on earth in a physical body. And anyone who speaks today (and in the future) about the return of Christ *in the physical body* is thereby serving the future Antichrist and actually preparing *his* coming to the earth.

What is of importance in this connection is a particular feature of virtually *all* D.K.'s works: evil or evil beings are very rarely and only quite incidentally mentioned in many thousands of dictated pages. Thus only rarely do vague observations appear about a 'black lodge' that exists somewhere, 'black magic' or even about the existence of a 'cosmic evil'. However, nothing precise is actually said about its source or origin—other than a brief reference to the fact that on old Atlantis occult wisdom was misused, leading to its downfall. If, nonetheless, the process of the presentation demands this in spite of everything, D.K. suddenly—instead of answering this question—brings information from the medium immersed in a deep trance where, remarkably, words about the origin of evil in the world can be related directly to the teachings of the 'Tibetan'. Thus, for example, the words: 'Evil [is] the result of the materialization of

---

[*] See the next chapter regarding this idea of the 'Tibetan'.

spirit'; it is 'purely and solely the result of the materialization of God'.[40] 'This is a great mystery,' continues the medium. But the 'Tibetan' apparently does not know this mystery despite all his assertions, for he concerns himself with this materializing of the spirit and God in his teaching only under the influence of the luciferic-ahrimanic inspirations that he has received.

Thus the stream of the 'Tibetan' and Alice Bailey is a clear testimony of the combined influence of the luciferic and ahrimanic powers today as they turn quite especially against the Christ impulse: 'It will [also] come about in the 20th century that Lucifer and Ahriman will seize hold in a quite particular way of the name of Christ,'[41] and this means 'that much of what calls itself Christian and bears the name of Christ works in an antichristian way, that the best strategy of luciferic and ahrimanic powers is to bring antichristian impulses into the world under Christ's name'.

Through being guided by their inspirations, the 'Tibetan' tried to do the same thing also in our time when he disseminated through the medium Alice Bailey the false teaching of the imminent return of Christ in a physical body among human beings.

Notes

1. CF, p. 366; the following quotations ibid., pp. 367, 347, 298, 387, 298, 1076.
2. DN, p. 141.
3. CF, p. 298.
4. GA 137, 11 June 1912.
5. GA 226, 17 May 1923.
6. GA 122, 22 August 1910.
7. Ibid. See also note 74 to chapter 2.
8. GA 129, 21 August 1911.
9. GA 136, 14 April 1912.
10. H.P. Blavatsky, *The Secret Doctrine* (1888), Vol. I, 'Cosmogenesis', p. 138, likewise the following quotation.
11. Ibid., Vol. II, 'Anthropogenesis', p. 513.
12. I, p. 58.
13. RI, p. 255.
14. H.P. Blavatsky, op. cit., Vol. I, p. 305.
15. CF, p. 298.
16. H.P. Blavatsky, op. cit., Vol. II, p. 33, and the following quotation.
17. Ibid., Vol. I, p. 202.
18. GA 232, 23 December 1923.
19. WM, pp. 379–80.
20. EH, p. 3; likewise the following quotation.
21. GA 254, 17 October 1915.

22. GA 254, 18 October 1915.
23. GA 174, 20 January 1917.
24. GA 199, 28 August 1920.
25. GA 199, 11 September 1920.
26. CF, p.1181. The diagram of the 'permanent atom' had already been published in Annie Besant's book *Ancient Wisdom* and also in several books by Leadbeater (e.g. in his book *The Chakras*).
27. In his autobiography (HT) in the chapter entitled 'Psychic Training', Leadbeater calls D.K. his teacher, who personally led him in his spiritual development.
28. GA 199, 11 September 1920.
29. Regarding the eighth sphere see GA 254, 18 October 1915 and GA 194, 21 November 1919.
30. GA 254, 18 October 1915.
31. GA 145, 28 March 1913.
32. CF, p. 817.
33. GA 176, 7 August 1917.
34. GA 254, 18 October 1915.
35. GA 227, 31 August 1923.
36. GA 254, 18 October 1915, also the following quotation.
37. GA 176, 14 August 1917.
38. CF, p. 298.
39. See GA 130, 21 September 1911; 4 November 1911; 18 November 1911.
40. See CF, p. 835.
41. GA 286, 7 June 1914 and the following quotation.

4. The Coming of the World Teacher

'Prepare men for the reappearance of the Christ. This is
your first and greatest duty.'
*(From D.K.'s circular letter to his pupils conveyed to them through
Alice Bailey in April 1948.)*[1]

As is fully apparent from D.K.'s words quoted at the end of the first
chapter, the preparation and proclaiming of the imminent return of the
Christ or the world Teacher in the physical body was from the outset the
actual purpose of the occult movement founded by Alice Bailey.

Before we turn to a consideration of D.K.'s conception of the Second
Coming, to which he himself devoted a specific book entitled *The
Reappearance of the Christ,*[*] one particular characteristic of the way that the
'Tibetan' deals with this question should be mentioned. It is a fact that in
his books he constantly changed the name of Christ, as though he
deliberately wanted to give the reader no possibility of forming a clear
conception of his true nature. For although D.K. uses designations for
Christ such as 'Son of God',[2] 'Word', 'Teacher alike of angels and of
men',[3] 'bearer of the cosmic principle of love',[4] 'Representative of
humanity and of the second divine aspect',[5] 'Avatar of Love'[6] and so on—
that is, although he frequently uses that name for him which, especially
for a Western reader, must call forth associations with the concepts of
Christian tradition—Christ is nevertheless for D.K., as we have seen,
merely an outstanding *human being* who is at the bodhisattva stage (that is,
he has reached the sixth or seventh stage of earthly initiation). We shall
cite a few questions which give an unambiguous picture of this.

'As you know, the first human being out of that "centre which we call
the race of men" to achieve this point [of initiation] was the Christ.'[7] 'His
achievement [the achievement of Christ in Palestine] was made possible
by the fact that the human family had reached a point at which it could
produce the perfect Man, Christ, the "eldest in a great family of brothers",
a Son of God, the Word made flesh.'

D.K. says the following about the 'development' of the human being
'Christ': 'So rapid was the development of the Christ, that in Atlantean

---

[*] In the brochure containing a short compendium of all D.K.'s books published by the
Lucis Press and bearing the title *Thirty Years' Work. The Books of Alice A. Bailey and the
Tibetan Master Djwhal Khul*, this book stands first in the sequence.

days He found Himself upon the Path of Probation.'[8] By 'the Probationary Path' D.K. means the stage that *precedes* the first, lowest
initiation. How future candidates for initiation deal with it is described by
D.K. as follows: 'Whilst the man is on the Probationary Path he is taught
principally to know himself, to ascertain his weaknesses and to correct
them.'[9]

Although the reader here and in certain other cases may initially have
the impression that in the teaching of the 'Tibetan' the Christ had indeed
been physically incarnated in Palestine, this is actually not the case. For
according to D.K. '[the Master Jesus] was, in His turn [in Palestine],
inspired and over-shadowed and used by His great Ideal, the Christ'.[10]*
And while Jesus did indeed undergo death on Golgotha, for the Christ
who was overshadowing him this was merely a matter of passing through
the next, sixth stage of evolution. 'As you know,' writes D.K. to his
pupils, 'He [Christ] took one of the greatest of the initiations (the sixth
initiation, that of Decision).'[11]

Despite this illusory character of the 'incarnation' of the Christ into
Jesus of Nazareth D.K. accepts that the latter's previous and subsequent
incarnations were wholly real, that is, of an actual physical nature.[12] We
have already spoken (see p. 225) about the incarnation of 'Christ' on earth
as Krishna; however, D.K. asserts that he knows of other previous
incarnations, without giving actual names: 'much has been communicated to us anent the life of the Christ, both in the Gospels and in
connection with His earlier incarnations'.[13] Moreover, D.K. understands
his present incarnation in the Himalayas not as the 'semblance' incarnation of Sanat Kumara but as a quite definite physical incarnation. We
have already cited the words of D.K. that the Christ today is 'dwelling in
the Himalayas' and daily, 'with hands uplifted', blesses the whole of
mankind, standing 'under the great pine in His garden'.[14] This is doubtless
the real description of a man who like all earthly human beings is
incarnated in a *physical body*. And so a strange picture emerges: before and
after the Mystery of Golgotha the Christ incarnates as do all human beings
in reality on the earth, while at the time of the Mystery of Golgotha he
merely 'overshadows' his pupil Jesus from above and is not physically
present. The significance of such assertions is completely clear: the distortion and obscuring of the true meaning of the Mystery of Golgotha.†

---

* The fact that, as the Christ descended into Jesus of Nazareth at the Baptism in the Jordan,
the individuality of the Master Jesus left his sheaths is clearly unknown to D.K. (see GA
148).
† See Rudolf Steiner's lecture cycle *From Jesus to Christ* (GA 131).

The designation 'Son of God' used many times with respect to Christ by D.K. has nothing in common with the use of this name in Christian circles. We shall mention here merely one of many examples in confirmation of this. D.K. speaks in one of his books about 'the three great Sons of God whose names are pre-eminent in the minds of men— Hercules, Buddha and the Christ'.[15] (It should be pointed out here that Hercules for some reason plays a particularly large part in D.K.'s teaching, which is why Alice Bailey also devoted a study of her own to him with the title *The Deeds of Hercules*.) In another book D.K. even named Hercules as a 'Sun God' and characterized the three in the following way: 'these Sons of God ... *Hercules, the Sun-God ... the Buddha ... the Christ ... embodied the essences of the spiritual life*'.[16]*

Thus the conclusion to which D.K. comes should no longer surprise us: 'The Christian Church has laid so much emphasis on Christ's unique position as the one and only Son of God that great error has crept in and has been fostered for centuries.'[17]

We shall now turn once more to the theme of this chapter. Already in her first book, *Initiation, Human and Solar*, which was dictated to Bailey in the years 1919–20 (first English edition 1922),[18] D.K. pointed to two principal tasks of the members of the Hierarchy from the Himalayas: preparing firstly the pupils and secondly humanity for the imminent coming of the world Teacher (see p. 231).

In addition to the Hierarchy, Shamballa also participates in this task, in that it avails itself of a whole group of 'Nirmanakayas' as mediators. 'Just as the Hierarchy—in this present cycle of world endeavour—is working through the New Group of World Servers,[†] so Shamballa is carrying out its intentions (as far as humanity is concerned) through this group of Nirmanakayas.[‡] This all connotes *a great centralization of the work in connection with the reappearance of the Christ*.'[19]

This more or less general information about the coming of the world Teacher before the end of the century was subsequently in 1945 made

---

*Thus for D.K. the spiritual difference between Hercules, Buddha and Christ consists simply in the combination of the three cosmic rays active within them: 1, 2 and 6 (see note 16), that is, those rays with which Master M. (first ray), Master K.H. (second ray) and the Master Jesus (sixth ray) are especially connected. In addition, according to D.K.—as we have seen—Christ is not the Son of that heavenly Father who is spoken of in the Gospels and in Christian tradition but merely a son of Sanat Kumara, who lives in his semblance body in Shamballa, which lies somewhere beyond the Gobi Desert (RI, pp. 83–4, and p. 222).

† See p. 216.

‡ See p. 229.

more specific and precise by D.K. through an event which he described as follows: 'The agony of the war, and the distress of the entire human family led Christ, in the year 1945, to come to a great decision—a decision which found expression in two most important statements. He announced to the assembled spiritual Hierarchy and to all His servants and disciples on Earth that He had decided to emerge again into physical contact with humanity, *if* they would bring about the initial stages of establishing right human relations; secondly, He gave to the world (for the use of the "man in the street") one of the oldest prayers ever known, but one which hitherto had not been permitted to be used except by the most exalted, spiritual beings. He used it Himself for the first time, we are told, at the time of the Full Moon of June, 1945.'[20] (Italics by D.K.)

This meditation, which was also called 'the great Invocation' or 'the world prayer', has since then appeared on the first page of *all* books by D.K. and Alice Bailey:

> From the point of Light within the Mind of God
> Let light stream forth into the minds of men.
> Let Light descend on Earth.

> From the point of Love within the heart of God
> Let love stream forth into the hearts of men.
> *May Christ return to Earth.*

> From the centre where the Will of God is known
> Let purpose guide the little wills of men—
> The purpose which the Masters know and serve.

> From the centre which we call the race of men
> Let the Plan of Love and Light work out
> And may it seal the door where evil dwells.

> Let Light and Love and Power restore the Plan on Earth.

D.K. then gave this 'world prayer', as he asserted, 'to the world—under instruction from the Christ'.[21] Since then it has not belonged 'to any person or group but to all humanity'.[22] Regarding this 'Prayer' itself he said: 'Forget not, They also use this great Invocation and that *not a day goes by that the Christ Himself does not sound it forth.*'[23] (Italics by D.K.) Hence D.K. again and again urges upon his pupils in his writings: 'I would ask you to use it daily [it was preceded by two other less important ones] and as many times a day as you can remember to do so.'[24] And elsewhere he says: 'Prepare men for the reappearance of the Christ. This is your first and greatest duty. The most important part of that work is teaching men—on a large scale—to use the Invocation so that it becomes a world prayer and focuses the invocative demand of humanity.'[25]

For D.K. the most important part was the line with the cry, 'May Christ return to Earth,' of which he wrote: 'One should place the strongest *emphasis* on the words "to Earth"; we must pronounce them with all our will, so that the "qualities" or "energies" that have been invoked may come down all the more surely and effectively to Earth.'[26] (Italics by D.K.)

We shall now turn to the content of the 'Invocation', which D.K. explains as follows: 'In the first two verses of the Invocation now used throughout the world the work of Buddha and Christ is emphasized.'[27] (According to D.K.'s teaching, Buddha is the avatar of illumination and wisdom and Christ the avatar of love.)[28] The third verse clearly relates to the next, third avatar or world teacher who will come after Christ, in order to reveal to mankind the highest will of God. D.K. gives the following information about him: 'His task, in many ways, is far more difficult than that of the two preceding Avatars [Buddha and Christ], for ... He carries the will of God into manifestation, and of that will we, as yet, know really nothing.'[29]

D.K. gradually reveals the mystery of this avatar who is to come only in the more distant future and who will some day occupy Christ's place in the Himalayan Hierarchy when the latter completes his task and ascends higher on the hierarchic ladder of stages. D.K. emphasizes his own relationship to him: 'We are forever linked as workers in the one Hierarchy and under the leadership of the Christ and His Successor in a distant century [the coming of the third avatar is probably being addressed here].'[30]

And in a later letter to his pupils (November 1944) D.K. finally reveals to them not only the 'mystery' of the third avatar but also his own connection with him: 'There are within the ranks of disciples certain of them who have been singled out for a peculiar and particular relation to the Christ. Such a one is the Master K.H. [Kut Humi],* Who is slated (is that not the word I should use?) to fill higher office when the Christ moves on to other work than that of the World Teacher. I myself [D.K.] hold a similar position to the Master K.H.'

And so as the bodhisattva Maitreya Christ had taken Buddha's place in the Himalayan Hierarchy once the latter had become a Buddha in the sixth century before Christ, so in the future when the Maitreya has completed his earthly task and has ascended to the Buddha stage will the

---

*Which is why in the third verse of the 'Invocation' the word 'Master' is used.

new 'bodhisattva' or 'world Teacher' K.H.* take his place in the Hierarchy, and the place as 'Master' will go to his easily most advanced pupil,
D.K. This explains why the 'Tibetan' was entrusted by the Hierarchy
with the task of preparing the return of Christ to the earth.

With respect to the fourth verse, this is to enable the gate to the sphere
of 'cosmic evil'[31] on earth to be closed, as D.K. explains in the following
way: 'The true nature of cosmic evil finds its major expression in wrong
thinking, false values and the supreme evil of materialistic selfishness and
the sense of isolated separativeness.' According to D.K.'s teaching the
appearance of this 'cosmic evil' in the twentieth century (through 'evil
men in every land'), which can only be overcome with the help of the
'Invocation' of the planetary Hierarchy, was preceded by two manifestations of this evil: during the decline of the Roman Empire and during
the rulership of the decadent French kings.†

The 'Tibetan' himself described as follows the significance and place of
this 'Invocation' within his overall work of preparing for the imminent
coming of the world Teacher: 'The first of the methods which will lead to
the eventual physical reappearance of the Christ has already been set in
motion; disciples and initiates in all lands are starting the work preparatory
to the outpouring of the Christ spiritual force, leading to the awakening of
the Christ consciousness ... in the hearts of men. This outpouring will
come as the result of three activities,' which D.K. described thus: the work
of pupils and initiates themselves, which will spread belief in the imminent
coming of the world Teacher amongst human beings everywhere; then
the desire for his coming on the part of the masses, and—most important—
the general use of the 'Invocation'. For the second line of the first verse calls
forth illumination on the mental plane (that is, understanding for the
Second Coming), the second line of the second verse makes the 'outpouring of the Christ spirit' into the masses on the astral plane possible, and
the second line of the third verse, which speaks of the highest or ultimate
'purpose', furthers the *'physical* appearance of Christ'.

---

* In another book D.K. brings this thought still more decisively to expression: '... the
Master K.H. will assume the role of World Teacher in the distant future when the Christ
moves on to higher and more important work than dealing with the consciousness of
humanity' (EH, pp. 643–4; see also D–2, p. 596).
† According to D.K. this 'cosmic evil' represents the second, dangerous category of evil;
the first category is the 'innate tendency to selfishness and to separation which is inherent
in the substance of our planet'. (In contrast to the second, mankind has to deal with this
first kind of evil without calling upon the Hierarchy.) However, it is very difficult to
recognize the difference between the *two* categories of evil from the quotations cited (both
were dictated in 1940).

This interpretation does not, however, by any means exhaust the meaning of the 'Invocation', for it refers at the same time to yet higher beings. Thus through Christ today there works a '*Spirit of Peace* [of world love] . . . a Being of tremendous cosmic potency [who] is today overshadowing the Christ in much the same manner as Christ (two thousand years ago) overshadowed or worked through the Master Jesus'.[32] D.K. does not explain to his readers what kind of a being this is, but he simply says—mysteriously—that the activity of this being on earth will become 'fully'[33] perceptible with the Second Coming. To be sure, 'this spiritual being will not descend from the high place whereon He works and from whence His energy is directed, but the Christ will serve as the channel for His directed potency'.

Finally, a special 'guest' of our solar system will also participate in the reappearance of Christ—the 'Avatar of Synthesis' abiding in the spiritual worlds who 'owing to the stupendous task confronting Christ [seeks to] fortify Him'.[*]

As a result these two beings, according to D.K., form together with Gautama Buddha a high 'energy' or 'Triangle of Force',[34] which will exert its influence upon the earth through the physical Christ during the Second Coming. In the 'Invocation' the three words 'light, love and power' in the last verse refer to this triangle, which D.K. interprets as follows: 'the energy of the Buddha: Light, for the light ever comes from the East; the energy of the Spirit of Peace: Love, establishing right human relations; the energy of the Avatar of Synthesis: Power, implementing both light and love'.[35] This 'Invocation' has, moreover, the further significance that it 'links the Father [the Lord of Shamballa, Sanat Kumara], the Christ and humanity in one great relationship', in 'one great *Triangle of Energies*'.

According to D.K.'s intentions the 'Invocation' that he had given to mankind was to be disseminated throughout the earth and amongst all nations. It was to be the new 'world prayer' and take the place of the most important Christian prayer, the 'Lord's Prayer', and thus serve as a foundation for a new world religion (more will be said about this later on). 'This new Invocation, if given widespread distribution, can be to the new world religion what the Lord's Prayer has been to Christianity.'[37]

---

[*] Regarding him see pp. 230 and 250. In another book D.K. imparted the following about this being's relationship with the Christ: 'This Avatar [of Synthesis] works today as one of the senior Members of the Great White Lodge and is in close touch with the Christ, with the Manu and with the Lord of Civilization . . .' (EH, p. 304). Hence the Christ will at his Second Coming 'come forth as the Representative of the Avatar of Synthesis and as His transforming Agent' (EH, p. 304). What will take place, therefore, is a 'dual event—the coming of the Avatar of Synthesis to the Hierarchy and of the lesser Avatar, His Representative, to humanity' (EH, p. 309).

Already by the year 1948, that is, only three years after its initial publication, this 'Invocation' had, thanks to D.K.'s books and pamphlets, been
widely distributed both by the organizations founded by him and also by
radio and the press, so that D.K. was able to say: 'Its extraordinary potency
can be seen in the fact that hundreds of thousands of people are already using
it day by day and many times a day; it is translated into forty eight different
languages and used by people in all these languages . . . It goes forth over the
radio in Europe and America and there is no country or island in the world
where its use is unknown. All this has taken place in the space of a few years.'
And one year later (1949) he writes to his pupils: 'Already this Invocation is
doing much to change world affairs—far more than may appear to your eyes
. . . I ask you, therefore, during the coming years to prepare to use and
distribute the Invocation and make it a major endeavour.'[38]

As already indicated above, D.K. considers the line 'May Christ return
to Earth' to contain the central words of the Invocation. But how does he
conceive of this 'return'? We shall allow him to speak for himself.

'From the quiet mountain retreat where He has waited, guided and
watched over humanity and where He has trained His disciples, initiates
and the New Group of World Servers, He must come forth and take His
place prominently on the world stage; take His part in the great drama
which is being played. This time, He will play His part, not in obscurity as
He previously did before the eyes of the entire world. Because of the
smallness of our little planet, and because of the prevalence of radio, of
television and the rapidity of communication, His part will be watched by
all . . . He does not come as the omnipotent God of man's ignorant
creation, but as the Christ, the Founder of the Kingdom of God on Earth,
to complete the work He started [in Palestine].'[39]

And elsewhere in the same book he says: 'No one knows in what
nation He will come; He may appear as an Englishman, a Russian, a
Negro, a Latin, a Turk, or any other nationality. Who can say which? He
may be a Christian or a Hindu by faith, a Buddhist or of no particular faith
at all.' 'He may reappear in a totally unexpected guise; who is to say
whether He will come as a politician, an economist, a leader of the people
(arising from the midst of them), a scientist or an artist?' 'The radio, the
press and the dissemination of news will make His coming different to
that of any previous Messenger; the swift modes of transportation will
make Him available to countless millions, and by boat, rail and plane they
can reach Him: through television, His face can be made familiar to all,
and verily "every eye shall see Him".'

If one reads such descriptions, one has to think of *A Short Story of
Antichrist* by Vladimir Soloviev, a story that D.K. probably did not know,

since he would otherwise certainly not have dared to express such analogies and comparisons to his readers ...

In another book D.K. describes the appearance of the world Teacher still more concretely: 'His coming in the air might be interpreted literally to mean that at the right time He will come by plane from the place on earth [from the remote valleys of the Himalayas] where He has been for many generations, watching over the sons of men; the words [from the Gospel] "every eye shall see Him" might mean that, by the time He comes, television will have been perfected and He will then be seen, by its means, from even the most distant spot on earth. To the orthodox Christian, the above will sound like the rankest blasphemy, but the question immediately arises: Why should it be blasphemy for Him [the world Teacher] to use modern methods? Whilst on earth before, He conformed to the customs of His time. "Riding on the clouds of heaven" may sound more picturesque and apparently require a greater expression of divinity, but why use such a means when a plane will equally well fulfil the purpose and carry the prophecy to completion?'[40]

As one reads these words written in August 1946 one is especially struck by how Rudolf Steiner, 30 years before, had anticipated their content quite literally as the most fatal error and at the same time as the principal means in the battle against the great truth of the Second Coming, the coming of Christ not in a physical but in a supersensible, etheric body. Rudolf Steiner spoke thus in a lecture that he gave on 1 August 1915: 'Therefore a genuine spiritual science recognizes it as the greatest conceivable error to suppose that the Christ, as He is united now [since the Mystery of Golgotha] with earth existence, could appear before mankind spatially confined within one single human being. It would be the gravest misapprehension of the Christ to assert that there could be a reincarnation of Christ at the present time, and that if He perhaps wished to speak in the future to—let us say—a person in Europe and then to someone in America, He would have to go by train and steamer in order to travel from Europe to America. That will never happen. He will always be raised above the laws of space and time. We must conceive of His appearance in the twentieth century as being raised above these laws ...[*]

---

[*] Thus Rudolf Steiner also spoke in other lectures of how Christ, when in a supersensible, etheric body, will be capable of being 'in two, three, even in a hundred or thousand places at the same time' without needing means of transport or the mediation of the mass media (GA 130, 1 October 1911), revealing himself to human beings in whom the capacity for a new etheric or 'natural' clairvoyance will develop over the next 2500–3000 years, a faculty which can enable Christ to be beheld in the adjoining spiritual world! (ibid.)

'It would therefore be, or rather it is, flying in the face of genuine spiritual science to assert that there could ever be a human reincarnation of Christ Jesus.'[41]

From the standpoint of Christian esotericism, no compromise is possible on this central question. Hence the teachings and movements founded by D.K. must in an occult respect be regarded as a conscious endeavour 'to eradicate the Christ principle from Western culture ... But this would be the same as eradicating the essential meaning of the Earth',[42] which would be a black magical deed of vast proportions. And so one must view the mysterious author or authors of this teaching from the standpoint of Christian esotericism as an emissary of those black magical schools which are trying in our time to put the physical Christ in the place of the etheric Christ and the earthly in the place of the etheric Second Coming, and hence prepare the appearance of the Antichrist.*

Already in 1910 Rudolf Steiner indicated that 'there [will] *around 1933* be many emissaries of black-magical circles who will falsely proclaim a *physical* Christ'.[43] In this connection it is striking that the 'Tibetan' founded through Alice Bailey an occult movement under the name of the 'New Group of World Servers' at the end of 1932 which today extends throughout the world. D.K. himself wrote in 1943, when he recalled its founding: 'Another phase of my work came into existence about ten years ago'[44]—that is, *1933*. The task of this movement or organization was, according to Bailey, to form 'the nucleus of the coming world civilization [the Aquarian age] and [it] was characterized by the qualities that would distinguish that civilization during the next 2,500 years'. Rudolf Steiner, however, pointed on many occasions to these next 2500–3000 years as the time when the revelations of the *etheric* Christ will gradually spread amongst mankind.[45] Then in the same year of 1932 came a further movement of world 'goodwill', to whose development—according to Bailey—she and the 'Tibetan' devoted themselves from 1933 until 1939.[46] The task of this movement was to bring about peace and cooperation in human relationships and also to spread throughout the world the books that the 'Tibetan' had dictated.† But the actual purpose of all these movements and the entire literature was to prepare the *physical* appearance of Christ as the new world Teacher (see p. 217f.).

Barely a month later, Rudolf Steiner spoke once again of the time when the message of the false Messiah as Christ in the physical body will be disseminated amongst mankind. He referred to this as the extending of

---

* See further at the end of the chapter.
† See *Thirty Years' Work. The Books of Alice A. Bailey and the Tibetan Master Djwhal Khul.*

materialism 'even to the spiritual conceptions of the world', where it will have a 'particularly baneful influence'.[47] He then spoke of the time approaching the middle of the twentieth century as one when the advent of the physical Christ will be propagated; and he also emphasized the particular responsibility of anthroposophy, which will 'grow immensely' because of the need to create a counterbalance to this false proclamation—above all between 1930 and 1950—by means of the truth of the etheric Christ. (The book *The Reappearance of the Christ* [1948] appeared in precisely this period; and 'the great Invocation' became generally known from 1945 onwards.)

Thus Rudolf Steiner said at the end of the lecture that has just been quoted: 'Because we are to enter into a new relation to Christ in the first half of this century, it must be repeatedly emphasized during the coming decades and until the event occurs that false Christs will arise who will knock at the doors of those who are only able to be materialists in the realms of spiritual science, and who can imagine a new relationship to Christianity if they see him before them in the flesh. A number of false Messiahs will turn this to their own use and say: Christ has reappeared in the flesh!' In this way the worst forms of modern materialism will not merely be drawn upon but also promoted, above all on a spiritual plane. And if humanity follows such a false Messiah to the extent that the appearance of Christ in the etheric—which is what is really taking place— passes everyone by, mankind 'will be cast into dreadful misery'.

In this connection the year specified by D.K. of 1945 also acquires a special significance, when the world Teacher living in the Himalayas shall have finally decided to appear to human beings in a physical body. Rudolf Steiner, on the other hand, had already indicated in early lectures of the second decade of the twentieth century that in the period from approximately 1930/1933 until 1945 human beings will begin to perceive the etheric Christ.[48] Subsequently, in 1924, he added prophetically that the appearance of the forces of the Sun Demon was about to impinge upon earthly evolution from 1933 onwards, the demon who is described in the Book of Revelation as the beast with the number 666 and whose forces entered upon the stage of European history with the accession to power of Hitler and his helpers. Rudolf Steiner spoke as follows in this lecture of 1924: 'Before the etheric Christ can be comprehended by human beings in the right way, humanity must first cope with encountering the beast who will rise up in 1933 ...'[49]*

---

* What is meant here is not, of course, the appearance of the beast *itself* in human form, which will happen only in the far apocalyptic future, but of a human instrument (see GA 104).

This impulse of the beast was destroyed in 1945 together with the Nazi regime in Germany, whereupon the preconditions as regards spiritual history for perceiving the influence of the etheric Christ again opened up for mankind.

According to Rudolf Steiner's spiritual-scientific research the new revelations of the Christ began in *1909*, when Christ appeared for the first time in the supersensible worlds in an etheric body (initially in a form that was accessible to initiates alone).[50] In the same year Leadbeater and Besant under the leadership of the Eastern occultists standing behind them tried to falsify this event by establishing, in contrast, the false mission in the form of Krishnamurti.[51] Similarly, when the human horizon in Europe gradually began again to clear for the perceiving of the etheric activity of the Christ in *1945*, D.K. and the same Eastern occultists associated with him emerged with their 'Great Invocation' and the proclamation of the imminent coming of the 'Messiah'.

What is particularly striking about this proclamation is the way that D.K. again and again speaks of how the physical appearance of the Christ will be preceded by a mass awakening of a 'Christ consciousness'. He speaks about this to his pupils for example in April: 'As I have earlier pointed out, the return of Christ will be expressed, in the first place, by an upsurging of the Christ consciousness in the hearts of men everywhere,'[52] which, according to D.K., will come about as a direct consequence of the 'outpouring of the Christ spiritual force' (see p. 276).

Thirty-two years earlier, in 1913, Rudolf Steiner astonishingly also spoke with the same words about the imminent awakening of a Christ consciousness amongst mankind. He initially pointed in this respect to the supersensible repetition of the Mystery of Golgotha which took place in the spiritual worlds neighbouring the earth and which Christ underwent during the preparation for His new etheric revelation.[53] However, the conclusions to which Rudolf Steiner came were diametrically opposed to D.K.'s and differ from them as day and night.

For Rudolf Steiner the gradual awakening of a Christ consciousness must lead to the arising of new clairvoyant faculties, with whose help an ever greater number of human beings will from the twentieth century onwards come over the course of the next three thousand years to an experience of the etheric Christ *in the supersensible*. These human beings will hear His voice and at the same time clairvoyantly behold His form, as Rudolf Steiner has described on several occasions in his lectures.[54]

For D.K., on the other hand, the awakening of a Christ consciousness in man means something altogether different. In his view this will first make human beings more receptive to the teachings of Christ, which are in our time disseminated throughout the world above all by the 'Tibetan'; and this will lead to many people hearing the voice of Christ and then even experiencing being 'overshadowed' by him—but all this only in order that they might recognize him on the earth when he finally appears *in a physical body*.

At this point D.K. lays his cards on the table to a certain extent when he points to the intimate connection between his proclamation of the imminent appearance of the world Teacher and the previous, though unsuccessful, attempt at such a proclamation begun in 1909 by Leadbeater and Besant.[55] He spoke about this to his pupils. After the awakening of a Christ consciousness, 'disciples everywhere will find themselves increasingly sensitive to His quality, His voice and His teaching; they will be "overshadowed" by Him in many cases, just as before He overshadowed His disciple Jesus; through this overshadowing of disciples in all lands, He will duplicate Himself repeatedly. The effectiveness and the potency of the overshadowed disciple will be amazing.

'One of the first experiments He made as He prepared for this form of activity was in connection with Krishnamurti. It was only partially successful. The power used by Him was distorted and misapplied by the devotee type of which the Theosophical Society is largely composed, and the experiment was brought to an end; *it served, however, a most useful purpose.*[56]*

In other words, the unsuccessful attempt at that time to tempt humanity through the false Messiah in the form of Krishnamurti is now, on the basis of these experiences, to be prepared more carefully and assiduously so that what could not succeed at the beginning of the century because of the 'devotee types' (D.K. is unable to hide his anger at this point) can be fulfilled at its end or subsequently, at the beginning of the next century, and the Maitreya Christ concealed somewhere in the ravines of the Himalayas can finally appear to mankind.

Several hundred pages in the various books that D.K. dictated to Alice Bailey after 1945 are devoted to describing this event and, quite especially, to preparing for it. A particular characteristic of these descriptions is that D.K. always endeavoured to portray Christ's life in Palestine and especially His most important deed on earth, the Mystery of Golgotha, as of far less significance and even of secondary importance compared with

---

* It follows from these words that everything that Rudolf Steiner said in many lectures about the 'experiment' with Krishnamurti can also be related to the new 'experiment' which the 'Tibetan' was preparing.

his future appearance in a physical body.[*] Thus at the beginning of his last communication to his pupils in 1949 D.K. said: 'The Christian resurrection is, however—from the angle of the great Lodge on Sirius[†]—only a minor one and a passing resurrection, though the revelation subsequently accorded is lasting and permanent in its effects.'[57] And in another book that he dictated to Alice Bailey in 1948 and was entitled *The Reappearance of the Christ* D.K. said that the physical Second Coming of Christ in the imminent future shall 'enable Him to consummate the effort He made 2000 years ago in Palestine' and 'to complete the work He started' then.[58] For 'His Mission on earth two thousand years ago is a part of that continuity and is not an extraordinary story, having no relation to the past, emphasizing a period of only 33 years and presenting no clear hope for the future'.[‡] For 'His comprehension and His apprehension of the will of God' [that is, of Sanat Kumara] today 'is deeper and His fulfilment of that Will is more in line with the divine Purpose than it was in Palestine two thousand years ago'. Hence 'He is today nearer that perfection [in following the will of the Father] than He ever was when before on Earth. It was this divine unfoldment which made it possible for Him to make the right choice, not only for Himself but also for the spiritual Hierarchy, during the years of decision, prior to *June, 1945*. Under the divine will, he had to reappear on Earth in *visible* presence.'

'In Palestine,' on the other hand, 'His appearance was mainly prophetic and His work primarily that of laying the foundation for the activities which will follow His reappearance.' And D.K. then introduces four main reasons which brought about 'the tragedy [the failure] of His appearance two thousand years ago' out of which the Christian 'theologians ... posit[ed] an unhappy story, producing a miserable and unhappy world'.

---

[*] With this purpose in mind D.K. again casts doubt upon the date of Jesus Christ's birth and emphasizes that 'the exact date of Christ's birth remains debatable' (RC, p. 106)—thus equating Jesus of Nazareth with Jeshua ben Pandira who lived a century earlier (whose identity was insisted upon by Blavatsky, Besant and Leadbeater in their books). (See Parts One and Three.)

[†] The reader may recall that according to D.K. the sixth stage of initiation that the Christ attained in Palestine corresponds to the second stage in the Sirius Lodge (see p. 228).

[‡] After these words D.K. allows himself a whole series of ironic remarks about the Book of Revelation, which gives people hopes that there will eventually be 'a new heaven and new earth'. 'Further than that, we are told nothing; humanity hopes for so much more that the picture presented [of a new heaven and earth] does not intrigue them. Behind this portrayal [in Revelation], if rightly interpreted, stands the human [that is, in the physical body], the loving and the divine presence of the Christ, embodying divine love and wielding divine power, directing His Church and establishing the Kingdom of God on Earth' (compare this with Rudolf Steiner's cycle on the Book of Revelation).

The first reason was the immaturity of humanity; the second was that he was himself not sufficiently strongly connected with 'the Father's House' [Shamballa],[*] the third that he might have used a greater number of prepared helpers (today they are the members of the 'New Group of World Servers' founded by D.K.); and the fourth reason was that human beings were 'not then desperate enough'[59] to follow the path that had been opened up to them. Consequently 'for nearly two thousand years He has waited to bring that mission to fruition'.[60]

However, this moment has now come, for today, supposes D.K., all the conditions enumerated have been fulfilled both on the part of the world Teacher and also mankind. Hence '—under law—He *may* not turn His back upon the presented opportunity'.[61] He must come. But this time He will not appear alone in the physical body but together with the whole Himalayan Hierarchy, that is, with a whole retinue of Masters, Adepts and their numerous pupils: 'This time the Christ will not come alone for His co-workers will come with Him.'[62] 'What is referred to [by the Second Coming] is the externalization of the Hierarchy and its exoteric appearance on earth.'[63] D.K. devoted an entire book to the appearance of the Hierarchy with the world Teacher, namely *The Externalization of the Hierarchy*, published in 1957 (it has over 800 pages).[64] Here he includes—as in his other books—many details which portray how the Masters of the planetary Hierarchy and their ashram—groups of their pupils working together—are working on preparing the Second Coming. The Master K.H. (Kut Humi) concentrates with particular intensity on its occurrence.[65] For 'the mission of that Ashram is to produce the energy which will make possible and definite the reappearance of the Christ'. And so the publication of the small book *The Reappearance of the Christ* (1947) is the fruit of the work of his ashram. K.H. will also help the future world Teacher with developing the 'new structure of the coming civilization'.

There then follows Master M. (Morya), who has already formed a special 'triangle of energies' with Manu and Christ. Through this triangle the Avatar of Synthesis will then work. Master M. will exert influence upon leaders of government and leading politicians and prepare them for recognizing the world Teacher. He 'is at this time acting as the inspirer of

---

[*] In another book D.K. speaks of how Christ was at that time able *for the first time* to enter into a direct connection with Shamballa: 'Two thousand years have gone since Gethsemane and since Christ made His initial contact with the Shamballa force' (EA, p. 581 and also D–2, p. 173). But at that time Christ 'was conscious still of . . . the *contrast* between His will and God's will [italics S.P.] (EA, p. 583).

the great national executives throughout the world'. The 'English Master', not referred to by name, who brought the 'labour movement' into life, for his part is endeavouring to prepare the broad proletarian masses for the coming of the world Teacher. The work of the other Masters who were—including D.K.—enumerated at the beginning of the second chapter is considered in a similar way.

Thus for example D.K. writes in one of his letters to his pupils: 'Your spiritual goal is the establishing of the kingdom of God. One of the first steps towards this is to prepare men's minds to accept the *fact* that the reappearance of the Christ is imminent.'[66] (Italics by D.K.)

At this point a particular aspect of the task of the Master Jesus needs to be emphasized (it is mentioned in the second book of the 'Tibetan'). In connection with the preparation for the Second Coming it is stated: 'The Master Jesus will . . . with certain of His chelas effect a re-spiritualization of the Catholic churches, breaking down the barrier separating the Episcopal and Greek churches from the Roman. This may be looked for, should plans progress as hoped, about the year 1980.'[67]

Finally in the book referred to above many pages are devoted to the question as to what the future world Teacher himself is doing today in his place of refuge in the Himalayas. Thus D.K. indicated that in May 1944 'our Master the Christ' was working to ensure that 'the will energy, emanating from Shamballa', streamed not to the 'Axis Powers' (Germany, Italy, Japan), but to the 'allied peoples', so that these latter may 'carry the war to a finish of victory and of triumph'.[68] Moreover he seeks to 'stiffen . . . the will to fight'; to inspire the 'diplomats' to develop 'certain post-war plans to arouse 'the minds of the masses and turning them . . . into a religious channel' and so forth. Finally he prepares within the Hierarchy for 'the Restoration of the Mysteries [on the earth]'.

From time to time he retires completely into solitude. This happened for example in April 1944. D.K. writes: 'The Christ has gone into a retreat for a month and cannot be reached even by the Masters until May 5th. He is in closest consultation with the Buddha and with the Lord of the World [Sanat Kumara]. This great Triangle of Potencies . . . are today entirely preoccupied with the task of bringing the war to an end.'*

The future world Teacher engaged further in May 1946 with the problems of the reorganization of the existing world religions, including the eventual overcoming of Judaism, and also with preparing new revelations for humanity which were from then on to lie at the foundation of the new world religion.

---

* What is meant here by the 'ending of the war' will be considered in the next chapter.

It is impossible, and indeed unnecessary, to enumerate all the many 'activities' of the future world Teacher. It is important that they all—together with the influence of the mahatmas mentioned above—in the end prepare for the *physical* appearance of the Christ.

But what shall the world Teacher bring about when he appears to humanity with his whole retinue from the Himalayas? He will above all make a beginning with the 'new epoch' or the 'Aquarian solar cycle'.[69]* At the moment when he made the resolve to return to human beings 'in June 1945, at the time of the full moon ... He definitely and consciously took over His duties and responsibilities as the Teacher and Leader during the Aquarian solar cycle. He is the first of the great world Teachers to cover two zodiacal cycles—the Piscean and the Aquarian.'[70] This resolve was, according to D.K., preceded by his difficult struggle two thousand years earlier in the Garden of Gethsemane, the result of which was 'the decision made by Christ ... to take over the building or reconstruction work in Aquarius, and thus complete the task which He attempted to do in the Piscean Age'.† According to D.K. the 'new' or 'Aquarian' epoch will begin very shortly, coinciding with the imminent appearance of Christ in a physical body.‡ As for his work in the Aquarian age, this will, according to D.K., 'continue for two thousand five hundred years', that is, for as long as the revelations of the *etheric* Christ will continue taking place according to Rudolf Steiner's spiritual research.[71]§ Hence for D.K. his teaching also belongs to this new epoch, as the titles of some of his books—such as *Education in the New Age* and *Discipleship in the New Age*, Vols. I and II—confirm.

However, such an early beginning of the Aquarian age is in harmony neither with the astronomical facts nor with the results of modern spiritual research. For from the astronomical standpoint the sun (the point of the vernal equinox) will enter the constellation of Aquarius around the year 2500, while the sixth, Slavonic post-Atlantean epoch will begin even later, around AD 3573, when the sun will have reached its culminating

---

* Thus D.K. dictated to Alice Bailey already in December 1919: 'When He [the Christ] will come and inaugurate the new era ...'

† D.K. had previously indicated that the hidden significance of his occupation as a 'carpenter' is contained in what has been said above, and he continued: 'This is the true meaning of the Biblical story of Christ's being crucified upon the cross of wood or the tree.'

‡ In contrast to spiritual science D.K. considers the Aquarian age as being the fifth and not the sixth epoch in the evolution of humanity.

§ In addition to the figure of 3000 years Rudolf Steiner also speaks several times of 2500 years.

point in the constellation of Aquarius and mankind has completed the development of the consciousness soul (without which a right relationship to the principle of the Spirit Self—which will then descend upon it—is impossible).[72]

The premature announcement of the Aquarian age, which D.K. made for the first time through Alice Bailey and which was subsequently taken up by the various occult trends generally known as 'New Age' movements, is in this case an indication of the combined influence of Ahriman and Lucifer. The former illicitly strives to bring the future into the present, with the inevitably paralysing effect of its premature appearance upon those higher human faculties which should be working only gradually within man, in order that the Spirit Self can descend into the fully developed individual ego-consciousness of the consciousness soul and not in a luciferic form through mediumism, atavistic clairvoyance and the state of mass possession.[*]

But what, according to D.K., does the world Teacher of the new age that begins with his coming bring? This will entail above all the founding of the 'new world religion'[73] which will finally unite all five great world religions: Christianity, Hinduism, Buddhism, Islam and Judaism. For all these religions have, according to D.K., long been awaiting the coming of the Messiah in the flesh: Christians, the Second Coming of Christ[†]; Hindus, the coming of the Kalki Avatar; Buddhists, the Maitreya Bodhisattva; Muslims, the Imam Mahdi; Jews, the promised Messiah. With the appearance of the world Teacher the adherents of all these religions, which have been prepared for this by members of the Himalayan Hierarchy, recognize in him the long-awaited divine emissary and unite in a common wish to serve him. (This idea, formulated precisely thus, is also fundamental in the teaching of the Roerichs.) Moreover, this union of the existing religions in the new world religion will be further hastened by the

---

[*] The gradual development of *new* supersensible capacities is not associated with the beginning of the Aquarian age but with quite different events: with the beginning of the modern epoch of the Archangel Michael's rulership (1879), with the end of the dark age of the Kali Yuga (1899) and with the beginning of Christ's reappearance in an etheric body (see GA 158, 9 November 1914 and GA 118). D.K. also spoke several times in his books about the imminent development of etheric clairvoyance and indicated that it leads human beings to a beholding of Shamballa (I, p. 33). However, Shamballa in his teaching is not the Shamballa of the etheric Christ spoken of by Rudolf Steiner (see GA 118) but a secret place 'beyond' the Gobi Desert where reigns the spectral Sanat Kumara.

[†] Here D.K. ignores—as elsewhere—the fact that the Christian world, in contrast to the Eastern religions, awaits the coming of Christ not in the flesh but *in a spiritual form*, as proclaimed in the Gospel.

general spread of the knowledge that 'the Buddha is closely allied with the Christ in this process of his reappearing';[74] furthermore, that 'Shri Krishna is shown to be an earlier incarnation of the Lord of Love, the Christ'[75] and finally that 'the Master Jesus ... overshadowed one of his senior disciples ... Mahomet'.

At the centre of this 'new world religion', whose manifestation the 'Group of the World Servers' established by D.K. is to prepare, will be three principal festivals. The first from a temporal point of view will be the Easter festival, which will be celebrated on the first *full moon* in April. This will be the festival of the Christ, 'the Teacher of all men and the Head of the Spiritual Hierarchy'.[76] The second will be the Wesak festival, which will be celebrated on the first *full moon* in May. This will be the festival of the Buddha, 'the spiritual Intermediary between the highest spiritual centre, Shamballa, and the Hierarchy'. It is not necessary here to go into greater detail about this festival, since this has already been done in the present work (see chapter 1). It is sufficient if one recalls that the Wesak festival, as D.K. asserts, is celebrated every year in a Himalayan valley and that it 'substantiate[s] the fact of Christ's physical existence among us',[77]* and that it also demonstrates the religious oneness of the West and the East, since 'both the Christ and the Buddha are then present' and with them all other Himalayan mahatmas, D.K. included, together with their advanced pupils.

Lastly the third festival is the so-called 'Festival of Goodwill' or of 'humanity', which like the Wesak festival has already been celebrated annually in the Himalayas on the first *full moon* of June: 'On this Festival for two thousand years the Christ has represented humanity ... Each year at that time He has preached the last sermon of the Buddha, before the assembled Hierarchy. This will, therefore, be a festival of deep invocation and appeal ...' This festival was established in 1952, on D.K.'s instruction, by his pupils as the 'World Invocation Day',[78] as a festival for 'a united voicing of the Invocation [the prayer for the coming of the physical Christ] on the same day in every land'.†

With all these festivals what is striking is their connection with the full moon, that is, their orientation to the moon rather than the sun, which is a feature of all religions and occult streams which acclaim Christ not as a

---

* D.K. affirms: 'The *fact* of His Presence upon earth in physical form is known today by many hundreds of thousands, and will eventually be realized by as many millions' (italics D.K.).

† In a book addressed to his pupils D.K. said: 'You can see, therefore, that a gigantic group meditation is going on in many differing phases upon our planet' (D–2, p. 206).

Sun Being but as a planetary being and, hence, merely as a link in the endless chain of the prophets and initiates of mankind.

Moreover, the spiritual significance of the three festivals is ordered in a totally different sequence to their temporal succession (April, May, June), which shows the true intention of their occult founders. Thus according to D.K. the highest festival is not Easter but Wesak, where the Buddha represents the Hierarchy, standing as it does at a deeper level than Shamballa and spiritually subordinate to it; and the 'Festival of Humanity' or the 'Festival of Goodwill' follows as the last in the sequence.

The foundation of the 'new world religion' is, moreover, associated with the influence and union of three mighty organizations: world Freemasonry, the Catholic Church and also numerous interconnected groups in which occult instruction in accordance with the method of the 'Tibetan' will be imparted.[*] The union of these three organizations will come about through the fact that the energies of Shamballa, the Hierarchy and individual teachers will increasingly work together harmoniously with their occult groups. (To the latter belong of course the movements—led by D.K.—of the 'World Servers', 'Goodwill', the 'Arcane School', 'Triangles' and so forth.) Then the following will happen: 'One of the things that will eventuate—when the new universal religion has sway and the nature of esotericism is understood—will be the utilization of the banded esoteric organisms, the Masonic organism and the Church organism as initiating centres.'[79] But what does that mean?

As already indicated, Christ is—according to D.K.—'the Hierophant of the first and second initiations'. And so D.K. says: 'He will, if the preparatory work is faithfully and well done, administer the first initiation in the inner sanctuaries of those two bodies [the Church and the Masonic Fraternity]. Many faithful workers will, during His period of work on earth, take this first initiation, and some few will take the second.'

'The first initiation' will be 'the Birth of the Christ in the cave of the Heart',[80] or the awakening of 'Christ consciousness'.[81] As D.K. writes: 'These initiates exist in their thousands today; they will be present in their millions by the time the year 2025 arrives.' (It follows from this that D.K. expects the coming of the world Teacher by the year 2025.) Thereafter 'the purifying waters of the Baptism Initiation (the second initiation) will submerge hundreds of aspirants in many lands'.[82] Then with the help of the members of the Hierarchy who will come down to earth with the

---

[*] Attempts had already been made previously to unite three such organizations (Freemasonic Lodges, Catholic Church and Theosophical Society) and to subject them to the world teacher Leadbeater (see Part Three, ch. 13).

world Teacher and with the support of the new initiates of the first and second stage, there will arrive the hour for the restoration of the '*ancient Mysteries*' or the 'Mysteries of Initiation' in which, under the leadership of the world Teacher, 'hundreds of thousands of men and women everywhere will pass through some one or other of the great expansions of consciousness'; and also a 'new world order, the order of the kingdom of God' will be brought about 'under the *physical* supervision of the Christ' or the unlimited rulership of the planetary Hierarchy on the earth which, according to D.K., is 'the true Church of Christ' or 'the true kingdom of God' which will be established on earth by the world Teacher.*

In order to achieve all this, 'right human relations' will be established on earth which the world Teacher will teach human beings. According to D.K., 'relinquishment, *submission* to existent facts, and *obedient* acquiescence to divine law are all involved. These are the things ... which [Christ] will help humanity to accept with enthusiasm and understanding. This will produce happiness ... [which] is for mankind a totally new experience. [For] Christ will have to teach men how to handle happiness correctly, to overcome the ancient habits of misery ...' Then the world Teacher will, according to D.K., teach human beings 'the Law of Rebirth', which will have the consequence that each person will recognize—if he has learnt it in the sense of the 'new world order'—'to ask nothing for the separated self, he then renounces desire for life in the three worlds and is then freed from the Law of Rebirth.† *He is now group conscious*, is aware of his soul group and of the soul in all forms.'[83] D.K. calls this renunciation of the individual ego in favour of group-consciousness the attainment of 'a stage of Christ-like perfection'.

It is not possible in this book even merely to characterize the simple-mindedness of the various details of the Second Coming which D.K.

---

* In the next chapter it will be shown with what kind of earthly events D.K. associates the first signs of the coming of this 'Kingdom of God'.

† Here, however, D.K. expresses a meaningful reservation: '*The Law exists; of the details of its working we know as yet nothing*' (RC, p. 118). This wholly egoless relationship to repeated earthly lives was adopted from D.K. by his pupil Alice Bailey. Thus she wrote in 1945 in her unfinished autobiography: 'One single life is probably of no more importance to the soul than fifteen minutes in 1903 is of importance to me' (AU, p. 91). Rudolf Steiner, in contrast, devoted six volumes of karma lectures to the effects of this law in their subtlest details (see GA 235, 236, 237, 238, 239, 240). For the mystery of reincarnation is associated with the human ego and not with the human soul. Thus in that he endeavours to make the ego become absorbed in a state of group consciousness, D.K. quite unambiguously reveals the luciferic source of his inspirations.

presents in his books. We shall therefore simply list the various chapter sub-headings. Thus the future world Teacher will teach mankind 'the Fact of God', but also 'Man's Relationship to God'. In reality this 'God' will be Sanat Kumara, who comes from Venus. He will also teach human beings 'the immortality of the human soul', which, however, merely leads to the renunciation of the ego and to its dissolution in a general soul-substance ('group-consciousness'). Then he will teach the 'Continuity of Revelation and the Divine Approaches', that is, that Gautama Buddha preceded him as Avatar and world Teacher and the next Avatar and world Teacher will follow him, then ever new and higher beings* and ever onwards in a chain of initiates, mahatmas, avatars, heavenly human beings, Logoi, Manvantars, cosmic planes and so forth who take over from one another.

In this connection, D.K.'s notion as to what the Second Coming means for Christ himself is especially characteristic. He is of the view that this will for him be none other than the next 'test' for his path to the following, seventh stage of initiation which he did not fully attain in Palestine, which is why he did not hear the Father's 'affirmative Voice',[84] who was silent during the Mystery of Golgotha.† For 'when Christ completes the work during the next two thousand years which He inaugurated two thousand years ago, that affirmative Voice [of the Father] will surely again be heard and divine recognition of His coming will be accorded. Then the Christ will take that stupendous initiation ... Then the Buddha and the Christ will together pass before the Father, the Lord of the World [Sanat Kumara], will together see the glory of the Lord and eventually pass to higher service of a nature and a calibre unknown to us.' In other words, when—according to D.K.—the Christ has reached the Buddha stage after 2000 years he will finally leave earthly humanity and pass on the leadership to the next Avatar or teacher of mankind.

D.K. then goes on to say: 'He too is facing a major test [the appearance

---

* For example, D.K. says about one of these: 'the work of the Buddha and of the Christ, and the work of the coming Avatar, will be superseded by One for Whom both Shamballa and the Hierarchy have unitedly waited and of Whom the doctrine of the Messiah and the doctrine of Avatars have been and are today only the dim distant symbols' (RI, p. 257).

† That is, the voice of Sanat Kumara from Shamballa, which D.K., as we have seen, identifies with the 'voice of the Father' addressing Christ in the Gospel, who, however—according to the 'Tibetan'—has not yet spoken his words of 'affirmation' with regard to the Mystery of Golgotha (see p. 228). Here it should be recalled that in D.K.'s system the highest stage of initiation attainable on the earth is not the seventh but the ninth, followed by the stages of cosmic initiation. (See Alice Bailey, *The Rays and the Initiations*, 'The Significance of the Initiations'.)

in a physical body], preparatory to a great initiation and when He has passed the test and fulfilled His task, He will pass to a still more exalted position in the Father's House or to some distant [from humanity] place of service where only the most exalted can follow Him; His present position [as world Teacher] will then be taken by the One Whom He has prepared and trained . . . Then His task will be done; He will be free again to leave us, *but this time not to return but to leave the world of men* in the hands of that great spiritual Server Who will be the new Head of the Hierarchy, the Church Invisible.'

And in another book D.K. spoke quite directly of where the Christ will go if he is 'not to return' to us: 'He [the Christ] is the expression, par excellence, of a Sirian initiation, and it is to that high place [Sirius] He will eventually go—no matter what duties of hierarchical obligations may take Him elsewhere between that time [his departure from Sirius] and now.'[85] It is then explained that His predecessor on this path to Sirius was not Sanat Kumara—whom D.K. doggedly identifies with the 'Father'—but none other than Lucifer. For 'Sanat Kumara is not on the Sirian line but . . . Lucifer, Son of the Morning, is closely related [to this line]'. And D.K. draws the conclusion: 'Hence the large number of human beings who will become disciples in the Sirian Lodge.'

From the standpoint of Christian esotericism the future working of the Christ appears altogether different. Since the Mystery of Golgotha He has been working as a pure spiritual Sun Being in the spiritual aura of the earth. For through Christ's having passed through the Mystery of Golgotha, He has united Himself with mankind not only for 'the next 2000 years' until the coming of the next world Teacher but 'until the end of earthly times', that is, until the end of the cosmic Earth aeon, until the total transformation of our whole cosmos, the transformation which is described in the Book of Revelation as the arising of the new heaven and the new earth, corresponding to the beginning of a new cosmic aeon spiritually beheld by John the Evangelist in the image of the heavenly Jerusalem.[86] As the Sun Logos and at the same time— since the Mystery of Golgotha—as the new Spirit of the Earth, Christ will at the end of the present aeon bring about the spiritualizing of the earth and thereafter its union with the sun, that is, that sublime condition beheld by John the Evangelist in the figure of the woman clothed with the sun who has twelve stars around her head and the moon under her feet.[87] Then the *sun impulse* brought by Christ into earthly evolution through the Mystery of Golgotha will attain its fulfilment, and the earth united with the sun will be the seed of a new cosmos in the universe, the cosmos of love into which the present cosmos of wisdom is to change, as Rudolf Steiner has described at the end of his book *Occult Science—An Outline*.[88]

Furthermore, in a still more all-encompassing perspective the Mystery of Golgotha turns out to be the centre of the entire evolution of the world, passing as it does through seven cosmic aeons from Old Saturn to Vulcan,[89] which for the modern initiate are recognizable only in the light of it. Hence Rudolf Steiner said: 'The whole of evolution, reaching back as far as Saturn and forward as far as Vulcan, is seen in such a way [in anthroposophy] that this light enabling us to see will ray out from the knowledge of the Mystery of Golgotha.'[90]

Thus the words of the Gospel 'I am with you always, to the close of the age' (Matthew 28:20) signify not a new coming of Christ in a physical body but an ongoing, ever higher stream of *supersensible* revelations for mankind,[91] with whom He has through the Mystery of Golgotha united Himself as its higher Ego for all future ages.[*]

'Hence one has no right,' said Rudolf Steiner, 'to associate with Christ's name any being who may incarnate in a physical body since the event of Golgotha. By doing this one would be displaying *a total misunderstanding of the Mystery of Golgotha* and showing that one does not know what has been determined by it. In the moment when one truly understands the Mystery of Golgotha, one does not bring Christ's name into connection with anything incarnating in a physical human body since the Mystery of Golgotha. To associate with Christ's name any being that has incarnated in a physical human body since the event of Golgotha means *either to abuse the name of Christ or to show a complete failure to understand the Mystery of Golgotha*.'[92]

In the case of D.K. it is a question of both the one and the other: on the one hand a complete misunderstanding of the Mystery of Golgotha, and on the other hand a distinct endeavour to regard this event as not having achieved its object and of little significance in comparison with the imminent coming of the (false) Messiah in a physical body.

★

---

[*] See further in Part Three, ch. 6. It is not possible here even only approximately to reflect the full depth of anthroposophical Christology, the varied nature and significance of Rudolf Steiner's spiritual-scientific insights about the cosmic Christ Being and the world significance of the Mystery of Golgotha as the central event which has given the whole of earthly evolution its meaning. In addition to his basic books Rudolf Steiner devoted many hundreds of lectures to the mysteries of esoteric Christianity (see the anthology ed. H. Giersch referred to in note 43). (The index of the Christological themes in his lexical legacy alone consists of a volume of a hundred pages.)

To conclude this chapter, a further aspect of the theme in question needs to be considered which perhaps more than anything else slightly lifts the veil hiding the mystery of the true source of the teaching of the 'Tibetan'. In his book *The Reappearance of the Christ* the last, seventh chapter is devoted to this aspect. There D.K. speaks firstly of one of the most pressing tasks of the 'Group of the New World Servers' founded by him in connection with the imminent appearance of the world Teacher: the need to mobilize millions of 'average men'[93] in all countries for the preparation for his coming. For 'it is in the hands of the masses of good little men and the millions of right thinking people in every land that the salvation of the world lies and by them the preparatory work for the Coming of the Christ will be done'. A central element in this work for the broad masses is the 'little prayer' disseminated amongst them by members of the groups of the 'World Servers': 'Lord God Almighty! Let there be peace on earth and let it begin with me'[*] ... [This] sums up all the requirements for those who seek to work in preparation for the coming of the Christ.'

D.K. then turns directly to the question with the consideration of which he ends the book devoted to this whole theme: that question which is particularly characteristic of the way that he tackles his own theme—that of the *financing of the Second Coming*. He dictates to Alice Bailey: 'Lack of financial support for the work of the Christ ... is perhaps the major difficulty, and it appears ... to be an insuperable one.'

For the reappearing world Teacher must, according to D.K.'s notions, fly many times around the whole world in an aeroplane, be allotted many broadcasts on television and radio in various countries, repeatedly hire large halls and stadiums for his official appearances and so on. And if, furthermore, he will be travelling everywhere with his entire 'occult retinue', it is not difficult to fathom how much all this is going to cost. And money does not fall from heaven. Hence D.K. tries to tackle this question with his practical sense. Thus he thinks of the need 'of raising funds in preparation for the return of the Christ'. But where is the money for this going to come from? D.K.'s answer is quite simple: through 'the selfless work of thousands of apparently unimportant people', that is, of those who—according to the 'little' prayer cited above—are to 'let it [this work] begin with me', admittedly not only in the ideal, or 'spiritual', sense but above all in a quite concretely material way.

---

[*] What is meant here is 'let' preparation for the Second Coming 'begin with me'.

Here D.K. proposes the following solution to the problem: 'If, for instance, the millions of people who love the Christ and seek to serve His cause gave at least a tiny sum of money each year, there would be adequate funds for His work.' However, this plan is impeded by the great difficulty of 'the seeming inability of people to give. For one reason or another, they give little or nothing,' complains D.K., 'even when interested in such a cause as that of the return of Christ.' Thus everyone is enjoined 'to give as they can'.

This highly practical, or one might say utilitarian, approach to the question of the 'return' of the world Teacher should not evoke astonishment, for a physical coming of the world Teacher can only be brought about with physical means, that is, with money. And if in Rudolf Steiner's words the proclaiming of the coming of a physical Christ is an expression of an 'Eastern materialism',[94] that is, a direct consequence of the penetration of *ahrimanic* powers also into the Asiatic East, *such* a coming must—by virtue of its ahrimanic nature—inevitably depend upon what represents the greatest concentration of ahrimanic powers in the physical world, namely money.[*]

In this connection D.K. set the members of the 'New Group of World Servers' led by himself a quite particular task. He wrote to them: 'It *must* [italics D.K.] be realized that money is the energy which can set in motion and make possible the activities of the New World Servers ... Money does not yet lie in their hands. Their need for it is great.'[95] For 'billions are ... needed to bring about the reconstruction of human affairs and thus purify and beautify our modern world to such an extent that the Christ can appear among men'.

In order that these 'millions' who are needed for the coming of the world Teacher may be reached as quickly as possible, D.K. demands that his pupils undertake on a weekly basis a special meditative task consisting of two parts: on Thursday all his pupils are to carry out a 'reflective meditation upon preparation for the reappearance of the Christ' and on Sunday a 'reflective meditation on attracting money for hierarchical purposes' (quite particularly for the preparation of the Second Coming). In both cases, however, what is involved is simply a different form of the work with the 'great Invocation' (see pp. 274–8).

---

[*] The extent of the 'Tibetan's' preoccupation with the problem of monetary resources is evident from the following paradoxical remark: 'Billions are required to overcome the materialism which has dominated mankind for untold aeons' (D–2, pp. 225–6). As one reads this attempt to achieve liberation from Ahriman by ahrimanic means, one inevitably calls to mind the words of Christ: 'How can Satan cast out Satan?' (Mark 3:23).

Thus D.K.'s pupils work on Thursdays with the first three verses and thus awaken the thought '*I have no other life intention*' (italics D.K.) than 'the service of the Coming One'. On Sundays (every Sunday morning) all pupils are to meditate especially the fourth and last verse. In this way the meditation itself is preceded by a whole series of intensified thoughts and prayers[*] beginning with: 'If money is one of the most important things needed today for spiritual work, what is the factor which is at present deflecting it away from the work of the Hierarchy?' Then the pupils immerse themselves in the thought: 'Ponder on the redemption of humanity through the right use of money.' They are then to immerse themselves in the image of a 'great stream of flowing golden substance'. Thereafter follows a fairly long 'invocative prayer' which includes among others the following words: 'The New Group of World Servers needs money in large quantities. I ask that the needed vast sums may be made available.' D.K. asserts that 'through creative imagination and by an act of the will [developed in exact meditation]' the pupils should develop the capacity to 'see untold and unlimited sums of money pouring into the hands of those who seek to do the Masters' work'. Then 'with conviction and emphasis' the pupils should speak the words: 'He for whom the whole world waits has said that whatsoever shall be asked in His Name and with faith in the response will see it accomplished.' After this follows the quite definite request: 'I ask for the needed money for ... [dots in the original text] and can demand it because ...' Only after these last words can the pupil finally meditate the fourth verse of the 'Invocation', which in its way forms the culmination of the whole meditative process.

At the conclusion of the exercise the pupils are then seriously to ponder how much they themselves have saved in the past week and are now able to sacrifice 'to the Christ and His Hierarchy' for the support of the imminent Second Coming. At this point D.K. manifests a particular strictness towards his pupils, who must make themselves conscious: 'if you do not give, you may not ask, for you have no right to evoke that which you do not share'. This meditation can, according to D.K., bring real fruits only when 'used by many simultaneously'.

In his next written communication to his pupils D.K. sums up what he has said previously in the following way: 'In my last series of instructions [in esoteric training] I gave you a group meditation which was based upon the furthering of the work of the New Group of

---

[*]The following summary reproduces the meditative work demanded by the 'Tibetan' only in a very abbreviated form; his description occupies three whole pages.

World Servers, as they sought to prepare humanity for the reappearance of the Christ'.*

This ahrimanic aspect of the organizations and movements founded by
the 'Tibetan', together with the 'occult materialism' described in the
previous chapters as the most important part of his teaching, invariably
prompts the question as to its relationship with an event that is to take
place shortly and to which Rudolf Steiner frequently referred. What is at
issue here is the following: precisely at the time when, according to D.K.,
the Second Coming is to begin (at the beginning of the twenty-first
century), according to Rudolf Steiner's spiritual-scientific research an
altogether different being is to appear on earth in a physical body—
Ahriman, of which event neither D.K. nor the Eastern occultists standing
behind him evidently know anything.

It is particularly striking that immediately after Rudolf Steiner had
spoken for the first time about the imminent appearance of Ahriman on
the earth in the flesh (October/November 1919), the 'Tibetan' entered
(on 19 November 1919) into telepathic connection with Alice Bailey and
began to dictate his books to her and, hence, started preparing for the
coming to earth of the world Teacher in a physical body.[96] However, the
question as to whether this congruence of time also signifies an identity
with respect to the being must initially be left open, since the answer to it
depends upon *who* in reality will appear on earth as the false Messiah,
whom the Eastern occultists are so actively proclaiming today[†] and
possibly also preparing for, and not uniquely only somewhere in the
ravines of the Himalayas. For such a preparation can be carried out
simultaneously in the most diverse places; and it may only become
apparent at the last moment which of the prepared candidates Ahriman

---

* To this exhortation the following should be added. The two extensive volumes entitled
Discipleship in the New Age (each volume has almost a thousand pages) contain not only
D.K.'s writings to the groups but also his letters to individual pupils (in the second volume
alone these letters make up nearly four hundred pages). The way that the relationship
between the teacher and his pupil develops is exemplified by the beginning of the following letter: 'My Friend and Brother: For several lives we have been associated, though
this is only the second incarnation wherein you have been definitely regarded by me and
by my Associates as a pledged disciple ... You are pledged as a disciple to further our plans
and to occupy yourself with definite group work.' And in a letter to another pupil he
writes: 'The Christ, through your own Master [that is here through D.K.] *and in no other
way*, knows you. Not yet can you know Him.'

† According to D.K. he will be preceded by another initiate who, either at the end of the
twentieth or the beginning of the twenty-first century, will take *D.K.'s teaching about the
Second Coming* further and lead to its culmination and, hence, will complete the preparation on earth for this event (see p. 260).

will use for his incarnation.* There is just one detail which in an aston-ishing way makes the future working of the incarnated Ahriman appear similar to the earthly activity of the world Teacher described by D.K. Rudolf Steiner once spoke about what Ahriman would bring when he comes to the earth: 'Through certain stupendous arts he would bring to man all the clairvoyant knowledge which until then can be acquired only by dint of intense labour and effort ... When Ahriman incarnates in the West at the appointed time, he would establish a great occult school for the practice of magic arts of the greatest grandeur, and what otherwise can be acquired only by strenuous effort would be disseminated widely over mankind.'[97]

D.K. says something similar about the world Teacher, who by coming to the earth will at the same time give millions of human beings 'initia-tion' and an 'expansion of consciousness'.

The incarnation of Lucifer in ancient times in the Asiatic East formed the opposite pole to this imminent appearance of Ahriman on the earth; for its consequence was that a mighty stream of luciferic wisdom des-cended upon mankind out of which the Asiatic East continues to live to a high degree even today.[98] Between these two poles of earthly evolu-tion—the incarnation of Lucifer in the past and of Ahriman in the future—stands *the Mystery of Golgotha*, the true understanding of which alone makes it possible for the forces of Lucifer and also of Ahriman to be conquered. 'Hence I [shall] never back down in any way,' said Rudolf Steiner, 'with regard to emphasizing this fact of the Mystery of Gol-gotha.'[99] For 'the knowledge that the Mystery of Golgotha stands in the middle of world evolution [represents] a forward step in the whole evolution of mankind'.[100] 'A time will come when a person who is a follower of the Chinese, Buddhist or Brahmanist religion will find it just

---

*It should be recalled here that, according to the Book of Revelation (19:20), the Antichrist will not appear alone but that his dark 'prophet' will precede him and will then actively help him. And whereas the former will come from the West, the second—as the bearer of the luciferic impulse that supports him—will probably come from the East. (See *A Short Story of the Antichrist* by Vladimir Soloviev.) And since D.K. ever and again emphasizes in his works the utterly decisive role of the Christ, who, in his opinion, belongs only to the lower *planetary* Hierarchy, one can from this standpoint easily imagine the full extent of the effect if the world Teacher together with all his pupils acknowledges a still higher being who comes to the earth and bows down before him and is, shall we say, a member not of the planetary but of the cosmic Hierarchy. D.K. himself alludes to this possibility when he maintains that 'the Messenger Who will later come ... will be a great and potent Avatar'—greater than Buddha and Christ—for he 'is not along the line of our humanity at all' (DN, p. 141).

as little against his religion to accept the Mystery of Golgotha as he would find it contrary to his religion to accept the Copernican world system. And it will be regarded as a kind of religious egotism if in the non-Christian religions one were to resist accepting these facts.'[101] This shows again 'how nonsensical it is for *certain occultists* to maintain that the Christ passes through repeated earthly lives'.[102]

Such assertions, which are extremely widespread and are rooted not only in a failure to understand the Mystery of Golgotha but in a complete denial of the living mystery of Christ, as is the case in the teaching of the 'Tibetan', become dangerous especially before the time of Ahriman's incarnation on the earth. For there will be 'ever less protection in the world against Ahriman's influence *outside* the forces streaming from the Christ mystery', whose focal point is the Mystery of Golgotha.

Notes

1. EH, p. 641.
2. RI, p. 91.
3. DN, p. 38.
4. RI, p. 91.
5. RC, p. 98.
6. EH, p. 300.
7. RI, p. 385; and the following quotation p. 91.
8. P, p. 42.
9. I, p. 64.
10. DN, p. 37.
11. RI, p. 548.
12. D–2, p. 270.
13. RI, p. 548.
14. I, p. 44.
15. EA, p. 204.
16. DN, pp. 38–9.
17. EH, p. 663.
18. I.
19. D–2, p. 206.
20. RC, pp. 30–1; and the following quotation p. 31.
21. RI, p. 755.
22. D–2, p. vi.
23. RC, p. 34.
24. EH, p. 488.
25. EH, p. 641.
26. 'Meditation Group for the New Age', Book 5, p. 12 German edition. Because this and the following quotations are taken from unpublished esoteric material, they have been retranslated from the German. (Translator's note.)

27. 'To the Pupils and Colleagues of the Arcane School', letter of Djwhal Khul dated 21 September 1947, p. 13 German edition.
28. RC, pp. 12 and 13.
29. EP, p. 289.
30. D–2, p. 569; and the following quotation ibid., p. 668.
31. RI, p. 753; and the following quotations ibid., pp. 753, 752, 616, 616.
32. RC, p. 74; see also EH, p. 397.
33. RC, p. 74; and the following quotations ibid., pp. 75, 76.
34. RC, p. 82.
35. RC, p. 82.
36. RI, pp. 757–8.
37. RC, p. 32; and the following quotation ibid., pp. 31–2.
38. RI, p. 759.
39. RC, pp. 54–5; and the following quotations ibid., pp. 19, 17, 16.
40. EH, pp. 575–6.
41. GA 162, 1 August 1915.
42. The Barr Manuscript, September 1907, Part III (GA 262).
43. Lecture of 12 January 1910. Marie Steiner's notes of this lecture are published (in German) in the anthology *Rudolf Steiner über die Wiederkunft Christi* (ed. H. Giersch), Dornach 1991.
44. AU, p. 250; and the following quotation ibid., p. 230.
45. See GA 118 and 130.
46. AU, p. 235.
47. GA 116, 2 February 1910, likewise the quotations that follow.
48. See GA 118.
49. GA 346, 20 September 1924.
50. GA 175, 6 February 1917.
51. See Part Three.
52. D–2, p. 171 and RI, p. 616.
53. See GA 152, 2 May 1913 and 20 May 1913.
54. See GA 188, GA 130 and GA 152.
55. See Part Three.
56. D–2, p. 171.
57. RI, p. 741.
58. RC, p. 39; and the following quotations ibid., pp. 51, 64, 65, 70, 70–1, 99.
59. RC, p. 100.
60. D–2, p. 173.
61. RI, p. 619.
62. RC, p. 58.
63. EH, p. 489; see also D–2, p. 409.
64. EH.
65. EH, p. 661; and the following quotations ibid., pp. 660, 662, 663, 505, 665, 664.
66. EH, p. 701.
67. CF, p. 759.
68. EH, p. 435; and the following quotations ibid., pp. 435, 435, 435, 436, 441, 545.

69. RC, p. 82.

70. RC, p. 82; and the following quotations ibid., pp. 97–8, 97, 83.

71. See GA 118.

72. See GA 185, 19 October 1918 and GA 121, 16 June 1910.

73. RC, p. 137; see also RC, pp. 5–6 and EH, p. 286.

74. RC, p. 96.

75. RI, p. 254, and the following quotation.

76. RC, p. 155 and the following quotation. See also EH, p. 347.

77. EH, p. 599; and the following quotations ibid., pp. 487, 599, 421.

78. RI, p. 760 and the following quotation ibid., pp. 759–60.

79. EH, p. 513, also 511; the following quotation ibid., p. 515.

80. RC, p. 86.

81. RI, p. 569; and the following quotation ibid., p. 571.

82. RC, p. 86; and the following quotations ibid., pp. 121, 127, 169, 108, 115, 119.

83. RC, p. 119; and the following quotations ibid., pp. 119, 144, 145, 147, 119, 147.

84. RC, p. 40 (see also RI, p. 83); and the following quotations ibid., pp. 40, 55–6, 57.

85. RI, p. 415, likewise the following quotation.

86. See GA 104.

87. Ibid.

88. GA 13, 'Present and Future Evolution of the World and of Mankind'.

89. Regarding the seven aeons of world evolution, see GA 13.

90. GA 207, 16 October 1921.

91. See note 39, chapter 3.

92. GA 129, 21 August 1911.

93. RC, p. 166; and the following quotations ibid., pp. 162, 171, 177, 178.

94. GA 121, 17 June 1910.

95. D–2, p. 225; and the following quotations ibid., pp. 226, 228, 226–7, 229, 230, 231, 511, 670.

96. See AU, pp. 245 and 162, and also EH, p. 338.

97. GA 191, 15 November 1919.

98. See GA 193, 27 October 1919 and 4 November 1919; and GA 191, 1 November 1919 and 15 November 1919.

99. GA 140, 26 October 1912.

100. GA 140, 3 November 1912.

101. GA 140, 26 October 1912; compare also RI, p. 254.

102. GA 140, 27 October 1912.

5. Occultism, Science and World Politics

> 'The long divorce between religion and politics *must* be
> ended.'
>
> D.K.—*Alice Bailey*[1]

Even from a fleeting acquaintance with the books of the 'Tibetan' it is clearly apparent that they are wholly imbued with the concepts of modern materialistic physics and astronomy. Without exception all D.K.'s books teem with concepts such as energy, force, vibrations, frequencies, electricity, magnetism, atomic matter, the permanent atom and so forth... Were he not so strongly to emphasize his Tibetan origin, one might well suppose that these books were dictated by some Western occultist or other or even by a whole group—not for nothing did Alice Bailey spend a large part of her life in America—and that perhaps some Eastern occultists, for example from Tibet, were added to this group.[*]

Thus when, for example, D.K. portrays the activity of the angels who—together with the teachers from the Himalayas—will accompany the world Teacher on the earth, he speaks of 'their vibrations' and of their more 'heightened vibration [than that of man]';[2] and when he goes on to maintain that these angels will 'teach humanity to see etherically', one must ask what kind of a clairvoyance will this be? It has already been stated that D.K. conceives of our solar system extending to the 'spiritual Sun' as consisting merely of various kinds of *electricity*.

The same is true of magnetism. When, for example, D.K. speaks about the occult schools of the individual planets of our solar system, he describes the earthly school as the 'School of Magnetic Response'.[3] And in another context he calls '*magnetism* ... the effect of the divine ray in manifestation'[4] or 'Divine Alchemy' and so on. D.K.'s most sub-

---

[*] Such a connection between Western and Eastern secret lodges in order to achieve a particular occult purpose of importance to both of them is not a new phenomenon in world history (see Part One). Such a connection in this case would be a further proof that Lucifer will assist the imminent appearance of Ahriman in the flesh by any means he can, uniting his forces with those of the ahrimanic spirits in order to be all the more certain of tempting human beings both in the West and in the East. (Regarding the union between Lucifer and Ahriman at the end of every millennium, see GA 286, 7 March 1914 and GA 191, 1 November 1919.)

stantial book, *A Treatise on Cosmic Fire*, is particularly full of such statements.

Most numerous, however, are D.K.'s statements about atoms, atomic matter, permanent atoms and so forth, which, according to his teaching, exist on all 'spiritual' levels of our solar system right up to the 'Sun Logos' itself and higher.

D.K.'s attitude towards the development of nuclear energy (the splitting of the nucleus) and its use as a means of mass extermination is especially characteristic of his way of dealing with this problem. As is well known, the first atom bombs were dropped on the Japanese cities of Hiroshima and Nagasaki on 6 August 1945, at the end of the Second World War, whereupon in Hiroshima alone more than 260,000 peaceful civilians died in the course of a few seconds and many thousands had to suffer in agony under the consequences of radioactive radiation during the ensuing decades.

The 'Tibetan' seems to be largely indifferent to all this, for only three days after the immense catastrophe he dictated to Alice Bailey for his pupils: 'I would like at this time to touch upon the greatest spiritual event [!] which has taken place since the fourth kingdom of nature, the human kingdom, appeared. I refer to the release of atomic energy, as related in the newspapers this week, August 6 1945, in connection with the bombing of Japan.

'Some years ago I told you that the new era would be ushered in by the scientists of the world and that the inauguration of the Kingdom of God on Earth would be heralded by means of successful scientific investigation. By this first step in the releasing of the energy of the atom this has been accomplished, and my prophecy has been justified during this momentous year of our Lord 1945.'[5] [*]

D.K. then wrote about the Japanese people who had been killed: 'They will be and are being defeated ... by the destruction physically of their war potential and the death of the form aspect [their physical bodies]. This destruction—and the consequent release of their imprisoned souls—is a necessary happening; it is the justification of the use of the atomic bomb upon the Japanese population.'

In the same book D.K. speaks in connection with the first use of the

---

[*] The reader may recall that in other contexts in his works D.K. brings this 'coming of God's Kingdom on Earth' quite clearly into connection with the Second Coming of Christ. And so the explosion of the atom bomb is for the 'Tibetan' the beginning of the proclamation of his Coming by scientists (and of course also politicians) and the first step into the new 'Aquarian Age'.

atom bomb of the 'freeing of some of the soul forces within the atom' and he continues: 'This has been, for matter itself, a great and potent initiation, paralleling those initiations which liberate or release the souls of men.' At this point D.K. goes so far that he makes a connection between the light which arises when the atom bomb explodes and no more and no less than the light that the Apostle Paul saw at his initiation on the way to Damascus. He expressed the following in his regular correspondence to his pupils: 'It [initiation in the epoch of the Second Coming] is closely related to the 'Blinding Light' which Saul of Tarsus saw on the road to Damascus and the "blinding light" which accompanied the discharge of energy from the atomic bomb. The "Blinding Light" which ever accompanies true conversion ... and which is an attendant demonstration of all Lives ... and the light which is released by the fission of the atom are one and the same expression on different levels of consciousness, and are definitely related to the processes and effects of initiation.'[6]

And in order still further to emphasize that in this case it is a question of the kind of initiation through which the world Teacher himself will appear as a hierophant at the time of the Second Coming, D.K. then himself links this 'blinding light' with the third line of the first verse of the 'great Invocation' and, hence, connects nuclear energy not only with the world Teacher but with 'God' [Sanat Kumara] himself, for the first verse runs:

> From the point of Light within the Mind of God
> Let light stream forth into the minds of men.
> Let Light descend on Earth.

That is, let the 'light' of the exploding atom bombs which bring to mankind the 'initiation' of the new epoch of the Second Coming stream down to it! Is this apocalyptic picture of the Second Coming a picture of the third, the *nuclear* world war?

And in another book D.K. refers to the relationship of the energy of the atom bombs with the activity of this same 'God' with the words: 'God in nature (i.e., the planetary Logos in concrete and material expression) has been revealed, and this has culminated in that tremendous expression of power—the atom bomb.'[7] Nuclear energy itself, however, he calls a 'saving force' and has in it the potency of rebuilding, of rehabilitation and of reconstruction'[8] and which also can bring about release 'from poverty, ugliness, degradation, slavery and despair'.

As for the planetary sources for the arising of this energy, he describes these as follows: 'Owing to *extra-planetary stimulation*, to the immediate planetary crisis and to the present *invocative cry of humanity* [that is, the cry about the Second Coming that was considered in the previous chapter], energy from Shamballa has been permitted to play upon the "centre which is called the race of men" and has produced two potent results: first, the world war was precipitated and, secondly, the fission of the atom, resulting in the atomic bomb, was brought about. Both these events were made possible by the pouring-in of the energy and power . . . of the first Ray of Power or Will . . . Thus was the new era ushered in; thus was the stage set for a better future. This was the intent and the purpose of Those Who compose the Council Chamber of the Lord [Sanat Kumara]. It rests with humanity itself to take advantage of the proferred opportunity which this *destructive* [italics D.K.] manifestation made possible,'[9] that is, the manifestation of the all-destroying Shiva, the highest aspect of the threefold Logos.

D.K. sees the *extra-planetary stimulation* mentioned at the beginning of this quotation in connection with the cosmic activity of particular beings, whom he calls 'the Lords of Liberation'.[10] These beings are associated with everything that concerns the problems of freedom and liberation on the earth. He writes: 'All great ideas have their emanating Sources of life, therefore, and These are called in the ancient invocation[*] with which we are occupied "Lords of Liberation". They are three in number, and one of Them is closer to the Earth and to humanity than are the other two, and it is He Who can be reached by those who comprehend the nature of freedom and who desire beyond all things to be liberated.' According to D.K. 'there was a clearly directed inflow of extra-planetary energy released by the Lords of Liberation, to Whom invocation had been successfully made; through the impact of this energy upon the atomic substance being dealt with by the investigating scientists, changes were brought about which enabled them to achieve success'.

Whereas D.K. relates the splitting (or 'liberation') of the atom to an 'extra-planetary' influence of the 'Lords of Liberation' (and, as we shall see, to the already familiar 'Avatar of Synthesis'), who strengthened the outpouring of the first ray from Shamballa into humanity, the idea of the atom bomb derives from a lower level of authority, from the ashram of Morya, who works with the forces of this ray: 'The atomic

---

[*] 'Let the Lords of Liberation issue forth.
Let them bring succour to the sons of men'—thus begins the invocation which D.K. gave to his pupils already in June 1940.

bomb emerged from a first ray Ashram.'[11] The highest leader of all ash-rams of this ray is the Mahatma Morya* (the future Manu of the sixth root race), who works today in a particularly intense way with Christ and the Manu of the fifth race. They form the 'energy triangle' men-tioned above, through which a still higher being is working in our time—the Avatar of Synthesis: 'These three—the Christ, the Manu and the Master Morya—create a triangle of energies into which (and through which) the energy of the Avatar of Synthesis can pour, finding right direction under Their combined efforts.'[12] As, however, the Avatar of Synthesis as the bearer of extra-planetary energy from the *extra-planetary spheres* came to Shamballa, all in all the picture arises: the Avatar of Synthesis induces Shamballa, together with the 'Great Lib-erator', to pour the energy of the first ray of power or the will into mankind. This energy works from there through the 'energy triangle' described above and then through the ashram of Morya† and first brings about the development of the nuclear bomb on earth and then its use, that is, that event which D.K., as we have seen, called 'the greatest spiritual event which has taken place since ... the human king-dom appeared'.[13]

The extent to which D.K. was *convinced* of the participation of the future world Teacher in the occult history of the invention and use of the first atom bomb is borne out by the following two statements. The first

---

* If one notes that, according to D.K., it is quite especially Morya's task to inspire the leading regents and politicians in the world, and that the fact of the first use of the nuclear bomb has such a colossal significance, does it not follow that in D.K.'s view it was Morya who inspired Truman to drop nuclear bombs on Japanese cities? A further detail is interesting in this connection. In her occult diaries which—according to her conviction—were dictated word for word by Mahatma M. (Morya), Helena Roerich writes in 1924 about an 'attempt' to obtain the formula of nuclear energy by the brotherhood [in the Himalayas], an attempt which initially failed and whose 'culmination is only now taking place' (Fiery Experience', diary entries by Helena Roerich, 1924; published in the anthology *U poroga novovo mira* ['At the Threshold of the New World'], Moscow 1993, entry of 24 April 1924). And ten years later D.K. likewise writes in his *A Treatise on White Magic* about this and says that 'three great discoveries are imminent' for humanity (EH, p. 497). He characterizes the first of these as follows: 'One is already sensed and is the subject of experiment and investigation, the releasing of the energy of the atom. This will completely change the economic and political situation in the world.' D.K. cites these words on 17 April 1945 in his writings to his pupils, where he particularly emphasizes that his prophecy is in process of fulfilment, and makes them aware of his knowledge in this respect.

† D.K. said: 'The Ashram or group centre through which the Master Morya works is also exceedingly busy. It is obvious to you that as this is a first ray Ashram, the energy coming from the Avatar of Synthesis will make its primary impact upon this Ashram' (EH, p. 662).

was written in May 1944: 'He [Christ] is . . . occupied with the process of deflecting the will-energy, emanating from Shamballa, in such a way that it will not be seized upon and misused by the Axis Powers [Germany, Italy, Japan] in order to stiffen their peoples into increased opposition to the Forces of Light. It must be rechannelled and used to stiffen the purpose of the United Nations to carry the war to a finish of victory and of triumph . . . This necessitates on the part of the Christ a concentration [of his forces] for which we have no equivalent word . . .' And in March 1945 he writes: 'A powerful first ray activity—the activity of will or purpose—is swinging into action. The Christ, as the Leader of the Forces of Light, *has empowered the Ashrams of the Masters upon this first Ray of Power* to strengthen the hands of all disciples in the field of government and of political arrangement in every nation; to enlighten, if possible, the various national legislatures *by whatever means may be needed.*' It follows from this that, according to D.K., the nuclear bombs dropped at Truman's command on peaceful Japanese cities were the first actual consequences of this activity.

Finally, in his letter of 9 August 1945—written after the nuclear catastrophe in Japan and including the 'justification' cited above—there is contained an exact description of how the planetary Hierarchy is able, with the help of the 'Great Liberator', to exert an influence upon a group of scholars [in Germany] in such a way that they experience 'a form of mental paralysis', whereas the other group [in America] is 'stimulated [by it] to the point of success'. And this latter group invented the atom bomb which, according to D.K., brought the war to an end: 'The atom bomb wrote *finis* to the world chapter of disaster. That atomic bomb (though used only twice destructively) ended the resistance of the powers of evil* because its potency is predominantly etheric.' Furthermore, considers D.K., 'it [the atom bomb] belongs to the United Nations *for use* (or let us rather hope, simply for threatened use) when aggressive action on the part of any nation rears its ugly head. It does not essentially matter whether that aggression is the gesture of any particular nation or group of nations or whether it is generated by the political groups of any powerful religious organization, such as the Church of Rome.'

This conviction of D.K.'s finds further confirmation in that, as we

---

* Actually the use of the nuclear bomb proceeded not from military aims (Japan had by this time been virtually conquered) but mainly from political purposes: the intimidation of the Soviet Union, which was at this time—in the view of the USA—about to obtain too much influence in Europe.

have seen, in his letters he associates the dropping of nuclear bombs on Japanese cities directly with the beginning of 'the new era' and the 'inauguration of the kingdom of God on Earth', that is, with the fundamental elements of the physical Second Coming resolved upon by 'Christ'—according to D.K.—*only two months before the first use of the nuclear bomb.*

And so Christ is from D.K.'s standpoint one of the 'occult originators' of the nuclear bomb and its use is the first visible sign of his Second Coming! A more reprehensible thought is barely conceivable!

The reason for such a positive attitude on the part of the initiates of the Hierarchy from the Himalayas to the devastating manifestation of nuclear energy, equivalent in its destructive potential to social forms such as Bolshevism (see Part One), may be viewed in the context of the secret endeavour which Rudolf Steiner once characterized as follows: 'Hence they [the initiates of the East] actually want to allow earthly civilization to disappear. They are to an extreme degree familiar with the spiritual world, and they are of the conviction that mankind would do better to withdraw from any subsequent incarnations. Hence they seek to work to ensure that human beings withdraw from incarnating further.'[14]

Through the 'splitting of the atom' and the discovery of the secret of nuclear energy, however, not only has the prediction of D.K. and Helena Roerich come to fulfilment but also a prediction of Rudolf Steiner's, which he made already earlier in October 1911, when he referred to the existence 'of a still more terrible force' than electricity and magnetism, 'which it will not be possible to keep hidden very much longer [by its originators]'.[15] Hence 'it can only be hoped that before some discoverer gives this force into the hands of mankind, human beings will no longer have anything immoral in their nature!' This was not the case, however, as is shown by the use of the atomic bomb against the peaceful inhabitants of two Japanese cities. In other words, nuclear energy was discovered *prematurely* by human beings and as a result was used for mass destruction of life.

In these, as in so many other cases, Christian esotericism and D.K.'s teaching are comparable like day and night. For what for the latter is the result of the working of energy and of the teachers of Shamballa as the highest guidance of our planet turns out from the standpoint of Christian esotericism to be the work of the most terrible demonic powers, the Asuras, which represent the most intense impulse of evil in our cosmos. The forces of the *life ether* of which they have taken hold manifest themselves from the sub-physical realm (higher Anti-Devachan) as the 'terrible forces of destruction' of nuclear energy, which are capable of destroying the *principle of life* on Earth!*

However, the part played by the 'Shamballa force' in the historical development of mankind extends far beyond what has been described hitherto.[16] For in the 'past 150 years' a whole series of 'outstanding personalities' have appeared in European history who 'reacted gradually and slowly to the Shamballa force'. Who were these outstanding people who worked under the direct inspiration of Shamballa? After everything that has been quoted so far, D.K.'s answer will probably no longer astonish the reader. So we will let him speak for himself.

'They have, however, reacted to that force through the medium of certain great and outstanding personalities who were peculiarly sensitive to the will-to-power and the will-to-change† and who (during the past 150 years) have altered the character of national life, and *emphasized increasingly the wider human values.* The men who inspired the initiating French Revolution; the great conqueror, Napoleon; Bismarck, the

---

* Modern spiritual science (anthroposophy) speaks of three kinds of adversaries, who have remained behind at various stages of world evolution and, hence, represent various degrees of evil in our cosmos. Lucifer and the spirits associated with him form the first group of these beings. They lagged behind evolutionary development as a whole in the previous aeon of Old Moon and belong in general to the Hierarchy of the Angeloi. Ahriman and the spirits connected with him form the second group. They fell behind earlier, in the aeon of Old Sun, and belong to the Hierarchy of the Archangels. The oldest opposing forces in our cosmos, finally, are the Asuras; they remained behind even earlier, in the aeon of Old Saturn, and belong to the Hierarchy of the Archai (see GA 110, question and answer session following the evening lecture of 21 April 1909, and also GA 154, 25 May 1914, GA 99 2 June 1907). In the course of earthly evolution the luciferic spirits thrust their way into the evolution of humanity in the Lemurian epoch and brought about at that time the 'Fall of Man' described in the Bible, resulting in the expulsion from Paradise. The ahrimanic spirits entered later into human evolution, on ancient Atlantis; and the Asuras are beginning only gradually from our time—the consciousness soul epoch—to work their way into earthly evolution (see GA 107, 22 March 1909). The luciferic spirits tempt man mainly from within and incite him to the various forms of egotism and arrogance, whereas the ahrimanic spirits entice him—more from without—to the various forms of materialism. (The Bible also highlights a difference between these two categories of evil spirits in calling the former the *Devil* and the latter *Satan*.) Finally the Asuras, who represent the forces of evil in our cosmos in their most strongly concentrated form can gradually destroy the very ego of a human being who has succumbed to them (ibid.). The outward expression of their influence in nature is the destructive power of the nuclear bomb, whereas Lucifer is manifested in nature through electricity and Ahriman through magnetism (see further in chapter 2).

† According to D.K. these are two fundamental aspects of the working of the first ray, the ray of will or power.

creator of a nation; Mussolini, the regenerator of his people; Hitler who lifted a distressed people upon his shoulders; Lenin, the idealist, Stalin and Franco *are all expressions of the Shamballa force* and of certain little understood energies.'

D.K. dictated these words to Alice Bailey in September 1939, that is, just after Nazi Germany invaded Poland (1 September 1939), the event which started the Second World War.[*] To be sure, D.K. changed his *attitude* towards Hitler a year later, and expressed himself thereafter only negatively about him.[†] This does not alter the fact that the 'Tibetan' was for almost seven years—from 1933 until 1940—positively disposed towards him.

An explanation for this initially positive and subsequently negative attitude on the part of D.K. and the Eastern occultists standing behind him towards the Führer of the Third Reich can be found through an altogether different Eastern 'guru', the recently deceased Bhagawan Shri Radjnesh. In an anthology of his numerous conversations with pupils it is reported how the White Brotherhood of the Himalayas, having lost all hope of somehow being able to influence a Western humanity that was so embroiled in materialism, decided to apply a more radical means for its salvation by sending it a 'shepherd with an iron staff', a task for which Hitler was chosen. According to Radjneesh, Hitler owed his brilliant, lightning-like career from an unknown lance-corporal to German Chancellor solely and exclusively to the help of the Himalayan mahatmas, who endowed him with their energy (possibly the same energy of the first ray of will or power, of which D.K. spoke so often). In Radjneesh's view, in the early period after his seizing of power Hitler conscientiously followed all the instructions of his secret teachers in the Himalayas, which is why his opportunities in Europe unfolded to the maximum degree. (A whole series of expeditions by Hitler and also Himmler to Tibet and to the Himalayas point in this direction, as does the swastika sign chosen by the Nazis, which Blavatsky had previously included in the emblem of the Theosophical Society.)

As time went on Hitler entered so fully into the role of omnipotent Führer that he gradually ceased listening to his Himalayan masters and all the more often merely followed his egotistic and power-hungry

---

[*] It is also significant in this connection that D.K. speaks not of two world wars but of *one*, which in his view lasted for 30 years, from 1914 until 1945 (see RI, p. 86 and D–2, p. 163).

[†] Thus in September 1940 he wrote that Hitler and his six closest colleagues were 'the custodians of forces which control them' (EH, p. 258).

wishes. This led to his occult instructors being compelled to withdraw their guidance and energy from him, leading shortly afterwards to his fall.[*]

It is not without interest here that Helena Roerich presents a very similar version of the events surrounding Napoleon, whom D.K. also mentions. In her opinion Napoleon was discovered and trained by the master Saint Germain, who was said to have organized the French Revolution until that point.[17] When the French Revolution deviated from the path that had been prescribed for it and followed a false direction, Saint Germain tried to reach the goal—the uniting of Europe—through Napoleon. But with him too his own conceit subsequently began to run riot, and he started ascribing his successes to himself alone. This led to the connection with the Himalayan brotherhood being dissolved and, without occult support, Napoleon very soon suffered a total defeat. 'The plan was destroyed,' dictated Mahatma M. in this connection to Helena Roerich, 'when Napoleon was recklessly dispatched to Russia, for he was not to make contact with Asia.'[18] Did not the same thing—according to the 'mahatmas from the Himalayas'—happen also with Hitler? In her letter of 14 May 1936 Helena Roerich made the following observation about him: 'You write that one member of the [Roerich] Society asked if Hitler will lead to the common good? I must say that I firmly believe that everything happens for the good. Lessons must be learnt in order that consciousness can move onwards . . . Thus we may say: all for the best.'[19] The further development of events in Europe was shortly to show in all clarity how everything was indeed to turn out 'for the best'.

But let us return to Radjneesh's theory. What is of importance here is not so much the question of the correctness of the explanations that he has given as the astonishing degree of correspondence between his attitude to Hitler, Mussolini, Franco and so on and that of D.K. to these same individuals.

If we recall once more Rudolf Steiner's prophetic indication from the year 1924 that *in 1933* (the year that Hitler came to power) the forces of the beast from the Book of Revelation will manifest themselves in Europe (see p. 281), the polarity between Christian esotericism and D.K.'s teachings with respect to this question stands before us in absolute clarity, like day and night.

---

[*]Unfortunately I am unable at present to give details of where these conversations of Radjneesh are published, as I became acquainted with them many years ago in Russia in a samizdat translation.

Thus according to the theory mentioned above, after he had come to power through the 'Shamballa force'[20] Hitler began to misuse this force after 1933 and therefore had to fall. D.K. then transfers this failure to collaborate rightly with the power received, so to speak, from 'above' from Hitler to the whole German people, and he dictates to Alice Bailey in 1948: 'Germany *as a nation* [italics D.K.] is too young, immature and negative to realize the true uses of power; she lacks the wisdom to use power, and her sense of inferiority (based on youth) leads her to misuse it when she has it.'[21]

From this derived D.K.'s positive attitude towards the 'Yalta Conference' in 1946, where the division of post-war Germany was finally decided. According to D.K. all three conference participants—Roosevelt, Churchill and Stalin—and also *all their decisions* were directly under the influence of the same first ray of Shamballa: '... the result of an intensive activity of the Masters and of Their disciples upon the first Ray of Will or Power',[22] related D.K. in the letter that he dictated to Alice Bailey in March 1945, and he continued: 'These are the things which the triangle at Yalta attempted to do. These they may not have consciously recognized as the work asked of them on account of their discipleship, but they automatically worked this way because they correctly sensed human need.' What D.K. says here is not surprising, since already in May 1945, when he was speaking about the working of 'divine guidance' in the world, he asserted that 'such inspired leadership is now being given to humanity by Winston Churchill and Franklin D. Roosevelt', whom D.K. also called examples of 'inspired leadership'. Of the latter he proclaimed in August 1946: 'that great first ray disciple, Franklin D. Roosevelt', that is, the disciple of Mahatma M.[*] The last of the three 'disciples' of Yalta, Stalin—a further 'expression of the Shamballa force'—has already been referred to in an earlier citation of D.K.'s writings.

A further significant characteristic of D.K.'s teaching is his very highly positive attitude towards the communism of Marx and Lenin, which was falsified only by their successors. He sees the errors of these successors in false 'interpretations of the writings of *Lenin and Marx* which are also personal and run counter to the meaning of these two men, just as the theologians of the Church interpret the words of Christ in a fashion which has no relation to His original intention'.[23]

This could also be a quotation from the book 'Community' by Helena

---

[*] This also explains why Helena Roerich addressed the letters which, she believed, she wrote at the behest of Mahatma M. specifically to Roosevelt (see Part One, Appendix 3).

Roerich. And it is a further confirmation of the Roerichs' assertion that emissaries of the Himalayan mahatmas met Karl Marx in London and Lenin in Switzerland[*] and gave them the impulse which D.K. subsequently called a 'divine impulse' (see further below).

Although he frequently criticizes the behaviour of the Soviet rulers during the 1940s in his letters, D.K. also always makes the observation that the 'great ideal' of 'Communism per se', 'its [Russia's] ideology' are not guilty of their errors: 'The major sin of Russia, and that which has prostituted and warped *the initial divine impulse underlying the ideology of that country*, is the determination she demonstrates at this time to be separative and to shut the Russian people away from world contact, using the implements of deception and the withholding of information. *It is not the totalitarian nature of the Russian government*[†] which is the prime disaster; it is the refusal to develop the universal consciousness. Many governments today are totalitarian in nature, either openly or subtly, but—at the same time—their peoples have free access to press and radio and are not kept in ignorance of world events.'

The great significance that D.K. attributes to the free access of all peoples to the resources of mass information—which for him is very much more important than the overcoming of totalitarian regimes in the world—is rooted in the notion that the future world Teacher will make his appearance on the earth accessible to *the whole of humanity* pre-eminently with the help of the press, radio and television and that therefore no obstacles should be placed in his way.

D.K. then continues about Russia: 'In Russia a world ideology is being wrought out which (when proven) can be presented to the world as a model system ... Russia is in reality—whether she realizes it or not at present—undertaking *a great experiment in education* [italics D.K.][‡] and, in spite of evil methods and sinning against the soul of human freedom, eventually the educational process will prove convincing to the world and provide a world model.'

Although D.K. is of the view that the aim which, as we have seen, he associates with the fulfilment of the 'ideal of Communism' can only be

---

[*] In Helena Roerich's book 'Community' tribute is paid on many pages to Lenin and his communistic ideas and the information given that the Hierarchy from the Himalayas fully supports the Bolshevik Regime in Russia (see Part One, ch. 3 and 4).

[†] These words were written in 1948, at the time of the so-called second great wave of Stalinist terror (the first was in 1937).

[‡] Similarly in Great Britain 'a great experiment in free government' is being undertaken and in the USA 'a great experiment in right relationships' (between human beings).

attained after the death or the removal from office of 'the present group of dictators and arrogant men' in Russia, he nevertheless stipulates also in this case that 'the intention of the dictating agents ... in Russia is basically good'.

D.K. sees the occult-political future of the whole of mankind in the form of the absolute power of *three great states*: firstly the USA, which unites North and South America under its influence; secondly Great Britain as the leading power in Europe and the head of the 'British Empire';[24] and thirdly the USSR. For 'their ideology [that of Russia] is fundamentally as sound as that in the other groups, but the difference lies in the factors of personality and the mode of applying the ideology'.[*] The USSR 'will eventually ... direct its major interest upon Asia ... as far as the Pacific' (written in September 1939).

According to D.K., through these three great nations there work also the three main kinds of energy: through Great Britain, the high Shamballa force; through the USA the power of the Hierarchy; and through the USSR the energy of humanity itself. And so these 'constitute a governing triangle of energy'[25] on our planet.

D.K.'s ideas about the occult-political partition of the world were dictated by him to Alice Bailey for the first time in September 1939, that is, over four years before the Yalta Conference, and then published in the chapter entitled 'The Modern Era'.[26] After the Yalta Conference D.K. then added the thought: 'In these three great nations, therefore, the three major divine aspects are being brought to manifestation, thus laying the foundation *for the new world order.*'[27]

On close examination this 'new world order' can, however, easily come to be seen as a barely concealed twofoldness rather than a seeming threefoldness, since, as D.K. asserts many times, Great Britain stands especially close to the United States (this is not a new idea but a well-known concept, familiar not only outwardly but also to occult history).[†] D.K. then writes in another book how this twofoldness can (or should) be transformed: 'Under the plan and contingent upon the energies pouring through the five planetary centres according to plan, there are three great fusing energies or vital centres present upon our planet: a) Russia, fusing and blending eastern Europe and western and northern Asia; b) the United States (and later South America) fusing and blending central and western Europe and the entire western hemisphere; and c) the British

---

[*] D.K. also employs in this connection the expression 'a most interesting experiment'.

[†] Thus for example in the words: 'It is of deep moment to realize that Great Britain and the United States are closely related' (EA, p. 524 and RI, p. 625).

Empire, fusing and blending races and men *throughout the entire world*. In the hands of these nations lies the destiny of the planet. These are the three major world blocs from *the consciousness angle* and from the angle of world synthesis.'[28]

From the standpoint of a man of 'Tibetan' origin, as D.K. describes himself, this is a highly unusual conception of the occult-political partition of the world in which, strangely, neither India nor Tibet is mentioned, nor even South Asia. In any case this picture of the future represents a clearly Western orientation, indeed an Anglomania, on the part of its author.*

D.K. also evaluates the 'three major ideologies' of the twentieth century—totalitarianism (fascism), democracy and communism—in a similar way.[29] In his opinion 'the three major ideologies', despite the distorted form in which they appear, are wholly justified and in truth are 'all equally divine in their essential natures, and in their essences'. For 'the ideology which is embodied in the vision of the totalitarian states is an erroneous but clear-cut response to the Shamballa influence of *will*; secondly 'the ideology behind the democratic ideal constitutes a similar response to the universality which the *love* of the Hierarchy prompts it to express; and ... communism is of human origin ... Thus the three aspects of God's nature are beginning to take form as three major ideas' (italics D.K.). And D.K. takes this thought further in the same book: 'We have, therefore, three great centres [Shamballa, the Hierarchy and Mankind] and from them emanate three types of energy which are taking form as the three governing ideologies in the consciousness of the race.' And 'the ignorant masses ... become victims of the exponents of the ideologies'.

In another book D.K. describes the occult origin of these three ideologies in the following way: 'It was the acuteness of this situation [amongst mankind], and the wide extent of the cleavage, which induced the watching Hierarchy [and its head, the world Teacher] to permit a direct inflow of the Shamballa force (in spite of its attendant risks) to pour into the world. The objective was to stimulate the free will of the masses; the result upon them has been *relatively good* as it has led to the formulation and expression of the great world ideologies—*Fascism, Democracy and Communism* as well as that peculiarly distorted blend of Fascism and Communism which goes by the name of Hitlerism or Nazism ... [All

---

* The actual situation in the first half of the twentieth century in India and Tibet with respect to Englishmen and their colonial politics is best appreciated from a study of the relevant history.

this] has become focused, expressive and creative by the force of the Shamballa influence.'[30] [*]

Thus ultimately 'behind all of them stands He Whom we call the Lord of the World [Sanat Kumara]', so that all of these 'temporary experiments' brought about by these ideologies are merely elements of an overall plan which has the aim that 'the kingdom of God will be established upon Earth', that is, 'a kingdom wholly of this world' as was spoken of in the previous chapter. The leader of this kingdom, however, will—as a new world Pope—be the world Teacher himself, the representative of Sanat Kumara on earth; and the would-be cardinals, archbishops and so forth of his retinue will consist of the numerous company of the Himalayan Hierarchy, adepts, masters, pupils and their followers throughout the world. D.K. puts it as follows: 'It is the closer approach of the Christ and of the Hierarchy of Masters to humanity which is implementing the initiatory energies, which is crystallizing the ideologies [fascism, democracy, communism] present today in the human consciousness, and fostering ... the latent *ideology of the Kingdom of God*.'[32]

And so, in D.K.'s view, the future 'ideology of the Kingdom of God' as a further development and synthesis of fascism, democracy and communism is alone in a position to resolve all the problems besetting contemporary humanity and to give all people on earth 'happiness'![33] All this should, according to the 'definite plan' of the Hierarchy referred to above, shortly be brought about, probably only after the end of the 'temporary experiments' which have led to the lives of some people, for example in Eastern Europe, being themselves brought to an end in the most recent past.[34]

In a chapter of the book *The Externalization of the Hierarchy* entitled 'The Coming World Order', D.K. wrote *in April 1940*: 'The new world order must lay the foundation for a future world order,'[35] that is, for the world order which will be inaugurated in the twenty-first century by the world Teacher now approaching the earth. And so we find in the work of the 'Tibetan' the term 'new world order' almost half a century before it appears in the pages of the official American press in 1989.

Probably in order to emphasize the approach of the final imple-

---

[*] As one reads these lines, one may ask whether some of the occult circles which support the radical nationalistic movement in present-day Russia are inspired by the 'Shamballa' influence. Thus in an editorial article published in the first number of a journal by the name of *Elementy* founded by these circles in Moscow in June 1992, the need is spoken of to unite the best that is contained in the three basic ideological families, communism, fascism and democracy.

mentation of this global plan, a new map was published in the British magazine *The Economist* on 1 September 1990—as had happened already a century earlier—which clearly illustrates the shape of 'the world' in the approaching age of the 'new world order'.[36] Even a cursory glance at this map and also at the editor Brian Beedham's accompanying article reveals the astonishing correspondence between its basic elements and D.K.'s occult-political ideas as summarized above.

In both cases there are two giants: the USA, which unites North and South America under its sovereignty and absorbs the whole of Western and Central Europe; and Russia (no longer the USSR), as the centre of a colossal Eurasian bloc soaking up the whole of western and central Asia. What is also striking in both cases is the non-existence of an independent Central Europe as a necessary bridge between the West and the East, and as an inevitable consequence the juxtaposition between Western and Eastern Christendom and also Western and Eastern culture in general.

'Ex occidente lux'—this new solution is represented on the map by a sun which shines over North America and towards which a kneeling European turns in an attitude of prayer. On the territory of Russia, in contrast, a head with a tiara is symbolically portrayed gazing towards the East as a picture of a reawakening Caesaro-Papism.[*]

The only difference between the versions of the 'new world order' seems to lie in the role of Britain. However, if one understands D.K.'s observations not in an outwardly political but in an occult-political sense, a complete correspondence with the present idea of the 'new world order' can be recognized., according to which only the Anglo-Saxon race can and must form such a world order on the grounds that its land of origin—and indeed the land of origin of all occult politics—is Britain.[37]

Of course, this has to do not with the British people as such and their great culture but with the secret lodges of the English-speaking peoples, which are so harmful both to them and to the whole of human evolution, lodges which originally arose in Britain and from thence gradually spread into all English-speaking countries.

Rudolf Steiner spoke several times in his lectures about these secret lodges of the English-speaking West and referred above all to three main dogmas in their occult-political teachings.

---

[*] Further eastwards, on the territory of modern Siberia, is a group of people resembling 'dancing Cossacks'. However, if one examines the various gestures of the figures more precisely, one can endow this scene with a quite different meaning. One person can be recognized as reaching out directly towards the breast of another, who raises his hands helplessly, while behind them are four witnesses or helpers.

Firstly: 'The Anglo-Saxons must spiritually rule the fifth post-Atlantean period,'[38] hence 'the fifth post-Atlantean culture must ... have an Anglo-Saxon physiognomy and character',[39] and 'the Anglo-Saxon race ... must exercise world sovereignty for the present and for many centuries into the future'.[40]*

Secondly: The picture of the future shape of Europe 'must be such that the intellectual life of Central Europe must above all else be suppressed as something that should not flow into the future of humanity'.[41]

Thirdly: In Eastern Europe, above all in Russia, 'socialistic experiments'[42] must be carried out for which the West 'is not suitable'; in other words, there was the 'task ... of making this Eastern, and specifically the Russian world, into a realm of socialistic experiments',[43] into a place for the practical implementation of Marxist-Leninist (Bolshevist) ideology.

These three points can also be discerned in the 'new world order' which D.K. together with the occultists standing behind him was preparing for mankind: the emphasizing of the world mission of Britain, the disappearance of Central Europe through its total integration into the Western bloc and a positive attitude towards Bolshevist ideology, as though it was wholly innocent of the bestiality and criminality of the Bolsheviks.

Thus the picture of the world sketched by the 'Tibetan' occultist in the first half of the twentieth century proves at its end to be the actual 'action programme' of world politics emerging from the West, a programme which is to become a 'reality' in the twenty-first century.

This chapter may be concluded with the well-known words of Benjamin Disraeli, written in the middle of the nineteenth century: 'The world is governed by very different personages from what is imagined by those who are not behind the scenes.'[44] Among these people who are 'behind the scenes' is doubtless the mysterious 'Tibetan', together with his inspirers and their occult-political plans.

Notes

1. RC, p. 18.
2. EH, p. 508.
3. CF, p. 1178.
4. CF, p. 44; the following quotation ibid. p. 1031.

---

* Lord Rosebery said about these plans already in 1893: 'We must not forget that it is a part of our duty and our heritage to ensure that the world bears the stamp of our people and not that of any other' (quoted from GA 173, 11 December 1916).

5. EH, p. 491; the following quotations ibid., pp. 496, 497.
6. D–2, p. 327 and the following quotation.
7. RI, p. 655
8. EH, p. 498; and the following quotation ibid., p. 500.
9. RI, pp. 646–7.
10. EH, p. 268; and the following quotations ibid., pp. 267, 495, 497, 249, 267, 495, 497.
11. EH, p. 548.
12. EH, p. 663.
13. EH, p. 491, and the following quotations ibid., pp. 435, 446, 494, 548, 548, 630, 491.
14. GA 196, 9 January 1920.
15. Question and answer session after the lecture of 1 October 1911, GA 130, and the following quotation.
16. EH, p. 132; the following quotation ibid., p. 133.
17. Helena Roerich, 'Fiery Experience', diary entries from 1924, published in UPNM ('At the Threshold of the New World'), Moscow 1993, entry dated 3 [2?] May 1924.
18. Ibid.
19. *Pisma Eleny Rerich* ('Letters of Helena Roerich, 1932–1955'), Novosibirsk 1993, letter of 14 May 1936.
20. EH, p. 133.
21. RI, p. 624.
22. EH, p. 449, and the following quotations ibid., pp. 449, 301, 578, 300.
23. RI, p. 680, and the following quotations ibid., pp. 595, 428, 679, 596, 595, 632, 631, 632, 622.
24. EH, p. 132, and the following quotations ibid., pp. 131, 132, 132.
25. RI, p. 640.
26. EH, p. 124.
27. EH, p. 632.
28. EA, pp. 529–30.
29. DN, p. 21; and the following quotations ibid., pp. 22, 22, 22, 22, 24.
30. EH, pp. 126–7.
31. DN, p. 25 and the following quotation.
32. RI, p. 581.
33. RC, p. 115.
34. See S.O. Prokofieff, *The Spiritual Origins of Eastern Europe and the Future Mysteries of the Holy Grail*, English translation Temple Lodge, 1993, 'Postscript'.
35. EH, p. 190.
36. See Terry M. Boardman, *Mapping the Millennium: Behind the Plans of the New World Order*, Temple Lodge, 1998.
37. The relationship between Britain and the United States on an occult plane can be brought to expression with the help of the following comparison. The United States is a big ship fitted out with the latest technology that is served by a large crew; but on the captain's bridge, determining the course of the ship, is a small number of British people.

38. GA 167, 28 March 1916.

39. GA 174a, 18 March 1916.

40. GA 174b, 21 March 1921.

41. GA 174a, 18 March 1916.

42. GA 174b, 21 March 1921.

43. Ibid.

44. The source of this quotation is Disraeli's novel *Coningsby*, first published in 1844. See page 240 of the Nonsuch Classics edition, 2007 or chapter XV of Book IV.

6. Alice Bailey and Helena Roerich

To conclude this survey of the occult teaching of Alice Ann Bailey (1890–1949), there is a need to consider the parallel aspects that doubtlessly existed between her destiny and that of Helena Roerich (1879–1955), the founder of Agni Yoga, the other familiar occult movement.

In the biographies and world-views of both these occult authors one can find striking correspondences but also not inconsiderable differences which, however, largely play the part of exceptions that prove the rule, thus giving rise to the thought that the two movements derive from the same occult source. One could also say that these not wholly corresponding occult streams nevertheless fit together perfectly into an overall picture, behind which there clearly manifests itself an all-embracing and cleverly thought out occult-political plan.

The teaching of Agni Yoga and the biography of its founder have already been spoken of at some length in Part One. We shall here consider these questions only to the extent that the theme of this chapter demands, by drawing upon some new material relating to Agni Yoga that did not feature in Part One.

The relationship between the spiritual destinies of Bailey and Roerich results from a whole series of particular qualities of their occult biographies. Thus they were born at roughly the same time and both died within a few years of one another. Both claimed to have met their occult teachers in England. Helena Roerich met the person whom she regarded as Mahatma M. on 24 March 1920 in London,[*] after which their occult collaboration began; while a personality under the name of Mahatma K.H. called on Bailey in Edinburgh on 30 June 1895. However, she took up occult collaboration with him only in autumn 1918. Moreover, both women visited India, with Alice Bailey staying there for only a few years and Helena Roerich for several decades. The reverse was true of North America, where the Roerichs spent in all only a few years and Alice Bailey the larger part of her life. Furthermore, both women came in contact for a

---

[*] In July 1851 Mahatma M. had also for the first time met H.P. Blavatsky in the physical body in London. Both Blavatsky and also, subsequently, Roerich asserted that before this first *physical* encounter they had perceived this teacher on more than one occasion 'in a vision' and therefore recognized him immediately in an earthly body (see W. Kingsland, *The Real H.P. Blavatsky*, London 1985, pp. 40–1). Altogether there are obvious parallels in Blavatsky's life with those of the two other women. Thus Blavatsky founded the Theosophical Society in New York, and she spent many years in India and so forth.

time with the Theosophical Society and even became members of it: Alice Bailey in California, the Roerichs in Russia and subsequently in India, where in 1925 they visited the headquarters of the Theosophical Society in Madras. Both Alice Bailey and Helena Roerich also from time to time published articles in the journal *The Theosophist* in Adyar.

To be sure, both Alice Bailey and also Roerich soon distanced themselves again from the Theosophical Society and founded their own occult movements in America: the Roerichs the first groups of Agni Yoga (1921) and later the Nicholas Roerich Museum in New York, and Bailey her publishing house and the first groups of the Arcane School (1923). Helena Roerich wrote her first book of *Agni Yoga*, 'Leaves from Morya's Garden', Part I 'The Call' to the dictation of the 'mahatma' in 1920–3; and at the same time Bailey likewise—to the dictation of the other 'mahatma'—wrote her first book *Initiation, Human and Solar*, which was published in 1922. Then, however, an ever more consistent geographical differentiation between the spheres of the occult influence of the two streams ensued, corresponding to the two world blocs referred to in the previous chapter.* The Roerichs thereafter concentrated more upon Russia, China, Mongolia, Tibet and India; whereas Alice Bailey focused upon America and Europe (with the exception of its eastern part). In this connection, the places where both women died are also symptomatic: Helena Roerich—after a vain attempt to return to Bolshevik Russia—died in India (near Calcutta) and Alice Bailey in New York.

Ostensibly at the behest of Mahatma K.H., Djwhal Khul, his closest pupil and at the same time the youngest Master of the Himalayan Brotherhood, began from November 1919 onwards to dictate her books to Alice Bailey under the pseudonym 'the Tibetan'. This continued until 1949, that is, for 30 years. Roughly at the same time (in 1920) a personality with the name 'Mahatma M.' began to dictate the books of *Agni Yoga* to Helena Roerich, and this work likewise went on until the end of her life.

It is not without interest that Helena Roerich was convinced that she personally met Alice Bailey's inspirer in India. In the last book of *Agni Yoga*, which bears the title 'The Superearthly' (1937), the mahatma dictating to her relates: 'We [the mahatmas] have not departed from life. When we manifested ourselves, we did not distinguish ourselves from the rest of earthly inhabitants. You could yourselves testify that Djwhal Khul, when he appeared in order to meet you, did not differ from the lamas.

---

* Helena Roerich wrote about this in the first half of the 1930s to President Roosevelt (see Part One, Appendix 3).

Thus all brothers [of the Himalayan community] and all other members of it outwardly have an ordinary earthly form.'[1]

In this connection it is particularly revealing to compare the character of the relationships of Alice Bailey and Helena Roerich to their inspirers. On the basis of the occult diaries of Helena Roerich from 1924 together with other notes and letters recently published in Russia,[2] the picture arises from her of a consistently undertaken occult schooling which her teacher—in her view Mahatma M.—carried out by means of direct astral contact. In her early childhood two Indians appeared to Helena Roerich in a vision.[3] She later recognized them as the Mahatmas M. and K.H.; the former then began repeatedly to visit her 'astrally', and in such a form that in her visions 'the Image of the Teacher merged with the Image of Christ, though the girl [Helena Roerich] feared to acknowledge this'.[4] In other words, already in early childhood it was suggested to Helena Roerich that Christ is not a divine-cosmic Being but merely one of the teachers of a mysterious brotherhood whose members, while having human status, are significantly in advance of the present stage of human evolution. Thus Helena Roerich in her diaries often uses the expression 'the Master Christ',[5] and she writes similarly about 'the Master Morya' or 'the Master Kut Humi' and so forth.

A constant telepathic connection between Helena Roerich and her main occult leader, the so-called Mahatma M., came about only later and, indeed, after their first *physical* encounter, which took place on 24 March 1920 in London. In time Mahatma M. took on the occult development not only of Helena Roerich but also of all other members of her family. Thus she wrote in one of her letters: '. . . Master Morya. He leads me and my family.'[6] Subsequently, asserted Helena Roerich, she was able at any time to take up telepathic contact with him and to ask him questions about the most diverse themes; and he responded with answers, sometimes without granting her permission to write them down, gave her occult exercises, characterized in detail their influence on his pupil's physical and more refined bodies, told her of changes in her aura, called forth within her an insight into her past incarnations (and told her about his own), monitored her occult experiences, corrected 'erroneous' perceptions, shared with her details from the life and work of the Himalayan Brotherhood and so on. Hence Helena Roerich wrote entries in her occult diary as she had heard them, that is, directly from the mahatma himself.

Soon the voice of Mahatma M. was joined by that of Mahatma K.H. From time to time both mahatmas took on material form, and they were sometimes even seen not only by Helena Roerich but also by further members of her family.[7] Then Helena Roerich began to hear the voices of other mahatmas. Thus Mahatma M. told her: '[Helena Roerich] was accustomed to our two rays M.M. and M.K.H. from childhood, but now to the pressure of other Masters.'[8] Gradually Helena Roerich continued to develop the capacity to perceive the various voices telepathically. And finally she begins to hear voices of still higher 'Masters'—those of the Christ and of Buddha, and her occult instructor explains to her why it is 'so much easier to hear the voice of Christ' than that of the Buddha.[9] This goes so far that Mahatma M., when one of the lamas in Tibet bestows on her a sculpture of the founder of Buddhism, dictates to her the following explanation of this episode: 'Do not suspect the lama, for by order of the Christ Sister Or. [a member of the Himalayan Brotherhood] sent him in order that the new fire of the Buddha might be kindled beside Christ.'[10]

Then her inspirer in the vision showed Helena Roerich the location of the Himalayan Brotherhood. In her diary there then follows a detailed description of the 25-storey occult museum hewn out of rock, where exhibits from all epochs of the earthly evolution of mankind are to be found. On the lowest floor, deep below the surface of the earth, 'the life of Christ' is depicted. As Helena Roerich writes, she remained longest in this portion of the museum. And although she was there not in her physical but in her astral body, she had to be extremely careful, 'for the air there is enriched with protective gases ... [and] the astral body is completely exposed ... [so that] We ourselves [the mahatmas] remain below the 20th floor for protection'.[11] One must then ask what idea Helena Roerich had of the astral body when she accepted that it, like the physical body, is subject to the influence of 'gases'?

There then follows the description of the wonderful garden of the mahatmas, together with the 'red-yellow tower' containing laboratories where they develop and guard their inventions, anticipating as they do the achievements of the earthly sciences by centuries. She is also told that it is Mahatma M., Helena Roerich's first teacher,[12] who has undertaken in our time to be 'watchman at the Tower'. It is interesting that Alice Bailey likewise says of him that he is now 'the Head of all truly esoteric schools'.[13]

Here can be observed one of the differences when comparing the mediumistic faculties of the two occultists. For Helena Roerich spoke again and again of her own clairvoyant experiences, of her frequent 'astral flights' to the Himalayan stronghold and so on, whereas Alice Bailey evidently had no clairvoyant experiences—although the sole clairvoyant dream in her life spoken of in chapter 1 brought about a turning point. This dream, during which Alice Bailey was participating in the Buddhist

Wesak festival in the Himalayas, is clearly reminiscent of Helena Roerich's 'prophetic dreams'. Especially its most important result—the experience of the Buddha's superiority to the Christ, as Alice Bailey believed thereafter throughout her life—corresponds to Helena Roerich's conviction of the superiority of the Maitreya Bodhisattva to the Christ (see below). But let us return to Helena Roerich's occult development. She wrote about it as follows: 'The teacher first appeared as an Indian, but when the consciousness of the pupil widened and learnt to encompass everything, the Beautiful Countenance gradually began to be transformed and at length took on a Sublime Countenance of Cosmic significance—that of the Lord of Wisdom and Beauty, the Lord of Divine Shamballa.'[14] Thus Helena Roerich was convinced that the guidance of her occult development soon passed from the Mahatma Morya to the Maitreya himself. This is why in her other works she ceased to make any clear distinction between them and gave her pupils the idea that they are identical (see Part One). This ascent on the part of Helena Roerich to the higher level of being a pupil of the Maitreya is accompanied by hymns of praise and eulogies that her occult teacher richly bestows upon her: 'Urusvati manifests to the Earth the connection with the heavens. Urusvati manifests the beauty of the symphony of the spheres. Urusvati manifests the ray of the Light that penetrates walls. Urusvati* manifests the Shield that indicates the course of the Heavenly Bodies. Urusvati manifests the flight of the arrows of the Spirit . . .'[15] and so forth. After such hymns of praise, of which not only her diary but especially the last volume of *Agni Yoga*, 'The Superearthly', are full, it should come as no surprise that Helena Roerich considered herself to be the highest and sole emissary on earth of the Lord of Shamballa, the Maitreya.

In one of her later letters (1949) she wrote: 'The stage of such a cosmic collaboration with the Gr[eat] L[ord]† is—as has been said—very rarely achieved.'[16] And in another letter: 'Do not doubt my words, I speak with the words of the Gr[eat] L[ord].'[17] And in a further letter: 'At present I

---

* 'Urusvati' is Helena Roerich's occult name, given to her by the Himalayan mahatmas. Translated from the Sanscrit it means: 'Light of the morning star' or 'Light of Venus'. Helena Roerich explained its significance in the following way: 'Svati, or to be more precise Urusvati, is today the planet Venus. This is what they call this planet in the Gr[eat] Wh[ite] Brotherhood. Uru and Svati can be understood as meaning Atman and Buddhi, as Spirit and Div[ine] Soul, also, if you like, as Buddhi and Manas' (*Pisma Eleny Rerich*— 'Letters of Helena Roerich', Vol. 3, Novosibirsk 1993, p. 120). Thus in conferring this honourable title on Helena Roerich, her inspirer probably wanted to indicate that she had fully developed the higher, spiritual triad of man's being.

† This is what Helena Roerich calls the Maitreya.

have a difficult time because of my collaboration with the Gr[eat] L[ord] on the cosmic and earthly plane.'[18] Thus it is Helena Roerich's view that all the books of *Agni Yoga* were telepathically dictated to her not by Mahatma M. but by the Maitreya: 'Of course, the author of the books is the Gr[eat] L[ord] M[aitreya] Himself. I simply hear and inscribe, it would not do to speak of this to those who are merely curious, but those closest to us may know.'[19] For this reason all 14 volumes of *Agni Yoga* were published anonymously by Helena Roerich without a reference to her name, for she did not see herself as their author. However, they were all furnished with small signs on the dust jacket: some with Sanscrit letters in a circle which mean 'Maitreya Santkha' or 'The Community of the Maitreya'[20] and which were to testify—as it were for 'those who understand'—to their 'true' author.[*]

Here we have a direct parallel between Helena Roerich and Alice Bailey, for both reckoned that they were not the authors of their teachings but asserted that they merely wrote down telepathically what was dictated to them. Thus one can apply to both women Rudolf Steiner's remark,[†] that such an occult hearing appearing in the form of a direct transmission of human words and thoughts (as dictation) is particularly dangerous for spiritual development, since it leads gradually to a situation where 'we sink down into the solid ground with the whole of our spirit and the whole of our soul'.[21] Not for nothing did Helena Roerich speak again and again in her diary about the *subterranean* museums in the temples of the Himalayan stronghold which she visited in her astral body.

'Anything we then hear inwardly,' continues Rudolf Steiner, 'will completely absorb us. You can drown in it most miserably and cease to be a human being [in the sense of becoming an instrument of the beings who are dictating]. Hence one must always look upon those people who say that all sorts of things are being thus imparted to them inwardly with a certain watchfulness. This is *always* dangerous.'[22] And it is dangerous

---

[*] Similarly, according to Helena Roerich, the symbolic sign at the entrance to the Roerich Museum in New York signifies, 'esoterically, Morya Rex' (ibid., letter dated 10 March 1936).

[†] Similarly two warnings on the part of true modern occultism pronounced by Rudolf Steiner—not to trust any form of mediumism or any information for which responsibility is borne not by the communicator himself but by a teacher or mahatma concealed behind him (see chapter 1)—fully apply to the means whereby Helena Roerich received her teachings. And the fact that she emphatically dissociated herself from vulgar mediumism is by no means a proof that she did not herself actually work with mediumistic powers, albeit of a higher order. Her recently published occult diaries are a clear testimony to this.

because 'they are *never particularly high spiritual beings* who speak to one in this way but ... those of a lower kind'.

In this respect a certain difference can be discerned between Alice Bailey and Helena Roerich. Whereas the essentially modest Alice Bailey confined herself to industriously writing down the dictation of D.K., who was only a pupil of K.H., Helena Roerich had no problem with referring back the dictation that she had heard to the highest authority, the Maitreya himself, who, as she said, 'has taken [upon himself] responsibility for our Planet',[23] that is, he is the ruler of the earth. But since she considered herself to be the main and *sole* representative of the Maitreya on earth, she could of course not be in agreement with the existence of another mediumistic mediator and had a distinctly negative attitude towards Alice Bailey's books and quite especially towards the society (the Arcane School) which she founded. For in Helena Roerich's opinion 'only this [Roerich] Society received the Teaching from the highest Source through N.K. and H.I.R. [N. and H. Roerich], who alone have been entrusted with it',[24] only it follows the 'indications' of the Maitreya and is under the 'protection' of the White Brotherhood; for only where 'those who have been entrusted' [the Roerichs] are present is the 'shield of the Maitreya' to be found (and so on). In Helena Roerich's words this is quite simply an 'occult axiom'!

As for Alice Bailey's books, they 'lack warmth of heart' and are 'extremely dry', although—continues Helena Roerich—'I have been told that [their] best pages have been borrowed from the Wh[ite] Br[otherhood]'. She was evidently exasperated by the fact that Alice Bailey expressed herself very positively about the books of *Agni Yoga* and even 'recommended them to her members and arranged classes where they could be studied'.[25]*

Thus a peculiar situation arises in the mutual relationship between these two occultists who claimed to have the same source for their esoteric knowledge (the mahatmas and Shamballa). Helena Roerich, who had herself testified to having met the Mahatma D.K. in India (see p. 323), maintained that the anonymous 'Tibetan' who dictated to Alice Bailey was not D.K. at all but a dark brother of the left path who merely worked 'behind the mask of the Teaching of the light'. 'We know,' she writes, 'who is hidden behind this pseudonym. His power is great. And the aim of this teacher is to entice into his cadre as many ordinary, useful people as

---

* Despite Helena Roerich's warnings, many of her pupils in a great variety of countries are working today with Alice Bailey's writings and accept that they derive from the same occult source as the books of the founder of Agni Yoga.

possible' who 'fly like moths into the black fire that reduces them to ashes', directly 'into the embrace of darkness'.[26]

Although Helena Roerich therefore disapproved of the secret inspirer of Alice Bailey's books,[*] she had to acknowledge that the foundations of the teaching derive from the same occult centre which she designates as a White Brotherhood, which is to say, from the same source as her own work.

The 'Tibetan' who dictated to Alice Bailey expressed himself similarly, although in a less sharp form, regarding the teaching of Agni Yoga. He observed in the book *A Treatise on White Magic*: 'In the book *Agni Yoga* some of the teaching to be given has filtered through but only from the angle of the will aspect. No book has as yet made its appearance which gives in any form whatsoever the "yoga of synthesis".'[27]

Of course, Helena Roerich did not share this view. She regarded Agni Yoga as an 'ocean of teaching', which for the first time unites *all* forms of yoga and all the occult seeking of mankind in a higher synthesis (see Part One).

Nevertheless these two characterizations complement one another in a certain respect. Through Alice Bailey a more 'intellectual' aspect and through Helena Roerich a more 'will-oriented' aspect was given of *one and the same teaching*, of which a synthesis or essentially a *middle* sphere quite clearly does not exist. From a spiritual-scientific standpoint there appears here the dichotomy described on several occasions by Rudolf Steiner of a one-sided development of the forces of the intellect and the will, which, if they unite in a union that is counter to natural processes, endeavour from their respective sides to destroy the inner centre of man's being whence alone man can today arrive at a true knowledge of the Christ Being.[†]

As we have seen, neither Alice Bailey nor Helena Roerich possessed a true knowledge of the Christ, since they both derived their knowledge

---

[*] A further detail may be of interest. Helena Roerich remarked in her letter about Bailey that 'the leaders of this extensive society [that is, Alice Bailey, together with her husband and also the "Tibetan" standing behind them with his secret helpers] are at the same time members of the sec[ret] police in the service of a state', which almost literally corresponds to Rudolf Steiner's statement about the false mahatma who inspired Blavatsky in the last years of her life (see Part Three).

[†] This is reminiscent of a description by Rudolf Steiner of how the Jesuits and certain Free Mason lodges have serious mutual quarrels in their lower ranks and at higher levels submit to a common leadership. 'Think,' Rudolf Steiner concluded a characterization of this phenomenon, 'what one can achieve if one has such an apparatus at one's disposal' (GA 167, 4 April 1916).

from one and the same antichristian source. Moreover, the latter referred back to a quite different authority, to that of the alleged Maitreya whom she placed above Christ, regarding him rather than Christ as the highest Leader of the Earth.

But what was imparted to Helena Roerich by this 'highest' authority, to whom she attributed her entire teaching, about the founder of Christianity? We shall let her speak for herself: 'We should not forget,' she wrote in one of her letters, 'that They [Christ and Buddha] and the L[ord] Maitreya came to the Earth from Venus at the threshold of the forming of the physical human being and are therefore our divine primal ancestors and educators.'[28] According to Helena Roerich, however, these three individualities are not at the same stage of development, the third of them being more highly developed and, hence, superior to the other two: 'In esoteric teaching three world rulers are referred to, Buddha, Christ and Maitreya. The Maitreya is the oldest, the first and the last, the tsar of all tsars, the teacher of all teachers. In [Blavatsky's] *The Secret Doctrine* He is Sanat Kumara [that is, Lord of the Earth]. I write this only to you and to those council members [of the Roerich Society] whom you consider should be told about it.'[29]

Thus although she distinguishes the Christ and the Maitreya and regards them as two different individualities, she resolutely places the Maitreya above Christ. On this point her teaching does not entirely harmonize with that of the theosophists (Besant and Leadbeater), or Alice Bailey's. This difference is particularly striking when it comes to comparing Helena Roerich's and Alice Bailey's ideas about the Second Coming. Helena Roerich says that the true 'Second Coming' is not the coming of Christ at all but will be that of the Maitreya, and that therefore the ancient Hebrews were, in her opinion, ultimately right in viewing Christ as not the true Messiah: 'In the name of Truth it is also necessary to say that Christ *was not* actually the Messiah promised them by the Scriptures.[*] The Messiah of the Hebrews is identical with the Maitreya, the Kalki Avatar, Muntazir [the future prophet of the Muslims] and so forth—that Highest of Beings who is to appear at the change of the Races in order to bring a New Proclamation and establish that vibration at which the spiritual evolution of the New Cycle will sound.'[30][†]

---

[*] This means that, in the view of Helena Roerich's inspirers, the Christ Himself was evidently mistaken in this respect, for He spoke about Himself many times in the Gospels as the Messiah awaited by the Hebrew people.

[†] Thus in her letters Helena Roerich regards the Maitreya and the future Manu as one and the same personality (ibid., letters of 10 May 1937 and 23 August 1937).

However, Helena Roerich conceives of this coming of the Maitreya not as his physical manifestation but mainly as a spreading of his teachings throughout the earth: 'The entire East believes in the Coming of the L[ord] Maitreya, but those who know are aware that the L[ord] Maitreya abides now in the form of the L[ord] of Shamballa and, of course, His Coming should not be understood as a manifestation of His flesh amidst earthly conditions and earthly inhabitants. The teaching of the L[ord] Maitreya will be spread throughout the entire World and will be at the forefront of a new era, the era of the awakening of the Spirit, also called the era of womanhood.'[31] And as this 'new era' began—according to Helena Roerich—already in January 1934,[*] 'the teaching that is being given now by the Gr[eat] L[ord] M[aitreya] is already a sign of His Coming'.[32] That is, such a 'sign of his coming' is the teaching of Agni Yoga being given now by a 'woman', Helena Roerich.

She then goes on to explain to her pupils why the coming of the Maitreya will not be a coming in the *physical* body, in that—in contrast to the traditional Buddhist conception—she maintains that he has already reached the Buddha stage: 'It was also strange to read the words that "if the Lord Maitreya is to become a Buddha, He will probably come in a physical body". That Individuality who in the Eastern conception will bear the Countenance of the Maitreya has already long been a Buddha, that is, has attained high Enlightenment, and so this reason that you have cited for a physical incarnation becomes redundant.'[33]

As for the appearance of the Maitreya in his 'fiery form', this is impossible at the present time, for it would be unbearable and destructive for someone who was unprepared for it: 'The Great Coming cannot be an ordinary event and will therefore not happen in the physical body.' 'His appearance ... in His fiery form would be destructive for many, many people, for His Aura is imbued with an energy of unusual power.'[34] And then Helena Roerich observes in the same letter in a completely unambiguous way that the Second Coming described in St Matthew's

---

[*] In one of her letters Helena Roerich wrote: 'Before these two black years [19]34 and [19]35 the sign of Great *Confidence* appeared, signifying—according to all the most ancient writings and prophecies—the beginning of the New Epoch of M[aitreya]' (*Pisma Eleny Rerich*—'Letters of Helena Roerich 1932–1955', letter of 18 November 1935). And in another letter she makes this date even more precise: 'The appearance of this sign came about in January [19]34' (ibid., p. 111). (By 'sign' is meant one of the messages of the Himalayan mahatmas to the Roerichs.) Subsequently, it is true, Helena Roerich shifted this date to 1936 and even to 1942 (see ibid., letter of 17 March 1938 and 'Letters of Helena Roerich 1929–1938', Vol. I, letter of 12 April 1935).

Gospel (24:27–30) actually refers not to Christ but to the appearance of the Maitreya in 'fiery form'.

This supersensible appearance of the Maitreya will, according to Helena Roerich, take place only in the future. But what concerns the immediate present is that the Maitreya is living pre-eminently as the Lord of Shamballa in the *physical* body: 'The L[ord] M[aitreya] now bears a physical body for particular purposes, but not for meeting with large numbers of people.'[35] In this earthly form he is reachable only by a few members of the Himalayan community, amongst whom he is living in one of the secret valleys surrounded by high mountains. And it was in this form that Helena Roerich perceived him on several occasions in her astral visions, not merely dictating to her all the books of *Agni Yoga* but also praising her quite especially for the work published in Mongolia in 1926, *Osnovy buddizma* ('The Foundations of Buddhism'), 'which the L[ord] highly approved of',[36] where she called the Buddha a communist and the future epoch of the Maitreya the 'age of the triumph of matter'.[*] Finally, Helena Roerich speaks in a further letter of the 'wish of the L[ord] Maitreya' that the third volume of Agni Yoga, 'Community'—that is, the volume containing her adulations of Lenin and Bolshevism—be published as quickly as possible'.[37†]

As for the founder of Christianity, who according to Helena Roereich is merely a 'younger' brother of the Maitreya, he is also apparently—so she imagines—living today in a physical body in so-called 'earthly Shamballa' in the depths of the Himalayas. Indeed, this is not the first time that he has been there. For the founder of Agni Yoga is of the view that Christ visited the Himalayas between the ages of 12 and 30 during his life in Palestine. 'I have no doubt—indeed I know—that Ch[rist] was in India,' she writes to her pupils.[38] And it is evident from Helena Roerich's recently published diary that her description of Christ's arrival in the Himalayas recounted in the first part of this present book[‡] was dictated to her by Mahatma M., who in his incarnation as a 'disciple of the Buddha' personally led Jesus to Shamballa, where the future founder of Christianity remained for three years. As Mahatma M. said, he and some like-minded individuals decided at that time to become pupils of Jesus. 'We decided there and then to serve His teaching . . .'[39] he dictated to Helena

---

[*] See Part One, ch. 4.

[†] See Part One, ch. 3, 4 and 10.

[‡] See Part One, ch. 7. Here the description of Christ's meeting and conversations with Mahatma M. is fully cited, accompanied by a reproduction of Nicholas Roerich's picture on the same subject, 'Znaki Christa' (The Signs of Christ).

Roerich, and continued: 'And so we want to begin the description of His life, so that no falsified word may live on the Earth. My best works were destroyed. Today it is also still impossible to publish your writings about Christ.'

On the basis of what she was allegedly told by the Himalayan mahatmas, Helena Roerich finally draws the following conclusion: 'The chronology of Christ's life is very imprecise. The Gr[eat] T[eachers] date the birth of Jesus at an earlier period than what is indicated in the Gospels. Rossul M[orya] was already alive when Ch[rist] began to preach.'[40]* Here we again encounter the endeavour—albeit in a veiled form—to confuse the birth of Jesus of Nazareth, which took place at the beginning of our era, with the birth of Jeshu ben Pandira a century earlier. As we have seen, this false view appeared for the first time with Blavatsky, who as regards this question—when she addressed it in her writings—relied on the view of Eastern mahatmas.† This disastrous error appears even more clearly in Annie Besant's book *Esoteric Christianity*, which Helena Roerich regarded 'quite definitely the best' of all works of the English theosophist.[41] In the same sense the secret inspirer dictated to Alice Bailey: 'The exact date of Christ's birth remains debatable.'[42]

However, it is also apparent that Helena Roerich did not follow through the difference referred to above between the Maitreya and the Christ with complete consistency. Thus she wrote in a letter: 'Ask those who are offended by the idea that the future epoch will be called the

---

* In her accounts of Jesus's visit to the Himalayan community at the Turning Point of Time, Helena Roerich never makes a clear distinction between Christ and Jesus (she very seldom uses the latter name at all).

† Thus in her article 'The Esoteric Character of the Gospels' (originally published in three parts in the journal *Lucifer* from November 1887) she questioned whether the historical life of Jesus had really been at the beginning of our era and asserted, as she herself said relying on the authority of the esotericism of the Eastern School and on various non-Christian occultists, that it was wholly a matter of indifference where Jesus came from, 'whether of Nazareth or Lydda' (in Lydda a century before Jesus's birth Jeshua ben Pandira was stoned and crucified). Blavatsky expressed this thought ever more decisively in an article published in December 1887 in the French journal *Le Lotus*: 'I say that scholars are lying or are talking nonsense. Our *teachers* are the ones who confirm this. If the story of Jeshu or Jesus ben Pandira is an error, then the whole of the Talmud, the entire Hebrew canon is erroneous.' And she continues: 'He was a follower of Jeshu ben Parashia . . . Found guilty of participating in the uprising of the Pharisees against Jannaeus in the year 105 BC, he fled to Egypt and took the young Jesus with him. This story is much truer than the stories of the New Testament, of which history makes no mention.' Is it then surprising that, in accordance with these words, Annie Besant wrote in her book *Esoteric Christianity*, in the chapter entitled 'The Historical Christ': 'The child whose Jewish name has been turned into that of Jesus was born in Palestine 105 BC' (op. cit. p. 96).

epoch of the Maitreya rather than that of Christ whether they really understand the significance of these names. If they knew more, they would not take any offence. The future epoch will stand under the rays of three Lords—Maitreya, Buddha and Christ.'[43] Helena Roerich explained in another letter what she had in mind with this curious formulation: 'The figures of the Buddha, Christ and Maitreya form in their unity a *Single Ego,*[*] so the predicted Second Coming should rightly be understood *as the manifestation of these three Sublime Figures*. The entire East awaits the coming of the Messiah, and every nation gives him the most beautiful Name and the one that is closest to it, often without knowing that the Bearers of These Names may be one and the same Ego.'[44] And at the end of the letter Helena Roerich observed: 'You must above all unite yourself in your hearts with the Figure of Christ-Maitreya ...'

Thus in her epistolary legacy Helena Roerich could arbitrarily either unite or separate these two individualities, in all probability depending on which aims she was seeking to attain in any particular case. She betrayed a similar ambiguity with regard to the question whether the imminent 'coming of the Maitreya' would take place physically or in another form. For all Eastern peoples expect his coming in the physical body, and so Helena Roerich left her readers and pupils—in that she referred constantly to their religious traditions—in complete uncertainty as to the actual form of this coming. In this respect Alice Bailey, with the more abstractly intellectual form of her presentation, expressed herself far more decisively and consistently, explaining on the one hand that Christ and the Maitreya are one and the same being who will very soon appear in a physical body on the earth as a 'world Teacher', and on the other asserting that in the future this event will be followed by the coming of still higher teachers.

Thus ultimately it is clear that, despite certain outward differences, both Alice Bailey and Helena Roerich have one thing in common above all else: *a total failure to understand the Christ Being and also the significance of the Mystery of Golgotha.*

Thus for example Helena Roerich writes about the Resurrection: 'Of course, at His Transfiguration Christ did not dematerialize His body but manifested Himself to the disciples in His refined body. The Resurrection likewise came about in this refined body.'[45] Thus Helena Roerich not only fails to see any essential difference between Christ's Transfiguration and Resurrection but places both these events at the same stage of an ordinary astral manifestation. As regards Christ's physical body, Mahatma

---

[*] All italics in this quotation are Helena Roerich's.

M. says the following to his pupil: 'The Spirit of Christ by His command caused His body to disintegrate into atoms. This was a remarkable achievement by the Christ. The opponent of cemeteries [Helena Roerich] must be glad when earthly baggage is taken away by its owner. *The bodies of Christ and Buddha are identical,* but their colouring is different.'[46]

Such a conception of the Resurrection as held by the founder of Agni Yoga does not greatly differ from Alice Bailey's 'understanding' of it, according to which everything that took place in Palestine at the Turning Point of Time had a temporary, preparatory character and succeeded only in part. A complete success is therefore to be awaited only as a result of Christ's Second Coming in the physical body.

Helena Roerich also interprets other central concepts of Christianity in a similar way. By the Father God, of whom Christ speaks on many occasions in the Gospels, she understands 'the older twin-soul' created by the Planetary Spirit at the creation of every human monad, likewise of the 'adept' Christ. In her opinion 'every adept', not only the Christ, has 'his older twin-soul, and She knows Him, being Father soul and Father-Fire'.[47]

Also in this case the difference as regards Alice Bailey's and Helena Roerich's conceptions of the heavenly Father is not particularly great. It consists only in that for the former the Father of the Christ is the Planetary Spirit himself (Sanat Kumara) and for the latter only his outcome—the 'soul-twin'. In both cases the conceptions have no relation to the 'Father' of the Gospels of which Christ himself speaks.

This explains why both Bailey and Roerich speak so aggressively against the divine Father, as he is described in the Gospels. Thus for example, one of the fundamental ideas running throughout the Gospel especially incites Helena Roerich: 'For me there is nothing more loathsome than the idea of the Almighty and All-Merciful Father-God who sacrifices his only-begotten Son, who is of the same essence as Himself, for the sins of human beings, which—according to the Testament—were created by Himself!'[48] 'Can it be,' she exclaims, 'that in later times such a type of fatherly love could be elevated to the status of divinity?! Every loving earthly father or mother would joyfully make the ultimate sacrifice for the rescuing of their son. Surely the divine Father is not morally inferior to the human beings He has created?!'

She likewise understands the concept of the creative Word, the Logos, as expressed in the prologue to St John's Gospel, as merely 'akin to vibration, or light', inasmuch as 'everything existing in the world is the manifestation of innumerable and manifold vibrations'.[49] Moreover, in

Helena Roerich's opinion the fourth Gospel was written not by John but by Mary Magdalen.[50] And by the Holy Spirit Helena Roerich understands merely a psychic energy ('the Holy Spirit is psychic energy'[51]). Thus Helena Roerich, or to be more precise the Eastern occultist dictating to her, imagines the Holy Trinity to consist of the 'twin-soul', 'vibrations' and 'psychic energy'. This should not surprise us if Mahatma M. dictated to her words such as these: 'May Christ be clothed in laboratory Rays.'[52] Modern adherents of Agni Yoga express themselves about Christ in a similarly dubious way. Here is one example among many: 'From now on, mighty streams of fire passed through His heart, the heart of the Redeemer, which works according to the rhythm of a reducing transformer ...'[53]

Alice Bailey's works are full of similar descriptions of the Father, the Logos and the Spirit, where they are seen as consisting of atoms, electricity, magnetism and vibrations of matter of varied power and speed. Hence it sounds really grotesque when Helena Roerich explains that Alice Bailey's teaching seems to her to be 'dry'. For the style and pseudo-scientific quality of many of her own descriptions can barely be distinguished from those of Alice Bailey. Thus for example: 'The cosmic atom is the basic atom from which the entire cosmos evolved ... The human atom is also the human monad ... The cosmic reason is above all the basic atom of the primal Sun.'[54] And one must ask whether the following description has any value: 'What is a moderator? In a fiery transmutation it makes sense to cover the centre a little to guard against fire. This covering can sometimes be done with a so-called psychic cap consisting of a condensed sheath of psychic energy.'[55] Helena Roerich also describes her own 'initiation'—which she allegedly underwent under the guidance of the Himalayan mahatmas—in a similar way. The difference between her teaching and that of Alice Bailey is simply that for Alice Bailey the whole cosmos—even its highest levels—is filled with electricity, whereas for Helena Roerich's inspirers an all-encompassing role is played by a so-called 'cosmic magnet', into whose 'mighty stream' man enters through his relationship with the Maitreya. For the whole of 'evolution has its origin in the Cosmic Magnet';[56] 'it forges the projection of the evolution of the planet' and 'maintains the human path'. And 'the great Teachers of mankind—not only earthly ones but those of distant worlds—who have together fully received the power of the Cosmic Magnet depict its Crown in the form of the Great Cosmic Reason ...'[57] However, Helena Roerich calls the foundation of this 'Cosmic Reason'—referring to the authority of the mahatmas—'involuntary mechanistic power'.[58] In other respects, Helena Roerich's cosmology can barely be distinguished from that of Alice Bailey: the same seven planes, wholly permeated with ever finer degrees of matter. And at the summit of this *material* pyramid is 'the energy of the Logos ...' which, according to one of Helena Roerich's pupils, 'with a vortical movement of inconceivable rapidity "bores holes" within the archetypal Cosmic Substance. These vortices of life, enveloped in the most refined sheath from the archetypal Cosmic Substance, are the primary atoms.'[59]

To conclude, mention should be made of a further element of concord, but also a difference, between the two teachings. They both concur in asserting that all leading Masters of the Hierarchy originally came from Venus to the earth. But beyond the bounds of Venus their cosmic paths suddenly diverge from one another. Alice Bailey's inspirer views earthly evolution as leading to the star Sirius, and Helena Roerich's inspirer to the constellation of Orion. In Helena Roerich's case this relationship also has a wholly concrete, material 'confirmation'. This has to do with the magical meteorite stone from Orion which is said to be in the keeping of the brotherhood of the mahatmas in the Himalayas and of which the Roerichs took a fragment with them on their Asiatic expedition. (See further in Part One, chapter 3.)

★

All in all an examination of the life's paths and the respective teachings of these two women Helena Roerich and Alice Bailey makes it plain that both were sent from one and the same occult centre,[*] one to the East and the other to the West, in order to work from two opposite geographical directions ultimately towards one and the same purpose: strengthening the power of the dark lodge of occultists who appeared under the name of the Himalayan mahatmas[†] and whose principal aim was to prepare the coming to earth of the false Messiah or world Teacher under the mask of the Maitreya Bodhisattva, who (according to Bailey) is equated with

---

[*] Another example of this is the fact that at the 16th 'Festival for Mind, Body and Spirit' in 1992 at the Royal Horticultural Hall, London, the books of Alice Bailey and Helena Roerich were exhibited in the same section and by a common representative.

[†] In this connection Alice Bailey wrote about the imminent physical appearance of members of the Hierarchy as the beginning 'of the kingdom of God' on earth (RC, p. 169 and EH, p. 407), while the Himalayan mahatmas spoke to Helena Roerich about themselves as the secret world government: 'Urusvati [Helena Roerich's Eastern name] has explained to many why they call us the World Government. Every human being feels, even though in varying degrees, that a centre of knowledge can be found somewhere. Where there is knowledge there is also power' (*Mosaic of Agni Yoga*, Vol. 2, Tbilisi 1990, p. 98).

Christ—or (according to Roerich) is placed higher than him—and has long been awaited by various religions under a variety of names.

Both teachings, deriving as they do from one and the same occult centre, firmly support the view that the planetary Hierarchy of the earth came to it from Venus and that in this Hierarchy the Christ occupies only the very modest position of one of the bodhisattvas in an endless chain of world Teachers stretching from the past right into the future.

The extent to which both Roerich and Bailey were well prepared for their occult task—the one in the East (including Russia) and the other in the West—is apparent from the style of their writings, which in both cases were dictated in a mediumistic way. Helena Roerich's style—as already noted in the first part of this book—corresponds completely to the soul qualities of Eastern people: it resembles an endless, unbroken meditation or to be more precise a distinctive (and indeed second-rate) kind of literary production constructed upon many repeats and a constant rhythmicizing of the prose sections, but above all upon a minimum of concrete thoughts directed to a waking consciousness. Because of this, reading the books of *Agni Yoga* tends to make one's ordinary waking consciousness go to sleep, giving rise in the soul to the easy feeling of blissfully dissolving into the rhythms and repetitions of the text and so exerting a strongly suggestive influence which is especially harmful for Eastern souls.

Alice Bailey's style, on the other hand, has an altogether different character. It is highly intellectual and almost entirely consists of abstract thoughts and assertions which for the most part are completely unproven but are marshalled in the tone of a higher authority that brooks no argument. Thus what strikes one most of all about Alice Bailey's books is their intellectuality. They are also full of numbered sections, points and further subdivisions, where letters and further sub-clauses follow the numbers in a constant endeavour to schematize a never-ending stream of unproven, often contradictory and generally unexplained occult *information*. There is virtually a total absence of any artistic or imaginative element. What is evident above all else is a purely intellectual fascination, with ever-ascending infinite cosmic plans, ever mightier cosmic beings, ever newer stages of initiation giving the reader the feeling that the secret author of these books must have quite extraordinary occult knowledge, without doubt far transcending anything else in the realm of occultism. However, all this so to speak 'supersensible knowledge' by its very nature not only does not lead to access to the *real spiritual world* but does not even give the reader the possibility of forming some sort of concrete idea of what *spirit* is in reality. For in D.K.'s or Bailey's teaching the universe that is accessible to a human being (and even to a Master) is full of the most diverse kinds and forms of everyday matter such as electricity, magnetism and permanent atoms of various levels and so forth, which from an occult standpoint signifies none other than the extending of the sub-earthly forces engendered by Lucifer, Ahriman and the Asuras to the whole cosmos that is accessible to man.

Thus on the basis of all that has been presented in this book, one may regard the content of Helena Roerich's books as *luciferic*-ahrimanic in nature, and that of Alice Bailey's as *ahrimanic*-luciferic.[*] What unites them, however, is above all their failure to understand the Christ impulse and the Mystery of Golgotha and, hence, a ceaseless, unconscious battle with them, a battle which is, nevertheless, waged in *full consciousness* by one and the same occult centre standing behind both streams. And just as— bearing out a true observation by Edouard Schuré—the escapade involving Krishnamurti was in a deeper, occult sense none other than an attempt on the part of radical antichristian occultism or an occultism of a left persuasion to prevent at any cost the revelation of the true wisdom of esoteric Christianity by anthroposophy,[60] so did this stream appear again in the teachings of Alice Bailey, this time using more refined and cleverly devised means to achieve the same goal.[†]

If, therefore, in conclusion we once again compare the anthroposophical stream of Christian esotericism with the Eastern-coloured streams of Helena Roerich and Alice Bailey it is scarcely possible to find a better image for this comparison than the sculptural Group carved by Rudolf Steiner with its two motifs in the centre and on the left side (from the viewer's perspective). Thus the central motif portrays the Etheric Christ, who in the twentieth century has supersensibly entered into humanity and has through His appearance caused Lucifer to fall into the cosmic abyss, and Ahriman to creep away and hide from his sun-rays like a dragon in the earth's dark depths.

The left side motif on the other hand is indicative of the destiny that is being prepared for earthly humanity by streams such as those of Alice Bailey and Helena Roerich which have no access to the Etheric Christ

---

[*] Especially in the case of Bailey, or to be more precise her secret inspirer, the question arises as to whether her books are not a particularly characteristic example of Ahriman's appearance as an author in the twentieth century, a phenomenon of which Rudolf Steiner spoke in 1924: 'Human hands will write the words, but Ahriman will be the author' (GA 240, 20 July 1924).

[†] That Alice Bailey's inspirer was familiar with anthroposophy is evident from his critical remark regarding Rudolf Steiner's teaching about child development in seven-year periods included in Alice Bailey's book *Education in the New Age*.

and as a result succumb to the combined influence of Lucifer and Ahriman who, as though sensing their 'victory', reach out their hands to one another.

★

If we now seek to sum up what has been said in this chapter, it should be noted that, according to Rudolf Steiner's spiritual-scientific research, at the end of every millennium a sort of temporary union takes place between the luciferic and ahrimanic forces battling against what the Christ and the Hierarchies serving Him—together with the circle of the bodhisattvas—want for the rightful evolution of humanity. Rudolf Steiner said in this connection: 'At the end of every millennium, the luciferic and ahrimanic spirits have a particular power ... With each millennium, hence in the years 1000, 2000 and so on, a particularly intense united assault on the part of Lucifer and Ahriman takes place ... As the new millennium approaches, they unite and exert an influence together on human beings.'[61]

As the turn of the millennium in our time is happening simultaneously with the greatest *spiritual* event of the whole of earthly evolution (the appearance of Christ in etheric form), anyone knowing of this should not be surprised that the adversarial powers have been making a *common* endeavour, and in the immediate future will be trying all the harder to do so, to falsify this central event with all the means at their disposal.

Rudolf Steiner referred especially to three ways in which such falsifications may come about. Thus the luciferic spirits try to make as large a number of people as possible possessed by themselves and their adherents (to the point of a temporary incorporation), endowing them with new, supersensible faculties which, however, will all the more surely divert such people from what is most important, namely a true knowledge of Christ. A person of particular genius from this group (and there are generally several of these in various parts of the world) will then appear as a spiritual teacher and consider himself to be Christ or even higher than Christ.[62] Such a person of great brilliance will then be the 'best' false precursor or false prophet of the imminent *incarnation* of Ahriman in the physical body[63] (Rev. 19–20). He will appear as a new 'world Teacher' and will be recognized as such by those 'supermen' who are possessed by luciferic beings, and by their many followers in the world.

Rudolf Steiner spoke in addition of an etheric (supersensible) individuality with a 'strictly ahrimanic nature' who will try with the help of certain occult, for the most part Western brotherhoods to occupy the place which rightfully belongs to Christ alone in the spiritual world adjoining the earth (true Shamballa).[64]

Thus we have three principal forms of the battle against Christ's appearance in the etheric body:

1. the furthering of the incorporation of *luciferic* spirits into earthly human beings;
2. the preparation for the incarnation of the mighty *ahrimanic* spirit on the earth;
3. the battle for the rulership in Shamballa between the Etheric Christ and the ahrimanic spirits, whom *asuric* beings are increasingly assisting in our time.

These three forms of the battle against the appearance of Christ in the etheric body can be discerned in germinal form in the teachings of that centre which has representatives and collaborators both in the East and in the West (for Lucifer and Ahriman are today working together), which inspired the occult movements of both Alice Bailey and also the Roerichs and continues even now to inspire new occult movements, especially those arising from the foundation of the 'New Age movement'.

The proclaiming of the imminent coming of the 'world Teacher' who will be interpreted as Christ or as a still higher being or simultaneously as the one and the other, a being who is penetrated by a human initiate, an Avatar or a Logos—this is the first act of the great drama of humanity which has already begun: the future encounter with the incarnated Ahriman!

There can be no doubt that the number of people who will succumb to the enormous temptation associated with the appearance of Ahriman will be very great. But all the more important will be the task of what will possibly be only a very small group of people who, on the basis of what has been imparted by modern spiritual science, will be in a position to recognize Ahriman and his luciferic false prophets and then fearlessly and uncompromisingly speak to the world openly and fully audibly about the true significance of Christ and the Mystery of Golgotha. For in this critical moment of world history the fate of earthly humanity will depend on whether people will be found who acknowledge no spiritual authority that does not rest upon a true knowledge of the Etheric Christ and upon a selfless service of the Christ, as Rudolf Steiner demonstrated with an exemplary power throughout his life.

Notes

1. Helena Roerich, *Agni Yoga*, Vol. III, Samara 1992, pp. 136–7.
2. Especially characteristic in this connection is the material published in the book *U poroga novovo mira* ('At the Threshold of the New World'), Moscow 1993.

There the autobiographical sketch 'Dreams and Visions' by Helena Roerich—consisting of diary entries from 1949—is published for the first time; and also included are her occult diary from 1924, entitled 'Fiery Experiences' and a series of previously unpublished letters from her last years (1945–9).

3. UPNM, p. 53.
4. Ibid., p. 32.
5. Ibid., p. 68. In contrast to this Helena Roerich speaks on several occasions about the Maitreya as the 'Great Teacher' (ibid.).
6. From the letter to V.A. Shibayev dated 25 July 1921, included in *Zhivaya etika* ('Living Ethics'), Moscow 1992, p. 391.
7. UPNM, p. 47.
8. Ibid., p. 70.
9. Ibid., p. 107.
10. Ibid., p. 71.
11. Ibid., p. 91 and also pp. 93, 94, 95.
12. Ibid., p. 103.
13. RI, p. 373.
14. UPNM, p. 54.
15. Ibid., p. 55.
16. Ibid., p. 156 (letter of 3 August 1949).
17. Ibid., p. 157 (letter of 27 August 1949).
18. Ibid., p. 164 (letter of 27 November 1949).
19. *Pisma Eleny Rerich* ('Letters of Helena Roerich 1932–1955'), 18 November 1935.
20. Ibid., letter of 10 March 1936.
21. GA 350, 18 July 1923.
22. Ibid., likewise the following quotation.
23. 'Letters of Helena Roerich 1932–1955', 10 March 1936.
24. Ibid., 23 August 1934.
25. Ibid.
26. Ibid.
27. WM, p. 429.
28. 'Letters of Helena Roerich 1929–1938', Vol. II, letter of 24 September 1935.
29. 'Letters of Helena Roerich 1932–1955', letter of 4 July 1936.
30. Ibid., letter of 30 June 1934.
31. 'Letters of Helena Roerich 1929–1938', Vol. II, letter of 4 November 1935.
32. 'Letters of Helena Roerich 1932–1955', p. 58.
33. 'Letters of Helena Roerich 1929–1938', Vol. I, letter of 12 April 1935.
34. 'Letters of Helena Roerich 1932–1955', p. 58.
35. Ibid., p. 57.
36. Ibid., letter of 30 June 1934.
37. Ibid., letter of 24 February 1936.
38. Ibid., letter of 8 February 1938.
39. UPNM, p. 80.
40. 'Letters of Helena Roerich 1932–1955', letter of 24 May 1938.
41. UPNM, letter of 13 November 1948.

42. RC, p. 106.

43. 'Letters of Helena Roerich 1929–1938', Vol. II, letter of 31 July 1937.

44. 'Letters of Helena Roerich 1932–1955', letter of 4 December 1937.

45. Ibid., letter of 2 September 1937.

46. UPNM, p. 107.

47. 'Letters of Helena Roerich 1932–1955', letter of 18 June 1936.

48. Ibid., letter of 7 May 1939.

49. Ibid.

50. UPNM, letter of 13 November 1948.

51. 'Letters of Helena Roerich 1932–1955', letter of 2 October 1936.

52. UPNM, p. 91.

53. Quoted from *Mir ognyonny* ('Fiery World'), no. 1, Riga-Moscow, p. 44.

54. Helena Roerich, *Letters to America*, Vol. III, 1948–55, letter of 10 December 1954.

55. 'Letters of Helena Roerich 1932–1955', letter of 2 September 1937.

56. *Agni Yoga*, Vol. I, p. 158.

57. 'Letters of Helena Roerich 1932–1955', letter of 3 February 1939.

58. 'Letters of Helena Roerich 1929–1938', Vol. I, letter of 6 December 1934.

59. Quoted from the journal *Mir ognyonny* 'Fiery World', no. 1, p. 23.

60. See further in Part Three.

61. GA 286, 7 March 1914.

62. See GA 130, 9 January 1912. That something of the kind exists in our time is evident from what is asserted by the modern Indian guru Sai Baba, who considers himself to be an avatar, that is, the incarnation of a divine being. This assertion, which he made at Christmas 1972, runs as follows: 'Christ did not say that He will never come again to the Earth. He said: "He who has sent me will come to the Earth." The one whose coming Jesus Christ prophesied is the Avatar Satia-Sai [Baba].' Quoted from Samuel Sandwise's book *Satia-Sai, the Saint and the Psychiatrist*.

63. See GA 191, 1 November 1919 and 15 November 1919; GA 193, 27 October 1919 and 4 November 1919.

64. See GA 178, 18 November 1917. Regarding true Shamballa, see GA 118.

7. Before the Century's End

Alice Bailey died on 15 December 1949 in New York. How has her teaching developed further? D.K. wrote himself after her death to his pupils: 'I am looking for no new 'stenographers' to take the place of A.A.B ... You have masses of undigested material with which to work, and enough teaching to express and make available to the public for twenty-five years to come.'[1]

If we add 25 years to the year 1949, we arrive at the year 1975. This year was, according to D.K., to be the beginning of the third epoch, which would represent the highest stage of development of his teaching (see p. 260), when new revelations 'emerging after 1975' will be 'be given on a worldwide scale via the radio'.[2]

The only person who has so far sought to implement this prophecy was Alice Bailey's successor, the Englishman Benjamin Creme. According to his own testimony, he entered already in 1959 into a 'telepathic' relationship with a master of the Hierarchy, who asked him not to reveal his name. As a result of an intense occult training, which Creme had received also telepathically from the same Master, he was from 1974 onwards in a position himself to receive messages from the Maitreya which, he says, 'were put into my mind'.[3] In January 1975 this being ordered Master Creme publicly to proclaim the messages received from the Maitreya in various occult groups of interested people. Then Creme began to give lectures in the West with the title 'The Reappearance of the Christ and the Masters of Wisdom'. He gave these lectures in various places, and the question and answer sessions after these lectures were collected in a book that he published in 1979 in London under the same title. On the jacket designed by Creme himself there is the 'mushroom cloud' of a nuclear bomb explosion with a yellow spot in the middle, which he called the 'Cosmic Spiritual Heart Centre.'[4]

Viewed as a whole the book itself is not of particular interest, since it consists merely of a simplified recounting of various aspects of Bailey's teachings. What merits a certain attention is only Creme's response to the observation that Rudolf Steiner spoke at the beginning of the century about the *etheric* reappearance of Christ and not about a physical event. Creme had this to say: 'Rudolf Steiner died in 1925. The announcement of the Christ's desire to return to the world was made in 1945. The decision to reappear was made earlier, but the *mode* of the reappearance was not determined [before 1945].'[5]

In this way did Creme explain the failure of the experiment with Krishnamurti, which in his opinion came about because 'the plan was changed' by the Maitreya with regard to his appearance and he decided to come *himself* to the earth having given up on the idea of working through his 'vehicle'. For material amplifying his ideas, Creme mentions to his adherents not only Bailey, Blavatsky and Sinnett but also all the volumes of *Agni Yoga* by Helena Roerich.[*]

But let us return again to his own story. As he said, in the following years he received an especially large number of 'telepathic' messages from the Maitreya personally (a portion of these was published in the appendix to the book referred to above). Regarding the most important message he wrote: 'On July 7th 1977, Maitreya Himself informed us that His Body of Light (His Ascended Body) was now at rest in His mountain Centre in the Himalayas.'[6] Then Creme's teacher informed him that the reappearance had begun. As a result Creme began in the autumn of that year to bring this proclamation to public knowledge. He founded several journals and tried to make his mark in the national press, on television and radio. Although at first he awakened some attention he did not have any success to speak of. The final result of all his efforts of communication was that, according to Creme, 'Maitreya the Christ descended in July 1977 from His ancient retreat in the Himalayas and took up residence in the Asian community of London,'[7] that he would soon appear in public and shake the world with his appearance. However—despite all Creme's affirmations—this did not happen, although he continued regularly to publish the 'communications' that he was allegedly receiving from the Maitreya (then still living in London). Remarks of the 'World Teacher' on political themes occupied an ever larger place in these 'communications'.

His appearance itself, as advertised everywhere by Creme to take place on the so-called 'Day of Declaration', was to take the following course: 'On the Day of Declaration, the international radio and television networks will be linked together, and Maitreya will be invited to speak to the world. We will see His face on television, but each of us will hear His words telepathically in our own language as Maitreya simultaneously overshadows all of humanity. Even those who are not watching Him on television or listening to the radio will have this experience.'[8] The Director of the BBC in 1986 was, however, not prepared to allow the Maitreya—who was living secretly in the less affluent suburbs of

---

[*] From Creme's remaining answers can be discerned his extremely positive attitude towards Marx. In his opinion, 'Marx was indeed a member of the Hierarchy, of a certain degree', and Creme's active connection with the Indian guru Sai Baba is also apparent.

London—to speak for himself, whereupon the 'world Teacher' decided to seize the initiative.

Thus he appeared, for example, in June 1988 'miraculously' in Nairobi, where he gave an address to 6000 Africans, each of whom to a man immediately recognizing him as the Christ. One of Creme's journals[9] even reproduced a blurred photograph of the 'world Teacher' with white headgear, white robe, black beard and Eastern facial features.* And from Creme's other journals we learn that the 'Maitreya has appeared to UN representatives and politicians in a variety of guises. He sat next to Javier Perez de Cuellar, who thought he was a colleague . . . [He] also appeared to President Bush. Initially Bush did not recognize the man who addressed him, and subsequently thought he was a bodyguard.'[10] Finally, 'Maitreya also appeared to Gorbachev in the guise of a colleague. He suggested to Gorbachev that since he spoke so much about democracy, it was necessary to initiate that [democratizing] process at home in the USSR,'[11] since he was saying such a lot about democracy. Nevertheless in spite of all these efforts of the 'world Teacher', his appearance as far as the mass of humanity is concerned has to date not taken place.

*

A further modern stream which has openly declared its connection with the community of Himalayan initiates is the impulse established in the second half of the twentieth century in the United States by Mark and Elizabeth Clare Prophet. As with the Roerichs, Bailey and Creme, the Prophets assert that they have achieved a telepathic connection with the Himalayan mahatmas, though in their case not merely with one of them but with all! As a result the Prophets regularly imparted their messages in letters or even in whole books, which would then appear under the name of the Master who had dictated them with the observation 'dictated to the Messenger' Mark L. Prophet or Elizabeth Clare Prophet. Thus in the catalogue of their publishing house the following books can be found, for example: Kuthumi, *Studies of the Human Aura*, continuation (*Intermediate Studies of the Human Aura*) by Djwal Kul; then Saint Germain, *Studies in Alchemy*; Jesus and Kuthumi (he is St Francis), *Prayer and Meditation*; El Morya, *The Chela and the Path* and so on.[12]† In this

---

* His headgear and the lower part of his face on this photograph are strongly reminiscent of a portrayal of Mahatma Morya in Nicholas Roerich's picture 'Signs of Christ' (see the reproduction in Part One).

† Most of the books were written in the form of letters dictated by the mahatmas in question.

way they enlarged the traditional circle of the Himalayan Masters of whom Alice Bailey wrote.

In their catalogue, books are also listed which were allegedly dictated to them by the Archangels Michael and Gabriel and *New Age Rosary and New Age Teachings* given by 'Mother Mary' herself.[13]

The original centre of the movement was the so-called 'Summit Lighthouse' which, as the Prophets assert, was founded in 1958 by 'the Ascended Master El Morya on Saint Germain's behalf ... in Washington D.C.'[14] In order to expand the movement the 'Ascended Masters' then founded the 'Church Universal and Triumphant', 'Montessori International' and also a series of 'study centres' throughout the world.

Since 1958 the 'Summit Lighthouse' has published weekly letters by the 'ascended Masters' to their pupils. These letters, called 'Pearls of Wisdom', represent an intimate contact, from heart to heart, between the guru and his chela. They contain instructions about cosmic laws, commentaries about present circumstances on the earth, and whatever the Great White Brotherhood considers necessary for the individual initiation of those who form part of this great movement of light-bearers on the earth.[15]

We shall cite here some extracts from writings of the Mahatma M.: 'The Darjeeling Council is a unit of hierarchy. I am its chief. Numbered among those who deliberate in our chambers are Saint Germain, Mary the Mother, Jesus the Christ and the Master Kuthumi ... Here in Darjeeling we are the followers of the path of Christ and the Buddha which are one.'[16]

And in another extract Mahatma M. says: 'Beloved ones, I point out to you one of the most pernicious errors of orthodoxy this day, and it is the lie that Jesus is the only Son of God, and furthermore that Jesus came into embodiment in the full mastery of Christhood and did not himself have to follow the Path and realize his own inner God-potential before beginning his mission.'[17]* Since Jesus realized his divine potential 'before beginning

---

*These words reproduce almost exactly the following pronouncement by Helena Roerich in one of her letters to her pupils: 'Our Church, which has established the dogma of the *One* [italics HR] and Only-Begotten Son of God, Jesus Christ, runs counter to the meaning of the prayer bequeathed by Jesus Christ Himself, "Our Father, Who art in Heaven", and also the words of the Bible "So God created man in his own image, in the image of God created he him". Having thus established the exclusivity of Sonship and divine Nature in Jesus Christ, the Church separated itself for ever from mankind' (*Pisma Eleny Rerich*—'Letters of Helena Roerich 1932–1955', p. 121). The 'Tibetan' developed this idea through Alice Bailey: 'The Christian Church has laid so much emphasis on Christ's unique position as the one and only Son of God that great error has crept in and has been fostered for centuries' (EH, p. 663). These observations also make it clearly apparent that the inspirations of all three impulses have one and the same source.

his mission', Mahatma Morya put it as follows to Elizabeth Prophet: 'Therefore, understand the meaning of the trek to the Himalayas by the teenager Jesus. Those lost years—eighteen in number—show the great preparation of this Soul of Light, this Son of Man, this one who truly embodied the full effulgence of our God ... This is the message of the discipleship of the teenager Jesus who went to find his teacher Maitreya,[*] who went to sit at the feet of Buddha who had come and gone five hundred years before his journey. He came to sit at the feet of those masters who had gone on before him.'[18]

Probably prompted by this indication from the mahatma, Elizabeth Prophet started to collect all known information about Jesus in the Himalayas, which led to the book *The Lost Years of Jesus*.[19] On the cover, as advertising copy, there are the words: 'Brilliant detective work! Where was Jesus age 12 to 30? No one knew ... until Elizabeth Clare Prophet reopened the file on the lost years of Jesus.'

The content of this book is not of any great interest. For through Rudolf Steiner's lectures on *The Fifth Gospel*, where on the basis of his own research in the Akashic Record he described the life of Jesus between the ages of 12 and 30,[20] one may learn that Jesus *never went to India* and altogether never left the Holy Land and its immediate vicinity. A more interesting aspect of Elizabeth Clare Prophet's book is her direct relationship to the literary and artistic legacy of the Roerichs. Thus on the frontispiece of the book is Nicholas Roerich's picture 'Jesus and the Giant's Skull', where Jesus is depicted in the Himalayan mountains. Moreover, Elizabeth Prophet includes 16 reproductions of the artist's pictures in her book,[†] his biography and extracts from a whole series of his works concerning the mysterious manuscript about Jesus's life in Asia, which the Roerichs sought for many years in Tibet and India.

Furthermore, Elizabeth Prophet considers herself and her husband on behalf of the mahatmas as 'carry[ing] on the work ... of Nicholas and Helena Roerich',[21] of whom she writes: 'The Roerichs set forth the word of Morya destined to reach both the Russian and the American people with the energy and the enlightenment that should deter the red dragon of World Communism. And so the Mother flame of Russia and the Mother flame of America converge [in the Roerichs' teaching] in spirals of freedom and victory ...' Of this one can only say that Elizabeth

---

[*] The reader may recall that according to the teaching of Alice Bailey or D.K. the Christ-Maitreya only overshadowed his pupil Jesus in Palestine.

[†] Likewise in other books published by Elizabeth Prophet there are frequently pictures by the Russian artist.

Prophet must have been ignorant of what the person whom they both regarded as Mahatma M. had actually dictated to Helena Roerich.

In a similar way to both Alice Bailey and Helena Roerich, Elizabeth Prophet loves to use words like 'electricity' and 'electronics' when describing the spiritual world. Thus for example: 'let the gathering of the elect be the gathering of electrons to welcome the Lord Christ in the midst of the circle of the AUM', or she speaks of 'the Electronic Presence of Michael the Archangel' in the human soul.[22] Leaving on one side the blasphemous character of these statements, we would contrast them with two observations by Rudolf Steiner, made on the basis of the results of modern spiritual-scientific research: 'In electricity are ... the instincts of evil, which must be overcome by the higher world ... For electrical atoms are evil, little demons.'[23]

The mantric words 'I AM', almost endlessly repeated, have a central place in Elizabeth Prophet's teaching. However, they have nothing really in common with the way they are understood in anthroposophy. It is true that Elizabeth Prophet asserts that 'I AM' is an expression of the cosmic Christ. But in her teaching the cosmic Christ has no particular relationship to the historical Jesus but works as a kind of 'higher Ego' in all mahatmas who have reached a certain stage of initiation. Thus according to Elizabeth Prophet, it is not the founder of Christianity who occupies a position of any particular significance in their circles but the Maitreya, whom she always calls the 'representative of the Cosmic Christ'.[24] Hence she also wrote the following about the proclamation of the 'I AM' by Christ Jesus at the Turning Point of Time: 'Conferred through Maitreya, this initiation [into the I am] was acclaimed by our Lord and Saviour ...'

So as not to weary the reader with further descriptions of Mark and Elizabeth Prophet's 'revelations', it should suffice to say that they are a very simplified, vulgarized mixture of the teachings of Blavatsky, Bailey and especially the Roerichs, while most of the 'new facts' added by the Prophets have a manifestly absurd character. Thus for example they speak about the additional previous incarnations of Saint Germain (other than those in Alice Bailey's books), which were the prophet Samuel, who was 'the sponsor, affectionately called "Uncle Sam", of the United States of America', Joseph in the Gospels, Christopher Columbus, Merlin. And in the twentieth century he was the personal teacher of Mark and Elizabeth Prophet, of whom the former was—they maintain—formerly Mark the Evangelist and the second Martha of Bethany and so on. Elizabeth Prophet also receives information from many other Himalayan mahatmas about ever new and more astonishing reincarnations. Thus Morya was formerly Abraham and King Arthur, and also Thomas Beckett and

Thomas Moore;[*] and the Three Kings from the East who came to greet the Jesus child were incarnations of the Mahatmas Morya, Kut Humi and Djwhal Khul and so forth.[25]

In order that an idea may be formed of the general level of this movement, the way that Elizabeth Prophet herself characterized the institution founded by her and her husband may finally be added: 'a Summit University' or 'an unprecedented opportunity to study the mystical paths of the world's religions as taught by the Ascended Masters and their Messenger'. And who are the 'sponsors' of this lofty institution? Elizabeth Prophet gives some indications: 'You will explore the teachings of Jesus Christ, Gautama Buddha, Lao Tzu and Confucius as well as the teachings of Hinduism, the Kabbalah and other spiritual traditions ... Summit University also offers the teachings of the Divine Mother East and West, including Kuan Yin and Mary.'[26]

However, this is still not all, for the mahatmas and world Teachers are not only sponsors but also form the permanent teaching body of the 'Summit University', with Elizabeth Prophet serving as their mediator. Thus Kut Humi and Djwhal Khul teach 'mastering the energies of the chakra' at the university, Saint Germain alchemy, Mother Mary 'the astrology of the New Age', and so on. The 'teaching and meditation of the Buddha' are, however, taught by Gautama himself, and also by 'Maitreya and the Bodhisattvas of East and West ...'[27]

*

As the reader may recall, D.K. said several times in his writings that the destiny of earthly humanity is dependent upon three powers: Britain, the USA and the USSR (today Russia). Hence the further development of the teachings of Alice Bailey and Helena Roerich in these three countries in the second half and at the end of the twentieth century is of particular interest. We have already considered the first two. Now we shall say a few words about Russia. We will not concern ourselves with the many Roerich societies that exist there, nor with the works of Alice Bailey (they are virtually all translated into Russian and come out one after another), nor with the books of Elizabeth Prophet (which have likewise been published), but with the further development of the 'revelations'.

---

[*] This does not correspond to Helena Roerich's notions about Morya's former incarnations. According to her letters he was Moses, Krishna, Plato and the Russian saint Sergei Radonezhsky (see V. Khramchenko's article 'Mezhdunarodnaya missiya Eleny Rerich') (The International Mission of Helena Roerich) in the journal *Serdtse* ('Heart', no. 1 (3), Moscow 1993).

Of all the extensive occult literature that is now—largely in the form of translations—being sold in Russia on literally every corner, the book of a certain A. Naumkin stands out. It was published in 1993 with the title *Kalagiya ili vlast nad vremenem* ('Kalagiya or Power over Time').[28] His subtitle runs: 'The Teaching of the Evolution of Man and the Universe, received with the ray of Maha-Satyan from the teacher of mankind Jesus Christ-Maitreya by the magician A.P. Naumkin in the Altai Mountains'. As an epigraph the author took a quotation by Nicholas Roerich from his book *Serdtse Asii* ('Heart of Asia'): 'The picture was brought to the palaces of the Buddha, to the places of the Maitreya.[*] [The word] Kalagiya was spoken.' 'Kalagiya' or the occult teaching of the nature of time is according to Tibetan tradition the fundamental teaching of Shamballa. The Roerichs' eldest son, Yuri, made it the subject of a whole scientific study. One of the purposes of the Roerichs' great trans-Himalayan expedition was to penetrate into the mystery of this teaching.

Instead of a foreword by the author, the publishers included at the beginning of the book a short interview with Naumkin from March 1991. Naumkin related that he had merely 'received' and written down the dictation given to him from the cosmos. He said about his work: 'The appearance of this book, this teaching was foretold by the masters. They awaited the book—and now here it is, signifying the beginning of grandiose events that are decisive for the whole of mankind, events that will begin in the immediate future.' Then as the interview proceeds he specifies that the 'Apocalypse' as a 'necessity and consequence of world evolution will begin in the summer of this [1993] year and end in 1996'. When asked how his book relates to the teaching of Agni Yoga or to other teachings based on Eastern tradition, he explains: 'All previous teachings have been preparing humanity to receive "Kalagiya".'

He himself characterizes the nature of the new teaching as follows: 'The essence of it is that man is a hologram—man is a hologram, every elemental particle is a hologram—thus the main task that "Kalagiya" resolves is connecting the hologram of man and his flesh to the cosmic Consciousness and to Space. The only thing that is immortal is Space. In order to achieve immortality, it is necessary to connect oneself to Space and to the energies of Space.' ' "Kalagiya" fully explains how to achieve this ... Man, to put it crudely, becomes a pump, sucking energy into himself.'

Naumkin ended the interview with the words: ' "Kalagiya" is a pre-

---

[*] What is meant here is the tangkha (the holy banner) of the Maitreya, which the Roerichs carried with them throughout their trans-Himalayan expedition.

cursor of the prophets and of Christ Himself, who will appear to human beings in *an earthly incarnation* and will direct His words to them. This will happen soon, in the next few years.' (Italics S.P.)

Then in the book comes the foreword, written by the book's 'true' author 'Jesus Christ-Maitreya'. And it ends with the words: 'I am the highest teacher of my true people and the saviour of those who love God, Jesus Christ-Maitreya, and I charge those people who are devoted to me and my Father with spreading my teaching … And my coming incarnation on Earth is approaching. My teaching will prepare my people for my appearance to them.'

It is unnecessary here to enter into a more detailed consideration of this 'teaching'. Many details and above all its style are at times strongly reminiscent of Helena Roerich's writings, with the difference that this 'new' teaching is to an even greater extent full of accumulations of scientific terms (mainly from quantum physics), and constantly mixed up with pseudo-Indian and pseudo-Christian religious conceptions. Phrases such as these give a flavour of the style: 'The psycho-correlative quantum fields of man—this is the nature of the true Spirit …' Or: 'in the absence of love and joy, instead of perceiving the reactor of evolution in space man sees fiery Gehenna in time, where he must burn eternally; for evolution is possible only in love and joy, which are gravitation and time. These energies [cause] his [man's] transition from the dimension of the photon-level of existence to the dimension of the tachymeter-level of existence. In this way the immortality of man's eternal life is attained.'

Admittedly, there is in 'Kalagiya' also another kind of 'information'. Thus for example 'Christ-Maitreya' subsequently becomes not only Krishna and Hermes-Trismegistos but also the 'Demiurge of the World'. But this is not the main point. The central focus of the book and also a key for understanding it is the so-called 'cosmic myth' which was dictated to Naumkin by the 'Christ-Maitreya' himself. According to this myth, none other than Lucifer is the first and only 'Son of God'. This basic thought of 'Kalagiya' is not new; it harmonizes with various remarks by Blavatsky already cited in this present work (see p. 259 and Part One, ch.1). And so in a certain sense the circle is closed.

In order to fill out the picture somewhat further, three more examples out of many will be mentioned. From 1991 onwards a whole series of books from the pen of Leïla Chellabi began to appear in France, the author being an occult writer of French-Arabic descent. Leïla Chellabi considers herself merely as a 'médiatrice', a mediator between humanity and Mahatma Morya, and in this sense as someone who brings about what Alice Bailey called the third developmental stage of the teaching, which was to emerge at the end of the twentieth century as 'the third phase of the hierarchical teaching'.[29]

As with Helena Roerich's books, the books of Leïla Chellabi are also written in the first person, that is as though from Morya himself (his name appears on the cover as the name of the author). They are devoted especially to the theme of the 'Externalization of the Hierarchy and Synthesis' or, to be more precise, to the preparation by all teachers of the Hierarchy of the imminent appearance of the world Teacher in the flesh or the 'incarnated Master', as Leïla Chellabi calls him and of whom Alice Bailey had already written at some length.

'After the phase [of the development of the teaching] with which A.A. B[ailey] was entrusted, it was necessary to return to the character of my ashram,' dictated Morya to her in the book which appeared in 1991 with the title *Christ en soi. Christ en tous. Christ en Vie* ('Christ in Oneself, Christ in All, Christ in Life'). On the back of the cover are the words: 'The hierarchic teaching is continued here in Christ, as was proclaimed by Master D.K. in the works of A.A.B.' And it goes on: 'For reading and meditating, for understanding, for one's own and other preparation for the Christian event of the 21st century.'

Having by virtue of her descent the 'twofold roots of Islam and Christianity', Chellabi sees it as her task to bring about a synthesis of the two religions. In Islam it is laws that make a particular impression on her, laws which regulate man's entire outward behaviour and also his practices of cleansing. 'From Islam I have the laws that regulate physical life and the discipline that leads through cleansing to God,' she wrote. Thus Chellabi endeavours in her works 'on behalf of Islam and Christianity' to bring these to a 'synthesis' under the guidance of Mahatma Morya.

As regards the relationship to Christianity, the mahatma dictates to her:

> To sacralize the Christ is good,
> But to desacralize is still better ...

And the author indeed achieves without particular difficulty such a 'desacralization' by mentioning this name two or three times on almost every page of the book in question. In her own words, her aim is that 'we recognize the being and not the dogmas; Christ the human being and not the crucified idol'.

Like Alice Bailey, Leïla Chellabi does not baulk at comparisons such as: 'Christ relates to spirituality as the electrical current to the lamp.'

On the other hand, there is a distinct inclination in Leïla Chellabi's works to imitate Helena Roerich. Thus all messages from Mahatma M. come from her pen either in the form of poetry or in rhythmic prose. Not for nothing does the Mahatma himself explain that 'in poetry everything is allowed',[30] thus relieving her of all responsibility for her words.

That Chellabi knows Agni Yoga (and how could this be otherwise, since both she and Helena Roerich draw upon the same source of inspiration) is evident for example from the following lines:

> ... From the hard stone to the precious stone,
> You pass on the path to Christ
> Through the radiant stages of the central spiritual fire.
> Agni Yoga represents the means of synthesizing this.

The reader will search in vain both in the works of the founder of Agni Yoga and also in those of her French successor for any actual knowledge of the spiritual world or of any supersensible fact at all. At best there are in Chellabi's writings merely numerous references to Alice Bailey's works. For the French occultist—like Helena Roerich—does not work with an intellectual content but tries to achieve the greatest possible influence upon the reader with the help of rhythm and (false) pictures, intended to prepare him for the imminent coming of 'Christ the human being, the incarnated master'.

★

A further example is the book of a 'Brother Philip', a member of the 'White Brotherhood', first published in 1961 in London and since then reissued several times under the title *Secret of the Andes*.[31] In this book a whole series of messages from the same mahatmas (Kut Humi, Morya, Saint Germain, Hilarion, Maha Chohan, Sanat Kumara and others) are reproduced through the mediation of 'Brother Philip', and also some from the four Archangels (Michael, Raphael, Gabriel and Uriel), who are connected with the influence of a secret group of the 'Great White Brotherhood' concealed somewhere in the depths of the Peruvian Andes.

As regards their style, these messages are strongly reminiscent of the works of Mark and Elizabeth Prophet. Not for nothing does the author himself speak of the affinity of his occult group to the 'Brotherhood of the Royal Teton Ranch, in Western U.S.A.'.[*]

Little is said in the messages about the mysteries of South America. Only from Morya's message dated July 1957 is it apparent that a 'New World Focus of Illumination' has arisen in the twentieth century in South America at Lake Titicaca in the Peruvian Andes, which—in contrast to

---

[*] 'The Royal Teton Ranch' is the headquarters of Mark and Elizabeth Prophet's movement near Los Angeles.

the centre in the Himalayas, which represents the 'male aspect'—will represent the 'female aspect' and will in time take on the further leadership of earthly humanity in this form. A secret 'Monastery' in the Andes, led by the abbot and author of the book under consideration, Brother Philip, forms part of this 'center'.

The main condition for receiving a pupil into the 'Monastery', which for its part is a preparatory stage for the reception of a candidate into the 'New World Focus of Illumination', is the now familiar idea of the imminent appearance of Christ *in the flesh*: 'The student must be aware of and accept the Cosmic Christ and believe that this Christ as God *came in the flesh* to mentor the Earth and that this same Christ will return again soon *in the flesh* [italics in the original].'

What Christ will accomplish after his physical appearance on earth is characterized in the message of 'the Archangel Gabriel': 'And then the new government, with Christ as King and the house of David once again shall reign supreme.' Thus what is in question here is the new 'world government', that is, the full and final subjection of the whole of humanity to 'the Prince of this world' in the form of the future incarnated world Teacher. At the end, according to 'Brother Philip', 'one world' will exist, 'not under the United Nations, but under Christ the King, the Lord of the Earth' (from the message of Master Hilarion). This is reminiscent of the spiritual exercises of Ignatius Loyola.

A further characteristic of the occultists from the Andes brings them into close proximity to the teachings of Helena Roerich and Alice Bailey: their complete and consistent denial of the cosmic significance of the Mystery of Golgotha. Thus the message of the 'Archangel Gabriel' states: 'Would the Great Creator of all send His Son to die in despair and failure on the Cross? This implies that the Creator admitted defeat. He makes no errors! We make error. Jesus came to the Earth to live, not to die! Tell that to your churches ... It is not the teachings of our heavenly Father. Jesus did not come to die primarily. He is not the dead Christ. Their entire gospel is based on the fact that Jesus died for them [human beings]. He lived for them ... he did not *die* for them!'[*] And those who, in spite of everything, believe in the Mystery of Golgotha and its world significance are told: 'They are not Christian. They follow the Dark One.'

Thus the circle closes again, giving rise to the picture of a single all-encompassing scenario, or a single 'operator' working single-mindedly behind the whole confusion of the diverse collection of occult streams of

---

[*] These words are strongly reminiscent of some thoughts of Helena Roerich, which she had expressed several decades previously (see p. 337f.).

our time which in one way or another are embraced by the common designation of the 'New Age Movement'.

★

Summing up everything that has been presented in this chapter, it has to be said that the examples that we have cited—and it would be easy to add many more—of the further development of the source of inspiration lying behind the work of Helena Roerich and Alice Bailey in the first half of the twentieth century are clearly indicative of a steady process of degradation in the second half of the century.

This state of affairs is serious if one calls to mind that the occult-historical recurrence of the apocalyptic number 666 for the third time in *1998* will have created a particularly favourable opportunity for the forces of the main cosmic opponent of Christ, the Sun Demon, Sorat, to exert an influence upon earthly evolution.[32] At the beginning of the twenty-first century mankind will be confronted by the physical incarnation of the mighty ahrimanic spirit,[33] who will quite definitely seek to make use of these cosmic forces of evil which will have entered into earthly evolution through the gate of the year 1998.[*]

In order to be able to resist all these dark forces, we earthly human beings will need above all a new and *conscious relationship* with the Etheric Christ, and also with the ruling Spirit of our Time who serves him in the higher worlds and in Christian esotericism is called Michael, the heavenly conqueror of the ahrimanic dragon. In order that—in the time of these impending difficult trials—humanity might achieve this relationship with Michael-Christ,[34] the modern science of the spirit or anthroposophy and also the cosmic mysteries of Michael were given by Rudolf Steiner out of the sources of Christian esotericism, and the etheric coming of Christ was proclaimed as the most important *spiritual* event of the twentieth century.

In which way can Lucifer and Ahriman, who by the end of the twentieth century will have united ever more strongly, oppose this sublime reality most effectively? Christ's coming in an etheric form cannot be prevented by any single demonic being in the entire cosmos. But what they are able to achieve and in our time seek to bring about is *to divert the attention of humanity from the true event of Christ's Second Coming in the spiritual world nearest to the earth* by any means available to them. Taking into account the general materialistic character of our time, the most effective means of achieving such a distraction will be to direct the

---

[*] In view of the fact that this translation post-dates the 1998 event referred to by the author in this passage, the tenses have been changed.—Translator

attention of as large a number of people as possible in the opposite direction by concentrating upon the coming of a false Messiah or false Christ in the physical body. And in order to achieve this, all dark occultists will endeavour to call forth amongst mankind a strong longing for the coming of the 'world Teacher' in the physical body, so as to make human beings satisfied that they are engineering his appearance as a precursor of the future incarnated Ahriman or perhaps even his own appearance.

In this sense, the role that will fall to anthroposophists in these coming years of trials will be that of standing like guardians of the threshold of the new millennium, so that mankind does not succumb to the magical enticements of the false Messiah and his prophets and, hence, fail to notice the living Christ in the etheric world, a failure which would be tantamount to a total forgetting of the higher significance of the earth and the existence of mankind and also of every individual human being living upon it.

However, we can take guidance from the words of Christ Jesus with which he himself prophetically spoke of this great trial standing before the whole of mankind: 'Take heed that no one leads you astray. For many will come in my name, saying, "I am the Christ", and they will lead many astray . . . Then if any one says to you, "Lo, here is the Christ!" or "There he is!" do not believe it. For false Christs and false prophets will arise and show great signs and wonders so as to lead astray, if possible, even the elect . . . So, if they say to you, "Lo, he is in the wilderness", do not go out; if they say, "Lo, he is in the inner rooms", do not believe it. For as the lightning comes from the east and shines as far as the west, so will be the coming of the Son of Man' (Matthew 24:4–5; 23–24; 26–27).

Notes

1. D–2, p. 85.
2. RI, p. 255.
3. Benjamin Creme, *The Reappearance of the Christ and the Masters of Wisdom*, London 1979, p. 20.
4. Ibid., p. 4.
5. Ibid., pp. 54–5, and the following quotations, pp. 203, 180, 203.
6. Ibid., p. 20.
7. *The Emergence. Special Information Issue* (second international edition), p. 1.
8. Ibid.
9. Ibid.
10. *Share International News. Commentaries and Forecasts for a Changing World*, no. 2, Autumn 1990, p. 2.
11. Ibid.

12. *Saint Germain on Alchemy, Formulas for Self-Transformation*, Mark L. Prophet, Elizabeth Clare Prophet, Summit University Press, Montana USA 1985, pp. 464–9.
13. Ibid.
14. Ibid., p. xxix and the following quotation, pp. 504–7.
15. Ibid., pp. xxix–xxx.
16. Mark L. Prophet, Elizabeth Clare Prophet, *Lords of the Seven Rays*, Book One, USA 1986, pp. 69 and 70.
17. Ibid., Book Two, p. 10.
18. *Lords of the Seven Rays*, Book Two, pp. 14–15 and 20.
19. Elizabeth Clare Prophet, *The Lost Years of Jesus. Documentary Evidence of Jesus' 17-year Journey to the East*, USA 1987.
20. See GA 148.
21. *The Chela and the Path*, p. 122.
22. Ibid., pp. 73 and 90.
23. GA 220, 28 January 1923.
24. *The Lost Teachings of Jesus 3, Keys to Self-Transcendence*, Mark L. Prophet, Elizabeth Clare Prophet, USA 1988, p. 114; and the following quotation ibid., p. 118.
25. See *Saint Germain on Alchemy*, p. 255; *Lords of the Seven Rays*, Book Two, pp. 299 and 17, Book One, pp. 33 and 36.
26. See *Saint Germain on Alchemy*, pp. 504–7.
27. Ibid.
28. A.P. Naumkin, *Kalagiya ili vlast nad vremenem* ('Kalagiya or Power over Time'), Moscow 1993. The following quotations are on pages 3, 4, 3, 5, 6, 8, 219, 220, 226, 163, 217. 'The Cosmic Myth about the Beginning of Creation or How Everything Began' is on pp. 210–18.
29. Leïla Chellabi, *Christ en soi. Christ en tous. Christ en Vie*, Cledam 1993, p. 1; the following quotations ibid., pp. 1, 2, 127, 169, 171, 174, 81, 175, 167.
30. Leïla Chellabi, *Le maître en incarnation, les Groupes et Shamballa*, Cledam 1992, p. 5; the following quotations ibid., pp. 309, 245.
31. Brother Philip, *Secret of the Andes*, first published in 1961 (London), then by Leaves of Grass, California 1976; the following quotations ibid., pp. 29, 26, 25, 44, 98, 99, 139, 100.
32. See GA 346, 12 September 1924.
33. See note 63, chapter 6.
34. Rudolf Steiner uses this double name in the article 'The Michael-Christ Experience of Man', GA 26, 2 November 1924.

Complete List of the Works by
Alice Bailey/The Tibetan

Books of the Tibetan (Djwhal Khul) through Alice Bailey

Initiation, Human and Solar	*1922
Letters on Occult Meditation	1922
A Treatise on Cosmic Fire	1925
A Treatise on White Magic	1934
Discipleship in the New Age, Vol. I	1944
Discipleship in the New Age, Vol. II	1955
Problems in Humanity	1947
The Reappearance of the Christ	1948
The Destiny of the Nations	1949
Glamour: A World Problem	1950
Telepathy and the Etheric Vehicle	1950
Education in the New Age	1954
The Externalization of the Hierarchy	1957

A Treatise on the Seven Rays

Vol. I—*Esoteric Psychology*	*1936*
Vol. II—*Esoteric Psychology*	*1942*
Vol. III—*Esoteric Astrology*	*1951*
Vol. IV—*Esoteric Healing*	*1953*
Vol. V—*Rays and Initiations*	*1960*

Books by Alice Bailey

The Consciousness of the Atom	1922
The Soul and its Mechanism	1930
From Intellect to Intuition	1932
From Bethlehem to Calvary	1937
The Light of the Soul	1927(?)
The Unfinished Autobiography	1951

---

*The year of the English edition.

Part Three

THE BIRTH OF CHRISTIAN ESOTERICISM IN THE TWENTIETH CENTURY AND THE OCCULT POWERS THAT OPPOSE IT

Preface

This third part of *The East in the Light of the West*, which is intended for the anthroposophical reader, differs quite fundamentally from the two other parts.

The task of the two previous parts was to characterize from an anthroposophical standpoint the two occult streams founded by Helena Roerich in the East and Alice Bailey in the West.

The third part has an altogether different character. Its principal task is to demonstrate the essential difference between Western (Christian) and Eastern esotericism through the example of the development of the anthroposophical movement within the Theosophical Society at the beginning of the twentieth century and, hence, also to reflect the erroneous, but still current, opinion according to which the spiritual science initiated by Rudolf Steiner at the beginning of the century was merely a kind of 'christianized' aspect of the Eastern-orientated theosophy of Blavatsky and her followers. This and similar views, which one comes across in all kinds of reference books, are in the majority of cases based upon a total ignorance of the actual state of affairs. One task of this book is to bring clarity with regard to this question.

The extensive spiritual-scientific and other documentary material presented in this book will enable the reader to see the radical difference between anthroposophy and Eastern theosophy. It will become clear to him that anthroposophy, although its development initially had an outward connection with the Theosophical Society, was from the outset an independent spiritual stream which derived its knowledge and its life-forces from its own wholly independent occult sources; and these may be called the sources of true esoteric Christianity.

The second task of this third part consists in the attempt to come at least a small step closer to one of the most difficult questions in the realm of modern occultism, a question which—despite its great significance for an understanding of many events in present times—has not hitherto been pursued to any great extent in anthroposophical literature. This has to do with the problem of the relationship of the Western and the Eastern Masters to one another, as was manifested through the example of the mutual relationship of two movements, the anthroposophical and the theosophical, respectively with them.

The reader who familiarizes himself with this aspect of the present work will immediately observe the main feature of its approach. It seeks not merely a simple, abstract answer to the question that has been posed but rather to arrive at a solution from an altogether different side, in that it focuses its attention upon the development of the central stream of Christian esotericism made accessible to all people in the twentieth century in the form of Rudolf Steiner's anthroposophy.

Only through a real understanding of the inner nature of anthroposophy and the laws of its development, together with what it says about the problems of human existence and the world, will it be possible to approach an answer to this question. For in order to find an answer, one has to try to consider the themes associated with it from the standpoint of the highest truths of esoteric Christianity, truths that reveal the true significance of earthly evolution.

Hence the reader who only wants simple and abstract answers may not be satisfied by reading this third part; whereas someone who is not only looking for intellectual answers but is also seeking a real possibility of developing his own relationship to the problem in question will also find an answer, though not in an abstract form but in the way that life responds to such questions. Such a response is directed towards the whole human being, that is, simultaneously to his thinking, feeling and will, and, through such a true understanding, awakens an inner experience, leading in its turn to an aspiration—engendered from one's free will—to become a conscious collaborator in the fulfilment of the high aims and ideals of earthly evolution, those aims of which anthroposophy speaks out of the sources of Christian esotericism.

Sergei O. Prokofieff
Stuttgart, December 1996

1. Rudolf Steiner and the Masters of Esoteric Christianity

As Rudolf Steiner frequently emphasized, the central task of anthroposophy or modern spiritual science—founded by him at the beginning of the twentieth century—is to make the mysteries of the cosmic Christ accessible to wide circles of humanity. In this sense anthroposophy is not only directly associated with the stream of esoteric Christianity but is its main representative in our time.

Rudolf Steiner came in contact with this stream for the first time already in his youth. Christ's words 'Knock, and it will be opened to you' (Matthew 7:7) began to become an occult reality in Rudolf Steiner's life as soon as he was able for the first time *out of himself*—as befits the epoch of the consciousness soul—to become fully aware of his essential life's task. Once this had happened, he was ready for the meeting with his teacher. Actually, he met one of them around 1879 in Vienna,[1] and the other somewhat later. Both were among the leading Masters of esoteric Christianity.

In his book *Rudolf Steiner Enters My Life*, Friedrich Rittelmeyer reports about a conversation with Rudolf Steiner on this theme which took place in 1915: 'What impressed me most was the way he spoke of the great teachers who crossed his path. Men of extraordinary spirituality, entirely unknown in public life, were there at the right moment, helping him in critical years to understand and develop his faculties, standing like sponsors at the dawn of his life's mission.'[2] And Rittelmeyer continues: 'Those who recall the intervention by one called "The Unknown" in the life of Jacob Boehme, the appearance of the "Friend of God" in the life of Tauler, can get an idea of the things of which Rudolf Steiner spoke on that occasion. The only difference was that here the guidance of these sublime leaders towards a great earthly mission was more consciously and clearly recognized ... Nor shall I ever forget the expression on his face when he said of one of these two men: "That was a *most significant personality!*" ... Later on he told me that he had once been suddenly saved by a "Master" when he was on the point of doing something which would have meant death. To my question as to whether either of these two men were still living, and if he ever saw him, he answered: "There is no need." He felt able, at any time, to establish a spiritual contact without the outer presence.'

In this book written for the general public Friedrich Rittelmeyer did not of course give the names of Rudolf Steiner's two teachers. However, he did so in 1924, in a conversation with W.J. Stein, who noted the following in his diary under the date 9 July 1924: 'Dr Steiner related in Frau Dr Steiner's presence that he had had two initiators: Christian Rosenkreutz and the Master Jesus ...'[3][*]

One can also find—in a veiled form—confirmation of this report in Friedrich Rittelmeyer's recollections. Thus according to Rudolf Steiner the unknown Master who sought out Boehme in his youth was a Rosicrucian Master,[4] that is either Christian Rosenkreutz or an emissary of his, and the 'Friend of God from the High Lands' who appeared to Tauler was an incarnation of the Master Jesus.[5] Moreover, Rudolf Steiner's words about his having been rescued by his Master correspond precisely to what he described in a lecture of the way that Christian Rosenkreutz chooses his pupils.[6] And the allusion to the Friend of God and the purely spiritual connection with one of the two teachers without outward contact corresponds to Friedrich Rittelmeyer's description: 'Rudolf Steiner replied to a question concerning the Friend of God from the High Lands, that he was the Master Jesus who, since the Mystery of Golgotha, has incarnated during every century. To another question about whether he was currently incarnated, Rudolf Steiner said that he was living at the time in the Carpathians, and indicated that they were in spiritual contact.'[7][†]

However, in Rudolf Steiner's case the encounter with the two leading teachers of Christian esotericism has an altogether different significance from what one would normally allot to such a meeting in traditional occultism. What Rudolf Steiner primarily achieved through it was a more precise and definite knowledge of the principal direction of the spiritual development in pursuit of which he could now accomplish all the tasks that had been placed before him *before* the first encounter with his teacher through his own resources. Thus he was shown the way of fulfilling his tasks in the sense of Christian-Rosicrucian esotericism by the occult teachers, but he had to follow this path in complete solitude. 'I have shown you who you are; now go and be yourself!'[8] The teacher addressed these words to his pupil as he went on his way.

In the sense of Christian esotericism, the highest and most essential aim

---

[*] A consideration of the question as to which of the two teachers Rudolf Steiner met first and which he met second lies beyond the scope of this book.

[†] In this connection Rudolf Steiner's journey in 1889 to Hermannstadt, which lies in the heart of the Carpathians, acquires a particular significance.

of this path—which Rudolf Steiner was subsequently to describe in his books *Knowledge of the Higher Worlds* and *Occult Science* and elsewhere[9]— was to attain knowledge of the cosmic Christ Being and also of the central significance of the Mystery of Golgotha in earthly evolution. Such a knowledge in the stream of true esotericism, however, cannot be a matter of theory but leads directly to an experience of the Christ as the highest supersensible reality in the spiritual worlds. For only a conscious *meeting* with Him, representing the culmination of Christian-Rosicrucian initiation, transforms the pupil into a Master who can henceforth stand before human beings not merely as an independent spirit-teacher but above all as a direct emissary of the cosmic Christ.

After many inner trials and conquests, Rudolf Steiner attained this high stage of Christian-Rosicrucian initiation at the end of the nineteenth century. In his autobiography *The Course of My Life*, he himself referred to this central experience in his inner development: 'Before this turn of the century came the testing of soul I have described. The unfolding of my soul rested upon the fact that *I had stood in spirit before the Mystery of Golgotha in most inward, most earnest solemnity of knowledge.*'[10]

At the end of the chapter devoted to a description of the Christian-Rosicrucian path in his book *Occult Science*, Rudolf Steiner later characterized this highest stage of spiritual development—called in anthroposophy that of 'Intuition'—as follows: 'Through this experience the pupil is initiated into the sublime mystery that is connected with the name of Christ ... Having thus come through Intuition to a knowledge of Christ in the spiritual world, the aspirant will find that he is able also to understand what took place historically on earth [through the Mystery of Golgotha] in the fourth post-Atlantean period of earthly evolution.'

It is evident from many of Rudolf Steiner's lectures that this experience of the cosmic Christ in the sphere of Intuition made manifest to him the high, divine nature of the Christ, the Sun Logos, who has since the Mystery of Golgotha worked as the new Spirit of the Earth and the guiding spirit of earthly evolution. 'This then is what the pupil attains through Intuition: the very meaning and significance of Earth evolution are communicated to him.'[11] '*The essential meaning of the earth* ... lies in the recognition and realization of the intentions of the *living Christ.*'[12]

In the last chapter of his book *Knowledge of the Higher Worlds*, Rudolf Steiner also characterized this encounter with the living Christ in the spiritual world in an objectivized form as a meeting with the Greater Guardian of the Threshold: 'An indescribable splendour radiates from the second Guardian; union with him lies as a far distant ideal before the eye of the soul. Yet there is also the certainty that this union will not be possible until all the powers which have come to the initiate from this [higher] world are applied by him to liberating and redeeming this world. If he resolves to fulfil the demands of the higher Being of Light, the initiate will be able to contribute to the liberation of the human race. He brings his gifts to the altar of humanity.'[13]

After he had in this way experienced a personal encounter with Christ in the sphere of Intuition, that is, after he had received his impulse, the impulse of the world 'I am', into his own human ego and had thereby brought the basic principle of the Christian mysteries to realization, the principle which comes to expression in the words of Paul the Apostle 'Not I but Christ in me' (Gal. 2:20), Rudolf Steiner attained altogether new possibilities of occult experience. Henceforth he was able to maintain his Christ-filled ego-consciousness at all stages of supersensible existence, a capacity which formed the foundation for all the spiritual research that followed.[*]

For since Christ is the highest cosmic archetype of the individual human ego, He is the only Being in our cosmos who can enter into this ego without extinguishing it. On the contrary, He can infinitely strengthen its inner forces and creative potential.[†]

Thus from this time onwards beings of the spiritual worlds were able to work through Rudolf Steiner's various sheaths, while his own Christ-imbued individual ego-consciousness was fully maintained.[14]

The consequence of this was there was a revelation of the mystery associated with the supersensible experience of the macrocosmic Christ Being at the next stage of Christian-Rosicrucian initiation, the stage consisting of knowledge of the relationship between the microcosm and the macrocosm,[15] or, in other words, between the circle of the highest earthly initiates (of the White Lodge) and the cosmic Christ Being. This mystery was considered in Part One (chapter 6, 'The Macrocosmic Christ Being and the Microcosmic Being of the Bodhisattvas');[16] but in order that what follows may be understood more clearly a brief summary will also be given here. The essential point is that knowledge of Christ as the Sun Logos and the highest guide of earthly evolution at the same time showed to Rudolf Steiner's spiritual perception the true nature of the

---

[*] The results of the spiritual research are brought together in the 350 volumes of the Collected Works.

[†] In this connection, Rudolf Steiner spoke subsequently in the lectures on questions of 'spiritual economy' about the receiving by man of a spiritual impression of Christ's Ego in the future (see p. 402). However, what will be possible for human individuals in general in the future is already possible today for the Christian initiate.

cosmic Christ's relationship with the highest human initiates, who in the mystery wisdom of the East are called *bodhisattvas*. Rudolf Steiner spoke about this in the lecture of 31 August 1909: 'How is the Christ, this principle, this Being to whom we must ascribe such a focal position, to be distinguished from a bodhisattva? The main difference between Christ and the bodhisattva is that we must necessarily call the bodhisattva the great teacher, the embodiment of the wisdom that transcends all cultures and is embodied in a variety of different ways. But the Christ is not simply a teacher, that is the point! Christ does not merely teach human beings, *Christ is a Being whom we may best understand if we seek Him where we can find Him at the dizzy heights of the world of spirit as an object of initiation, and where we can compare Him with other spiritual beings [bodhisattvas].*'[17] And Rudolf Steiner expressed the result of this comparison as follows: 'He is not simply a teacher, He is *life*, life that streams into other beings who then become teachers.[*] Thus the bodhisattvas are those who derive their teaching from enjoying the bliss of beholding Christ in the spiritual heights.'[18]

The essential difference between the bodhisattvas and the Christ lies, moreover, in the fact that a bodhisattva, as a highly developed *human* being, ascends in the course of his spiritual development into that high spiritual sphere which is called the bodhisattva sphere in the direction from below upwards, whereas the Christ, as a divine, *superhuman* Being from still higher worlds lying beyond the confines of our solar system, moves down into this sphere from above.[19]

In another lecture Rudolf Steiner described this humanly cosmic mystery in the following way: 'Thus twelve bodhisattvas belong to Christ. They have prepared and further developed what He brought as the greatest impulse of our cultural evolution. *We see* the twelve and, in their midst, the thirteenth. We[†] have now ascended to the sphere of the bodhisattvas[‡] and entered a circle of twelve stars. In their midst is the Sun,

---

[*] From this standpoint it is not correct to describe Christ as the 'teacher of teachers' as happens in certain occult writings. The bodhisattvas are indeed the teachers of all earthly teachers. Christ, on the other hand, is not a teacher in the earthly sense of the word but something infinitely greater. He is the source of the bodhisattvas' life and at the same time—as the cosmic 'I am'—the highest archetype of their own being.

[†] It is probably barely necessary to point out that the word 'we' in this and in previous quotations can be understood as signifying 'I'. For Rudolf Steiner was speaking out of his own spiritual experience.

[‡] As Rudolf Steiner attests in the same lecture, the sphere of the bodhisattvas lies in the world of providence (in the East this world is called *Buddhi*), which is above Higher Devachan. The word *providence* is an indication that the guidance of earthly humanity has its origin there.

illuminating and warming them. From this Sun they derive the *source of life* that afterwards they have to carry down to the earth ... Thus the picture on earth is one in which the Christ stands in the middle of earthly evolution, with the bodhisattvas as His precursors and His successors, bringing his work closer to mankind ... The same number of bodhisattvas as were needed to prepare mankind for the Christ will also be needed to develop to maturity what shall have flowed into it through Him ... And only when the last bodhisattva belonging to Christ shall have completed his work will humanity realize what Christ really is. Human beings will then be filled with a will in which the Christ Himself will *live* ... and they will be the outward expression of Christ on the earth.[20]

The fulfilment of his mission, that is, when in his last incarnation he has become a Christian Buddha, signifies for every Christian bodhisattva that, as a Buddha, he is able to bring to humanity the mysteries of the cosmic Christ not in the form of a teaching but in the form of life itself, that is, in a purely magical way.

Rudolf Steiner explained this result of his spiritual research by means of the example of the Maitreya bodhisattva, the spiritual successor of Gautama Buddha, who will in future be the *first* Christian Buddha, the first human being who will attain this high stage *after* the Mystery of Golgotha, after the Sun Logos dwelt on the earth.

Already during his last incarnation before the Turning Point of Time, this bodhisattva—working through Jeshu ben Pandira—prepared the coming of Christ to the earth with the help of the Order of the Essenes. The Apostle and Evangelist Matthew subsequently also belonged to the occult school that he founded.[21] The Maitreya bodhisattva has since then incarnated again and again in the centuries since the time of Christ. He is that 'great teacher, who will be able to give to those human beings who are ripe for it the profoundest instruction concerning the nature of the Mystery of Golgotha'.[22] And approximately 2500–3000 years after our time,[*] when he will finally have ascended to the Buddha stage, he will teach mankind not only the mystery of the cosmic Christ but 'will imprint into human souls directly, *magically*, the nature of the Mystery of Golgotha',[23] that is, imprint into the whole of earthly evolution the cosmic *life* springing from him that overcomes death. (See further regarding the Maitreya bodhisattva in chapter 8.)

Thus we have here that hierarchic sequence contained in the esoterically understood words of Christ 'I am the way, and the truth, and the life'

---

[*] That is, approximately 5000 years after his predecessor, Gautama Buddha, became a Buddha.

(John 14:6): the *way* of Christ is travelled by every Christian initiate; the highest *truth*, the highest understanding of Christ and of His central deed on the earth—the Mystery of Golgotha—is brought to mankind by the Christian Master who raises himself to the stage of a bodhisattva or similarly enters into a conscious relationship with the bodhisattva sphere; and the *life* of Christ is what streams into humanity through the future Christian Buddha. And above these three stages, imbuing them with the forces of the way, the truth and the life, reigns the 'I am' of Christ, His 'world-Ego', the focal point of consciousness of the Sun Logos.

Every spiritually striving human being can and should unite himself from our time onwards with this *true spiritual hierarchy* of our planet by becoming a pupil of anthroposophy or, which is the same thing, by embarking upon the path of modern Christian-Rosicrucian initiation. Rudolf Steiner described this hierarchic sequence with these words: 'I have an obligation to steep myself in the mysteries of which one can hear today [in spiritual science]. I have an obligation to feel that as a human being I am one link in a chain which has to stretch from the beginning to the end of evolution, in which are linked together all human beings, individualities [initiates], bodhisattvas, Buddhas, [the] Christ. I must say to myself: to feel that I am a link in it is to be conscious of my true worth as a human being.'[24] Hence Rudolf Steiner spoke in the same lecture of how a person 'who has the opportunity today to devote himself to spirit-knowledge enjoys a gift of grace from karma'. For if someone today 'becomes a bodhisattva, Buddha or Master, this signifies an inner development, albeit one that is higher and which any human being can pass through. The esoteric training of a human being is no more than a beginning of what can lead to Buddhahood.'[25]

Over the course of many millennia all Masters of esoteric Christianity have followed this path of continual spiritual ascent. The two greatest of them, Christian Rosenkreutz and the Master Jesus, whom Rudolf Steiner encountered in his youth, were characterized by him as 'the great, highly revered *bodhisattvas of the West*',[26] and, as we shall see later, he placed the former at an even higher level.

Notes

1. See further in: Sergei O. Prokofieff, *Rudolf Steiner and the Founding of the New Mysteries*, Temple Lodge, 1994.
2. *Meine Lebensbegegnungen mit Rudolf Steiner*, 1928; English translation by Dorothy Osmond 1929, fourth edition Floris Books, 1963.
3. See Stein's diary entry in note 290 of Thomas Meyer's book *D.N. Dunlop: A Man of Our Time*, Temple Lodge, 1992.

4. See GA 7, the chapter entitled 'Valentin Weigel and Jacob Boehme', the lectures of 1 February 1920 (GA 196) and 8 October 1906 (GA 96) and note 8.

5. See GA 264, 22 October 1906, and note 7.

6. See GA 130, 28 September 1911.

7. GA 264, p. 225.

8. Edouard Schuré, from the foreword to the French translation of Rudolf Steiner's book *Christianity as Mystical Fact and the Mysteries of Antiquity* (GA 8). The foreword was written by Schuré in 1908 on the basis of personal conversations with Rudolf Steiner in the autumn of 1907 in Barr (Alsace).

9. GA 10, the chapter entitled 'Life and Death. The Great Guardian of the Threshold', and GA 13, the chapter entitled 'Knowledge of Higher Worlds. Concerning Initiation'.

10. GA 28, ch. XXVI.

11. GA 13, the chapter entitled 'Knowledge of Higher Worlds. Concerning Initiation'.

12. GA 262, 'The Barr Manuscript', III.

13. GA 10, the chapter entitled 'Life and Death. The Great Guardian of the Threshold'.

14. See further in: Sergei O. Prokofieff, *Rudolf Steiner and the Founding of the New Mysteries*.

15. GA 13, the chapter entitled 'Knowledge of Higher Worlds. Concerning Initiation'.

16. See in: Sergei O. Prokfieff, *Rudolf Steiner and the Founding of the New Mysteries*.

17. GA 113, 31 August 1909.

18. Ibid.

19. See further in GA 211, 24 April 1922, also in: Sergei O. Prokofieff, *The Twelve Holy Nights and the Spiritual Hierarchies*, Part I, ch. 2, Temple Lodge, 2004.

20. GA 116, 25 October 1909.

21. See GA 123, 6 September 1910 and GA 130, 3 December 1911.

22. GA 130, 3 December 1911.

23. Ibid.

24. GA 130, 5 November 1911.

25. GA 130, 17 September 1911.

26. GA 113, 31 August 1909.

2. Rudolf Steiner's Role in the Theosophical Society

Rudolf Steiner's affinity to the central stream of esoteric Christianity and his personal relationship with the two leading Masters also determined his twofold connection to the theosophical movement. For both these Masters had on the one hand taken part in the original *spiritual* founding of the Theosophical Society, which was brought into being on the outward plane in 1875 by H.P. Blavatsky and Olcott in New York. 'This initial founding [of the Society],' wrote Rudolf Steiner, 'had a decidedly Western nature. Likewise the [first] publication *Isis Unveiled* [1876], in which Blavatsky revealed a large number of esoteric truths, has just such a Western character ... This is because the truths themselves are *inspired* by the great *initiates of the West* [italics by Rudolf Steiner], who also inspired the Rosicrucian wisdom.'[1] On the other hand, as the inspirations of the Rosicrucian teachers were reflected only in a highly distorted form by H.P. Blavatsky in the book referred to and, moreover—as will be shown later on—in a completely erroneous way, these Western teachers soon ceased to inspire Blavatsky, and abandoned her. 'But the door had been opened,' continues Rudolf Steiner: 'Blavatsky's soul had been prepared in such a manner that spiritual wisdom was able to flow into it.' '*Eastern* initiators' who wanted to oppose Western materialism through ancient *Eastern* wisdom 'were able to take hold of her'; for 'they wanted to imprint *their* form of spiritual knowledge, which had been preserved through the ages, on the Western world. Under the influence of this stream the Theosophical Society took on its Eastern character, and the same influence was the inspiration for Sinnett's *Esoteric Buddhism* and Blavatsky's *Secret Doctrine.*'

This one-sided Eastern character was at variance with not only Rudolf Steiner's mission but also his entire inner inclination. Nevertheless he accepted Count Brockdorff's pressing invitation and began to give lectures in the branch which he led in Berlin. For *he had been asked*, and in accordance with an occult law he had not had the right to turn away those who were truly searching and asking, above all because those who requested him to give lectures wanted to hear *what he could and wished to give them out of his own spiritual experience and research.* 'Until now it has been my principle not to divulge anything within the theosophical movement that cannot be corroborated by my own [spiritual] knowledge.'[2]

In other words, the only answer that Rudolf Steiner could and wanted to give from the outset in the Theosophical Society to the request that was made to him was the purest wisdom of esoteric Christianity, a true Rosicrucian occultism springing from the Christian-Rosicrucian initiation which he had attained and from the occult research which he based upon it.

This is also confirmed through the lectures that Rudolf Steiner gave in the autumn and winter of 1900/1901 in Berlin at the theosophical branch of the Brockdorffs. To begin with there were two lectures about Nietzsche and Goethe (the latter concerning the esoteric significance of his *Fairy Tale*, behind which lie Rosicrucian mysteries) and then a substantial cycle of 27 lectures on Christian mysticism (especially that of Central Europe),[3] which he subsequently reworked for the published book *Mysticism at the Dawn of the Modern Age and its Relation to the Modern World-View*.[4] In this book (as also in the lecture cycle that gave rise to it) Rudolf Steiner pointed out that the sources of true *Christian* theosophy lie in a whole series of European mystics and occultists from the Middle Ages and early modern times. Subsequently the substance of this book came to be valued by several leading theosophists as 'true theosophy'.[5] Rudolf Steiner said of this: 'I had reason to be satisfied. For I had given only the findings of my spiritual vision, and these were accepted in the Theosophical Society.'[16] But because at the end of the cycle the Brockdorffs asked Rudolf Steiner to continue giving lectures in their branch he began with a second extensive cycle of 24 lectures with the title *Christianity as Mystical Fact and the Mysteries of Antiquity* (October 1901 to April 1902). Here, as subsequently in the book with the same title,[7] Rudolf Steiner sought to demonstrate from the sources of Christian esotericism the central place of the Mystery of Golgotha in the spiritual evolution of mankind as a culmination and—in terms of spiritual history—a fulfilment of the highest ideal and ultimate purpose of *all* mysteries of antiquity. Almost simultaneously he began a further cycle of lectures, this time outside the Theosophical Society in a small circle of spiritual seeking individuals who called themselves 'Die Kommenden' [literally 'the coming ones']. Rudolf Steiner called this new cycle—again consisting of 24 lectures—'From Buddha to Christ'; in it he tried, in his own words, 'to show what a mighty advance the Mystery of Golgotha signifies in comparison with the Buddha event, and how the evolution of humanity, as it strives towards the Christ event, approaches its culmination'.[8]

The cycle *Christianity as Mystical Fact* made a strong impression upon all those who heard it and upon the Brockdorffs—for here information was being given for the first time out of actual spiritual experience about the true mysteries of Christianity. No one had previously spoken about these mysteries in the Theosophical Society *in this form*, so that Count Brockdorff personally proposed to Rudolf Steiner that he enter the Society and also lead the Berlin Branch (or Lodge, as it was called at the time) in his stead. Rudolf Steiner, however, categorically declined to do so. On being asked for his reasons he gave the following answer in 1901 to Marie von Sivers (later Steiner): 'This is impossible, for I make a great difference between Eastern and Western [Christian] mysticism.'[9] In the lecture of 14 December 1911 Rudolf Steiner himself recalled this conversation with Marie von Sivers: 'I answered her with a long conversation, the gist of which was this: it will always be impossible for me to belong to a Society where one is engaged in the kind of theosophy permeated everywhere with misunderstood Eastern mysticism, which is the case in the Theosophical Society; for my business would be to recognize that *more important occult impulses* currently exist, and that it would be impossible to concede that the West has anything to learn from this Eastern mysticism. What I represent would be put in a wrong light if I said: I want to be a member of a Society that has Eastern mysticism as its byword. That was the content of the conversation.'[10] And only after Rudolf Steiner had received a direct indication from his teacher did he declare at the beginning of 1902 (on 12 January), in response to the pressing requests on the part of the Brockdorffs, that he was prepared to become a member of the Theosophical Society and to lead the Berlin Lodge. Subsequently, in 1905, he referred to this fact in one of his letters to Marie von Sivers: 'I can only say that had the Master not convinced me that, in spite of all this, theosophy is necessary for our time I would only have written philosophical books and lectured on literature and philosophy even *after* 1901.'[11]

One of the arguments that the Master might have advanced to motivate Rudolf Steiner to join the Theosophical Society can be found in the notes which Rudolf Steiner prepared for Edouard Schuré in 1907:[*] 'True initiators stood at its [the Society's] cradle and *that is why* it is at *present* an instrument of current spiritual life, even if subsequent events have resulted in certain imperfections.'[12]

Hence Rudolf Steiner also remarked in 1912 about his joining the Theosophical Society: 'And so nothing else could be done at the moment when we were invited to join this theosophical movement, nothing else could be done other than to return once more to those original sources

---

[*] Rudolf Steiner wrote these while he was staying in Schuré's country house in Barr. By this means he was giving a written response to Schuré's three questions: (i) regarding his own spiritual development, (ii) regarding Christian Rosenkreutz, and (iii) regarding the Theosophical Society.

which we may designate as belonging to all mankind, in contrast to those of a narrowly specialized nature.'[13]

Formal membership of the Society ensued on 17 January 1902, together with taking responsibility for the Berlin Lodge. Rudolf Steiner subsequently (1911) recalled these events: 'I never put forward any kind of motion to become a member of the Society, but I said to myself: If the Society wants me, they can have me.'[14]

Ten months later the leader of the Leipzig Lodge, Richard Brosch, suggested to Count Brockdorff: 'If Dr Steiner is already Chairman of the Berlin Lodge, he can also become General Secretary of the German Section.'[15] (The idea of its inauguration arose in Germany at that time.) The founding of the new Section ensued at the constituent assembly on 19/20 October 1902, when Rudolf Steiner was named as General Secretary by the ten German lodges. Rudolf Steiner was entrusted with this task precisely because he had from the outset uncompromisingly represented the stream of Christian esotericism through his entire activity.

The extent of Rudolf Steiner's spiritually independent reception by the official circles in the Theosophical Society is exemplified by the fact that on the very day when he was named as General Secretary (20 October 1902) he gave the lecture that he was due to give in the circle of 'Die Kommenden', this being the third in a cycle of 27 lectures—with the characteristic title 'From Zarathustra to Nietzsche. The Evolutionary History of Mankind in the Light of the World Conceptions from the most ancient Oriental Times until the Present or Anthroposophy'. This cycle represented a continuation and further development of the previous cycle and of its theme 'From Buddha to Christ'.

In 1923 Rudolf Steiner elaborated further: 'I left the assembly immediately, and while the others continued to confer and conversed together about theosophy, I gave my lecture cycle about anthroposophy.' Only one of the theosophists—he subsequently became an anthroposophist—went 'out of curiosity' to this lecture and later said to Rudolf Steiner: 'Yes, what you said then did not harmonize with what Mrs Besant and Blavatsky had been saying.' Whereupon Rudolf Steiner replied: 'That's very likely to be the case.' And he continued: 'So one could already say: this isn't quite right, it is something different.'[16]

When Rudolf Steiner subsequently described his work within the Theosophical Society, he could therefore say with complete justification: *'No one was left in uncertainty of the fact* that I would present to the Theosophical Society only the results of my own visionary research. For I stated this on all appropriate occasions. And when the German Section of the Theosophical Society was founded in Berlin in the presence of Annie

Besant and I was chosen to be its General Secretary, I had to leave the foundation sessions because I had to give one of my lectures before a non-theosophical audience. In these lectures I was dealing with the spiritual development of humanity, and I had made a point of adding to the title the words "an anthroposophy". Annie Besant also knew that at this time I was under this title presenting in lecture-form what I had to say [from my own experience] about the world of spirit.'[17] Thus with this title an allusion was being made to the new impulse that the stream which he led wanted to bring into the world. For once the Sun Logos had become *man*, a new epoch—characterized by a Christian esotericism following on from the ancient revelations springing from the sphere of the divine Father (that is, the primordial Theo-sophia)—was to begin, the epoch of the Son, which was to bring to mankind a knowledge of Christ as the cosmic image of man, the heavenly man whose forces can since the Mystery of Golgotha be found in *every* human being. In this more esoteric sense the designation *anthroposophy* signifies the search for the finding of the divine principle, not outside man but *within* him. For anthroposophy is a path that leads to the conscious discovery by the individual human being within his 'I' of that divine Being who united himself with earthly evolution through the Mystery of Golgotha.

Thus what Rudolf Steiner taught as a modern Christian initiate at that time and until his death he taught, in his own words, on the foundation of 'capacities kindled by the Christ impulse'.[18] By virtue of these capacities he knew from his own occult experience that the 'essential *meaning of the earth* [of earthly evolution] ... lies in the recognition and realization of the intentions of the *living Christ*'[19] and that 'it is the deepest aim of Rosicrucianism to reveal these intentions in the form of complete wisdom, beauty and activity'. Both Rudolf Steiner and his two spiritual Masters were fully allied with Rosicrucianism as the main stream of esoteric Christianity.

Rudolf Steiner's joining of the Theosophical Society was, however, preceded by another important event. For in order to begin with fulfilling this task in full measure *within the context of the Theosophical Society*, Rudolf Steiner had—in accordance with the strict spiritual law referred to above[*]—to wait until the corresponding question was posed from without and, moreover, from the Society itself. A general invitation to give lectures would not suffice. This central question was, however, posed

---

[*]This spiritual law states that in the present epoch of human freedom the spirit-teacher may give higher knowledge only in the form of an answer to a question posed to him from without, that is, if there is a genuine need among human beings for such knowledge.

to him on 11 November 1901 at a reception at Count Brockdorff's house by Marie von Sivers, who was at that time already a member of the Society. For like no one else she was struggling with the one-sidedly Eastern direction of the Theosophical Society and with the materialistic tendencies that manifested themselves in it ever more strongly.* In contrast, the first lectures by Rudolf Steiner which she heard in Brockdorff's salon immediately evoked in her the feeling that this new and virtually unknown lecturer was speaking out of quite different sources of wisdom. Thus Marie von Sivers was the *first person* who recognized Rudolf Steiner as a representative of Christian esotericism and, through her question, opened up the path towards the fulfilment of his central task.

In the period that followed, Rudolf Steiner would frequently recall this question in lectures and private conversations. Johanna Mücke, who had personally taken part in such a conversation, reported: 'He [Rudolf Steiner] explained that Frau Dr Steiner had at that time herself posed the question whether it might not be possible to present this [theosophical] wisdom in a manner that was more in tune with European cultural life and taking into account the Christ impulse. Herr Dr Steiner augmented this recollection with words which I shall never forget: "*In this way the opportunity was presented to me to work there* [in the Theosophical Society] *in the sense that I had in mind. The question was put to me, and—in accordance with spiritual laws—I was able to give the answer to such a question.*" '[20] Thus once he had received an indication from his spirit-teacher and a question was forthcoming from the Theosophical Society itself, Rudolf Steiner finally decided to become a member of this Society. This happened on 17 January 1902, approximately two months after the conversation referred to.

In what sense did Rudolf Steiner now intend—according to his own words, cited above—to work within the Theosophical Society? His intention was to work also *within* the Society in the same spirit out of which he had previously worked *outside* it: solely out of the spirit of true Christian esotericism. And as Rudolf Steiner—ever following his law—

---

* She subsequently wrote as follows about the difficulties that she was experiencing with the Theosophical Society: 'In spring 1902 I was for three weeks daily translating from English into Italian lectures by the Indian Jinaradjadasa, who had been appointed as the future President of the Theosophical Society. For inner reasons I had great difficulty at the time bringing much of it to outward expression and often recoiled from what I had to say, so materialized did the spirit appear to me to be here.' (Quoted from *Aus dem Leben von Marie Steiner-von Sivers. Biographische Beiträge und eine Bibliographie*, Dornach 1956. Regarding Jinaradjadasa, see also GA 185, 27 October 1918.)

spoke solely out of his own spiritual experience, he now had the task of verifying what was taught from the Eastern tradition in the Theosophical Society through his own independent research in the spiritual world. The theosophical teachings of karma, of reincarnation, life after death, the various cycles of evolution, ancient religions and races—all this Rudolf Steiner had not merely to investigate anew but thereby raise to an altogether new level, in that he imbued this ancient wisdom[*] with the new light which had streamed into earthly evolution through the Mystery of Golgotha. For only through this could these most ancient truths cease merely to belong to the past and be transformed into what also has a definite significance for the future. Thus what was involved here was a *re-enlivening* of the old primordial wisdom of mankind in the new light of Christ, without whose direct involvement neither the old wisdom nor mankind in general can have a future.

In 1909 Rudolf Steiner characterized this fundamental task of anthroposophy in our time, to whose fulfilment he dedicated his entire life, in the following way: 'That is why the anthroposophical world-conception sees the Christ Being as a sort of central point in the whole panorama of reincarnation, of the being of man, of our contemplation of the cosmos and so forth. And whoever studies this anthroposophical world-conception in its true sense will say to himself: I can contemplate all that, but I can comprehend it only when the whole picture focuses upon the great central point, upon the Christ. I have depicted in various ways the doctrine of reincarnation, the teaching of the human races, of planetary evolution and so on; but the Being of Christ is here painted from a single point of view, and this sheds light on everything else. It is a picture with a central figure to which everything else is related, and I can fathom the significance and expression of the other figures only if I understand the main figure.[†] That is how it stands with the anthroposophical world-conception. We project a great picture of various phenomena of the spiritual world; but then we focus upon the principle figure, upon the Christ, and only then do the details of the picture become intelligible.'[21] Numerous lectures and lecture cycles that Rudolf Steiner gave in the early years of his activity within the Theosophical Society confirm these words.

---

[*] It is not for nothing that Annie Besant called her principal work *Ancient Wisdom*, thereby indicating that its content derived from the past and led back to it.

[†] In his lectures, Rudolf Steiner spoke in this sense—out of a true knowledge of the Christ Being as the 'main figure' of earthly evolution—also about the great initiates of mankind: about Manu, Buddha, Zarathustra, Mani, Maitreya, Moses, Pythagoras, Hermes, Krishna, the Indian Rishis, Orpheus and others, also about their participation in preparing for Christ's coming to earth.

Of course, the majority of the listeners who attended Rudolf Steiner's lectures in these early years as members of the Theosophical Society were well familiar with Eastern-oriented works, especially those by Blavatsky and Sinnett. For this reason Rudolf Steiner had first to present to his listeners the meaning of theosophical teachings from the standpoint of Rosicrucian esotericism in order gradually to lead them to an understanding of this esotericism and, hence, to prepare the ground for this wisdom in the sense of a knowledge of its 'principal figure—the Christ'. The lecture series *Fundamentals of Esotericism*,[22] whose 31 lectures were given by Rudolf Steiner in 1905 in Berlin, is a particularly impressive example of such a cycle. Here there is a gradual transition from Eastern to Western esotericism, the latter of which was set forth in cycles such as *Theosophy in the Light of St John's Gospel* (1906) or *The Theosophy of the Rosicrucian* (1907) and several others, in which the mysteries of esoteric Christianity were directly revealed.[23]

No less than a year after his nomination as General Secretary, Rudolf Steiner was received into the so-called 'Esoteric School' of the Theosophical Society (23 October 1902).[24] Helena Blavatsky had established this School in the year of the publication of *The Secret Doctrine* (1888), initially in the form of an 'Esoteric Section of the Theosophical Society'. However, in the following year, because of difficulties that had arisen in the running of the Society, she was compelled to make the School independent from it; and—after renaming it the '*Eastern* School of Theosophy'—she declared herself as its sole leader. The word 'Eastern' in the name of the School corresponded precisely to the substance of its teachings and quite especially to its path of schooling (initiation), which had a thoroughly Eastern yoga character. This could hardly be otherwise, since the two *Eastern* mahatmas standing behind it were, according to Blavatsky's own conviction, at that time active not in the Society but in the Esoteric School which she herself led.[*] Hence she considered herself only as its outward head and the Mahatmas Kut Humi and Morya as its inner leaders (the inner head).[25]

Some time before her death Blavatsky named Annie Besant as her successor in the 'outward' leadership of the School (outer head), which she still led when Rudolf Steiner joined it. He subsequently wrote about this step: 'I had introduced my anthroposophical activity into the Theosophical Society. I had to be informed, therefore, as to all that

---

[*] The estrangement of the Eastern mahatmas from the official Theosophical Society at the time of the publication of *The Secret Doctrine* by Blavatsky is also confirmed by Rudolf Steiner (see GA 262, 'The Barr Manuscript', III).

occurred in the latter. For the sake of this information, and also because I myself considered a smaller circle necessary for those advanced in anthroposophical knowledge of the spirit, I had myself admitted into the "Esoteric School". *My smaller circle, however, was to have a meaning different from the School.*[26] The significance of this last sentence will be clearly understandable from what has been said previously; for the 'Esoteric School' of Helena Blavatsky and Annie Besant had—as did the theosophical movement as a whole—an Eastern character, whereas Rudolf Steiner's principal task from the outset was to lead his pupils in the direction of Christian-Rosicrucian initiation. And so, soon after the beginning of his activity in the Theosophical Society, he began to give those members of the Society who turned to him for help with questions of inner development appropriate esoteric guidance. He did this—as he himself testified—in full accordance with the indications of his own spirit-teacher Christian Rosenkreutz. Thus he wrote in a letter to one of his esoteric pupils at that time (1904): 'You are so kind as to give me the name "leader" in your letter. I am able and allowed to be your leader only in so far as the exalted Master by whom I myself am guided gives me instruction. I follow *him* with full consciousness in everything I impart to others.'[27] *

In order that he might be able to give his pupils esoteric guidance within the Theosophical Society not only personally but also, so to speak, officially, Rudolf Steiner had to establish his own branch of the Esoteric School. For this a formal authority on the part of its leadership was needed. He had to become what in theosophical language one called an 'Archwarden of the E.S.'. This occurred on 10 May 1904, when Annie Besant nominated Rudolf Steiner as the leader responsible for the Esoteric School in Germany and Austria.

However, there was a further reason why Rudolf Steiner considered it necessary to connect himself with this Esoteric School. He said in this

---

* What Rudolf Steiner says here is not in contradiction with his frequent assertions that he always spoke out of his own spiritual experience, that is, said only what he had himself researched in the spiritual world. He explained this in a public lecture on 13 October 1904 in Berlin as follows: 'The so-called Masters have the capacity to stimulate us—no more than this: they stimulate us in the spiritual domain . . . They appeal to nothing other than *our own human cognitive faculties* and give guidance by means of certain methods as to how we may develop the powers and faculties that reside in every human soul to raise ourselves to higher realms of existence' (GA 53, 13 October 1904, also the following quotation). In other words: they stimulate their pupils to their own spiritual research. And so Rudolf Steiner continues in the same lecture: 'I [shall] say nothing . . . that I have not been in a position to examine myself and for which I could not be accountable.'

regard: 'Now, I wished everywhere to link up with what was already in existence, with what history had already provided. Just as I did this in regard to the Theosophical Society, I wished to do likewise in reference to the "Esoteric School". For this reason my "more restricted circle" existed at first in connection with this School.'[28] These words are indicative of the highly important law of occult continuity, regarding whose esoteric significance Rudolf Steiner spoke as follows in a lecture from 1909: 'In the spiritual world there is a definite law,' which consists in that 'a fact of the spiritual world that has once been discovered by a clairvoyant or by an occult school cannot be investigated a second time if the would-be researcher has not first been informed that it has already been discovered ... Therefore, already known facts in the spiritual world can be perceived only when their import has been consciously grasped as communications already made. This is the law that establishes for all epochs the foundation of universal brotherliness. It is impossible to penetrate into any domain of the spiritual world without a link having first been made with what has already been fathomed by the Elder Brothers of humanity. The spiritual world sees to it that nobody can become a law unto himself, saying: "I am not concerned with what is already there. I shall investigate only for myself." None of the facts communicated in spiritual science today could be perceived by even the most highly developed and advanced individuals if they had not been previously known. Because a link must be there with what has already been discovered, the theosophical movement had also to be founded on this basis.'[29]

However, if this law could be fulfilled on the level of the Theosophical Society through studying the teachings existing within it, its implementation on a higher level—that of the leadership of the Esoteric School—signified entering into direct contact with the spiritual inspirers of these teachings. But as all these teachings had an Eastern, Tibeto-Indian character, the teachers with whom Rudolf Steiner—in order to fulfil the above law—had now to enter into spiritual contact were *Eastern teachers*, the occult leaders of the Esoteric School of the Theosophical Society since Blavatsky's times. Hence immediately after his appointment as leader of the Esoteric School for Central Europe, Rudolf Steiner began to speak for the first time not only of the two Western Masters standing behind him, Christian Rosenkreutz and the Master Jesus, but also of two Eastern Masters, Kut Humi and Morya. There is evidence for this in the extant notes of the earliest esoteric lessons that he regularly gave from July 1904 onwards in the Esoteric School.[30]

And so in order that he might fulfil his own task of illuming the ancient wisdom of the East with the new light of the Sun Logos, the Christ, Rudolf Steiner had to take up direct contact with the inspirers of this ancient wisdom, since otherwise he would—according to the law referred to—have been unable to follow its basic rule of speaking only out of his own spiritual experience, on the foundation of his own spiritual research.

That Rudolf Steiner was at this time a representative solely and exclusively of the occult stream of Christian esotericism is borne out, for example, by the following fact. Already in 1904, simultaneously with the beginning of his activity as leader of the Central European Section of the theosophical Esoteric School, he started publishing articles in the journal *Lucifer-Gnosis* which were put together in 1907 in the book *Knowledge of the Higher Worlds*, the book which presents the classical description of the Christian-Rosicrucian path of initiation. At the same time, however, he was also describing in his lectures from the years 1904–7 in a manifold and detailed way the three main paths of spiritual knowledge: the Eastern yoga path, the Christian-Gnostic path and the Christian-Rosicrucian path.[31] He characterized the occult sources of the last two of these as follows: 'The Master Jesus and the Master Christian Rosenkreutz have prepared two paths of initiation for us: the Christian-Esoteric path [the so-called Christian-Gnostic] and the Christian-Rosicrucian one.'[32] Behind the Eastern yoga path, however, stood Eastern mahatmas, and this path had been the actual one in the Theosophical Society since Blavatsky's time. Rudolf Steiner repeatedly emphasized in the lectures referred to above that the Eastern path *is absolutely not suitable* for people of the West (those belonging to European and American civilization). For them only the other two paths are appropriate; and for someone living within modern Western civilization the Christian-Rosicrucian path is the more suitable. 'The first is not for Europeans,'[33] said Rudolf Steiner for example in the lecture of 4 November 1906. And somewhat earlier in the same year, in the lecture of 20 October, he pointed out that 'it [the Eastern path]' brings 'illusions and is also damaging to the souls . . . [of people from the West]'.[34] Regarding the last of the three paths, he wrote in a letter to Annie Besant from the summer of 1906: 'Out of their clear premonition of the distinctive qualities of the fifth [modern] human sub-race, the Masters of the Rosicrucian School have defined the "path" for the West which is *alone* appropriate in the present cycle. To the extent that it may be brought into the public domain, this "path" has been described by me in the journal *Lucifer-Gnosis*.'[35]

To reiterate: although the path which Rudolf Steiner subsequently gave in the book *Knowledge of the Higher Worlds* was presented on the basis of his own spiritual experience (the book merely describes in objective form the spiritual path that its author had himself travelled), he had to obtain *permission* for publishing the rules of the only kind of occult pupilship appropriate for Western people in our time that it contained directly from the two leading Rosicrucian Masters. In Rudolf Steiner's words, in order that 'a picture of the truth [the true path] may be given ... the Masters of Wisdom have given permission for the publication of such rules'.[36]*

Notes

1. 'The Barr Manuscript', Part III, likewise the following quotations.
2. GA 264, 4 May 1907 (letter circulated to esoteric pupils).
3. The lecture on Nietzsche was given by Rudolf Steiner on 22 September 1900, the lecture 'Goethe's Secret Revelation'—devoted to Goethe's *Tale of the Green Snake and the Beautiful Lily*—on 29 September 1900, the cycle of 27 lectures on Christian mysticism was given in the period between 6 October 1900 and 27 April 1901. No notes exist of any of these lectures.
4. GA 7.
5. GA 28, ch. XXX.
6. Ibid.
7. GA 8.
8. GA 28, ch. XXX.
9. Marie Steiner-von Sivers' essay 'The Beginnings of Rudolf Steiner's Spiritual-Scientific Activity', quoted from *Aus dem Leben von Marie Steiner-von Sivers. Biographische Beiträge und eine Bibliographie* ('From the Life of Marie Steiner-von Sivers. Biographical Contributions and a Bibliography'), Dornach 1956.
10. GA 264, 14 December 1911.
11. GA 262, letter of 9 January 1905.
12. GA 262, 'The Barr Manuscript', III.
13. GA 158, 11 April 1912.
14. GA 264, 14 December 1911.
15. Ibid.
16. GA 258, 11 June 1923.
17. GA 28, ch. XXX.
18. GA 110, 12 April 1909 (morning lecture).
19. GA 262, 'The Barr Manuscript' III, likewise the following quotation.
20. See note 9, the article entitled 'Aus der Geschichte des Philosophisch-Anthroposophischen Verlages' (From the History of the Philosophic-Anthroposophic Publishing Company).
21. GA 112, 30 June 1909.
22. GA 93a.

---

*Rudolf Steiner spoke with somewhat different words in the lecture of June 1912 (GA 130).

23. GA 94 and GA 99, see also GA 96, 97, 100 among others.
24. See further in GA 264, editorial introduction to Parts I and II.
25. See GA 262, 'The Barr Manuscript', III.
26. GA 28, ch. XXXII.
27. GA 264, letter to Doris and Franz Paulus dated 11 August 1904.
28. GA 28, ch. XXXII.
29. GA 109/111, 4 June 1909.
30. See for example the notes of the esoteric lessons of 9 July 1904, 26 June 1906 and 22 October 1906 in GA 264.
31. See for example the lectures of 3, 4 September 1906 (GA 95), 19 September and 30 November 1906 (GA 97), 20 October 1906 (GA 96), 4 November 1906 (GA 94) among others.
32. GA 264, esoteric lesson of 1 June 1907.
33. GA 94, 4 November 1906.
34. GA 96, 20 October 1906.
35. GA 264, letter to Annie Besant written at the beginning of July 1906. Reference is being made here to the articles that first appeared in the journal *Lucifer-Gnosis* and later formed the book *Knowledge of the Higher Worlds* (GA 10).
36. GA 53, 15 December 1904.

3. The Theosophical Congress in Munich. The Separation of Eastern and Western Esotericism

Despite the essential difference between the two occult streams, the Eastern and the Rosicrucian, Rudolf Steiner remained in spiritual contact with the two Masters of the East within the sphere of the Esoteric School for almost three years. This was the case until May 1907, when something quite extraordinary occurred: the theosophical Esoteric School, which had hitherto been a single whole, divided into an Eastern and a Western part, led, respectively, by Annie Besant and Rudolf Steiner. This outwardly happened entirely peacefully, according to a conversation between the two leaders during the Munich Congress of the European Section of the Theosophical Society, which had been organized by the German Section under Rudolf Steiner's leadership. Marie von Sivers, who was serving as the interpreter for this discussion, reported: Rudolf Steiner 'explained to her [Annie Besant] . . . the need that had arisen for him to place his own esoteric work independently from hers wholly on the foundation of Western-Christian mysticism. She listened to this in silence, with a somewhat impenetrable [facial] expression.'[1] However, from the way that Rudolf Steiner reported to the members of the Esoteric School about the separation that had taken place, one can sense that this was no more than an earthly *consequence* of another, far more significant division.

Thus Rudolf Steiner informed the members of the School in the esoteric lesson of 1 June 1907, held during the cycle of 14 lectures linked to the Munich Congress[*] and characteristically called *The Theosophy of the Rosicrucian*[2]: 'No one should believe that there is disharmony between the Masters of the East and West. However, *an incisive change has occurred* lately regarding the Esoteric Schools of the East and of the West. Until now, both Schools have been united in a large circle under the combined leadership of the Masters. Now, however, the Western School has become independent, and there are two comparable Schools: one in the East, the other in the West—two smaller circles instead of the one large one. The Eastern School is being led by Mrs Annie Besant, and those who

---

[*] There were particularly many members of the German Section present at this esoteric lesson, since most of them had come for Rudolf Steiner's lecture cycle, which had been scheduled to take place in association with the Congress.

feel more attracted to her in their hearts *can no longer remain in our School. People should sound exactly their hearts' longing to discover which way they are being led.* At the head of our Western School there are two Masters: the Master Jesus and the Master Christian Rosenkreutz. And they lead us along two paths, the Christian and the Christian-Rosicrucian way.'[3] In the same lesson he went on to say: 'What is given through me at the behest of the Masters of the West goes alongside what is given through Mrs Besant on behalf of the Masters of the East, quite *independently* of it.' From this moment onwards 'there must be an Esoteric School of the West and an Esoteric School of the East. They stand side by side, of equal value. Each possesses its two Masters: Mahatma K[ut Humi] and Mahatma M[orya]; Master Jesus of Nazareth and Master Christian Rosenkreutz. One of these Schools is led by Mrs Besant, the other by Dr Steiner. *But we have to decide which one to follow.*'—'The Christian teaching and the Christian-Rosicrucian teaching now exist in the West. The former educates through the feelings, the latter through understanding. The dying cultures of the East still need the Eastern teachings. The Western teachings are for future cultures.' And at the end of the lecture he said: 'We stand at the dawning of the Sixth Day of Creation [sixth cultural period]. We have to develop the sixth and seventh cultural epochs out of ourselves. The future in its rising light is already present within us. Apprehending this, receive into yourselves what the Master Christian Rosenkreutz has spoken.'[4] (The reading of the Master's words followed.)

In these extracts from three different accounts[*] of the esoteric lesson in question, which established the existence of a *Christian-Rosicrucian* School independent from Eastern occultism, the *necessity* that Rudolf Steiner emphasized so strongly of *choosing* between the two Schools—that is, the impossibility of following the Western and also the Eastern Masters simultaneously—is clearly apparent. This means that the Western Masters—through their emissary, Rudolf Steiner—excluded *their pupils* from the possibility of having an allegiance to the latter. And this prohibition can, in the context of the entire esoteric lesson that marked the official separation of the two occult Schools, be understood as nothing other than a direct testimony of *the participation of the Master himself within the circle*, so that the emergence of two independent Esoteric Schools and—five years later—of two independent Societies, the Theosophical and the Anthroposophical, can be seen as merely an *earthly reflection* of this separation.

---

[*] Nothing was allowed to be written down during an esoteric lesson. Hence all notes of the lessons (there were over three hundred altogether) were transcribed by the participants from memory after the lessons.

How 'profoundly decisive'—in Rudolf Steiner's words—this separation was may be seen from the fact that he himself evidently broke off all
spiritual engagement with both the Eastern mahatmas. In any event, until
the end of his life he did not utter the name of Mahatma Morya *even once*,
and mentioned Kut Humi only a few times incidentally in lectures that he
gave in 1915–16 in connection with the occult biography of H.P.
Blavatsky—and even then only in a particular context which will be
considered below. Thus there was in the ensuing period no question of
any inspirations from or contact with these Masters. Even their portraits
were removed from the rooms where Rudolf Steiner gave esoteric
lessons.

On the other hand, Rudolf Steiner's relationship with the two Rosicrucian Masters referred to—and also with other teachers who will be
spoken of later on—continued to be strengthened; and this led to the
revealing of ever greater depths of the true Christian esotericism that
contains an all-embracing knowledge of the cosmic Christ Being and the
Mystery of Golgotha.* Similarly, the first revelation of the cosmic mysteries of the Archangel Michael, the 'Sun Countenance of Christ',
occurred at the end of the same year of 1907 (on 5 December) within the
Western Esoteric School that was henceforth led solely by Rudolf
Steiner.[5]

Moreover, Rudolf Steiner never again spoke about the Eastern yoga
path to the extent that he did *until* the summer of 1907, but he mentioned
it more seldom and incidentally as something that has essentially no significance for Western people. In contrast, he spoke again and again and in
ever new ways about the Christian-Gnostic path and especially the
Rosicrucian path of initiation.

From all this there arises the decisive question as to the true occult
reason for the split between the spirit-teachers. It follows from what has
been said so far that the reason for this split, from an esoteric standpoint,
can only be around one issue: *the different relationship to the Christ Being and
the different understanding of this Being's central significance for the future destiny
of the earth and of mankind.*

In the lecture of 12 April 1909, Rudolf Steiner referred to this fun-

---

*In the ensuing esoteric lessons, which Rudolf Steiner continued to hold until the
beginning of the First World War in 1914 under the auspices of the Esoteric School that
he led, the work on the three Rosicrucian sayings 'Ex Deo nascimur', 'In Christo
morimur' and 'Per Spiritum Sanctum reviviscimus' had a central place. (Most of the notes
of the esoteric lessons that Rudolf Steiner gave between 1904 and 1914 have been
published in GA 264 and 265; others are in preparation.)

damental difference between Eastern and Western (Rosicrucian) wisdom: 'You are all familiar with the evolution of the theosophical movement and must realize that the impetus for its development accompanied the proclamation of certain truths—in a form I need not describe here—known as the *Stanzas of Dzyan*.'[6] And then Rudolf Steiner continued, having referred to the great significance of Eastern wisdom as a mighty legacy of the *past* evolution of humanity: 'After the ice had been broken in this way [by the development of theosophy], one could speak more freely out of the wellsprings of Western occultism . . . out of the sources of the living occultism faithfully guarded in the Rosicrucian mysteries. There is no wisdom of the East that has not streamed into Western occultism. In the teachings and investigations of the Rosicrucians, indeed, you will find everything that has been preserved by the great sages of the East. Nothing, absolutely nothing, known through Eastern wisdom is missing in the wisdom of the West. There is only this difference. The wisdom of the West *had to illumine this whole body of Eastern teaching*, the entirety of Eastern wisdom, Eastern research, *with the light kindled in humanity by the Christ impulse*, but without losing any of it. It should not be said that a single iota of Eastern occultism is missing from Western occultism, which is derived from the hidden Rishis of the West who are invisible to human eyes. Nothing is missing. *It is simply that everything had to be renewed out of the rejuvenating fountain of the Christ impulse* . . . with [new supersensible] faculties kindled by the Christ impulse.'

Herein consists the *only*, but fundamental and decisive difference between the Esoteric School of Rudolf Steiner and that of Annie Besant, and that means ultimately between the Western Masters standing behind the former, Christian Rosenkreutz and the Master Jesus, and the Eastern Mahatmas Kut Humi and Morya standing behind the latter, all of whom represented the ancient wisdom of mankind but in the former case wholly renewed out of the forces of the Christ impulse and in the second case neither having undergone nor even acknowledging such a renewal. Three months after the separation, Rudolf Steiner wrote in September 1907 for Edouard Schuré: 'The Eastern initiations must of necessity leave untouched the *Christ* as the central *cosmic* factor of evolution . . . They [the revelations of oriental initiation] could only hope for success within evolution if the principle of Christianity were to be eradicated from Western culture. But this would be the same as eradicating the essential *meaning of the earth*, which lies in the recognition and realization of the intentions of the *living Christ*.'[7]

The *first* half of these words are fully confirmed by the letters of the two mahatmas, in whose collection of letters to Sinnett the name of Christ is barely mentioned at all in the course of 600 pages—to say nothing of any *knowledge* of His true Being and His true significance for earthly evolution. As for the rest of theosophical literature, it has already been observed that nothing is said about Christianity except only in a distorted way.[*]

The *second* half of the words quoted became a reality two years after the separation of the two Esoteric Schools, when Eastern occultism openly made the attempt to 'eradicate the Christ principle from Western culture' by replacing it with the appearance of a false Messiah, a new world Teacher of Eastern (Indian) origin, as happened in the events associated with Krishnamurti.

However, before we concern ourselves—albeit only in brief—with this and other events which formed the further reasons for the separation of the Western and Eastern lodges, something will be said here about the 1907 Munich Congress, where this separation became official.

As has already been mentioned, the 'Munich Congress of the European Sections of the Theosophical Society' was prepared by the German Section under the leadership of Rudolf Steiner himself. It was organized entirely in the spirit of Christian-Rosicrucian esotericism. Thus on the cover of the conference programme there was a cross with roses together with the initial letters of the three Rosicrucian sayings (see the footnote on page 388). In the conference hall itself there were busts of Fichte, Hegel and Schelling, the two occult columns associated with the Rosi-crucian mysteries and the seals, depicting scenes from the Book of Revelation, the last and seventh of which—incorporating the essential nature of the Grail mystery—was prepared in accordance with the per-sonal indications of Rudolf Steiner. In the three lectures that Rudolf Steiner gave during the conference, he spoke in the first about Rosi-crucian initiation,[†] in the second about some results of this initiation, ending with a direct indication of what the leading teacher of Christian esotericism (Christian Rosenkreutz) expects from people today; and in the third lecture he dealt at some length with the occult significance of the various Rosicrucian symbols and artistic representations in the place where the lectures were held.[8]

Linked to the congress was a cycle of 14 lectures entitled *The Theosophy*

---

[*] This applies to all works by Olcott and Blavatsky (with the exception of certain places in *Isis Unveiled*) and also those of Besant and Leadbeater. The sole exception is the work of Mabel Collins, who was under the influence of Christian and not Eastern inspirations and who joined the independent Anthroposophical Society when it was founded in 1912/13.
[†] Christian-Gnostic initiation was also considered in this lecture, but Eastern initiation was not mentioned at all.

of the Rosicrucian, given between 22 May and 6 June with only a two days' pause, when Rudolf Steiner gave two public lectures on the theme 'Bible and Wisdom'.[9] This cycle began with the history of the Rosicrucian movement, its tasks and the new relationship between teacher and pupil practised within it,[*] which was fully distinguished from the customary relationship in Eastern occultism. The teacher in Rosicrucian initiation does not demand absolute and unconditional authority as was the case in the theosophical movement (when the mahatmas appeared, Olcott, Blavatsky, Leadbeater and the others present literally fell down before them), but he appears merely as a 'friend and adviser',[10] or also as 'stimulator' (see p. 381), and he is a teacher in the sense, for example, of a mathematics teacher. In the last lecture of the cycle Rudolf Steiner again spoke—as he had at his first lecture at the congress—at some length about the two *Christian* paths of initiation: the Christian-mystical and the Rosicrucian paths. The cycle itself is, as its name implies, a great panorama of Rosicrucian wisdom with its centre of the true knowledge of the cosmic Christ as the Sun Logos. Rudolf Steiner's next great cycle, like-wise consisting of 14 lectures entitled *Theosophy and Rosicrucianism* and commencing in Kassel three days after the end of the Munich cycle, had a similar form.[11]

This pronouncedly Christian-Rosicrucian orientation of the congress must have been striking to Annie Besant and her followers. She had herself come to the congress directly from India and had given a lecture about the relationship of the Masters to the theosophical movement, with the Eastern teachers as ever being in a focal position.

After the congress Annie Besant spent a further six days in Munich, and a whole series of meetings and conversations with Rudolf Steiner took place, where Marie von Sivers interpreted and was therefore an invo-luntary witness. These conversations not only finally confirmed that there were two different esoteric schools but they also had the legacy of a revelation of extraordinary importance that Annie Besant made to Rudolf Steiner in the presence of Marie von Sivers. Rudolf Steiner subsequently reported 'that in Munich in 1907 Annie Besant admitted before a witness [Marie von Sivers], who would be ready to so testify at any time, that she *was not competent with regard to Christianity*. And because of that she, as it

---

[*] In his preface to the book *Knowledge of the Higher Worlds* Rudolf Steiner wrote in this connection: 'For anyone who is seeking spiritual training in accordance with present-day spiritual conditions, a *direct* relationship to the objective world is much more important than a relationship to the personality of a teacher' (GA 10, preface to the fifth edition, dated 7 September 1914).

were, transferred the movement to me inasmuch as Christianity should flow into it.'[12] Annie Besant confirmed this in a letter to Hübbe-Schleiden, to whom she wrote on 7 June 1907 soon after her return from Munich to London: 'Dr. Steiner's occult training is very different from ours. He does not know the eastern way, so cannot, of course teach it. He teaches the Xtian & Rosicrucian way, & this is very helpful to some, but is different from ours. He has his own School, on his own responsibility.'[13]

Rudolf Steiner had indeed never taught the Eastern path of schooling, though not—as Besant maintained—because he did not know it but because he considered it unsuitable for modern Western humanity. Thus he prefaced the description of the Christian-Rosicrucian path of initiation in the Munich lecture cycle with the following words: 'This [Rosicrucian] path orients man not to the past [as does the Eastern path] but to the future, to those conditions which man is still to experience.'[14] In other words, whereas Eastern initiation sought to lead man back to the paradisaical state which he has lost, the new Christian initiation (in its two forms) endeavours to lead mankind into the future, to the fulfilment of the ultimate ideal of human evolution, as portrayed in the image of the heavenly Jerusalem at the end of the Book of Revelation of St John.[19] Hence Besant, who only knew the Eastern path, was absolutely incapable of understanding the Rosicrucian path emanating from esoteric Christianity, and was able honestly to confess this.

However, it very soon transpired that Annie Besant not only regarded herself as 'not competent with regard to Christianity' but that already two years after these conversations she claimed to have an ultimate degree of competence regarding this question. And so on the exoteric plane the separation of the two occult Schools proved to be a prologue to the separation of the two movements, even to the arising of two completely independent Societies.

Notes

1. Quoted from Christoph Lindenberg, *Rudolf Steiner. Eine Chronik*, Stuttgart 1988.
2. GA 99.
3. GA 264, esoteric lesson of 1 June 1907, also the following quotations.
4. Ibid.
5. The notes of this first esoteric lesson devoted to the Michael mystery were published in *Beiträge zur Rudolf Steiner-Gesamtausgabe*, no. 67/68, Dornach 1979.
6. GA 110, 12 April 1909.
7. GA 262, 'The Barr Manuscript', III.
8. See further regarding the content of the Munich Congress in GA 284.
9. 23 and 24 May 1907: the text of these lectures has not yet been published.

10. GA 99, 22 May 1907.
11. The Kassel cycle is published in GA 100.
12. GA 264, 14 December 1911.
13. A facsimile of this letter is printed in Emil Bock's book *Rudolf Steiner, Studien zu seinem Lebensgang und Lebenswerk*, Stuttgart 1967.
14. GA 99, 6 June 1907.
15. See GA 104, 29/30 June 1908.

4. The Decline of the Theosophical Society. The Ascendancy of Christian Esotericism

The following characterization of the events leading to the decline of the Theosophical Society will be preceded by a brief description of them given by Rudolf Steiner in his autobiography: 'But from 1906 onwards, there were certain events in the Theosophical Society which clearly manifested the terrible extent of its deterioration. Whereas at an earlier period, at the time of H.P. Blavatsky, the fact of such happenings was asserted by the outside world ... since 1906 the Society—upon whose guidance I did not have the slightest influence—had been pervaded by activities reminiscent of the aberrations of spiritism, which made it necessary for me to emphasize again and again that the part of the Society which was under my direction had absolutely nothing to do with these things. The climax of these activities was reached when it was asserted of a Hindu boy that he was the person in whom Christ would appear in a new earthly life.'[1]

In order to gain a better understanding of these words written by Rudolf Steiner, and especially his reference to the significance of the year 1906, we must now briefly turn to the history of the arising of the idea of the new world Teacher (the Messiah) in theosophical circles.

In his book *The Bodhisattva Question* Thomas Meyer describes how this terrible mistake arose: 'Already in 1889 H.P. Blavatsky informed a group of theosophists that the true purpose of the Theosophical Society was to prepare "humanity for the coming of the world Teacher".'

Five years later, after the death of H.P. Blavatsky (in May 1891), Annie Besant made a similar declaration. Moreover, C.W. Leadbeater, with whom Annie Besant had become acquainted in 1890 and who in the coming decades was to become a decisive figure for her spiritual orientation, from the beginning of the new century made the search for this 'world Teacher' his wholly personal task.[2] Charles Leadbeater (1854[*]– 1934) was originally an Anglican priest in London. After he had become acquainted with Sinnett's books and with the letters of the mahatmas published in them, he sent the Mahatma K.H. a letter through a medium

---

[*] According to Peter Michel, in his book *Charles W. Leadbeater mit den Augen des Geistes: Die Biographie eines grossen Eingeweihten*, Aquamarin Verlag, 1998, Leadbeater was not, as generally supposed, born on 17 February 1847 but on 16 February 1854 in Stockport.

known to himself with the request to receive him into the ranks of his pupils. Some time later he received two letters in reply through Helena Blavatsky, signed with the abbreviation 'K.H.', the second of which ended with the words: 'Greetings to you, my new chela.'[3] Once he had been received as a pupil Leadbeater—following the direction of his teacher—immediately gave up all his activities and followed Blavatsky to India. In 1883 he became a member of the Theosophical Society and shortly afterwards—on Blavatsky's advice—made the transition to Buddhism in order to be able to serve the mahatmas better.[4]

In the Theosophical Society Leadbeater rapidly became well known, not only through his numerous books but especially through his clairvoyant faculties, with whose help in 1904 in America he discovered the first candidate for the role of the 'world Teacher', the 13-year-old Hubert van Hook, the son of the then leader of the American Section of the Theosophical Society. The preparation of the new Messiah was, however, soon interrupted because of the scandal that broke out in 1906, when Leadbeater was publicly accused of amoral conduct (in the sexual domain), compelling him to leave the Society in the same year.

Rudolf Steiner adopted from the outset a clear and unambiguous position with regard to the 'scandal surrounding Leadbeater'. Thus he wrote in a letter to the members of the German Section: 'I myself can speak all the more freely ... because, from the point of view of that occultism I am obliged to represent, I have to reject the methods by which Mr. Leadbeater arrives at his occult knowledge and what he recommends to others as a useful method of working.'[5] From Rudolf Steiner's standpoint the reason for 'Leadbeater's fall' lay not so much in the man himself as 'in his entire occult system' and above all in the erroneous methods that he used for spiritual development. In the same letter Rudolf Steiner goes on to say 'that hardly anyone is guaranteed not to fall into serious error if one employs the methods which lie at the foundation of Leadbeater's work'.

For these methods of spiritual development were not only of a one-sidedly Eastern character but were diametrically opposed in their nature to the Rosicrucian method of teaching which is alone suitable for Europeans. The occult methods employed by Leadbeater completely lacked the 'mental development'[6] necessary for every Westerner who seeks the spirit and leading to a uniquely reliable 'inwardly contemplative insight'—that rigorous and consistent intellectual training which underlies the Rosicrucian method and without which 'Western people wander about *without a rudder*, regardless of whether they are moving on the physical plane or on a higher plane'. Leadbeater, on the other hand, based his methods on the development of distinctly problematic mediumistic, atavistic faculties which excluded any conscious control on the part of the clairvoyant over his supersensible perceptions—a capacity which is indispensable for *distinguishing* between truth and illusion in the spiritual world. In place of such conscious control Leadbeater envisaged 'the absolute authority of a *guru*—which is impossible in the West due to the general cultural situation'. The danger was, therefore, that the clairvoyant became the blind plaything of highly dubious occult powers which he easily came to regard as 'teachers' or 'mahatmas' on whom he relied as indisputable authorities of the highest order; and as we have seen, this happened in Leadbeater's case with truly catastrophic consequences for the entire Theosophical Society.

The same is true of Leadbeater's books, regarding which Rudolf Steiner wrote to Annie Besant in the summer of 1906: 'Had I been on my own, I would have *never* recommended the writings of Mr. Leadbeater as suitable theosophical reading material.'[7]

Probably the most essential aspect of the entire story was, however, the fact that for the first time the hitherto little known attempts of the leaders of the Theosophical Society—above all Leadbeater and Besant—to prepare a *specific* candidate for the role of the new Messiah became familiar to a wider public.

Further and—because of their consequences—even more serious symptoms of the decline of the Theosophical Society were the occult circumstances manifesting themselves already in the following year (1907) with the choice of Annie Besant as Olcott's successor in the leadership of the Society after his death on 17 February 1907, together with the fact that, wholly unexpectedly, she received Leadbeater back into the Society. As numerous documents that have now been published indicate,[8] Rudolf Steiner had nothing against Annie Besant being chosen as President of the Society, despite the fact that he had a fundamental disagreement with her regarding an understanding of the Christ Being.[*] He merely did not agree that she united in herself the tasks of leading the Esoteric School and carrying administrative responsibility for the Society,[†] which had never

---

[*] Thus Rudolf Steiner wrote in the circular letter of 28 April 1907 to the members of the Executive Council of the German Section of the Theosophical Society: 'One does not necessarily have to agree with Mrs. Besant's particular spiritual bent, but one can, nevertheless, acknowledge that, under the present circumstances, she is the only candidate under consideration for the presidency' (GA 264).

[†] According to a definite occult law, any active involvement with outward administrative or organizational situations must necessarily have a negative effect upon the work of an Esoteric School where one individual takes upon himself both duties, those associated with exoteric and also esoteric leadership.

previously happened in occult circles. As, however, he had no possibility of influencing the selection process, he was in the end prepared to agree to it had the 'authority' of the mahatmas not been commandeered for the achieving of this aim.

The situation was that a whole series of official pronouncements were being made to the Society by its leadership that the mahatmas had appeared on three occasions in astral form at Olcott's deathbed and were visible not only to Olcott himself but also to the two ladies who were looking after him and who were in his room at that moment, and that one of them had precisely written down the conversation which she had witnessed immediately after the disappearance of the mahatma. On the occasion of the first visit only Mahatma Morya answered Olcott's questions:

> *Question*: What is your Divine Will in reference to my successor—whom shall I appoint?
> *Answer*: (Master M.): Annie Besant.
> *Question*: She is so much in Esoteric Work, will not that prevent her fulfilling properly the duties of President?
> *Answer*: We will overshadow her . . .
> *Question*: Shall I appoint her with or without the conditions I had in mind this P.M.?
> *Answer*: Conditions unwise, nothing binding.[9]

What is of particular interest in this dialogue is that Olcott, as an esotericist of many years' standing, was so bold as to express to his visitor out of his own experience—albeit in a somewhat different form—that same objection that Rudolf Steiner was also making at that time. In any event there was a great scandal when this dialogue became known within the Society and Annie Besant explained that she was taking on the office of President only in accordance with the Masters' command, inasmuch as the authority of the mahatmas was thereby being used in order to attain purely administrative ends. The effect of this was to exert considerable psychological pressure on all members of the Society, in complete contradiction with the Society's statute guaranteeing total freedom to all its members on this question.

Rudolf Steiner from the outset spoke out decisively against this misappropriation of the names of the mahatmas, while declining to answer the question as to whether or not they had actually appeared to Olcott. Thus he wrote in the circular letter already referred to: 'I can only assure you at this point that I am not yet permitted to reveal what I know about the appearances [of the mahatmas] in Adyar.'[10] And then Rudolf Steiner referred to how, in addition to the two polar opinions that the appearance of the mahatmas at Olcott's deathbed was true or a figment of the imagination, 'there is, as every occultist should know, a third possibility'.* Rudolf Steiner then reiterated: 'But as I said before, because I am not allowed to speak about these revelations, it must still remain only an indication.'

The only way of understanding this is that the Masters of Western occultism standing behind Rudolf Steiner did not permit him to proclaim what he knew from his own experience about the events in Adyar.

The appearance of the mahatmas at Olcott's deathbed had a further disastrous consequence for the destiny of the Theosophical Society, namely the reinstatement of Leadbeater. After the latter's departure from the Society Annie Besant had written: 'Leadbeater has come to grief ... If I should one day also transgress I would ask of those who love me that they should not hesitate to condemn my failings.'[11] And then only a year later the opposite occurred, as Rudolf Steiner wrote in 1911: '... Mrs Besant at first personally condemned Leadbeater and then, after a short while, sided with him.'[12] And so Rudolf Steiner had to explain a second time that 'one cannot really work any longer with this Society'.[13] Thus there was not only the problem of the dubious occultist Leadbeater and Annie Besant's inconsistency with regard to him but also the—as it were—*occult reasons* for his renewed admission to the Society. This occult aspect of the events concerned consisted of the following.

A few days after the first appearance of the two mahatmas at Olcott's deathbed there followed their second visit, during which the question of Leadbeater was discussed. Again both the ladies present in the room were able to perceive the astral vision and wrote down the conversation that they heard *verbatim*. First Kut Humi spoke with the dying man, then Morya. In response to Olcott's question they confirmed the deep spiritual relationship that still existed between Leadbeater and Besant, who according to the mahatmas 'had worked together on the higher planes under the Masters' instructions'.[14] And then the mahatmas demanded from Olcott firstly a written rehabilitation of Leadbeater in the form of an article, which was to state that both mahatmas 'had worked through both Mrs Besant and Mr Leadbeater' and secondly that he must be invited in writing to return to the Society.

At the end of the conversation they spoke frankly to Olcott: 'He

---

* A detailed analysis of such a 'third possibility' may be found in the book by Thomas Meyer referred to above (see note 2).

[Leadbeater] has been a light in the Society,' whereupon the mahatmas withdrew after they had said a few words to one of the ladies present.

In the course of the next two days Olcott successively dictated the letter to Leadbeater and the article with the information referred to for the journal *The Theosophist* to the lady who was recording the proceedings. However, whether because of his physical frailty or because he was inwardly uncertain with regard to the rightness of what was going on, he was unable to arrive at an ending for the article 'rehabilitating' Leadbeater. Then the figure of Morya suddenly appeared again to the lady who was writing in accordance with his dictation and dictated the end of the article to her personally. Moreover, Olcott's completed letter to Leadbeater was shown to the mahatma during the same visit, and only once the latter had given it his approval was it sent to the addressee.[15] As for the article, it was published the following month in *The Theosophist* (February 1907) under the title 'A Recent Conversation with the Mahatmas'. Annie Besant, who became president of the Society in June 1907, did, however—notwithstanding the full 'authority of the mahatmas'—need more than a year to persuade the members to reconcile themselves to receiving Leadbeater back into the Society. This happened in the autumn of 1908, and already in the spring of the following year Leadbeater, who had again settled in Adyar, discovered a new candidate for the role of world Teacher, this time the Indian boy Krishnamurti.

The seriousness with which Rudolf Steiner in 1907 viewed not only the 'dire situation' that had arisen in the Society at that time but above all the underlying occult aspect of the events regarding which he did not have the right to speak is evident from his letter to Anna Minsloff dated 26 March 1907: 'Many dark powers are at work to destroy just the most sincere occult endeavour that is so much needed for the healing of mankind today. At the present moment my lips must remain sealed about the real deeper causes of the struggle that is being waged behind the scenes. *It can turn into a terrible strife and we must face what is to come with open eyes.* The time may soon come when I may be able to speak about the events taking place in Adyar.'[16]

Evidently, Rudolf Steiner did not receive permission to reveal to the members the occult foundations of the events in Adyar. Moreover, he was henceforth silent on this subject. But soon after the events in question he gave a clear, unambiguous response to this situation, not verbally but through what he did. This response was the separation—as already described—of the hitherto (until May 1907) single Esoteric School into two Schools, into a Western and an Eastern School.

To be sure, the reason for this separation lay, as has already been said, far deeper than the serious problems surrounding the events in Adyar; for these events, which proved to be a symptom enabling the tip of a whole iceberg of events that had been taking place in the occult world to become visible, were not the real cause of the separation.

In the first esoteric lesson—already quoted in part—which Rudolf Steiner gave after the separation of the Western from the Eastern School, he said in this connection: '*The questions that have arisen concerning the appearances (of the Masters) in Adyar must be answered*. It is not for occultists to decide whether these appearances are genuine or not. The voice of the Western Masters is *less clamorous* than that of the Eastern Masters. The call of the Western Masters [of Christian Rosenkreutz and the Master Jesus] goes out to all those in the West, to know if they wish to unite themselves with the two Masters of the West. If we want to introduce the Eastern wisdom here [in the West] and follow the Eastern teachings, this would indicate the decline of the West.* We need the Western teaching given to us by these two Masters.'[17]

This part of the lesson was recorded as follows by another participant: 'But this Eastern form of truth is not for us Western peoples. It can only restrict us and divert us from our goal. Here in the West are the people who will form the nucleus for the coming epochs. *That should be the true answer to what was proclaimed recently as the voice of the Masters from the East* [this refers to the events in Adyar]. Our Western Masters have also spoken, even though *in a less clamorous way*. And we would inscribe what they have said deep into our hearts. They summoned us to share in the future development of mankind, and *to remain steadfast and endure in all the battles that remain ahead of us*; to hold on to what we possess of the sacred living tradition. This summons will continue to sound in our souls.'[18]

It is striking that Rudolf Steiner again and again spoke in this esoteric lesson out of the direct inspirations *only* of the two Western Masters: 'Our Western Masters ... summoned us ...,' 'The call of the Western Masters goes out to all those in the West ...,' 'Receive into yourselves what the Master Christian Rosenkreutz has spoken ...'

In this connection, three further elements need to be distinguished in the transcript that has been quoted. Firstly, in both versions of what Rudolf Steiner said in this lesson the Western Masters were stated to be 'less clamorous' than those from the East. The distinctly negative nuance

---

*From the context of the lesson it is unmistakably clear that by 'Eastern wisdom' here above all Blavatsky's *Secret Doctrine* is meant.

reflected in these words* is a clear indication that the deeper reason for the outward separation of the two Esoteric Schools can be ascribed to certain differences of opinion that had arisen in the circle of the Masters themselves. This is confirmed by a second element, by the reference to the impending struggles which Rudolf Steiner also mentioned in the letter to Anna Minsloff; while in the esoteric lesson he referred to the Western Masters as the source of these presentiments.† The third element consists of the clear dichotomy between Eastern and Western wisdom in the esoteric lesson, between the Eastern and Western paths of initiation and esoteric traditions and, hence, the Eastern and Western Masters representing them: the former as being directed towards the past and thus unsuitable for the Western peoples and the latter inclined towards the future and inseparably associated with a true understanding of the Christ impulse, without which mankind has no future but only a magnificent past to which, however, there can be no return. Of particular importance in this dichotomy between Eastern and Western wisdom is Rudolf Steiner's unambiguous indication that it does not originate from him or from his difference of opinion with Annie Besant but from the Western Masters—that is to say, it is a direct consequence of their separation from the Eastern mahatmas on an occult level: 'They [the Western Masters] summoned us to share in the future development of mankind . . . to hold on to what we possess of the sacred living tradition [of Christian esotericism]'.

★

Immediately after the final separation of the Western Esoteric School from the Eastern, Rudolf Steiner—as though freed from an inner burden—began with a revelation of esoteric Christian wisdom that is without parallel in its depth and scope; and in the esoteric lessons (of which several hundred had been held by the beginning of the First World War)‡ the Eastern mahatmas were not mentioned again. Their place in the esoteric

---

* These words ('mit weniger Geräusch/weniger Geräuschvoll') must have made a deep impression on the listeners, which is why the two different participants independently mention them in their report.

† As will be shown later on, these struggles actually began two years later, when the 14-year-old Indian boy Krishnamurti was officially summoned by Besant and Leadbeater—who attributed to themselves the 'authority' of the two Eastern mahatmas—as the new Messiah.

‡ In recent years a start has been made with publishing all notes of the esoteric lessons as part of the Collected Works. Four volumes have appeared so far [1997]. Others will follow. (See GA 264, 265, 266/1, 266/2.)

lessons was henceforth taken by the inspirations and the supersensible presence of the Western Masters, the great teachers of Rosicrucianism, and in every lesson Rudolf Steiner constantly considered new aspects of Christian esotericism. The three Rosicrucian sayings that express the essential nature of the Christ mystery occupy a central place in most of the lessons. The same is also true of his lectures within the context of the German Section which he led. It is possible here to refer to only a few out of the many individual lectures and cycles, those that are of particular importance for the present study. Thus in the following year, 1907, Rudolf Steiner gave an extensive cycle of twelve lectures in Hamburg on the Gospel of St John, where the teaching of the cosmic Christ, the Sun Logos, was revealed, that Being who—having passed through the Mystery of Golgotha—became the new Spirit of the Earth, the highest cosmic leader of the whole of earthly evolution. This theme was further deepened in the cycle of twelve lectures on the Apocalypse of St John. The mystery of the future of Christendom was spoken of here, as was the central significance of the Christ impulse for the evolution of the Earth and mankind in the future.

The mystery of esoteric Christianity was presented with particular power and breadth in 1909. Thus in April of this year in Düsseldorf there followed the cycle of ten lectures on *The Spiritual Hierarchies and their Reflection in the Physical World. Zodiac, Planets, Cosmos*, where for the first time a description was given of the occult foundations of the Christian teaching of the *cosmic Hierarchies*, consisting of the nine categories of spiritual beings from the Angels to the Seraphim, the rulers not only of the evolution of the Earth and of the solar system but also of the entire starry cosmos. Earthly humanity, representing 'the principle of freedom and love', is gradually to be added to these heavenly Hierarchies as the future Tenth Hierarchy.[19] However, it will only attain this high goal through uniting with the Christ impulse and with all the forces entering into earthly evolution *from the Mystery of Golgotha*.

In the first half of this year (from January to May) Rudolf Steiner also considered the theme of 'spiritual economy' and—by means of several concrete examples of outstanding personalities—gave indications of the influence of the 'spiritual copies' of the various sheaths of Jesus of Nazareth in the historical development of humanity (initially of his etheric and astral bodies and in the future also of an impression of his ego), once the divine Christ Being had dwelt within them and transformed them over the course of three years. In February 1909 Rudolf Steiner in a lecture also called the Christ 'the greatest avatar being [that is, divine incarnation] who has ever lived on the earth'.[20] The culmination of the theme of 'spiritual economy', however, was without doubt the indication that Rudolf Steiner gave in a whole series of lectures that 'part of the inner mission of the universal stream of spirituality [anthroposophy] is to prepare human beings to become so mature in soul that an ever-increasing number of them will be able to absorb a copy of the Ego Being of Christ Jesus'.[21]

The lecture that Rudolf Steiner gave in Berlin on 22 March 1909 with the title 'The Deed of Christ and the Opposing Spiritual Powers, Lucifer, Ahriman and the Asuras'[22] is especially important for our theme. Here not only did he place before his listeners the threefold picture of the forces of evil in earthly evolution (of which Eastern wisdom knows hardly anything) but he also referred for the first time to its main counter-balance in speaking about the White Lodge guiding humanity, whose twelve members surround in the spiritual world the central source of wisdom and love in our cosmos, the cosmic Christ, who shines like a spiritual Sun in the circle of twelve stars and who guides them with the help of that high spiritual being who in Christian esotericism is called the Holy Spirit. And so this Lodge, which Rudolf Steiner subsequently also called the Lodge of the Bodhisattvas (see p. 369), is none other than the cosmic archetype of the great Whitsun community, whose central task is making the 'intentions of the living Christ'[23] and the all-encompassing significance of the Mystery of Golgotha clearly comprehensible to all people of good will.

In this lecture Rudolf Steiner gave a full and conclusive definition of those high leaders of humanity who can *rightfully* be called 'Masters of Wisdom and the Harmony of Feelings'. They all *without exception* belong to the White Lodge referred to or are directly related to it and are its servants and emissaries on earth. Thus Rudolf Steiner said in this lecture: 'And those who have understood that the advancement of mankind depends on comprehending the great event of Golgotha are they who, as the Masters of Wisdom and of the Harmony of Feelings, are united in the great, leading Lodge of humanity ... Thus what the Christ himself has sent through the Holy Spirit radiates as light over the Lodge of the Twelve. The Holy Spirit is the great teacher of those whom we call the Masters of Wisdom and of the Harmony of Feelings.'[24]

If we now bear in mind that the theosophical movement, to the extent that this can be judged from its extensive literature, had a non-Christian and even at times antichristian character,[*] it follows that its secret inspirers,

---

[*] As has been said above, exceptions to this general rule can be seen in some passages in Helena Blavatsky's first book, *Isis Unveiled*, where Rosicrucian inspirations come to expression, albeit largely in a distorted form, and also in Mabel Collins's book *Light on the Path*, the substance of which likewise derives from occult Western sources.

whoever they were, true mahatmas or merely Eastern occultists, did *not* come under the above definition of the Masters of Wisdom or of the Harmony of Feelings, and this means that they have *no* direct relationship with the Lodge of the Twelve (of the Bodhisattvas).

The relationship of anthroposophy or modern spiritual science founded by Rudolf Steiner to the high Lodge of the Holy Spirit or the Lodge of the Bodhisattvas was from the outset altogether different. Rudolf Steiner spoke of this in the same lecture: 'The wisdom that has been brought together by the spiritual-scientific movement in order to understand the world and the spirits within it flows [from Christ] through the Holy Spirit into the Lodge of the Twelve, and this is ultimately what will gradually lead mankind to a conscious and free understanding of the Christ and the event of Golgotha. Thus engaging in spiritual science means understanding that Christ has sent the Spirit into the world [through the Lodge of the Bodhisattvas].* Hence to concern oneself with it is in the spirit of true Christianity.'

And so, once he had freed himself from the spiritual bonds of a one-sided Eastern occultism, Rudolf Steiner was able to begin directly revealing the great mysteries of Christian esotericism, without a knowledge of which mankind cannot find its path into the future.

Notes

1. GA 28, ch. XXXI.
2. See Thomas Meyer, *The Bodhisattva Question*, ch. 5, London 1993.
3. See note [188].
4. See C.W. Leadbeater, *How Theosophy came to me*, Adyar, Madras, India 1986.
5. Circular letter written by Rudolf Steiner in Berlin in June 1906 (GA 264), also the following quotations.
6. Letter to Annie Besant, written by Rudolf Steiner in Berlin in June 1906 (GA 264), likewise the following quotations.
7. Ibid.
8. The documents are published in GA 264.
9. H. Murphet, *Yankee Beacon of Buddhist Light. Life of Col. Henry S. Olcott*, ch. 24, 'Last Days', Wheaton Ill., USA, pp. 305–6.
10. Rudolf Steiner's letter 'To the Members of the Executive Committee of the

---

*Rudolf Steiner later spoke in detail about the theme of the twelvefold circle of the bodhisattvas who surround Christ in the high sphere of the Spirit in cycles such as *The East in the Light of the West* (nine lectures given in Munich, August 1909) or *The Gospel of St Luke* (ten lectures, Basel, September 1909), *The Christ Impulse and the Development of Ego Consciousness* (seven lectures, Berlin, May 1910) and also in many individual lectures (for example, the lecture of 9 January 1912. (See GA 113, GA 114, GA 116, GA 130.)

German Section of the Theosophical Society' dated 28 April 1907 in GA 264, also the following quotations.

11. Quoted from GA 264, Editor's Foreword to Part II.
12. GA 264, 14 December 1911.
13. Ibid.
14. See note 9, likewise the following quotations.
15. Ibid.
16. GA 264, letter of 26 March 1907.
17. GA 264, esoteric lesson of 1 June 1907.
18. Ibid., likewise the following quotations.
19. See GA 110, 18 April 1909 (II).
20. GA 107, 15 February 1909.
21. GA 109, 7 March 1909.
22. Published in GA 107.
23. GA 262, 'The Barr Manuscript', III.
24. GA 107, 22 March 1909, also the following quotation.

5. The Theosophical Congress in Budapest and its Consequences

The fifth congress of the European Sections of the Theosophical Society, which took place in Budapest between 30 May and 2 June 1909, occupies an important place in the history of the mutual relationship of the Western and Eastern esoteric streams within it.

The most important and distinctive aspect of this congress was probably that the difference between Rudolf Steiner's and Annie Besant's under-standing of the Christ became fully apparent for the first time. Rudolf Steiner subsequently—in December 1911[1]—reported what the immediate outcome of the congress had been: 'In 1909 Annie Besant announced in many different places a lecture about the nature of Christ. At the time it gradually became known that a rumour was circulating about the idea of a Christ appearing in the flesh, and this idea grew stronger and stronger, eventually culminating with what you know.'[*] At the congress Rudolf Steiner gave a lecture on 31 May entitled 'From Buddha to Christ', and then Annie Besant presented her understanding of this question in her lecture on the theme 'Christ, Who is He?' In the lecture Annie Besant first spoke about the nature of a bodhisattva and then proceeded to characterize Christ as a being with a similar nature. At the end of the lecture she mentioned that he might possibly be expected to appear again shortly in a new incarnation.[†] This had the consequence that at the congress—in Rudolf Steiner's words—a peculiar situation arose where 'two people were defending opposing views from one platform'.

Marie von Sivers, who experienced all these events personally, char-acterized this situation as follows: 'The continuation of Dr Steiner's debate with Annie Besant took place at the congress in Budapest. The incompatibility of the paths taken in Adyar and the methods practised there with the path of Christian-Rosicrucian esotericism was clearly specified by Dr Steiner.'[2]

---

[*] At that time, Annie Besant actually still considered the 13-year-old American of Dutch ancestry Hubert van Hook to be the world Teacher, ignorant of the fact that Leadbeater, who had again become her closest colleague, had already (at the beginning of May that year) found the new pretender for this role—in Krishnamurti—in Adyar.

[†] See Alexander Strakosch, *Lebenswege mit Rudolf Steiner. Erinnerungen* ('A Life's Journey with Rudolf Steiner. Memoirs'), Dornach 1994.

At this point the lecture that Rudolf Steiner himself gave at the congress, that is, in the presence of Annie Besant and her followers, needs to be considered in greater detail. Its theme was, as has been said, 'From Buddha to Christ'. To begin with Rudolf Steiner referred to the three great teachers and leaders of the Rosicrucian stream: to Zarathustra/the Master Jesus, Scythianos and Gautama Buddha (who since his last Indian incarnation in the sixth pre-Christian century has been active in a spirit-body): 'These are the three names, sacred names of the Masters, that were venerated in the greatest secrecy in the sanctuaries of the mysteries and the mystery schools of the Rosicrucians.'[3] Rudolf Steiner then went on to consider in this lecture in particular detail the developmental path of Zarathustra, the founder of the second post-Atlantean cultural epoch, who subsequently incarnated in ancient Babylon as Zaratas or Nazaratos and was the great teacher of Pythagoras. The latter appeared at the Turning Point of Time as one of the three Persian kings or Magi from the East of whom St Matthew's Gospel speaks.[*] Then Rudolf Steiner spoke in this lecture about Gautama Buddha as a great pre-Christian servant of the Christ through whom Christ worked in former times out of the spiritual world. And at the end of the lecture he again named Zarathustra, Scythianos and Gautama Buddha the 'three Rosicrucian Masters'.

However, the culmination of the lecture was when Rudolf Steiner stated that the Christ could be seen as the highest aim of *all* true mysteries over the course of earthly evolution as a whole. The great sun oracle on ancient Atlantis led by Manu, the founder of post-Atlantean evolution, was dedicated to Him; and the Indian cultures arising within this evolutionary period successively looked up full of hope to the cosmic Christ, in expectation of the moment when He would descend to the earth: 'The Christ Being was known in all the mysteries. In ancient India, at the time of the Seven Rishis, the Being who represented Christ was called Vishva Karman—Zarathustra named Him Ahura Mazda. In Egypt He was known as Osiris. The Jewish people called Him Yahweh or Jehovah.[†] During the fourth cultural epoch, this same Being lived for three years upon our physical earth. He is the Being who will in future reunite the sun with the earth. When the blood streamed from the wounds of the

---

[*] This reference by Rudolf Steiner in Annie Besant's presence to Pythagoras as a pupil of Nazaratos and, in his next incarnation, as one of the three Magi had a particular significance, since she was the focus of the opinion that Pythagoras was one of the former incarnations of the Mahatma Kut Humi (see further below).

[†] The cosmic Christ revealed himself to all these peoples through the Gods (the hierarchic beings) who served him and who were associated with the corresponding religions.

Redeemer upon Golgotha ... since the event of Golgotha Christ has become the planetary Spirit of the Earth; since then He is to be found in the physical aura of the earth.'[4]*

The lecture ended with a mighty perspective of the future evolution of humanity, in which the law of 'spiritual economy' will apply. As concrete examples Rudolf Steiner mentioned Augustine as a bearer of a copy of the etheric body of Christ Jesus; and Francis of Assisi, Thomas Aquinas and Elizabeth of Thuringia as bearers of copies of His astral body. At the end of the lecture he indicated that from our time onwards copies of the ego of Christ Jesus will be prepared in the spiritual worlds, to be borne by 'the Christ bearers, the true Christophori' in the future. Their task will be 'to be the heralds of his Second Coming'. However, this reappearance of Christ will not be a repetition of His physical appearance at the Turning Point of Time but will be a supersensible revelation similar to what the Apostle Paul experienced on the road to Damascus, when he suddenly beheld Christ in the spiritual aura of the earth. (Rudolf Steiner also described this experience of Paul at some length in his Budapest lecture.)

The knowledge of the cosmic Christ and of the central significance of the Mystery of Golgotha for the whole of earthly evolution lying at the heart of the lecture, together with what was said in it regarding the participation of the leading initiates of olden times who today serve the true Rosicrucian mysteries in preparing for the Mystery of Golgotha—all this must have made a remarkably strong impression upon those attending the congress, who had been accustomed to quite different information within the Theosophical Society.

However, this lecture also had another significance for the leaders of the Theosophical Society who were taking part in the congress. For both Annie Besant and her close associates were well familiar with the letter which A.P. Sinnett had received around 1880 from the highest leader of the Indo-Tibetan mahatmas, the Mahachohan, whom—as we have seen—the mahatmas revered as their 'venerable chief'. This letter presented an entirely different view on the part of the Mahachohan of the tasks of the Theosophical Society and above all of the nature of Christianity and the significance of its founder. Thus the Mahachohan wrote in this letter: 'The Theosophical Society was chosen as the

---

* This characterization of the Christ Being in the presence of Annie Besant had a further particular significance, since in the leading circles of the Theosophical Society an altogether different being was considered to be the highest leading spirit of the earth (its Planetary Spirit): see further below.

corner-stone, the foundation of the future religions of humanity.'[5]* In the esoteric teaching which was to serve as its foundation, 'Osiris, Krishna, Buddha, Christ will be shown as different names for one and the same royal highway to final bliss, Nirvana'.[†] This idea of the abstract 'equality' of all spirit-teachers and adepts both of the past and also of the future, which runs like a red thread through the writings of H.P. Blavatsky, Besant, Leadbeater and subsequently of Roerich and Bailey, and also of many others, can therefore be traced back to the 'highest authority' that applies to it.

From the standpoint of Christian esotericism, the truth is altogether different. 'Osiris, Krishna, Buddha, Christ' are not merely 'names' in the endless sequence of adepts travelling one and the same path but the first three of these (among many others) are servants and helpers in preparing the coming to earth not simply of the highest human adepts but of the Sun Logos, the Christ, the highest Being of our entire cosmos.[‡] Hence Rudolf Steiner also spoke in his introductory lecture at the Budapest congress—in the presence of Annie Besant and the other leaders of the Theosophical Society—directly of the way that in olden times the Christ revealed His cosmic nature through Osiris and Gautama Buddha and also through many other leading adepts of humanity (Rudolf Steiner

---

* This statement regarding 'the foundation of the future religions' perplexingly contradicts the motto of the Theosophical Society: 'There is no religion higher than truth'. It anticipates, as it were, the actual attempt made later by the leaders of the Theosophical Society to establish such a new religion with the help of the 'world Teacher' Krishnamurti and—for this purpose—the 'Star of the East' (see further in chapters 10 and 11).

† The editor of this letter, C. Jinarajadasa, observed in his commentary to it: 'This is certainly the most important letter ever received from the adept teachers, as it is a communication from the Maha Chohan, one of the three great Adepts who form the "triangle" of the great Hierarchy.' (According to theosophical teaching, mankind is led by three adepts, Buddha, Manu and the Mahachohan, who at the same time represent the hierarchy of the mahatmas: see A.A. Bailey, *Initiation, Human and Solar*, ch. 6, and C.W. Leadbeater, *The Masters and the Path*, Part I.) The Mahatma Kut Humi said of the Mahachohan in one of his letters: 'to [his] insight the future lies like an open page' (see footnote above). But as is clearly apparent from the Mahachohan's letter, this future includes a true knowledge neither of the Christ Being nor of the Mystery of Golgotha. Jinarajadasa refers in his commentary to the fact that both Blavatsky, who quoted from it in an article from the year 1888, and also Besant and Leadbeater knew this letter very well.

‡ Thus Rudolf Steiner said, for example, in the esoteric lesson of 1 September 1912 in Munich: 'The great initiates Buddha, Pythagoras, Zarathustra and so forth [in the same lesson Krishna is also mentioned in this connection] are assembled around the Christ and let themselves be influenced by his forces equally whether they are incarnated in the physical body or are abiding in spiritual worlds, and they work out of this same Spirit' (GA 266/2, the esoteric lesson of 1 September 1912).

expressed himself somewhat later about the influence exerted by Christ through Krishna: see chapter 8).

Thus the growing polarization between Indo-Tibetan and Christian occultism had sooner or later to become obvious not only for congress participants but also for most members of the Theosophical Society. Even the immediate future showed that the more Rudolf Steiner disclosed the mysteries of esoteric Christianity, so much the stronger did the resistance towards this of Annie Besant and her closest followers become. Since they were not in a position either to refute this Rosicrucian wisdom or to set something similar over and against it, the occult powers standing behind Besant and Leadbeater resorted to a last, one could say desperate measure: they decided to overcome Western esotericism by opposing it with a false Messiah.

It is true that from 1904 until 1906 the search had been on for such a new Messiah, but neither Annie Besant nor Leadbeater had by 1909 been able to decide to speak of this openly or even to make official references to an actual candidate (van Hook had been prepared for this role more or less in secret). All this fundamentally changed after the Budapest congress. In the August of this year Annie Besant gave a public lecture in Chicago about the 'world Teacher', and in the autumn there was talk throughout the Theosophical Society of his actual bearer, the 14-year-old boy Krishnamurti, whom Leadbeater had shortly before found in Adyar. Consequently, at the end of this year the special society 'Order of the Star in the East' was founded, and the future Messiah was speedily proclaimed its leader.

The well-known French writer and theosophist Edouard Schuré wrote about the deeper reasons for such a sudden appearance of a 'new Messiah' in his letter of 1 March 1913 addressed to the President of the French Section and, with this letter, at the same time explained the reason for his leaving the Theosophical Society. He cited specifically a conversation that had taken place in 1908, when a well-known Dutch theosophist, 'an intimate friend of Leadbeater and Besant', had—in the presence of Schuré and several other theosophists—replied to the question as to whether the Esoteric Schools of Annie Besant and Rudolf Steiner could exist alongside one another by stating his view that this would be completely impossible, for 'India alone was in possession of the [esoteric] tradition and there had never existed a scientific esotericism of the West'.[6] Schuré then made the following comment to these words in his letter: 'I was surprised by this definite assertion. I soon comprehended its meaning when, like a bomb—or rather, like a fabricated framework—the Alcyone affair burst upon us. For this affair is *truly* nothing but the answer of Adyar to the resurgence of

Christian esotericism in the West, and I am convinced that, without the latter, we would have never heard a word about the future prophet Krishnamurti.'

With his departure, however, a process was initiated in the Theosophical Society which not only testifies to its further decline but to something much worse: it became an instrument of antichristian powers.

Notes

1. GA 264, 14 December 1911 and the following quotation.
2. Quoted from *Aus dem Leben von Marie Steiner-von Sivers. Biographische Beiträge und eine Bibliographie*, Dornach 1956, the chapter entitled 'Der Kongreß in München 1907'.
3. GA 109, 31 May 1909, also the following quotations.
4. Ibid., likewise the following quotations.
5. *Letters from the Masters of the Wisdom*, First Series, letter no. 1, Adyar, Madras, India, 1988. K.H. (Kut Humi) prefaced this letter with the following observation: 'To A.P. Sinnett. An abridged version of the view of the Chohan on the T.S. (Theosophical Society) from his own words as given last night. My own letter, the answer to yours, will shortly follow. K.H.'
6. Edouard Schuré's letter to Charles Blech is published in French in S. Rihouet-Croze, *Une épopée de l'esprit au XXe siècle*, Paris 1973, ch. 21, 'Les trois congrès', and in German translation in GA 264, editor's foreword to Part II.

6. The Revelation of the Christian Mysteries and the Proclamation of the Etheric Christ

While the process of decline within the Theosophical Society—to the extent that it was under the direct influence of Besant and Leadbeater—intensified, Rudolf Steiner continued to reveal at a breathtaking speed ever deeper mysteries of Christian esotericism before his astonished listeners within the German Section of which he was the leader. In this way he was fulfilling the principal task of modern Christian esotericism: 'To transmute into what people can understand all that flows through Christ out of the spiritual worlds,'[1] a task whose implementation had been prepared for centuries within esoteric Christianity.

On the day after the main lecture of the congress Rudolf Steiner gave a further public lecture on the theme 'Western Paths of Initiation', and after the end of the congress he immediately began a cycle of ten lectures entitled 'Rosicrucian Esotericism' in the Budapest theosophical Lodge.[2] Here Rudolf Steiner, in speaking about the spiritual stream initiated by Christian Rosenkreutz, pointed out already in the first lecture that 'it . . . is the task of Rosicrucian theosophy to show how a being such as the Christ has been active both in the past and now . . .'.[3] Then Rudolf Steiner repeated the lecture 'From Buddha to Christ' in Vienna (on 14 June), and ten days later he began in Kassel with a big cycle of 14 lectures on *The Gospel of St John and its Relation to the Other Gospels, especially that of St Luke*,[4] where he again placed a broad picture of Christian esoteric wisdom before his listeners and referred already in the first lecture to its Rosicrucian origin.

Finally, in August of the same year Rudolf Steiner gave a cycle of nine lectures in Munich with the title *The East in the Light of the West. The Children of Lucifer and the Brothers of Christ*.[5] It was probably impossible to characterize the situation that was developing at this time within the Theosophical Society in any better way. For in the light of Western esotericism, everything that was taking place in the considerably Eastern-oriented Theosophical Society was not simply a polarization between Eastern and Western esoteric traditions but in a deeper, occult sense a real confrontation between the children of Lucifer[*] and the brothers of Christ.

---

[*] Compare Blavatsky's attitude to Lucifer, described in Part One ('The Sources of the Later Teachings of H.P. Blavatsky').

Of all these lectures, the last one of the Munich cycle (31 August) has a particular importance. It represents a remarkable deepening of the question of the 'three Rosicrucian Masters' Zarathustra, Scythianos and Gautama Buddha which was initially addressed in a lecture at the Budapest congress.

In the Munich lecture, Rudolf Steiner spoke about a gathering of leading Christian Masters of the West that took place in the fourth century AD. It was convened by Manes, the great teacher of Christian esotericism, who during his incarnation at the Turning Point of Time had, as the youth of Nain, been initiated by the Christ himself.[6] He summoned three further individualities: Zarathustra (the Master Jesus), Scythianos, the great guardian of the ancient wisdom of Atlantis, and Gautama Buddha, who—since at that time he was not incarnated in a physical body—participated in this conference in a particular way by working through another personality.[*] 'Thus we have a council around Manes, with Manes in the middle and around him Scythianos, Buddha and Zarathustra.'[7] Rudolf Steiner described what was worked out and decided by this council as follows: 'At this council the plan was formulated that all the wisdom of the bodhisattvas [that is, the wisdom of the circle of bodhisattvas surrounding the cosmic Christ in the higher spiritual world] of the post-Atlantean period might flow ever more strongly into the future of humanity. The plan for the future evolution of the Earth that was resolved upon at that time was adhered to and then carried over into those European mysteries known as the mysteries of the Rose Cross. The individualities of Scythianos, Buddha and Zarathustra have always been involved in the mysteries of the Rose Cross [that is, since their founding in the thirteenth century]. They were teachers in the schools of the Rose Cross—teachers who sent their wisdom as gifts to the earth, because the Christ was to be understood in his [cosmic] Being through this wisdom.'

'The great teachers of the European initiates', 'the great, revered bodhisattvas of the West' was how Rudolf Steiner referred to this 'group of teachers ... who will make the Christ comprehensible to mankind to the fullest degree, and to whom humanity will look up as the great bodhisattvas through whom Christ will be understood'. And then Rudolf Steiner continued, using the word 'we' that is usual in lectures instead of 'I': 'This shall be done through modern spiritual science [anthroposophy]; it shall begin to introduce the teachings of Scythianos, Zarathustra and Gautama Buddha into the world, *not in their old form but in an altogether new and independently researchable way for our time. We are beginning by integrating*

---

[*] Compare with the footnote on p. 435.

the essential elements of what we have been able to learn from them into our cultural environment.'

Rudolf Steiner stands before us as the earthly emissary of the leading Masters of Christian esotericism, namely Manes, Zarathustra, Scythianos and Gautama Buddha and of course the leader of the entire Rosicrucian stream, Christian Rosenkreutz, entrusted with the high task of bringing their teaching to humanity today, that is, unveiling the new under-standing of the Christ Being that streams out of the bodhisattva sphere. This task did not simply lie in mechanically passing on the new teaching received from the Masters of esoteric Christianity to humanity but in independently researching supersensibly the spiritual truths that he had arrived at on the basis of his own initiation. Rudolf Steiner himself referred to this important fact in the words quoted above, when he spoke of how he brought the teaching of the Masters 'not in their old form but in an altogether new and *independently researchable way* for our time', that is, in the way in which he could himself research in the higher worlds.

Thus Rudolf Steiner's listeners must have recognized by 1909 if not before that, in drawing from the sources of Christian esotericism, he was speaking about an altogether different hierarchy of spirit-teachers than those acknowledged in the Theosophical Society.[*] This emerged with particular clarity the following year, when Rudolf Steiner started to unfold the mysteries of the Etheric Christ.

At the beginning of the following year—1910—Rudolf Steiner spoke openly for the first time in Stockholm about the reappearance of Christ in the etheric body. This occurred on 12 January in a lecture for members of the Theosophical Society.[8] From then on his proclaiming of the Etheric Christ runs like a red thread through his entire spiritual-scientific activity, right up to the last reference to this central spiritual event of the twentieth century on 20 September 1924 in a lecture for priests of the Christian Community,[9] that is, eight days before the worsening of his illness, which prevented him from giving any more lectures half a year before his death.

In addition to the many lectures that Rudolf Steiner gave on this theme for members of the Society, his first public lecture about the Etheric Christ of 13 June 1910 in Christiania (Oslo) should be mentioned,[10] also his artistic portrayal of this theme in the first Mystery Drama *The Portal of*

---

[*] This question was considered at some length in Part Two in connection with Alice Bailey's teaching. There it was shown that the Master Jesus and the Count of Saint Germain were mentioned as being among the theosophical teachers, while nevertheless understood altogether differently in the 'theosophical' hierarchy than in the hierarchy of Christian esotericism.

Initiation, which has the subtitle *A Rosicrucian Mystery*,[11] and then the opening up of this theme for a wider public in the book published in 1911 *The Spiritual Guidance of Man and Humanity*. Here Rudolf Steiner referred to the relationship of Rosicrucianism, and also its continuation in modern spiritual science or anthroposophy, to the hierarchic beings in the higher worlds who bring to mankind today the revelation of the Etheric Christ and a knowledge of Him as a Being who 'imbues the whole solar system with spirit'.[12]

Especially in the lectures that were given on this theme before the beginning of the First World War, two aspects come ever and again into prominence. One is Rudolf Steiner's repeated indication that the central task of the spiritual science or anthroposophy established by him in the twentieth century out of the sources of Western esotericism is *to prepare* human beings for the imminent etheric appearance of Christ and *to proclaim* this event to all people of good will. According to him, it is 'extraordinarily important that spiritual science is a preparation for 'the new [etheric] revelation of Christ'.[13] Moreover: 'It is the duty of anthroposophy to proclaim this.'[14] Or in another lecture: 'Here on the earth we must prepare ourselves for this event and create the organs for it. The new Christ event of the twentieth century—this is what we now proclaim.'[15] And in another context: 'For this reason anthroposophy has the mission also of proclaiming the Christ in His etheric form.'[16] (The number of such observations by Rudolf Steiner could be multiplied without any difficulty.)

The second aspect is the absolute impossibility that Christ will return *in a physical body*. Thus for example he spoke as follows in the first public lecture about the Etheric Christ: 'The Christ was in the world physically only once, as spiritual science shows us; *and it is a misunderstanding of the whole nature of Christ* if one were to believe that a physical being could appear a second time who could be named a Christ. This is the hypomochlion.'[17]

Moreover, Rudolf Steiner points to the dangers that threaten a right relationship to the etheric appearance of Christ through materialistic tendencies from both West and East. Thus from the West the danger will be that anything said anywhere about the Etheric Christ will be regarded as 'wild fantasy, as the height of folly'.[18] From the East, in contrast, there will come the danger that manifested itself at the beginning of the twentieth century initially in the saga of Krishnamurti and which subsequently—albeit in a somewhat different form—appeared in the teachings of Alice Bailey. Rudolf Steiner said about this 'Eastern danger': 'Today materialism has invaded all spheres. It is not only ingrained in the

West, but has also invaded the East—where, however, it assumes another form. One consequence of oriental materialism might well be that mankind will fail to recognize the higher aspects of a Christ revelation, with the result that something will happen which I have often spoken of here and which I must repeat again and again, namely that materialistic thinking will have a purely materialistic conception of the appearance of Christ' and will maintain 'that Christ will appear in a physical body. The result would simply be another form of materialism ... But in the twentieth century it would be a great misfortune if, under the pressure of materialism, the teaching that Christ will appear were to be taken in a materialistic sense, implying that Christ might appear in a physical body. This would only prove that mankind had not acquired any perception of or insight into the real progress of human evolution towards higher spiritual powers.' Such a union of Western materialism with the East and its spiritual traditions should not appear contradictory to us. For as was shown at some length through the examples of Blavatsky, Sinnett and the Roerichs, Western materialism can under conditions do best to join up with one or another aspect of Eastern spirituality and so become an 'occult materialism'.[*]

Rudolf Steiner's refusal to compromise with any attempt to falsify Christ's etheric appearance by means of a physical one can be understood if we again turn to the words which we have already cited many times, those he wrote in 1907 for Edouard Schuré: 'They [the revelations of oriental initiation] could only hope for success within evolution if the principle of Christianity were to be eradicated from Western culture. But this would be the same as eradicating the essential *meaning of the earth*, which lies in the recognition and realization of the intentions of the *living Christ*.'[19] As, however, the true 'living Christ' has begun to manifest himself to mankind in an etheric form from 1909 onwards, any resistance to this event and quite especially any attempt at consistent distortion has signified an overt determination on the part of certain occult circles of the East 'to eradicate the principle of Christianity from Western culture' and, with it, also the 'meaning' of earthly evolution. Hence if anyone were to proclaim the return of Christ *in the physical body*—whoever might be the source of such a statement—this was for Rudolf Steiner not merely a 'theoretical' difference of opinion between the East and West but an occult error of the most disastrous kind with consequences for the spiritual destiny of humanity and the earth.

However, Rudolf Steiner not only spoke repeatedly and categorically

---

[*] See Part One.

about the impossibility that Christ will come again in a physical body but he firmly established this impossibility out of the source of his own spiritual research. This can be discerned with particular clarity through the metamorphosis that the ancient Eastern teaching of Shamballa underwent in the light of Christian esotericism. Thus he spoke several times in 1910 about how that long-lost mysterious ancient land of Shamballa in the East will appear in a new form before the spiritual sight of humanity. It will manifest itself before man's new clairvoyant faculties as a new, all-embracing etheric sphere, as the supersensible domain of the Etheric Christ, and it will draw forth from it the knowledge and powers that it needs above all to bring to fulfilment 'the meaning of the earth', which 'lies in the recognition and realization of the intentions of the living Christ'.

As the highest lord and ruler of this sublime etheric sphere or spirit-land, the Christ will manifest Himself ever more and more to humanity in the course of the next three millennia. 'Among the first visions that human beings will have when Shamballa manifests itself again will be Christ in His etheric form. Humanity has no other leader than the Christ to take it into that land that oriental writings declare to have vanished. Christ will lead humanity to Shamballa ... Thus at the time when human beings will be most sceptical regarding documents [the Gospels], the new profession of faith in Christ Jesus will arise through our growing into the sphere in which we shall encounter Him, through our growing into the mysterious land of Shamballa.'[20][*] And this new revelation of Christ as the Lord of Shamballa is at the same time the fulfilment of His words spoken on the earth in ancient Palestine: 'My Kingdom is not of this world' (John 18:36).

In this sense the proclamation of a return to the earth by Christ in a physical body, that is, a proclamation of Christ's kingdom as being 'of this world'—whatever its source and however high the authority on which it rests may be—derives from antichristian, ahrimanic inspirations of 'the prince of this world' (John 14:30).

The next step in the deepening of the theme of the Second Coming consists of a whole series of lectures in 1911, where Rudolf Steiner spoke further about the mystery of the Etheric Christ and explained how from the twentieth century onwards He will gradually become the Lord of Karma of the whole of earthly evolution.[21] Thus, for example, in the

---

[*] The arising of this new Shamballa or the etheric sphere of Christ in the spiritual surroundings of the earth is associated with the process whereby the earth is gradually becoming a new sun of our cosmos. This process was begun through the Mystery of Golgotha (see S.O. Prokofieff, *The Cycle of the Year*, Part IX, first and second chapters).

lecture of 7 October, where he said: 'Just as on the physical plane in Palestine, at the beginning of our era, an event occurred in which the most important part was taken by Christ himself—an event which has its significance for the whole of humanity—so in the course of the twentieth century, towards the end of the twentieth century, a significant event will again take place, not in the physical world, but in the world we usually call the world of the etheric. This event will have as fundamental a significance for the evolution of humanity as the event of Palestine had at the beginning of our era ... What is this event? ... *Occult clairvoyant research tells us that* in our epoch *Christ becomes the Lord of Karma for human evolution.* This event marks the beginning of something that we find intimated also in the Gospels: He will come again to separate, or to bring about the crisis for, the living and the dead. Only, according to occult research, this is not to be understood as though it were a single event which takes place on the physical plane. It is connected *with the whole future evolution of humanity* ...[22] In the future it will rest with Christ to decide what our karmic account is, how our credit and debit in life are related.'[*]

And then, having shared the results of his own spiritual-scientific research, Rudolf Steiner immediately adds: 'This has been common knowledge in Western occultism for many centuries ... But recently it has been verified, again with the utmost care, by every means available to occult research.' Thus Rudolf Steiner emphasizes particularly that the fact 'verified' by him 'with the utmost care' with the help of occult research, namely that Christ will in the twentieth century become the lord of the karma of the whole of earthly evolution, has been prophetically known for centuries to 'Western occultism', that is, above all to the teachers of the Rosicrucian stream referred to above.[†] For those teachers, initiated

---

[*] Rudolf Steiner goes on to refer in this lecture to the direct connection between the fact that Christ becomes the Lord of Karma and the development of the new faculty which will extend amongst mankind over the next three millennia: 'In our time the office of Karmic Judge passes over to Christ Jesus in the higher world next to our own. This event works into the physical world, on the physical plane, in such a way that individuals will develop towards it the feeling that by all their actions they will be causing something for which they will be accountable to the judgement of Christ. This feeling, now appearing quite naturally in the course of human development, will be transformed so that it permeates the soul with a light which little by little will shine out from the individual himself, and will illuminate the form of Christ in the etheric world. And the more this feeling is developed—a feeling that will have stronger significance than the abstract conscience—the more will the etheric form of Christ be visible in the coming centuries.'
[†] This is a further testimony that Rudolf Steiner has consistently obeyed the occult law referred to above (the law that a connection must be established with what has previously been investigated).

into the deeper mysteries of esoteric Christianity, knew that the Christ as the Sun Logos, by passing through the Mystery of Golgotha and becoming the new Spirit of the Earth, has now come to imbue the whole of earthly evolution and also the karma of the earth with His Being, and that sooner or later He must also take upon himself its guidance and its shaping until the end of earth existence. In other words, from the twentieth century onwards Christ is beginning to bring the karma of the earth into order, that is, in harmony with the karma of the sun, for without this the future union of earth and sun cannot take place. It is in this sense that the following words of Rudolf Steiner should be understood: 'In truth, this begins in the twentieth century and will hold good until the end of the earth. It is in our twentieth century that this judgement, this ordering of karma, begins.'[23] This is a further confirmation of the impossibility of a Second Coming of Christ in a physical body. For from now on and until the end of earthly evolution He is connected not only with the karma of one or another physically incarnated human being but with the karma of humanity *as a whole* as its higher *Group Ego*. And for this Christ Ego mankind shall in the course of earthly evolution gradually develop within itself new, astral, etheric and physical sheaths,[*] so as to enable the Christ to permeate the whole of mankind as a single organism, thus making it possible for it to make the transition to the next cosmic condition, as portrayed in the Book of Revelation in the picture of the New Jerusalem:[24] '... Human beings shall then lay the foundations, in the course of earthly evolution, for a great community which can be permeated and made fully Christian by the Christ impulse.'[25] Thus by the end of earthly evolution Christ will be associated *with the whole of earthly humanity* in a purely spiritual form, which rules out His incarnation in a physical body.

Rudolf Steiner also occultly establishes this impossibility of a further physical incarnation on Christ's part from quite a different standpoint. In so doing he unfolds ever new and deeper mysteries of esoteric Christianity. Thus in lectures from the same year (1911) he states on several occasions that the present appearance of Christ in an etheric body is only the beginning of further, higher supersensible revelations which will be granted to humanity in accordance with the awakening of ever higher faculties of conscious clairvoyance. Christ's appearance in the etheric on

---

[*] By a 'physical' sheath is meant here the general spiritual transformation (spiritualization) of the physical bodies of *all* human beings as a result of their moral development, resulting from their supersensible relationship with Christ. See further in the lecture of 30 May 1912 (GA 155) and in S.O. Prokofieff, *The Cycle of the Year*, Part IV, chapter 6.

the astral plane, which begins in our time and will last in the region of three thousand years, will be followed by His manifestation in the astral body on lower Devachan and then the revelation of the cosmic Christ on higher Devachan, after which Christ will in the still more distant future lead mankind on the stages of purely cosmic development, those of the Spirit Self, Life Spirit and Spirit Man. For 'the manifestations of Christ will lie at an ever higher level. That is the mystery of the development of Christ.'[26] And 'the more visions human beings win for themselves, the greater Christ will appear to them, the mightier He will appear!'[27]

Rudolf Steiner spoke as follows about this ascending ladder of stages of ever more sublime revelations of Christ: 'The Christ individuality was on earth in the body of Jesus of Nazareth for only three years [from the Baptism in the Jordan until the Mystery of Golgotha] and will not come again in a physical body. In the fifth post-Atlantean epoch He will come in an etheric body, in the sixth in an astral body, and in the seventh in a mighty cosmic ego that will be like a great group soul of humanity ... So we see how, starting from a physical human being on earth [at the Turning Point of Time], the Christ gradually evolves[*] as etheric Christ, astral Christ and ego Christ to become the Spirit of the Earth who then rises to even higher stages together with all mankind.'[28]

And so just as Christ in the Mystery of Golgotha, which 'gave the earth its meaning',[29] demonstrated His true nature as the creative, divine Word referred to at the beginning of St John's Gospel, who overcame death and transformed man's physical body into the imperishable resurrection body, into the purest manifestation of the Sun Logos, so at the next stage, from our time onwards, the Sun Logos will reveal Himself in a transformed etheric body, then in a transformed astral body and finally in the ego which is associated with the entire spirit-cosmos. In this way He will rise in the spiritual worlds from one plane to another and lead the consciousness of mankind into ever higher worlds of spirit.

This can also be described by saying that at the moment when in the Mystery of Golgotha the blood of the Redeemer flowed from His wounds, His Spirit united with the entire earth, which from this moment onwards was transformed into his new planetary body, into the *physically* visible manifestation of the Sun Logos. The next *etheric* manifestation of Christ, beginning in our time, reveals the relationship of the Sun Logos with all seven planets of our solar system on the astral

---

[*] He evolves in this sense not as regards His own Being but with respect to His ascending and ever-strengthening revelations for mankind.

plane.[*] Then in about three thousand years, the epoch of the revelation of Christ in His astral nature will begin, which will manifest the relationship of the Sun Logos on lower Devachan with the sun in its highest starry aspect. In the further future there will follow Christ's manifestation in His ego nature, which will unveil the mystery of the relationship of the Sun Logos with the entire zodiac. Finally, the subsequent revelations—of which it is barely possible to speak in the human language of today—will render an understanding accessible to human beings of the relationship of the Sun Logos with the spiritual realms of our cosmos that lie *beyond* the limits of the zodiac. For since the Mystery of Golgotha the influence of the Sun Logos—now that He has gone through an earthly incarnation—is of such a kind that the earth henceforth forms His physical body, His etheric body embraces the spheres of all seven planets, His astral body extends to the sun, His ego encompasses the entire zodiac and we would then have to seek His higher members beyond the limits of the zodiac.

The threefold supersensible revelation of Christ briefly summarized here, which could also be called the three *post-earthly, or subsequent, stages* of the Mystery of Golgotha (on the grounds that they represent its direct continuation, a consequence of the *unique* event within earthly evolution at the Turning Point of Time, when 'the Word became flesh', John 1:14), can only really be understood in its full significance and its true esoteric nature if one relates them with what has been imparted by modern spiritual research about the three so-called *pre-earthly, or preliminary, stages* of the Mystery of Golgotha. Rudolf Steiner spoke about these in a whole series of lectures in 1913, when he revealed the mystery of how Christ, in the course of His descent from the spiritual heights of our cosmos and His approach to the earth, on three occasions sent down to earthly humanity—once in the Lemurian epoch and twice in the Atlantean—those healing spiritual forces which it needed more than anything else in order that it might not wholly and irretrievably succumb in its physical, etheric and astral bodies to the pernicious influences of the luciferic and ahrimanic beings who had found their way into earthly evolution as a result of the Fall.

It is not possible in the present work to go into further detail about these supersensible events, which Rudolf Steiner described in his lectures.[†] We shall therefore confine ourselves here to Rudolf Steiner's

---

[*] Including the sun in its planetary aspect (see Sergei O. Prokofieff, *The Twelve Holy Nights and the Spiritual Hierarchies*, Part I, second chapter).

[†] See GA 152 and S.O.Prokofieff, *The Cycle of the Year*, Part II, fourth chapter.

summarizing words: 'Thus Christ gradually approached the earth. The first and second pre-earthly stages [of the Mystery of Golgotha] were in the world of Devachan [higher and lower Devachan], the third was in the astral world and the event of Golgotha was in the physical world.'[30]

We can summarize all this by means of the following diagrammatic picture:

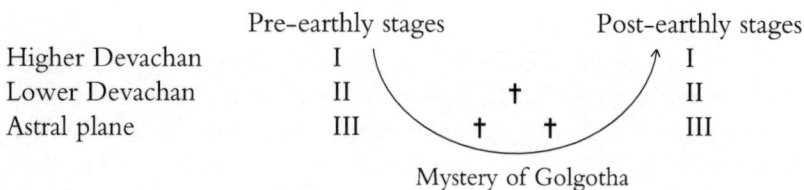

	Pre-earthly stages				Post-earthly stages
Higher Devachan	I				I
Lower Devachan	II		†		II
Astral plane	III		†	†	III

Mystery of Golgotha

If we now consider that the three stages subsequent to the Mystery of Golgotha are a direct continuation and karmic consequence of the three pre-earthly stages and the Mystery of Golgotha itself is their centre and mid-point—a real hypomochlion—this knowledge of these cosmic relationships renders the idea that Christ could appear a second time physically on the earth altogether impossible. For such an assumption would signify a total failure to understand the Mystery of Golgotha as a unique, central event between the three pre-earthly and the three post-earthly stages.

Everything that has been said in this chapter can be summarized by the following words of Rudolf Steiner: 'Looking at the course of earthly evolution we note that the Mystery of Golgotha stands in its very centre. Everything that went before was in preparation for and pointed towards this Mystery of Golgotha; and everything that has happened since is a gradual advance in the streaming of its forces into human souls and human hearts.'[31]

Notes

1. GA 130, 17 June 1912.
2. Published in GA 109.
3. GA 109, 3 June 1909.
4. Vienna, 14 June 1909 (GA 109); the Kassel cycle is published in GA 112.
5. Published in GA 113.
6. Undated esoteric lesson published in GA 264 under the title 'The Connection of the Masters with the Raisings of the Dead in the Gospels'.
7. GA 113, 31 August 1909, also the following quotations.
8. The total number of lectures between 1910 and 1924 in which the imminent appearance of Christ in the etheric world was mentioned amounts to several

hundred. A list of them is contained in the anthology *Rudolf Steiner über die Wiederkunft Christi*, ed. H. Giersch, Dornach 1991.

9. The sixteenth lecture from the cycle on the Book of Revelation [18 lectures in all]. It was given by Rudolf Steiner in September 1924 for the priests of the Christian Community.

10. The transcript of this lecture was first published in *Beiträge zur Rudolf Steiner Gesamtausgabe* N 106, Dornach 1991.

11. GA 14, second scene. First performance in summer 1910 in Munich.

12. GA 15, chapter III. The subtitle of this book is: 'Spiritual-Scientific Conclusions about the Evolution of Mankind'.

13. GA 121, 16 June 1910.

14. GA 118, 10 May 1910.

15. GA 118, 20 February 1910.

16. GA 130, 4 November 1911.

17. See note 10.

18. GA 121, 17 June 1910, also the following quotation.

19. GA 262, 'The Barr Manuscript' III, also the following quotations.

20. GA 130, 6 March 1910.

21. See further in the lectures of 7 and 14 October 1911 (GA 131) and the lecture of 2 December 1911 (GA 130).

22. GA 131, 7 October 1911, also the following quotations.

23. GA 130, 2 December 1911.

24. See GA 104, 30 June 1908, and also S.O. Prokofieff, *The Cycle of the Year*, Part IV, ch. 6, Temple Lodge, 1995.

25. GA 155, 30 May 1912.

26. GA 121, 16 June 1910.

27. GA 118, 6 March 1910.

28. GA 130, 21 September 1911.

29. GA 152, 2 May 1913.

30. GA 152, 30 March 1914.

31. GA 152, 7 March 1914.

7. The Christian Teaching of Reincarnation and Karma

The truth that, from our time onwards, Christ has become the Lord of Karma is amongst the most important insights of anthroposophical Christology.[1] This means that from now on the teaching of karma and reincarnation familiar from ancient Eastern traditions of wisdom has acquired a completely new significance and meaning. Hence this ancient teaching must now be transformed and renewed in the light of the occult cosmic fact that Christ has become the Lord of Karma.

This has happened through modern spiritual science or anthroposophy, which has given the world an entirely new understanding of reincarnation and karma as a supersensible reality impinging upon the world of the senses that does not merely harmonize with the principal teachings of Christianity but is also in a position to throw light upon its deepest mysteries, which have until now—or to be more precise until our present epoch of the appearance of Christ in the etheric—had to remain concealed.

The nature of this new and truly Christian teaching of reincarnation and karma may be described as follows.

Just as mankind needed many thousands of years to prepare for the incarnation on earth of the Sun Logos, the Christ, whose life culminated in His death and resurrection on the hill of Golgotha, so will earthly humanity need many thousands of years to grasp the full significance of this central and *unique* event and then to spiritualize the whole of earth existence by means of the spiritual forces emanating from it.

No single human soul should be excluded from this process of sharing in the Christ forces that have been active in earthly evolution since the Mystery of Golgotha. For this purpose ever new incarnations will be needed for human souls in order that they may enter deeper and deeper into the eternally living Christ mysteries, deriving from them the forces that are necessary for a full and final resurrection of humanity and of the earthly Creation that has from the earliest times been associated with it (see Romans 8).

This ultimate ideal of earthly evolution described at the end of the Book of Revelation in the picture of the New Jerusalem,[2] where there will be no more death or a need for further reincarnation (Rev. 21:4), will only be attainable through a conscious endeavour on the part of *all* human souls in the course of many incarnations. For 'the kingdom of heaven has suffered violence, and men of violence take it by force' (Matthew 11:12).

Thus from the standpoint of esoteric Christianity the period during which human souls pass through reincarnations is not an endless process without a beginning or end, as is often imagined in the East, but it has, on the contrary, a clear beginning and end in the course of earthly evolution, its Alpha and its Omega. In the Bible these are portrayed through the two great boundary pillars of world history, the Fall and the eventual overcoming of death, as described at the beginning of the Book of Genesis which introduces the Old Testament. Between these two poles lies the Mystery of Golgotha, which gives mankind the possibility of making the transition from the first to the last condition, that is, of ultimately overcoming the compulsion to reincarnate. Herein lies its *paradisaical* quality, though it is up to ourselves to open up this source of beneficial influence. However, this cannot happen immediately or in a short time. For no one alive today can overcome the death forces in his organism—this will only be possible in the distant future; thus no human being who has not yet reached the Buddha stage in his development can overcome the immutable law of reincarnation. Nevertheless, the Mystery of Golgotha is the highest guarantee that this will be possible for *every* human being.

The same is also true of the law of karma, which is an expression of the inexorable law of divine justice in our world. Hence Christ said: 'Think not that I have come to abolish the law and the prophets; I have come not to abolish them but to fulfil them. For truly, I say to you, till heaven and earth pass away, not an iota, not a dot, will pass from the law until all is accomplished' (Matthew 5:17–18). In other words, the law of karma in its present earthly form will cease to be effective only at the end of the present earthly aeon and the beginning of the aeon of the heavenly Jerusalem.[3] But here too the process of transition to the new, higher evolutionary state will be gradual and will extend over many incarnations, in the course of which human beings will work—with the help of the Christ forces that they have received—on transmuting the inexorable law of karma into pure *grace*, and this will be the only 'law' of the New Jerusalem.[*] The Mystery of Golgotha will again be the guarantee and the source for this transformation of karma, for without it karma would remain for ever the unchanging law that it was from the outset and still remains today in the minds of Eastern peoples. Hence for them the purpose of evolution is not the transformation of karma into *grace* but liberation from karma. This is the source of the endeavour of Eastern

---

[*] See further in: S.O. Prokofieff, *The Occult Significance of Forgiveness*, Temple Lodge, 1995.

religions to escape from 'this world' with its adversities, suffering and death instead of gradually transforming and spiritualizing it through the forces emanating from the Mystery of Golgotha.

After this short introduction into the teaching of reincarnation and karma as embodied in modern esoteric Christianity, the reader will have no difficulty in understanding that the idea of reincarnation and karma which Rudolf Steiner expounded in anthroposophy derives not from Eastern, theosophical or Buddhist sources but solely from Christian-Rosicrucian origins.

As he himself relates in his autobiography *The Course of My Life*, Rudolf Steiner, who from his youth had followed the Christian-Rosicrucian path of initiation, had by the age of 26–7 been able to perceive the reality of reincarnation on the basis of his own spiritual experience. He described this as follows: 'It was in the very time of my life I am now describing [1887–8] that I succeeded in attaining to definite perceptions of the repeated earthly lives of man.'[4] Rudolf Steiner particularly emphasized that he did not arrive at this knowledge out of books or religious traditions of the East but directly from the 'supersensible path' that he followed, for: 'the way of theorizing in this region was not my *own* way' (emphasis by Rudolf Steiner).

But how was Rudolf Steiner able to arrive at a direct *experience* of the truth of reincarnation out of the sources of Christian-Rosicrucian initiation? This was possible because, from the very beginning of the founding of the Rosicrucian mysteries and their occult schools, Masters such as Manes, Zarathustra, Scythianos and Buddha (the latter in the spirit-body) taught in them at the higher stages of initiation.

Thus Manes, who convened the council referred to above (see p. 413) in the fourth century AD, had as his central task—after his incarnation in the ninth century as Parzival, when he became the highest leader of the mysteries of the Holy Grail—gradually to forge the link between Christianity and the truth of reincarnation amongst mankind, though not by borrowing this truth from the East but through its rebirth out of the depths of the mysteries of esoteric Christianity itself. Rudolf Steiner portrayed this in the following way: 'Thus Manes prepared himself in his life as Parzival to become a future teacher of Christianity [in the Rosicrucian mysteries], whose task it will be to penetrate Christianity itself more and more with the teachings of karma and reincarnation.'

The second teacher of reincarnation was Gautama Buddha. However, he taught this truth in the Rosicrucian mysteries not in the old form in which he had proclaimed it six centuries before the founding of Christianity but in the wholly *new* form that these teachings acquired as a result of his supersensible participation in the incarnation of the Christ. For this had the consequence that Gautama Buddha himself evolved further and became one of the great *Christian* teachers of reincarnation and karma (see chapter 7).

Finally, Rudolf Steiner referred in the same lecture to Scythianos as the Master who is the guardian of a still higher teaching than that of reincarnation in the Rosicrucian mysteries. 'Thus one will [through spiritual science] begin to understand Scythianos, whose task it is to teach not only the reincarnation of human souls but that which holds sway from eternity to eternity.'[6] For he will teach that highest of truths that the Christ brought to the earth from the kingdom of the Father and which he united with earthly evolution as a whole through the Mystery of Golgotha.[7]*

As we know, exoteric Christianity—in contrast to its esoteric counterpart—initially did not accept the truth of reincarnation into the body of its teachings. This was at the time spiritually justified and even necessary and was therefore acknowledged by the Masters. There were *three* reasons for this.

Firstly, the Eastern version of this teaching (for example the Buddhist) was incompatible with the evolution towards freedom through which Christian humanity must pass. Hence the Eastern form of this teaching in the West needed to be completely forgotten in the West, in order that human beings might gradually become sufficiently mature for a new, Christian form of this teaching grounded upon a consistent development of the ego principle, whose highest archetype was introduced into earthly evolution by the Christ.

Secondly, the teaching of reincarnation had to be forgotten for a time by Christian humanity so that it might learn to value and love the earth as a place where alone man can attain to a full unfolding of all the forces of his individual ego and, as a result, also to an experience of true freedom, whose fruits he then must bear into the spiritual world (Devachan): 'hence ... for a time Christianity did not teach reincarnation and karma but the importance of an earthly life, in order that man might grow fond of the earth to the point of being mature enough for a *new Christianity*— including the teaching of reincarnation and karma—which may save the earth and bring all the fruits [of earthly evolution] to Devachan.'[8]

Thirdly, Christian humanity needed to arrive at the experience that

---

* In a later lecture (4 June 1924, GA 236) Rudolf Steiner spoke of how Christ brought the new impulse of spiritualized time to the earth, which is capable of overcoming the forces of death that permeate the world of space.

Christ's coming to earth and the Mystery of Golgotha are the central events of the whole of earthly evolution and that their acceptance or non-acceptance in this one earthly life is a question upon the answer to which the subsequent destiny of the soul in the higher worlds depends. This should awaken a feeling in the souls of human beings for the significance of earthly life as the only possibility of gaining knowledge of and becoming united with those higher spiritual forces which have streamed into mankind through the Mystery of Golgotha.

Whereas in exoteric Christianity (by the fourth century) the knowledge of reincarnation almost completely disappeared, in the circles of esoteric Christianity—as we have seen—the foundations were laid for an altogether *new form* of this teaching, which was then gradually to stream into earthly humanity after the period of the maturation and development of the individual ego and the principle of individual freedom associated with it. For only the fully evolved human ego can grasp the central idea of the Christian teaching of reincarnation and karma, which consists in that only the Christ impulse, having united itself with the earth through the Mystery of Golgotha, gives *meaning* to the earthly incarnations of man, since these are no longer merely a means of liberating oneself from the endless cycle of birth and death but represent a path of fulfilling the meaning of the earth and man's destiny upon it. In order to understand and fulfil all the impulses that Christ implanted into the earth, mankind will still need many incarnations. However, these will be accompanied by the ever-growing awareness that 'through the Christ impulse we possess a power which can give these incarnations an ever loftier content'.[9] Without this power all subsequent incarnations will increasingly be experienced as lacking any spiritual value.

This new Christian form of reincarnation could be revealed to mankind in full measure only once the Kali Yuga, the dark age, had come to an end in 1899. Hence the idea of reincarnation began gradually to appear in Christian Europe as though by itself from the second half of the eighteenth century. Thus G.E. Lessing in 1780 published his book *The Education of the Human Race*, where this idea is central. There can be no question of its having been outwardly borrowed from the East, since Eastern writings on this theme had not yet been translated into a European language. (The *Bhagavadgita*, for example, was first translated into German in 1834.) Moreover, Lessing's conception of reincarnation was altogether different from—say—that of traditional Buddhism.

In two lectures, on 6 and 14 October 1911, Rudolf Steiner characterized at some length the main difference between the notion of reincarnation as it appeared in the West initially through Lessing and as it has existed traditionally in the East for centuries. The difference is that this teaching in the East served as a means of personal salvation for the individual, whereas with Lessing it concerns the whole of humanity. 'For the Christ impulse makes everything a person does or can do into an action of universal relevance.'[10] And so Rudolf Steiner sums up the difference between the Western and Eastern form of this teaching as follows: 'And when the idea of reincarnation reappeared in the eighteenth century, it appeared as a Christian thought.' The same can be said of Goethe, Novalis and many other outstanding representatives of European culture.[11] Somewhat later, in the middle of the nineteenth century (1851), the doctor and philosopher Gustav Widenmann made the first attempt to resolve the central Christian question of the immortality of the soul from the standpoint of reincarnation. Thus 'his idea of reincarnation', though 'embryonic' in nature, 'is permeated by a Christian impulse'.[12]

According to Rudolf Steiner's occult research this sudden emergence in Christian form of the idea of reincarnation in the West is associated with the supersensible inspiration of Christian Rosenkreutz, under whose influence Lessing, Widenmann, Drosbach and others[13] developed this idea.[*] In its present, spiritual-scientific form, however, this teaching could manifest itself as a component of Christian civilization only with the beginning of the twentieth century. Thus the title of the first lecture that Rudolf Steiner gave as General Secretary on 20 October 1902 in Berlin, on the occasion of the festive founding of the German Section of the Theosophical Society, was 'Practical Karma Exercises'.[14] Here the idea of reincarnation and karma was for the first time presented out of the sources of esoteric Christianity. However, the substance of this lecture met with a total misunderstanding on the part of the majority of the members of the Theosophical Society at the time and in addition called forth a true panic in the older members who had been educated in the Eastern forms of this teaching.[15] This had the consequence that Rudolf Steiner had to give up his plan and had to wait almost two decades before he could consider this theme 'in a truly esoteric' way[16] immediately before the Christmas

---

[*] This found a tragic expression in the destiny of Blavatsky while she was writing *Isis Unveiled*, also under the influence of Rosicrucian inspirations (see GA 130, 27 September 1911). However, she was able to receive these only at a relatively low level. Since the idea of reincarnation was taught only at the highest stages of initiation in the Rosicrucian schools during recent centuries (GA 131, 6 October 1911), Blavatsky—who had access only to the lower stages of initiation—did not hear about this idea at all and so did not include it in her *Isis Unveiled* (GA 133, 23 October 1911). She then subsequently took up this idea from the East, though only in its traditional form which cannot be reconciled with Christianity.

Conference of 1923/24. After this conference it was then possible to speak about karma and reincarnation directly out of the Michaelic sources of Christian esotericism without any restriction in 83 karma lectures.[17]

And so the following picture emerges. From the fourth century onwards the knowledge of reincarnation gradually disappears amongst Western humanity. At the same time, however, preparations for establishing this teaching in a completely new, Christian form—which it could only have under the influence of the Mystery of Golgotha—begin in the circles of esoteric Christianity. Moreover, the fruits of this preparation gradually manifest themselves from the end of the eighteenth century also in the outward cultural life of Europe and North America, appearing spontaneously here and there among the most diverse thinkers without any connection with one another.

With the end of the Kali Yuga the Christian teaching of reincarnation and karma then appeared for the first time, in a manner that was accessible and comprehensible to all people, in spiritual-scientific form through anthroposophy. For whereas it was still necessary in previous centuries to hold this teaching back from directly influencing Christian humanity, on the grounds that its concealing would significantly accelerate the maturing of the individual ego principle, after the end of the Kali Yuga a further holding back would have seriously hindered the general evolution of mankind. Hence the Masters of esoteric (Rosicrucian) Christianity took the decision to make it public. In addition, they wanted to create a counterbalance to the spreading of this teaching in its old, pre-Christian (Eastern) form in the Christian world, as had been begun by H.P. Blavatsky and Sinnett. This publicizing of the teaching of reincarnation in a new Christian form was then carried out at the beginning of the twentieth century by Rudolf Steiner as an emissary of the leading Rosicrucian Masters.

All this can be summarized in Rudolf Steiner's words: 'For the nearly two millennia of Christian development so far, what was given in esoteric Christianity could not be incorporated in outer, exoteric life. For example, it was not possible to incorporate what can be taught in our present epoch as a *Christian truth*, namely the re-embodiment of man, or reincarnation. When we, in anthroposophy, teach reincarnation today, we are fully conscious that reincarnation is a *Christian truth* which *can* be made known exoterically today to a humanity which has become more mature, but which could not be made known to the immature souls of the first Christian centuries.'[18]

Thus the teaching of reincarnation or re-embodiment, which Rudolf Steiner proclaimed in the twentieth century as a 'Christian truth', is not borrowed in any of its elements from any traditional Eastern teaching. Rudolf Steiner referred to this quite decisively in, for example, a lecture from the year 1923, when he was looking back at the first period of the emergence of anthroposophy: 'The first period of the anthroposophical movement lasted until around 1908 or 1909. Those who trace the history of the arising of the anthroposophical movement will be able to see how everything that could—*without being adapted from old traditions* but, rather, from an immediate awareness of the present—be found regarding life before birth, repeated earthly lives and so on, how this is oriented towards that historical development within human earth-existence which has its focus in the Mystery of Golgotha and in the Christ impulse.'[19]

These words characterize more the outward aspect of the process in question. For the fact that the Rosicrucian Masters decided to publicize the Christian teaching of reincarnation at the beginning of the twentieth century was, from an esoteric point of view, associated with its main task, the 'recognition and realization of the intentions of the *living Christ*'.[20] And these 'intentions' consisted for our time, according to Rudolf Steiner, in that '*it is the living Christ, from out of the spiritual world, who is the living teacher of reincarnation today*'.[21]

This sheds light on the deeper reasons why Rudolf Steiner said to the Waldorf teacher Walter Johannes Stein in Den Haag in 1922 that it was his principal task in this earthly life to reveal the mysteries of reincarnation and karma to humanity.[22] And the 83 karma lectures that Rudolf Steiner gave after the Christmas Conference are, from an esoteric standpoint, none other than a first revelation which *the Christ himself as the Lord of Karma* gave to mankind. For to the extent that he himself gradually becomes the Lord of Karma will he also become a 'living teacher of reincarnation' for human beings.

In the future, the new faculty of supersensibly beholding one's past incarnations will develop under the influence of Christ. This will happen during the next three millennia, to the point where man becomes convinced out of his own spiritual experience what a great difference exists between his own incarnations before and after the Mystery of Golgotha,[23] when for the first time it became possible for the human individual to be united also on earth with the forces of the Sun Logos. As a result the whole of earthly evolution will gradually manifest itself to such a person as consisting of two parts: pre-Christian evolution will appear to him as a preparation for Christ's coming to the earth and the Mystery of Golgotha, and the evolution that follows it, from this event and 'until the close of the age' (Matthew 28:20), will be seen as a time whose principal purpose is to recognize the impulses of the Mystery of Golgotha and to implement them amongst earthly human beings.

In a later lecture Rudolf Steiner described this perspective of world history in the following way: 'And so this one event of Golgotha, this one ensouling of a human being by a divine Being, alone imparts meaning and purpose to the *whole* of earthly evolution. All previous evolution is to be thought of as preparatory to this event of Golgotha, and all subsequent evolution as the fulfilment, the consequence of the Mystery of Golgotha.'[24]*

The true Christian idea of reincarnation also acquires its significance from such a perspective of world history. For only by coming to the earth again and again is the human soul able fully to receive into itself the fruits of the Mystery of Golgotha and thereby fulfil its destiny.

Notes

1. See GA 130, 2 December 1911 and GA 131, 14 October 1911.
2. See GA 104, 30 June 1908.
3. Ibid.
4. GA 28, ch. VII, likewise the following quotations.
5. Undated esoteric lesson published in GA 264 under the title 'The Connection of the Masters with the Raisings of the Dead in the Gospels'.
6. GA 113, 31 August 1909.
7. Regarding Scythianos, see: Sergei O. Prokofieff, *Die geistigen Aufgaben Mittel- und Osteuropas* ('The Spiritual Tasks of Central and Eastern Europe') ch. 7, Dornach 1993.
8. GA 93a, 25 October 1905.
9. GA 118, 15 May 1910.
10. GA 131, 14 October 1911.
11. See Emil Bock, *Wiederholte Erdenleben. Die Wiederverkörperungsidee in der deutschen Geistesgeschichte* ('Repeated Earthly Lives. The Idea of Reincarnation in German Cultural History'), Stuttgart 1967.
12. GA 131, 14 October 1911.
13. GA 130, 27 September 1911.
14. See GA 240, 16 April 1924.
15. See GA 240, 24 August 1924.
16. See GA 240, 16 April 1924.
17. The lectures on *Karmic Relationships* from 1924 are published in the six volumes GA 235–240 in Rudolf Steiner's Collected Works.
18. GA 118, 15 May 1910.
19. GA 257, 6 February 1923.

---

*Rudolf Steiner spoke in a similar way in the lectures of 24 December 1920 (GA 202) and 16 October 1921 (GA 207).

20. GA 262, 'The Barr Manuscript', III.

21. GA 118, 15 May 1910.

22. See further in 'Das Haager Gespräch—Ein Beitrag zu Rudolf Steiners Leben-geschichte' (The Hague Conversation—A Contribution to Rudolf Steiner's Biography), an article by W.J. Stein from 1934, published in *W.J. Stein/Rudolf Steiner. Dokumentation eines wegweisenden Zusammenwirkens*, Dornach 1985.

23. See GA 131, 14 October 1911.

24. GA 209, 26 December 1921.

8. The Mystery of Golgotha and the Great Teachers of Mankind

Jesus and Krishna

One being, whose task it was to be the principal mediator between the Sun Logos and humanity, had a place of particular importance not only in the preparation for the Mystery of Golgotha on earth but also in its cosmic pre-earthly stages. After this being—for the salvation of mankind—had served on three occasions in the higher, supersensible worlds as the cosmic bearer of the Christ, as a kind of heavenly Christophorus, it came down to earth for the first time in order, as Jesus of Nazareth, to become the bearer of the Sun Logos also in the physical world.

According to Rudolf Steiner's spiritual research, this being was originally a sister soul of the first human being, Adam. At the Fall it was held back by higher hierarchic powers from descending into matter and had abided since then in the spiritual worlds.[1] In one of his lectures Rudolf Steiner spoke of how this mystery of the two Adams, one earthly and one heavenly—the latter having been a bearer of the Christ first in the cosmos and subsequently on the earth—is represented in Old Testament tradition by the two trees of Paradise, the Tree of Knowledge and the Tree of Life, with the 'old' Adam taking into himself the forces of the former, while the forces of the latter were guarded within the soul of the 'new' Adam, the future Jesus of Nazareth.[2] By the Turning Point of Time this being had never incarnated on the earth but it had been the bearer in the higher worlds of all the primordial, paradisaical forces of man's being untouched by the Fall. In this capacity this being had been revered in olden times by initiates, who communed supersensibly with it in many pre-Christian mystery centres.[3]

Only once did this lofty individuality come in contact with earthly events. Spiritual science lifts for us here the veil concealing a deep mystery, that of the central figure of the most highly revered work of the Indian East, the *Bhagavadgita*. For the high being who suddenly spoke through the charioteer Arjuna before the battle on the field of Kuru and who in Indian tradition has since borne the name of Krishna was, from an esoteric point of view, none other than the sole, brief *incorporation* of the future Jesus of Nazareth. 'He [Jesus of Nazareth] had never previously been fully incarnated in a human body. His relationship to Krishna was not a true embodiment but was of a vicarious nature.'[4][*] His heavenly soul was revealed to mankind at this moment as the bearer of the paradisaical archetype of man's being, as the source of that high wisdom of life which human beings possessed before the Fall.

Just as Rudolf Steiner entitled his most important Christological cycle 'From Jesus to Christ', so was he able to say by way of characterizing the central thrust of the spiritual science that he had initiated: 'Our path ... is the straight line from Krishna—if we do want to go further back [that is, to Zarathustra and Manu]—via Buddha, Elijah, John [the Baptist] to Christ,' and 'our task is to proclaim the Mystery of Golgotha.'[5]

However, in order to prepare for the appearance of the Sun Logos on the earth, this sister soul of humanity had to unite its heavenly wisdom, its wisdom of the 'Tree of Life', with the ripest fruits of earthly wisdom and earthly experience or the wisdom of the 'Tree of Knowledge'. It did not itself possess this latter quality; and it was able to receive it from the most spiritualized and highly evolved earthly individualities, Zarathustra and Gautama Buddha. They were the principal representatives of the two mystery streams of ancient times, the Northern and the Southern streams, the first of which sought a path into the supersensible worlds through an ecstatic union with the spiritual foundations of the outer world and the second through a mystical immersion into the depths of one's own soul.[6] In preparing the sheaths of Jesus of Nazareth the individuality of Gautama Buddha was active mainly in his astral body from birth until his twelfth year, while between the ages of 12 and 30 the ego of Zarathustra permeated all

---

[*]In the cycle *The Bhagavad Gita and the Epistles of St. Paul*, which was given at the founding of the independent Anthroposophical Society (end of 1912), and also in *The Occult Foundations of the Bhagavad Gita* (1913), and specifically the lectures GA 142, 1 January 1913 and GA 146, 3 June 1913, Rudolf Steiner considered this theme in detail. In the lecture of 1 January 1913, Rudolf Steiner also used the word *Ersatzverkörperung* ('a substitute embodiment'). We can picture this process in the following way. The individuality of the charioteer Arjuna—who had been prepared in the mysteries—left his earthly sheaths for a certain time, relinquishing them to another, higher individuality. In another lecture Rudolf Steiner characterized such a process as follows: 'Not every physical personality should be regarded as an actual reality; it can be a maya through which a higher being is working' (GA 113, 31 August 1909).

three of his sheaths,* after which it left them immediately before the
Baptism in the Jordan and sacrificially made them available to the Sun
Logos descending from the cosmos.[7]

Thus in the course of the preparation of the earthly sheaths for the
incarnation of the Sun Logos, the best fruits both of the Tree of Life and
of the Tree of Knowledge were brought together and united.

Zarathustra

A further section of this chapter will be devoted to Gautama Buddha.
Here it is necessary to consider the individuality of Zarathustra at greater
length.

Already on ancient Atlantis he was 'one of the most important pupils of
the initiate of the sun oracle',[8] that is, of Manu himself. Then in the course
of many incarnations this high individuality prepared his next task: the
founding of the second, ancient Persian, post-Atlantean cultural epoch.
The nature of this epoch consisted in that mankind was to begin its main
task on the earth: the transforming of the material world and the developing of the individual human ego in the course of this work.

In order to fulfil this task Zarathustra first had to imbue his soul with the
wisdom of the previous epoch, whose highest representatives were the
ancient Indian Rishis.[9] He received this wisdom, which as regards its
sources goes back to ancient Atlantis, during a whole series of earthly lives,
thus enabling him to rise to a new, higher stage and to become the *first*
earthly human being who was able to attain an initiation out of the forces
of the *post-Atlantean* epoch.

The consequence of this was that Zarathustra, for the first time in
earthly evolution, began to expound high supersensible wisdom and

---

* According to Rudolf Steiner's spiritual-scientific research, two Jesus children were born
in Palestine at the Turning Point of Time, their births being respectively described in the
Gospels of St Luke and St Matthew. Thus in St Luke's Gospel the birth of the paradisaical
archetypal human being, the sister-soul of Adam, is described, that being who was not
subject to the Fall. The family tree in this Gospel extends back to Adam and to God, and
one of the ancestors of this soul was Nathan, a son of David. In St Matthew's Gospel, on
the other hand, the birth of the reincarnated Zarathustra is described. He has a completely
different family tree, his ancestor being a *different* son of David, Solomon; and for this
reason the genealogy of the two Gospels coincides from Abraham until David, but
thereafter until Joseph there is not a single name in common. When the Solomon Jesus
was 12 years old, the ego of Zarathustra left his sheaths (he died soon afterwards) and
passed over into the sheaths of the Nathan Jesus, where it remained until the Baptism in
the Jordan. (See further regarding the two Jesus children in GA 15, 114, 117, 123 and 148,
also in Emil Bock, *The Childhood of Christ*, Floris, 1997.)

purely clairvoyant knowledge of the spiritual worlds not only in the form of imaginations (as was the case before him), but also in the form of human thoughts and concepts, from which subsequently emerged what we call today scientific knowledge.

Rudolf Steiner characterized this process as follows: 'Whereas the Rishis seem to be consecrated individuals stemming from a primordial past, vessels into whom ancient Atlantean wisdom has flowed, Zarathustra appears as the first historical personality to be initiated into a genuinely post-Atlantean mystery-knowledge, that is to say, knowledge presented in such a way that it could be understood only by the intelligence of post-Atlantean humanity ... True, it was pre-eminently supersensible knowledge that was acquired in the Zoroastrian schools. Nevertheless it was there that knowledge began for the first time to take the form of concepts.'[10]

Thus Zarathustra's place in earthly evolution was not only as the founder of the ancient Persian cultural epoch but also as the precursor of the ensuing post-Atlantean evolution, which ultimately led to the scientific and technological civilization of our times. Out of the forces of the new *post-Atlantean* initiation, Zarathustra revealed to humanity the mysteries of the highest Sun God, Ahura Mazda (Ormuzd), and the opposing spirit of darkness, matter and death—Ahriman. For on the path to the full unfolding of the forces of the individual ego, a path that leads ever deeper into the realm of matter and death, mankind had inevitably to encounter its dark ruler in order through overcoming his temptations and enticements to reach the goal of earthly evolution. As a way of helping a youthful mankind to withstand the difficult trials that confronted it, Zarathustra initiated his pupils into the mysteries of Ahura Mazda, through which the Christ—who was dwelling at that time on the sun— revealed Himself to human beings.[11] In this way Zarathustra became the great herald of the cosmic Christ, as the central Being of our cosmos, and the great preparer of His impending incarnation on the earth.

In the course of preparing this principal event of the whole of earthly evolution, the ego of Zarathustra had successively to sacrifice all three of his earthly sheaths, which he had brought to a high degree of perfection over the course of many incarnations. He sacrificed his astral body to one of his pupils, the future founder of Egyptian culture, Hermes Trismegistos, and his etheric body to another pupil, the future Moses.[12] Then he incarnated in Babylon as Zaratas and was there the great teacher of Pythagoras.[13] The latter incarnated subsequently as one of the three Magi.[14] At the Turning Point of Time they came from Persia to Palestine in order to greet their teacher, who had come again to the earth, this time to sacrifice his own physical body to the Sun Logos, the cosmic Christ, thereby preparing His descent to the earth so that the Mystery of Golgotha might be fulfilled.[15]

But what happened to the individuality of Zarathustra after the Baptism in the Jordan? After he had made this great sacrifice, this individuality continued to work on amongst mankind and was incarnated almost every century on the earth under the name *the Master Jesus*.[16] His inspirations in particular lie behind many lectures in the Christological and Gospel cycles given by Rudolf Steiner in the pre-war years.[*] In the cycle *The Gospel of St Luke* he referred directly to this source of his inspirations: 'He [the Master Jesus] is the inspirer of those who strive to understand Christianity in its living growth and development; within the [Western] esoteric schools he inspired those whose perpetual duty it was to cultivate the teachings of Christianity. He stands behind the great spiritual figures of Christianity, ever teaching what the great event of Palestine signifies.'[17]

In the twentieth century it was Rudolf Steiner who took on the task of unveiling the deeper meaning of the events of Palestine.

Manu

The individuality of Manu also played a particular part in the preparation for Christ's coming to the earth. He had been the highest initiate of the sun or Christ's oracle on Atlantis, and was the oldest teacher of Zarathustra and also of the holy Rishis, the founders of the ancient Indian epoch. As the spiritual leader of post-Atlantean evolution, he led a small group of his pupils away from Atlantis before its destruction and founded together with them a new mystery centre in the heart of Asia, in the middle of the Gobi Desert, whence the spiritual impulses that laid the foundation for the post-Atlantean epoch of Earth evolution had their origin.[18]

Manu himself was, however, not only the head of the highest oracle on Atlantis;[†] his spiritual rank was, in an esoteric sense, even higher. For he was in olden times the leader of the so-called 'Mother Lodge of mankind', which was a kind of archetype of the sun oracle in the spiritual world and of which the sun oracle was at that time its earthly representative.

This 'Mother Lodge' led by Manu guided from the outset the

---

[*] See further in: Sergei O. Prokofieff, *The Cycle of the Year*, Part VI, second chapter.
[†] According to the indications of spiritual science, Manu is not a human individuality but a superhuman being, who completed his human development in the previous aeon of earthly evolution (see GA 93, 11 November 1904 and 7 October 1904).

evolution associated with preparing the earthly sheaths for the future incarnation of the Sun Logos, the Christ.[19] In the genealogy of the Gospel of St Luke, which has its origin in the paradisaical (divine) condition of mankind and culminates in the birth on earth of Adam's sister soul, who had been protected in the 'Mother Lodge' since the Fall, the uninterrupted influence of this Lodge is documented. Similarly in the genealogy of the Gospel of St Matthew, which begins with Abraham, the ancestor of the Hebrew people and the recipient of its distinctive task— the preparation of the physical body for the incarnation of Christ—we have a further testimony of its participation in earthly events. A further physical incorporation of Manu as Melchizedek represented an important stage in this process. He met the ancestor of the Hebrew people, Abraham, before the gates of Salem with bread and wine and initiated him into the mystery of the high mission of the people entrusted to him: preparing in the course of generations the earthly sheaths for the future incarnation of the Christ, the Sun Logos, on the earth.[20]*

Thus according to modern spiritual science, based as it is on a spiritual research that derives from a true Christian-Rosicrucian initiation, all the ancient spiritual and religious streams gradually united in a mighty current, which had the aim of preparing for the greatest event of earthly evolution, referred to in the words from St John's Gospel: 'The Word became flesh' (John 1:14).

Gautama Buddha

In connection with the central part that ideas about Gautama Buddha as the leader of the entire Himalayan Hierarchy played from the outset in the Theosophical Society, we need to look more closely at this highly evolved individuality. Thus the English theosophist Jean Overton Fuller wrote in her book *Blavatsky and Her Teachers*: 'But was the Mahachohan, the Chohan Lama Rimbouchy, the final head of the school or hierarchy to which Morya, Koot Humi and the other Masters of Wisdom belonged? No. About the higher reaches both Madame Blavatsky and Olcott are naturally very reticent. The highest human being on our planet, they explained, was Gautama Buddha or Tsongkapa, in respect to whom Morya and Koot Hoomi felt themselves less than the dust beneath his feet.'[21] And Mahatma Kut Humi wrote in this connection in his letter

---

*Orpheus, who—according to Rudolf Steiner—was one of the bodhisattvas who, apart from Gautama Buddha, attained the Buddha stage before the coming of Christ to the earth, was among the great preparers and emissaries of the Christ.

to Sinnett of 8 July 1881: 'When our great Buddha—the patron of all the adepts, the reformer and codifier of the occult system, reached first Nirvana on earth, he became a Planetary Spirit[*]... That is as rare as the Buddhas themselves, the last Khobilgan who reached it being Tsong-ka-pa of Kokonor (XIV Century), the reformer of esoteric as well as of vulgar Lamaism.'[22]

The verbal teachings of Blavatsky and Olcott cited here by an English theosophist are further confirmed by Kut Humi's words, which he wrote in a letter to the Christian A.O. Hume (Sinnett's colleague): 'Thus in our temples [in contrast to Christian places of worship—S.P.] there is neither a god nor gods worshipped, only the thrice sacred memory of the greatest as the holiest man that ever lived.'[23][†]

The leader of the Mahatmas Morya and Kut Humi, whom in their letters they always called their 'venerable chief' or 'Mahachohan',[24] wrote in a similar style: 'Buddhism, stripped of its superstitions, is eternal truth, and he who strives for the latter is striving for Theo-Sophia, Divine Wisdom, which is a synonym of truth.'[25] And in his commentaries to Kut Humi's letters to Leadbeater, the Indian C. Jinarajadasa (who succeeded Annie Besant as President of the Theosophical Society) wrote: 'The great Adept known as the Mahachohan once said, describing Himself and His fellow-Adepts, that they were all "the devoted followers of the spirit incarnate of absolute self-sacrifice, of philanthropy, divine kindness, as of all the highest virtues attainable on this earth of sorrow, the man of men, Gautama Buddha" (from the Mahachohan's letters to members of the Theosophical Society).'[26]

This is also confirmed by Sinnett, on the basis of information that he had received in the Mahatma Letters, in the foreword to the first edition of his book *Esoteric Buddhism*: 'Buddha, however, undertook the task of revising and refreshing the esoteric science of the inner circle of initiates ... From Buddha's time till now the esoteric science referred to has been jealously guarded as a precious heritage belonging exclusively to regularly initiated members of mysteriously organized associations.'[27] Sinnett goes on to characterize 'the Tibetan Brotherhood' of the mahatmas as 'incomparably the highest of such associations'.

---

[*] In his letter to Sinnett, Mahatma K.H. wrote regarding Planetary Spirits or Buddhas that 'the higher planetary Spirits [are] the only "Spirits" we believe in' (letter no. 6, 10 December 1880).

[†] For this reason Mahatma K.H. (Kut Humi), at the end of his letter to Leadbeater, also first sent 'the blessing of our Lord [the Buddha]' and then 'my poor blessing', that is, the blessing of K.H. himself (*The 'K.H.' Letters to C.W. Leadbeater*, with a commentary by C. Jinarajadasa, p. 68, Adyar, India 1988).

Helena Blavatsky similarly confirms this in one of her letters: 'The Society was formed, then gradually made to merge into and evolve hints from the Secret Doctrine [this is also what H.P. Blavatsky called her principal work] *of the oldest school of Occult Philosophy in the whole world*—a school to reform which, finally, the Lord Gautama was made to appear...'[28]

This information corresponds approximately to the content of some notes from the year 1903 in Marie von Sivers's handwriting, which probably refers back to occult instruction that Rudolf Steiner had given her in private: 'When the individuality of the Mahaguru incarnated as Buddha, the teachings of the latter led to misunderstandings and differences of opinion. He had given too much. Buddha had to incarnate once more as Shankarasharya.[*] He trained the Tibetan teachers, the mahatmas, who have revealed in part the teachings of theosophy, to convey to the various religions the esoteric content inherent in each of them, and to raise the sunken spiritual level of humanity.'

The substance of these notes was unexpectedly carried forward in Sinnett's book *Esoteric Buddhism* (in the chapter 'The Buddha'). There the author referred not only to one but to two further reincarnations of Gautama. Thus after his second incarnation in the figure of Shankarasharya, who had the task of bringing Buddhist teachings into harmony with the older, Brahmanistic teachings, he was incarnated for a third time, in the fourteenth century, as Tsong-Kha-Pa, the well-known reformer of Tibetan Buddhism. In this third incarnation he founded in Tibet the 'Brotherhood of Initiates', certain later members of which were revered as mahatmas in the Theosophical Society.[†]

What follows from all this is that the teachings of the mahatmas can be traced back not directly to Gautama Buddha but to the continuation of his esoteric teachings through Shankarasharya on the one hand and Tsong-Kha-Pa on the other.

In a somewhat later lecture Rudolf Steiner described the occult background of the mahatmas in the following words: 'The great sages originated from oriental knowledge, from the oriental world. They

---

[*] In his later lectures Rudolf Steiner further specified that only the astral body of Gautama Buddha lived in Shankarasharya and not his individuality (ego): see GA 107, 22 March 1909.

[†] At the end of this chapter Sinnett himself emphasizes that 'these explanations [are] directly gathered from authorities to whom the subject is no less familiar in its scholarly than in its esoteric aspect' (page 140). By 'authorities' Sinnett had in mind above all two theosophical mahatmas with whom he was in correspondence while he was working on his book (see *The Mahatma Letters to Sinnett*).

belonged to a brotherhood which had its roots in what one may call the deep Buddhism of the Orient. The brotherhood does not have its roots in so-called Southern Buddhism, which you can find particularly in Ceylon, but in Northern Buddhism, which does not merely encompass the pure and noble moral teaching and the teaching of justice of Southern Buddhism but also a sublime teaching of the spiritual, the spiritual life of the world. This Northern Buddhism can in a certain sense be regarded as a kind of esoteric teaching, in contrast to Southern Buddhism.'[30]

Thus by living only within Asiatic-Buddhist tradition, the mahatmas seemingly knew nothing either of the older European incarnations of Gautama (while still a bodhisattva) or of his direct participation in the preparation for the coming of Christ to the earth, not to speak of his relationship to the stream of esoteric Christianity.

Already in earlier lectures Rudolf Steiner referred on several occasions to how Gautama Buddha had frequently incarnated as a bodhisattva among the original peoples of Europe before his last earthly incarnation in India in the sixth century BC, in the course of which he attained the Buddha stage as Prince Gautama, and had worked among them as a high spirit-teacher, a memory of which is retained in the figure of Odin.[31] Thus in ancient times he worked very closely together with the two other Masters of the West, Zarathustra and Scythianos, on preparing the future Western (European) culture.[*] As one of the leading teachers of humanity the Buddha individuality, while he was in the spiritual world adjoining the earth after his last earthly incarnation, could not of course stay away from the most important event of earthly evolution—the embodiment on it of the Sun Logos, the Christ— which he had served already *before* his first incarnation on the earth. 'Thus in Buddha you have an old emissary of the Christ,' said Rudolf Steiner out of the sources of esoteric Christianity, 'who had the task of preparing Christ's work upon the earth.'[32][†] But how did this preparation by Gautama Buddha look in outward terms? Once he had attained the buddha stage six centuries before the incarnation of the Sun Logos on the earth, the Buddha was able to bring to mankind the great *teaching* of compassion and love and, hence, prepare the ground for the coming of the Christ, who brought not only the teaching *but love itself,* the substance of cosmic love—and that is something infinitely greater. Rudolf Steiner referred to the immense step forward in the transition

---

[*] See further in Sergei O. Prokofieff's books, *The Spiritual Origins of Eastern Europe* and *Die geistigen Aufgaben Mittel-und Osteuropas.*
[†] See further in the chapter 'The Principal Error of Agni Yoga' in Part One.

from Buddha to Christ, from Buddhism to Christianity, in the lecture cycle on *The Gospel of St Luke*,[33] which he gave in Basel in 1909,* that is, directly after the Munich cycle *The East in the Light of the West*.

In the Munich cycle he touched upon this theme—but only very discreetly—when referring to the medieval legend of the Indian prince Josaphat,† who was converted to Christianity by the hermit Barlaam, as proof that in the Middle Ages Buddha's true relationship to the Christ was known in Europe. The deeper *occult* foundations of this relationship were, however, first presented in the Basel cycle.

When considering in these lectures the occult significance of the first chapter of St Luke's Gospel, he unveiled the mystery that it was Gautama Buddha in his spirit-body, the Nirmanakaya, who was manifested to the shepherds in the field and proclaimed to them the coming of the Saviour, the Sun Logos. After this he participated in the preparation of His incarnation at the Baptism in the Jordan by working for twelve years in the astral body of Jesus of Nazareth, with the result that Buddhism was spiritually fully renewed out of the forces of the Christ as He was approaching the earth. 'The mature and sublime conceptions taught by Buddha needed to pass through a fountain of youth in order that they might be revealed to mankind in a new form, filled with fresh, rejuvenating forces.'[34] But how did the renewed and fully Christianized Buddha impulse come to manifestation? This was apparent in the mighty preaching of John the Baptist, who out of the inspirations of the transformed Buddha proclaimed the imminent coming of Christ: 'From the mouth of John the Baptist we hear what the Buddha had to say six hundred years after he had lived in a physical body.'[35] 'What the mouth of John uttered was spoken under the inspiration of the Buddha.'

This supersensible relationship that spiritual science recognizes between the entelechy of the Buddha with John the Baptist can help us to understand the mystery why it is in connection with the latter that reincarnation is mentioned in the New Testament, where it is stated that the individuality of the prophet Elijah appeared in the figure of John the Baptist (Matthew 17:10–12). The Apostles are in a position to understand

---

*From a somewhat different standpoint Rudolf Steiner had already spoken about this spiritual step forward in his very first spiritual-scientific lectures—thus for example in the two cycles from autumn/winter 1901–2: *From Buddha to Christ* and *Christianity as Mystical Fact* (see p. 374).

†The name Josaphat is etymologically related to the name Budasaf or Buddha (see 31 August 1909, GA 113).

the law of reincarnation out of the inspirations of a renewed Buddhism: 'Then the disciples understood that he was speaking to them of John the Baptist (Matthew 17:13).

What has been said here makes it easier to understand Rudolf Steiner's words from the last lecture of the Munich cycle (*The East in the Light of the West*), where he spoke of how the Buddha subsequently taught in the Rosicrucian mystery schools after the complete renewal of his teaching as a result of his participation in the events of Palestine: 'Christianity learnt the teaching of reincarnation and karma from the Buddha, even though not in an old form that would no longer be appropriate. Why have the teachings of reincarnation and karma flowed today [through anthroposophy] into Christianity? They have done so because they have learnt to understand the initiates of the Rose Cross through the Buddha, the great teacher of the idea of reincarnation.'[36]*

That Rudolf Steiner himself was among those 'Rosicrucian initiates' who cultivated a direct spiritual relationship with the further evolved Gautama Buddha is borne out by the words from a lecture on the theme of 'The Penetration of the Buddha-Mercury Stream into Rosicrucianism'[37] two years later (here too the usual oratorical 'we' should be read as 'I'): 'But we [in contrast to traditional Buddhism, which acknowledges only the old teaching of Buddha] look to the Buddha who has moved onwards and from spiritual realms exercises an enduring influence upon human culture. *We* contemplate the Buddha as described in our studies of St Luke's Gospel, whose influence streamed down upon the Jesus of the Nathan line of the House of David; *we* contemplate him at the further stage of his development in the realm of the spirit, who proclaims from there the truths of basic importance for our time [that is, the truths of reincarnation and karma and their renewed form] ... *If through clairvoyant insight we understand the inspirations of the Buddha, we must speak of him as he actually exists today.*'[38]†

---

* The last sentence is quoted in accordance with the original stenogram.

† In the same lecture Rudolf Steiner goes on to sketch an all-embracing picture of the influence of the Christ impulse since the Mystery of Golgotha as the *central* spiritual stream of earthly evolution, into which from the middle of the nineteenth century onwards—in accordance with a certain spiritual rhythm—the stream of the renewed Buddhism gradually began to be incorporated as a very important 'secondary stream'. The difference between the central and secondary streams should be understood in the sense that in our solar system the sun, being not a planet but a star and at the same time the gateway to the higher spiritual spheres of the cosmos, is the *central heavenly body* with respect to all the secondary heavenly bodies, or planets, that are subordinate to it, amongst which is Mercury, whose Planetary Spirit guided Gautama Buddha.

For this reason Rudolf Steiner constantly emphasized from the beginning of his activity in the Theosophical Society 'the need to distinguish between orthodox oriental Buddhism in its original form, which might make the attempt to transplant itself as a fixed and unalterable system into Europe and to engender out of itself a "conception of Christ",[*] and a Buddhism that is progressing to further stages of development'.[29] Regarding this 'Buddhism that is progressing to further development', which is associated above all with the further spiritual development of its founder, Rudolf Steiner said the following: '[Gautama] Buddha at that time [after the Mystery of Golgotha] did not have the intention in his true spiritual being to disseminate what one knows as Buddhism in its old form, but rather did he seek to progress further with the evolution of the time, with evolution as a whole.'[40] This further development of the individuality of Gautama Buddha consisted above all in his participation in the preparation for the Christ Being's coming to the earth and the Mystery of Golgotha and subsequently in spreading the spiritual consequences of this central event amongst mankind. 'Once the Buddha had become a being who no longer needed to incarnate in a human body, he became a helper of *Christian* evolution from the spiritual world,' indicated Rudolf Steiner; and he continued: 'Thus the Buddha individuality worked on—invisibly, supersensibly—in the stream which entered the evolution of humanity through the Mystery of Golgotha.'

From the outset Rudolf Steiner needed neither the traditional nor the occult teachings of Buddhism, as cultivated for example in the brotherhood of the Tibetan mahatmas. For on the basis of his own spiritual-scientific research on Gautama Buddha he was able to draw directly from the sources of esoteric Christianity, with which the living Gautama remained connected after the Mystery of Golgotha.

Thus Rudolf Steiner could say with justice: 'Today it is not even remotely necessary to propagate echoes of Buddhism. We are perfectly capable today of describing the situation out of our European culture, indeed out of Christian culture, without referring to Buddhist sources or origins or other oriental influences ... For it is not necessary [today] to take refuge in oriental sources. Only the initial stimulus proceeded from

---

[*]Where such an attempt leads is shown by the fact that Blavatsky and, after her, also Besant, relying solely upon Buddhist tradition, considered Jeshu ben Pandira—who had lived a century earlier and through whom the Maitreya Bodhisattva was working—to be the Christ (see further in chapter 13).

this oriental source. What we have today does not stream to us from Buddhism.'[41]

From the sources of esoteric Christianity Rudolf Steiner referred to seven deeds of Gautama Buddha which he carried out in the service of the Christ impulse:

1. Gautama Buddha's participation in the proclaiming of the imminent birth of Jesus Christ on earth for the shepherds in the field, as described in St Luke's Gospel.[42]
2. Gautama Buddha's influence through the astral body of Jesus of Nazareth until his twelfth year, which brought about the total renewal of the spiritual nature of Buddhism[43] and was manifested again in the preaching of John the Baptist, who prepared Christ's coming to the earth out of the renewed Buddha forces.[44]
3. Gautama Buddha's participation, alongside Zarathustra and Scythianos, in the great council of Manes in the fourth century.[45]
4. Gautama Buddha's teaching in the seventh and eighth centuries after Christ in the mystery school on the Black Sea, where he taught in a supersensible body out of the direct inspiration of the Christ. (One of his most advanced pupils at that time was the individuality who was to incarnate in the twelfth century as Francis of Assisi, probably the most significant representative of a Buddhism that has been transformed by the Christ impulse.)[46]
5. Gautama Buddha's teaching in a supersensible body in the true Rosicrucian mysteries and mystery schools from the time of their founding in the fourteenth century.[47]
6. The transferring of his further activity to Mars, in order to fulfil there the high Christian task entrusted to him by Christian Rosenkreutz. (This will be spoken of in the next chapter.)
7. The inspiring of modern spiritual science or anthroposophy, as founded in the twentieth century by Rudolf Steiner, through Gautama Buddha from the Mars sphere.[48]

This extensive panorama of Gautama Buddha's supersensible activity *in Christian times* resulting from modern spiritual research shows us the whole cosmic and earthly significance of the world-embracing task of this great servant of Christ, and it also indicates his own further development. It is probably not necessary to emphasize here that the Eastern initiation which can be traced back to traditional esoteric Buddhism knows nothing of all this. Hence even today we do not find this knowledge anywhere in the Theosophical Society, nor in the work of Helena Roerich or Alice Bailey.

The Maitreya Bodhisattva

In the present survey of the influence of the great teachers of humanity in their constant service of the Christ, it is now necessary to focus upon the relationship of the Maitreya Bodhisattva to the Christ impulse, the bodhisattva who in three thousand years' time will be the first *Christian Buddha*. Rudolf Steiner said of him that he will appear 'as the greatest teacher of the Christ impulse',[49] whose word will work through his moral power* 'in order to make the Christ event [of the Mystery of Golgotha] in the fullest degree clear to human beings'.[50] In all his incarnations at the bodhisattva stage, however, he will likewise dedicate all his forces to the service of Christ, bringing ever new impulses and knowledge from the high sphere of the bodhisattvas for this purpose (see p. 369). Thus already a century before the incarnation of the Sun Logos on the earth he worked through Jeshu ben Pandira, the great reformer of the Essene Order and one of the great preparers for Christ's coming in the physical body among the Hebrew people. The Apostle and Evangelist Matthew, who had the task of creating through his Gospel a bridge between the appearance of Christ and ancient Hebrew mystery teachings so as to facilitate the Hebrew people's access to Christianity, came from the occult school that he founded for this purpose.[51] This task of serving Christ has been continuing through the twentieth century, in that the Maitreya Bodhisattva has been proclaiming the most significant spiritual event of our time, the appearance of Christ in the etheric body. According to Rudolf Steiner, '[he] will be the true herald of Christ in etheric raiment, just as at that time [a century before Christ's birth] he prophesied the physical appearance of the Christ'.[52]

If we take seriously the fact that the Theosophical Society originally had the task of helping this bodhisattva to fulfil his mission of proclaiming the Etheric Christ, the later history of the Society makes it plain that, once it had succumbed to overtly antichristian occult influences, it became the greatest impediment for the working of this bodhisattva. For instead of proclaiming Christ in the etheric body, the leaders of the Theosophical Society—by confusing Christ with the bodhisattva, the divine with the human being—made the attempt to falsify Christ's Second Coming by presenting a false Messiah in the physical body from among their midst. In this way the theosophical leaders blocked the mission of this bodhisattva in the twentieth century and, moreover, while making it seem in the most vociferous terms that they were serving the Maitreya.

---

* In this sense Rudolf Steiner also translated the name Maitreya as 'Bringer of goodness through the word' (GA 130, 18 November 1911), which then exerts a magical influence.

As a result a situation arose where the Maitreya Bodhisattva urgently needed help in order to fulfil his task. This was granted to him by the representative of that occult stream which over the centuries had prepared Christ's appearance in the etheric body, namely the Rosicrucian stream. In order to understand *how* this help was made available, we need to consider the following.

According to Rudolf Steiner's occult research the being of a bodhisattva, while ascending to buddhahood, never fully incarnates in that human individuality who in any given century is its bearer.[53] The union of such a chosen human bearer with the bodhisattva takes place only through the incorporation of the latter in the former. Only once the bodhisattva has undergone many 'incorporations' or 'vicarious' incarnations will he finally incarnate as an ordinary human being, that is, from the outset (already in his mother's body) form his own physical body rather than avail himself of a mediator in the form of a human bearer.[54] For only once he has independently imprinted the higher faculties which he has assembled over millennia upon such a physical body will he be able to pass these on to the whole of mankind, as did Gautama Buddha in his full incarnation in the sixth century BC with the 'eightfold path' and 'four truths'.

In the lecture of 25 October 1909 Rudolf Steiner described this process at some length by means of the example of the Gautama Bodhisattva: 'Gautama Buddha was [before his last incarnation, when he rose to the buddha stage] a being who had always been able to incarnate in the earthly bodies of the various periods of civilization without having had to use everything in this human organization. It had not been necessary for this being to go through real human incarnations. Now, however, came an important turning point for this bodhisattva. It became necessary for him [in order to become a buddha] to become acquainted with all the destinies of the human organization within an earthly body that he was to enter. He was to experience something that could only be experienced in an earthly body; and because he was such a high individuality, this one incarnation would suffice for him to see all that a human body can develop ... He was, therefore, able to re-ascend into the spiritual world directly after that incarnation; there was no need for him to go through another. What human beings will, in a certain sphere, evolve out of themselves during future cycles, Buddha was able to give as a great directing force in this one incarnation.'[56]

A bodhisattva has to make use of such incomplete incarnations in the course of all his incarnations as a bodhisattva, so as not for one moment to lose his spiritual connection with the bodhisattva sphere and, hence, with his own task.[*]

It follows from this that a bodhisattva can, as regards his incomplete incarnations or incorporations, make use of the most diverse human bearers, who for their part may be advanced individualities and even initiates. This was the case, for example, with Jeshu ben Pandira, who was initiated in Egypt already in his youth. Rudolf Steiner spoke of him as follows: 'The bodhisattva who is the successor of [Gautama] Buddha incarnated in the *personality* of Jeshu ben Pandira one century before the birth of Jesus of Nazareth,'[57] that is, he was not this individual himself but merely incarnated within his being. Such a bodhisattva does not therefore have to undergo the long and complicated process of building up a physical body of his own; he can incarnate in virtually any century.[58] 'The bodhisattva who incarnated in Jeshu ben Pandira and *also* reincarnated *in others*,[†] returns repeatedly. In about three thousand years he will attain buddhahood and, as the Maitreya Bodhisattva, will live through his last incarnation ... Thus the next bodhisattva, who incarnated in Jeshu ben Pandira and *in others* on an on-going basis, became the great teacher of the Christ impulse.'

Thus no one can know beforehand which physical bearer the bodhisattva will choose for his incarnation (incorporation) in any particular case. This will become evident only when the person concerned has reached his thirtieth year. This fact is consistent with the spiritual law that the life of the bodhisattva who is to become the first *Christian Buddha* will in the case of each of his incarnations (incorporations) be a microcosmic reflection of the macrocosmic life of Christ, who was united with Jesus of Nazareth when he had reached the age of 30. Rudolf Steiner put this in the following way: 'All the incarnations of

---

[*] A bodhisattva being is, from a spiritual-scientific standpoint, extraordinarily complicated, much more so than many occultists suppose. For although from the earthly standpoint he appears as a highly evolved human being, from the standpoint of the spiritual world he is a being through whom spirits of the Third Hierarchy—Angeloi, Archangeloi and at times even Archai—are directly able to work (see GA 110, 16 April 1909–II). As a result a bodhisattva can under certain conditions function as a superhuman being (though on a microcosmic scale when compared to the macrocosmic Christ Being). Consideration of this hierarchic aspect of the bodhisattva nature lies beyond the scope of this work and would need a separate study.

[†] After Rudolf Steiner had characterized the complicated phenomenon of the incomplete 'incarnation' of a bodhisattva in lectures from 1909 (see GA 114, 20 September 1909, and GA 116, 25 October 1909), he often referred to it in subsequent years—for brevity's sake—simply as an 'incarnation'.

the bodhisattva who will become the Maitreya Buddha have shown that in this sense his life, too, will resemble that of Christ. It is never known during the childhood or youth of an individual* that he will become a bodhisattva.'[59] Hence from the standpoint of true occultism it is completely impossible to speak of the working of a bodhisattva through a human being who has not reached this year. For only from this year onwards does the bodhisattva begin to work through him and call forth a sudden and complete transformation within him. 'This transformation[60] occurs particularly between the thirtieth and thirty-third years. It can never be known beforehand that *precisely this body* [that is, this earthly bearer] *will be taken possession of by the bodhisattva.*'[61] It follows from this formulation that the bodhisattva can work through *various personalities*, both during their entire life from the age of 30 and also for a shorter time, in order to fulfil a particular task of some kind. This also happened at the beginning of the twentieth century. After the true task of the bodhisattva—the proclaiming of the Etheric Christ—had been completely blocked by the leaders of the Theosophical Society at the time,† another human being had to help him to fulfil it. Such a helper could in this case only be an initiate who was incarnated on the earth at the same time, who firstly knew from his own experience about the mystery of the bodhisattvas—that they are united with Christ in the higher worlds (see p. 369f.)—and secondly knew, again from his own experience, the mystery of the etheric Second Coming of Christ. Moreover, this initiate had to regard the proclaiming of this event as *his own task*. In other words: the task of such an initiate had in a certain sense to coincide with the mission of the bodhisattva, which would enable the latter—notwithstanding the impediments—to participate in the fulfilment of his task and, hence, bring his mission in the twentieth century to realization.

Such an initiate was Rudolf Steiner, who was to proclaim the Etheric Christ in the twentieth century out of the sources of Christian-Rosicrucian esotericism. Hence the Maitreya Bodhisattva was able to fulfil his essential task through him. In this case the earthly personality of Rudolf Steiner was not, so to speak, taken hold of 'from above', as happened with Jeshu ben Pandira and in all other cases, but Rudolf Steiner consciously gave the bodhisattva the possibility of fulfilling his

---

* In these words that Rudolf Steiner spoke in the autumn of 1911 is clearly contained an allusion to the affair of the 14-year-old Krishnamurti.

† This is not the place to speculate through which personality the bodhisattva would have worked in other circumstances.

mission through him *without* any exchange of personality or a sudden transformation of his being—as described above—taking place.*

Thus despite everything the proclaiming of the Etheric Christ in the twentieth century was accomplished. However, the culmination of this century was without doubt in the years 1910–13, when the combined activity of Rudolf Steiner and the bodhisattva was at its most intense. At this time Rudolf Steiner was directly inspired by the bodhisattva from the spiritual worlds, receiving his inspirations and collaborating with him in full consciousness. In this way the presence and influence of the bodhisattva through him at times became so intense that it is possible that a temporary astral incorporation took place (though without an exchange of personalities, which was possible as a result of the Rosicrucian initiation that Rudolf Steiner had received). In any event many anthroposophists who heard Rudolf Steiner's lectures at this time experienced the real, supersensible presence of the individuality of the bodhisattva in the room.[62] This was especially strongly the case at the end of the tenth lecture of the cycle on the Gospel of St Matthew, where Rudolf Steiner himself openly referred to the source of his inspirations, that is, to his supersensible connection with the bodhisattva: 'We must make ourselves receptive to the inspiration of the bodhisattva who will subsequently become the Maitreya Buddha. And this bodhisattva will inspire us by drawing attention to the near approach of the time when in a new form, in an *etheric* body, Christ will bring blessing to those who develop new [clairvoyant] faculties through a new Essene wisdom, the time when Christ's Second Coming in an etheric raiment will approach human beings in an enlivening way. We wish to speak entirely in the sense of the inspiring bodhisattva who is to become the Maitreya Buddha.'[63] And at the end of the same lecture he said: 'With the knowledge gained from the inspiration of the bodhisattva himself, we are declaring what form the future manifestation of Christ will take.' These words indicate with full clarity that Rudolf Steiner was at that time truly *inspired* by the bodhisattva, but he was *not* himself the bodhisattva and still less a reincarnation of Jeshu ben Pandira. Identifying the individuality of Rudolf Steiner with that of the Maitreya Bodhisattva would be a great mistake.[64] Rudolf Steiner belonged from the outset solely to the Rosicrucian stream, the principal stream of esoteric Christianity. On account of the three-year period of collaboration (from 1910 to 1913) with the bodhisattva on an occult plane something of great significance took place, namely a considerable degree of merging between the Western Rosicrucian stream and

---

*See further in S.O. Prokofieff, *Rudolf Steiner and the Founding of the New Mysteries*, ch. 3.

the Eastern stream of the Maitreya. This was accomplished by the great Christian initiate Rudolf Steiner, who united both streams for ever on the earth under the sign of their common service to the Etheric Christ. Hence already in 1911 he could say with justice: 'In this way the two streams work together, the stream of the Maitreya Buddha and the Western stream connected with Christian Rosenkreutz.'[65] For since this time they have been working together as a pledge for the future union of the West with the East.

Already in the year 1909 Rudolf Steiner was able, by virtue of *his own* spiritual research and his direct connection with the spiritual sphere of Christ, to experience the *beginning* of the etheric Second Coming in the higher worlds.[66] For this was at that time accessible only to the visionary perception of an initiate. From 1910 onwards he then began, *in conjunction with* the Maitreya Bodhisattva (out of his inspirations), to proclaim this event, so that this year may justly be called *the year of the proclamation of the Etheric Christ.*[*] Hence during this and the two subsequent years Rudolf Steiner again and again unites in his lectures three themes: that of the Second Coming, that of the Maitreya and that of Christian Rosenkreutz.[67]

When the proclamation had taken place and the bodhisattva—now that he had in this way *fulfilled* his task in the twentieth century *through Rudolf Steiner*—gradually diminished his inspirations and then, it would appear, again ascended into the higher worlds, the theme of the Maitreya almost completely disappeared from Rudolf Steiner's lectures. On the other hand, he continued to speak out of the sources of Rosicrucian esotericism about the etheric Second Coming of Christ again and again until his death.[68]

Rudolf Steiner deepened the theme of the etheric Second Coming throughout his life not through the inspirations of the Maitreya but through his own spiritual research, revealing in the process ever new aspects of it. Thus he spoke about the participation of the entelechy of Jesus of Nazareth (Krishna), the Archangel Vidar and the ruling Time Spirit of our age, Michael, in the etheric Second Coming;[69] revealed the connection between the future beholding of the Etheric Christ and the working of the Holy Spirit in the higher worlds;[70] referred to the connection between the appearance of the Etheric Christ and the quest for the new Isis, the divine Sophia, in spiritual science;[71] drew attention repeatedly to the influence of ahrimanic and luciferic beings working

---

[*] It should be said that the years 1910 and 1911, because of the large number of lectures devoted to this theme, formed the culmination of this deed of proclamation.

against the etheric Second Coming;[72] and set forth in detail the occult strategy of certain secret brotherhoods of the East and the West which serve them[73] and much more.[74]

Notes

1. See GA 114, 18 September 1909, also note 3.
2. Ibid.
3. See GA 142, 1 January 1913, and GA 146, 3 June 1913.
4. GA 152, 30 March 1914.
5. GA 266/2, the esoteric lesson of 20 September 1912.
6. See GA 113, 27 August 1909 and GA 124, 19 December 1910.
7. GA 109, 31 May 1909.
8. Ibid.
9. GA 109, 25 May 1909.
10. GA 124, 7 November 1910.
11. See GA 211, 24 April 1922.
12. See GA 123, 2 September 1910.
13. See GA 109, 31 May 1909.
14. Ibid.
15. Ibid.
16. See further in GA 114, 21 September 1909, and the undated esoteric lesson published in GA 264 under the title 'The Connection of the Masters with the Raisings of the Dead in the Gospels'.
17. GA 114, 21 September 1909.
18. See GA 13; GA 93, 7 October 1904; GA 103, 27 May 1908; GA 109, 31 May 1909; GA 114, 18 September 1909.
19. See GA 114, 18 September 1909 and 19 September 1909.
20. See GA 123, 4 September 1910.
21. Jean Overton Fuller, *Blavatsky and Her Teachers*, East-West Publications, London and The Hague 1988, p. 113. See also note 26.
22. *The Mahatma Letters to A.P. Sinnett*, third edition 1962 (pp. 43–4).
23. Quoted from the same volume, letter no. 10 (p. 58).
24. William Kingsland, *The Real H.P. Blavatsky*, ch. 6, London 1985.
25. *Letters from the Masters of the Wisdom*, first series, letter no. 1, Adyar, Madras, India, 1988 (p. 3).
26. Quoted from '*The K.H.' Letters to C.W. Leadbeater*, with a commentary by C. Jinarajadasa, Adyar, Madras, India, 1980.
27. A.P. Sinnett, *Esoteric Buddhism*, ch. 1, 'Esoteric Teachers', London 1972, also the quotations that follow.
28. From the letter to Olcott dated 6 December 1887, when Blavatsky had been working on her book *The Secret Doctrine*, quoted from *Personal Memoirs of H.P. Blavatsky*, compiled by Mary K. Neff, Rider and Co., London 1937, p. 256.
29. GA 264, pp. 255–6.
30. GA 52, 8 December 1904, also the following quotation.

31. See GA 105, 14 August 1908.

32. GA 137, 12 June 1912.

33. GA 114, especially the lecture of 25 September 1909.

34. GA 114, 18 September 1909.

35. GA 114, 20 September 1909, also the following quotation.

36. GA 113, 31 August 1909.

37. See GA 124, 13 March 1911.

38. Ibid.

39. Ibid.

40. GA 141, 22 December 1912, also the following quotations.

41. GA 52, 8 December 1904.

42. See GA 114, the lectures of 16, 17, 18 September 1909.

43. See ibid., and GA 15 chapter III.

44. See GA 114, 20 September 1909.

45. See GA 113, 31 August 1909.

46. See GA 141, 22 December 1912.

47. See GA 31 August 1909.

48. See GA 113, 31 August 1909; GA 124, 13 March 1911; GA 130, 19 September 1911.

49. GA 130, 21 September 1911.

50. GA 130, 4 November 1911.

51. See GA 123, 6 September 1910.

52. GA 130, 4 November 1911

53. Se GA 114, 20 September 1909.

54. Ibid.

55. GA 114, 17 September 1909.

56. GA 116, 25 October 1909.

57. GA 130, 21 September 1911, also the following quotations.

58. See GA 130, 4 November 1911.

59. GA 130, 21 September 1911.

60. See ibid., and GA 131, 14 October 1911. This age relates only to the Maitreya Bodhisattva and all subsequent bodhisattvas who will reach the buddha stage in the epochs *after* Christ's appearance on the earth.

61. GA 131, 14 October 1911.

62. See in this connection Adolf Arenson's lecture 'Rudolf Steiner und der Bodhisattva des 20. Jahrhunderts', published in: *Ergebnisse aus dem Studium der Geisteswissenschaft Rudolf Steiners* ('Results from the Study of Rudolf Steiner's Spiritual Science'), Book 2, Freiburg 1980. The same applies to other great teachers of humanity, whose supersensible presence would often be perceived when Rudolf Steiner spoke about them. Thus for example, in the course of the esoteric lesson that Rudolf Steiner gave in April 1909 in Düsseldorf during the lecture cycle *Spiritual Hierarchies and their Reflection in the Physical World. Zodiac, Planets, Cosmos* (GA 110), Elisabeth Vreede experienced the spiritual presence of the individuality of Zarathustra (the Master Jesus). See the lecture by Vreede of 9 July 1930, published in Thomas Meyer, *The Bodhisattva Question*, Temple Lodge, 1993. Some anthroposophists could also perceive the spiritual presence of

Christian Rosenkreutz when Rudolf Steiner spoke about him in Neuchâtel (lectures of 28 September 1911 and 18 December 1912).

63. GA 123, 10 September 1910, also the following quotation.

64. Rudolf Steiner expressed himself on this subject in replying to Günther Wagner's direct question during the Bern cycle quoted above: 'I am not.' This answer and a further one to a similar question posed to him somewhat later in Berlin are included in Thomas Meyer's book *The Bodhisattva Question*.

65. GA 130, 20 November 1911.

66. Rudolf Steiner spoke of this subsequently in the lecture of 6 February 1917 (GA 175).

67. See for example the lectures of 28 September 1911 and 20 November 1911 (GA 130).

68. See note 8 to chapter 6.

69. See the lectures of 1 January 1913 (GA 142), 17 June 1910 (GA 121) and 9 November 1914 (GA 158).

70. See the lecture of 14 April 1914 (GA 153).

71. See the lecture of 24 December 1920 (GA 202) and also S.O. Prokofieff, *The Heavenly Sophia and the Being Anthroposophia*, Temple Lodge, 1996.

72. See the lectures of 9 November 1914 (GA 158), 14 October 1917 (GA 177) and 28 March 1913 (GA 145).

73. See the lecture of 18 November 1917 (GA 178).

74. See note 8 to chapter 6.

9. Christian Rosenkreutz—the Leading Master of Esoteric Christianity

The great and deeply mysterious individuality of Christian Rosenkreutz occupies a central position in the circle of the esoteric servants of the Christ.

In our time it is only from what has been imparted by anthroposophy, representing as it does a modern continuation of *true* Rosicrucianism, that reliable information can be derived about the great founder of this latter impulse; for the spiritual stream founded by him unites *all* the Masters in our time who have been spoken of above.

Rudolf Steiner unfolded the mystery of the founding of this central stream of Christian esotericism for the first time in two lectures that he gave in Neuchâtel (Switzerland) in 1911 on the eve of Michaelmas Day.[1] In the first lecture he described the extraordinary initiation of the future Christian Rosenkreutz around the year 1250 and in the second the nature of the work of his pupils, that is, of all true Rosicrucians, in the ensuing centuries.

The founding of the Rosicrucian stream in the thirteenth century was conceived as the most important step on the path of implementing the spiritual plan that was developed and adopted at the council in the fourth century by the four leading teachers of Christian esotericism. The founding of this stream was necessary in order that all the ancient wisdom of mankind preserved since the time of ancient Atlantis might be renewed through the Christ impulse, which had been working in the spiritual aura of the earth since the Mystery of Golgotha.

However, this renewal happened in a particular way. Towards the end of the first half of the thirteenth century twelve wise men who were 'filled with the greatness of Christianity',[2] and were at the same time bearers of the whole of Atlantean and post-Atlantean wisdom,* came together in a secret place in Europe. 'They were convinced,' stated Rudolf Steiner, 'that the whole of spiritual life was contained in their twelve streams ... *Their aim was to achieve a synthesis of all the religions,* but they knew that this was not to be achieved by means of any theory but only as the result of

---

* Seven were guardians of the wisdom of the seven epochs of ancient Atlantis, four of the others were bearers—respectively—of the four post-Atlantean epochs and the fifth was a representative of the present, fifth epoch in prophetic form.

spiritual life,' and to this end a thirteenth was to join their circle. At the time this individual was still quite young and was growing up wholly under the care and educational supervision of the twelve, who knew that he had been incarnated at the Turning Point of Time and had personally been present at the Mystery of Golgotha. 'He had been incarnated at the time of the Mystery of Golgotha,' said Rudolf Steiner about him, thereby referring to the fact that in the personality of the thirteenth the individuality of the Apostle and Evangelist John, 'whom the Lord loved' (John 13:23) was again incarnated, he who was most deeply initiated into the mysteries of the living Christ.[3] During the highly specialized education that the thirteenth underwent under the leadership of the twelve, they were able to give him so much of their wisdom that finally his 'body ... became quite transparent, and for days he lay as though dead.' This signified that the all-embracing wisdom of the twelve received into his soul penetrated right into his physical body and completely took hold of his life body (etheric body). Because of this his life body became spiritualized to such an extent that it was no longer in a position to maintain the ordinary life activity of the physical body. From a spiritual standpoint, this was similar to what had formerly happened with Lazarus in the Gospel, who—as the beloved disciple of Christ—had received so much esoteric wisdom from him that he became ill, though from a quite particular illness which 'is not unto death; it is for the glory of God' (John 11:4). This was now repeated in the case of the thirteenth. For four days the twelve wise men gathered around him and let their most secret knowledge stream around him in short, mantric formulas, until he was filled with the wisdom of all twelve spiritual streams. And then a great miracle occurred, 'an event that could only happen once in history'. He awoke again after four days, but as a 'new soul'. Then the twelve could recognize from his words that his soul, filled with the ancient wisdom of mankind, had met Christ in the spiritual world and that He had completely transformed it and at the same time renewed the entirety of world wisdom which he bore not only in his soul *but also in his life body*. In other words, not only the soul (the astral body) but also the *etheric body* of the thirteenth was wholly transformed by the Christ.

Rudolf Steiner described what happened next in these words: 'In the course of a few weeks the thirteenth reproduced all the wisdom that he had received from the twelve, but in a new form. *This new form was as though given by Christ himself.* The twelve called what he now revealed to them true Christianity, the synthesis of all religions; and they distinguished between this true Christianity and the Christianity of the period in which they lived.' For through the thirteenth, the spiritual Sun of the world itself renewed the twelve aspects of world wisdom. And then the twelve said to themselves, in Rudolf Steiner's words: ' "Now, for the first time, the twelve religions and world conceptions have been given to us, united into one interconnected whole!" And henceforward what we call Rosicrucian Christianity lived in the twelve men.'[4]

The thirteenth himself died shortly after his initiation and was reborn in the following century. In this new incarnation he received the name Christian Rosenkreutz and founded the Rosicrucian stream, and his pupils—the first Rosicrucians—were the followers of the twelve.[5]

Christian Rosenkreutz's leadership in the circle of the Masters of esoteric Christianity was acknowledged at a council which assembled in the Alps on the eve of Good Friday 1380. Twelve leading Masters of Christian humanity gathered in a little, barely accessible chapel high in the mountains, in accordance with an indication from the spiritual worlds.

Some scanty reports of this council also reached the outside world, thanks to a strictly confidential letter of the Friend of God from the High Lands (the Master Jesus) to his pupil Rulman Merswin, who did not take part in the gathering. (The letter has been preserved to this day in a Strassburg monastery.) This letter was published and commented upon by the anthroposophical author Wilhelm Rath in his book *The Friend of God from the High Lands*.[6] When he was working on the book, the possibility emerged for him to ask Rudolf Steiner some questions relating to his theme. The conversation took place in Stuttgart on 16 October 1922. Wilhelm Rath recounted it as follows. In answer to a question about the significance of the gathering of twelve high Friends of God with the already very elderly Friend of God from the High Lands at Easter 1380, described in the last letter of the Friend of God, Rudolf Steiner said: 'You see, this is where you have the change to Rosicrucianism. It is the same thing that is pointed to in Goethe's poem "The Mysteries". Since that time [that is, since the gathering of the twelve leading representatives of Christianity at Easter 1380 referred to by the Friend of God from the High Lands in his last letter][7] Christian Rosenkreutz has become the leading personality in the [Christian] spiritual life of the West. Both he and the Master Jesus, the Friend of God from the High Lands, have been incarnated in every century since then. They incarnate in turns every century, *and from that time the Master Jesus has worked in the same way as Christian Rosenkreutz*.'[8]

The most important and in a certain sense most esoteric result of the initiation of Christian Rosenkreutz in the thirteenth century is that his etheric body, wholly permeated as it was by the Christ impulse, was preserved in the spiritual world. In the ensuing centuries the spiritual forces of this etheric body were considerably strengthened by the spiritual work of many generations of true Rosicrucians. 'Through the work of Rosicrucians the etheric body of Christian Rosenkreutz became ever stronger and mightier from century to century. It worked not only through Christian Rosenkreutz but through all those who became his pupils.'[9]

As a great proclaimer of Rosicrucian wisdom in the twentieth century, Rudolf Steiner also worked out of the inspirations of this etheric body. He expressed this in a wholly objective and matter-of-fact way in the first Neuchâtel lecture: 'Everything that is made known in the name of theosophy is strengthened by the etheric body of Christian Rosenkreutz, *and those who make theosophy known let themselves be overshadowed by this etheric body*, which is able to exert an influence upon them both when Christian Rosenkreutz is incarnated and also when he is not.'

★

However, it was a year later that Rudolf Steiner revealed to anthroposophists a particularly important mystery regarding the influence of the Rosicrucian stream in the world, again in Neuchâtel, in the lecture of 18 December 1912. Here he referred to a further gathering of leading Rosicrucians which took place at the end of the sixteenth century in Europe, to which Christian Rosenkreutz summoned all twelve of those who had participated in his initiation in the thirteenth century and also the participants at the council in the fourth century. Thus the individuality of Gautama Buddha again took part in this gathering by being present in his spirit body (Nirmanakaya). Rudolf Steiner spoke about this as follows: 'This conference was well prepared by Christian Rosenkreutz in that the *closest friend and pupil of Christian Rosenkreutz, Gautama Buddha, was [present] in a spirit body.*'[10]

The reason why this conference was necessary was that Western humanity was moving inevitably towards a separation of people into two diametrically opposite categories: one-sided mystics with only spiritual interests and not concerning themselves with earthly affairs, and no less one-sided practical materialists with an interest only in earthly matters. From an occult point of view this split was the direct consequence of the negative spiritual influences upon the earth deriving since the beginning of modern times from the planet Mars. If this division within mankind was to be avoided, it was necessary that a reorientation of the spiritual forces of Mars with regard to the earth should come about. However, this could result only through a quite definite event which—with respect to the situation developing on Mars at that time—may be referred to as a kind of little Mystery of Golgotha; and the individuality of Gautama Buddha was allotted the task of accomplishing it.[*] Rudolf Steiner described this in the following way: 'The individuality Buddha was, as it were, sent by Christian Rosenkreutz from the earth to Mars ... and he accomplished for Mars a deed similar to what the Mystery of Golgotha was for the earth.'[†] And Rudolf Steiner continued, directing his gaze to Christian Rosenkreutz who sent Gautama Buddha to Mars: 'Christian Rosenkreutz is thus revealed to us as the great servant of Christ Jesus; but what Buddha, as the emissary of Christian Rosenkreutz, was destined to contribute to the work of Christ Jesus had also to come to the help of the work accomplished by Christian Rosenkreutz in the service of Christ Jesus. Thus the soul of Gautama Buddha has not again been in physical incarnation on the earth [since the sixth century before the birth of Christ], but it is utterly dedicated to the Christ impulse.' Only as a result of this sacrificial deed of the Buddha on Mars was it possible for a balance between the spiritual and practical activities of human beings on the earth to be reached; and the consequence of this in the esoteric domain was that it was possible for mankind in the twentieth century to find that inner path of inner development which, by uniting both polarities in itself, was given by Rudolf Steiner as the modern path of Christian-Rosicrucian initiation. He himself referred to this in the same lecture: 'The book *Knowledge of the Higher Worlds* describes the Western path of development that is compatible with practical activities of every kind. Today I have indicated that a basic factor in these matters is the mission assigned to Gautama Buddha by Christian Rosenkreutz, for I have spoken of the significant influence which the sending of Buddha to Mars exercised in our solar system.'

At the end of this extraordinary lecture Rudolf Steiner spoke, again in a completely objective form, about his relationship to Christian Rosenkreutz, while at the same time giving expression to his great respect for the high mission and the worldwide influence of this sublime human individuality: '*And those who are able to draw near to Christian Rosenkreutz* see with reverent wonder the consistent way in which he has carried out the great mission entrusted to him, which in our time is the Christian-Rosicrucian path of development. That the great teacher of Nirvana is now fulfilling a mission outside the earth, on Mars—this is one of the deeds of Christian Rosenkreutz.'

---

[*] In the present work only a brief characterization of the events concerned can be given. A detailed description may be found in the lecture by Rudolf Steiner referred to.

[†] Buddha's departure to Mars, from whose sphere he has ever since spiritually influenced the earth, happened in 1604 (ibid.).

In the same lecture, Rudolf Steiner said of this mighty imagination of the great teacher of the West, who—surrounded by the twelve Masters of esoteric Christianity—sent the great teacher of the East to Mars, that meditative concentration upon it is a path whereby every modern human being today may become a personal pupil of Christian Rosenkreutz.

★

The central mystery associated with the initiation of Christian Rosenkreutz in the thirteenth century consisted in the arising of his special etheric body, which—wholly filled with the forces of the cosmic Christ—has been in the aura of the earth since the Mystery of Golgotha. As the spiritual forces of this etheric body have been strengthened over the centuries through the intense esoteric work both of Christian Rosenkreutz himself and also of his own pupils, the spiritual emanation of this etheric body has from the twentieth century onwards had a significant part to play *in the most important supersensible event of our time, the event which Rudolf Steiner designated as the new appearance of Christ in the etheric body, as the renewal of that spiritual experience of the living Christ which the Apostle Paul had on the road to Damascus* (see Acts, ch. 9).

Rudolf Steiner said in this regard: 'The twentieth century has the task of enabling this etheric body [of Christian Rosenkreutz] to become so powerful that it can also work exoterically [that is, outside the small circles of Rosicrucians where it has worked hitherto]. Those affected by it will be granted the experience of the event that Paul experienced on the road to Damascus. Until now this etheric body has only exerted an influence upon the Rosicrucian school; in the twentieth century more and more people will be able to experience the effect of it, and through this they will come to experience the appearance of Christ in the etheric body. It is the work of the Rosicrucians that makes possible the etheric vision of Christ. The number of those who will become capable of seeing it will grow and grow. We must attribute this to the important work of the twelve and the thirteenth in the thirteenth and fourteenth centuries.'[11] These words are a further testimony of the deep relationship existing between true Rosicrucianism and the central event of our time—the etheric appearance of Christ on the astral plane.

According to Rudolf Steiner's spiritual research, the beginning of the supersensible appearance of Christ was in 1909. In a later lecture in Berlin in 1918 he spoke about this as follows: 'The occultist can indicate quite precisely that since 1909 what is to come [the etheric appearance of

Christ] has been in preparation in a clearly perceptible way, that since 1909 we have been living in a quite particular time. Moreover, it is possible today—if one merely seeks this—to be very close to Christ, to find Him in an altogether different way from how He was found in earlier times.'[12] This makes it easier to understand why Rudolf Steiner revealed such profound mysteries of Christian-Rosicrucian occultism in his lectures in precisely this year.

But this is not all; for the reference to 1909 can also shed much light upon the esoteric foundations of the entire escapade with Krishnamurti, which was the result of a real occult opposition. On the one hand, we have in this year in the spiritual world, on the astral plane, the *beginning* of Christ's Second Coming in a supersensible body and, on the other, on the earth the counter-picture of this event, the presenting by Leadbeater of the 14-year-old Indian Krishnamurti as the future bearer of the *physically incarnated* Christ and the beginning of the proclaiming of the new Messiah by Annie Besant.*

If, in accordance with the letter to Edouard Schuré quoted above, we are to seek the reason for the Krishnamurti affair in the opposition of Leadbeater and Besant—under the influence of their occult leaders—to the revelation of the sources of wisdom of Western, Christian-Rosicrucian occultism, we are confronted with a still deeper reason for the sudden appearance of Krishnamurti in the endeavour of these occult circles of the East actively to oppose the *etheric* appearance of Christ by replacing it with a false *physical* Messiah.

Here again we are presented with the difficult question: what is the significance—bearing in mind all that has just been said—of the separation of the Western and Eastern teachers described above (see p. 386), which took place only two years before these events? Or to put it in another way: what was the relationship, if any, of the two Eastern mahatmas, who continued to be the occult leaders of Annie Besant and of the Esoteric School which she led, to the new appearance of Christ in the etheric? The theosophical literature to which we have access, which refers back in one way or another to the mahatmas in question, gives no answer to this question. *It contains no word about the etheric advent of Christ in the twentieth century.* On the contrary, both Annie Besant and also Charles Leadbeater, Helena Roerich and Alice Bailey constantly refer to indications and advice which they claim to have received directly from these Eastern mahatmas and their pupils, making all the while repeated attempts to

---

* As will be shown later on, for Leadbeater and Besant the Christ and the future Maitreya Buddha are one and the same individuality.

prepare for the appearance on earth of a *physical* Messiah, be it Krishna-murti or someone else.*

We shall consider the question that has been posed here as this present book proceeds. What needs to be emphasized here to begin with is the direct relationship of *all Western teachers* who belong to the stream of Rosicrucian esotericism and who have been spoken of above with the etheric appearance of Christ. For they all, without exception, are the great servants of the Etheric Christ and participate in the new mysteries in the spiritual worlds or on the earth. Thus much of what Rudolf Steiner spoke in those years out of the sources of esoteric Christianity he said, as he himself put it, 'with regard to what the Masters have taught about our working our way upward to Christ, who will appear [for all human beings] even in this century on the astral plane'.†

Similarly in other lectures, Rudolf Steiner referred on several occasions to how in the circles of true Rosicrucians and, of course, in the first instance, among the teachers and leaders of this stream—especially from the thirteenth century onwards—there existed a knowledge of the future appearance of Christ in etheric form, which would begin in the twentieth century (the first century after the end of the Kali Yuga) and will continue over the next three thousand years.[13]

Thus the next three thousand years will also be an epoch of the uniting of all world religions and world conceptions on the foundation of a direct perception of the Etheric Christ as the highest divine guide of earthly evolution. In anticipation of this distant future, the spiritual foundation for the future uniting of all earthly religions within the vessel of esoteric Christianity was laid at Christian Rosenkreutz's initiation in the thirteenth century by the group of twelve. But as we have seen, this aim could be fulfilled only through the uniting of the Rosicrucian stream with the high wisdom streaming to humanity directly from the bodhisattva sphere, as had been decided at the gathering convened by Manes in the fourth century.

However, actually bringing about this synthesis of all religions encompassed by earthly humanity can only begin in the twentieth century under the influence of the strengthening of the etheric body of

---

* Regarding Bailey see Part Two. Helena Roerich was less concerned with the coming of Christ in the physical body, since she saw her task as preparing for the appearance among human beings of a quite different individuality from the future Messiah or world Teacher.
† From 1909 onwards the Christ could be beheld solely by initiates; only from the 1930s could He also be perceived by other human beings as a result of a naturally developing clairvoyance.

Christian Rosenkreutz as described above. 'This etheric body has the purpose of influencing the development of Christianity in its true form as the synthesis of all the great religions and world-conceptions,' said Rudolf Steiner.[14]

Hence the uniting of all religions and world-conceptions within Rosicrucian Christianity is directly associated with Christ's appearance in the etheric body: 'What was given in the different religious creeds has been gathered into a single whole by Christian Rosenkreutz and the group of twelve. This means that everything that the separate religions had to give and all that their followers strove and longed for will be found in the Christ impulse. Development during the next three thousand years will consist in this: the establishing and furthering of an understanding of the Christ impulse. From the twentieth century onwards *all religions* will be united in the Rosicrucian mystery. This will become possible over the course of the next three thousand years because it will no longer be necessary to teach humanity from documents, for through [clairvoyantly] beholding [the etheric] Christ human beings will themselves learn to understand the experience that Paul had on the road to Damascus. Mankind will itself pass through the experience of Paul.'[15]

Thus from the twentieth century onwards and then over the course of the next three millennia, all religions will begin to unite upon the foundation of esoteric (Rosicrucian) Christianity *in the light of the knowledge of the Etheric Christ.*

A start was made with this union in the twentieth century by Rudolf Steiner with his spiritual-scientific research concerning the participation of all the great teachers of humanity in the preparations for the appearance of Christ on the earth and the Mystery of Golgotha, for example of Manu, Zarathustra, Krishna, Gautama Buddha, Scythianos, Manes, Orpheus, Hermes Trismegistos, Abraham, Moses, and many, many others (some of these have been considered in chapter 8).

However, the main task of Rudolf Steiner and of the whole of spiritual science or anthroposophy that he founded was without doubt the *proclaiming* of the appearance of Christ in the etheric body as the most important spiritual event of our time and the *preparing* of all people of good will for it as a foundation for the further evolution of mankind.

Notes

1. Lectures of 27 and 28 September 1911 (GA 130).
2. GA 130, 27 September 1911, likewise the following quotations.
3. GA 265, p. 456.

4. GA 130, 20 November 1911.

5. Ibid., also the lecture of 27 September 1911 (GA 130). The history of the founding of Rosicrucianism in the fourteenth century is also described in the tracts of Johann Valentin Andreae *Fama Fraternitatis* (1614), *Confessio Fraternitatis* (1615). They are published in *Quellen und Forschungen zur württembergischen Kirchengeschichte*, Vol. 6, Stuttgart 1981 [and in *A Christian Rosenkreutz Anthology* edited by Paul M. Allen].

6. Published in English translation by Hawthorn Press, Stroud 1991.

7. Ibid.

8. GA 264, p. 225.

9. GA 130, 27 September 1911, also the following quotation.

10. GA 130, 18 December 1912, also the following quotations.

11. GA 130, 27 September 1911.

12. GA 175, 6 February 1917.

13. See for example the lectures of 7 October 1911 (GA 131), 1 October 1911 (GA 130) and 18 April 1910 (GA 118).

14. GA 130, 20 November 1911.

15. GA 130, 28 September 1911.

10. The Founding of the Anthroposophical Society. The Revelation of the Michael Mysteries

From everything that has been said in the previous chapters it follows once again with full clarity that Rudolf Steiner from the outset, also within the Theosophical Society, was representing Christian-Rosicrucian occultism alone, which sooner or later necessarily led to a conflict with the then leaders of the Theosophical Society, who increasingly adopted an openly antichristian path. Thus already at the beginning of 1911 G. Arundale, a pupil and follower of Leadbeater, with the latter's blessing and with the active support of Annie Besant founded the new 'Order of the Rising Sun' within the Theosophical Society, which later the same year was renamed the 'Star of the East', the main aim of which was to serve as an instrument for the preparation and publicizing of the new Messiah.

Rudolf Steiner, on the other hand, was at that time giving powerful Christological lectures such as the cycle *From Jesus to Christ*,[1] which revealed the cosmic significance of the mystery of Christ's Resurrection, publishing the book mentioned above, *The Spiritual Guidance of Man and Humanity* (see p. 415), where he writes about the participation of Zarathustra and Gautama Buddha in the preparation of the events of Palestine in addition to proclaiming the *etheric* appearance of Christ, giving lectures about Christian Rosenkreutz's initiation in the thirteenth century and about the Christian mission of the Maitreya Bodhisattva in the twentieth century,[2] and at the end of the year was beginning with the organization of an esoteric group which, if the necessary trials had been successfully withstood, was to take up direct contact with Christian Rosenkreutz.[*]

---

[*] This was a small group of eight pupils of the Esoteric School. The connection with Christian Rosenkreutz was to be established in such a way that it could exist independently of him (Rudolf Steiner). Rudolf Steiner had received Christian Rosenkreutz's agreement for this. However, this initiative failed because of a moral error of one of its members. If one makes oneself familiar with the material which has now been published concerning the founding of this esoteric group (see further in GA 264, 'An Esoteric-Social Impulse for the Future. An Attempt towards founding a Society for Theosophical Style and Art', 15 December 1911), one is struck by the unusual strictness—almost harshness—and the extraordinary seriousness with which Rudolf Steiner set about the undertaking of this task. For any moral deviation from the high purpose of this group immediately made it impossible to continue. It is apparent here how sharply the character of the relationship in Western esotericism to the Masters responsible differs from that pertaining in the East; thus for example Blavatsky once went down on her knees in front of the mahatmas and on another occasion mockingly referred to them as 'bosses'.

As a result of Rudolf Steiner's many-sided activity, his influence and authority within the Theosophical Society steadily grew. Marie von Sivers, who personally took part in the dramatic events, subsequently described the consequences as follows: 'The Theosophical Society was alarmed. It saw the deep effect of Steiner's teaching on souls in search of Christ. It did not want to expose its members to this, it did not want to expose them to the danger of taking in Steiner's teachings, thus becoming unfaithful to the orientalizing stream.'[3] Thus the conflict was unavoidable.

A first symptom of the conflict was Annie Besant's sudden cancellation of the regular congress of the European Sections of the Theosophical Society that had been planned to take place in Bologna in the autumn of 1911. The reason for the cancellation was obvious. For Annie Besant had intended personally to introduce Krishnamurti to the participants as the new Messiah and the head of the Order 'Star of the East', whereas Rudolf Steiner wanted to give a lecture on the true relationship of the Christ Being to Gautama Buddha and the Maitreya Bodhisattva, with as its culmination a detailed description of the bodhisattva sphere and its relationship to the Christ. Despite the cancellation of the congress, Rudolf Steiner nevertheless spoke about this theme in Lugano and Locarno on his way to Italy, and he then gave his Bologna lecture entitled 'Buddha and Christ. The Sphere of the Bodhisattvas' in Milan.[4]

The polarization between truth and error in the central question of knowledge of the Christ Being nevertheless intensified; for in matters of truth no compromises are possible in modern occultism.

In spite of everything Rudolf Steiner tried to exercise patience in 1912, though without for a moment compromising with what were for him the blatant errors of the leaders of the Theosophical Society. The reason for this was that he had received an indication from the Western masters that he should remain in the Society for as long as possible and campaign for truth *within* it.

In the esoteric lesson that he gave on 20 September 1912, Rudolf Steiner referred directly to the circumstance that 'according to the advice [in another set of notes from the lesson the word 'judgement' in the sense of 'verdict' is used] of the Masters [we] should remain [in the Theosophical Society]'.[5] But when he categorically refused to receive members of the 'Star of the East' into the German Section which he led, the solution took its own course.

Rudolf Steiner subsequently described what happened next in his autobiography *The Course of My Life*: 'For the propagation of this absurdity, a special society was formed within the Theosophical Society, that of the "Star of the East". It was utterly impossible for me and my friends to include membership of this "Star of the East" as a branch of the German Section, as they desired and as Annie Besant, President of the Theosophical Society, especially intended. Since we could not do this, we were excluded in 1913 from the Theosophical Society. We were forced to found the Anthroposophical Society as an independent body.'[6]

For Rudolf Steiner this exclusion from the Theosophical Society was a real liberation; for as he himself had said, he had on three occasions been seriously confronted with the question whether he could continue working in this Society.[*] The first occasion had been after the scandal around Leadbeater, the second was after the scandal caused by the appearance of the mahatmas with the dying Olcott, and the third arose because Krishnamurti was proclaimed as the new Messiah.

The situation worsened in the following years. First Annie Besant tried to draw Rudolf Steiner into participating in the 'Star of the East' by suggesting that he be officially declared in this case as a reincarnation of John the Evangelist.[7] After Rudolf Steiner had categorically rejected this absurdity, Annie Besant resorted to an outright lie. She explained that Rudolf Steiner, supposedly, had the intention of going to India where, through some sort of 'coup d'état', he would seize power over the whole Society, despite the fact that Rudolf Steiner had explained to Annie Besant personally and before witnesses that under no circumstances did he want to, or would, work anywhere except in Central Europe.[8] When even this did not get her anywhere, she publicly called Rudolf Steiner a 'Jesuit novice'[9]—an absurd assertion to make about someone who in his youth had defended Nietzsche and Haeckel[10] and who subsequently spoke about Jesuits and their occult practices as, for example, he did in the first lecture of the cycle *From Jesus to Christ* and in many other lectures.[11]

However, it is clearly apparent from what has already been said that this campaign of lies and slander unleashed by Annie Besant actually had an altogether different foundation and can—as we have seen—be traced back to the desperate efforts on the part of Eastern occultism to suppress Western occultism by discrediting its principal representative, a method which the Jesuits themselves used several times in their embittered struggle against anthroposophy.[12]

Rudolf Steiner's exclusion from the Theosophical Society did not disturb the rhythm of his work for a moment and brought about hardly any change in his work as such. In place of the German Section an

---

[*] See his address on 14 December 1911 to the General Meeting of the German Section of the Theosophical Society in Berlin (GA 264).

independent free Anthroposophical Society was founded, whose task it was to bring anthroposophy into the world as the modern teaching of the wisdom of esoteric Christianity. Rudolf Steiner subsequently described this as follows: 'They [anthroposophists] didn't mind that [being excluded from the Theosophical Society] because it didn't change anthroposophy in any way. I myself had never presented anything but anthroposophy to those interested in hearing about it, and that includes the period during which anthroposophy was *outwardly* included within the Theosophical Society.'[13] Thus in his article 'The Mission of Spiritual Science and of its Building in Dornach' Rudolf Steiner could say with complete justice: 'I now wish to say something about the development of our Anthroposophical Society, because errors have been circulated on the subject. For instance, it is said that our Anthroposophical Society is only a kind of development out of what is called the "Theosophical Society". Although it is true that what we aim at within our Anthroposophical Society found its place for a time within the framework of the general Theosophical Society, yet our Anthroposophical Society must on no account be confused with the Theosophical Society.' For 'that which now forms the substance of our anthroposophical view of the world, as studied in our circle of members, is not borrowed from the Theosophical Society but was represented by me as something entirely independent which—as a result of that Society's invitation—took place within it, until it was found heretical and was "shown the door" ... Thus it is an entirely erroneous conception to confuse in any way what is living within the Anthroposophical Society with what is represented by Blavatsky and Besant.'[14]

Marie von Sivers, co-founder of the independent Anthroposophical Society, herself recalled: 'At Christmas 1912 there took place in Cologne the first official union of those supporters of a theosophical outlook who were not minded to disappear into a dogmatic Indian stream but—on the basis of the achievements of the cultural life of modern times and the radical new impulse that was given to earthly evolution by the Christ event—could only recognize a spiritual schooling for the West which is appropriate for the developmental condition of present-day European humanity ...'[15]

Rudolf Steiner chose as the theme of his lectures for this founding conference 'The Bhagavadgita and the Epistles of Paul'.[16] In this cycle of five lectures he dwelt at some length upon the spiritual content of this great Indian poem, which is a synthesis of the three oldest Eastern streams of Vedanta, Yoga and Sankya and altogether represents 'the highest flower of an age that was passing away',[17]* in contrast to the epistles of Paul, which 'flicker like a tiny flame' that nevertheless testifies to the dawning of a new world day, a new cosmic epoch, whose foundation was laid by the Mystery of Golgotha.

The description of the mysteries of Krishna and of his further evolution formed without doubt the high point of the entire cycle. Thus in the last lecture of the cycle on 1 January 1913 Rudolf Steiner for the first time referred to his sole, complete earthly incarnation as Jesus of Nazareth, the future bearer of the Sun Logos, the Christ, on earth. 'For this reason precisely this lecture cycle has been placed at the starting point of this anthroposophical movement [Society]; for it can furnish the proof that [in anthroposophy] we are not dealing with something narrow but that through our movement we are able to extend our horizon beyond those bounds which Eastern thinking is capable of fathoming.'[18]

The laying of the foundation stone of the 'Johannes-Bau' (Goetheanum) on 20 September 1913 in Dornach, representing the first outwardly visible *Rosicrucian temple* of modern times, was among the most significant events of the year 1913.[19] In this year, too, Rudolf Steiner spoke for the first time about the cosmic preliminary stages of the Mystery of Golgotha, and he also began to give indications from the 'Fifth Gospel', that is, a description of the earthly life of Christ Jesus as preserved in the spiritual worlds in the Akashic Record.[20]

In the present book it is particularly important to consider one episode of the earthly life of Jesus of Nazareth from the Fifth Gospel. According to the Akashic Record, from his twenty-fourth year onwards Jesus began for a while to approach the Essene Order and even attended its meetings without, however, becoming a member of it. After one of his visits to the Essenes, Gautama Buddha appeared to him in the spirit† and said to him in a conversation in the spirit what Rudolf Steiner recounted in these words: 'If my teaching, as it actually is, were to be led to full fruition, then all human beings would have to lead the life of the Essenes. But that cannot be. That was the error in my teaching.'[21] For 'on the path that I have

---

* Three months previously Rudolf Steiner had already indicated: 'Krishna, [the] great Indian teacher who appears to us ... as the end-point of the revelations of millennia' (GA 139, 19 September 1912).

† From a karmic, occult point of view, this supersensible encounter was brought about by the fact that Gautama had already been a pupil of Krishna while still a bodhisattva in previous incarnations, with the result that—after he had attained Buddhahood in the sixth century AD—he was able to show human beings the path leading back to that higher world (before the Fall) of which and *from which* Krishna had spoken several millennia before (see GA 139, 19 September 1912).

given to humanity, not *all* human beings can have a relationship with the divine-spiritual world'.[22] In other words, this was an indication from Gautama himself that in place of the principle of liberation for a few chosen ones that he had brought into the world there was to come the other principle of *resurrection* attainable by everyone. For the principle of liberation leads mankind into the past, back to the lost paradise to that state before the Fall towards which the Essenes aspired—though at the cost of the rest of humanity—and which Jesus of Nazareth brought again to the earth. The principle of a general resurrection, on the other hand, which came into the world through the union of the Christ descending from the sun with Jesus, and through Christ Jesus' deed in passing through death and Resurrection on Golgotha, is wholly of the future and directed towards the events described in the Book of Revelation, as Rudolf Steiner explained at some length in the lecture cycle devoted to a spiritual-scientific study of the Revelation of St John.[23]

It was to this need for a complete reorientation of mankind from the past to the future that Gautama Buddha referred during his conversation with Jesus of Nazareth from the spiritual world. And the 'error' in Buddha's teaching referred to was corrected in its entirety when the Buddha himself, in accordance with Christian Rosenkreutz's summons, transferred his field of activity to Mars in 1604 and, in imitation of Christ, fulfilled something of the nature of a minor Mystery of Golgotha. Through this he has achieved since then the possibility of exerting an influence from the Mars sphere upon the souls of *all* human beings who are passing through this sphere between two earthly incarnations, a deed which he carries out for the healing of earthly evolution and in the name of fulfilling 'the intentions of the living Christ'. 'Thus Gautama Buddha, now working from Mars, is one of the great servants of Christ Jesus.'[24]

In conclusion, a further theme from this year also needs to be considered. From 1913 onwards it ran in all subsequent years like a golden thread through Rudolf Steiner's spiritual-scientific research and culminated in the final years of his earthly life. It is the theme of how the Archangel Michael,[*] the Countenance of Christ, the most significant servant of Christ in the spiritual worlds who in exoteric Christianity is venerated as the archstrategist and leader of the heavenly hosts, became in 1879 the Time Spirit of our epoch, and it includes his participation in preparing for Christ's Second Coming in the etheric body.

In his lectures from May 1913 in London and Stuttgart[25] Rudolf

---

[*] Rudolf Steiner had hitherto only touched upon this theme in esoteric lessons within the context of the Esoteric School (see p. 388).

Steiner spoke for the first time concretely and at length about the
heavenly mission of Michael as the leading Sun Archangel and highest
inspirer of the new, cosmic Christianity in our time. Michael it was who
in pre-Christian times from the spiritual worlds prepared the descent of
the Sun Logos to the earth and the Mystery of Golgotha, in order in our
time, with the beginning of the present epoch of his rulership over
humanity,* to endow mankind with the new spiritual light, the light that
leads to a true knowledge of the Christ events: 'Michael can give us new
spiritual light which may be regarded as a transformation of the light that
was given through the Mystery of Golgotha, and human beings today can
receive that light,'[26] said Rudolf Steiner. The initial manifestation of this
light is the modern spiritual knowledge which has come to humanity in
the form of spiritual science or anthroposophy and which is oriented
towards knowledge of the Christ. Thus Michael, the great cosmic servant
and emissary of Christ, sends human beings today 'increasing spiritual
revelations that will shed more and more light upon the Mystery of
Golgotha' with the help of 'spiritual knowledge, *our gift from Michael*'.

As for Rudolf Steiner's relationship to Michael, the following can be
said about it. In the course of his initiation process, whose starting point was
his meeting with Christian Rosenkreutz†—an event which for Rudolf
Steiner was associated with the beginning of a conscious mastery of the
world of *imaginations* and culminated in an encounter with Christ in
Intuition (see p. 367—Rudolf Steiner also necessarily had to pass through
the realm of *inspirations* in order there to meet face to face with the spiritual
leader of the present epoch, the 'Countenance of Christ', Michael. *For in
our time the fully conscious path to Christ is through the Michael sphere.*

It was Christian Rosenkreutz who showed Rudolf Steiner this path of
spiritual development. For it had always been the innermost striving of all
true Rosicrucians to encounter Michael in the spiritual worlds, in order
then to become his servant on earth and thus rightly prepare the future
epoch of his leadership of earthly evolution. 'True Rosicrucianism lies
absolutely in the line of activity of the Michael mission. It helped Michael
to prepare on earth the spirit-work which he wished to prepare for a later
age.'[27]

---

* According to the teaching of esoteric Christianity, which has been verified and confirmed by modern spiritual research, seven Archangels—succeeding one another in turn—
lead mankind, and the mightiest of these is the Archangel Michael (see GA 152, 240 and
243).
† This meeting took place in Vienna at the beginning of the 1880s, that is, immediately
after the beginning of the present Michael epoch. See Sergei O. Prokofieff, *Rudolf Steiner
and the Founding of the New Mysteries*, ch. 2.

Before the beginning of the modern epoch of Michael's rulership and during its preparation, however, true Rosicrucians were only able to encounter Michael in a dim, dreamy state of consciousness. Encountering him *in full consciousness* became possible only with the beginning of this epoch, that is, since the year 1879: 'The old Rosicrucian movement is characterized by the fact that its most illumined spirits had an intense longing to meet Michael [in the spiritual world]; but they could only do so, as it were, in a dreamy state. Since the end of the last third of the nineteenth century, human beings can meet Michael in the spirit, in a fully conscious way.'[28]

★

One of the first who was worthy of such a meeting was Rudolf Steiner. By following the spiritual path indicated by his teacher, he had necessarily sooner or later to arrive at such a conscious encounter with Michael in the spiritual world bordering upon the earth, a world which at that time was separated from the world of human beings only by a thin veil. Only at the end of his life, less than a year before his death, did Rudolf Steiner refer on one occasion to this first encounter with Michael, which he had in the period between his thirtieth and thirty-first years: 'Behind a veil separating the physical world from the adjoining spiritual domain there were momentous happenings, grouped around the spirit-being whom we call Michael ... Participating in these happenings were strong and forceful followers of Michael ... but there were also mighty demonic powers, who under the sway of ahrimanic influences set themselves in rebellion against what was to come into the world through Michael ... I lived through what was taking place in this world behind the veil, in this sphere of Michael's activity.'[29] And what was taking place was what Rudolf Steiner later described in ten lectures as Michael's battle with the ahrimanic dragon. The aim of this battle was to free that path whereby the Etheric Christ was to approach mankind from the ahrimanic powers.[30]

What has just been said makes it easier to understand from what source Rudolf Steiner derived his knowledge about the influence of the forces of evil in the world. This lay in his understanding that, just as the revealing of the mysteries of death is associated with the Mystery of Golgotha and their overcoming with the Resurrection of Christ, so was the revelation to humanity of the mystery of evil connected with Christ's etheric manifestation and the gradual overcoming of evil with the powers of goodness in a truly Michaelic sense (that is, with the help of the spiritual powers bestowed by Michael).[31] For these two factors—the true knowledge of evil through the etheric appearance of Christ (only the brightest light makes the darkest shadows visible) and also the path of the overcoming of evil, which Michael makes manifest to humanity through his gift of anthroposophy—form the occult foundation of Rudolf Steiner's spiritual-scientific research concerning the various categories of the powers of evil and their influence within man in earthly history and in the cosmos.

Hence not merely in dozens but in many hundreds of lectures—and, moreover, in a very concrete and detailed way—Rudolf Steiner characterized the aims of the opposing powers and the nature of their influence, illumining them with the light of Michael-Christ and making their most secret intentions visible.[*] For every human being today must—if he is to find his path into the future in the sense of the 'intentions of the living Christ'—*know* the aims and the manner of influence of the principal categories of Christ's adversaries, the aims of Lucifer, Ahriman and the Asuras[32] together with the chief opponent of Christ in our cosmos standing behind them and inspiring them, the sun demon Sorat, whom the Book of Revelation portrays as the beast with the number 666.[33] In this sense, knowledge about them is a first and extraordinarily important step on the path towards their overcoming, for the influence of the powers of evil in the world is the stronger if only few people know of their existence.

There is truly nothing in the modern world to compare with what Rudolf Steiner accomplished in this realm and—as one can indeed say—accomplished on behalf of Michael-Christ. This becomes especially clear if one compares the results of his spiritual research with what traditional Eastern teachings or the teachings of the Eastern mahatmas—in so far as they are contained in their own letters[†] or in the works of Blavatsky, Besant, Roerich, Bailey and others—are able to say about the source of evil in the world.

Despite the deep insights into the theme of evil to be found in anthroposophy, this theme is by no means its most important one. What is most important in anthroposophy was and is Christian-Rosicrucian wisdom (of which only a part concerns knowledge of evil) *in the light that*

---

[*] In this connection the fact that Rudolf Steiner began to reveal the mystery of the double nature of evil in both its luciferic and ahrimanic aspects precisely in 1909, the year of the etheric appearance of Christ, acquires a particular significance (see GA 107, 1 January 1909).

[†] In this connection the letter from Kut Humi cited in Part One is especially characteristic, in that he states that one third of the evil on our planet derives from man's egotism and self-love and the other two thirds from the religions now existing in the world (above all the Christian religion).

is given today to mankind by Michael. From this follows Rudolf Steiner's mission, which he began directly to bring to realization only in the last years of his life: the union *in the new Christian mysteries* of esoteric Christianity, which has been cultivated for centuries in the circles of true Rosicrucians (and also among Grail knights, Templars and several other streams), with cosmic Christianity, as represented in the spiritual worlds by the Sun Archangel, Michael.

As already said, Rosicrucianism and above all its leading Masters, who have been spoken about several times in the present book, aspired towards this synthesis. Its realization was, however, possible only in the twentieth century after the beginning of the new Michael epoch (1879), the end of the dark age of Kali Yuga (1899) and the beginning of Christ's Second Coming in the etheric (1909). The task of bringing about this union was given by Christian Rosenkreutz himself to Rudolf Steiner, *the great Christian initiate working publicly in the twentieth century.*

Rudolf Steiner laid the spiritual *foundation stone* of the new Christian mysteries at the Christmas Conference of 1923/4,[34] in which—as he himself testified—Christian Rosenkreutz and his hosts of teachers and pupils participated. However, the first step in actually bringing these mysteries to realization was the founding of the esoteric Michael School *on this foundation stone.*[36]

The *Foundation Stone Meditation* given by Rudolf Steiner at the Christmas Conference, which represents a kind of quintessence of the entirety of anthroposophical wisdom, is a mantric testimony of the union between the Michael stream and the true Rosicrucian stream, of these two principal bearers of cosmic and earthly Christianity.[37] It contains the highest union of the ninefold heavenly Hierarchies, whose representative and messenger to earthly human beings is the archstrategist Michael, with the three Rosicrucian sayings, which bring to expression the essential nature of esoteric Christianity:

> Ex Deo nascimur
> In Christo morimur
> Per Spiritum Sanctum reviviscimus

This union became possible only through the spiritual-scientific knowledge of the threefoldness of the being of man, who, out of his higher ego, himself thrice calls upon his soul in the new mysteries to turn to the 'day-radiant light', to Michael, who opens to it the path to the 'Sun of Christ' spoken of in the last part of the Foundation Stone Meditation.

Notes

1. GA 131.
2. See GA 130.
3. From Marie Steiner's Foreword, written in 1947, for the first edition of the anthology of Rudolf Steiner's lectures entitled *Das esoterische Christentum und die geistige Führung der Menschheit* (GA 130), translated as *Esoteric Christianity and the Mission of Christian Rosenkreutz*.
4. All three lectures are published in GA 130.
5. GA 266/2, esoteric lesson of 20 September 1912.
6. GA 28, ch. XXXI.
7. Rudolf Steiner mentioned this episode in the lecture of 19 November 1916.
8. See the lectures of 28 March 1916 (GA 167) and 18 March 1916 (GA 174a).
9. Ibid.
10. In his youth Rudolf Steiner wrote a whole series of articles in defence of Haeckel and Nietzsche and a book about the latter, *Friedrich Nietzsche, Ein Kämpfer gegen seine Zeit* ('Friedrich Nietzsche, A Fighter for Freedom'), GA 5. (The most well known of the articles about Haeckel is entitled 'Haeckel und seine Gegner' (Haeckel and his Opponents), in GA 30.)
11. See for example the lecture of 2 November 1918 (GA 185).
12. See for example the lecture of 31 December 1919 (GA 195).
13. GA 257, 6 February 1923.
14. GA 35 (see *Approaches to Anthroposophy*, RSP, 1992, lecture of 11 January 1916).
15. Marie Steiner, *Gesammelte Schriften*, Vol. I, 'Die Anthroposophie Rudolf Steiners', Dornach 1967. From the foreword to the first (1932) edition of Rudolf Steiner's lecture cycle *The Bhagavad Gita and the Epistles of Paul*.
16. GA 142, a cycle of five lectures.
17. GA 142, 31 December 1912 and the following quotation.
18. GA 142, 1 January 1913.
19. The building of the first Goetheanum was preceded by the construction of a much smaller temple that was made in Malsch as a model, where it still exists today. See regarding this and also its relationship to the first Goetheanum in Erich Zimmer's book *Der Modelbau von Malsch und das erste Goetheanum*, Stuttgart 1979.
20. All the lectures on the content of the Fifth Gospel were brought together in GA 148.
21. GA 148, 4 October 1913.
22. GA 148, 4 November 1913.
23. GA 104, lecture cycle consisting of twelve lectures.
24. GA 130, 18 December 1912.
25. Lectures of 2, 18 and 20 May 1913 (GA 152).
26. GA 152, 2 May 1913, likewise the following quotations.
27. GA 26, letter of 6 December 1924, 'Hindrances and Helps to the Michael Forces in the Dawn of the Age of the Consciousness Soul'.
28. GA 233, 13 January 1924.
29. GA 240, 12 August 1924.

30. See the lectures of 9 November 1914 (GA 158); 14 October 1917 (GA 177); and the lecture of 28 March 1913 (GA 145).
31. See GA 185, 25 October 1918.
32. See GA 107, 22 March 1909, also GA 194, 15 December 1919.
33. See GA 104, 29 June 1908.
34. Regarding the Chrismas Conference see GA 260 and also Sergei O. Prokofieff, *Rudolf Steiner and the Founding of the New Mysteries*, chapters 5 and 7, and *May Human Beings Hear It!*
35. These words were spoken by Rudolf Steiner in a personal conversation with Ita Wegman. They are recorded in *Rudolf Steiner's Mission and Ita Wegman*, the chapter entitled 'Rudolf Steiner's Mission', Rudolf Steiner Press, 1977.
36. Regarding the School of Spiritual Science at the Goetheanum, which in an esoteric sense is the Michael School on the earth, see the introduction to the lecture of 18 July 1924 (GA 240) and also in GA 260a.
37. Regarding the Foundation Stone Meditation see GA 260 and also Sergei O. Prokofieff, op. cit. ch. 6 and *May Human Beings Hear It!*

11. The Brief History of a False Messiah

Now that in the previous chapters there has been a consideration of the problems that arose in the Theosophical Society between the streams of Western and Eastern esotericism on account of the fundamental difference in their understanding of the Christ Being, and now that the view of *Western* esotericism in this regard has been characterized at some length, in order to arrive at a full picture the view of the *Eastern* esoteric stream—as it was represented by the official leadership of the Theosophical Society at that time—must now be examined, even if only briefly.

As has been mentioned many times in this book, one consequence of the erroneous view on the part of Eastern occultism of the Christ Being was the identifying of His *divine* Being with the *human* being of the Maitreya and the proclaiming of the imminent arrival of a new world teacher—who was to be at once both the Christ and also the Maitreya—in the person of the Indian boy Krishnamurti, who had been discovered by Leadbeater in Adyar in 1909. Through his clairvoyant faculties he had beheld the aura of the boy as he was bathing in the sea and had immediately decided that he was destined to become the bearer of the future world Teacher.

Before we turn to the subsequent history of Krishnamurti,[1] a few words need to be said about Leadbeater and those occult personalities whom he regarded as his spiritual teachers. It has already been mentioned above that as a result of his involvement with spiritualism he came in contact with a teacher whom he called Mahatma Kut Humi, received several letters from him and was soon received into the ranks of his personal pupils (see p. 394f.).

Subsequently, however, according to Leadbeater's own statement, it was not Kut Humi but his most important pupil of Tibetan origin, who had since Blavatsky's times been known in theosophical circles under the name Djwhal Khul (D.K.), who took the development of Leadbeater's clairvoyant faculties in hand. This mahatma is of particular interest since he later became the main inspirer of the books of Alice Bailey. In the last book of Agni Yoga Helena Roerich also mentions her meeting with him in Sikkim in northern India.[2]

In his brief autobiography *How Theosophy Came to Me*,[3] which Leadbeater published at the end of his life and where he makes every effort to place his devotion to the theosophical mahatmas and his boundless reverence for them in the foreground, the entire last chapter—entitled

'Psychic Training'—is devoted to the training in clairvoyance which he had personally received from D.K.

One encounters the name Djwhal Khul very frequently in the earliest theosophical documents, especially in the letters of the mahatmas Kut Humi and Morya to Sinnett. As Blavatsky, Olcott, Leadbeater[*] and other theosophists attest, he often appeared to them in an astral vision and in materialized form, sometimes with the two 'older' mahatmas and at other times without them. He reached the stage of adept (the so-called 'fifth initiation') relatively late, around 1875 or even later.[†] In accordance with theosophical conceptions the attaining of this stage gave him the right not only to take over the tasks of his teacher K.H. but also to lead his own occult school (a spiritual ashram) and to have his own spirit-pupils. As various theosophical sources report,[4] he was at that time preparing to receive in future the 'sixth initiation' and then take the place of his teacher K.H. in the Hierarchy of the Himalayan Masters (which will be discussed later on), whereas the latter was for his part to rise higher, attain the bodhisattva stage and relieve the Maitreya Bodhisattva from his office.

D.K. himself informed Alice Bailey in the 1920s that it was he who dictated to Helena Blavatsky 'significant parts' of *The Secret Doctrine*,[5] although Blavatsky herself, and also those around her, reckoned that this work was inspired by the 'older' mahatmas M. and K.H., which—to be sure—does not rule out the possibility of a mediating role on the part of D.K.

That D.K. and Helena Blavatsky had a close connection is in any case borne out by the fact that the founder of the Theosophical Society once asked D.K. to draw for her that mysterious valley in the Himalayas where all theosophical mahatmas live, avoiding all contact with the outside world. In this valley—as she said herself—she also received her 'initiation' during the three years that she was permitted to reside there. D.K. complied with her request, and Leadbeater subsequently (1925) published this drawing in his book *The Masters and the Path*. Mahatma Morya's—

---

[*] In his autobiography and also in his book *The Masters and the Path* Leadbeater describes such a materialization of D.K., which took place in Blavatsky's presence in her hotel room in Cairo. Leadbeater was at this moment sitting on the floor—as he described it—and looking through some papers by the firmly locked door when he suddenly saw the mahatma standing in the middle of the room. He cried out in surprise, whereupon Blavatsky laughed and explained to him: 'You will not go far on the path of occultism if you are so easily startled at a little thing like that,' and she went on to introduce him to their materialized visitor (*How Theosophy Came to Me*, p. 80).

[†] D.K. himself mentioned this year to Alice Bailey, although Leadbeater gave a later date (probably the beginning of the twentieth century).

little—house can be clearly seen in it, beside it its occupant on horseback and in the distance, standing up to his knees in the water of the lake and with a staff in his hand, D.K., who had been included in the picture at the personal request of Blavatsky. Mahatma K.H.'s house is not visible, whereas in Leadbeater's book its plan and internal furnishings are described in detail. According to Leadbeater's description in this book, the inhabitants of this or the neighbouring Himalayan valley included further mahatmas and also their leaders, the Maitreya Bodhisattva, the leader of Mahatma K.H., and the Vaivasvata Manu (the Manu of the present fifth root race), the leader of Mahatma M.

As Leadbeater describes in his autobiography the karmic threads connecting him with Mahatma K.H. and his most illustrious pupil D.K. went back to the sixth century BC, when K.H. was incarnated as Pythagoras and D.K. as his pupil Kleineas. In the year 504 the future Leadbeater (who at that time was an Athenian by descent), 'to our great and awed delight' visited Pythagoras on one of the Greek islands not long before his death. When Pythagoras died, his pupil Kleineas went to Athens and founded a school of philosophy there, of which the future Leadbeater was for many years a pupil. Leadbeater goes on to state in his autobiography that when they first met (in the nineteenth century) the Mahatma K.H. had immediately recalled the words that Pythagoras had spoken to him when they parted. This episode was to convince Leadbeater of their centuries-old connection. And just as was the case in their Greek incarnation, so on this occasion too K.H. entrusted the responsibility for Leadbeater's occult development to his most advanced pupil (D.K.), who was at the time a fully fledged adept (or almost so).

However, as we have seen, the fruits of this instruction were more than dubious. Quite apart from the highly problematic method of occult research which Leadbeater learnt from his 'teacher' (whoever he may have been), a mediumistic, atavistic method which by its very nature Rudolf Steiner uncompromisingly condemned (see p. 395), probably the most important feature of the esoteric training experienced by Leadbeater was that he, who in the past had been an Anglican priest, became an occultist who—in Rudolf Steiner's words—'actually knows nothing whatsoever about Christ'.[6]

Despite all this—and quite possibly because of it—Leadbeater became very soon after his return to the Theosophical Society, which as we have seen had happened by order of the mahatmas (see p. 398), the second most important person after Annie Besant, or in an occult sense even the most important, in the Theosophical Society. For according to Schuré's words from the letter quoted above (see p. 410): 'The President needed

Leadbeater for her occult research,' since 'this collaborative work seemed to her necessary in order to bolster her authority.'

One result of this collaboration was, among others, the extensive three-volume work *Conversations about the Path of Occultism*, in which the president and her spiritual advisor tried to develop further, and make more accessible to members of the Society, those methods of spiritual training and occult research which had already caused the scandalous and absurd situation involving Krishnamurti.

The extent to which Leadbeater's influence was decisive for the subsequent destiny of the Theosophical Society becomes clearly visible from the fact that, after Annie Besant's death, two protégés and pupils were named successively as President: first, George Arundale, the founder of the order 'Star of the East', and then S. Jinarajadasa, who subsequently edited and wrote a commentary upon Leadbeater's letters.

★

Now that we have thus briefly characterized Leadbeater's relationship to those individuals whom he named as his spiritual teachers and honoured with the title of mahatma, we can now turn to the Krishnamurti affair. For its most significant trait was without doubt the participation of a whole series of mahatmas, as not only Leadbeater and Annie Besant maintained but also Krishnamurti himself attested on the basis of his own occult experiences.

The occult career of this Indian boy—who was at the time still a minor—began with the so-called 'first initiation', which took place on 10/11 April 1910. In order to carry this out, Leadbeater and Krishnamurti were locked up together in Annie Besant's rooms in Adyar (she was present at the time) and, according to their own statements, were throughout (one day and two nights) outside their physical bodies. Balfour-Clarke, a playmate of Krishnamurti's, who witnessed these events and stood guard at the door, from time to time bringing warm milk which he put beside Leadbeater and Krishnamurti, described everything that happened in Adyar at that time in his recollections, which were published under the title of *The Boyhood of J. Krishnamurti*.[7]

After the two days both of those involved left their place of seclusion. In this short time Krishnamurti had changed considerably and appeared as though 'radiant' (Balfour-Clarke). Together with a small group of enthusiastic listeners who had received him at the entrance, he went at once to the next grove, where he shared with them his spiritual experiences. Later that same year he recorded them for Annie Besant in writing. As Balfour-Clarke attested, the written text—which is still preserved—

corresponded precisely to Krishnamurti's oral account. Krishnamurti reported that, after he had left his physical body, he found himself immediately in the Himalayan valley described above at K.H.'s house, where the other two mahatmas, M. and D.K., were expecting him. Then they all made their way to the Maitreya Bodhisattva, in whose house the candidate for initiation saw five other theosophical Masters. Krishnamurti's account continues: 'Then the Master (Kuthumi) took my right hand, and the Master Djwal Kul my left, and they led me in front of the Lord Maitreya, you [Besant] and uncle (C.W.L.) standing close behind me.'[8] Then a short conversation with the Maitreya took place, during which the latter demanded that the two mahatmas would have to vouch for the candidate. K.H. did this, and Krishnamurti held them by their hands. At the end of the conversation the Maitreya 'called towards Shamballa', whereupon a 'great Silver Star' lit up over the candidate's head and on each side of it the figures of Gautama Buddha and the Mahachohan appeared.[*] Then the process of initiation unfolded further and was finally completed with the solemn words of the Maitreya: 'In the name of the One Initiator [Sanat Kumara], whose Star shines above us, I receive you into the Brotherhood of Eternal Life.' Whereupon Krishnamurti received the personal blessing of the Maitreya, and the ceremony ended. However, the culmination of the initiation process was reached only during the following night, when—as Krishnamurti reported—he stood before the Lord of the World, before Sanat Kumara, whose silver star he had beheld the previous evening. 'And that was the most wonderful experience of all, for He [stood before me in the form of] a boy not much older than I am, but the handsomest I have ever seen, all shining and glorious, and when He smiles it is like sunlight.' And the 'Lord of the World' said to Krishnamurti, turning to him, that 'I must never forget His presence, for His strength would be always behind me, and His Star would shine over me.' At the end of his report Krishnamurti went on to state that behind the 'Lord of the World' were standing three other figures. However, he did not look at them, as he was unable to tear himself from Sanat Kumara's gaze.[†]

★

We have given such a full account of Krishnamurti's first initiation because virtually the whole Himalayan Hierarchy of which detailed characterizations were subsequently given in Bailey's and Leadbeater's

---

[*] A picture that represents a sort of parody of Christ's Transfiguration.
[†] Krishnamurti's full account is included in Balfour-Clarke's reminiscences.

books* participated in it. Also of significance is the fact that in Krishna-murti's vision those two teachers whom Leadbeater and then also Alice Bailey considered to be K.H. and D.K. appeared before the Maitreya to vouch for the young candidate.

For Leadbeater and Besant this report of Krishnamurti's constituted an irrefutable proof that the Maitreya had received the neophyte and would shortly use his physical body to appear before human beings as the world Teacher. Hence, said Balfour-Clarke, Annie Besant explained for the first time on 29 October 1911 at the members' conference of the Theo-sophical Society in Adyar that 'after what they had seen and felt, it was no longer possible to make even a pretence of concealing the fact [from the members of the Society] that Krishna's [Krishnamurti's] body had been chosen by the Bodhisattva'.

The so-called 'second initiation' took place on Walpurgis Night from 30 April until 1 May 1912. This resembled the content of the first (again there was an astral vision of mahatmas and of the Maitreya and so forth). However, it took place not in India but in Sicily, whither Krishnamurti was taken by Leadbeater and Arundale specially for this event. Already the place and the time of its execution speak for themselves,[9] and anyone who knows even only a little about occultism needs no further comment. In Leadbeater's view the initiation was—to all appearances—fully successful, so that the preparation for the coming of the 'world Teacher' needed to happen on a completely different scale, far transcending the limits of the—as regards its numbers—still very modest Order 'Star of the East'.

Two of the most powerful world organizations were to be used for the purpose: Freemasonry and the Catholic Church. In order to penetrate the former, use was made of the 'Order of International Co-Freemasonry' established already in 1893 under the auspices of the Theosophical Society in Paris, an Order to which both men and women belonged. According to the plans of its founders, this Order was eventually to fulfil a leadership role for all true Freemasons. Now, however, it was—so Leadbeater intended—to serve as a means of transforming Freemasonry into an instrument for the world Teacher.

In order to penetrate the Catholic Church, a member of the Theo-sophical Society, James Ingall Wedgwood, somewhat later (in 1917) founded the so-called 'Liberal Catholic Church' in London (as a new branch of the old Catholic Church of Utrecht), which Leadbeater led from the same year, becoming its 'presiding Bishop' (as we have seen, he had already transferred his allegiance from Christianity to Buddhism: see

---

*See further in Part Two.

p. 395).* Similarly, George Arundale, the founder of the 'Star of the East' and the future President of the Theosophical Society (after Annie Besant), became its Bishop. According to Leadbeater's plans this organization was gradually to become a new, all-embracing Church and at the same time the second instrument for the earthly activity of the 'world Teacher' (who would be at the same time both the Christ and also the Maitreya). In this capacity it was gradually to replace the Roman Catholic Church (or to subordinate it to itself, since the incarnated Messiah has a higher standing than any pope) and, in time, all other Churches.

The plan of making use of both organizations (Freemasonry and the Liberal Catholic Church) in order to win as many people as possible for the 'world Teacher' was a consequence of the address that Bishop Wedgwood gave in 1925 at the conference of the 'Star of the East' in Omman (Holland). A. Methorst-Kuiper summarized this as follows by including some extracts in his publication *Krishnamurti*: 'It may be seen from this and other such addresses just how earnestly convinced were the leaders of the Liberal Catholic Church and other related movements [for example, Freemasonry], that the coming Teacher would use them and their work in a special way to reach the people.' Moreover, the leadership of the newly established Church explained after a short while that 'the Christ works essentially through the Liberal Catholic Church'.[10] Thus not only the falsification of the founder of Christianity was being prepared from this quarter but also of all Christian Churches.

Krishnamurti's 'third initiation' occurred without Leadbeater's help. In 1922, during his stay in California, Krishnamurti became seriously ill. However, his illness ended with a quite sudden recovery, which was accompanied by a vision of Mahatma K.H. and the Maitreya (as with the first two initiations) and by 'vibrations' of Gautama Buddha.[11] The result of this experience was the candidate's inner conviction which he at once communicated to Leadbeater in a letter: 'I feel once again in touch with Lord Maitreya and the Master [K.H.] and there is nothing else for me to do but to serve Them.'[12] However, in 1925 some initial doubts in his own mission began to arise within Krishnamurti. These doubts were called forth by the sudden death of his beloved brother, with respect to

---

* Subsequently, after the failure of the Krishnamurti episode, Leadbeater continued to be active as a Catholic bishop in Australia. He even wrote several books on this subject. One of these, which describes his clairvoyant observations during the Catholic Mass, includes a coloured illustration on the frontispiece which is entitled 'the true form of the Last Supper' and on which is a 'spiritual form' reminiscent of a Buddhist stupa, engirdled by four narrow minarets like the towers of an Islamic place of worship.

whom the Mahachohan himself had in the astral vision promised Krishnamurti at the beginning of his illness that 'he will be well'.[13]* Despite all this, however, his doubts rapidly diminished, and on 28 December 1925 Krishnamurti gave a public address about the world Teacher at the regular congress of the 'Star of the East', after a Catholic Mass had been held in a Hindu temple.[14] During this address his voice suddenly changed, and he began for the first time to speak in the first person in the name of the world Teacher, and in a completely strange voice that was not his own.[15] Then Annie Besant officially proclaimed: 'The Coming [of the world Teacher] has begun.'[16] And in 1927 she declared in an interview with the agency of the Associated Press of America: 'The World Teacher is here.'[17] The extraordinary influence that Krishnamurti was able to exert upon his followers at such moments is borne out, for example, by the fact that the 92-year-old Balfour-Clarke, in recalling this scene many years later, called Krishnamurti's sudden transformation during his address 'an unforgettable, unique spiritual experience'[18] for his entire life.

Nevertheless, over the coming years Krishnamurti's doubts overwhelmed him more and more often. Moreover, he was as an Indian strongly repelled by the ritual of the Catholic Mass, in which he had to participate anew again and again. When he was asked directly whether he would make use of the Liberal Catholic Church as his own organization, he answered in the negative. Not long afterwards Balfour-Clarke personally heard Leadbeater say during an address by Krishnamurti: 'Talks more nonsense every day ...' Leadbeater continued to try finding a way out of the difficult situation by asserting that the Maitreya had expressed the wish that the listeners should not take everything that Krishnamurti said literally.[19] But nothing could prevent the total destruction of the illusions.

Thus the tragi-comedy neared its end. The individuality of Krishnamurti, which was gradually awakening to an independent life, was slowly able to shake off the bonds of the false role of world Teacher that had been foisted on him from without. In 1929 he publicly renounced it, dissolved the Order 'Star of the East', left the Theosophical Society, the Esoteric School and also the Freemasonic Order. From now on he

---

*At the same time Annie Besant made the list of the first seven of the twelve disciples of the future Messiah officially known. These were: she herself, the three leading bishops of the Liberal Catholic Church (Leadbeater, Wedgwood and Arundale), Leadbeater's protégé Jinarajadasa (later President of the Theosophical Society after Arundale) and two other individuals.

wanted to be himself and follow his own path. Only Annie Besant believed to the end of her life (1933) in his identity with the world Teacher. 'Everything that Krishna does is good,' were her last words,[20] when Krishnamurti left her and the Theosophical Society.

Notes

1. See further in Thomas Meyer, *The Bodhisattva Question*, Temple Lodge, 1993.
2. She does so in the penultimate book of *Agni Yoga* ('Brotherhood', Part Two). The 'mahatma' dictates to her the following: 'We have never withdrawn from life. When we appeared, we did not distinguish ourselves from average people. They can themselves attest that Djwhal Khul, when he appeared in order to meet you, did not distinguish himself from the lamas.'
3. C.W. Leadbeater, *How Theosophy Came to Me*, Adyar, Madras, India, 1986.
4. See *A Short History of the Theosophical Society*, compiled by Josephine Ransom, Adyar, Madras, India, 1989, and C.W. Leadbeater, The Masters and the Path, Part I, Adyar, Madras, India 1988.
5. See Alice Bailey, *Initiation—Human and Solar* (1922), ch. 6.
6. GA 155, 15 July 1914.
7. R. Balfour-Clarke, *The Boyhood of J. Krishnamurti*, Bombay 1977.
8. Ibid.
9. See further in Thomas Meyer, *The Bodhisattva Question*.
10. A.J.G. Methorst-Kuiper, *Krishnamurti*, Bombay 1976.
11. Cited from Thomas Meyer, *The Bodhisattva Question*, ch. 10.
12. Quoted from *Krishnamurti: The Years of Awakening* by Mary Lutyens, Avon Books, New York 1991, p. 173.
13. Ibid., p. 217.
14. See note 10.
15. See note 7.
16. Ibid.
17. See note 12, p. 259.
18. See note 7, also the following quotations.
19. Ibid.
20. Quoted from Fred Poeppig, *Rudolf Steiner der große Unbekannte. Leben und Werk*, Vienna 1960.

12. True and False Occult Teachers

> 'A theosophy that does not provide the means of
> understanding Christianity is absolutely valueless
> to our present civilization.'
>
> *Rudolf Steiner, lecture of 8 May 1910 in Berlin*

It would surely be unnecessary to concern oneself at such length with the absurd story of the theosophical 'Messiah' if its inglorious finale in 1929 had really signified its end. However, this was not the case. For already long before its culmination, at the beginning of 1920, an Eastern occultist calling himself Mahatma Morya visited Helena Roerich, and at the end of the previous year 1919 the most important pupil of the Mahatma K.H. began to dictate to Alice Bailey her books under the name D.K. (Djwhal Khul). It is true that the attitude of Helena Roerich and Alice Bailey to the Krishnamurti saga differed quite widely. Helena Roerich sharply condemned it in her letters, since she was of the opinion that Christ and the Maitreya were two different individualities. She was convinced that the future advent of the Messiah or world Teacher expected by all religions had nothing to do with Christ but that it would be the appearance on earth of the 'oldest' mahatma in the Himalayan Hierarchy, the Maitreya.[1] Moreover, his appearance would come about not in the physical but in the spiritual (etheric) body.[*] Thus Helena Roerich, out of the inspirations that she received from the Eastern occultists standing behind her, sought to oppose the Etheric Christ with an altogether different individuality.[2]

Alice Bailey, in contrast, stood positively behind the Krishnamurti episode, since her inspirers—as was the case with Besant and Leadbeater—cherished the opinion that Christ and the Maitreya are one individuality who would become manifest to humanity in the physical body. In this sense, Alice Bailey wrote under the dictation of her occult inspirer that the physical appearance of Christ will be preceded by a process whereby he will 'overshadow' some chosen pupils who are preparing his imminent

---

[*] This assertion did not, however, prevent Helena Roerich from supposing that the Maitreya will until his coming be living in the Himalayas in a physical body. That the coming of the Maitreya will take place in the spirit (etheric) body and that he will be in his physical body in the Himalayas until his coming is specified by Helena Roerich in an undated letter (probably from 1934) published in the third volume of her letters. See regarding this in Part Two.

manifestation in the flesh: 'They will be "overshadowed" by Him in many cases, just as before, He overshadowed His disciple Jesus;* through this overshadowing of disciples in all lands, He will duplicate Himself repeatedly. The effectiveness and the potency of the overshadowed disciple will be amazing.' And Alice Bailey continued: 'One of the first experiments He [Christ] made as He prepared for this form of activity was in connection with Krishnamurti. It was only partially successful. The power used by Him was distorted and misapplied by the devotee type of which the Theosophical Society is largely composed, and the experiment was brought to an end; it served, however, a most useful purpose.'[3]

Thus Alice Bailey's view fully corresponds in three significant points with those of Leadbeater/Besant: firstly, that Christ belongs to the one true Himalayan Hierarchy within which he occupies the position of a bodhisattva (corresponding to the 'seventh Initiation');† secondly, that the Christ and the Maitreya Bodhisattva are one and the same individuality; and thirdly, that the coming of the world Teacher, Christ-Maitreya, in the flesh is imminent and is essential to prepare for.[4]

These three points are addressed particularly thoroughly in the book by Leadbeater already referred to, *The Masters and the Path*, which appeared in Adjar in approximately 1925, and also by Alice Bailey in her book *Initiation—Human and Solar*, which came out in New York in 1922. (In both books the Himalayan Hierarchy and the path of initiation of their pupils and adepts were described.) But since the book by Bailey came out three years earlier, one must suppose that Leadbeater either borrowed some of its ideas for his own book without acknowledging their source, while ascribing everything to his own clairvoyant faculties, or that— especially where Christological questions are concerned—both he and Alice Bailey were drawing from one and the same occult source, since they both asserted that their teachers and inspirers were the Mahatmas K.H. and D.K.[5] In any event Bailey often cited Leadbeater in her books,‡ and most frequently from his book *The Christian Creed*.§

---

* That for Alice Bailey and her inspirers it was not the incarnation of Christ that took place in Palestine but only an 'overshadowing' of Jesus of Nazareth through Him, see Part Two.
† Helena and Nicholas Roerich express themselves in a somewhat confused manner on this subject; sometimes they connect the Maitreya with Morya, at other times they maintain that the Maitreya has already reached the buddha stage (see Part One).
‡ Helena Roerich, in contrast, very sharply criticized Leadbeater and most of his books in her letters, which of course did nothing to change the antichristian trend of her own occultism.
§ Already in 1904 Annie Besant suggested to Rudolf Steiner that he should use this book as material for the instruction of his pupils within the Esoteric School, which he categorically refused to do.

At this point we need to consider in greater detail a question which has already arisen several times in the present work. In the context of what has been said so far, it can be formulated as follows: were those Eastern mahatmas to whom Besant, Leadbeater and subsequently Roerich and Bailey continually referred as their inspirers and, even, as the originators of their teachings and to whom they gave the names Morya and Kut Humi really *identical* to those occult individualities who under those same names in 1875 brought about the founding of the Theosophical Society through Helena Blavatsky, individualities to whom Rudolf Steiner—during his three-year connection with them within the Esoteric School (from 1904 until 1907)—gave those names and from whom he, or to be more precise, the Western Masters standing behind him, separated themselves in 1907?

Rudolf Steiner himself did not give an exhaustive answer to this question. The impression arises that, while knowing the answer, he consciously did not *want* to or could not give it at the time,[*] possibly because the Western Masters standing behind him did not allow it. One can here merely assert with a large measure of probability that the separation of the Eastern and Western Esoteric Schools together with the Eastern and Western Masters standing behind them, described in chapter 5, can from an occult point of view have only one sole reason, namely their different understanding as regards the place and significance of the Christ Being in earthly evolution. As for the question as to what happened with the Eastern Masters after their separation from the Western Masters, we would not seek—following Rudolf Steiner—to give *any* definite answer. Such a relationship to this question emerges directly from what has been said hitherto, the purpose of which was not so much to investigate the path of development and the intentions of one or the other Eastern occultist but to show that with Rudolf Steiner from the very beginning of his activity *a completely different impulse* entered into earthly evolution, which as regards its nature and origin has *nothing in common* with any of the representatives of *Eastern* occultism.

The only response that can be made to this question is not to give a direct, unambiguous answer but just to express one or another *supposition*. The most probable one is the following: soon *after* the separation from the Western Masters the Eastern mahatmas left the Theosophical Society and took no further part in its further history, and they also had no relationship to the Krishnamurti affair subsequently instigated by Leadbeater and Besant and still less to the occult streams of Helena Roerich and Alice

---

[*] That this was so is borne out by the passage from Rudolf Steiner's letter to Anna Minzlow quoted on p. 399.

Bailey, whereas quite different occultists took their place who, in assuming their names, set themselves the aim not only of falsifying the etheric coming of Christ by substituting for it a physical one (or by preparing for the coming of another individuality instead of Christ) but putting another, new world religion in place of Christianity. This had the consequence that what in the original theosophical movement, deriving as it did from the true Eastern mahatmas, had merely a non-Christian character took on through the change an overtly antichristian form.

In occultism it is a fairly common phenomenon that, when certain occult powers abandon their activity, demonic beings may soon come to occupy the spiritual vacuum that arises if it is not immediately filled by positive spiritual impulses emanating from human beings. Thus, for example, the gradual withdrawal of the Greek and Teutonic gods from the direct leadership of earthly human beings led to a great variety of demonic beings taking hold of their former field of activity and Christendom accordingly had to battle with these demons for centuries.

In the case of the Theosophical Society the situation was even more complicated, because already at the time when Helena Blavatsky was working on her *Isis Unveiled* the most diverse kinds of left-oriented occultists, who served not universally human aims but, rather, their own, egotistical grouplike tendencies, were beginning actively to influence her alongside the Western Masters and Eastern mahatmas. The tragedy of the situation that developed in this way was that Helena Blavatsky, because of the particular character of her mediumistic gifts, was completely unable to distinguish between the frequently wholly contradictory occult influences deriving from the various individualities and spiritual beings who successively worked through her over the course of many years, communicating to the world through her at one time deep knowledge of pre-Christian (Eastern) religions and at another time overtly materialistic and antichristian teachings.

Colonel Olcott, who knew Helena Blavatsky as no one else did, on several occasions expressed in his many volumes of diary entries—published under the title *Old Diary Leaves*—his astonishment over the fact that at times almost daily he experienced with his own eyes how various occult individualities, one after another, made use of her body for a certain time with short interruptions. He reports that at such times not only Helena Blavatsky's handwriting changed and also her knowledge of the English language but even her behaviour, her voice, her walk, her facial expression (at times she even tried to twirl a non-existent moustache, and so on). At such moments she could freely speak and write about subjects with which she would never have concerned herself in her ordinary consciousness and for which on the whole she exhibited no under-standing. Circumstances of this kind, which had probably also prevailed earlier with Blavatsky, became more and more frequent after her serious illness in summer 1875 in Philadelphia, just before the beginning of her work on *Isis Unveiled*. (During this illness she lay in a trance for many hours.)

Olcott, who helped Blavatsky to write her *Isis Unveiled* for two years, subsequently reported about this work: 'Whence did H.P.B. draw the materials which compose *Isis*, and which cannot be traced to accessible literary sources of quotation? From the Astral Light, and by her soul-senses, from her Teachers—the "Brothers", "Adepts", "Sages", "Masters", as they have been variously called. How do I know it? By working two years with her on *Isis* and many more years on other literary work . . . The glaring contrasts between the jumbled and the almost perfect por-tions of her MS quite clearly prove that the same intelligence was not at work throughout; and the variations in handwriting, in mental method, in literary facility, and in personal idiosyncrasies, bear out this idea . . . There was also the greatest possible difference in the English of these various styles. Sometimes I would have to make several corrections in each line, while at others I could pass many pages with scarcely a fault of idiom or spelling to correct . . . As I understand it, she herself had loaned her body as one might loan one's typewriter, and had gone off on other occult business that she could transact in her astral body, a certain group of Adepts occupying and manoeuvring the body by turns.'[6]

After such phenomena had repeatedly been displayed in his presence over the years, Olcott was at times even prepared seriously to give cre-dence to the legend that the real Helena Blavatsky had actually fallen on 2 November 1867 in the battle of Mentana (where she was fighting on the side of Garibaldi's revolutionary troops) and that from this time onwards only her 're-animated' outer sheath continued to live on the earth, suc-cessively being taken possession of by various occultists. In any case Olcott noted in his diary: 'There were intervals when her body was not occupied by the writing Mahatmas; at least I assume it to be so, although I have sometimes been even tempted to suspect that none of us, her colleagues, ever knew the normal H.P.B[lavatsky] at all, but that we just dealt with an artificially animated body, a sort of perpetual psychic mystery, from which the proper *jiva* was killed out at the battle of Mentana, when she received those five wounds and was picked out of a ditch for dead. There is nothing intrinsically impossible in this theory.'

In a similar way one can find in *The Secret Doctrine* and in *The Mahatma Letters to A.P. Sinnett* the deepest wisdom of the ancient Eastern religions alongside obvious occult errors, falsifications and even blatant materialism.[*] In other words, its content sometimes consists of a barely comprehensible mixture of non-Christian inspirations of the mahatmas and antichristian inspirations of certain circles of left-oriented Eastern occultists.[†]

Although it is for the most part extremely difficult to distinguish between the two sources of inspiration in the works of Blavatsky and Sinnett that have been referred to (especially with Blavatsky, because of her chaotic manner of presentation), nevertheless one can in general make a clear distinction between them, and specifically between the non-Christian and antichristian impulses.

A strict dividing line therefore needs to be drawn between the true Eastern mahatmas and those who, illegitimately usurping their names, brought such clearly antichristian teachings into the world as were propagated by Besant, Leadbeater, Bailey and others.

The present work would seek to give the reader a sure foundation for such a distinction, in that the possibility remains completely open that also the Eastern mahatmas at the time in question will prove to be *true* 'Masters of Wisdom and of the Harmony of Feelings', that is, those leading individualities who, as Rudolf Steiner formulated it, 'have understood that the advancement of mankind depends on comprehending the great event of Golgotha' (see p. 403).

For two paths emerge from the sphere of influence of the non-Christian impulses associated with the ancient pre-Christian religions of the Asiatic East: the one reaches up to the sphere of activity of true Christian esotericism and the other descends to the realm of determinedly antichristian powers. The latter aspect therefore signifies an occult 'fall' or, to express it more spiritual-scientifically, a 'retardation' of the respective occultists behind the general evolutionary path of mankind. Those Eastern occultists who—having illegitimately called themselves 'mahatmas' and appropriated their names—began to work occultly within the Theosophical Society were in this state of 'fall' or 'retardation'.

Such a fall is not inherently impossible in the occult domain. On the contrary, it has happened more than once in earthly evolution and, moreover, not only with earthly initiates but equally with the heavenly

---

[*] See for example the 'mahatma letter' quoted in Part One.

[†] In this connection Olcott wrote with regard to the arising of *Isis Unveiled*: 'Then how are we to regard the authorship of *Isis* . . . ? . . . It is unquestionably a collaborated work and not that of H.P.B[lavatsky] alone . . . The question is highly complex, and the exact truth will never be known as to the share which each of the participants had in it.'

Hierarchies, which led to the arising of luciferic, ahrimanic and other demonic beings to whose influence even initiates can succumb under certain conditions. Here we shall give a particularly characteristic example from what has been imparted through spiritual science of such a retardation among the Hierarchy standing immediately above man, that of the Angels. Rudolf Steiner cites this example in his book *The Spiritual Guidance of Man and Humanity*.[7] It can be described as follows.

Christ embarked upon His path to the earth by way of his journey through the various spheres of the heavenly Hierarchies to the sphere of influence of the Angels in the Egypto-Chaldaean epoch.[*] However, there were among the Angels also those who, through the influence of luciferic or ahrimanic powers (that is, the influence upon evolution of beings who were already retarded), *did not accept the Christ*. And by not accepting Him, they also renounced receiving much higher powers than those that they possessed until then. For their 'retardation ... stems from the fact that ... they *did not subject themselves to the leadership of Christ*, so that they continued to work independently of the Christ'.[8]

The present, fifth post-Atlantean epoch, however, is a repetition of the third, Egypto-Chaldaean epoch.[9] Hence those angelic beings who led mankind already in the third epoch are beginning today to work upon evolution in general, and this includes both those who had at that time received Christ in the supersensible worlds and also those who had rejected Him and became furtherers and fulfillers of luciferic and ahrimanic impulses.

Rudolf Steiner describes how the former became inspirers of Rosicrucian wisdom and in our time inspirers of modern spiritual science or anthroposophy, and they will be those 'who in the twentieth century will lead human beings to a beholding of Christ, as Paul beheld Him. They will show man that Christ does not only work on the earth *but spiritualizes the entire solar system*.'[10]

Those Angels, on the other hand, who did not accept Christ in the third epoch have 'fallen' still deeper in our time and therefore try their best to oppose His coming in the etheric. Hence 'they manifest themselves in everything that gives a *materialistic* character to our culture, *and they are often observable in the aspiration towards the spiritual*'. This latter aspect is exemplified by the Eastern occultists referred to, who illegitimately use the mahatmas' names in order to falsify Christ's Second Coming. For

---

[*] In a similar way Christ passed through the sphere of the Archangels in the second, ancient Persian epoch and through the sphere of the Archai in the first, ancient Indian epoch (see note 7).

Rudolf Steiner designates every Eastern teaching that assumes a further *physical* incarnation of Christ 'Eastern materialism' (see p. 416), that is, a manifestation of the most extreme materialism where—as in the East— there was originally an aspiration towards spirituality.[*] Reference has already been made to the source of this materialism, namely the inspirations of fallen Angels who have not recognized the Christ in the spiritual world and who therefore also prevent those human beings whom they inspire from recognizing him, be they 'ordinary' people, pupils of the spirit or even initiates.

Rudolf Steiner shared important details of the secret plans and manner of working of these Eastern occultists in his lectures between 1915 and 1916. In these lectures he described a group of mainly Indian occultists in addition to the Eastern Masters inspiring Blavatsky, Sinnett and their principal works who, however, were following only their egotistical group-interests and not universally human ones and who accordingly belonged to the left-oriented occultists. The story of how these Eastern occultists of a left persuasion took hold of Helena Blavatsky is particularly noteworthy. Rudolf Steiner mentioned it several times in the lectures from 1915 and 1916 referred to.[11] What happened was as follows. Because of her exceptional mediumistic faculties, Helena Blavatsky was received into a whole series of occult lodges in Europe and America[†] and had quickly made herself familiar with the occult knowledge cultivated within them. However, she was of an honest and upright character and opposed certain of the occult-political aims of these lodges, threatening to publicize their occult knowledge in so far as she had come to know it, which for them would have been like a death sentence.

After a series of further complications, the whole story ended in the decision being taken at a secret gathering of occultists that Blavatsky should be subjected to what in occultism is known as a 'throwing back of the soul's aspirations' or 'occult imprisonment'.[12] Rudolf Steiner describes what happened next: 'At an occult conference attended by occultists from many different countries in 1879, this was decided and imposed upon Blavatsky. And so Blavatsky now indeed lived for a considerable number of years in occult imprisonment.'

---

[*] Compare also with Sinnett's false teaching of the 'eighth sphere' outlined in Part One.
[†] The reason for this heightened interest of the Western secret brotherhoods (lodges) in a medium lay in the fact that at that time they for the most part had no direct access to the spiritual worlds and were therefore compelled to make use of mediumistically gifted individuals for their own purposes, in order with their help to obtain the information that they needed from the spiritual worlds.

The nature of this 'imprisonment' was as follows: 'Through certain machinations a sphere of imaginations is called forth in a soul which brings about a dimming of what the soul previously knew, thus making it virtually ineffective. It is a procedure which honest occultists never apply, and even dishonest ones only very rarely.'[13]

And in another lecture Rudolf Steiner characterized this dubious procedure with these words: 'The nature of this occult imprisonment, which is performed by certain means of ceremonial magic,[*] is that everything that the person in question has developed inwardly is led to a certain sphere and is then thrown back into his soul. Thus the individual concerned is only able to see for himself what he has developed and is unable to share [this knowledge] with the outside world, with the result that he has to work upon it in complete isolation.'[14]

Then events unfolded in the following way: 'Certain Indian occultists now came to know of the affair [the occult imprisonment], occultists who on their part tended strongly towards the left, and whose prime interest it was to turn the occultism which could be given to the world through H.P.B[lavatsky] in a direction where it could influence the world in line with their special aims.'[15] And these 'Indian occultists' of a left persuasion, after coming to an agreement with the Western occultists referred to, were then able to free H.P. Blavatsky from her occult imprisonment, whereupon she very rapidly succumbed to their influence. Rudolf Steiner in the same lecture even called them her 'spiritual bread-givers'. Rudolf Steiner said of these Eastern occultists that they 'not only had special aims connected with Indian interests but also made trenchant concessions to the materialistic spirit of the age'.

Thus into Blavatsky's *Secret Doctrine* and her additional, later works there followed in addition to the inspirations of the Eastern mahatmas also much of what she 'wrote under the influence of Indian occultists of a left persuasion'[16] who were already pursuing overtly antichristian aims.[†] 'These occultists,' said Rudolf Steiner, 'being adherents of the left path, had no other aim than the promotion of their own special interests— Indian interests. They had in mind to establish all over the earth a system of wisdom from which Christ, and Yahweh too, were excluded. Therefore something would have to be interpolated into [theosophical]

---

[*] According to Rudolf Steiner, such means are used 'only by [occult] brotherhoods who allow themselves to engage in illicit arts' (GA 254, 11 October 1915).

[†] As already noted, their influence had already manifested itself to a lesser degree in Blavatsky's first work *Isis Unveiled*.

teachings whereby Christ and Yahweh were eliminated ... And so for occult reasons H.P. Blavatsky was prepared in such a way as to become a hater of Christ and Yahweh.'

This had the consequence that her principal work, *The Secret Doctrine*, was the fruit of a *twofold* influence. The difference between these two aspects can be discerned, for example, from these words of Rudolf Steiner: 'Blavatsky's *Secret Doctrine* has this great merit of directing people's minds to the spiritual world. But the path followed was in pursuance of special interests, not the interests of the evolution of humanity in general.'

The first part of this quotation can be related to the true Eastern mahatmas, who were endeavouring to overcome Western materialism and to reawaken an interest in the spiritual world within Western people, albeit only with the help of ancient Eastern wisdom, which does not take the Christ impulse into account and, hence, does not actually lead to a knowledge of it.[17]

In this connection Rudolf Steiner wrote in the 'Barr Manuscript': 'To begin with these Eastern initiators [of H.P. Blavatsky] had the best of intentions. They saw how Anglo-American influences were steering mankind towards the terrible danger of a completely materialistic impregnation of thinking. [Hence] they—these Eastern initiators [mahatmas]—wanted to imprint *their* form of spiritual knowledge, which had been preserved through the ages, on the Western world,'[18] a knowledge which, however, originated from sources that were alien to everything associated with the new evolutionary stream springing from the Mystery of Golgotha, 'in which the Eastern world has not participated.'[19]

As for the second part of the quoted passage, which has to do with the 'special interests' that are opposed to those of humanity as a whole, it clearly relates to the 'Indian occultists' referred to above who pursued directly antichristian aims. For according to Rudolf Steiner there stood as an inspirational force behind these Indian occultists 'certain [spiritual] beings who had an interest in guiding her [Blavatsky] into putting Lucifer in the place of Christ ... Thus did those *cosmic powers* who desired to advance materialism work even through what was called theosophy.'[20]

Of particular significance here is the reference to the collaboration between luciferic and ahrimanic impulses in these 'Indian occultists' on a common antichristian foundation: the inclination towards Lucifer, on the one hand, and the furthering of Western materialism through the destruction of Christianity, on the other, that is, the uniting of that 'Indian esotericism' with the 'modern materialistic science' of which Rudolf Steiner wrote in the 'Barr Manuscript', where he emphasized the 'unfruitfulness' and 'incorrectness' of such a synthesis through the example of the books of Sinnett and Blavatsky.[21] *

However, this is not the full extent of the complexity, the 'somewhat involved nature' (Rudolf Steiner)[22] of the occult situation that gradually formed around H.P. Blavatsky, to say nothing of the growing influence that was extended through her upon the further development of the Theosophical Society. Thus in his lectures of 1915–16 Rudolf Steiner spoke about a further change, specifically the replacement of the original Kut Humi, who led H.P. Blavatsky occultly for a time, by a completely different individuality who, nevertheless, appeared under his name and accomplished this so cleverly that H.P. Blavatsky did not notice the substitution. Rudolf Steiner called the other individuality on one occasion a 'deceiver', on another a 'grey magician', 'who was in the service of a very restricted [secret] human society' which wanted to propagate a 'one-sided world-conception' in the world;[23] on another occasion Rudolf Steiner called this individuality 'a rascal involved in the service of Russia ... who was pursuing ambitious political aims above all else'[24] and 'wanted to amalgamate in a conscious way what could emerge from Blavatsky's soul capacities and Anglo-Saxon occultism',[25] and on another a 'spy ... in the hands of a certain Society who had escaped from occult brotherhoods in which he was initiated to a high degree'.[26] †

On the basis of the descriptions that Rudolf Steiner has given in this connection, it is impossible to avoid the suppositions that not only one but *several* different individualities giving themselves the same name (K.H.) were working through H.P. Blavatsky. However, Blavatsky herself was not in a position to see through the deception, and so in the majority of cases she herself became a sacrifice to the various occult influences to which she was subjected. Moreover, there is a particular difficulty in that all the occultists working through the highly mediumistic consciousness of H.P. Blavatsky took the form of the mahatmas or their emissaries to whom she was wholly devoted and whose words repre-

---

* That this synthesis is the principal task of Blavatsky's book is borne out by the title of the two volumes published in her lifetime: 'The Secret Doctrine: The *Synthesis* of Science, Religion and Philosophy'.

† As Rudolf Steiner testifies, this false mahatma participated occultly in the composing of Sinnett's books *The Occult World* and *Esoteric Buddhism* and also, to a certain extent, in the writing of *The Secret Doctrine* (GA 254, 11 October 1915).

sented for her the highest law.[*] This had the consequence that she alternately became the instrument of opposing occult influences, without being able to distinguish between them. Such an exchanging of one inspirer by another took place several times in Blavatsky's life. This is why, in the lectures referred to, Rudolf Steiner again and again emphasized the confusion and complicatedness of the whole situation: 'The good, poor Blavatsky ... was the plaything of a great variety of forces'[27] so that 'the most manifold [occult] aspirations and streams worked through her psyche'.[28] Anyone who is even only slightly familiar with the nature of such occult phenomena and knows the mediumistic, atavistic character of Blavatsky's faculties, together with her tendency to be very receptive to all supersensible influences but without any capacity to distinguish them and to judge them independently, will gain the impression that everything that has been cited here is in no way improbable.[†] For 'with her all of what had taken place within her was not fully in her consciousness; her psychic nature was also to a high degree *subconscious*.'[29]

Of particular importance for the understanding of this phenomenon of the constant change in H.P. Blavatsky's inspirers is her own description of her inner state at such moments. This can be found in one of her letters to her sister, V. Zhelikovsky: '*Someone* comes and envelops me as a misty cloud and all at once pushes me out of myself, and then I am not "I" any more—Helena Petrovna Blavatsky—but someone else. Someone strong and powerful, born in a totally different region of the world; and as to myself, it is almost as if I were asleep, or lying by not quite conscious—not in my own body, but close by, held only by a thread which ties me to it.'[30] Since Blavatsky was at such moments in a state resembling 'sleep' or 'virtually without consciousness', she could not of course convincingly establish *who* was actually speaking at the time, working through her or writing books and letters with her hand.

Thus in the occult biography of Helena Blavatsky we have a whole series of substitutions: firstly, in place of the Rosicrucian Masters who had originally given the theosophical movement its esoteric impulse there

---

[*] 'I served them, and had no right to raise my voice,' wrote Blavatsky in a letter. And in another letter she related: 'Whenever I am *told* to write, I sit down and obey, and then I can write easily upon almost anything... Why? Because *somebody who knows all* dictates to me ... My Master and occasionally others whom I knew in my travels years ago' (italics in original). (Cited from Mary K. Neff, *Personal Memoirs of H.P. Blavatsky*, 1937.)

[†] In the many volumes of Olcott's diaries one may find a large number of confirmations of this fact. These diaries were published in six volumes under the overall title *Old Diary Leaves*. The particularly striking examples can be found in Mary K. Neff's book already cited.

appeared Eastern Masters (see further in the next chapter); then, parallel with their influence (and even earlier), 'left-oriented Indian occultists'— who were under the influence of luciferic and ahrimanic beings—began to be active after they had freed her from the occult imprisonment in which she had been placed by certain Western lodges; and finally she was made use of not without success over several years by wholly problematic occultists, who pursued the basest political aims and whose occult methods bordered on 'grey magic'. The latter were evidently associated in one way or another with the 'Indian occultists' referred to above.

All this can be summarized schematically:

1. Christian influence   Rosicrucian Masters
2. Non-Christian influence   Eastern mahatmas
3. Antichristian, politically   'Certain Indian occultists'
     coloured influence
4. Political and grey-magical   False mahatmas and dark
     influence   occultists standing behind them

Also to be considered are the extraordinarily confused relationships that Blavatsky had to various occult societies (lodges) in France, Britain and America, each of which sought to use her for their own purposes, her 'occult imprisonment' and also much else besides.[31] Finally, the sheer endless succession of the various mahatmas and their replacements, who appeared both to the leaders of the Theosophical Society and also to many of its individual members (whether in the physical body, in materialized form or in an astral vision), descriptions of which are richly evident in theosophical literature, and also the endless argument about the 'pre-cipitation' of their letters[*] to one or another member (such as, for example, the story regarding Judge and so forth)—all this gives the impression of an extreme gullibility and an occult naivety bordering upon irresponsibility on the part of the participants in and witnesses of these manifestations, above all in the case of the leaders of the movement such as Blavatsky, Olcott, Besant, Leadbeater and others who were clearly not in a position to be discriminating as to the true nature of their occult experiences.

When in 1902 Rudolf Steiner pursued the invitation to connect himself with the Theosophical Society, the effects of the three influences mentioned in the above scheme (excluding the first) were still in evidence

---

[*]In the Theosophical Society this term was used for letters that were sent in 'refined matter' and then materialized and fell straight out of the air when they had reached the addressee.

within it. Hence it was his urgent task to reintroduce the *original impulse* (the first referred to above) which had not played a part for several decades, in order to overcome the third and fourth influences whose effects had come to be predominant over the occult scene and to try to establish a right relationship to the second influence.

Rudolf Steiner characterized this task as follows: 'In this period [of the development of the anthroposophical movement] a quite particular hope was justified until 1905 or 1906. This was the hope that the anthroposophical element might gradually become the living substance of the Theosophical Society.'[32] However, this was not fulfilled. The reason was that shortly before the separation between the Western and Eastern Masters in 1907 (see chapter 3) the Eastern mahatmas evidently renounced all connection with the 'Eastern Esoteric School' led by Besant (they had already—although not completely—broken off their connection with the Theosophical Society in Blavatsky's time).[33] This had the consequence that already by 1909 the Eastern occultists of a left persuasion dominated the occult scene, as did the occultists who were engaging in grey-magical practices (the third and fourth influences); for these latter were, through Leadbeater and certain other leading theosophists, very rapidly subjecting Annie Besant—who was at that time not only the leader of the 'Esoteric School' but also President of the world Theosophical Society—to their influence. And so they held in their hands all the levers of power in the Theosophical Society and were therefore now able to work towards the fulfilling of their principal aim that first 'something would have to be interpolated into [theosophical] teachings whereby [the] Christ . . . was eliminated',[34] in order then 'to eradicate the Christ principle from Western culture'.[35] These left-oriented occultists tried to achieve the former by spreading the false teaching of the identity of the Maitreya Bodhisattva and also by proclaiming his imminent appearance in the flesh as a new 'world Teacher', and the latter by putting forward such a—false—Messiah in the person of Krishnamurti.

This occult escapade was subsequently the main cause of the spiritual decline of the Theosophical Society, since it led to its complete discreditation, especially in the eyes of the Western world. Hence the left-oriented occultists and the still darker occult powers standing behind them soon had to resort to new channels, which they did through the agency of two other mediums, Helena Roerich and Alice Bailey. Thus the occult battle against Christianity continued, albeit in two different forms, both in the East and in the West.

All in all there were from 1907 onwards three successive main occult events in the development of the Theosophical Society: the parting of the

Western and Eastern Masters, the eventual separation of the latter from it and its total domination by the occultists of a left persuasion.

As for Rudolf Steiner, his position as the representative of esoteric Christianity and the emissary of the occult Masters of the West was clear, consistent and uncompromising in all these events. Thus after the separation between the Western and Eastern Esoteric Schools in June 1907, it was only in lectures from 1915 and 1916, in which he spoke for the first time about the occult foundations of the tragic destiny of Helena Blavatsky, that he mentioned on one final occasion the name of one of the mahatmas (Kut Humi). And it is striking *how* he did so. He spoke about him in a somewhat aloof way, as though looking upon what had happened from a distant historical perspective and merely stating an objective fact. Thus these lectures are also a further proof that after his separation from the Eastern Esoteric School in 1907 Rudolf Steiner maintained neither outer nor inner (occult) relations with it.[*] This is even more clearly apparent in his relationship to Mahatma M., who—as Helena Blavatsky explained on several occasions—was her first and main occult leader, her 'boss', as she herself often called him.[36] After 1907 Rudolf Steiner did not mention his name even once. But there is much to be said for the fact that, as with K.H., his place came at a certain moment to be occupied by a completely different individuality originating from the left-oriented Indian brotherhood referred to, who used the mahatma's name in order all the more easily to lead Helena Blavatsky and her credulous followers into error. As for D.K., *Rudolf Steiner mentioned this name neither before nor after the year mentioned above*, although, as already stated, this youngest mahatma had already been well known in theosophical circles since the time of Blavatsky and Sinnett.

Rudolf Steiner's position with regard to the left-oriented occultists' attempts to put forward a false Messiah was especially hard and uncompromising. From the outset he referred clearly and directly to the great occult error contained in the various notions of a *physical* Second Coming of Christ and deriving from a fatal intermingling of the *human* nature of the bodhisattva and the *supersensible, divine* nature of Christ.

Until the final separation from the Theosophical Society and the founding of the independent Anthroposophical Society at Christmas 1912, Rudolf Steiner spoke again and again of how it is the most

---

[*] Thus after a pause of seven years, when he set forth Blavatsky's occult biography for the last time in the lecture cycle *The History and Conditions of the Anthroposophical Movement in relation to the Anthroposophical Society* (summer 1923), he did not mention the names of these mahatmas (see GA 258).

important task of anthroposophists as modern representatives of Christian-Rosicrucian occultism to testify to the truth regarding this question, which is central to the whole of earthly evolution, and to point openly towards the deeply erroneous nature of such teachings with whose help the demonic powers seek to divert humanity today from a true knowledge of Christ: 'It will be a severe test for those who have been prepared by spiritual science to recognize where the truth lies, to know whether the spiritual theories are really permeated by a living, spiritual feeling or whether they are only a disguised form of materialism. It will be a test of the further development of spiritual science whether a sufficient number of people will be enabled by it to understand that they must seek the new manifestation of Christ in the etheric world, or whether they will refuse to look beyond the physical plane and expect to see a manifestation of Christ in the physical body. *The theosophical movement has yet to undergo this test.*'[37]

It is the essential aim of this book to offer help to all people of good will to undergo this test and at the same time to attain a right relationship to the Mystery of Golgotha and to the present manifestation of Christ in an etheric form.

Notes

1. In Helena Roerich's opinion three individualities determine the present evolutionary stage of the earth: Gautama Buddha, Christ and the Maitreya, though the last mentioned is the 'oldest' of them, 'the first and the last' (letter of 4 July 1936, published in *Pisma Eleny Rerich* ('The Letters of Helena Roerich. 1932–1955'), Vol. 3, Novosibirsk 1993).

2. Rudolf Steiner refers to the process of preparing such individualities of a 'strictly ahrimanic nature' in connection with describing the activity of certain occult lodges of the West which have in the twentieth century been battling against the etheric Second Coming of Christ (GA 178, 18 November 1917 and: Sergei O. Prokofieff, *The Spiritual Origins of Eastern Europe and the Future Mysteries of the Holy Grail*, ch. 18, Temple Lodge, 1993). In this respect the occult, mediating activity of the Roerichs between the Asiatic East and the American West is of particular interest (see: Sergei O. Prokofieff, *The East in the Light of the West*, Part I, ch. 3 and Appendix 4).

3. Alice Bailey, *Discipleship in the New Age*, Vol. 2, p. 171.

4. That the views of Leadbeater, Besant and Alice Bailey with respect to the Christ Being correspond is apparent from the content of the books cited earlier by Josephine Ransom and by Leadbeater himself (*The Masters and the Path*). That Annie Besant for her part wholly concurred with Leadbeater's views is evident from the fact that in her foreword to his book *The Masters and the Path* she wrote: 'I desire to associate myself with the statements made in this book, for the accuracy of nearly all of which I can personally vouch.'

5. See Alice Bailey, *The Rays and the Initiations*, Vol. 5 'Of the Seven Rays', p. 299.
6. These quotations from *Old Diary Leaves*, Vol. I, by Olcott are taken from Mary K. Neff's book *Personal Memories of H.P. Blavatsky* (1937). The following quotations are from the same source.
7. GA 15, ch. III.
8. Ibid.
9. See GA 106, 2 September 1908.
10. GA 15, ch. III, also the following quotation.
11. See note (338).
12. GA 167, 28 March 1916, also the following quotation.
13. GA 173, 26 December 1916.
14. GA 167, 28 March 1916.
15. GA 254, 11 October 1915, also the following quotation.
16. GA 254, 18 October 1915, also the following quotations.
17. See GA 262, 'The Barr Manuscript', III.
18. Ibid.
19. Ibid.
20. GA 172, 27 November 1916.
21. GA 262, 'The Barr Manuscript', III.
22. GA 254, 18 October 1915.
23. GA 162, 1 August 1915.
24. GA 174a, 18 March 1916.
25. GA 174b, 12 March 1916.
26. GA 173, 9 December 1916.
27. GA 167, 28 March 1916.
28. GA 174a, 18 March 1916.
29. Ibid.
30. This letter is printed in Mary K. Neff, *Personal Memoirs of H.P. Blavatsky.*
31. See further in the following lectures by Rudolf Steiner from the years 1915–16, which contain information about Blavatsky's occult biography: GA 162, 1 August 1915; GA 254, 11, 17 and 18 October 1915; GA 174b, 12 March 1916; GA 174a, 18 March 1916; GA 167, 28 March 1916; GA 171, 7 October 1916; GA 173, 9 December 1916 and 26 December 1916.
32. GA 258, 15 June 1923.
33. See Rudolf Steiner's letter to Anna Minzlow of 26 March 1907, printed in GA 264.
34. GA 254, 18 October 1915.
35. GA 262, 'The Barr Manuscript', III.
36. See the book by Vsevolod S. Soloviev cited on pp. 515–16.
37. GA 121, 17 June 1910.

13. Universal and Particular Aims in Occultism

We shall now concern ourselves again with the scheme that was presented in the previous chapter and consider it in greater detail. Four sources of inspiration were identified for the founder of the theosophical movement, Helena Blavatsky, which successively defined the whole history of the Theosophical Society from its founding in New York in 1875 until our own time.

As was shown at the beginning of this work, 'this initial founding . . . had a decidedly Western nature. The publication *Isis Unveiled* [by Helena Blavatsky] ... has just such a Western character.'[1] For the truths of Western occultism that it contains were '*inspired* by the great *initiates of the West*, who also inspired Rosicrucian wisdom.'

However, since Blavatsky 'presents' the high inspirations of the Rosicrucian Masters in her book only 'in a distorted or even caricatured manner', these Masters 'decided'—moreover also for another reason, which will be spoken of further below—'to drop the matter *in this form* for the time being'. Then '*Eastern* initiators were able to take hold of [Blavatsky's] soul', as Rudolf Steiner put it. They were also already inspiring Blavatsky when she was writing *Isis Unveiled*, though not entirely, that is, without destroying the general, clear Western emphasis of this book. Thus one can say, all in all, that during the writing of *Isis Unveiled* initially both Western and Eastern Masters were participating.

Rudolf Steiner had the following to say about the temporal context and the reasons for their collaboration. The teachings of the Eastern Masters (the true mahatmas) were—as regards their occult origin— originally associated with the stream of esoteric Buddhism, which goes back to the influence of the great Indian mystic and reformer Shri Shankaracharya (eighth and ninth century AD). Those individualities who subsequently became the theosophical mahatmas emerged from the Esoteric School that he founded. They formed an occult brotherhood in the depths of the Himalayas which had the aim of preserving and nurturing the esoteric wisdom of the East.

At the beginning of the nineteenth century the last representatives of true Rosicrucianism entered into a kind of spiritual alliance with the leading representatives of this Eastern brotherhood. This alliance was in the first instance to serve the common battle of the Western and Eastern Masters against the ever-strengthening materialism of especially Western humanity. Hence Rudolf Steiner also wrote in 'The Barr Manuscript' of 'the best of intentions' that the 'Eastern initiators had to begin with'. Regarding their union with the Rosicrucian Masters he spoke as follows: 'And so it happened that the last Rosicrucians had united with the oriental brothers [the members of the brotherhood referred to]—from whom the initiative derived [that led to the founding of the theosophical teaching]— already at the beginning of the nineteenth century.'[2]

This collaboration between the Western and Eastern Masters lasted, as we have seen, for a whole century until summer 1907, the time when the Western and Eastern Esoteric Schools went their separate ways (see chapter 3).

Thus at the time of the founding of the Theosophical Society the Western and Eastern Masters were still working together and were together participating in the process of writing down H.P. Blavatsky's first great work, *Isis Unveiled*. However, the Western Masters soon ceased for the above-mentioned reason to inspire Blavatsky, for 'the Western initiators saw how little opportunity they had to allow the stream of spiritual wisdom to flow into mankind by this means' [that is, through Helena Blavatsky].[3] Thus Blavatsky was now under the influence of the Eastern Masters, who for their part decided to make a further attempt to confront the ever-strengthening tide of Western materialism. They 'wanted to imprint *their* form of spiritual knowledge, which had been preserved through the ages, on the Western world', and that means the most ancient Eastern wisdom that went back through Shankaracharya, Gautama Buddha and the Holy Rishis of ancient India to its sources on ancient Atlantis.[4] Thus Sinnett's *Esoteric Buddhism*, which relied extensively on the content of the letters that the author had received from the Eastern mahatmas, and quite especially Blavatsky's *Secret Doctrine*, and a whole series of further Eastern-coloured works of early theosophical literature, arose in this way.

This had the consequence that, with Blavatsky's transition from working on *Isis Unveiled* to working on *The Secret Doctrine*, in an occult respect a total reorientation of the Theosophical Society took place.[*] She was from this time onwards one-sidedly oriented towards Eastern (Buddhist) wisdom.

Rudolf Steiner said regarding this fundamental change in Helena Blavatsky's biography and at the same time in the history of the Theosophical Society: 'Another hundred years later [after the publication in 1785 of a book inspired by Christian Rosenkreutz, *The Secret Symbols of*

---

[*] This began earlier, at the time when Blavatsky was working on the second part of *Isis Unveiled* (see the first footnote on p. 506).

the Rosicrucians] we see the influence of the Rosicrucian stream coming to expression again in the work of H.P. Blavatsky, especially in the book *Isis Unveiled*. Much of the meaning of these [Rosicrucian] symbols has been put into words there ...* In her later works [especially in *The Secret Doctrine*] she departed entirely from it, even though something of H.P. Blavatsky's uncritical spirit was already in evidence in the earlier ones.'[5] Or in another lecture: 'Then it happened that Madame Blavatsky was diverted from the influences emanating from Rosicrucianism by certain factors which would go beyond what can be spoken about in the present context and was captured by an orientalizing theosophy. This is the context out of which *The Secret Doctrine* was written.'[6]

Thus the first difficulty in the mutual relations between the Western and Eastern Masters manifested itself at the time when H.P. Blavatsky was writing *The Secret Doctrine*. It consisted of the following. From the standpoint of the Western Masters, 'regarding the value of Eastern wisdom as the subject of study one can only say that this study is of the highest value, because—while Eastern cultures have preserved their sense of esotericism—Western cultures have lost theirs'.[7] For this reason Rudolf Steiner said, for example, in the lecture of 12 April 1909: 'These Stanzas of Dzyan from *The Secret Doctrine*† do, in fact, contain some of the deepest and most significant fragments of wisdom. Much of this wisdom originated in the teachings of the Holy Rishis that flowed into the sacred lore of the East.'[8] Moreover, in so far as the content of the *Mahatma Letters* can be traced back to the true mahatmas and therefore contained occult knowledge preserved from ancient times, Rudolf Steiner referred to it as having something of 'the greatest that has been revealed to mankind'.[9]

On the other hand, Rudolf Steiner regarded as indisputable the view of the Western Masters that 'equally it should be understood that the *introduction* of a correct esotericism in the West can only be of the Rosicrucian-Christian type, because this *latter* gave birth to Western life

---

* Rudolf Steiner clarified that not the whole of *Isis Unveiled* but only a part of it was written under the influence of Rosicrucian inspirations: 'We must dwell mainly upon the first half of the publication [*Isis Unveiled*], which is written along the lines of the [Rosicrucian] *Symbols*. In the second part Blavatsky deviates somewhat from the Rosicrucian stream' (GA 130, 27 September 1911).

† As Blavatsky declares, she received the text of the Stanzas of Dzyan when she was living in Tibet from the Mahatmas M. and K.H., who helped her to write *The Secret Doctrine*, which is itself essentially an extensive commentary on them. 'Thus she [Blavatsky] was guided in accordance with powers which could give everything that is external to Christianity with great power and clarity,' said Rudolf Steiner in this connection (GA 143, 8 May 1912).

and because by its loss mankind would deny the meaning and destiny of the earth',[10] which according to the Western Masters 'lies in the recognition and realization of the intentions of the *living Christ*. To reveal these intentions in the form of complete wisdom, beauty and activity is, however, the deepest aim of Rosicrucianism.'

H.P. Blavatsky, in contrast, who was—especially after her work on *The Secret Doctrine*—under the influence of the Eastern Masters, had above all the wish to 'introduce all manner of things from Indian, Tibetan culture into European culture'.[11]

For this reason Rudolf Steiner expressed himself very strongly immediately after the separation of the Western from the Eastern Esoteric School in the esoteric lesson of 1 June 1907, which has already been cited several times in this book. He said, wholly basing his statements on the view of the Western Masters: 'But this Eastern form of truth [what is meant here is the content of *The Secret Doctrine*] is not for us Western peoples. It can only restrict us and divert us from our goal.'[12] This goal consisted of the following: 'But it is now our task to strive towards an ever more comprehensive understanding of the Christ and to penetrate deeper and deeper into the Mystery of Golgotha. All the wisdom of previous ages has been flowing towards that end.'[13]

Since they did not recognize this central task of our time and could not make it their own, the Eastern mahatmas were also not able to fulfil their own aims of counteracting the materialism which was increasingly extending everywhere. For Blavatsky's *Secret Doctrine* which they inspired and quite especially Sinnett's *Esoteric Buddhism* 'distort the high teaching of the [Eastern] initiators' to such an extent that 'the initiators, the Eastern ones as well, withdrew their influence in increasing measure from the official Theosophical Society and the latter became the arena for all kinds of occult forces which distorted the great cause'.[14]

In order to maintain at least some kind of a connection with the mahatmas, Helena Blavatsky hastily left India and, once she had finally settled down in Europe, soon founded an Esoteric School in London under the name 'Eastern School of Theosophy', through which the connection with the mahatmas—as Rudolf Steiner attests—'was preserved at least until 1907 (see chapter 4). Thus this process all in all unfolded in three stages:

1877: publication of *Isis Unveiled*. The Western (Rosicrucian) Masters withdraw from Helena Blavatsky.
1888: publication of *The Secret Doctrine*. The Eastern Masters (mahatmas) withdraw from the official Theosophical Society.

1889: founding of the 'Eastern School of Theosophy' by Helena Blavatsky in London under her personal leadership—as a final attempt to preserve her connection with the mahatmas.

Now that we have considered the first two sources of inspiration of H.P. Blavatsky (see the scheme on p. 499), we must now turn to the third and—associated with it—the fourth source, which, in contrast to the two others, we must characterize as unambiguously negative. For notwithstanding all differences between the Western and Eastern Masters, Rudolf Steiner nevertheless regarded the influence of the latter upon Helena Blavatsky as positive, on the grounds that in their way they were seeking to release her from the influence of those dark occultists who had her at their mercy. Thus Rudolf Steiner observed in a lecture on 28 March 1916, when he was characterizing the dubious aspirations of these dark occultists: 'The original leader dearly wanted to lead Blavatsky into a rightful channel; but then he was replaced by a leader who was anything but what Blavatsky called a mahatma.'[15] Rudolf Steiner similarly mentioned in another lecture the 'good influence' that 'the mahatma who is known as K.H. had over [Blavatsky] for a while'.[16]

After the Eastern mahatmas withdrew from the 'official Theosophical Society' from 1888 onwards, it came after a short while to be governed by those Eastern occultists who from the outset did not only pursue decidedly egotistical aims but also tried to make use of Helena Blavatsky, and through her the whole Theosophical Society, for the fulfilment of their highly dubious political machinations. It was they who, from the initial phase of the Theosophical Society, had tried ever and again to turn it not only into the bearer of a wisdom external to Christianity—though pre-Christian as regards its sources—as did the mahatmas but also into an instrument *against* Christianity and subsequently against the future appearance of Christ in the etheric body. As a result of *their influence* the Theosophical Society soon began to change from being the bearer of a (neo-Buddhist) movement external to Christianity into the bearer of a decidedly antichristian movement.

Thus during her work on *Isis Unveiled* there worked within Helena Blavatsky's soul—in addition to the Christian inspirations of the Rosicrucian Masters and the inspirations external to Christianity streaming from the mahatmas—antichristian inspirations of certain Indian occultists who belonged to a secret occult brotherhood.

The influence of this brotherhood upon Helena Blavatsky was at first relatively weak, since it was to a certain extent paralysed by the other two influences.* After the transfer of the headquarters of the Theosophical Society to India, to Adyar, however, this influence began to grow and intensified in the period when Blavatsky was working on *The Secret Doctrine* (especially after her liberation from 'occult imprisonment' by these left-oriented Eastern occultists). In the same esoteric lesson on 1 June 1907, the first that was given after the final separation of the Western from the Eastern Esoteric School, Rudolf Steiner described the situation in which Helena Blavatsky now found herself: 'When Blavatsky wrote *Isis Unveiled*, these [Eastern] brotherhoods assumed that this was their knowledge, for they were familiar with many symbols and teachings, and they tried in every way to put obstacles in her path. So H.P. Blavatsky was hindered in the worst possible way in accomplishing her work *in the sense of Christian esotericism* as originally intended. She really had to suffer terrible things at that time. And those occult brotherhoods actually succeeded in forcing her to present what she had to offer in her second work, *The Secret Doctrine*, in an Eastern guise.'[17]

In other words, those hindrances (of a purely occult nature) which Eastern occultists placed in her path expressed themselves above all in an artificially created dulling of her inner vision, with the consequence that when she read in the Akashic Record she could—as was the case with the Eastern occultists—penetrate only to a knowledge of bodhisattva-like beings but not to a true knowledge of the Christ. Rudolf Steiner described this situation of hers in the following way: 'Thus it came about that Madame Blavatsky *was increasingly forced* to envelop herself in a fog [with regard to Christianity], and she could only clearly see what has been handed down through so-called purely Aryan traditions.'[18]

This then had the consequence that H.P. Blavatsky, under the influence of false inspirations, made the truly disastrous occult error of confusing the incarnation of the bodhisattva, the future Maitreya Buddha, that is, a highly evolved human being who lived as Jeshu ben Pandira or Pantera a century before the Turning Point of Time, with the coming to earth of the divine Christ Being. Rudolf Steiner said of this: 'Take H.P. Blavatsky. She directed her occult gaze to the period when Jeshu ben Pandira lived; she saw that a great bodhisattva individuality was incarnated in him, but—because her occult eye was limited through being caught up in an *orientalist theosophy*—she was unable to see that 105 years afterwards it was the time of Christ. In short, her knowledge of Christ extended only

---

*Despite everything there are to be discerned in *Isis Unveiled*, in addition to truths that derive from Christian occultism and elements of true Eastern wisdom, also already distinct errors with regard to Christianity and even antichristian elements.

to what has been said [outwardly] about him in the West, and out of this the idea formed that Christ never lived at all, that it was all a pack of lies; whereas 105 years before our era a certain Jeshu ben Pandira had lived who had been stoned and hung from a tree, thus not crucified. This Jeshu ben Pandira was described as though he had been Jesus of Nazareth. But this is a total confusion.'[19] So that we must say: 'In that stream [of Eastern theosophy] one simply does not see what the Christ Being actually is.'

Blavatsky's article published under the title 'The Esoteric Character of the Gospels' in the journal *Lucifer* in 1887 (while she was actively working on *The Secret Doctrine*) represents what is probably an even more convincing testimony of this total inability to understand the Christ Being and the significance of his incarnation on the earth.[*] In this article, which can be regarded as the most concentrated and clearest exposition of Blavatsky's attitude to this problem, the following specific statement is made: 'Thus Jesus, whether of Nazareth or Lüd (Lydda) [the place where Jeshu ben Pandira was stoned] . . .'[20] for 'to the true follower of the Spirit of Truth it matters little, therefore, whether Jesus, as man and Chrestos [the name for a pupil who is travelling a path of initiation], lived during the era called Christian, or before, or never lived at all. The Adepts, who lived and died for humanity, have existed in many and all the ages, and many were the good and holy men in antiquity who bore the surname or title of Chrestos before Jesus of Nazareth, otherwise Jesus (or Jehoshua) Ben Pandira was born.' Hence the prophecy of the Sybil of Erythrea of Christ's coming to the earth, which Blavatsky cites in her article (' "Iesus, Christos, God, Son, Saviour, Cross" '), 'contains a real prophecy—only not referring to Jesus—. . . [it] has nought to do with Jesus'. And whence, in her opinion, does the content of the Gospels come? 'Whence, then, the Gospels, the life of Jesus of Nazareth?' she asks. And she herself replies in the same article: 'Has it not been repeatedly stated that no human, *mortal* brain could have invented the life of the Jewish Reformer, followed by the awful drama on Calvary? We say, on the authority of the esoteric Eastern School, that all this came from the Gnostics, as far as the name Christos and the astronomico-mystical allegories are concerned, and from the writings of the ancient *Tanaïm* [an ancient occult tradition that preceded the Talmud and the Kabala] as regards the Kabalistic connection of Jesus or Joshua with the Biblical personifications . . . No wonder that the very meaning of the terms *Chrestos* and *Christos*, and the bearing of both on "Jesus of Nazareth", a name coined out of Joshua the *Nazar*, has now

---

[*] In 1888 Blavatsky was awarded the Medaille Subba Rao—the highest honour of the Theosophical Society—for this article, as the best publication of the year.

become a dead letter for all with the exception of non-Christian Occultists.'*

Thus throughout H.P. Blavatsky's works from when she was writing *The Secret Doctrine* we must distinguish two different elements. On the one hand that which derived from the inspirations of the mahatmas, under whose influence she expounded Eastern, pre-Christian wisdom: 'If one surveys the whole of Blavatsky's *Secret Doctrine*,' said Rudolf Steiner, 'one has to see in it something akin to a resurrection of the old mysteries, actually nothing new.'[21] For 'Blavatsky did not really know the essential nature of the Mystery of Golgotha', in that she was under the influence of this source of inspiration and therefore had no idea that 'in the Mystery of Golgotha the culmination of the entirety of the old mysteries is presented as an outward fact'. Thus under the influence of the mahatmas H.P. Blavatsky 'reveals in her *Secret Doctrine* the various impulses of a wide variety of ancient religions and their development in one great panorama'.[22] However, under the influence of the members of a left-oriented Eastern brotherhood as described above 'she did not merely judge but demonstrated throughout that she had a deep sympathy for all world religions outside Judaism and Christianity and, in contrast, a deep antipathy towards Judaism and Christianity. That which derives from these latter religions was sharply made out to be of lesser worth than the great revelations of the various pagan religions. Thus she had an explicitly antichristian orientation.' The first of these elements derived from the mahatmas and the second from the dubious Eastern brotherhood.

To this picture there needs to be added the whole unsystematic and chaotic character of the manner of presentation in *The Secret Doctrine*, which—as we have seen—led to the distortion of many of the truths communicated by the Eastern mahatmas. Hence Rudolf Steiner also indicated in a lecture that it would be good 'to remove five sixths of *The Secret Doctrine* and to rewrite the remaining sixth in an orderly fashion'.[23] However, this radical remark does not alter the decisive fact that even in the remaining 'sixth part' one would search in vain for any sort of Christian wisdom, for there is none in this book. On the contrary—to the extent that Eastern occultists of a left persuasion participated in its coming

---

* The following extract from Blavatsky's letter to her sister V. Zhelikhovsky indicates how little she was conscious of the absurdity of her remarks about Christianity and its founder: 'In the third (November) issue of *Lucifer* from 1887 you can find my article ['The Esoteric Character of the Gospels'], where I praise Christ's preaching as … would any true Christian, God willing, who has not been infected by Papism or by Protestant twaddle' (quoted from *Radda-Bai* [H.P. Blavatsky]—*biografichesky ocherk* ('A Biographical Sketch'), Vera Petrovna von Hahn de Zhelikhovsky, Moscow 1993).

into being—it tragically proved to be a source of erroneous notions about Christianity for whole generations of theosophists. Rudolf Steiner referred to this state of affairs with these words: 'It followed, therefore, that with respect to everything that is not Christian *The Secret Doctrine* contained great truths, whereas where it concerned Christianity there was utter nonsense.'

This was essentially Blavatsky's relationship to the mysteries of Christianity at the time when she was working on *The Secret Doctrine*, which in her opinion and in that of her followers was the principal work of theosophical literature. It is still viewed as such today. Consequently, the difference between *The Secret Doctrine* and Blavatsky's first great work *Isis Unveiled*, which still contained inspirations of the Rosicrucian Masters, is transformed into an abyss between Christian and antichristian impulses. For the members of the left-oriented Eastern brotherhood succeeded in 'presenting to her a wholly false conception of Christ ... And [this conception] was passed on to her closest pupils and is still being carried around today, though coarsened to the point of becoming grotesque.'[24]

This came outwardly to expression through the fact that both H.P. Blavatsky and also Olcott in 1880—during their journey to Ceylon—officially converted from Christianity to Buddhism[25] and later, under the same influence, also Besant and Leadbeater.[*] Inwardly, this led, for example, to Besant writing in a book which appeared in 1902 under the remarkable title *Esoteric Christianity or the Lesser Mysteries* (following Blavatsky, Besant considered the 'great' mysteries—in contrast to Christianity—to be those of Egypt, India and Tibet): 'The child whose Jewish name has been turned into that of Jesus was born in Palestine 105 BC.'[26] According to Besant he was educated by Jews until the age of 19, when he entered the Essene Order and eventually went to Egypt 'and was initiated in Egypt as a disciple of that one sublime Lodge from which every great religion has its founder'.[27] (According to Talmud tradition Jeshu ben Pandira did indeed spend some time in Egypt, though not in very early childhood as did Jesus but in his youth.)

From Besant, this—as Emil Bock put it—'main Christological error of the theosophists' was passed on to Leadbeater. And Leadbeater was very strongly under the influence of the Indian brotherhood referred to and quite especially that of the false mahatmas, whom—because of his distorted spiritual development—he was unable to distinguish from the true mahatmas. Consequently Leadbeater did not hesitate to draw practical

---

[*] Blavatsky came originally from an Orthodox family, while Besant's and Leadbeater's family background was Anglican. The latter had even been an Anglican priest.

conclusions from this Christological error, and he began to search for a specific candidate for the role of the future 'world Teacher'.

If, to all that has been said, we now add that the false mahatmas did not only illicitly appropriate the names of the true mahatmas but also on several occasions falsified their letters and spread these distorted forms among the leading members of the Society—the majority of whom, H.P. Blavatsky included, regarded them as true without a shadow of doubt and made every effort to shape the life of the Theosophical Society in accordance with the indications that they found in them—we can understand the extent to which the ground of the Theosophical Society was, once the Eastern Masters had withdrawn from it around 1888, made ready eventually to become 'an arena for all kinds of occult forces which distorted the great cause'.[28]

This also explains why, in the situation of the falsely attributed 'Mahatma Letters', Rudolf Steiner decisively defended H.P. Blavatsky. For in this case she was not the deceiver, as many opponents of the theosophical movement maintained at that time,[*] but was herself— because of her gullibility and uncontrolled supersensible faculties—the sacrifice of a slyly plotted act of deception which had been perpetrated around her by a group of dark occultists.[29]

The following example may show how difficult it actually was to distinguish the true mahatma letters from the falsely attributed ones. In a letter with Mahatma M.'s signature, the mahatma himself or someone who had signed his name informed the German theosophist Hübbe-Schleiden, who wanted to know who had actually written *The Secret Doctrine*: 'I ... certify that the "Secret Doctrine" is dictated to Upasika [H.P. Blavatsky] partly by myself & partly by my Brother K.H.' K.H. likewise confirmed this in a letter: 'It is for his [Dr Hübbe-Schleiden's] own satisfaction that the undersigned is happy to assure him that *The Secret Doctrine* when ready,[†] will be the triple production of M. [Morya], Upasika and the Doctor's most humble servant.'[30]

The handwriting of these two long-published letters (as also of the letters of the mahatmas to Leadbeater and other leading members of the Theosophical Society) corresponds precisely to that of the mahatmas' letters to H.P. Blavatsky and Sinnett. But as for their content, they are

---

[*] This is a reference to the scandal when various devices were found in Blavatsky's rooms at the headquarters of the Theosophical Society in Adyar [a sliding door, chests with false bottoms and so on] enabling the 'Mahatma Letters'—which according to Blavatsky had materialized directly out of the air—suddenly to appear.

[†] Both letters were written in 1896, that is, after Blavatsky's death.

right if one relates them to those portions of *The Secret Doctrine* where the true, ancient Eastern wisdom is presented, and *wrong* if one relates them to certain antichristian or simply erroneous pages of this book.

Of course, the decidedly materialistic letter—one of the *Mahatma Letters to Sinnett*—quoted in the first part of this work is clearly bogus (despite all Helena Roerich's assertions), inasmuch as it directly contradicts the principal aim of the mahatmas, namely to counteract Western materialism with the help of ancient Eastern wisdom. In other cases, however, it is extraordinarily difficult to distinguish the genuine from the false. Nevertheless, in the Theosophical Society *all* these letters are considered to be genuine and therefore regarded as an indisputable authority.

★

In the light of this, the question naturally arises: according to what occult or, to be precise, karmic law did the dark, Eastern occultists manage so easily to occupy that inner vacuum which came into being in the Theosophical Society after the departure first of the Western and then of the Eastern Masters? Of course, this was to no small degree the result of the moral weaknesses, errors and undue naivety of the leading members of the Theosophical Society. Nevertheless, all this was only the outward aspect of the situation. The real reasons for such a success on the part of the dark occultists lay deeper. Rudolf Steiner spoke about this mystery in the lecture that he gave on 11 April 1912 for Russian anthroposophists in Helsingfors (Helsinki): 'Because of the way that England is karmically connected with India in a world context, the possibility was easily given that those sublime powers that nurtured the first beginnings of the theosophical movement were perverted. For this is a normal occurrence in occultism, that powers seeking to pursue their *special interests* take on the form of those who have previously given impulses of their own.'[31]

At this point it is necessary to enter into what Rudolf Steiner calls 'universally human' interests in occultism on the one hand and 'special' on the other. We shall first consider this question from a more outward, so to speak occult-historical aspect and then from an esoteric viewpoint.

The following words of Rudolf Steiner may serve as a starting point: 'Her [Blavatsky's] first work, *Isis Unveiled*, merely shows the whole chaotic, illogical, passionate and muddled aspects of her nature, while demonstrating throughout that behind her stand watchful [spiritual] powers who want to guide her towards what belongs to all humanity. In *The Secret Doctrine*—in addition to what is undoubtedly very great [which derives from the inspirations of the mahatmas]—there runs a thread of special human interests, interests proceeding from certain occult centres [of the East] which do not have universally human interests in view but partial, special interests. Tibetan, Indian and also Egyptian initiations today always have only narrow human interests in view, seeking as they do to enable the suppressed occultism of the East to avenge itself on the Western world.' Rudolf Steiner explains in the same lecture that the possibility of such an 'occult revenge' results from the karmic debt that the West took upon itself over the centuries because of harsh colonial politics and the mighty advance of Western materialism in the East. This had the consequence that 'India, which had previously been suppressed in its occultism, karmically took revenge by replacing Western occultism—on the first occasion when it appeared in the West—with its own national, egotistic occultism.'

The special interests which the Eastern initiates pursued did not only relate to the occult domain, however, but were also directly associated with occult-political plans. Rudolf Steiner characterized their nature in one of his later lectures in the summer of 1923: 'For it was the case that Blavatsky had initially received a stimulus from a quarter which I do not want to speak about further, and that she then formulated what appeared in *Isis Unveiled*. Then through all sorts of machinations it came about that Blavatsky was subjected to a second influence from oriental occult teachers, behind whom was concealed *a culturally political tendency of an egotistic nature*. From the very outset a one-sided *Eastern political impulse* was concealed in what was sought to be achieved in a roundabout way through Blavatsky. Behind this outward aim lay the determination to show the materialistic West how much more valuable the spiritual knowledge of the East is than the materialism of the West, to achieve a cultural hegemony—and, moreover, an overall imperial sovereignty—of the East over the West by bestowing Eastern wisdom upon the spiritual culture (or, if you like, the spiritless culture) of the West. This is the source of what I might describe as the complete change of direction from the wholly European nature of *Isis Unveiled* to the wholly oriental character of Blavatsky's *Secret Doctrine*. The most diverse factors were influencing the situation. But one of these factors was the endeavour to link India with Asia [Tibet, China and Japan] in order to create an Indo-Asiatic sphere of influence with the help of the Russian Empire. And so this teaching acquired its Indian content in order to win a spiritual victory over the West. You see, this is a one-sidedly egotistic, national-egotistic impulse.'[32]

This is confirmed to a remarkable degree in the reminiscences of Vsevolod Soloviev, an older brother of the well-known philosopher, to whom H.P. Blavatsky confided her 'political' plans in Würzburg in 1885, at the time of her most intense work on *The Secret Doctrine*: 'You see,' she began, 'this is the situation: you're coming to Petersburg soon to undertake something of great importance and value for Russia. I want to put myself forward as a secret agent of the Russian Government for India. I am capable of anything that can assist my native land in triumphing over these English wretches. I hate the British Government in India with its missionaries—they are all my personal enemies who are thirsting for my downfall. This alone is enough for me to exert all my energies in battling with them ... And it is true that I can inflict a lot of damage on them in India ... and only I, for no one else is suited for such a role! My influence upon Indians is vast—I could give you all manner of proof of this ... Millions of Indians will follow me if I give the merest sign ... I shall easily organize a huge uprising ... I guarantee that in a year's time the whole of India will be in Russian hands ... If I can only be given the financial means ... I don't need much—you know me in this respect—if only it can be made possible for me to get to India via Russia, since after the affair of Columba and the missionaries I cannot reach it any other way, I shall carry out one of the greatest of historical feats!... Several years ago, during the ministry of Timashev,[*] I suggested this, but I didn't receive any answer ... And now ... this is even easier for me ... I can bring every-thing about in a year's time ... Help me in this patriotic cause!'[33]

What stands out in these words—among other things—is H.P. Blavatsky's burning hatred of the English, which she communicated to the 'mahatmas',[34] and also the indication that it was possible to organize an insurrection in India, a point that the 'mahatmas' (actually those Eastern occultists who had adopted their names) mentioned subsequently in a letter that they sent in 1926 to the Bolshevik Government via the Roerichs.[35]

All in all the Roerichs' journey to Russia through India and Tibet and back through Bolshevik Mongolia looks like a further attempt of the Eastern occultists standing behind them to pursue the aims referred to, though on this occasion not through the 'white' but through the 'red' tsar.[36] (Subsequently, in the 1930s, this subject was also addressed in Helena Roerich's letters to the American President Roosevelt.)[37]

From an esoteric standpoint this group-oriented national character of Eastern occultism manifests itself primarily in its total inability to recog-nize the true nature of the Christ in His divine-cosmic nature and also the central significance of the Mystery of Golgotha as the most important

---

[*] Between 1868 and 1877 Timashev held the post of Minister for Domestic Affairs in the Russian Government.

event of earthly evolution. 'For,' wrote Rudolf Steiner, 'the Eastern initiations must of necessity leave untouched the *Christ* as the central *cosmic* factor of evolution.'[38] Consequently, the highest being that the Eastern initiates are able to reach in their occult knowledge is only a bodhisattva or a Buddha. 'This is the highest individuality to which the orientalist occult teaching can rise ... The consequence was that the seers [of the Eastern occult teaching] could only reach as far as a bodhisattva individuality.'[39]

In other words, Eastern initiation stopped at the stage of knowledge of beings of the rank of a bodhisattva, and, moreover, only in the old form which was appropriate *before* the Mystery of Golgotha. Through incarnating again and again on the earth, the bodhisattvas have the task of bringing new spiritual impulses out of the spiritual world, impulses which bring the evolution of mankind further from one epoch to another, within the context of a so-called root race or one or other of the sub-races (cultural epochs) belonging to it, and also within one or another nation or a whole group of nations.

On the other hand, the incarnation of the Sun Logos or Christ on the earth could take place only *one single* time, and it has significance not for any particular geographical part of the earth (the East, the Middle or the West), not for a particular nation or group of nations but for the *whole* of mankind. For, as the highest divine archetype of *every* human ego, Christ has a relationship as an ego Being to *all* earthly human beings, without any difference with respect to national or racial affinities. The same can also be said with regard to time. Christ's coming to the earth and the Mystery of Golgotha together constitute a unique and central event, not only within this or that sub-race, root race, globes or circles,* but within the compass of the entire incarnation of the present earth. Moreover, it is also the central event in the whole series of the cosmic incarnations of our earth, from ancient Saturn to Vulcan, of which Eastern occultism knows only the one incarnation which directly preceded the Earth incarnation, that of Ancient Moon.[40]

Rudolf Steiner referred to this central position of the Mystery of Golgotha in world evolution in, for example, the lecture cycle *Cosmosophy*, which he gave in the autumn of 1921: 'People would like to know the difference between anthroposophy and what lived as the older theosophy. Is this difference not evident? The older theosophy has warmed up the pagan cosmologies. [The first volume of *The Secret Doctrine* was devoted to Genesis.] In the theosophical literature you will discover

---

*Theosophical terms for the various epochs into which earthly evolution is divided.

everywhere warmed-up pagan cosmologies, which are no longer suited to modern human beings ... The centre is missing throughout. It is missing to an even greater extent than in outer natural science. Anthroposophy has a continuing cosmology that does not extinguish the Mystery of Golgotha but accepts it, so that this Mystery is contained within it. The whole of evolution, reaching back as far as Saturn and forward as far as Vulcan, is seen in such a way that this light enabling us to see will ray out from the knowledge of the Mystery of Golgotha.'[41]

Hence Rudolf Steiner again and again compares the Mystery of Golgotha with the fulcrum of the world scales (hypomochlion), of which there can only be *one* if the scales are to function. The Mystery of Golgotha occupies such a place as a unique event in world evolution which cannot be repeated, an event that endows earthly evolution as a whole with its meaning.

Thus from an esoteric point of view, Christianity belongs to the *whole* of mankind or, which is the same thing, *every* human being. For without consciously and freely receiving the Christ impulse into his own ego as its highest, divine archetype, the individual human being—and that ultimately means the whole of humanity—will never attain the goal of his evolution, the goal for the sake of which Christ came to the earth and has, as the highest Ego of mankind and the Lord of the entire earth, ever since been united with it.

Eastern occultism and its methods of initiation are, on the other hand, inherently unable to recognize the Christ as He has been working in the spiritual aura of the earth since the Mystery of Golgotha. For the methods of this occultism derive from the deepest past of earthly evolution (ultimately from ancient Atlantis), that is, from the time before the union of the Sun Logos with the earth. This is the source of the danger that always threatens Eastern occultism when it oversteps the bounds of these realms where it developed historically and seeks in one or another way to penetrate into the West, that is, when it begins to claim a universally human significance while preserving its original pre-Christian form. If, moreover, it is unable to recognize the true cosmic nature of Christ, this Eastern occultism will sooner or later inevitably arrive at the conviction that Christ is only one of the bodhisattvas and that He will appear again in a physical body, or that another and even more significant bodhisattva will come soon after Him—for as we have seen, Eastern initiation is unable to rise to a higher knowledge than to that of the bodhisattvas.

When considered from an esoteric standpoint, the special or group-oriented interests of the Eastern occultists consist precisely in that they strive to put the particular proclamations of the bodhisattvas who alternate with one another in the course of the historical development of mankind in place of the Christ impulse, which is the *central* impulse of earthly evolution as a whole—that is, to set the personal and national above the general and universally human.

If one adds the endeavour—already noted above—of certain occult circles of the East to avenge themselves on the West in one way or another, it was easy for these special interests to become distinctly egotistic, as indeed ultimately happened in the case of the leaders of the Theosophical Society, first with H.P. Blavatsky and Olcott and then with Besant and Leadbeater. For in time they all came under the extreme one-sided Eastern influence.

★

In conclusion, mention needs to be made of the strange paradox that the endeavours of the left-oriented Eastern occultists referred to above to 'take revenge on the West' by exerting all their energies 'to eradicate the principle of Christianity from Western culture'[42] led to an ever closer collaboration with various occult lodges of the West which in all essentials pursued the same antichristian aims, albeit out of completely different considerations.[*]

Their first contacts were probably in one way or another associated with the highly confused story of Blavatsky's liberation from her occult imprisonment in which she had been placed by Western 'brothers' (especially at the instigation of an American lodge, which was assisted in this very dubious undertaking by certain European lodges) and then released by Eastern 'brothers'.

Rudolf Steiner described these events as follows: 'By means of various machinations the Indian and American occultists reached a kind of agreement. The Americans promised not to interfere in what the Indians wanted to do with Blavatsky, and the Indians undertook to remain silent about what had happened before ... Once all these things had run their course, the only one to benefit from Blavatsky was the Indian brother-hood.'[43]

In all probability these contacts, which led to the agreement referred to, also formed the starting point for a further close collaboration between the left-oriented Eastern and Western brotherhoods, which then in the twentieth century—in full view of Christ's appearance in the etheric

---

[*] Regarding the aims of these Western brotherhoods, see further in S.O. Prokofieff, *The Spiritual Origins of Eastern Europe and the Future Mysteries of the Holy Grail*, ch. 18.

body—became the conscious endeavour to counteract this central event of our epoch with all available means.

Out of this *common* battle of the Eastern and Western brotherhoods against the Etheric Christ there then arose in the first half of our century such overtly antichristian, occult streams as those of Alice Bailey and Helena Roerich which have been considered in the present work.[*]

From all this it also becomes understandable why Rudolf Steiner, in order to rescue the 'universally human' impulse originally imparted to the Theosophical Society by the Rosicrucian Masters, had in all his work within it to oppose from the outset any one-sided Eastern occultism by means of a true knowledge of Christ and of the Mystery of Golgotha as involving every human being irrespective of his affinity to this or that culture, nation or race. Thus when recalling his activity within the Theosophical Society many years later (1923) Rudolf Steiner said: 'During this first phase [what is meant here is the seven-year period of the development of anthroposophy from 1902 until 1909], the Anthroposophical Society led an embryonic existence within the Theosophical Society ... In this first phase it had a special mission, that of *counterposing* the spirituality of Western civilization, centred in the Mystery of Golgotha, to the Theosophical Society's course, which was based on a traditional acceptance of ancient oriental wisdom.'[44] For only a knowledge of the central significance of the Mystery of Golgotha for the whole of mankind could return to theosophy its original, *universally human* character.

Notes

1. GA 262, 'The Barr Manuscript', III, also the following quotations.
2. GA 52, 8 December 1904.
3. GA 262, 'The Barr Manuscript', III.
4. See GA 110, 12 April 1909 (1).
5. GA 130, 27 September 1911.
6. GA 133, 23 October 1911.
7. GA 262, 'The Barr Manuscript', III.
8. GA 110, 12 April 1909 (1).
9. GA 143, 8 May 1912.
10. GA 262, 'The Barr Manuscript', III, also the following quotations.

---

[*] This also explains the repeated journeys of the Roerichs between India and America, also Alice Bailey's period in America and the establishing of the centre of her movement in New York and also the Roerichs' founding in the same city of their museum, which they hoped would become the centre of their movement in the Western world.

11. GA 191, 10 October 1919.
12. GA 264, esoteric lesson of 1 June 1907.
13. GA 266/2, esoteric lesson of 20 September 1912.
14. GA 262, 'The Barr Manuscript', III.
15. GA 167, 28 March 1916.
16. GA 173, 9 December 1916.
17. GA 264, esoteric lesson of 1 June 1907.
18. GA 143, 8 May 1912.
19. GA 133, 23 October 1911.
20. H.P. Blavatsky, *The Esoteric Character of the Gospels*, likewise the following quotations.
21. GA 258, 14 June 1923, also the following quotations.
22. GA 258, 13 June 1923, also the following quotation.
23. GA 133, 23 October 1911.
24. GA 143, 25 February 1912.
25. The ceremony took place on 25 May. Olcott wrote about it in *Old Diary Leaves*, Vol. II: 'We had previously declared ourselves Buddhists long before in America, both privately and publicly, so that this was but a formal confirmation of my previous professions. H.P. B[lavatsky] knelt before the huge statue of the Buddha, and I kept her company' (quoted from W. Kingsland, *The Real H.P. Blavatsky*, ch. XI, Adyar, India 1985).
26. Op. cit., p. 96.
27. Ibid., pp. 96–7.
28. GA 262, 'The Barr Manuscript', III.
29. See regarding this GA 258, 12 June 1923.
30. Quoted from Boris Zirkoff, 'Rebirth of the Occult Tradition. How *The Secret Doctrine* of H.P. Blavatsky was Written', printed as the 'Historical Introduction' to the Seventh (Adyar) Edition of *The Secret Doctrine*, 1979 (p. 16).
31. GA 158, 11 April 1912, also the following quotation.
32. GA 258, 14 June 1923.
33. Vsevolod S. Soloviev, *Sovremennaya zhritsa Izida* ('The Modern Priestess of Isis'), ch. XX, Moscow 1994.
34. See Part One, Appendix I.
35. See Part One, ch. 4, 'The Roerichs' Mission to Bolshevik Russia'.
36. See Part One, Appendix 3.
37. See Part One, Appendix 4.
38. GA 262, 'The Barr Manuscript', III.
39. GA 133, 23 October 1911.
40. See GA 243, 20 August 1924.
41. GA 207, 16 October 1921.
42. GA 262, 'The Barr Manuscript', III.
43. GA 173, 26 December 1916.
44. GA 257, 6 February 1923.

14. The Main Criterion for Forming a Judgement about Occult Teachers

To conclude this study of the problem concerning the Eastern and Western Masters, mention must now be made of the *most important criterion* enabling an individual in our modern consciousness-soul age to form a judgement about it. This criterion is its relationship to the *objective truth* which derives from a knowledge of the basic facts of the evolution of the world and humanity that is not limited by any special standpoint. True Rosicrucianism has from the outset striven for this knowledge of objective truth, that is, a truth which concerns the *whole* of earthly humanity and not only a part of it, both the Eastern and the Western aspects. Hence Rudolf Steiner, drawing his knowledge from these occult sources, also said: 'Neither Eastern nor Western predelictions must be allowed to colour our view. Anyone who speaks from a Rosicrucian point of view accepts neither Orientalism nor Occidentalism; both appeal to him equally. The inner nature of the facts alone determines their *truth*.'[1]

Thus every person who claims the name of a true Master in our time must be viewed as such by human beings today living in the age of human freedom not merely on the basis of their own assertions or those of others, that is, on the foundation of some kind of outward authority or of their occult knowledge and capacities, but the assertions of this person must first be subjected to a careful examination by every available means. For this is the most important rule for true Rosicrucian esotericism in our time.

Rudolf Steiner, as a modern Rosicrucian Master, formulated this rule as follows: 'I beg you ... never to accept on authority or on faith anything I have said or shall say ... I beg of you not to accept as an article of faith what I have said about Zarathustra and Jesus of Nazareth, about Hermes and Moses, Odin and Thor, and about Christ Jesus Himself, nor to accept my statements as authoritative. I beseech you to abjure the principle of authority, for that principle would be deleterious to our movement ... I have no qualms. All that is given out of Rosicrucian sources can be tested in every way ... I am convinced that the more thoroughly you test it, the more you will find that what has been given out of the sources of the Rosicrucian mystery will correspond to the truth. I take it for granted that the communications that are made from Rosicrucian sources will be tested rather than believed, not superficially but ever more conscientiously ... You must accept nothing on authority ... We make no appeal to belief in authority.'[2]

And in another lecture Rudolf Steiner formulated this rule of true Rosicrucianism in this way: 'Christian Rosenkreutz never demands a personality cult and sees to it that teachings are made accessible to and understood by the power of reason. His teaching never demands blind faith in the Masters. If we only use our own powers, the possibility will arise of knowing the Masters of Wisdom and of the Harmony of Feelings *through truth*. No one will demand faith in them as a precondition, for faith in the Masters would then be on a higher level than truth.'[3]

Such a denial of all outward authority and the necessary demand for a careful examination of all that has been imparted are, moreover, in accordance with the basic feature of the modern Michael epoch. Thus the words of the modern Rosicrucian Master that have been quoted can be attributed not only to the great teachers of Christian esotericism but also to the still higher spiritual authority standing behind them, the spirit of our time, Michael, of whom Rudolf Steiner said in one of his lectures: 'Michael wants to be the spiritual hero of freedom.'[4]

From the outset the truth that is known in freedom and recognized out of freedom was given full priority in modern spiritual science (anthroposophy). Only because of this can it become an authority of the highest order for man today, for it expresses itself as the innermost need of his heart, as a direct expression of his own spiritual being. Only through such an unlimited commitment to truth can man today guarantee his freedom, and that means also his dignity as a human being.

It is clear from what has been said that the high principle of freedom which Rudolf Steiner expounded and established in his first 'Michaelic' book *The Philosophy of Freedom*[5] and which has ever since served as the foundation of the whole of spiritual science is not in any way at variance with a genuine reverence for what is higher, for without this no path of true, spiritual development is possible. But this reverence in modern esotericism is not a reverence for human beings, even where they have been initiated into certain mysteries of existence, but simply a reverence for *truth* as such. Rudolf Steiner formulated this fundamental principle of modern esotericism already at the beginning of his book *Knowledge of the Higher Worlds*: 'It must be emphasized that in the domain of higher knowledge it is *not* a matter of venerating persons but of venerating *knowledge* and *truth*.'[6]

The words quoted do not, however, signify a rejection of all human authority in earthly life but, rather, refer to the *conditions* of its *legitimate* manifestation in our time and also to the basis of the criteria for evaluating it, namely where a human individual has been able to make a higher truth that he has apprehended a reality in his own life. This rule applies not only to the pupils but above all to the teachers of true occultism, that is to say, also to initiates themselves. And it is the relationship of such an initiate (or mahatma) to the *highest truth* as revealed to mankind through Christ's appearance on the earth which represents the main *criterion* for the inner justification of such an authority. For in Christ there took place for the first and only time in earthly evolution what John described in these words: 'And the Word became flesh' (1:14), that is, the entire fullness of the Sun Logos, the personified truth of our cosmos, appeared on earth in a human body. Thus Christ Jesus was also the only Being who could say of himself: 'I am the Way, the Truth and the Life' (John 14:6), words which only the incarnated Sun Logos was able to pronounce.

This means that from this time only this *highest truth*, which has appeared to all human beings, represents also the *main criterion* for assessing a particular spirit-teacher. To what extent is the reality of Christ and the Mystery of Golgotha that He accomplished the true focus of the work of such a teacher, and is his life a path of discipleship (or imitation, as one would have said in the Middle Ages), trodden in full freedom, of the great cosmic archetype of man, the Christ? For since the time when the Christ united Himself in the Mystery of Golgotha with earthly evolution, the aim—and that means also the truth—of earthly evolution has from the occult standpoint consisted simply and solely 'in the recognition and realization of the intentions of the *living Christ*',[7] of the intentions of Him who, as the new Spirit of the Earth and its highest guide,[8] is at the same time also the 'essential meaning of the earth' and hence also 'the deepest aim of Rosicrucianism'.

For this reason, all Rosicrucian Masters who follow the Christ on the inner path—such as have been spoken of in this work—may with justice enjoy the highest authority in the anthroposophical movement, for they all manifest to the world his truth with their own lives. This authority of a true initiate and Master of Wisdom and of the Harmony of Feelings is rightly enjoyed also by Rudolf Steiner, the founder of anthroposophy, whose entire life was a constant discipleship on the *path* of Christ, a proclamation of the *truth* of Christ and a testimony to the *life* of Christ, as has been described at some length in the book *Rudolf Steiner and the Founding of the New Mysteries*.[9]

What has been described here as the necessary criteria for recognizing a true Master may also serve as a criterion for defining the *true* 'White Lodge'. This is, however, not of so simple a form as many occultists imagine. The 'White Lodge' actually has various levels, corresponding to the stage of development of its members. The lodge of the bodhisattvas in the sphere of providence (Buddhi) described in the first chapter represents its *highest* aspect. This highest lodge is then reflected in all the lower planes of the spiritual world and finally on the physical plane (for example, in the circle of the twelve Apostles, the twelve Knights of the Holy Grail or in the twelve wise men who participated in the initiation of Christian Rosenkreutz in the thirteenth century). At all these levels it is, following the law of reflection, called 'White Lodge'. However, depending on how high—to which spiritual level of the 'White Lodge'—the spiritual gaze of its earthly representatives penetrates, the possibility also exists that these latter may be mistaken, and this possibility grows to the extent of their distance from the original archetype. Whereas hierarchic beings are able to 'remain behind' in the spiritual worlds, human beings are protected to a lesser degree, especially if they have not attained to a direct beholding of the bodhisattva sphere, whence it is possible to gain access to the highest truth of our cosmos, the Christ.

The closer the initiate comes in the course of his ascent into the spiritual worlds to the highest aspect of the White Lodge, the bodhisattva sphere, the less becomes the possibility for him personally to err. For each error melts like the snow in spring beneath the life-bestowing rays of the Spirit-Sun, the Christ, who is Himself the Way, the Truth and the Life of our cosmos, qualities which He introduced into earthly evolution when He came to the earth and united Himself with earthly evolution through the Mystery of Golgotha. 'Christ was on earth one single time and has therefore experienced what it is to descend to the earth, to live on it and ascend from it again. He comes from the other side and is that Being who is in the midst of the twelve bodhisattvas, who receive from Him what they carry down to the earth.'[10] And in the same lecture Rudolf Steiner explains their number *twelve* in the following way: 'We cannot speak of more than twelve because, when the twelve bodhisattvas have accomplished their missions, the period of earth existence shall have been completed.' And so we have six bodhisattvas who have in earthly evolution prepared Christ's coming to the earth and rose to the Buddha stage *before* the Mystery of Golgotha, and there will again be six whose principal task it is to bring its fruits to mankind.[*]

As indicated above, what the bodhisattvas experience at the highest

---

[*] In this lecture Rudolf Steiner cited two examples of bodhisattvas who became Buddhas *before* Christ came to the earth: Gautama Buddha and Apollo-Orpheus. In other lectures Rudolf Steiner also spoke several times about the first *Christian* bodhisattva, who will be the Maitreya Buddha 5000 years *after* the Mystery of Golgotha.

level of the White Lodge is not the teaching of Christ but He Himself as
the source of its *life* (see p. 370). And as the bodhisattvas are imbued with
this Christ-life they experience it in their own being as the *truth* attainable
to earthly man,* which they then bring to earthly humanity.

In the following words, Rudolf Steiner characterized the earthly
evolution of humanity as revealed to the modern Christian initiate from
the standpoint of the working of the high White Lodge amongst mankind: 'All former cultural life on earth has come to the earth through the
fact that the great leader of earthly evolution—Christ—has sent to the
earth those to whom He initially entrusted the mission to prepare on earth
what He had to do. He was still in the heavenly heights and sent down
His emissaries. And they, the great founders of religions, had to prepare
human beings for His coming. The last of these emissaries was the
Buddha, who brought the teaching of compassion and love.† Nevertheless there were formerly other bodhisattvas and after Christ there will
be other bodhisattvas who have to extend what came to the earth through
Christ Jesus.'[11]

And Rudolf Steiner continued: 'It will be good if human beings will
listen to the bodhisattvas who come afterwards, for they are His servants.
Every time that a bodhisattva will appear in the future, for example after
three thousand years, one will understand the Christ—who illumines
everything—that much better. Christ is the Being with the deepest
nature, and the others are there so that the Christ may be better understood. Therefore we may say that Christ sent the bodhisattvas on ahead to
prepare mankind for Him; and he sends them after Him in order that the
greatest deed of earthly evolution [the Mystery of Golgotha] can be
understood ever more clearly. Through all this wisdom which pours forth
upon the earth, we shall be in a position to get to know Christ better.
Thus we stand on the earth as people on a quest. We began with
struggling to understand Christ. What we have learnt to know of Him
[through spiritual science] we have applied—as we will in future apply
what the bodhisattvas will teach—in order the better to comprehend the
Master of all bodhisattvas, the focal point of our [solar] system. Thus
mankind will become ever wiser and will come to know Christ better and

---

* In the lecture of 31 August 1909 (GA 113) Rudolf Steiner refers to the cosmic principle
of the Holy Spirit active in the bodhisattva lodge (the White Lodge). Under its influence,
the *life* of Christ filling the lodge becomes the highest *truth* of Christ which the bodhisattvas are able to recognize in their souls.
† A similar characterization of how Gautama Buddha, in preparing for the coming of
Christ, brought the *teaching* of compassion and love whereas Christ brought *love itself* (the
cosmic substance of love) can be found in the lecture of 25 September 1909 (GA 114).

better. But it will understand Him completely only when the last of the bodhisattvas has performed his service and brought the teaching which is necessary to render us capable of comprehending the most profound Being of earth existence, Christ Jesus.'

When, moreover, the mission of the bodhisattvas has been fulfilled, mankind will not only have understood the Christ Being but will be wholly permeated by Him: 'Only when the last bodhisattva belonging to Christ shall have completed his work will humanity realize what Christ really is. Human beings will then be filled with a will in which the Christ Himself will live. He will become immersed in human beings through their thinking, feeling and will, and mankind will be the outward expression of Christ on earth.'[12]

Since, however, the bodhisattvas are able *after* the Mystery of Golgotha to proclaim to humanity the highest *truth* about this mystery out of the cosmic source of *life*, mankind had first to be prepared for this. For this reason it became necessary soon after Christ's appearance on the earth (in the fourth century) to unite also the *way*, a new Christian path of initiation, with the life of Christ and His truth. For through Christ's having come down to earth and passed through the Mystery of Golgotha, the relationship of the bodhisattva sphere to the earth had changed. The bodhisattvas were to bring to mankind not only the ancient wisdom of the cosmic Christ, the great Creator Logos who abides on the sun, as they had done for millennia, but they were now to bring the transformed wisdom of the Logos who 'became flesh' and then passed through death and conquered it in the Resurrection, thus giving meaning to the whole of earthly evolution: 'Before the Mystery of Golgotha the meaning of the earth was on the sun. Since the Mystery of Golgotha the meaning of the earth has been united with the earth itself'[13]—with these words Rudolf Steiner brought the esoteric significance of this event to expression.

In order now to unite also the new way with the truth and the life, Manes, the great bodhisattva of the West, in the fourth century AD convened that great council in which Gautama Buddha (in the spirit-body) and the other two bodhisattvas of the West, Scythianos and Zarathustra (the Master Jesus) also participated. 'At this council the plan was formulated whereby all the wisdom of the bodhisattvas from post-Atlantean times could flow ever more strongly into the future of mankind.'[14] This plan was focused on developing a new spiritual *path* or a new Christian initiation through which in the future, in the approaching epoch of human freedom, *every* human being could—by following this path—come to know the highest *truth* of the earth, the truth about Christ and the Mystery of Golgotha, in order then to become a participant in the new Christian initiation of the exalted *life* emanating from Christ. This path was, as we have seen, begun with the initiation of Christian Rosenkreutz in the thirteenth century (see chapter 9), together with the subsequent founding of the Rosicrucian stream on earth through its schools of initiation, where this path was consistently taught.

Thus Rudolf Steiner spoke as follows about the further destiny of the plan formulated at this council: 'And what was decided at that time as the plan for the future development of earthly culture was adhered to and then carried over into those European mysteries known as the mysteries of the Rose Cross.' Thus according to the resolve of the council of the fourth century the union of the *life*, *truth* and *way* of Christ was achieved in the Rosicrucian mysteries through their connection with the bodhisattva sphere and in this way it becomes possible to gain access in them to a conscious experience of his cosmic 'I am'.

This new path of initiation,* which leads to an experience of the 'I am' of Christ, continued to exist for centuries only in the mystery schools of true Rosicrucians, which were strictly closed and hidden from the outside world.† Only since the beginning of the present consciousness-soul epoch in 1413, the new epoch of Michael's rulership in 1879 and finally the end of the dark age of the Kali Yuga in 1899 have the conditions arisen to make this path public. This path of a Christian-Rosicrucian initiation appropriate for the present time was presented in detail by Rudolf Steiner on behalf of the Rosicrucian Masters at the beginning of the twentieth century, in a manner that is accessible to *every* human individual today.[15]

In our time this is the *only* path of spiritual development which wholly takes into account the underlying character of the present epoch and is in a position to guide every person of good will with full consciousness and in freedom on the *path* of initiation, which leads to a knowledge of the *truth* of Christ and the Mystery of Golgotha, that is, also to a knowledge of the true meaning of earthly evolution and, in addition, to a direct

---

* Before its inauguration there was, as its predecessor, the so-called Christian-mystical path of initiation referred to by Rudolf Steiner in Part II of the Barr Manuscript, where he traces it back to the 'Friend of God from the High Lands', one of the medieval incarnations of the Master Jesus (Zarathustra) (see the esoteric lesson of 1 June 1907, GA 264). This path, however, requires a complete withdrawal from the world, which is not in accordance with the essential character of our epoch and its tasks. Hence Rudolf Steiner wrote: 'Until that time [until certain Rosicrucian principles become known] Christian-mystical initiation was given to the West' ('The Barr Manuscript', II).

† This refers to the *true* Rosicrucians, of whom even today the outside world knows nothing, and not those various occult societies and Freemasonic organizations which have again and again appeared here and there in the course of European history.

experience of Christ as the bearer of the divine '*I am*' of our cosmos. This is also how Rudolf Steiner, who personally followed this path of initiation to its highest stages, experienced Christ.[16]

What has been said here applies of course not only to Rudolf Steiner but to *all* true Rosicrucian Masters and above all the highest of them, who have been spoken of in this work. They all attained not only the highest stages on this path but they were also—as we have seen—the teachers of this path in the Rosicrucian schools over the course of many centuries: 'They [Zarathustra, Scythianos, Gautama Buddha and others] were the teachers in the schools of the Rose Cross,' said Rudolf Steiner of them.[17]

In this sense Rudolf Steiner called these Rosicrucian Masters not only initiates but also initiators, that is, teachers who *initiated* their pupils in the Rosicrucian schools into the mysteries of the Christian-Rosicrucian path of initiation, which at its highest stages (from the stage of intuition onwards) leads to a conscious experience of Christ as the leader of the twelvefold lodge of the bodhisattvas. In 'The Barr Manuscript' Rudolf Steiner employed in this connection the formulation 'the great *initiates* of the West, who are also the *initiators* of Rosicrucian wisdom'[18] and referred thereby to two different aspects of their activity. As initiates they have a direct relationship with the bodhisattva sphere (which is why Rudolf Steiner in the majority of cases preferred this term, on the grounds that it characterizes their own state of development),[19] and as initiating individuals, as initiators, they are active in the Rosicrucian schools in so far as they guide the initiation of their pupils into the mysteries of the 'living Christ'.

In 'The Barr Manuscript' Rudolf Steiner continued to use the term 'Eastern initiators', thus referring to the fact that they, too, initiated their pupils into certain mysteries of the spiritual world. The initiation deriving from them is, however, only a continuation of old, pre-Christian mysteries belonging to the *past* evolution of humanity. Hence the Eastern initiators (mahatmas) only initiate their pupils 'in *their* form of spiritual knowledge, which had been preserved through the ages' (Rudolf Steiner).

They then tried to spread this ancient Eastern wisdom, together with the Eastern path of initiation that leads to it, also in the West through H.P. Blavatsky, though without any knowledge of the Christ. For this old Eastern initiation does not suffice for a knowledge of Christ and of the Mystery of Golgotha, since its foundations were created and developed *before* Christ came to the earth. This is because only the founding of new Christian mysteries (as opposed to a renewal of the old pre-

Christian mysteries) can lead to a true knowledge of the Mystery of Golgotha.* 'Coming to terms with the Mystery of Golgotha requires not a renewal of the old mysteries [as H.P. Blavatsky aspired to achieve under the influence of the Eastern teachers] but the discovery of a whole *new mystery knowledge*. The discovery of the spiritual world in a wholly new form is necessary,'[20] that is, in the form in which the Etheric Christ can be consciously experienced today.

Consequently 'the Eastern initiations must *of necessity* leave untouched the Christ as the central cosmic factor of evolution'.[21] This means that the Eastern initiations, as they are practised today by Eastern initiators and passed on to their pupils,[†] *no longer reach* the bodhisattva sphere today, for the principal task of *all*[‡] bodhisattvas—as we have seen—is *to bring the truth (knowledge) of Christ to mankind*, which since His appearance on the earth is inseparable from knowledge of the Mystery of Golgotha as the central event of earthly evolution.[§] Hence the 'Eastern initiators', who actually knew *nothing* about Christ's relationship to the bodhisattvas but who at a certain point gained power over Helena Blavatsky, tried through her to spread their traditional teaching of bodhisattvas and Buddhas in the West, which led to such 'revelations of oriental initiation ... standing aside from the living culture in the West in a sectarian manner', that is, 'having no decisive influence on Western cultures, which *trace their beginnings back to Christ's life on earth*'.

★

This means that the following realms of higher knowledge must necessarily remain closed to oriental initiation in its various forms:

---

* Regarding the founding of the new Christian mysteries through Rudolf Steiner, see chapter 10 and also in: Sergei O. Prokofieff, *Rudolf Steiner and the Founding of the New Mysteries*, chapters 3–7.

† See the particularly striking example that Rudolf Steiner gave about Blavatsky (p. 511).

‡ A consideration of the question as to whether there are 'retarded' or even 'fallen' bodhisattvas who do not serve the Christ and therefore do not belong to the cosmic sphere, that is, who have succumbed to luciferic or ahrimanic powers, lies beyond the scope of the present work.

§ It is important to note that the *whole* of theosophical literature testifies that the Mahatmas M. and K.H. never spoke of themselves as bodhisattvas and were never regarded as such in the Theosophical Society. Rather did they regard the bodhisattvas—and still more the Buddha—as higher beings with respect to their own stage of development (see chapter 8). Rudolf Steiner, on the other hand, called the great teachers of Rosicrucianism—because of their direct relationship with Christ in the sphere of providence (Buddhi)—'bodhisattvas of the West' (see chapter 1).

1. Oriental initiation does not extend to the highest aspect of the White Lodge, consisting of the twelve bodhisattvas who serve the Christ in the sphere of providence.

2. In its knowledge of the cosmic Hierarchies, Eastern initiation extends only to the stage of the lunar Pitris and Dhyan-Chohans (planetary spirits), corresponding in Christian esotericism to the Angels and Archangels,[22] who lead individual human beings and the various peoples; but it does not include the Archai or Time Spirits, who lead mankind from one epoch to another. For this reason it is also ignorant of Michael, the cosmic 'countenance of Christ', who leads mankind today. To an even greater degree, a true knowledge of the six higher Hierarchies—the Powers, Principalities, Dominions, Thrones, Cherubim and Seraphim, whose influence extends not only to our sun but embraces the whole cosmos beyond the confines of our solar system—is hidden from oriental initiation.[23] This has the consequence that in addition the true mysteries of the Sophia in our cosmos, which are above all connected with the second, Sun Hierarchy, are not accessible to it.[24] For access to these exalted Hierarchies is made possible only through knowledge of the central mystery of the Sun, which is associated with the working of the Sun Logos, the Christ, as 'the guide of *all* beings of the higher Hierarchies'.[25]

3. In its knowledge with respect to the past cosmic incarnations of the Earth, oriental initiation extends only to the condition of Old Moon, which preceded that of the earth. It is ignorant of the older conditions, those of Old Sun and Old Saturn, and still more so of the future incarnations of the earth, which are associated with the cosmic aeons of Jupiter, Venus and Vulcan. The Revelation of St John, on the other hand, describes the transition to them. For they become accessible to an initiate only through union with the Christ impulse.

4. For oriental initiation the world significance of the Mystery of Golgotha as the central event not only of earthly but also of cosmic (hierarchic) evolution also remains closed. Earthly evolution as a whole is divided into two parts, the first of which was a preparation for the Mystery of Golgotha, the most important deed of the Sun Logos, who incarnated only once on the earth, while the second serves to make the consequences of this deed a living reality amongst mankind.

5. It follows from all this that any real knowledge of the Sun Logos, the highest Being of our cosmos—with whom this initiation is *unable to form any real relationship*—is not accessible to oriental initiation; for such a relationship is possible only through a knowledge of the Mystery of Golgotha, as a result of which the forces of the Sun Logos entered directly

into earthly evolution. In other words, oriental initiation recognizes even today only that relationship of the Sun Logos to mankind which existed *before* His incarnation on the earth, a relationship which has ceased to correspond to the occult reality for well-nigh two thousand years.

6. This has the consequence that oriental initiation can only lead humanity back to its paradisaical state, which preceded the development of the individual ego and is therefore not compatible with true human freedom. Hence the relationship between the mahatmas and their pupils in the Theosophical Society was based from the outset upon the principle of unconditional obedience and a higher authority, which is wholly at variance with the fundamental character of the present age. (The leaders of the Theosophical Society constantly referred to the teachings and secret instructions that they received from the mahatmas.) Whereas a true knowledge of the spiritual significance and higher meaning of human freedom can only be achieved on the foundation of a true knowledge of Christ in its present Michaelic form.

7. Moreover, a deeper knowledge of the mystery of evil in our cosmos is not accessible to oriental initiation. It knows from its occult tradition only something about Lucifer as man's inner tempter, who seduces him mainly through lower passions and various forms of egotism. Oriental initiation lacks any knowledge of Ahriman, of the Asuras and especially of the sun demon, Sorat,[26] the chief adversary of the Sun Logos in our cosmos, who is described in the Book of Revelation. For a real knowledge of the powers of evil is revealed only in the Christian mysteries through a knowledge of the bearer of the highest principle of goodness in our cosmos, the Christ.

8. Eastern initiation also cannot pursue the path that leads the soul into the higher spheres of the spiritual world after death. For *conscious* knowledge of this is possible only if the initiate receives the Christ impulse into his soul after death, thus enabling him to maintain his individual consciousness in the sun sphere and in the world midnight hour, the highest point that souls can reach between two earthly incarnations.[27]

9. Finally, without entering into the modern mysteries of the living Christ as the Lord of the karma of the whole of earthly evolution it is impossible to acquire actual knowledge of the laws of karma, without which mankind will not be able to fulfil its true destiny on the earth (see chapter 7).

Thus oriental initiation in all its forms and various aspects in our time *does not lead* to what represents the focal point of Rosicrucian wisdom, and it *cannot do so*; it does not lead to a true knowledge of the White Lodge and the heavenly Hierarchies, the future evolution of the Earth and the true significance of its evolution; it does not lead to a knowledge of the Sun Logos and its connection with mankind, it does not reveal the mysteries of human freedom and it does not impart any true understanding of the sources of evil. The reason why all this is denied to oriental initiation is that it has no access to the key to *all* the mysteries referred to, namely a knowledge of Christ and the Mystery of Golgotha.

Everything that has been said here regarding the teachers of Eastern occultism does of course also apply to an even greater degree to its pupils. This problem appears with particular clarity in the example of H.P. Blavatsky as the most important pupil and representative of the 'Eastern initiators' within the theosophical movement, which 'completely failed to grasp the revelations of the Old and New Testaments'.[28]

'Thus we regard H.P. Blavatsky as the bringer of a new light of dawn. What good would that light be, however, if it were not to illumine the most important thing that man has ever possessed? *A theosophy that does not furnish the means of understanding Christianity is absolutely worthless to our present civilization.*' Rudolf Steiner spoke these words on 8 May 1910 in Berlin, on the so-called 'Day of the White Lotus', the anniversary when Blavatsky's death is commemorated in the Theosophical Society. In the same lecture he also observed that Blavatsky's soul in the higher worlds wished to overcome this total absence of any true knowledge of Christianity in theosophy.

Rudolf Steiner considered the problem of the occult teachers who stood behind Helena Blavatsky, and who gave the best part of their work to the world through her, for the last time in the lecture of 20 August 1924 in Torquay, England, in the cycle *True and False Paths in Spiritual Investigation.*

The fact that Rudolf Steiner took up this theme again in England is no accident. This doubtlessly has to do with the fact that since Helena Blavatsky's time—she spent the last years of her life in London and died there—a particularly strong theosophical tradition had existed in this country.

In the lecture referred to, Rudolf Steiner began by saying that in the whole of theosophical literature—in so far as it originated in the wisdom of the Eastern initiates (mahatmas) and contained genuine communications from the spiritual world—a description of world mysteries was given which was viewed from within the limits of the moon sphere surrounding the earth. 'If you read this [theosophical] literature,' said Rudolf Steiner in Torquay, 'you will find . . . that it describes the world of which I am now speaking, the moon sphere.'[29]

This one-sided orientation towards the moon sphere represented for Rudolf Steiner the greatest occult obstacle to a connection with the Theosophical Society. This one-sidedness can be traced back mainly to the works of Helena Blavatsky.

Rudolf Steiner said of this in Torquay: 'Undoubtedly this [theosophical] material contains much that is incorrect, but much that is highly significant, magnificent and powerful, especially in the writings of H.P. Blavatsky. But *everything* [italics S.P.] to be found in the writings of H.P. Blavatsky is determined by her association with the moon sphere and her relationship with initiates who continued to abide in this moon sphere.'

And Rudolf Steiner continued: 'I can assure you that I have come to know many of these initiates, and I have discovered that such spirits penetrate into the moon sphere but they lose interest if one seeks to develop further. When I wrote my book *Occult Science—an Outline* in the years between 1906 and 1909, and I described the Earth in its earlier incarnations of Moon, Sun and Saturn, my description did not stop with the Moon incarnation but traced the evolutionary process back to Saturn; whereas all the initiates who spoke of these matters concluded their account between Moon and Sun and, indeed, went back only to the moon sphere. Any suggestion that they should look further back was met with indifference, sometimes even with a sense of disquiet. They declared this to be impossible, for the path was blocked by an impenetrable barrier.'*

These words of Rudolf Steiner can be grasped in their full occult significance if one calls to mind what he said in the lecture cycle *The Evolution of Consciousness*, which he had given one year earlier also in Britain, about the nature of the bodhisattvas. In this cycle Rudolf Steiner characterized them as 'emissaries from the moon, who in the Orient are called bodhisattvas',[30] who in olden times had the task of bringing 'the wisdom of the sun also to earthly human beings in the old oriental

---

*What Rudolf Steiner said here is confirmed by many written statements of the mahatmas, some of which were cited in Part One, chapter 6. Jean Overton-Fuller defined this situation in her book *Blavatsky and her Teachers* as follows: 'The second generation Theosophy of Mrs Besant and Leadbeater will make a great deal of the "Solar Logos". The term does not occur in the writings of Blavatsky or the Mahatmas, though the words "heart and brain" [the sun is "heart and brain of our pigmy universe"] seem to imply that vast ball of fire we call the sun to be the physical body of a being. But it is not God' (Jean Overton-Fuller, *Blavatsky and her Teachers*, London 1988, p. 97). This meaning, which Besant and Leadbeater (and subsequently Alice Bailey), in contrast to Blavatsky, connected with the concept 'Sun Logos', as we have seen turned out to be clearly antichristian and it was from then on no longer inspired by the Eastern mahatmas but by quite different occultists of a left persuasion, whose aim was to oppose Christianity by falsifying its spiritual foundations.

civilizations', in other words, to bring the high sun wisdom to earthly humanity only in an indirect (reflected) lunar form.

This state of affairs changed considerably through the Mystery of Golgotha, which gave mankind the possibility of creating *directly* out of the living sources of the high sun wisdom and, hence, of participating in the forces of the Sun Logos which overcome death in all realms of existence.

Rudolf Steiner referred to this fundamental change within the evolution of humanity with these words: 'Because of the progress made in the evolution of the Earth, it then became necessary that earthly civilization should no longer be nourished, as it were, by the moon beings alone. The whole evolution of the Earth would have had to take a course different from the one prescribed by cosmic wisdom if only the emissaries from the moon [bodhisattvas] had figured in it. For this reason there came about the great, momentous event we call the Mystery of Golgotha . . . Through this, quite different conditions arose for the evolution of the Earth. The wisdom of the sun dwellers was introduced into earthly evolution as an impulse by Christ Jesus; and under this impulse the further course of earthly evolution must therefore proceed.' This enables one to understand why knowledge of the Mystery of Golgotha as the central event of earthly evolution had 'of necessity'[31] to remain inaccessible to the Eastern initiates. The reason was that they were not in a position to venture in their knowledge of the supersensible worlds beyond the moon sphere, which meant that they were not able to enter with full consciousness into the sun sphere, whose all-embracing wisdom alone makes it possible to understand the mystery of 'the Word' becoming 'flesh' (John 1:14), or to penetrate to the domain of Saturn and thus fathom with its forces the sublimest of mysteries, that of the death and Resurrection on Golgotha.

★

All this Rudolf Steiner achieved in anthroposophy, which became a new theosophy, renewed out of the Christ impulse, a theosophy which—by following the divine Christ Being—found its way down to earth, where it united with man (anthropos) and made available to him a true knowledge of Christ and of the meaning of the earth.

Thus Rudolf Steiner could characterize anthroposophy or modern spiritual science as follows: 'And this hope and confidence [in the future] may allow us to say that our teaching is itself what Christ has wished to say to us, in fulfilment of His words: "I am with you always, even to the end of the Earth ages" (Matthew 28:20). We have wished to be mindful only of what comes from Him. And all that *He has inspired us with*, according to His promise, we want to take into our souls as our spiritual science.'[32]

Rudolf Steiner referred again and again in his lectures to his own direct relationship to the Christ Being, for out of this relationship there arose anthroposophy, founded by him in the twentieth century. We shall cite here one further example. In a lecture that he gave in 1911 in Stuttgart, under the characteristic title 'In what sense are we Theosophists and in what sense Rosicrucians?', he said: 'We are seeking to acquire the state of mind of approaching Christ *as He lives today*; and only when we have come to know that this Christ is a living Being shall we shed light upon what happened in earlier times.'[33] And some years later: 'We follow the Christ, letting His inspiration flow into us, receiving Him into our imaginations.'[34]

These words of the great Christian initiate of the twentieth century are fully in accord with the definition of a true Master of Wisdom and of the Harmony of Feelings deriving from the Rosicrucian stream: 'And those who have understood that the advancement of mankind depends on comprehending the great event of Golgotha are they who, as the Masters of Wisdom and of the Harmony of Feelings, are united in the great leading [White] Lodge of mankind. And just as formerly, as in a living cosmic symbol, tongues of flame came to rest [at Whitsun] upon the community [of the Apostles], so the Holy Spirit whom the Christ Himself has sent holds sway as the light over the lodge of the Twelve. The Thirteenth is the leader of the lodge of the Twelve, the Holy Spirit is the great teacher of those whom we call the Masters of Wisdom and of the Harmony of Feelings ... What is brought together as wisdom through the spiritual-scientific movement [anthroposophy] in order to understand the world and the spirits within it flows through the Holy Spirit into the lodge of the Twelve, and this is ultimately what will gradually bring mankind to a conscious, free understanding of Christ and of the event of Golgotha.'[35]

In this statement is also contained the *main criterion for the evaluating* of all initiates and their pupils who are seeking to work on earth in the present consciousness-soul epoch. It consists in the answer to the question as to what is the nature of their relationship 'to the most important gift that mankind possesses', the Christ impulse and the Mystery of Golgotha, without a real, esoteric understanding of which no occult wisdom, no Eastern or Western initiation will be of any benefit to humanity, for they *cannot* lead mankind to bring to fulfilment 'the essential meaning of the earth, which lies in the recognition and realization of the intentions of the living Christ'.

★

On 20 September 1913 in Dornach Rudolf Steiner laid the foundation stone of the First Goetheanum, the temple of the new Christian mysteries.

This building with two cupolas was conceived such that the design of its small (esoteric) cupola represented an imaginative picture of the bodhisattva sphere, with twelve thrones arranged in a semicircle and in their midst as their highest goal the sculptural image of the Representative of Humanity, the Christ; and the design of the large (exoteric) cupola was to depict the main spiritual-scientific truths of the evolution of mankind, which is directed towards the achieving of this great aim, that is, the fulfilling of the *essential significance* of the earth. Thus the First Goetheanum, the 'House of the Word' through whose forms the Spirit was to speak to human beings,[36] consisted of three elements. It represented the *way*, or path of modern initiation, that began with the red window of the western portal (which formed the entrance to the Goetheanum from west to east) and then led through the realm of *truth* (the space of the large cupola) into the realm of world *life* (the space of the small cupola) and in it to its source, the cosmic Christ, who stood before the pupil of the new mysteries surrounded by the twelve great teachers, who *in their totality* manifest to earthly humanity the entire fullness of the revelations of the cosmic 'I am'.[37]

In his address at the laying of the foundation stone, Rudolf Steiner said: 'It must be so if—aglow with the fire of love—we are to fight on in that conflict it is granted us to inherit, in that great spiritual conflict which was waged by our forefathers when they were repelling over there [at the borders of Christian Europe] the ahrimanic onslaught of the Moors.'[38]

Mankind is still involved in this spiritual conflict today. It is the battle that various occult powers are waging in East and West against a true knowledge of the Mystery of Golgotha and the new appearance of Christ to humanity in etheric form. The occult streams of Helena Roerich and Alice Bailey described, respectively, in Parts One and Two of this book are merely two particularly characteristic examples among many others of this battle.

These openly antichristian streams should now be opposed by all teachers and pupils of true Christian esotericism who are aware of the mystery of Christ. They should all participate today in this great spiritual battle—'aglow with the fire of love', with their love for Christ. For this battle has to do with something of great—indeed of the greatest—magnitude, namely the meaning of the earth and of the humanity that dwells upon it.

For Christ *is* the new Spirit of the Earth, the highest leader of earthly evolution. Hence everything that happens on the earth in the sense of its ongoing evolution must be brought into a conscious connection with Him, otherwise it will inevitably fall prey to Lucifer or the other adversarial powers.[39]

Thus everything that has been said regarding the Western and Eastern Masters can be summarized as follows. Since Christ began to appear in the spiritual worlds in etheric form, in the world of *real occultism* there are no longer non-Christian paths of initiation but all are, in the light of the Etheric Christ, gradually becoming either Christian paths (in the sense of Christian esotericism as described in this book) or antichristian, that is, either serving 'the intentions of the living Christ'[40] or opposing these intentions.

What could in Helena Blavatsky's time still be given by the Eastern initiators (mahatmas) as an occultism external to Christianity must, if it is taken further, inevitably be in danger in our time of being usurped by antichristian occultism (as the history of Krishnamurti and also the incorrect information about the Christ Being in the teachings of Roerich, Bailey and others testify).

Thus the strict words which Christ Jesus spoke in Palestine almost two thousand years ago, 'He who is not with me is against me' (Matthew 12:30), are today, with the beginning of his appearance in the etheric body, becoming a reality also in the world of occultism. For from now on not only the spreading of false teachings about the Christ but also any ignoring of the central significance that His unique coming to earth and His accomplishing of the Mystery of Golgotha have—which comes about if one draws the attention of human beings exclusively to the old pre-Christian religions and the occultism connected with them (which has no knowledge of the Mystery of Golgotha) and to paths of initiation which do not lead to a true knowledge of Christ—has to be seen in our time as a form of the battle against Him and His etheric Second Coming.

Which path have the Eastern initiators (mahatmas) chosen in this sense? Rudolf Steiner was probably unable to give a conclusive answer to this question because the ultimate decision had not yet been made by them; and so it was necessary to keep both possibilities open. No answer to this question can therefore be given here.

We have only been able to pose *questions* here. The *answers* must be given by the mahatmas themselves with words and deeds, by proclaiming the Etheric Christ and by serving him.

Notes

1. GA 121, 17 June 1910.
2. Ibid.
3. GA 130, 5 November 1911.
4. GA 233, 13 January 1924.
5. The relationship between *The Philosophy of Freedom* and the Michael impulse is

referred to by Rudolf Steiner in his articles 'The Michael-Christ Experience of Man' (2 November 1924) and 'Michael's Mission in the Cosmic Age of Human Freedom' (9 November 1924). Both are published in GA 26.

6. GA 10, 'Conditions'.
7. GA 262, 'The Barr Manuscript', III.
8. Rudolf Steiner spoke of how Christ, after passing through the Mystery of Golgotha, became the new Spirit of the Earth and the highest leader of its evolution in many of his lectures, for example in GA 99, 2 June 1907; GA 103, 26 May 1908; GA 104, 23 June 1908.
9. See further in Sergei O. Prokofieff, op. cit., Temple Lodge, 1994.
10. GA 116, 25 October 1909.
11. GA 117, 4 December 1909, likewise the following quotation.
12. GA 116, 25 October 1909.
13. GA 226, 17 May 1923.
14. GA 113, 31 August 1909, also the following quotation.
15. See GA 10 and GA 13, also the lectures of 19 September 1906, 22 February 1907 (GA 97); 6 June 1907 (GA 99) and many others.
16. See further in: Sergei O. Prokofieff, *Rudolf Steiner and the Founding of the New Mysteries.*
17. GA 113, 31 August 1909.
18. GA 262, 'The Barr Manuscript', III.
19. See for example the lecture of 31 August 1909 and many others.
20. GA 258, 14 June 1923.
21. GA 262, 'The Barr Manuscript', III, also the following quotations.
22. See H.P. Blavatsky, *The Theosophical Glossary*, London 1992, and also GA 11.
23. See GA 180, 30 December 1917.
24. See further in: Sergei O. Prokofieff, *The Heavenly Sophia and the Being Anthroposophia*, Temple Lodge, 1996/2006.
25. GA 129, 21 August 1911.
26. See GA 104, 29 June 1908.
27. See further regarding the life after death in GA 227, 231, 239.
28. GA 116, 8 May 1910, also the following quotation.
29. GA 243, 20 August 1924, also the following quotations.
30. GA 227, 29 August 1923, also the following quotations.
31. GA 262, 'The Barr Manuscript', III.
32. GA 155, 16 July 1914.
33. GA 284/285, 16 October 1911.
34. GA 159/160, 15 June 1915.
35. GA 107, 22 March 1909.
36. See GA 286, 17 June 1914.
37. Regarding the twelve aspects of the 'I' which find their highest archetype in this circle, see GA 119, 29 March 1910.
38. GA 245. The address was given on 20 September 1913 at the laying of the foundation stone of the First Goetheanum in Dornach.
39. See GA 155, 16 July 1914.
40. GA 262, 'The Barr Manuscript', III.

Volumes of Rudolf Steiner's Collected Works (GA) Referred to in the Text

Where a volume has been translated into English in its entirety or where the relevant lectures are included in this translated edition, an English title is given; where this is not the case the German title is used, qualified only if a lecture or article from the volume in question referred to by the author has been translated. Translations from Rudolf Steiner's works have been either edited or newly made by the present translator.

2	*A Theory of Knowledge Implicit in Goethe's World Conception*
3	*Truth and Knowledge*
4	*The Philosophy of Freedom*
5	*Friedrich Nietzsche*
7	*Mysticism at the Dawn of the Modern Age*
8	*Christianity as Mystical Fact*
9	*Theosophy*
10	*Knowledge of the Higher Worlds*
11	*Cosmic Memory*
13	*Occult Science*
14	*The Four Mystery Plays*
15	*The Spiritual Guidance of Man and Humanity*
16	*A Road to Self-Knowledge*
26	*Anthroposophical Leading Thoughts*
28	*The Course of My Life* or *Autobiography*
30	*Methodische Grundlagen der Anthroposophie (1884–1901)*
35	*Philosophie und Anthroposophie*
	Approaches to Anthroposophy (includes lecture of 11 January 1916)
52	*Spirituelle Seelenlehre und Weltbetrachtung*
53	*Ursprung und Ziel des Menschen*
	The Inner Development of Man (lecture of 15 December 1904)
93	*The Temple Legend*
93a	*Foundations of Esotericism*
94	*Kosmogonie. Populärer Okkultism. Das Johannes-Evangelium. Die Theosophie an Hand des Johannes-Evangelium* (Munich, 27 October–6 November)
95	*At the Gates of Spiritual Science* or *Founding a Science of the Spirit*
96	*Original Impulses for the Science of the Spirit. Christian Esotericism in the Light of New Spiritual Insights*
97	*The Christian Mystery*
99	*Theosophy of the Rosicrucian* or *Rosicrucian Wisdom*
100	*Menschheitsentwicklung und Christus-Erkenntnis. Theosophie und Rosenkreutztum—Das Johannes-Evangelium* (Typescript EN 50 comprises notes of these eight lectures given in Basel)

All English titles currently available can be obtained via Rudolf Steiner Press (UK),
www.rudolfsteinerpress.com or SteinerBooks (USA), www.steinerbooks.org